CLYMER™

YAMAHA

XV700-1100 Virago · 1981-1997
XV535 Virago · 1987-1997

The world's finest publisher of mechanical how-to manuals

INTERTEC PUBLISHING

P.O. Box 12901, Overland Park, Kansas 66282-2901

Copyright ©1997 Intertec Publishing Corporation

FIRST EDITION
First Printing February, 1986

SECOND EDITION
Revised to include 1985 and 1986 models
First Printing November, 1986

THIRD EDITION
Revised to include 1987 models
First Printing September, 1987
Second Printing April, 1988
Third Printing October, 1988
Fourth Printing September, 1989
Fifth Printing April, 1990

FOURTH EDITION
Revised by Ed Scott to include 1988-1990 models
First Printing February, 1991
Second Printing December, 1991

FIFTH EDITION
Revised by Ed Scott to include 1992 models
First Printing November, 1992

SIXTH EDITION
Revised by Ed Scott to include 1987-1993 XV535 models
and 1993 XV750 and XV1100 models
First Printing October, 1993
Second Printing June, 1994

SEVENTH EDITION
Revised to include 1994-1995 models
First Printing April, 1995
Second Printing March, 1996

EIGHTH EDITION
Revised to include 1996-1997 models
First Printing June, 1997
Second Printing January, 1998

Printed in U.S.A.

ISBN: 0-89287-692-1

Library of Congress: 97-70697

MEMBER

MOTORCYCLE INDUSTRY COUNCIL, INC.

Technical photography by Ron Wright and Ed Scott.

Technical illustrations by Steve Amos and Robert Caldwell.

COVER: Photographed by Mark Clifford, Mark Clifford Photography, Los Angeles, California.

The following books and guides are published by Intertec Publishing.

CLYMER SHOP MANUALS
Boat Motors and Drives
Motorcycles and ATVs
Snowmobiles
Personal Watercraft

**ABOS/INTERTEC/CLYMER BLUE BOOKS
AND TRADE-IN GUIDES**
Recreational Vehicles
Outdoor Power Equipment
Agricultural Tractors
Lawn and Garden Tractors
Motorcycles and ATVs
Snowmobiles and Personal Watercraft
Boats and Motors

AIRCRAFT BLUEBOOK-PRICE DIGEST
Airplanes
Helicopters

AC-U-KWIK DIRECTORIES
The Corporate Pilot's Airport/FBO Directory
International Manager's Edition
Jet Book

I&T SHOP SERVICE MANUALS
Tractors

INTERTEC SERVICE MANUALS
Snowmobiles
Outdoor Power Equipment
Personal Watercraft
Gasoline and Diesel Engines
Recreational Vehicles
Boat Motors and Drives
Motorcycles
Lawn and Garden Tractors

CONTENTS

QUICK REFERENCE DATA
XV700-1100

FUSES

	Amperage
Main	
XV920J, XV1100	30
All others	20
Headlight	15
Signal	15
Ignition	10
Tail	10
Reserve	
XV700, XV1000, XV1100	20
XV920J	30
All other models	Not specified.

APPROXIMATE REFILL CAPACITIES

Engine oil	
With filter change	3.3 quarts (3,100 cc)
Without filter change	3.2 quarts (3,000 cc)
Engine rebuild	3.8 quarts (3,600 cc)
Front forks	
XV700 (1984-1985)	13.2 oz. (389 cc)
XV700 (1986-1987)	13.4 oz. (396 cc)
XV750 (1981-1983)	9.4 oz. (278 cc)
XV750 (1988-on)	13.4 oz. (396 cc)
XV920 (1981-1982 chain drive)	8.9 oz. (264 cc)
XV920 (1982-1983 shaft drive)	10.2 oz. (303 cc)
XV1000, XV1100	12.6 oz. (372 cc)
Final gear case (if so equipped)	0.21 qt. (200 cc)

RECOMMENDED LUBRICANTS

Engine oil	
40° F and above	SAE20W/40, SE-SF
40° F and below	SAE10W/30, SE-SF
Brake fluid	DOT 3 or DOT 4
Battery refilling	Distilled water
Fork oil	SAE 10
Cables and pivot points	Yamaha chain and cable lube or SAE 10W/30 motor oil
Fuel	Regular
Final gear oil (if so equipped)	
All weather	SAE 80W/90, GL4
Above 40° F	SAE 90, GL4
Below 40° F	SAE 80, GL4
Drive chain (if so equipped)	Shell Alvania 1 or lithium-base EP2 grease

TIRE INFLATION PRESSURE (COLD)

Load	XV700, XV750, XV1000, XV1100 psi (kg/cm²)	XV920 psi (kg/cm²)
Up to 198 lb. (90 kg)		
Front	26 (1.8)	26 (1.8)
Rear	28 (2.0)	28 (2.0)
198-353 lb. (90-160 kg)		
Front	28 (2.0)	
Rear	32 (2.3)	
353-529 lb. (160-240 kg)		
Front	28 (2.0)	
Rear	40 (2.8)	
198-470 lb. (90-213 kg)		
Front	—	28 (2.0)
Rear	—	32 (2.3)
High-speed riding		
Front	32 (2.3)	28 (2.0)
Rear	36 (2.5)	32 (2.3)

REPLACEMENT BULBS

Item	Wattage
Headlight	12V 60/55W
Tail/brakelight	12V 8/27W
Meter light	
XV920J	12V 2W
All other models	12V 3.4W
Indicator lights	
1981-1983	12V 3.4W
1984-on	12V 4.0W
License light	
XV750	12V 8W
XV920J	12V 3.8W
All other models	Not specified
Flasher/running light	
XV700, XV1000, XV1100	12V 27W
XV920J	12V 27W X 4/8W
All other models	Not specified

TUNE-UP SPECIFICATIONS

Ignition timing	Fixed
Valve clearance (cold)	
1981-1983	
Intake	0.004 in. (0.10 mm)
Exhaust	0.006 in. (0.15 mm)
1984-on	
Intake	0.003-0.005 in. (0.07-0.10 mm)
Exhaust	0.005-0.007 in. (0.12-0.15 mm)
Spark plug	
Type	NGK BP7ES
Gap	0.028-0.032 in. (0.7-0.8 mm)
Tightening torque	14.5 ft.-lb. (20 N•m)
Idle speed	950-1,050 rpm
Compression pressure (warm @ sea level)	
Standard	156 psi (11 kg/cm²)
Minimum	128 psi (9 kg/cm²)
Maximum	171 psi (12 kg/cm²)
Maximum difference between cylinders:	14 psi (1.0 kg/cm²)

CLYMER™

YAMAHA

▶ ## *XV700-1100 Virago • 1981-1997*

XV535 Virago • 1987-1997

INTRODUCTION

This portion of this detailed and comprehensive manual covers all 1981-on Yamaha XV700-XV1100 V-Twins. Two versions of the Model 920 have been produced, chain-driven and shaft-driven. The Euro-style, chain-drive models were offered in 1981 and 1982 and are identified by an R proceeding the model number. In addition, Yamaha also offered a shaft-driven Model 920 during 1982. For 1983, however, all 920 models, including all other models covered in this manual, are shaft-driven.

The expert text contained within this manual gives complete information on maintenance, tune-up, repair and overhaul. Hundreds of photos and drawings guide you through every step. The book includes all you need to know to keep your Yamaha running right.

Where repairs are practical for the owner/mechanic, complete procedures are given. Equally important, difficult jobs are pointed out. Such operations are usually more economically performed by a dealer or independent garage.

A shop manual is a reference. You want to be able to find information fast. As in all Clymer books, this one is designed with this in mind. All chapters are thumb tabbed. Important items are extensively indexed at the rear of the book. All the most frequently used specifications and capacities are summarized on the *Quick Reference* pages at the front of the book.

Keep the book handy in your tool box and take it with you on long trips. It will help you to better understand your Yamaha, lower repair and maintenance costs and generally improve your satisfaction with your bike.

CHAPTER ONE

GENERAL INFORMATION

This detailed, comprehensive manual covers Yamaha XV700-1100 models. The expert text gives complete information on maintenance, tune-up, repair and overhaul. The book includes all you need to know to keep your Yamaha running right.

A shop manual is a reference. You want to be able to find information fast. As in all Clymer books, this one is designed with you in mind. All chapters are thumb-tabbed. Important items are extensively indexed at the rear of the book. All procedures, tables, photos, etc., in this manual assume that the reader may be working on the bike or using this manual for the first time. All the most frequently used specifications and capacities are summarized in the *Quick Reference Data* pages at the front of the book.

Keep the book handy in your tool box. It will help you to better understand how your Yamaha runs, lower repair and maintenance costs and generally improve your satisfaction with the bike.

Table 1 lists engine serial numbers for all models covered. **Table 2** lists general specifications. **Tables 1-4** are at the end of this chapter.

MANUAL ORGANIZATION

All dimensions and capacities are expressed in English units familar to U.S. mechanics as well as in metric units.

This chapter provides general information and discusses equipment and tools useful both for preventive maintenance and troubleshooting.

Chapter Two provides methods and suggestions for quick and accurate diagnosis and repair of problems. Troubleshooting procedures discuss typical symptoms and logical methods to pinpoint the trouble.

Chapter Three explains all periodic lubrication and routine maintenance necessary to keep your Yamaha running well. Chapter Three also includes recommended tune-up procedures, eliminating the need to constantly consult chapters on the various assemblies.

Subsequent chapters describe specific systems such as the engine, clutch, transmission, fuel, exhaust, suspension, steering and brakes. Each chapter provides disassembly, repair and assembly procedures in simple step-by-step form. If a repair is impractical for a home mechanic, it is so indicated. It is usually faster and less expensive to take such repairs to a dealer or competent repair shop. Specifications concerning a particular system are included at the end of the appropriate chapter.

Some of the procedures in this manual specify special tools. In most cases, the tool is illustrated either in actual use or alone. Well equipped mechanics may find they can substitute similar tools already on hand or fabricate their own.

The terms NOTE, CAUTION and WARNING have specific meanings in this manual. A NOTE provides additional information to make a step or procedure easier or clearer. Disregarding a NOTE could cause inconvenience, but would not cause equipment damage or personal injury.

A CAUTION emphasizes areas where equipment damage could result. Disregarding a CAUTION could cause permanent mechanical damage; however, personal injury is unlikely.

A WARNING emphasizes areas where personal injury or even death could result from negligence. Mechanical damage may also occur. WARNINGS *are to be taken seriously.* In some cases, serious injury and death have resulted from disregarding similar warnings.

Throughout this manual keep in mind 2 conventions. "Front" refers to the front of the Yamaha. The front of any component, such as the engine, is the end which faces toward the front of the vehicle. The "left-" and "right-hand" sides refer to the position of the parts as viewed by a rider sitting on the seat facing forward. For example, the throttle control is on the right-hand side and the clutch lever is on the left-hand side. These rules are simple, but even experienced mechanics occasionally become disoriented.

SERVICE HINTS

Most of the service procedures covered are straightforward and can be performed by anyone reasonably handy with tools. It is suggested, however, that you consider your own capabilities carefully before attempting any operation involving major disassembly of the engine.

Some operations, for example, require the use of a press. It would be wiser to have these operations performed by a shop equipped for such work, rather than to try to do the job yourself with makeshift equipment. Other procedures require precise measurements. Unless you have the skills and equipment required, it would be better to have a qualified repair shop make the measurements for you.

There are many items available that can be used on your hands before and after working on your bike. A little preparation prior to getting "all greased up" will help during clean-up.

Before starting out, work Vaseline, soap or a product such as Pro-Tek (**Figure 1**) onto your forearms, into your hands and under your fingernails and cuticles. This will make clean-up a lot easier.

For clean-up, use a waterless hand soap such as Sta-Lube and then finish up with powered Boraxo and a fingernail brush.

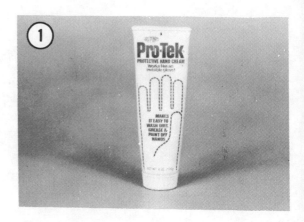

Repairs go much faster and easier if your machine is clean before you begin work. There are many special cleaners, such as Gunk or Bel-Ray Degreaser (**Figure 2**), for washing the engine and related parts. Just follow the manufacturer's directions on the container for the best results. Then rinse it away with a heavy spray of water from a garden hose. Clean all oily or greasy parts with cleaning solvent as you remove them.

> *WARNING*
> *Never use gasoline as a cleaning agent. It presents an extreme fire hazard. Be sure to work in a well-ventilated area when using cleaning solvent. Keep a fire extinguisher, rated for gasoline fires, handy in any case.*

Special tools are required for some repair procedures. These may be purchased at a dealer, rented from a tool rental shop or fabricated by a mechanic or machinist (often at considerable savings).

Much of the labor charges for repairs made by dealers are for the labor hours involved during the removal, disassembly, assembly and installation of other parts in order to reach the defective part. It is frequently possible to perform the preliminary operations yourself and then take the defective unit to the dealer for repair.

Once you have decided to tackle the job yourself, read the entire section in this manual which pertains to the job, making sure you have identified the proper section. Study the illustrations and text until you have a good idea of what is involved in completing the job satisfactorily. If special tools or replacement parts are required, make arrangements to get them before you start. It is frustrating and time-consuming to get partly into a job and then be unable to complete it.

Simple wiring checks can be easily made at home, but knowledge of electronics is almost a

necessity for performing tests with complicated electronic testing gear.

During disassembly keep a few general cautions in mind. Force is rarely needed to get things apart. If parts are a tight fit, such as a bearing in a case, there is usually a tool designed to separate them. Never use a screwdriver to pry apart parts with machined surfaces such as crankcase halves. You will mar the surfaces and end up with leaks.

Make diagrams (or take an instant picture) wherever similar-appearing parts are found. For instance, crankcase bolts are often not the same length. You may think you can remember where everything came from, but mistakes are costly. There is also the possibility that you may be sidetracked and not return to work for days or even weeks and the carefully laid out parts may get moved.

Tag all similar internal parts for location and mark all mating parts for position. Record number and thickness of any shims as they are removed. Small parts such as bolts can be identified by placing them in plastic sandwich bags. Seal and label them with masking tape.

Wiring should be tagged with masking tape marked as each wire is removed. Again, do not rely on memory alone.

Protect finished surfaces from physical damage or corrosion. Keep gasoline and hydraulic (brake) fluid off painted surfaces.

Frozen or very tight bolts and screws can often be loosened by soaking with a penetrating oil, such as WD-40 or Liquid Wrench, then striking the bolt head sharply with a hand impact driver. Avoid heat unless absolutely necessary, since it may melt, warp or remove the temper from many parts.

No parts, except those assembled with a press fit, require unusual force during assembly. If a part is hard to remove or install, find out why before proceeding.

Cover all openings after removing parts to keep dirt, small tools, etc., from falling in.

When assembling 2 parts, start all fasteners, then tighten evenly.

Wiring connections and brake shoes should be kept clean and free of grease and oil.

When assembling parts, be sure all shims and washers are installed exactly as they came out.

Whenever a rotating part butts against a stationary part, look for a shim or washer. Use new gaskets if there is any doubt about the condition of the old ones. A thin coat of oil on non-pressure type gaskets may help them seal more effectively.

Heavy grease can be used to hold small parts in place if they tend to fall out during assembly. However, keep grease and oil away from electrical and brake components.

High spots may be sanded off a piston with sandpaper, but fine emery cloth and oil will do a much more professional job.

Carbon can be removed from the head, the piston crowns and the exhaust ports with a dull screwdriver. *Do not* scratch the surface. Wipe off the surface with a clean cloth when finished.

The carburetors are best cleaned by disassembling them and soaking the parts in a commercial carburetor cleaner. Never soak gaskets and rubber parts in these cleaners. Never use wire to clean out jets and air passages; they are easily damaged. Use compressed air to blow out the carburetor *after* the float has been removed.

A baby bottle makes a good measuring device for adding oil to the front forks and final drive. Get one that is graduated in fluid ounces and cubic centimeters. After it has been used for this purpose, do not let a small child drink out of it as there will always be an oil residue in it.

Take your time and do the job right. Do not forget that a newly rebuilt engine must be broken in in the same manner as a new one. Keep the rpm within the limits given in your owner's manual when you get back on the road.

TORQUE SPECIFICATIONS

Torque specifications throughout this manual are given in foot-pounds (ft.-lb.) and Newton Meters (N•m). Newton meters are being adopted in place of meter kilograms (mkg) in accordance with the International Modernized Metric System. Tool manufacturers now offer torque wrenches calibrated in Newton meters.

Existing torque wrenches calibrated in meter kilograms can be used by performing a simple conversion. All you have to do is move the decimal point one place to the right; for example, 4.7 mkg = 47 N•m. This conversion is sufficient for use in this manual even though the exact mathematical conversion is 3.5 mkg = 34.3 N•m.

General torque specifications are listed in the individual chapters. For those components that are not listed, refer to **Table 2** for a general listing of nut and bolt tightening torques. To use the table, first determine the size of the nut or bolt. **Figure 3** and **Figure 4** show how this is done.

SAFETY FIRST

Professional mechanics can work for years and never sustain a serious injury. If you observe a few rules of common sense and safety, you can enjoy many safe hours servicing your own machine. If you ignore these rules you can hurt yourself or damage the bike.

1. Never use gasoline as a cleaning solvent.
2. Never smoke or use a torch in the vicinity of flammable liquids, such as cleaning solvent, in open containers.
3. If welding or brazing is required on the machine, remove the fuel tank(s) (and any gas-filled shock absorber) to a safe distance, at least 50 feet away.
4. Use the proper sized wrenches to avoid damage to nuts and injury to yourself.
5. When loosening a tight or stuck nut, think about what would happen if the wrench should slip. Be careful; protect yourself accordingly.
6. Keep your work area clean and uncluttered.
7. Wear safety goggles during all operations involving drilling, grinding or the use of a cold chisel.
8. Wear safety goggles when using chemicals, such as solvent, and when using compressed air to clean and dry parts.
9. Never use worn-out tools.
10. Keep a fire extinguisher handy; be sure it is rated for gasoline and electrical fires.

SPECIAL TIPS

Because of the extreme demands placed on an bike several points should be kept in mind when performing service and repair. The following items are general suggestions that may improve the overall life of the machine and help avoid costly failures.

1. Use a locking compound, such as Loctite Lock N' Seal No. 2114 (blue Loctite) on all bolts and nuts, even if they are secured with lockwashers. This type of Loctite does not harden completely and allows easy removal of the bolt or nut. A screw

or bolt lost from an engine cover or bearing retainer could easily cause serious and expensive damage before its loss is noticed.

When applying Loctite, use a small amount. If too much is used, it can work its way down the threads and stick parts together not meant to be stuck.

Keep a tube of Loctite in your tool box; when used properly it is cheap insurance.

2. Use a hammer-driven impact driver to remove tight screws, particularly engine cover screws. These tools help prevent the rounding off of screw heads and ensure a tight installation.
3. When straightening out the "fold-over" type lockwasher (usually used on the clutch nut), use a wide-blade chisel such as an old and dull wood chisel. Such a tool provides better contact on the folded tab, making straightening out easier.
4. When installing the "fold-over" type lockwasher, always use a new washer if possible. If a new washer is not available, always fold over a part of the washer that has not been previously folded.

Reusing the same fold may cause the washer to break, resulting in the loss of its locking ability and a loose piece of metal adrift in the engine.

When folding the washer over, start the fold with a screwdriver and finish it with a pair of pliers. If a punch is used to make the fold, the fold may be too sharp, thereby increasing the chances of the washer breaking under stress.

These washers are relatively inexpensive and it is suggested that you keep several of each size in your tool box for field repairs.

5. When replacing missing or broken fasteners (nuts, bolts and screws), especially on the engine or frame components, always use Yamaha replacement parts. They are specially hardened for each application. The wrong 50-cent bolt could easily cause serious damage and rider injury.

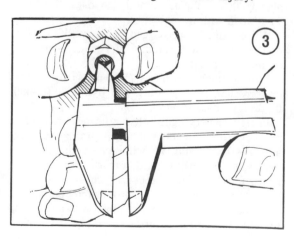

6. When installing gaskets in the engine, always use Yamaha replacement gaskets *without* sealer, unless designated. These gaskets are designed to swell when they come in contact with oil. Gasket sealer will prevent the gaskets from swelling as intended, which can result in oil leaks. These Yamaha gaskets are cut from material of the precise thickness needed. Installation of a too thick or too thin gasket in a critical area could cause engine damage.

EXPENDABLE SUPPLIES

Certain expendable supplies are required. These include grease, oil, gasket cement, shop rags and cleaning solvent (**Figure 5**). Ask your dealer for the special locking compounds, silicone lubricants and lube products which make maintenance simpler and easier. Cleaning solvent is available at some service stations.

PARTS REPLACEMENT

Yamaha makes frequent changes during a model year, some minor, some relatively major. When you order parts from the dealer or other parts distributor, always order by engine and frame

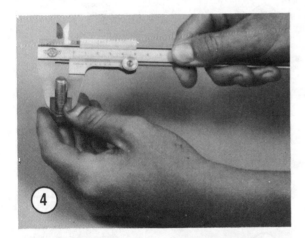

number. Write the numbers down and carry them with you. Compare new parts to old before purchasing them. If they are not alike, have the parts manager explain the difference to you.

SERIAL NUMBERS

You must know the model serial number for registration purposes and when ordering replacement parts.

The frame serial number and the vehicle identification number (VIN) are stamped on the right-hand side of the steering head. The engine number is located on the lower right-hand side of the crankcase.

BASIC HAND TOOLS

A number of tools are required to maintain your Yamaha in top riding condition. You may already have some around for other work like home or car repairs. There are also tools made especially for bike repairs; these you will have to purchase. In any case, a wide variety of quality tools will make bike repairs more effective and easier.

Top quality tools are essential; they are also more economical in the long run. If you are now starting to build your tool collection, stay away from the "advertised specials" featured at some parts houses, discount stores and chain drug stores. These are usually a poor grade tool that can be sold cheaply and that is exactly what they are—*cheap*. They are usually made of inferior material and are thick, heavy and clumsy. Their rough finish makes them difficult to clean and they usually don't last very long. Also be careful when lending tools to "friends"—make sure they return tools promptly; if not, your collection will soon disappear.

Quality tools are made of alloy steel and are heat treated for greater strength. They are lighter and better balanced than cheap ones. Their surface is smooth, making them a pleasure to work with and easy to clean. The initial cost of good quality tools may be more but it is cheaper in the long run. Don't try to buy everything in all sizes in the beginning; do it a little at a time until you have the necessary tools.

Keep your tools clean and in a tool box. Keep them organized with the sockets and related drives together, the open-end and box wrenches together, etc. After using a tool, wipe off dirt and grease with a clean cloth and put the tool in its correct place. Doing this will save a lot of time you would have spent trying to find a socket buried in a bunch of clutch parts.

The following tools are required to perform virtually any repair job on a bike. Each tool is described and the recommended size given for starting a tool collection. **Table 4** includes all the tools that should be on hand for simple home repairs or major overhauls. Additional tools and some duplications may be added as you become more familiar with the bike. Almost all motorcycles and bikes (with the exception of the U.S.-built Harley and some English bikes) use metric-size bolts and nuts. If you are starting your collection now, buy metric sizes.

Screwdrivers

The screwdriver is a very basic tool, but if used improperly it will do more damage than good. The slot on a screw has a definite dimension and shape. A screwdriver must be selected to conform with that shape. Use a small screwdriver for small screws and a large one for large screws or the screw head will be damaged.

Two basic types of screwdriver are required to repair the bike—a common (flat blade) screwdriver and the Phillips screwdriver.

Screwdrivers are available in sets which often include an assortment of common and Phillips blades. If you buy them individually, buy at least the following:

    a. Common screwdriver—5/16×6 in. blade.
    b. Common screwdriver—3/8×12 in. blade.
    c. Phillips screwdriver—size 2 tip, 6 in. blade.

Use screwdrivers only for driving screws. Never use a screwdriver for prying or chiseling. Do not try to remove a Phillips or Allen head screw with a common screwdriver; you can damage the head so that the proper tool will be unable to remove it. Keep screwdrivers in the proper condition and they will last longer and perform better. Always keep the tip of a common screwdriver in good condition. **Figure 6** shows how to grind the tip to the proper shape if it becomes damaged. Note the parallel sides of the tip.

Pliers

Pliers come in a wide range of types and sizes. Pliers are useful for cutting, bending and crimping. They should never be used to cut hardened objects or to turn bolts or nuts. **Figure 7** shows several pliers useful in bike repairs.

Each type of pliers has a specialized function. Gas pliers are general purpose pliers used mainly for holding things and for bending. Locking pliers are used as pliers or to hold objects very tight like in a vise. Needlenose pliers are used to hold or bend small objects. Channel lock pliers can be adjusted to hold various sizes of objects; the jaws remain parallel to grip around objects such as pipe

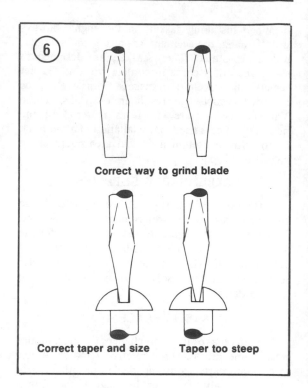

Correct way to grind blade

Correct taper and size   Taper too steep

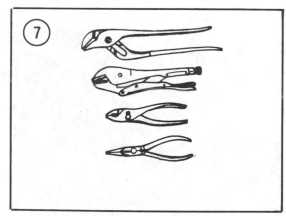

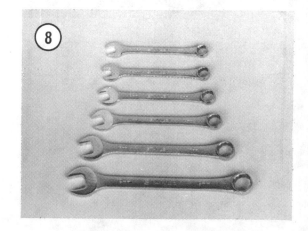

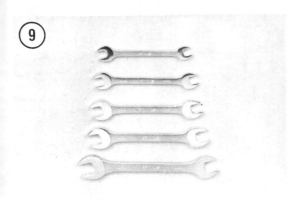

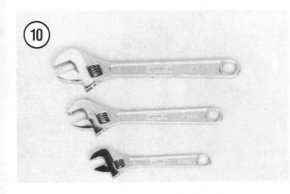

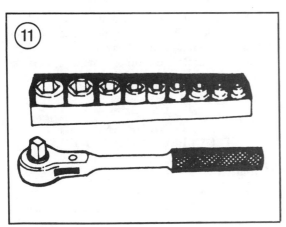

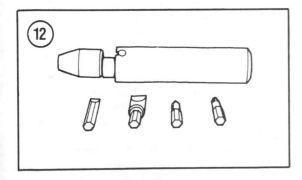

or tubing. There are many more types of pliers. The ones described here are the most commomly needed for bike repairs.

Box and Open-end Wrenches

Box and open-end wrenches are available in sets or separately in a variety of sizes. See **Figure 8** and **Figure 9**. The size number stamped near the end refers to the distance between 2 parallel flats on the hex head bolt or nut.

Box wrenches are usually superior to open-end wrenches. An open-end wrench grips the nut on only 2 flats. Unless it fits well, it may slip and round off the points on the nut. The box wrench grips on all 6 flats. Both 6-point and 12-point openings are available on box wrenches. The 6-point gives superior holding power; the 12-point allows a shorter swing.

Combination wrenches which are open on one side and boxed on the other are also available. Both ends are the same size.

Adjustable (Crescent) Wrench

An adjustable wrench (also called Crescent wrench) can be adjusted to fit nearly any nut or bolt head. See **Figure 10**. However, it can loosen and slip, causing damage to the nut and maybe to your knuckles. Use an adjustable wrench only when other wrenches are not available.

Crescent wrenches come in sizes ranging from 4-18 in. overall. A 6 or 8 in. wrench is recommended as an all-purpose wrench.

Socket Wrenches

This type is undoubtedly the fastest, safest and most convenient to use. See **Figure 11**. Sockets which attach to a ratchet handle are available with 6-point or 12-point openings and 1/4, 3/8 and 3/4 inch drives. The drive size indicates the size of the square hole which mates with the ratchet handle. The 3/8 inch drive is most commonly used for bike repair.

Torque Wrench

A torque wrench is used with a socket to measure how tight a nut or bolt is installed. They come in a wide price range and with either 3/8 or 1/2 in. square drive. The drive size indicates the size of the square drive which mates with the socket. Purchase one that measures 0-100 ft.-lb. (0-140 N•m).

Impact Driver

This tool might have been designed with the motorcyclist in mind. See **Figure 12**. It makes

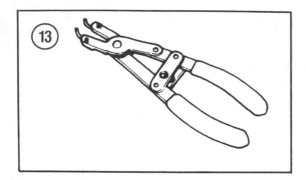

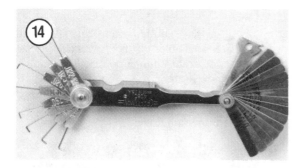

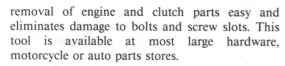

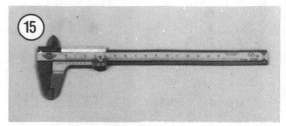

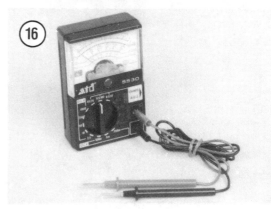

removal of engine and clutch parts easy and eliminates damage to bolts and screw slots. This tool is available at most large hardware, motorcycle or auto parts stores.

Circlip Pliers

Circlip pliers (sometimes referred to as snap ring pliers) are necessary to remove the circlips used on the transmission shaft assemblies. See **Figure 13**.

Hammers

The correct hammer is necessary for bike repairs. Use only a hammer with a face (or head) of rubber or plastic or the soft-faced type that is filled with buckshot. These are sometimes necessary in engine teardowns. *Never* use a metal-faced hammer on the bike as severe damage will result in most cases. You can always produce the same amount of force with a soft-faced hammer.

Ignition Gauge

This tool has both flat and wire measuring gauges and is used to measure spark plug gap. See **Figure 14**. This device is available at most auto or motorcycle supply stores.

Vernier Caliper

This tool is invaluable when reading inside, outside, depth and step measurements to close precision in either metric or inch scales. Some calipers are manufactured with both scales. The

vernier caliper can be purchased from large dealers or mail order houses. See **Figure 15**.

Other Special Tools

A few other special tools may be required for major service. These are described in the appropriate chapters and are available either from a Yamaha dealer or other manufacturers as indicated.

TUNE-UP AND TROUBLESHOOTING TOOLS

Multimeter or VOM

This instrument (**Figure 16**) is invaluable for electrical system troubleshooting and service. A few of its functions may be duplicated by homemade test equipment, but for the serious mechanic it is a must. Its uses are described in the applicable sections of this book.

Compression Gauge

An engine with low compression cannot be properly tuned and will not develop full power. A compression gauge measures engine compression. The one shown in **Figure 17** has a flexible stem which enables it to reach cylinders where little clearance exists between the cylinder head and frame.

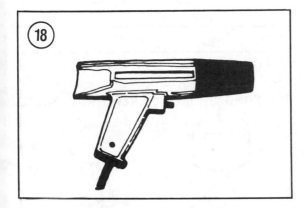

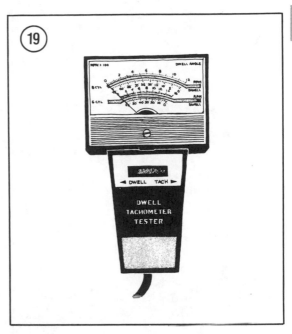

Strobe Timing Light

This instrument is necessary for tuning. By flashing a light at the precise instant the spark plug fires, the position of the timing mark can be seen. Under the flashing light marks on the alternator flywheel line up with the stationary mark on the crankcase while the engine is running.

Suitable lights range from inexpensive neon bulb types to powerful xenon strobe lights. See **Figure 18**. Neon timing lights are difficult to see and must be used in dimly lit areas. Xenon strobe timing lights can be used outside in bright sunlight. Both types work on the Yamaha; use according to the manufacturer's instructions.

Portable Tachometer

A portable tachometer is necessary for tuning. See **Figure 19**. Ignition timing and carburetor adjustments must be performed at the specified engine speed. The best instrument for this purpose is one with a low range of 0-1,000 or 0-2,000 rpm and a high range of 0-4,000 rpm. Extended range (0-6,000 or 0-8,000 rpm) instruments lack accuracy at lower speeds. The instrument should be capable of detecting changes of 25 rpm on the low range.

MECHANIC'S TIPS

Removing Frozen Nuts and Screws

When a fastener rusts and cannot be removed, several methods may be used to loosen it. First, apply penetrating oil such as Liquid Wrench or WD-40 (available at hardware or auto supply stores). Apply it liberally and let it penetrate for 10-15 minutes. Rap the fastener several times with a small hammer; do not hit it hard enough to cause damage.

For frozen screws, apply penetrating oil as described, then insert a screwdriver in the slot and rap the top of the screwdriver with a hammer. This loosens the rust so the screw can be removed in the normal way. If the screw head is too chewed up to use this method, grip the head with locking pliers and twist the screw out.

Remedying Stripped Threads

Occasionally, threads are stripped through carelessness or impact damage. Often the threads can be cleaned up by running a tap (for internal threads on nuts) or die (for external threads on bolts) through the threads. See **Figure 20**. To clean or repair spark plug threads, a spark plug tap can be used (**Figure 21**).

Removing Broken Screws or Bolts

When the head breaks off a screw or bolt, several methods are available for removing the remaining portion.

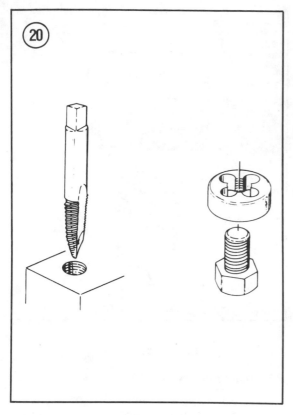

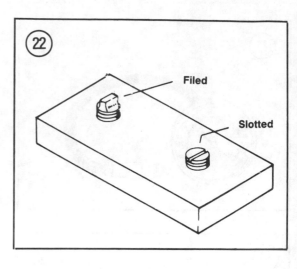

Filed

Slotted

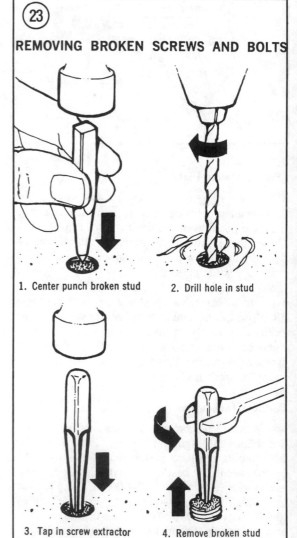

REMOVING BROKEN SCREWS AND BOLTS

1. Center punch broken stud

2. Drill hole in stud

3. Tap in screw extractor

4. Remove broken stud

If a large portion of the remainder projects out, try gripping it with locking pliers. If the projecting portion is too small, file it to fit a wrench or cut a slot in it to fit a screwdriver. See **Figure 22**.

If the head breaks off flush, use a screw extractor. To do this, centerpunch the exact center of the remaining porton of the screw or bolt. Drill a small hole in the screw and tap the extractor into the hole. Back the screw out with a wrench on the extractor. See **Figure 23**.

Table 1 ENGINE SERIAL NUMBERS

Model number and year	Engine serial No. start to end
1981	
XV750H	4X7-000101 to 4X7-200100
XV920RH	5H1-000101 to 5H1-100100
1982	
XV750J	4X7-200101 to 4X7-300100
XV920J	10L-000101 to *
XV920RJ	5H1-100101 to *
1983	
XV750K	4X7-300101 to *
XV750MK	20X-000101 to *
XV920K	24M-000101 to *
XV920MK	27Y-000101 to *
1984	
XV700L	42W-000101 to *
XV700LC	42X-000101 to *
XV1000L	42G-000101 to *
XV1000LC	42H-000101 to *
1985	
XV700N	56E-000101 to *
XV700NC	56F-000101 to *
XV1000N	56V-000101 to *
XV1000NC	56W-000101 to *
1986	
XV700SS	1RR-000101 to 1RR-010100
XV700SSC	1TU-000101 to 1TU-005100
XV700CS	1RM-000101 to 1RM-014100
XV700CSC	1RV-000101 to 1RV-015100
XV1100S	1TE-000101 to 1TE-015100
XV1100SC	1TA-000101 to 1TA-005100
1987	
XV700ST	1RR-010101 to *
XV700STC	1TU-005101 to *
XV700CT	1RM-014101 to *
XV700CTC	1RV-005101 to *
XV1100T	1TE-015101 to *
XV1100TC	1TA-005101 to *
1988	
XV750U	3AL-000101 to *
XV750UC	3CM-000101 to *
XV1100U	1TE-029101 to *
XV1100UC	1TA-007101 to *
1989	
XV750W	3AL-007101 to *
XV750WC	3CM-002101 to *
XV1100W	1TE-035101 to *
XV1100WC	1TA-009101 to *
1990	
XV750A	3AL-01301 to *
XV750AC	3CM-005101 to *
XV1100A	1TE-040101 to *
XV1100AC	1TA-012101 to *

(continued)

Table 1 ENGINE SERIAL NUMBERS (continued)

Model number and year	Engine serial No. start to end
1991	
XV750B	3AL-019101 to *
XV750BC	3CM-007101 to *
XV1100B	1TE-043101 to *
XV1100BC	1TA-014101 to *
1992	
XV750D	3AL-024101 to *
XV750DC	3CM-008101 to *
XV1100D	1TE-047101 to *
XV1100DC	1TA-015101 to *
1993	
XV750E	3AL-029101 to *
XV750EC	3AL-009101 to *
XV1100E	1TE-050101 to *
XV1100EC	1TE-016101 to *
1994	
XV750F	3AL-034101 to *
XV750FC	3AL-014101 to *
XV1100F	1TE-054101 to *
XV1100FC	1TE-020101 to *
1995	
XV750G	3AL-039101 to *
XV750GC	3CM-015101 to *
XV1100G	1TE-059101 to *
XV1100GC	1TA-021101 to *
1996	
XV700H1 3JLN (except California)	3AL-047101-on
XV750HC1 3JLP (California)	3CM-017101-on
XV1100H 3JKR (except California)	1TE-064101-on
XV1100HC 3JKN (California)	1TA-022101-on
XV1100SH 3JKS (except California)	1TE-069101-on
XV1100SHC 3JKT (California)	1TA-024101-on
1997	N/A

* Not specified.

Table 2 GENERAL SPECIFICATIONS

Engine type	Air-cooled, 4-stroke, SOHC, V-twin
Bore and stroke	
XV700	3.16 × 2.72 in. (80.2 × 69.2 mm)
XV750	3.27 × 2.72 in. (83 × 69.2 mm)
XV920	3.62 × 2.72 in. (92 × 69.2 mm)
XV1000	3.74 × 2.72 in. (95 × 69.2 mm)
XV1100	3.74 × 2.95 in. (95 × 75 mm)
Displacement	
XV700	42.64 cu. in. (699 cc)
XV750	45.64 cu. in. (748 cc)
XV920	56.14 cu. in. (920 cc)
XV1000	59.86 cu. in. (981 cc)
XV1100	64.86 cu. in. (1,063 cc)
Compression ratio	
XV700	9.0:1
XV750	8.7:1
XV920, XV1000, XV1100	8.3:1
Ignition	Transister control ignition (TCI)
Carburetion	2 Hitachi carburetors
(continued)	

Table 2 GENERAL SPECIFICATIONS (continued)

Air filter	Dry type element
Fuel type	Gasoline: regular
Fuel tank capacity	
XV700 (1984-1985)	3.3 gal. (12.5 l)
Reserve	0.6 gal. (2.5 l)
XV700 (1986-1987)	3.9 gal. (14.7 l)
Reserve	0.6 gal. (2.5 l)
XV750	3.2 gal. (12 l)
Reserve	0.7 gal. (2.6 l)
XV920RH, RJ	5.0 gal. (19 l)
Reserve	0.8 gal. (3.2 l)
XV920J, K, MK	3.8 gal. (14.5 l)
Reserve	0.5 gal. (2.0 l)
XV1000	3.8 gal. (14.5 l)
Reserve	0.79 gal. (3.0 l)
XV1100	4.4 gal. (16.8 l)
Reserve	0.79 gal. (3.0 l)
Clutch	Wet, multi-plate
Transmission	5 speeds, constant mesh
Transmission ratios	
1981-1983	
1st	2.35:1
2nd	1.67:1
3rd	1.29:1
4th	1.03:1
5th	0.9:1
1984-1985	
1st	2.35:1
2nd	1.67:1
3rd	1.29:1
4th	1.03:1
5th	0.85:1
1986-on	
XV700, XV750	
1st	2.35:1
2nd	1.67:1
3rd	1.29:1
4th	1.03:1
5th	0.85:1
XV1100	
1st	2.29:1
2nd	1.67:1
3rd	1.28:1
4th	1.03:1
5th	0.85:1
Final reduction ratio	
XV700	3.42:1
XV750	3.21:1
XV920RH, RJ	3.17:1
XV920J, K, MK	3.14:1
XV1000, XV1100	3.00:1
Starting system	Electric starter only
Battery	
XV700, XV750	12 volt/16 amp hour
XV920, XV1000, XV1100	12 volt/20 amp hour
Charging system	AC alternator

(continued)

Table 2 GENERAL SPECIFICATIONS (continued)

Chassis dimensions	
XV700, XV1000, XV1100	
Overall length	88.0 in. (2,235 mm)
Overall width	33.1 in. (840 mm)
Overall height	46.1 in. (1,170 mm)
Seat height	28.1 in. (714 mm)
Wheelbase	60.0 in. (1,525 mm)
Ground clearance	5.7 in. (145 mm)
XV750 (1981-1983)	
Overall length	87.8 in. (2,230 mm)
Overall width	33.7 in. (850 mm)
Overall height	46.7 in. (1,160 mm)
Seat height	Not specified
Wheelbase	60.0 in. (1,525 mm)
Ground clearance	5.7 in. (145 mm)
XV750 (1988-on)	
Overall length	90.0 in. (2,285 mm)
Overall width	33.1 in. (840 mm)
Overall height	46.9 in. (1,190 mm)
Seat height	28.1 in. (714 mm)
Wheelbase	60.0 in. (1,525 mm)
Ground clearance	5.7 in. (145 mm)
XV920RH, RJ	
Overall length	89.0 in. (2,260 mm)
Overall width	36.6 in. (930 mm)
Overall height	46.1 in. (1,170 mm)
Seat height	Not specified
Wheelbase	60..6 in. (1,540 mm)
Ground clearance	5.5 in. (140 mm)
XV920J, K, MK	
Overall length	87.4 in. (2,220 mm)
Overall width	33.1 in. (840 mm)
Overall height	47.4 in. (1,205 mm)
Seat height	29.5 in. (750 mm)
Wheelbase	59.8 in. (1,520 mm)
Ground clearance	5.7 in. (145 mm)
Basic weight	
XV700 (1984-1985)	496 lb. (225 kg)
XV700 (1986-1987)	505 lb. (229 kg)
XV750	496 lb. (225 kg)
XV920RH, RJ	493 lb. (224 kg)
XV920J, K, MK	496 lb. (225 kg)
XV1000	520 lb. (236 kg)
XV1100	527 lb. (239 kg)
Steering head angle	
XV700, XV1000, XV1100	32°
XV750, XV920J, K, MK	29°, 30 minutes
XV920RH, RJ	28°, 30 minutes
Trail	
XV700, XV1000, XV1100	5.1 in. (129 mm)
XV750, XV920J, K, MK	5.4 in. (133 mm)
XV920RH, RJ	4.96 in. (126 mm)
Front suspension	Telescopic fork
Travel	5.9 in. (150 mm)
Rear suspension	
1981-1983	Monoshock
1984-on	Dual shock

(continued)

Table 2 GENERAL SPECIFICATIONS (continued)

Rear suspension (continued)	
Travel	
XV700 (1984-1985)	3.8 in. (97 mm)
XV700 (1986-1987)	2.8 in. (70 mm)
XV750	3.94 in. (100 mm)
XV920RH, RJ	4.13 in. (105 mm)
XV920J, K, MK	Not specified
XV1000, XV1100	3.8 in. (97 mm)
Front tire	
XV700, XV1000, XV1100	100/90-19 57H
XV750, XV920J, K, MK	3.50H-19-4PR
XV920RH, RJ	3.25H-19-4PR
Rear tire	
XV700, XV1000, XV1100	140/90-15 70H
XV750, XV920J, K, MK	130/90-16 67H
XV920RH, RJ	120/90-18 65H

Table 3 GENERAL TIGHTENING TORQUES*

Fastener size	ft.-lb.	N·m
6 mm	4.5	6
8 mm	11	15
10 mm	22	30
12 mm	40	55
14 mm	51	85
16 mm	94	130

*This table lists general torque for standard fasteners with standard ISO pitch threads. Use these specifications only if specific values are not provided for a given fastener.

Table 4 HOME WORKSHOP TOOLS

Tool	Size or Specification
Screwdrivers	
Slot	5/16 × 8 in. blade
Slot	3/8 × 12 in. blade
Phillips	Size 2 tip, 6 in. blade
Pliers	
Gas pliers	6 in. overall
Vise Grips	10 in. overall
Needlenose	6 in. overall
Channel lock	12 in. overall
Snap ring	–
Wrenches	
Box-end set	10-17, 20, 32 mm
Open-end set	10-17, 20, 32 mm
Crescent (adjustable)	6 and 12 in. overall
Socket set	1/2 in. drive ratchet with 10-17, 20, 32 mm sockets
Allen set	2-10 mm
Cone wrenches	–
Spoke wrench	–
Other Special Tools	
Impact driver	1/2 in. drive with ass't tips
Torque wrench	1/2 in. drive—0-100 ft.-lb.
Tire levers	For moped or motorcycle tires

CHAPTER TWO

TROUBLESHOOTING

Diagnosing mechanical problems is relatively simple if you use orderly procedures and keep a few basic principles in mind.

The troubleshooting procedures in this chapter analyze typical symptoms and show logical methods of isolating causes. These are not the only methods. There may be several ways to solve a problem, but only a systematic approach can guarantee success.

Never assume anything. Do not overlook the obvious. If you are riding along and the bike suddenly quits, check the easiest, most accessible problem spots first. Is there gasoline in the tank? Has a spark plug wire fallen off?

If nothing obvious turns up in a quick check, look a little further. Learning to recognize and describe symptoms will make repairs easier for you or a mechanic at the shop. Describe problems accurately and fully. Saying that "it won't run" isn't the same as saying "it quit at high speed and won't start" or that "it sat in my garage for 3 months and then wouldn't start".

Gather as many symptoms as possible to aid in diagnosis. Note whether the engine lost power gradually or all at once. Remember that the more complicated a machine is, the easier it is to troubleshoot because symptoms point to specific problems.

After the symptoms are defined, areas which could cause problems are tested and analyzed. Guessing at the cause of a problem may provide the solution, but it can easily lead to frustration, wasted time and a series of expensive, unnecessary parts replacements.

You do not need fancy equipment or complicated test gear to determine whether repairs can be attempted at home. A few simple checks could save a large repair bill and lost time while the bike sits in a dealer's service department. On the other hand, be realistic and do not attempt repairs beyond your abilities. Service departments tend to charge heavily for putting together a disassembled engine that may have been abused. Some won't even take on such a job—so use common sense and don't get in over your head.

OPERATING REQUIREMENTS

An engine needs 3 things to run properly: correct fuel-air mixture, compression and a spark at the correct time. If one or more are missing, the engine will not run. Four-stroke engine operating principles are described in Chapter Four.

The electrical system is the weakest link of the 3 basics. More problems result from electrical

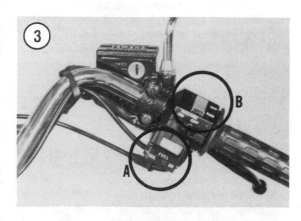

breakdowns than from any other source. Keep that in mind before you begin tampering with carburetor adjustments and the like.

If a bike has been sitting for any length of time and refuses to start, check and clean the spark plug and then look to the gasoline delivery system. This includes the fuel tank, fuel shutoff valve, fuel line to the carburetor and the fuel pump and filter on XV1000 and XV1100 models. Gasoline deposits may have formed and gummed up the carburetor jets and air passages. Gasoline tends to lose its potency after standing for long periods. Condensation may contaminate the fuel with water. Drain the old fuel (fuel tank, fuel lines and carburetors) and try starting with a fresh tankful.

TROUBLESHOOTING INSTRUMENTS

Chapter One lists the instruments needed. Follow the instrument manufacturers' instructions for their use.

EMERGENCY TROUBLESHOOTING

When the bike is difficult to start or won't start at all, it does not help to wear down the battery using the starter. Check for obvious problems even before getting out your tools. Go down the following list step by step. Do each one; you may be embarrassed to find your kill switch off, but that is better than wearing down the battery. If the bike still will not start, refer to the appropriate troubleshooting procedure in this chapter.

1. Is there fuel in the tank? Open the filler cap (**Figure 1**) and rock the bike. Listen for fuel sloshing around.

> *WARNING*
> *Do not use an open flame to check in the tank. A serious explosion is certain to result.*

2. On models except XV1000 and XV1100, is the fuel shutoff valve in the ON position. Turn the valve to the reserve position to be sure you get the last remaining gas. See **Figure 2**.
3. On XV1000 and XV1100 models, make sure the fuel pump switch is on the reserve position (A, **Figure 3**). If there is doubt about the fuel pump operation, refer to Chapter Seven.
4. Make sure the kill switch is not stuck in the OFF position (B, **Figure 3**) or that the wire is not broken and shorting out.
5. Are the spark plug wires (**Figure 4**) on tight? Push both spark plugs on and slightly rotate them to clean the electrical connection between the plug and the connector.
6. Is the choke (**Figure 5**) in the right position?

ENGINE STARTING

An engine that refuses to start or is difficult to start is very frustrating. More often than not, the problem is very minor and can be found with a simple and logical troubleshooting approach.

The following items show a beginning point from which to isolate engine starting problems.

Engine Fails to Start

Perform the following spark test to determine if the ignition system is operating properly.

1. Remove one of the spark plugs.
2. Connect the spark plug wire and connector to the spark plug and touch the spark plug base to a good ground such as the engine cylinder head (**Figure 6**). Position the spark plug so you can see the electrodes.
3. Crank the engine over with the starter. A fat blue spark should be evident across the spark plug electrodes.

> *WARNING*
> *Do not hold the spark plug, wire or connector or a serious electrical shock may result. If necessary, use a pair of insulated pliers to hold the spark plug or wire. The high voltage generated by the ignition system could produce serious or fatal shocks.*

4. If the spark is good, check for one or more of the following possible malfunctions:
   a. Obstructed fuel line or fuel filter.
   b. Leaking head gasket(s).
   c. Low compression.
5. If the spark is not good, check for one or more of the following:
   a. Weak ignition coil(s).
   b. Weak TCI module.
   c. Loose electrical connections.
   d. Dirty electrical connections.
   e. Loose or broken ignition coil ground wire.
   f. Broken or shorted high tension lead to the spark plug.

Engine is Difficult to Start

Check for one or more of the following possible malfunctions:
   a. Fouled spark plug(s).
   b. Improperly adjusted choke.

   c. Contaminated fuel system.
   d. Improperly adjusted carburetor.
   e. Weak TCI module.
   f. Weak ignition coil(s).
   g. Poor compression.

Engine Will Not Crank

Check for one or more of the following possible malfunctions:
   a. Blown fuse.
   b. Discharged battery.
   c. Defective starter motor.
   d. Seized piston(s).
   e. Seized crankshaft bearings.
   f. Broken connecting rod.
   g. Locked-up transmission or clutch assembly.

ENGINE PERFORMANCE

In the following check list, it is assumed that the engine runs, but is not operating at peak performance. This will serve as a starting point from which to isolate a performance malfunction.

The possible causes for each malfunction are listed in a logical sequence and in order of probability.

Engine Will Not Idle

   a. Carburetor incorrectly adjusted.
   b. Fouled or improperly gapped spark plug(s).
   c. Leaking head gasket(s).
   d. Obstructed fuel line or fuel shutoff valve.
   e. Obstructed fuel filter on XV1000 and XV1100 models.
   f. Ignition timing incorrect.
   g. Valve clearance incorrect.

Engine Misses at High Speed

   a. Fouled or improperly gapped spark plugs.
   b. Improper carburetor main jet selection.
   c. Ignition timing incorrect.
   d. Weak ignition coil(s).
   e. Obstructed fuel line or fuel shutoff valve.
   f. Obstructed fuel filter on XV1000 and XV1100 models.
   g. Clogged jets in carburetors.

Engine Overheating

   a. Incorrect carburetor adjustment or jet selection.

b. Ignition timing incorrect.

c. Improper spark plug heat range.

d. Damaged or blocked cooling fins.

Smoky Exhaust and Engine Runs Roughly

a. Clogged air filter element.

b. Carburetor adjustment incorrect (mixture too rich).

c. Choke not operating correctly.

d. Water or other contaminants in fuel.

e. Clogged fuel line.

f. Clogged fuel filter on XV1000 or XV1100 models.

Engine Loses Power

a. Carburetor incorrectly adjusted.

b. Engine overheating.

c. Ignition timing incorrect.

d. Incorrectly gapped spark plugs.

e. Obstructed muffler.

f. Dragging brake(s).

Engine Lacks Acceleration

a. Carburetor mixture too lean.

b. Clogged fuel line.

c. Clogged fuel filter on XV1000 and XV1100 models.

d. Ignition timing incorrect.

e. Improper valve clearance.

f. Dragging brake(s).

ENGINE NOISES

1. *Knocking or pinging during acceleration—* Caused by using a lower octane fuel than recommended. May also be caused by poor fuel. Pinging can also be caused by a spark plug of the wrong heat range. Refer to *Spark Plug Selection* in Chapter Three.

2. *Slapping or rattling noises at low speed or during acceleration—*May be caused by piston slap (excessive piston-cylinder wall clearance).

3. *Knocking or rapping while decelerating—* Usually caused by excessive rod bearing clearance. bearing clearance.

4. *Persistent knocking and vibration—*Usually caused by worn main bearing(s).

5. *Rapid on-off squeal—*Compression leak around cylinder head gasket(s) or spark plugs.

EXCESSIVE VIBRATION

This can be difficult to find without disassembling the engine. Usually this is caused by loose engine mounting hardware. High-speed vibration may be due to a bent axle shaft or loose or faulty suspension components.

CLUTCH

The three basic clutch troubles are:

a. Clutch noise.

b. Clutch slipping.

c. Improper clutch disengagement.

All clutch troubles, except adjustments, require partial engine disassembly to identify and cure the problem. Refer to Chapter Five for procedures.

TRANSMISSION

The basic transmission troubles are:

a. Excessive gear noise.

b. Difficult shifting.

c. Gears pop out of mesh.

d. Incorrect shift lever operation.

Transmission symptoms are sometimes hard to distinguish from clutch symptoms. Be sure that the clutch is not causing the trouble before working on the transmission.

FRONT SUSPENSION AND STEERING

Poor handling may be caused by improper tire pressure, a damaged or bent frame or front steering components, worn wheel bearings or dragging brakes.

BRAKE PROBLEMS

Sticking disc brakes may be caused by a stuck piston(s) in a caliper assembly or warped pad shim(s).

A sticking drum brake may be caused by worn or weak return springs, dry pivot and cam bushings or improper adjustment. Grabbing brakes may be caused by greasy linings which must be replaced. Brake grab may also be due to an out-of-round drum. Glazed linings will cause loss of stopping power.

ELECTRICAL PROBLEMS

Rapid failure of bulbs may be caused by excessive vibration, loose connections that permit sudden current surges, or the installation of the wrong type of bulb.

The majority of light and ignition problems are caused by loose or corroded ground connections. Check these first prior to replacing a bulb or electrical component.

IGNITION SYSTEM

All models are equipped with a Transistor Controlled Ignition (TCI) system. This solid state system uses no contact breaker points or other moving parts. Because of the solid state design, problems with the ignition system are relatively few.

Refer to Chapter Seven for ignition system troubleshooting procedures.

CHAPTER THREE

LUBRICATION, MAINTENANCE AND TUNE-UP

Your bike can be cared for by two methods: preventive or corrective maintenance. Because a motorcycle is subjected to tremendous heat, stress and vibration (even in normal use), preventive maintenance prevents costly and unexpected corrective maintenance. When neglected, any bike becomes unreliable and actually dangerous to ride. When properly maintained, the Yamaha XV is one of the most reliable bikes available and will give many miles and years of dependable, fast and safe riding. By maintaining a routine service schedule as described in this chapter, costly mechanical problems and unexpected breakdowns can be prevented.

The procedures presented in this chapter can be easily performed by anyone with average mechanical skills. **Table 1** presents a factory recommended maintenance schedule. **Tables 1-6** are at the end of the chapter.

ROUTINE CHECKS

The following simple checks should be carried out at each fuel stop.

Engine Oil Level

Refer to *Engine Oil Level Check* under *Lubrication* in this chapter.

General Inspection

1. Quickly examine the engine for signs of oil or fuel leakage.
2. Check the tires for imbedded stones. Pry them out with a small screwdriver.
3. Make sure all lights work.

NOTE
At least check the brake light. It can burn out anytime. Motorists can not stop as quickly as you and need all the warning you can give.

Tire Pressure

Tire pressure must be checked with the tires cold. Correct tire pressure depends on the load you are carrying. See **Table 2**.

Battery

Remove the right-hand side cover and check the battery electrolyte level. The level must be between the upper and lower level marks on the case (**Figure 1**).

NOTE
*On 1984-on models, it is necessary to remove the battery (**Figure 2**) to check the electrolyte level.*

For complete details see *Battery Removal/Installation and Electrolyte Level Check* in this chapter.

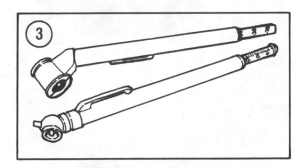

Lights and Horn

With the engine running, check the following.
1. Pull the front brake lever and check that the brake light comes on.
2. Push the rear brake pedal and check that the brake light comes on soon after you have begun depressing the pedal.
3. With the engine running, check to see that the headlight and taillight are on.
4. Move the dimmer switch up and down between the high and low positions and check to see that both headlight elements are working.
5. Push the turn signal switch to the left position and the right position and check that all 4 turn signal lights are working.
6. Push the horn button and note that the horn blows loudly.
7. If the horn or any light failed to work properly, refer to Chapter Seven.

MAINTENANCE INTERVALS

The services and intervals shown in **Table 1** are recommended by the factory. Strict adherence to these recommendations will ensure long life from your Yamaha. If the bike is run in an area of high humidity, the lubrication services must be done more frequently to prevent possible rust damage.

For convenient maintenance of your motorcycle, most of the services shown in **Table 1** are described in this chapter. Those procedures which require more than minor disassembly or adjustment are covered elsewhere in the appropriate chapter. The *Table of Contents* and *Index* can help you locate a particular service procedure.

TIRES AND WHEELS

Tire Pressure

Tire pressure should be checked and adjusted to accommodate rider and luggage weight. A simple, accurate gauge (**Figure 3**) can be purchased for a few dollars and should be carried in your motorcycle tool kit. The appropriate tire pressures are shown in **Table 2**.

NOTE
*After checking and adjusting the air pressure, make sure to reinstall the air valve cap (**Figure 4**). The cap prevents small pebbles or dirt from collecting in the valve stem, allowing air leakage or resulting in incorrect tire pressure readings.*

Tire Inspection

Check tire tread for excessive wear, deep cuts, imbedded objects such as stones, nails, etc. If you find a nail in a tire, mark its location with a light crayon before pulling it out. This will help locate the hole for repair. Refer to Chapter Eight for tire changing and repair information.

Check local traffic regulations concerning minimum tread depth. Measure with a tread depth gauge (**Figure 5**) or small ruler. Yamaha recommends replacement when the tread depth is 5/16 in. (0.8 mm) or less. Tread depth indicators appear across the tire when tread reaches minimum safe depth. Replace the tire at this point.

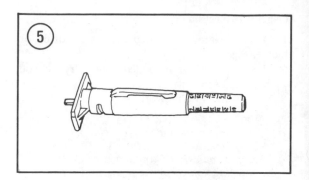

Wheel Spoke Tension

On wire wheels, tap each spoke with a wrench. The higher the pitch of sound it makes, the tighter the spoke. The lower the sound frequency, the looser the spoke. A "ping" is good; a "klunk" says the spoke is loose.

If one or more spokes are loose, tighten them as described in Chapter Eight.

Rim Inspection

Frequently inspect the wheel rims. If a rim has been damaged it might have been knocked out of alignment. Improper wheel alignment can cause severe vibration and result in an unsafe riding condition. If the rim portion of an alloy wheel is damaged the wheel must be replaced as it cannot be repaired.

BATTERY

CAUTION
*If it becomes necessary to remove the battery breather tube when performing any of the following procedures, make sure to route the tube correctly during installation to prevent acid from spilling on parts. Refer to the battery installation label fastened to one of the side covers (**Figure 6**).*

Removal/Installation and Electrolyte Level Check

The battery is the heart of the electrical system. It should be checked and serviced as indicated (**Table 1**). The majority of electrical system troubles can be attributed to neglect of this vital component.

In order to correctly service the electrolyte level it is necessary to remove the battery from the frame. The electrolyte level should be maintained

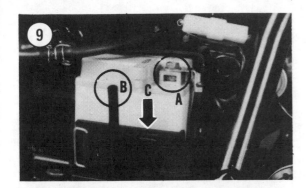

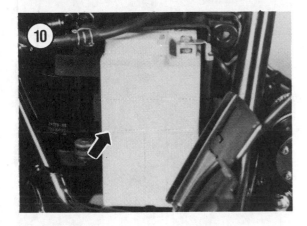

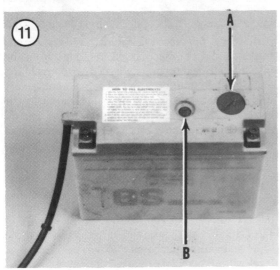

between the two marks on the battery case (**Figure 1**). If the electrolyte level is low, it's a good idea to completely remove the battery so that it can be thoroughly cleaned, serviced, and checked.

1. Remove the right-hand side cover.

2A. *1981-1983:*

   a. Disconnect the negative battery cable from the battery (A, **Figure 7**).

   b. Disconnect the positive battery cable.

   c. Remove the top battery cover (B, **Figure 7**).

   d. Disconnect the battery vent tube (**Figure 8**).

   e. Lift the battery out of the battery box and remove it.

2B. *1984-on:*

   a. Disconnect the negative battery cable from the battery (A, **Figure 9**).

   b. Disconnect the battery vent tube (B, **Figure 9**).

   c. Disconnect the battery hold-down strap (C, **Figure 9**) and slide the battery partway out of the box (**Figure 10**).

   d. Disconnect the positive battery cable.

   e. Remove the battery.

> *WARNING*
> *Protect your eyes, skin and clothing. If electrolyte gets into your eyes, flush your eyes thoroughly with clean water and get prompt medical attention.*

> *CAUTION*
> *Be careful not to spill battery electrolyte on painted or polished surfaces. The liquid is highly corrosive and will damage the finish. If it is spilled, wash it off immediately with soapy water and thoroughly rinse with clean water.*

3. Remove the caps from the battery cells and add distilled water. Never add electrolyte (acid) to correct the level. Some models have been equipped with a long-life type battery that uses a single filling plug (A, **Figure 11**). When filling the battery on these models, each cell will fill automatically. On all models, fill only to the upper battery level mark.

4. After the level has been corrected and the battery allowed to stand for a few minutes, check the specific gravity of the electrolyte in each cell with a hydrometer (**Figure 12**). On models equipped with the long-life battery, check the specific gravity through the single fill hole (A, **Figure 11**). See *Battery Testing* in this chapter.

5. After the battery has been refilled, recharged or replaced, install it by reversing these removal steps.

Testing

Hydrometer testing is the best way to check battery condition. Use a hydrometer with numbered graduations from 1.100 to 1.300 rather than one with color-coded bands. To use the hydrometer, squeeze the rubber ball, insert the tip into the cell and release the ball. Draw enough electrolyte to float the weighted float inside the hydrometer. Note the number in line with the electrolyte surface; this is the specific gravity for this cell. Return the electrolyte to the cell from which it came.

The specific gravity of the electrolyte in each battery cell is an excellent indication of that cell's condition (**Table 3**). A fully charged cell will read 1.275-1.280; a cell in good condition reads from 1.225-1.250; anything below 1.120 is practically dead.

> *NOTE*
> *Specific gravity varies with temperature. For each 10° that electrolyte temperature exceeds 80° F, add 0.004 to reading indicated on hydrometer. Subtract 0.004 for each 10° below 80° F.*

If the cells test in the poor range, the battery requires recharging. The hydrometer is useful for checking the progress of the charging operation. **Table 3** shows approximate state of charge.

Charging

> *WARNING*
> *During charging, highly explosive hydrogen gas is released from the battery. The battery should be charged only in a well-ventilated area, and open flames and cigarettes should be kept away. Never check the charge of the battery by arcing across the terminals; the resulting spark can ignite the hydrogen gas.*

> *CAUTION*
> *Always remove the battery from the motorcycle before connecting charging equipment.*

A typical battery charger for motorcycles is shown in **Figure 13**.

1. Connect the positive (+) charger lead to the positive battery terminal and the negative (-) charger lead to the negative battery terminal.
2. Remove all vent caps from the battery, set the charger at 12 volts and switch it on. If the output of the charger is variable, it is best to select a low setting—1 1/2 to 2 amps.

> *CAUTION*
> *The electrolyte level must be maintained at the upper level during the charging cycle; check and refill as necessary.*

3. After battery has been charged for about 8 hours, turn the charger off, disconnect the leads and check the specific gravity. It should be within the limits specified in **Table 3**. If it is, and remains stable for one hour, the battery is charged.
4. To ensure good electrical contact, cables must be clean and tight on the battery's terminals. If the

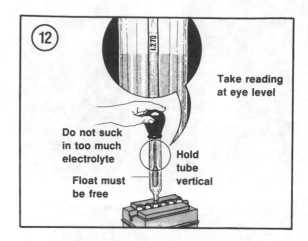

cable terminals are badly corroded, even after performing the above cleaning procedures, the cables should be disconnected, removed from the bike and cleaned separately with a wire brush and a baking soda solution. After cleaning, apply a very thin coating of petroleum jelly (Vaseline) to the battery terminals before reattaching the cables. After connecting the cables, apply a light coating to the connections also—this will delay future corrosion.

New Battery Installation

When replacing the old battery with a new one, be sure to charge it completely (specific gravity of 1.260-1.280) before installing it in the bike. Failure to do so or using the battery with a low electrolyte level will permanently damage the battery.

Battery Sensor Cleaning

Every 3,000 miles (5,000 km) the battery sensor (B, **Figure 11**) on XV920J models should be removed and cleaned of all corrosion to prevent microcomputer system malfunction.

LUBRICATION

Refer to **Figure 14** for major lubrication points.

LUBRICATION POINTS

1. Front wheel bearings
2. Steering head bearings
3. Control cables
4. Final drive unit splines
5. Front axle
6. Front forks
7. Speedometer cable
8. Engine oil
9. Side and center stand pivots
10. Swingarm
11. Final drive
    (Note: Drive chain Non XV920RH & RJ models)
12. Rear wheel bearing

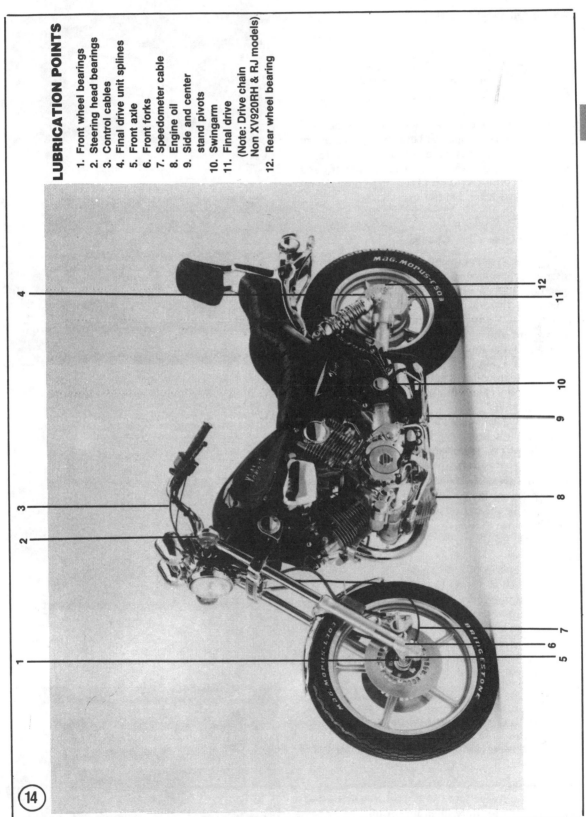

Engine Oil Level Check

Engine oil level is checked through the inspection window located at the bottom of the crankcase cover on the left-hand side (**Figure 15**).

1. Place the bike on the centerstand. Start the engine and let it reach normal operating temperature.

2. Stop the engine and allow the oil to settle.

3. The oil level should be between the maximum and minimum marks on the window (**Figure 15**). If necessary, remove the oil fill cap (**Figure 16**) and add the recommended oil (**Table 4**) to raise the oil to the proper level. Do not overfill.

Engine Oil and Filter Change

The factory-recommended oil and filter change interval is specified in **Table 1**. This assumes that the motorcyle is operated in moderate climates. The time interval is more important than the mileage interval because combustion acids, formed by gasoline and water vapor, will contaminate the oil even if the motorcycle is not run for several months. If a motorcycle is operated under dusty conditions, the oil will get dirty more quickly and should be changed more frequently than recommended.

Use only a detergent oil with an API rating of SE or SF. The quality rating is stamped on top of the can (**Figure 17**). Try always to use the same brand of oil. Use of oil additives is not recommended. Refer to **Table 4** for correct viscosity of oil to use under different temperatures.

To change the engine oil and filter you will need the following:

a. Drain pan.
b. Funnel.
c. Can opener or pour spout.
d. Wrench or socket to remove drain plug.
e. 4 quarts of oil.
f. Oil filter element.

There are a number of ways to discard the used oil safely. The easiest way is to pour it from the drain pan into a gallon plastic bleach, juice or milk container for disposal.

> *NOTE*
> *Some service stations and oil retailers will accept your used oil for recycling. Check local regulations before discarding the oil in your household trash.*

1. Place the motorcycle on the centerstand.
2. Start the engine and run it until it is at normal operating temperature, then turn it off.

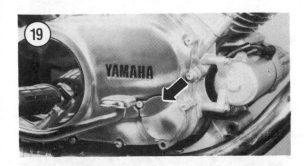

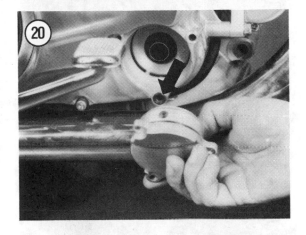

3. Place a drip pan under the crankcase and remove the drain plug (**Figure 18**). Remove the oil filler cap (**Figure 16**); this will speed up the flow of oil.

4. Allow the oil to drain for at least 15-20 minutes.

NOTE
Before removing the oil filter cover, thoroughly clean off all dirt and oil around it.

5. To remove the oil filter, unscrew the bolts securing the filter cover (**Figure 19**) to the crankcase.

CAUTION
*When removing the bottom oil filter cover bolt, make sure to completely unscrew the bolt all the way. If the bolt is pulled out, its threads may damage the O-ring (**Figure 20**) in the crankcase.*

6. Remove the cover and the filter (**Figure 21**). Discard the oil filter and clean out the cover and filter housing with cleaning solvent. Dry parts thoroughly.

7. Inspect the O-ring in the cover (**Figure 22**) and in the crankcase (**Figure 20**). Replace if necessary.

NOTE
Prior to installing the cover, clean off the mating surface of the crankcase—do not allow any dirt to enter the oil system.

8. Install the new oil filter.

9. Reinstall the filter cover to the crankcase and tighten the bolts securely. Install the drain plug and gasket and tighten to 31 ft.-lb. (43 N•m).

10. Fill the crankcase with the correct viscosity (**Table 4**) and quantity (**Table 5**) of oil.

11. Screw in the oil fill cap securely.

12. Check the engine oil pressure as described in this chapter.

13. After completing Step 12, start the engine and allow it to idle. Check for leaks.

14. Turn the engine off and check for correct oil level (**Figure 15**); adjust if necessary.

Engine Oil Pressure Check

This procedure should be performed whenever the engine oil is changed.

1. Slightly loosen an engine oil line union bolt at one of the cylinders; it does not matter which line or which cylinder. See **Figure 23**.

2. Start the engine and allow it to idle.

3. Observe the loosened oil line union bolt. Oil should seep from the bolt within one minute of starting the engine. If oil does not seep out after

one minute, stop the engine and locate the problem.

4. After completing the oil pressure check, tighten the oil line union bolt.

Front Fork Oil Change

To gain access to the fork caps, it is necessary to partially remove the handlebar assembly. The following procedure requires two persons.

1981-1983 XV750 (except Midnight Virago) and 1981-1982 XV920RH, RJ (chain-driven) models

1. Place the bike on the centerstand and disconnect the negative battery cable from the battery.
2. Remove the rear view mirrors.
3. Remove the fuel tank as described in Chapter Six.
4. Except XV920RH and XV920RJ—Using a small screwdriver, carefully pry the plastic emblem (A, **Figure 24**) from the handlebar cover. Remove the screw under the plastic emblem and remove the handlebar cover (B, **Figure 24**).
5. Remove the handlebar clamp bolts and remove the clamps (**Figure 25**). Lay the handlebar assembly aside without disconnecting any cables.
6. Unscrew and remove the plastic cap from the top of the fork tube.
7. Depress the valve stem (**Figure 26**) with a small screwdriver to release all air from the fork tube.
8. Loosen the top fork tube pinch bolt (**Figure 26**).
9. The spring seat and spring are secured in place with a wire stopper ring (**Figure 27**). To remove the wire stopper ring, have an assistant depress the spring seat (A, **Figure 28**) using a suitable punch or drift. Then pry the wire stopper ring (B, **Figure 28**) out of its groove in the fork with a small screwdriver. When the wire ring is removed, release tension from the spring seat and remove it together with the fork spring.
10. Place a suitable drain pan under the fork and remove the drain screw (**Figure 29**). Allow the fork oil to drain for at least 5 minutes.

> *WARNING*
> *Do not allow the fork oil to come in contact with any of the brake components.*

11. With both of the bike's wheels on the ground, have an assistant steady the bike. Then push the front end down and allow it to return. Perform this procedure until all the fork oil is expelled from the fork tube.
12. Install the drain screw (**Figure 29**).

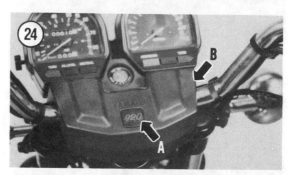

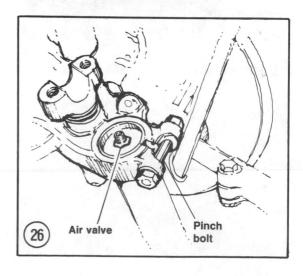

26 Air valve   Pinch bolt

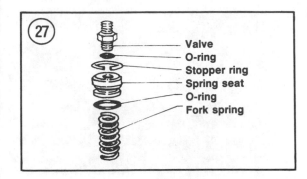

27

— Valve
— O-ring
— Stopper ring
— Spring seat
— O-ring
— Fork spring

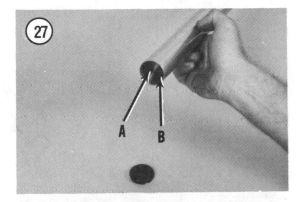

27

A   B

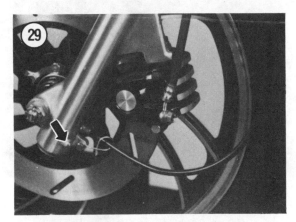

29

30

13. Fill the fork tube with the recommended oil (**Table 4**) in the correct amount (**Table 5**). Slowly pump the fork up and down to distribute the oil.

> NOTE
> *Use a baby bottle to measure the correct amount of fork oil. Baby bottles are incremented in fluid ounces (fl. oz.) and cubic centimeters (cc).*

14. Install the fork spring and spring seat. Have an assistant compress the spring seat and install a *new* wire stopper ring. Make sure the wire ring seats fully in its groove in the fork tube before releasing the spring seat.

15. Repeat Steps 6-14 for the opposite fork tube assembly.

16. Install the handlebar assembly and tighten the clamp bolts securely.

> NOTE
> *If the handlebar clamps have arrows stamped on them, the arrows must face toward the front of the bike.*

17. Fill the forks with air as described in Chapter Eleven.

18. Install all remaining components removed during disassembly.

19. Road test the bike, then check for oil and air leakage.

XV700, 1983 XV750 Midnight Virago, 1988-on XV750, 1983 XV920, 1983 XV920 Midnight Virago, XV1000 and XV1100

1. Place the bike on the centerstand and disconnect the negative battery cable from the battery.

2. Remove the rear view mirrors.

3. Remove the fuel tank as described in Chapter Six.

4. Remove the handlebar clamps (A, **Figure 30**). Lay the handlebar assembly aside without disconnecting any cables.

5. On XV750MK and XV920K and MK, carefully pry the plastic emblem (A, **Figure 24**) from the handlebar cover using a small screwdriver. Remove the screw under the plastic emblem and remove the handlebar cover (B, **Figure 24**).

6. Using a small screwdriver, carefully pry the cap (B, **Figure 30**) from the top of the fork tube.

7. If so equipped, remove the air valve cap and depress the valve stem (**Figure 31**) with a small screwdriver to release all air from the fork tube.

8. Loosen the top fork tube pinch tube bolt (A, **Figure 32**).

3

9. On XV750MK and XV920K and MK models, loosen the fork cap with a wrench and remove it. On all other models loosen the fork cap (B, **Figure 32**) with a 17 mm Allen wrench and remove it.

NOTE
If a 17 mm Allen wrench is not available, use a bolt with a 17 mm head and locking pliers as shown in **Figure 33**.

10. Place a suitable drain pan under the fork and remove the drain screw (**Figure 29**). Allow the fork oil to drain for at least 5 minutes.

WARNING
Do not allow the fork oil to come in contact with any of the brake components.

11. With both of the bike's wheels on the ground, have an assistant steady the bike. Then push the front end down and allow it to return. Perform this procedure until all the oil is expelled from the fork tube.

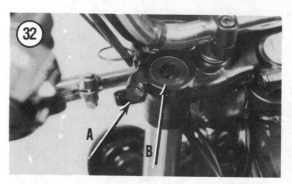

12. Reinstall the drain screw (**Figure 29**).
13. Fill the fork tube with the recommended oil (**Table 4**) in the correct amount (**Table 5**). Slowly pump the fork up and down to distribute the oil.

NOTE
Use a baby bottle to measure the correct amount of fork oil. Baby bottles are incremented in fluid ounces (fl. oz.) and cubic centimeters (cc).

14. Install the fork spring and fork cap. Tighten the fork cap securely.
15. Repeat Steps 6-14 to change the oil in the opposite fork assembly.
16. Install the handlebar assembly and tighten the clamp bolts securely.

NOTE
If the handlebar clamps have arrows stamped on them, the arrows must face toward the front of the bike.

17. On models equipped air-adjustable forks, fill the forks with air as described in Chapter Eleven. *Do not* exceed the maximum recommended air pressure in the forks.
18. Install all remaining components removed during disassembly.
19. Road test the bike, then check for oil and air leakage.

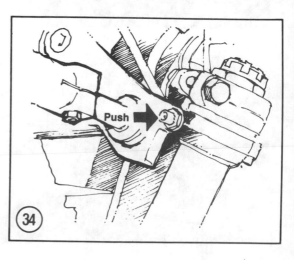

XV920J (1982 Shaft-drive)

1. Place the bike on the centerstand and disconnect the negative battery lead.
2. Remove the rear view mirrors.
3. Remove the fuel tank as described in Chapter Six.
4. Remove the master cylinder. See Chapter Ten.
5. Remove the center handlebar cover.
6. Remove the handlebar assembly as described in Chapter Eight.
7. Remove the air valve cap from the left fork tube. Use a screwdriver to depress the valve stem and release the air pressure from both fork tubes. See **Figure 34**.
8. Turn the adjuster cover (**Figure 35**) to the No. 1 position.
9. Loosen the fork tube cap pinch bolt.
10. Remove the fork tube cap.

CAUTION
*The fork tube cap is fitted with a damper adjustment rod (**Figure 36**). When handling the fork cap, make sure not to bend or damage the rod in any way as this will cause improper fork operation.*

11. Place a drip pan under the fork and remove the drain screw (**Figure 29**). Allow the oil to drain for at least 5 minutes.

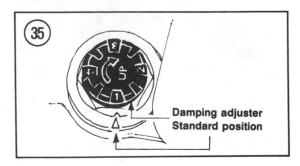

(35) Damping adjuster
Standard position

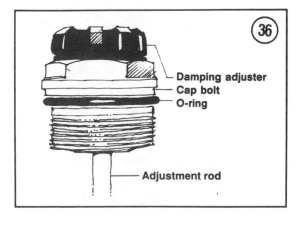

(36) Damping adjuster
Cap bolt
O-ring

Adjustment rod

WARNING
Do not allow the fork oil to come in contact with any of the brake components.

12. With both of the bike's wheels on the ground, have an assistant steady the bike. Then push the front end down and allow it to return. Perform this procedure until all the oil is expelled from the fork tube.
13. Install the drain screw.
14. Fill the fork tube with the correct amount (**Table 5**) and viscosity (**Table 4**) of fork oil.

NOTE
In order to measure the correct amount of fluid, use a baby bottle. These bottles have measurements in fluid ounces (oz.) and cubic centimeters (cc) imprinted on the side.

15. Insert the end of the cap/rod assembly into the semicircular hole in the top of the damper rod. Push the fork cap down and screw the cap on. Tighten to 22 ft.-lb. (30 N•m).

CAUTION
Do not force the cap/rod assembly during installation or when tightening the cap or you may damage it. If the cap/rod is not inserted into the top of the damper rod correctly, the cap/rod will protrude too far out of the fork tube. The cap/rod is inserted into the damper rod correctly when the cap/rod sits on the fork tube collar.

16. Repeat Steps 8-15 for the opposite fork.
17. Fill the forks with air as described in Chapter Eleven.
18. Install and adjust the handlebar position as described in Chapter Eight.
19. Install all components that were removed.

Final Drive Oil Level Check

Final drive gear oil must be checked when the engine is cold. If the bike has been run, allow it to cool down. When checking and changing the final drive gear oil, do not allow any dirt or foreign matter to enter the gear case opening.

1. Place the bike on the centerstand on a level surface.
2. Wipe the area around the filler cap clean and unscrew the cap (A, **Figure 37**).
3. The oil level should be at the bottom of the filler cap hole.
4. If the oil level is low, refill with the correct gear oil specified in **Table 4**.
5. Install the filler cap and tighten it securely.

Final Drive Gear Oil Change

The factory-recommended oil change interval is specified in **Table 1**.

To drain the oil you will need:

a. Drain pan.

b. Funnel.

c. Adjustable wrench.

d. One quart of gear oil (refer to **Table 4**).

Discard old oil in the same manner as outlined under *Engine Oil and Filter Change* in this chapter.

1. Place the bike on the centerstand.

2. Place a drain pan under the final drive gear housing drain plug.

3. Wipe the area around the drain plug clean of all road dirt and remove the drain plug (B, **Figure 37**). Loosen the filler cap (A, **Figure 37**) as this will speed up the flow of oil.

4. Allow the oil to drain for at least 10 minutes.

> *WARNING*
> *Do not allow the oil to come in contact with any of the brake components or drip onto the rear tire.*

5. Install the drain plug and tighten it securely.

6. Remove the filler cap and refill the case with the recommended amount (**Table 5**) and viscosity (**Table 4**) of oil.

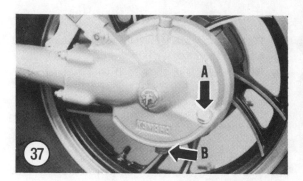

Control Cables

The control cables should be lubricated at the intervals specified in **Table 1**. At this time, they should also be inspected for fraying, and the cable sheath should be checked for chafing. The cables are relatively inexpensive and should be replaced when found to be faulty.

They can be lubricated with a cable lubricant and a cable lubricator or with a funnel and oil. The second method requires more time and the complete lubrication of the entire cable is less certain.

> *NOTE*
> *The main cause of cable breakage or cable stiffness is improper lubrication. Maintaining the cables as described here will assure long service life.*

Lubricator method

1. Disconnect the clutch (A, **Figure 38**) and choke (B, **Figure 38**) cables from the left-hand handlebar. Disconnect the throttle cable from the throttle grip (**Figure 39**).

> *NOTE*
> *It is necessary to remove the screws that clamp the housing together to gain access to the throttle cable ends.*

2. Attach a lubricator (**Figure 40**) to the cable following the manufacturer's instructions.

3. Insert the nozzle of the lubricant can into the lubricator, press the button on the can and hold it down until the lubricant begins to flow out of the other end of the cable.

> *NOTE*
> *Place a shop cloth at the end of the cable(s) to catch all excess lubricant that will flow out.*

> *NOTE*
> *If lubricant does not flow out the end of the cable, check the entire cable for fraying, bending or other damage.*

4. Remove the lubricator. Reconnect and adjust the cable(s) as described in this chapter.

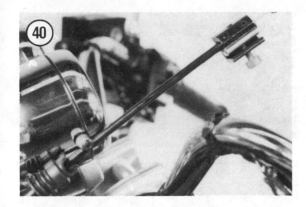

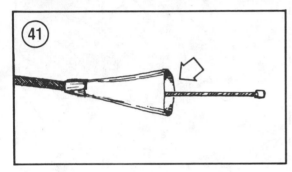

Oil method

1. Disconnect the cables as described under *Lubricator Method*.
2. Make a cone of stiff paper and tape it to the end of the cable sheath (**Figure 41**).
3. Hold the cable upright and pour a small amount of light oil (SAE 10W-30) into the cone. Work the cable in and out of the sheath for several minutes to help the oil work its way down to the end of the cable.
4. Remove the cone. Reconnect and adjust the cable(s) as described in this chapter.

Swing Arm Bearings

Repack the swing arm bearings every 10,000 miles (16,000 km) with a lithium-base, waterproof wheel bearing grease. Refer to Chapter Nine for complete details.

Rear Brake Cam Lubrication

Lubricate the brake cam whenever the rear wheel is removed (if required).
1. Remove the rear wheel as described in Chapter Nine.
2. Take out the brake backing plate.
3. Wipe away the old grease, being careful not to get any on the brake shoes.
4. Sparingly apply high-temperature grease to the camming surfaces of the camshaft, the camshaft groove, the brake shoe pivots and the ends of the springs (**Figure 42**). *Do not* get any grease on the brake shoes.

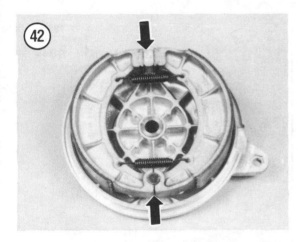

> *WARNING*
> *Use only a high-temperature brake grease. Temperatures created by braking conditions will cause other types of grease to thin and run onto the brake shoes, causing loss of rear braking power.*

5. Reassemble the rear wheel and install it. See Chapter Nine.

Speedometer Cable Lubrication

Lubricate the cable every year or whenever needle operation is erratic.
1. Remove the cable from the instrument cluster (**Figure 43**).
2. Pull the cable from the sheath.
3. If the grease is contaminated, thoroughly clean off all old grease.
4. Thoroughly coat the cable with a good grade of multi-purpose grease and reinstall into the sheath.

5. Make sure the cable is correctly seated into the drive unit.

NOTE
*If the cable won't seat into the drive unit, disconnect the sheath at its lower connection (**Figure 44**). Install the cable end into the drive unit, then reconnect the sheath.*

MAINTENANCE

Maintenance intervals are listed in **Table 1**.

Drive Chain
(XV920RH, RJ Models)

Inspection/Replacement

The drive chain on these models is completely enclosed in a special housing (**Figure 45**). Procedures commonly used to check drive chain wear cannot be used on these models. Instead, Yamaha recommends that the drive chain be replaced every 30,000 miles (50,000 km) or whenever abnormal noise or vibration occurs after adjusting the drive chain. The drive chain should always be replaced when all of the swing arm-to-drive chain adjustment is used up. Drive chain replacement is described in Chapter Nine.

Tension
Check/Adjustment

The drive chain tension should be checked and adjusted at the intervals specified in **Table 1**. When performing this adjustment, keep in mind that proper chain adjustment requires correct chain free play and alignment.

1. Place the bike on the centerstand and shift the transmission to NEUTRAL.
2. Remove the chain inspection cap (**Figure 45**) from the chain case.
3. Referring to **Figure 46**, check the drive chain tension by pushing the chain up and down. The tension is correct if the chain link pins do not go below or above the limit marks on the chain case. Correct free play is 1/4-7/16 in. (7-10 mm). If incorrect, proceed to Step 4.
4. Loosen the chain case holding bolts.
5. Remove the rear axle cotter pin. Loosen the axle nut and the chain adjusting locknuts (**Figure 47**).
6. Screw the adjusters (**Figure 47**) either in or out as required in equal amounts until the free play is as specified in Step 3.

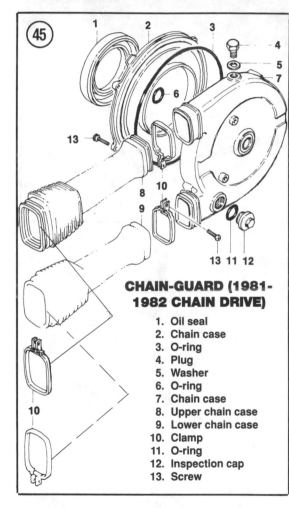

CHAIN-GUARD (1981-1982 CHAIN DRIVE)

1. Oil seal
2. Chain case
3. O-ring
4. Plug
5. Washer
6. O-ring
7. Chain case
8. Upper chain case
9. Lower chain case
10. Clamp
11. O-ring
12. Inspection cap
13. Screw

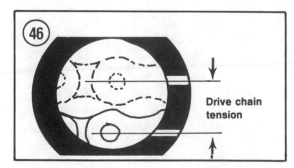

Drive chain tension

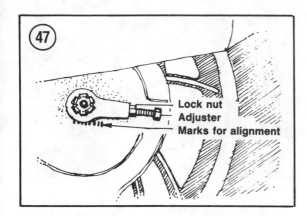

Lock nut
Adjuster
Marks for alignment

CAUTION
When performing the adjustment in Step 6, turn the left- and right-hand side adjusters the same amount to maintain correct axle alignment. If alignment is not maintained, rapid chain and sprocket wear will result. If alignment is correct but excessive chain and/or sprocket wear is experienced, the swing arm should be checked by a dealer or specialist for twisting or damage.

7. Tighten the adjuster locknuts and axle nut securely. Torque the axle nut to 77 ft.-lb. (105 N·m).

NOTE
Always install a new cotter pin—never reuse an old one.

8. Reinstall the drive chain inspection cap.
9. After adjusting the drive chain, adjust the rear brake pedal free play as described in this chapter.

Lubrication

Because the drive chain operates in a closed case, initial lubrication is provided at the factory. It is only necessary to replace the drive chain lubricant under the following circumatances:

a. The drive chain is replaced.
b. The drive chain case is disassembled.
To replenish the chain lubricant, remove the grease filler plug on the chain case and refill with the correct quantity (**Table 5**) and type (**Table 4**) of grease. Reinstall the filler plug.

Disc Brake Fluid Level

On models without a computerized monitor system, you must visually check the fluid level in the reservoir (**Figure 48**). On models with a computerized monitor system, the brake fluid level is automatically monitored by the system. If the brake fluid is low, the system will warn you by flashing the BRK light on the instrument panel. This light will remain on during engine operation until the brake fluid is brought to the correct level. If the BRK light should come on, the brake fluid level is low and should be serviced immediately.

The fluid level in the reservoir should be maintained above the lower level line (**Figure 48**). If necessary, correct the level by adding fresh brake fluid. Remove the cover screws and cover and lift the diaphragm out of the housing. Add fluid to bring the level above the lower level line. Reinstall the diaphragm and cover. Tighten the cover screws.

WARNING
Use brake fluid clearly marked DOT 3 only and specified for disc brakes. Others may vaporize and cause brake failure.

CAUTION
Be careful not to spill brake fluid on painted or plated surfaces as it will destroy the surface. Wash immediately with soapy water and thoroughly rinse it off.

If the brake fluid was so low as to allow air in the hydraulic system, the brakes will have to be bled. Refer to Chapter Ten.

Disc Brake Lines and Seals

Check brake lines between the master cylinder and the brake caliper. If there is any leakage, tighten the connections and bleed the brakes as described in Chapter Ten. If this does not stop the leak or if a line is obviously damaged, cracked or chafed, replace the line and seals and bleed the brake. Always replace the brake seals every two years; replace brake hoses every four years.

Disc Brake Pad Wear

Inspect the brake pads for excessive or uneven wear, scoring and oil or grease on the friction surface.

If any of these conditions exist, replace the pads as described in Chapter Ten.

NOTE
Always replace both pad sets (left and right sides) at the same time.

XV920RH and RJ

On these models, an inspection window is installed on the rear of each caliper housing. To inspect, flip the window cover open and observe the red wear line on each pad. If the pads are worn to the red line, they must be replaced.

All other models

On these models, each brake pad is fitted with a wear indicator tab (**Figure 49**). When the brake pads are new, the tabs are positioned well away from the brake disc. As the pads wear, the tabs are brought closer to the brake disc. When the tabs are very close to contacting the brake disc, the brake pads must be replaced as a set.

Disc Brake Fluid Change

Every time you remove the reservoir cap a small amount of dirt and moisture enters the brake fluid. The same thing happens if a leak occurs or any part of the hydraulic system is loosened or disconnected. Dirt can clog the system and cause unnecessary wear. Water in the fluid vaporizes at high temperatures, impairing the hydraulic action and reducing brake performance.

To maintain peak braking performance, change brake fluid every 10,000 miles (16,000 km) or two years, whichever comes first. To change brake fluid, follow the *Bleeding the System* procedure in Chapter Ten. Continue adding new fluid to the master cylinder and bleeding fluid out of the caliper(s) until the fluid leaving the caliper(s) is clean and free of contaminants.

WARNING
Use brake fluid clearly marked DOT 3 only. Others may vaporize and cause brake failure.

Front Brake Lever Adjustment

An adjuster is provided to maintain the front brake lever free play.

1. Loosen the rubber brake lever shield (**Figure 50**) and slide it away from the brake lever pivot.

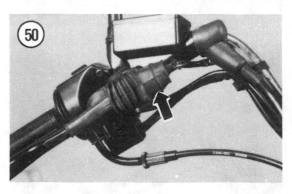

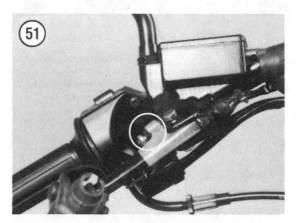

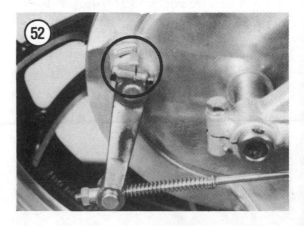

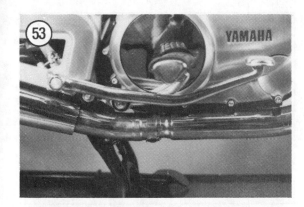

2. Loosen the adjuster locknut (**Figure 51**) and turn the adjuster (**Figure 51**) to obtain a free play measurement of 3/16-5/16 in. (5-8 mm). Tighten the locknut.

> *NOTE*
> *Free play is the distance the lever travels from the at-rest position to the applied position (the point at which the master cylinder is depressed by the lever adjuster).*

3. Rotate the front wheel and check for brake drag. Also operate the brake lever several times to make sure it returns to the at-rest position immediately after release.
4. Reposition the rubber shield.

Rear Brake Shoe Wear

Inspect the rear brake shoes for wear by depressing the brake pedal and checking the wear indicator on the brake hub (**Figure 52**). If the indicator reaches to the wear limit, replace the brake shoes as described in Chapter Ten.

Rear Brake Pedal Height Adjustment

The rear brake pedal height should be adjusted at the intervals specified in **Table 1** or anytime the brake shoes are replaced.
1. Place the motorcycle on the centerstand.
2. Check to be sure the brake pedal is in the at-rest position.
3. The correct height position below the top of the foot peg (**Figure 53**) is 3/4-1 1/4 in. (20-30 mm). To adjust, proceed to Step 4.
4. Loosen the locknut and turn the adjusting bolt to achieve the correct height. See **Figure 54** (1981-1983) or **Figure 55** (1984-on). Tighten the locknut securely and adjust the free play (described in this chapter) and brake light (described in Chapter Seven).

Rear Brake Pedal Free Play

Adjust the brake pedal to the correct height as described in this chapter. Then turn the adjustment nut on the end of the brake rod (**Figure 56**) until the brake pedal has 3/4-1 1/4 in. (20-30 mm) free play. Free play is the distance the pedal travels from the at-rest position to the applied position when the pedal is depressed lightly.

Rotate the rear wheel and check for brake drag. Also operate the pedal several times to make sure it returns to the at-rest position immediately after release.

Adjust the rear brake light switch as described in Chapter Seven.

Clutch Adjustment

The clutch cable should be adjusted to maintain a free play of 3/32-1/8 in. (2-3 mm).

1. At the hand lever, remove or slide back the clutch lever shield(s). Loosen the locknut (A, **Figure 57**) and rotate the adjuster (B, **Figure 57**) for free play adjustment (**Figure 58**).

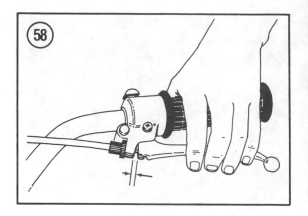

> *NOTE*
> *If sufficient free play cannot be obtained at the hand lever, additional adjustment can be made at the clutch mechanism adjuster as described in Steps 2-5.*

2. Completely loosen the clutch cable at the handlebar.

3. Remove the clutch mechanism adjuster cover (**Figure 59**).

> *NOTE*
> *When turning the adjuster in Step 4, slight resistance will be offered by an O-ring installed on the adjuster. Make sure, to turn the adjuster far enough to contact the pushrod.*

4. Loosen the adjuster locknut and turn the adjuster *clockwise* until it lightly seats against the clutch pushrod. See **Figure 60**.

5. Back out the adjuster 1/4 turn. Tighten the lock nut and install the clutch mechanism cover.

> *CAUTION*
> *Do not operate the clutch hand lever until the clutch mechanism adjustment is complete. Failure to observe this caution could cause the balls in the clutch mechanism adjuster to disengage. The adjuster would then have to be disassembled and the problem corrected.*

6. Readjust the clutch lever free play (see Step 1).

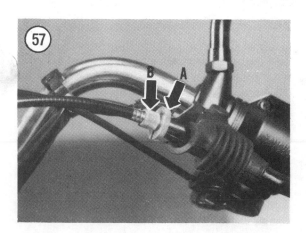

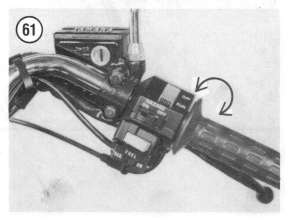

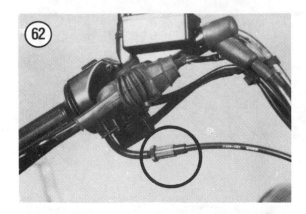

Throttle Operation/Adjustment (1981-1987)

The throttle grip should have 10-15° rotational play (**Figure 61**). Make sure there is free play in the cable so the carburetors will be able to close completely when the throttle is let off. If adjustment is necessary, loosen the cable locknut (**Figure 62**) and turn the adjuster (**Figure 62**) in or out to achieve the proper play. Tighten the locknut.

Check the throttle cable from grip to carburetors. Make sure it is not kinked or chafed. Replace it if necessary.

Make sure that the throttle grip rotates smoothly from fully closed to fully open. Check at center, full left and full right position of steering.

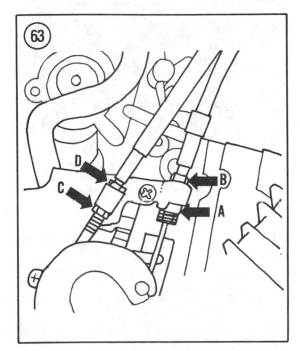

Throttle Cable Adjustment (1988-on)

The throttle should have 0.8-0.12 in. (2-3 mm) of rotational play (**Figure 61**). Make sure there is free play in the cables so the carburetors will be able to close completely when the throttle is let off. If adjustment is necessary, perform the following.

1. Remove the air cleaner as described in this chapter.
2. Loosen the front cable locknut (A, **Figure 63**) and turn the adjuster (B, **Figure 63**) in or out to achieve the proper play. Tighten the locknut (A).
3. Loosen the rear cable locknut (C, **Figure 63**) and turn the adjuster (D, **Figure 63**) in or out to achieve the proper play. Tighten the locknut (C).
4. If the correct amount of freeplay still cannot be achieved, loosen the cable adjuster locknut (A, **Figure 64**) next to the throttle grip. Turn the adjuster (B, **Figure 64**) in or out to achieve the proper play. Tighten the locknut (A).
5. Make sure all locknuts are tightened securely.
6. Check the throttle cable(s) from grip to carburetors. Make sure it is not kinked or chafed. Replace it if necessary.
7. Make sure the throttle grip rotates smoothly from fully closed to fully open. Check at center, full left and full right position of steering.
8. Install the air cleaner as described in this chapter.

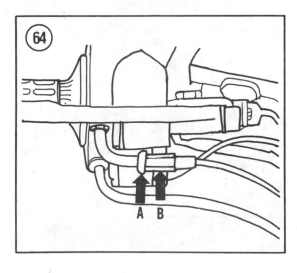

Fuel Shutoff Valve/Filter

Refer to Chapter Six for complete details on removal, cleaning and installation of the fuel shutoff valve.

Fuel Filter (1984-on XV1000 and XV1100)

Fuel filter replacement is described in Chapter Six.

Fuel and Vacuum Line Inspection

Inspect the condition of the fuel line and vacuum line for cracks or deterioration; replace if necessary. Make sure the hose clamps are in place and holding securely.

Exhaust System

Check for leakage at all fittings. Do not forget the crossover pipe connections. Tighten all bolts and nuts; replace any gaskets as necessary. Removal and installation procedures are described in Chapter Six.

Air Cleaner Removal/Installation

A clogged air cleaner can decrease the efficiency and life of the engine. Never run the bike without the air cleaner installed; even minute particles of dust can cause severe internal engine wear.

The service intervals specified in **Table 1** should be followed with general use. However, the air cleaner should be serviced more often if the bike is ridden in dusty areas.

1981-1983

1. Remove the left-hand side cover.
2. Remove the bolts securing the air filter housing to the frame (**Figure 65**). Remove the 2 housing bolt rods.
3. Remove the air filter housing (**Figure 66**).
4. Disassemble the air filter cover (A, **Figure 67**).
5. Remove the air filter (**Figure 68**).
6. Tap the element lightly to remove most of the dirt and dust then apply compressed air to the inside surface of the element.
7. Inspect the element and make sure it is in good condition. Replace if necessary.
8. Clean the inside of the air box with a shop rag and cleaning solvent. Remove any foreign matter that may have passed through a broken cleaner element.
9. Assemble the air filter housing assembly. When installing the air filter housing make sure that the rubber foam gasket (B, **Figure 67**) seats properly against the frame.
10. Install all parts previously removed.

1984-on

1. The air filter housing is shown in **Figure 69**. Remove the air housing attaching bolts and disconnect the air filter hose at the frame.

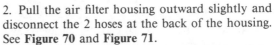

2. Pull the air filter housing outward slightly and disconnect the 2 hoses at the back of the housing. See **Figure 70** and **Figure 71**.

3. Remove the screws from the backside of the housing and remove the chrome plate and hose (**Figure 72**).

4. Remove the air filter (**Figure 73**).

5. Tap the element lightly to remove most of the dirt and dust, then apply compressed air to the inside surface of the element.

6. Inspect the element and make sure it is in good condition. Make sure the air filter sealing surface (**Figure 74**) is not torn. Replace if necessary.

7. Clean the inside of the air box with a shop rag and cleaning solvent. Remove any foreign matter that may have passed through a broken cleaner element.

8. Assemble the air filter housing assembly. When installing the air filter housing make sure that the 2 hoses (**Figure 71**) are connected to the filter housing (**Figure 70**).

Crankcase Breather Hose

Inspect the hose for cracks and deterioration and make sure that the hose clamps are tight (**Figure 75**).

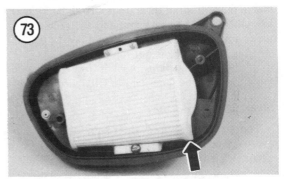

Wheel Bearings

The wheel bearings should be cleaned and repacked at the service intervals specified in **Table 1**. Refer to Chapter Eight and Chapter Nine for complete service procedures.

Starter Brushes

The starter brushes should be replaced at the intervals specified in **Table 1**. Complete service procedures are found in Chapter Seven.

Steering Play

The steering head should be checked for looseness at the intervals specified in **Table 1**.

1. Prop up the motorcycle so that the front tire clears the ground.

2. Center the front wheel. Push lightly against the left handlebar grip to start the wheel turning to the right, then let go. The wheel should continue turning under its own momentum until the forks hit their stop.

3. Center the wheel and push lightly against the right handlebar grip.

4. If, with a light push in either direction, the front wheel will turn all the way to the stop, the steering adjustment is not too tight.

5. Center the front wheel and kneel in front of it. Grasp the bottom of the 2 front fork slider legs. Try to pull the forks toward you and then try to push them toward the engine. If no play is felt, the steering adjustment is not too loose.

6. If the steering adjustment is too tight or too loose, adjust it as described in Chapter Eight.

Steering Head Bearings

The steering head bearings should be repacked every 10,000 miles (16,000 km) as described in Chapter Eight.

Front Suspension Check

1. Apply the front brake and pump the fork up and down as vigorously as possible. Check for smooth operation and check for any oil leaks.

2. Make sure the upper (**Figure 76**) and lower (**Figure 77** or **Figure 78**) fork bridge bolts are tight.

3. On XV920J models, refer to Chapter Eight for handlebar adjustment and service procedures. On all other models, check the tightness of the 4 Allen bolts (**Figure 79**) securing the handlebar.

4. Check that the front axle pinch bolt is tight (**Figure 80**).

5. Check that the front axle nut cotter pin is in place and that the axle nut is tight.

CAUTION
If any of the previously mentioned bolts and nuts are loose, refer to Chapter

*Eight for correct procedures and torque
specifications.*

Rear Suspension Check

1. Place the bike on the centerstand.
2. Push hard sideways on the rear wheel to check
for side play in the swing arm bushings or bearings.
3. Check the tightness of the upper and lower
shock absorber mounting nuts and bolts.
4. Check the tightness of the rear brake torque arm
bolts (A, **Figure 81**).

5. Make sure the rear axle nut is tight and the
cotter pin is still in place. See **Figure 82**.
6. Make sure the rear axle pinch bolt (B, **Figure 81**)
is tight.

> *CAUTION*
> *If any of the previously mentioned nuts
> or bolts are loose, refer to Chapter Nine
> for correct procedures and torque
> specifications.*

Nuts, Bolts and Other Fasteners

Constant vibration can loosen many fasteners on
a motorcycle. Check the tightness of all fasteners,
especially those on:

    a. Engine mounting hardware.
    b. Engine crankcase covers.
    c. Handlebar and front forks.
    d. Gearshift lever.
    e. Sprocket bolts and nuts (if so equipped).
    f. Final drive bolts and nuts (if so equipped).
    g. Brake pedal and lever.
    h. Exhaust system.
    i. Lighting equipment.

TUNE-UP

A complete tune-up restores performance and
power that is lost due to normal wear and
deterioration of engine parts. Because engine wear
occurs over a combined period of time and
mileage, the engine tune-up should be performed
at the intervals specified in **Table 1**. More frequent
tune-ups may be required if the bike is used
primarily in stop-and-go traffic.

Table 6 summarizes tune-up specifications.

Before starting a tune-up procedure, make sure
to first have all new parts on hand.

Because different systems in an engine interact,
the procedures should be done in the following
order:

a. Clean or replace the air cleaner element.
b. Adjust valve clearance.
c. Check engine compression.
d. Check or replace the spark plugs.
e. Check the ignition timing.
f. Synchronize carburetors and set idle speed.

To perform a tune-up on your Yamaha, you will need the following tools:
a. Spark plug wrench.
b. Socket wrench and assorted sockets.
c. Flat feeler gauge.
d. Compression gauge.
e. Spark plug wire feeler gauge and gapper tool.
f. Ignition timing light.
g. Carburetor synchronization tool (measure manifold vacuum).

Air Cleaner Element

The air cleaner element should be cleaned or replaced as described in this chapter.

Valve Clearance Adjustment

Valve clearance measurement must be made with the engine cool, at room temperature.
1. Remove the following parts:
a. Seat.
b. Fuel tank (see Chapter Six).
c. Air filter housing (as described in this chapter).
2. Disconnect the crankcase ventilation hose.
3. Remove the mixture control valve case on 1984 California models. See Chapter Six.
4. Remove the ignition (**Figure 83**) and crankshaft (**Figure 84**) covers.
5. Remove the spark plugs (this makes it easier to turn the engine by hand). See **Figure 85**.

6. Rotate the engine by turning the crankshaft *clockwise*. Use a socket on the nut located on the left-hand end of the crankshaft (**Figure 86**). Continue to rotate the crankshaft until the "T" mark for the *rear cylinder* (**Figure 87**) is aligned with the crankcase cover stationary pointer as viewed through the window in the crankcase cover.
7. Remove the intake and exhaust valve covers for both cylinders. See **Figure 88**.
8. Check that there is free play at both the intake and exhaust valve rocker arms for the rear cylinder. See **Figure 89**. If not, rotate the crankshaft 360°; recheck for free play at both rear cylinder rocker arms.

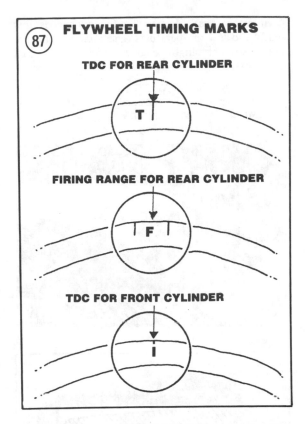

FLYWHEEL TIMING MARKS

TDC FOR REAR CYLINDER

FIRING RANGE FOR REAR CYLINDER

TDC FOR FRONT CYLINDER

9. Insert a feeler gauge between the exhaust valve rocker arm adjuster screw and the end of the valve (**Figure 90**). The clearance is correct when there is a slight drag on the feeler gauge when it is inserted and withdrawn. Repeat for the intake valve.

> *NOTE*
> *The correct valve clearance is specified in **Table 6**.*

10. To correct the clearance:
   a. Loosen the valve adjuster locknut (**Figure 90**).
   b. Turn the adjuster in or out to obtain the correct clearance.
   c. When the correct clearance is obtained, tighten the locknut and recheck the clearance.
   d. Repeat for the opposite valve.

11. Turn the crankshaft approximately 285° *clockwise* to bring the front cylinder to top dead center (TDC) on the compression stroke. Align flywheel "I" mark with the stationary pointer (**Figure 87**). Repeat Step 9 and Step 10 to adjust the front cylinder's intake and exhaust valves.

12. Install the valve, timing and crankshaft covers.

13. Install the mixture control valve on 1984 California models as described in Chapter Six.

14. Install the air filter housing as described in this chapter.

15. Install the spark plugs, fuel tank and seat.

Compression Test

At every tune-up, check cylinder compression. Record the results and compare them at the next check. A running record will show trends in deterioration so that corrective action can be taken before complete failure.

The results, when properly interpreted, can indicate general cylinder, piston ring and valve condition.

NOTE
The valves must be properly adjusted before performing a compression test.

1. Warm the engine to normal operating temperature. Ensure that the choke and throttle valves are completely open.
2. Remove the spark plugs.
3. Connect the compression tester to one cylinder following manufacturer's instructions (**Figure 91**).
4. Have an assistant crank the engine over until there is no further rise in pressure.
5. Remove the tester and record the reading.
6. Repeat Steps 3-5 for the other cylinder.
7. When interpreting the results, actual readings are not as important as the difference between the readings. Standard compression pressure is specified in **Table 6**. Pressure should not vary from cylinder to cylinder by more than 14 psi (1 kg/cm2). Greater differences indicate worn or broken rings, leaky or sticky valves, blown head gasket or a combination of all.

If compression reading does not differ between cylinders by more than 10 psi, the rings and valves are in good condition.

If a low reading (10% or more) is obtained on one of the cylinders, it indicates valve or ring trouble. To determine which, pour about a teaspoon of engine oil through the spark plug hole onto the top of the piston. Turn the engine over once to clear some of the excess oil, then take another compression test and record the reading. If the compression increases, the valves are good but the rings are defective on that cylinder. If compression does not increase, the valves require servicing. A valve could be hanging open but not burned or a piece of carbon could be on a valve seat.

NOTE
If the compression is low, the engine cannot be tuned to maximum performance. The engine should be disassembled and inspected.

Spark Plug Selection

Spark plugs are available in various heat ranges that are hotter or colder than the spark plugs originally installed at the factory.

Select plugs in a heat range designed for the loads and temperature conditions under which the engine will operate. Using incorrect heat ranges can cause piston seizure, scored cylinder walls or damaged piston crowns.

In general, use a hotter plug for low speeds, low loads and low temperatures. Use a colder plug for high speeds, high engine loads and high temperatures.

NOTE
In areas where seasonal temperature variations are great, the factory

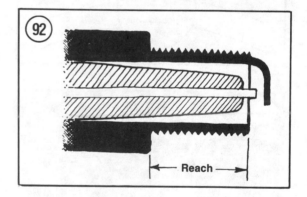

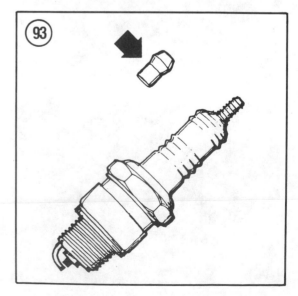

recommends a "two-plug system"—a cold plug for hard summer riding and a hot plug for slower winter operation.

The reach (length) of a plug is also important. A longer than normal plug could interfere with the valves and pistons causing permanent and severe damage (**Figure 92**). The standard spark plugs are listed in **Table 6**.

Spark Plug Removal/Cleaning

1. Grasp the spark plug leads (**Figure 85**) as near to the plug as possible and pull them off the plugs.
2. Blow away any dirt that has accumulated in the spark plug wells.

CAUTION
The dirt could fall into the cylinders when the plugs are removed, causing serious engine damage.

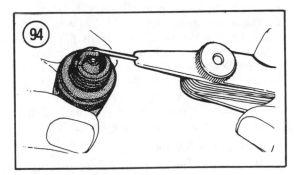

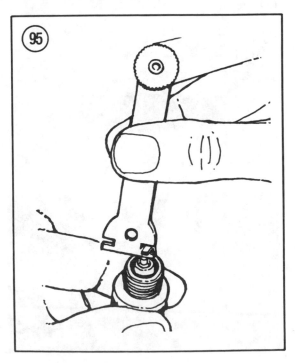

3. Remove the spark plugs with a spark plug wrench.

NOTE
If plugs are difficult to remove, apply penetrating oil such as WD-40 or Liquid Wrench around base of plugs and let it soak in about 10-20 minutes.

4. Inspect spark plug carefully. Look for plugs with broken center porcelain, excessively eroded electrodes and excessive carbon or oil fouling. Replace such plugs.
5. If you use a sand-blast type device to clean old plugs, be very careful. While this type of cleaning does a thorough job, the plug must be perfectly clean of all abrasive cleaning material when done. If not, it is possible for the cleaning material to fall into the engine during operation and cause piston-to-cylinder damage.

Spark Plug Gapping and Installing

New plugs should be carefully gapped to ensure a reliable, consistent spark. You must use a special spark plug gapping tool with a wire gauge.
1. Remove the new plugs from the box. Do *not* screw on the small terminals that are loose in each box (**Figure 93**); they are not used.
2. Insert a wire gauge between the center and the side electrode of each plug (**Figure 94**). The correct gap is found in **Table 6**. If the gap is correct, you will feel a slight drag as you pull the wire through. If there is no drag or the gauge won't pass through, bend the side electrode *with the gapping tool* (**Figure 95**) to set the proper gap.
3. Put a small drop of oil on the threads of each spark plug.
4. Screw each spark plug in by hand until it seats. Very little effort is required. If force is necessary, you have the plug cross-threaded; unscrew it and try again.

NOTE
If a spark plug is difficult to install, the cylinder head threads may be dirty or slightly damaged. To clean the threads, apply grease to the threads of a spark plug tap (Figure 96) and screw it carefully into the cylinder head. Turn the tap slowly until it is completely installed. If the tap cannot be installed, the threads are severely damaged and the head must be repaired by a specialist or replaced.

5. Tighten the spark plugs to a torque of 14 ft.-lb. (20 N•m). If you don't have a torque wrench, tighten an additional 1/4 to 1/2 turn after the gasket has made contact with the head. If you are reinstalling old, regapped plugs and are reusing the old gasket, only tighten an additional 1/4 turn.

> *NOTE*
> *Do not overtighten. Besides making the plug difficult to remove, the excessive torque will squash the gasket and destroy its sealing ability.*

6. Install each spark plug wire. Make sure it goes to the correct spark plug.

Reading Spark Plugs

Much information about engine and spark plug performance can be determined by careful examination of the spark plugs. This information is only valid after performing the following steps.
1. Ride the bike a short distance at full throttle in any gear.
2. Turn off the kill switch before closing the throttle and simultaneously pull in the clutch. Coast and brake to a stop. Do not downshift transmission with the engine not running.
3. Remove spark plugs and examine them. Compare them to **Figure 97**:
  a. If the electrodes are white or burned, the plug is too hot and should be replaced with a colder one.
  b. A too-cold plug will have sooty deposits ranging in color from dark brown to black. Replace with a hotter plug and check for too-rich carburetion or evidence of oil blow-by at the piston rings.
  c. If either plug is found unsatisfactory, replace them both.

Ignition Timing

Timing is set at the factory on all models and is not adjustable (the base plate screws have no slots for adjustment). The following procedure is used to check ignition timing only.

It is only necessary to check the timing on the rear cylinder. If it is found correct, the front cylinder will automatically be correct.

> *NOTE*
> *Before starting this procedure, check all electrical connections related to the ignition system. Make sure all connections are tight and free of corrosion and that all ground connections are tight.*

1. Place the bike on the centerstand.
2. Remove the timing cover (**Figure 83**).
3. Connect a portable tachometer following the manufacturer's instructions. The bike's tach is not accurate enough in the low rpm range for this adjustment.
4. Connect a timing light to the rear cylinder following the manufacturer's instructions.

> *CAUTION*
> *When attaching the timing light to the spark plug wire, do not puncture the wire or cap with the timing light probe. This would cause either excessive wire resistance or high-voltage leakage to ground. In either case, engine misfiring would result.*

5. Start the engine and let it warm up to normal operating temperature. Bring the engine speed to 950-1,500 rpm and aim the timing light at the marks on the timing plate (**Figure 98**).
6. The stationary pointer should align with the "F" mark on the timing plate (**Figure 87**). If not, remove the alternator cover as described in Chapter Seven and check the pick-up (A, **Figure 99**) and stator (B, **Figure 99**) assembly screws for tightness. If these are tight, refer to Chapter Seven for ignition system troubleshooting. Ignition timing cannot be adjusted on these models.

Carburetor Idle Mixture

Idle mixture is preset at the factory and it is *not* to be reset.

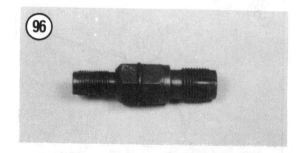

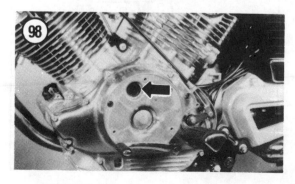

(97)

SPARK PLUG CONDITION

3

GAP BRIDGED
- Identified by deposit buildup closing gap between electrodes.
- Caused by oil or carbon fouling. If deposits are not excessive, the plug can be cleaned.

NORMAL
- Identified by light tan or gray deposits on the firing tip.
- Can be cleaned.

OIL FOULED
- Identified by wet black deposits on the insulator shell bore or electrodes.
- Caused by excessive oil entering combustion chamber through worn rings and pistons, excessive clearance between valve guides and stems, or worn or loose bearings. Can be cleaned. If engine is not repaired, use a hotter plug.

CARBON FOULED
- Identified by black, dry fluffy carbon deposits on insulator tips, exposed shell surfaces and electrodes.
- Caused by too cold a plug, weak ignition, dirty air cleaner, too rich a fuel mixture, or excessive idling. Can be cleaned.

LEAD FOULED
- Identified by dark gray, black, yellow, or tan deposits or a fused glazed coating on the insulator tip.
- Caused by highly leaded gasoline. Can be cleaned.

WORN
- Identified by severely eroded or worn electrodes.
- Caused by normal wear. Should be replaced.

FUSED SPOT DEPOSIT
- Identified by melted or spotty deposits resembling bubbles or blisters.
- Caused by sudden acceleration. Can be cleaned.

OVERHEATING
- Identified by a white or light gray insulator with small black or gray brown spots and with bluish-burnt appearance of electrodes.
- Caused by engine overheating, wrong type of fuel, loose spark plugs, too hot a plug, or incorrect ignition timing. Replace the plug.

PREIGNITION
- Identified by melted electrodes and possibly blistered insulator. Metallic deposits on insulator indicate engine damage.
- Caused by wrong type of fuel, incorrect ignition timing or advance, too hot a plug, burned valves, or engine overheating. Replace the plug.

Carburetor Synchronization (1981-1987)

A vacuum gauge must be used to synchronize the carburetors.

NOTE
Prior to synchronizing the carburetors, the ignition timing must be checked and the valve clearance properly adjusted.

1. Place the bike on the centerstand. Start the engine and let it reach normal operating temperature. Then turn it off.
2. Remove the seat.
3. Remove the fuel tank as described in Chapter Six.
4A. 1981-1983:
   a. Loosen the ventilation pipe-to-small air filter clamps as shown in A, **Figure 100**.
   b. Disconnect the rear cylinder vacuum line at the intake manifold (B, **Figure 100**). Connect one vacuum gauge line at this connection.
   c. The front cylinder has two vacuum lines. Disconnect the smaller diameter line (**Figure 101**); connect the vacuum gauge line at this point. Leave the larger vacuum line connected.
4B. 1984-on XV700:
   a. Disconnect the small diameter hose at the front carburetor joint.
   b. Disconnect the rubber cap from the rear carburetor joint.
   c. Connect the vacuum gauge to the front and rear carburetor joints.
4C. 1984-on XV1000 and XV1100:
   a. Remove the mixture control valve cover (**Figure 102**).
   b. Disconnect the vacuum hose at the mixture control valve (A, **Figure 103**).
   c. Disconnect the rubber cap from the rear carburetor joint (B, **Figure 103**).
   d. Connect the vacuum gauge to the mixture control valve and rear carburetor joint connections.
5. Place the fuel tank back onto the frame and reconnect the fuel lines. Raise the rear of the tank slightly to gain access to the carburetor synchronizing screw.
6. Turn the fuel petcock lever to the PRI position. On XV1000 and XV1100 models, no petcock is used. The fuel valve is electrically operated during engine operation.
7. Start the engine and allow it to warm up. Idle the engine at 950-1,050 rpm.

8. The carburetors are synchronized if they have the same gauge readings. If not, use a carburetor adjusting wrench with a screwdriver tip to turn the synchronizing screw (**Figure 104**) until the gauge readings are the same.

NOTE
***Figure 104** is shown with the carburetor assembly removed for clarity only.*

9. Remove the fuel tank and reconnect all vacuum lines. Reinstall all parts previously removed.

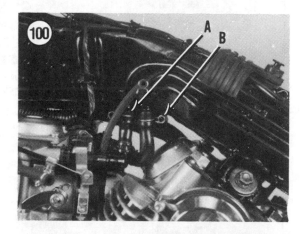

Carburetor Synchronization (1988-on)

A vacuum gauge must be used to synchronize the carburetors.

NOTE
Prior to synchronizing the carburetors, the ignition timing must be checked and the valve clearance properly adjusted.

1. Place the bike on the centerstand. Start the engine and let it reach normal operating temperature. Then turn it off.
2. Remove the seat.
3. Remove the fuel tank as described in Chapter Six.

4. Remove the frame left-hand side cover.
5. Remove the air filter as described in this chapter.
6. Disconnect the small diameter hose at the front carburetor joint.
7. Disconnect the rubber cap from the rear carburetor joint.
8. Connect the vacuum gauge to the front and rear carburetor joints.
9. Place the fuel tank back on the frame and reconnect the fuel lines. Raise the rear of the tank slightly to gain access to the carburetor synchronizing screw.
10. Restart the engine and again allow it to warm up. Idle the engine at 950-1,050 rpm.
11. The carburetors are synchronized if they have the same gauge readings. If not, use an offset screwdriver and turn the carburetor synchronizing screw (**Figure 105**) until the gauge readings are the same.
12. Remove the vacuum gauge lines and remove the fuel tank.
13. Reconnect all items disconnected.
14. Reinstall all parts previously removed.

Carburetor Idle Speed Adjustment

Before starting this adjustment, the air cleaner must be clean, the carburetors must be synchronized and the engine must have adequate compression (see *Compression Test* in this chapter). Otherwise this procedure cannot be done properly.

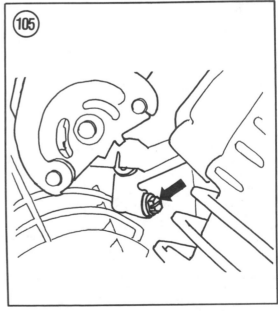

1. Attach a portable tachometer following the manufacturer's instructions.

NOTE
The bike's tachometer is not accurate enough in the low rpm range for this adjustment.

2. Start the engine and let it warm up to normal operating temperature.

3. Set the idle speed (**Table 6**) by turning the front cylinder's carburetor throttle stop screw in or out to achieve the proper idle speed. Refer to **Figure 106** for 1981-1987 models or **Figure 107** for 1988-on models.

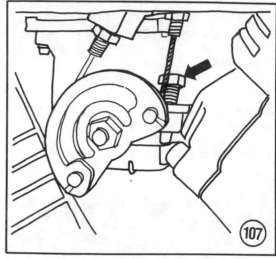

Table 1 MAINTENANCE SCHEDULE*

Initial 600 miles (1,000 km) or 1 month	• Change engine oil and filter • Check front and rear brake free play; adjust if required • Check front brake pad and rear brake shoe thickness; replace if required • Adjust clutch free play • Lubricate all control cables • Check drive chain tension and adjust if necessary** • Change final gear oil***
Initial 3,000 miles (5,000 km) or 7 months	• Check, clean and regap spark plugs
Initial 3,000 miles (5,000 km) or 6 months; then every 2,500 miles (4,000 km) or 6 months	• Check exhaust system mounting bolts and gasket • Check carburetor synchronization; adjust if required • Check engine idle speed; adjust if required • Change engine oil and filter • Check front and rear brake free play; adjust if required • Check front brake pad and rear brake shoe thickness; replace if required • Adjust clutch free play • Lubricate all control cables • Lubricate clutch and brake lever pivot points • Lubricate brake and shift lever pivot points • Lubricate centerstand and side stand pivot points • Check steering stem bearings for looseness; adjust if required • Check front and rear wheel bearings for smooth rotation; replace if required • Check battery fluid level and specific gravity
Initial 3,000 miles (5,000 km) or 7 months; then every 5,000 miles (8,000 km) or 12 months	• Check and adjust valve clearance • Check crankcase ventilation hose for cracks or damage; replace if required • Check fuel line and vacuum hoses for cracks or damage; replace if required • Clean air filter (replace if damaged) • Check drive chain tension and adjust if necessary** • Change final gear oil***
Initial 8,000 miles (13,000 km) or 18 months; then every 7,500 miles (12,000 km) or 18 months	• Replace spark plugs
Initial 8,000 miles (13,000 km) or 18 months; then every 10,000 miles (16,000 km) or 24 months	• Replace alternator brushes
Every 10,000 miles (16,000 km) or 24 months	• Repack steering stem ball bearing grease

* This Yamaha factory maintenance schedule should be used as a guide to general maintenance and lubrication intervals. Harder than normal use and exposure to mud, water, sand, high humidity, etc., will dictate more frequent attention to most maintenance items.
** Chain drive models only.
*** Shaft drive models only.

Table 2 TIRE INFLATION PRESSURE (COLD)

Load	XV700, XV750, XV1000 XV1000, XV1100 psi (kg/cm²)	XV920 psi (kg/cm²)
Up to 198 lb. (90 kg)		
Front	26 psi (1.8)	26 (1.8)
Rear	28 (2.0)	28 (2.0)
198-353 lb. (90-160 kg)		
Front	28 (2.0)	
Rear	32 (2.3)	
353-529 lb. (160-240 kg)		
Front	28 (2.0)	
Rear	40 (2.8)	
198-470 lb. (90-213 kg)		
Front	—	28 (2.0)
Rear	—	32 (2.3)
High-speed riding		
Front	32 (2.3)	28 (2.0)
Rear	36 (2.5)	32 (2.3)

Table 3 BATTERY STATE OF CHARGE

Specific gravity	State of charge
1.110-1.130	Discharged
1.140-1.160	Almost discharged
1.170-1.190	One-quarter charged
1.200-1.220	One-half charged
1.230-1.250	Three-quarters charged
1.260-1.280	Fully charged

Table 4 RECOMMENDED LUBRICANTS

Engine oil	
40° F and above	SAE20W/40, SE-SF
40° F and below	SAE10W/30, SE-SF
Brake fluid	DOT 3 or DOT 4
Battery refilling	Distilled water
Fork oil	SAE 10
Cables and pivot points	Yamaha chain and cable lube or SAE 10W/30 motor oil
Fuel	Regular
Final gear oil (if so equipped)	
All weather	SAE 80W/90, GL4
Above 40° F	SAE 90, GL4
Below 40° F	SAE 80, GL4
Drive chain (if so equipped)	Shell Alvania 1 or lithium-base EP2 grease

Table 5 APPROXIMATE REFILL CAPACITIES

Engine oil	
With oil filter change	3.3 qts. (3,100 cc)
With out oil filter change	3.2 qts. (3,000 cc)
Engine rebuild	3.8 qts. (3,600 cc)
Front forks	
XV700 (1984-1985)	13.2 oz. (389 cc)
XV700 (1986-1987), XV750 (1988-on)	13.4 oz. (396 cc)
XV750 (1981-1983)	9.4 oz. (278 cc)
XV750 (1988-on)	13.4 oz. (396 cc)
XV920 (1981-1982 chain drive)	8.9 oz. (264 cc)
XV920 (1982-1983 shaft drive)	10.2 oz. (303 cc)
XV1000, XV1100	12.6 oz. (372 cc)
Final drive case (if so equipped)	0.21 qt. (200 cc)

Table 6 TUNE-UP SPECIFICATIONS

Ignition timing	Fixed
Valve clearance (cold)	
1981-1983	
Intake	0.004 in. (0.10 mm)
Exhaust	0.006 in. (0.15 mm)
1984-on	
Intake	0.003-0.004 in. (0.07-0.10 mm)
Exhaust	0.005-0.006 in. (0.12-0.15 mm)
Spark plug	
Type	NGK BP7ES
Gap	0.028-0.032 in. (0.7-0.8 mm)
Tightening torque	14.5 ft.-lb. (20 N•m)
Idle speed	950-1,050 rpm
Compression pressure (cold @ sea level)	
Standard	156 psi (11 kg/cm^2)
Minimum	128 psi (9 kg/cm^2)
Maximum	171 psi (12 kg/cm^2)
Maximum difference between cylinders	14 psi (1.0 kg/cm^2)

3

CHAPTER FOUR

ENGINE

The engine used on all models is a V-twin air-cooled, 4-stroke design. The cylinders are offset (to improve rear cylinder cooling) and set at a 75° angle; the cylinders fire on alternate crankshaft rotations. Each cylinder is equipped with a single camshaft and 2 valves. The crankshaft is supported by 2 main bearings in the vertically split crankcase.

Both engine and transmission share a common case and the same wet-sump oil supply. The clutch is a wet-plate type located inside the right crankcase cover. Refer to Chapter Five for clutch and transmission service procedures.

This chapter provides complete procedures information for disassembly, removal, inspection, service and reassembly of the engine. Service procedures for all models are virtually the same. Where differences occur, they are identified.

Table 1 and **Table 2** provide complete engine specifications. **Table 3** lists engine tightening torques for all models.

Tables 1-5 are located at the end of this chapter.

Before starting any work, read the service hints in Chapter One. You will do a better job with this information fresh in your mind.

ENGINE PRINCIPLES

Figure 1 explains how the engine works. This will be helpful when troubleshooting or repairing the engine.

SERVICING ENGINE IN FRAME

Many components can be serviced while the engine is mounted in the frame:
a. Gearshift mechanism.
b. Clutch.
c. Carburetors.
d. Starter motor and gears.
e. Alternator and electrical systems.
f. Oil pump.

ENGINE REMOVAL/INSTALLATION

1. Place the motorcycle on its centerstand. Remove the left- and right-hand side covers and accessories such as fairings and crash bars.
2. Remove the battery from the frame as described in Chapter Three.
3. Remove the fuel tank as described in Chapter Six.
4. Drain the engine oil as described in Chapter Three.
5. Disconnect the spark plug wires.

4-STROKE OPERATING PRINCIPLES

①

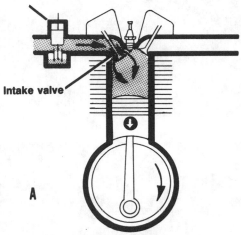

Carburetor

Intake valve

A

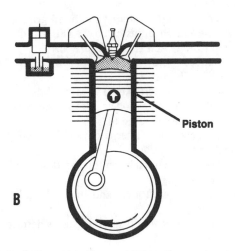

Piston

B

4

As the piston travels downward, the exhaust valve is closed and the intake valve opens, allowing the new air-fuel mixture from the carburetor to be drawn into the cylinder. When the piston reaches the bottom of its travel (BDC), the intake valve closes and remains closed for the next 1 1/2 revolutions of the crankshaft.

While the crankshaft continues to rotate, the piston moves upward, compressing the air-fuel mixture.

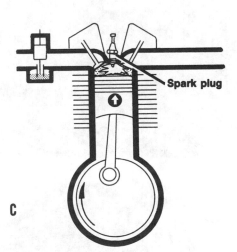

Spark plug

C

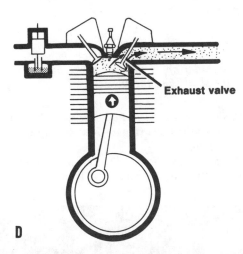

Exhaust valve

D

As the piston almost reaches the top of its travel, the spark plug fires, igniting the compressed air-fuel mixture. The piston continues to top dead center (TDC) and is pushed downward by the expanding gases.

When the piston almost reaches BDC, the exhaust valve opens and remains open until the piston is near TDC. The upward travel of the piston forces the exhaust gases out of the cylinder. After the piston has reached TDC, the exhaust valve closes and the cycle starts all over again.

6. Remove the air filter assembly bolts and remove the air filter assembly. See **Figure 2** (1981-1983) or **Figure 3** (1984-on).

7. Remove the exhaust system as described in Chapter Six.

8. Loosen the clutch cable at the hand grip. Then remove the clutch adjuster cover (**Figure 4**) and disconnect the clutch cable (**Figure 5**).

9. Disconnect the carburetor assembly as described in Chapter Six.

10. Disconnect the crankcase breather hose.

11. On 1984 and later models, remove the mixture control valve case (**Figure 6**).

12. Disconnect the alternator wiring at the electrical connector.

13. Remove the clutch assembly as described in Chapter Five.

14. Remove the shift lever and the left-hand rear crankcase cover.

15. Remove the gearshift mechanism as described in Chapter Five.

16. Remove the starter motor idler gears and shaft as described in this chapter. Then remove the starter motor attachment bolts and pull the starter motor out of the crankcase.

17. Remove the bolt attaching the ground wire to the engine. Position the wire back and out of the way.

18. Remove the alternator assembly as described in Chapter Seven.

NOTE
When performing Step 19A, have an assistant apply the rear brake to keep the shaft from turning.

19A. *Shaft-drive models*: Pull back the rubber boot and remove the bolts (**Figure 7**) securing the drive shaft coupling.

19B. *Chain-drive models*: Disconnect and remove the drive chain as described in Chapter Nine.

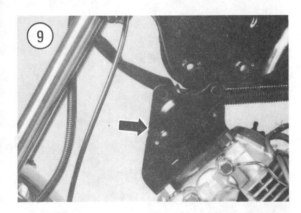

20. Examine the engine to make sure everything has been disconnected and positioned out of the way.

21. Place wooden blocks (**Figure 8**) under the crankcase to support the engine once the mounting bolts are removed.

22. Loosen, but do not remove, all engine mounting bolts and nuts.

23. Remove the front engine mount bolts, nuts and brackets (**Figure 9**).

4

NOTE
Rubber dampers are used on some engine mounts. Note their position for reassembly.

24. Withdraw the rear engine mount through bolt (**Figure 10**).

25. Have an assistant help you slide the engine forward (**Figure 11**) and remove it.

26. While the engine is removed for service, check all of the frame engine mounts for cracks or other damage. If any cracks are detected, take the chassis assembly to a dealer or frame specialist for further examination.

27. Install by reversing the removal steps; note the following.

28. After the engine is positioned correctly, install the rear through-bolt (**Figure 10**). Install the upper front bolts, plates and nuts. Start the nuts but do not tighten.

30. On shaft-drive models, install 4 *new* drive shaft bolts and tighten them evenly in two stages to specifications (**Table 4**). Reattach the rubber boot.

31. Tighten the front and rear top motor mount bolts to specifications (**Table 5**).

32. Fill the crankcase with the recommended type and quantity of engine oil. Refer to Chapter Three.

33. Start the engine and check for leaks.

CYLINDER HEADS
AND CAMSHAFTS

This section describes removal, inspection and installation procedures for the cylinder head and camshaft components. Valves and valve components are described under a separate heading.

Removal

1. Remove the engine from the frame as described in this chapter.

2A. *Rear cylinder:* Rotate the engine by turning the crankshaft *clockwise.* Use a socket on the nut located on the left-hand end of the crankshaft until the "T" mark for the *rear cylinder* (**Figure 87**, Chapter Three) is aligned with the crankcase cover stationary pointer as viewed through the window in the crankcase cover.

2B. *Front cylinder:* Turn the crankshaft approximately 285° clockwise to align the flywheel "I" mark with the stationary pointer.

> *NOTE*
> *Do not remove the rotor from the left-hand side of the engine (**Figure 12**) as it will be used during camshaft installation.*

3. Remove the bolts securing the cam chain tensioner (**Figure 13**) and remove the tensioner.

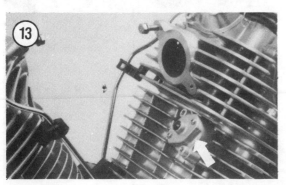

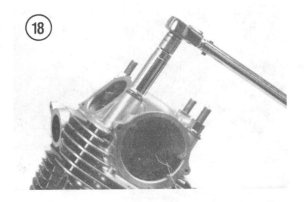

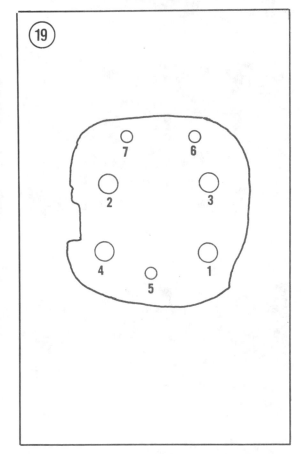

4. Disconnect the oil delivery lines (**Figure 14**) at both cylinders. Store the oil lines in a safe place to prevent damage.

5. Remove the valve adjustment cover and loosen the valve adjustment nuts (A, **Figure 15**).

6. Remove the cam sprocket covers (B, **Figure 15**).

7. Remove the camshaft sprocket bolt (A, **Figure 16**).

8. Remove the oil baffle plate (at the rear cylinder only). See B, **Figure 16**.

9. Attach a length of safety wire to the cam chain, then let the chain drop.

> *NOTE*
> *Before removing the cam sprocket in Step 10, note the position of the dowel pin between the camshaft and and cam sprocket. Remove the camshaft sprocket carefully so that the dowel pin does not pull out of the camshaft and fall into the crankcase cavity.*

10. Remove the camshaft sprocket (**Figure 17**) by pulling it off the camshaft. Remove the camshaft dowel pin.

11. Loosen all cylinder head nuts (**Figure 18**) 1/2 turn in the sequence shown in **Figure 19**. After all the nuts have been loosened, remove the nuts and washers.

12. Remove the rear frame engine mounts (**Figure 20**) from the rear cylinder head.

13. Loosen the head by tapping around the perimeter with a rubber or plastic mallet.

> *CAUTION*
> *Remember, the cooling fins are fragile and may be damaged if tapped on too hard. Never use a metal hammer.*

14. Remove the cylinder head (**Figure 21**) by pulling straight up and off the cylinder studs. Place a clean shop rag into the cam chain opening in the cylinder to prevent the entry of foreign matter.

NOTE
After removing the cylinder head, check the top and bottom mating surfaces for any indications of leakage. Also check the head and base gaskets for signs of leakage. A blown gasket could indicate possible cylinder head warpage or other damage.

NOTE
Do not remove the rubber sleeves from the front cylinder studs (Figure 22).

15. See **Figure 23**. Remove the bolt (A) securing the retaining plate (B) in the cylinder head and remove the plate. Then remove the bushing (**Figure 24**) and camshaft (**Figure 25**).

16. Repeat Steps 2-15 for the opposite cylinder head.

Camshaft Inspection

1. Check the inside and outside camshaft bushing surfaces for pitting or chatter marks (**Figure 26**). Replace if required. If the camshaft bushing is severely worn, check the cylinder head for wear where the bushing rides. The surface should be smooth with no visible wear marks. Replace the cylinder head if this surface is worn.

2. Check cam lobes (**Figure 27**) for wear. The lobes should not be scored and the edges should be square. Slight damage may be removed with a silicon carbide oilstone. Use No. 100-120 grit initially, then polish with a No. 280-320 grit.

3. Even if the cam lobe surfaces appear satisfactory, with no visible signs of wear, they must be measured with a micrometer as shown in **Figure 28**. Replace the shaft(s) if worn beyond the service limit (measurements less than those given in **Table 1** or **Table 2**).

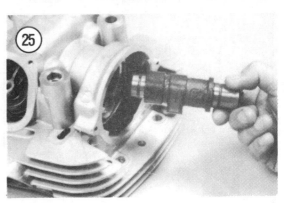

4. Place the camshaft on a set of V-blocks and check its runout with a dial indicator. Replace the camshaft if runout exceeds specifications in **Table 1** or **Table 2**.

5. Inspect the camshaft sprockets (A, **Figure 29**) and camshaft drive sprockets (B, **Figure 29**) for wear; replace if necessary.

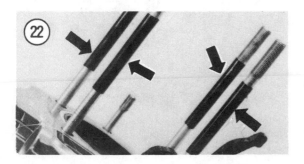

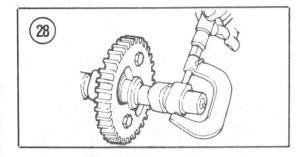

Cylinder Head Inspection

1. Remove all traces of gasket from head and cylinder mating surfaces. Do not scratch the gasket surface.

2. Without removing valves, remove all carbon deposits from the combustion chambers (**Figure 30**) with a wire brush. A blunt screwdriver or chisel may be used if care is taken not to damage the head, valves and spark plug threads.

> *CAUTION*
> *If the combustion chambers are cleaned while the valves are removed, make sure to keep the scraper or wire brush away from the valve seats to prevent damaging the seat surfaces. A damaged or even slightly scratched valve seat will cause poor valve seating.*

3. Examine the spark plug threads in the cylinder head for damage. If damage is minor or if the threads are dirty or clogged with carbon, use a spark plug thread tap (**Figure 31**) to clean the threads following the manufacturer's instructions. If thread damage is severe, refer further service to a dealer or competent machine shop.

4. After all carbon is removed from combustion chamber and valve ports and the spark plug thread holes are repaired, clean the entire head in solvent.

5. Clean away all carbon on the piston crowns. Do not remove the carbon ridge at the top of the cylinder bore.

6. Check for cracks in the combustion chamber and exhaust ports. A cracked head must be replaced.

7. After the head has been thoroughly cleaned, place a straightedge across the gasket surface at several points (**Figure 32**). Measure warp by inserting a feeler gauge between the straightedge and cylinder head at each location. Maximum allowable warpage is 0.010 in. (0.25 mm). If warpage exceeds this limit, the cylinder head must be replaced.

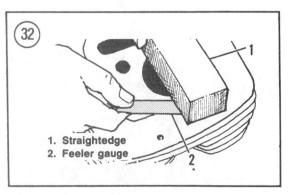

1. Straightedge
2. Feeler gauge

8. Inspect the valves and valve guides as described in this chapter.

Installation

1. Loosen the valve adjusters (**Figure 33**).
2. Apply engine assembly oil to all camshaft bearing surfaces (**Figure 34**) and carefully install the shaft into the cylinder head so that the pin on the end of the camshaft aligns with the cylinder head timing mark (**Figure 35**).
3. Apply assembly oil to the camshaft bushing surfaces and install it in the cylinder head so that the cut-out portion in the front of the bushing is flush with the cylinder. See **Figure 24**.
4. Install the bushing retaining plate (B, **Figure 23**) and bolt (A, **Figure 23**). Tighten the bolt to 14 ft.-lb. (20 N•m).
5. Install a new head gasket.
6. Slide the safety wire attached to the cam chain up through the cylinder head chain cavity and install the cylinder head.

> *NOTE*
> *Make sure the front cam chain is secured in the cylinder head cam chain guide slot.*

7. Make sure the rubber covers are installed on the front cylinder head studs (**Figure 22**). Lightly oil all cylinder head stud threads.
8. Install the engine mount brackets on the rear cylinder head (**Figure 20**).
9. Install the cylinder head nuts and bolts. The taller nuts fit onto the front cylinder head studs; the shorter nuts fit on the rear cylinder head studs. See **Figure 36** (front) and **Figure 37** (rear).
10. Tighten all nuts and bolts in the sequence shown in **Figure 19** to the specifications in **Table 3**.
11. Repeat Steps 1-10 for the opposite cylinder.

> *NOTE*
> *Steps 12-17 describe camshaft timing procedures for the rear cylinder. Pull up on the rear cylinder cam chain when performing Step 12 to prevent it from binding the timing gears.*

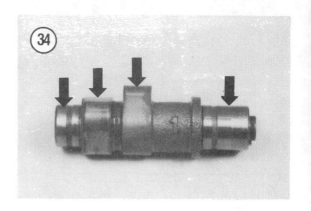

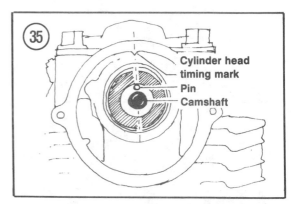

Cylinder head timing mark
Pin
Camshaft

12. Remove the rotor timing covers. Turn the crankshaft *clockwise* with a socket on the rotor nut (**Figure 38**) to align the "T" mark on the flywheel with the stationary pointer (**Figure 39**). The rear cylinder is now at TDC (top dead center).

13. Lift up on the cam chain and engage the cam chain sprocket with the chain. There should be no slack in the front run of the chain. If there is, reposition the sprocket in the cam chain. Then lift up the sprocket and chain and place the sprocket onto the end of the camshaft so that the sprocket hole fits onto the pin in the end of the camshaft. At this point, the timing mark on the cylinder head should be aligned with the hole in the camshaft sprocket. See **Figure 40**. Check the front run of the cam chain; it must be taut when the cam chain sprocket is installed on the end of the cam. If not, remove the sprocket and reinstall.

14. When the cam chain timing for the rear cylinder is correct as described in Step 13, proceed to Step 15.

15. Install the oil baffle onto the rear cylinder camshaft. Install the camshaft securing bolt and tighten to specifications (**Table 3**).

16. From a sheet of steel 0.039 in. (1 mm) thick, cut a plate to the dimensions in **Figure 41**. This plate is necessary to adjust the rear cylinder cam chain tension.

17. Adjust the rear cylinder cam chain tension as follows:

  a. Remove the rubber plug from the end of the tensioner body.

  b. Hold the tensioner in your hand as shown in **Figure 42** and insert a small screwdriver into the end of the tensioner body. Tighten the inner spring with the screwdriver while at the same time pushing the tension rod into the tensioner housing (**Figure 43**).

  c. Continue to tighten the tensioner spring until it is completely tight. Still holding the tension rod, remove the screwdriver and install the steel plate (fabricated in Step 16) into the slot in the end of the tensioner body (**Figure 43**).

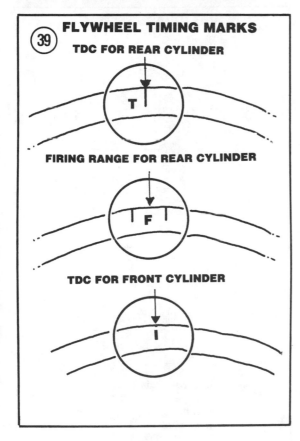

FLYWHEEL TIMING MARKS

TDC FOR REAR CYLINDER

T

FIRING RANGE FOR REAR CYLINDER

F

TDC FOR FRONT CYLINDER

I

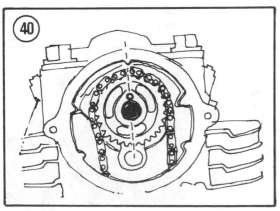

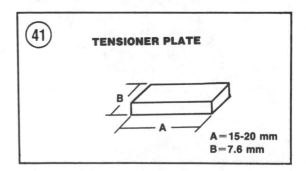

TENSIONER PLATE

B

A

A = 15-20 mm
B = 7.6 mm

d. Install the cam chain tensioner into the rear cylinder using a new gasket. Install the tensioner bolts and tighten to specifications (**Table 3**).

e. Remove the tensioner plate and reinstall the rubber plug. Store the tensioner plate for reuse.

NOTE
Step 18 and Step 19 describe camshaft timing procedures for the front cylinder.

18. Pull up on the chain and rotate the crankshaft *clockwise* with a socket on the rotor nut to align the "I" mark on the flywheel with the stationary pointer (**Figure 39**). The front cylinder is now at TDC (top dead center).

19. Repeat Steps 13-15 to install and align the front cylinder camshaft.

20. Install the front cam chain tensioner as described in Step 17, using a new gasket. Install the tensioner bolts and tighten to specifications (**Table 3**).

21. Check the camshaft timing as follows:

a. Rear cylinder: Turn the crankshaft *clockwise* with a socket on the rotor nut to align the "T" mark on the flywheel with the stationary pointer (**Figure 39**). The timing mark on the rear cylinder camshaft sprocket must be aligned with the cylinder head timing mark (**Figure 40**).

b. Front cylinder: Turn the crankshaft *clockwise* and align the "I" mark on the flywheel with the stationary pointer (**Figure 39**). The timing mark on the front cylinder camshaft sprocket must be aligned with the cylinder head timing mark (**Figure 40**).

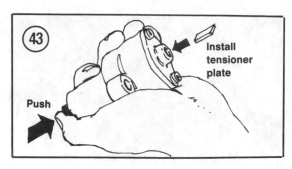

(43) Install tensioner plate

Push

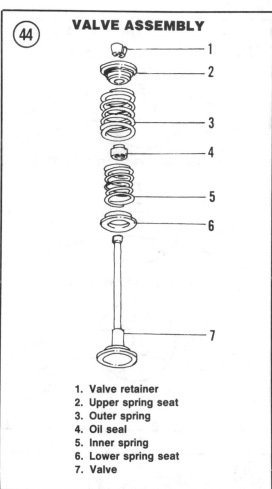

(44) **VALVE ASSEMBLY**

1. Valve retainer
2. Upper spring seat
3. Outer spring
4. Oil seal
5. Inner spring
6. Lower spring seat
7. Valve

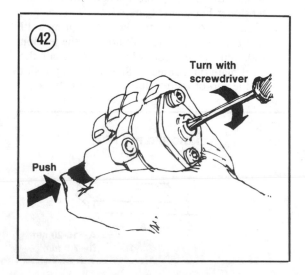

(42) Turn with screwdriver

Push

(45)

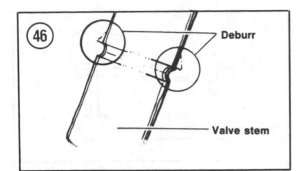

Deburr

Valve stem

c. If there is any binding while rotating the crankshaft, *stop*. Determine the cause before proceeding. If one or both cams are misaligned when the crankcase timing mark is aligned correctly, disassemble and reassemble until all alignments are correct. This alignment is absolutely necessary for correct valve timing and to prevent expensive damage to the pistons and valve train.

22. Install the oil pipes.

23. Reinstall the engine as described in this chapter.

24. Adjust the valves as described in Chapter Three.

25. Start the engine and check for leaks.

VALVES AND VALVE COMPONENTS

Removal

Refer to **Figure 44** for this procedure.

1. Remove the cylinder head as described in this chapter.

2. Install a valve spring compressor squarely over the valve retainer with other end of tool placed against valve head (**Figure 45**).

3. Tighten valve spring compressor until the split valve keepers separate. Lift out split keepers with needlenose pliers.

4. Gradually loosen valve spring compressor and remove from head. Lift off upper spring seat.

> *CAUTION*
> *Remove any burrs from the valve stem grooves before removing the valve (Figure 46). Otherwise the valve guides will be damaged.*

5. Remove the inner and outer springs and valve.

6. Remove the oil seal (**Figure 47**).

7. Remove the lower spring seat (**Figure 48**).

> *CAUTION*
> *All component parts of each valve assembly must be kept together (Figure 49). Do not mix with like components from other valves or excessive wear may result.*

8. Repeat Steps 2-7 to remove remaining valve(s).

Inspection

1. Clean valves with a wire brush and solvent.

2. Inspect the contact surface of each valve for burning (**Figure 50**). Minor roughness and pitting can be removed by lapping the valve as described in this chapter. Excessive unevenness on the contact surface is an indication that the valve is not serviceable. The contact surface of the valve may

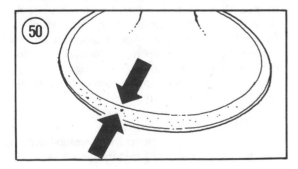

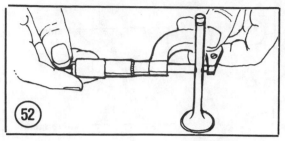

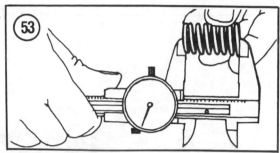

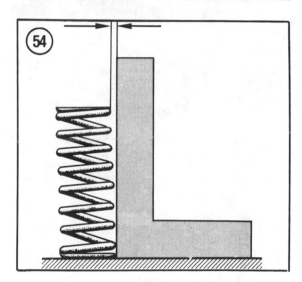

be ground by a specialist, but it is best to replace a burned or damaged valve with a new one.

3. Inspect the valve stems for wear and roughness and measure the vertical runout of the valve stem as shown in **Figure 51**. The runout should not exceed specifications (**Table 1** or **Table 2**).

4. Measure valve stems for wear using a micrometer (**Figure 52**). Compare with specifications in **Table 1** or **Table 2**.

5. Remove all carbon and varnish from the valve guides with a stiff spiral wire brush.

NOTE
Step 6 requires special measuring equipment. If you do not have the required measuring devices, proceed to Step 8.

6. Measure each valve guide at top, center and bottom with a small hole gauge. Compare measurements with specifications in **Table 1** or **Table 2**.

7. Subtract the measurement made in Step 4 from the measurement made in Step 6. The difference is the valve guide-to-valve stem clearance. See specifications in **Table 1** or **Table 2** for correct clearance. Replace any guide or valve that is not within tolerance. Valve guide replacement is described in this chapter.

8. Insert each valve in its guide. Hold the valve just slightly off its seat and rock it sideways. If it rocks more than slightly, the guide is probably worn and should be replaced. As a final check, take the head to a dealer and have the valve guides measured.

9. Measure the valve spring heights with a vernier caliper (**Figure 53**). All should be of the length specified in **Table 1** or **Table 2** with no bends or other distortion. Replace defective springs.

10. Measure the tilt of all valve springs as shown in **Figure 54**. Compare with specifications in **Table 1** or **Table 2**.

11. Check the valve spring retainer and valve keepers. If they are in good condition, they may be reused.

12. Inspect valve seats (**Figure 55**). If worn or burned, they must be reconditioned. This should be performed by your dealer or local machine shop, although the procedure is described in this chapter. Seats and valves in near-perfect condition can be reconditioned by lapping with fine carborundum paste. Lapping, however, is always inferior to precision grinding.

Installation

1. Coat the valve stems with molybdenum disulfide paste and insert into cylinder head.

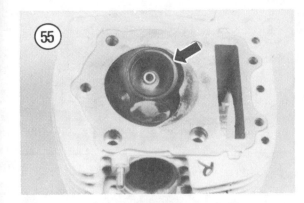

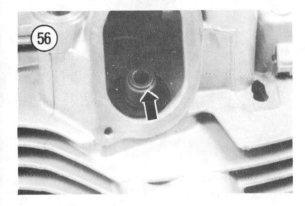

2. Install the lower spring seat (**Figure 48**) and a new seal (**Figure 56**).

NOTE
Oil seals should be replaced whenever a valve is removed or replaced.

3. Install valve springs with the narrow pitch end (end with coils closest together) facing the cylinder head (**Figure 57**).
4. Install the upper spring seat.
5. Push down on the upper spring seat with the valve spring compressor and install valve keepers. After releasing tension from compressor, examine valve keepers to make sure they are seated correctly.
6. Repeat Steps 1-5 for remaining valve(s).

Valve Guide Replacement

When guides are worn so that there is excessive stem-to-guide clearance or valve tipping, they must be replaced. Replace all, even if only one is worn. This job should only be done by a dealer or qualified specialist as special tools are required.

Valve Seat Reconditioning

This job is best left to your dealer or local machine shop. They have the special equipment and knowledge for this exacting job. You can still save considerable money by removing the cylinder head and taking just the head to the shop.

Valve Lapping

Valve lapping is a simple operation which can restore the valve seal without machining if the amount of wear or distortion is not too great.
1. Smear a light coating of fine grade valve lapping compound on seating surface of valve.
2. Insert the valve into the head.
3. Wet the suction cup of the lapping stick and stick it onto the head of the valve. Lap the valve to the seat by spinning the lapping stick in both directions. Every 5 to 10 seconds, rotate the valve 180° in the valve seat; continue lapping until the contact surfaces of the valve and the valve seat are a uniform gray. Stop as soon as they are, to avoid removing too much material.
4. Thoroughly clean the valves and cylinder head in solvent to remove all grinding compound. Any compound left on the valves or the cylinder head will end up in the engine and will cause excessive wear and damage.
5. After the lapping has been completed and the valve assemblies have been reinstalled into the head, the valve seal should be tested. Check the seal of each valve by pouring solvent into each of the intake and exhaust ports. There should be no leakage past the seat. If leakage occurs, the combustion chamber will appear wet. If fluid leaks past any of the seats, disassemble that valve assembly and repeat the lapping procedure until there is no leakage.

ROCKER ARM ASSEMBLIES

The rocker arms are identical (same Yamaha part No.) but they will develop different wear patterns during use. It is recommended that all parts be marked during removal so that they can be assembled in their original position.

Removal/Inspection/Installation

1. Remove the cylinder head(s) as described in this chapter.

2. Remove the rocker arm bolts (**Figure 58**).

3. Thread a M6×1.00 threaded bolt into the end of one rocker arm shaft and remove the shaft and rocker arm. If the shaft is difficult to remove, use a special knock puller as shown in **Figure 59**. Repeat for the opposite rocker arm shaft.

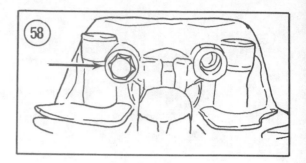

NOTE
*The knock puller used in Step 3 (**Figure 60**) can be easily fabricated from a long bolt with M6×1.00 threads and a heavy piece of round metal stock with a hole drilled through it.*

4. Wash all parts in cleaning solvent and thoroughly dry.

5. Inspect the rocker arm pad where it rides on the cam lobe and where the adjuster rides on the valve stem. If the pad is scratched or unevenly worn, inspect the cam lobe for scoring, chipping or flat spots. Replace the rocker arm if defective. Replace the adjusting screw if worn.

6. Measure the inside diameter of the rocker arm bore (A, **Figure 61**) with an inside micrometer and check against dimensions in **Table 1** or **Table 2**. Replace if worn to the service limit or less.

7. Inspect the rocker arm shaft for wear or scoring. Measure the outside diameter (B, **Figure 61**) with a micrometer and check against dimensions in **Table 1** or **Table 2**. Replace if worn to the service limit or greater.

8. Coat the rocker arm shaft and rocker arm bore with assembly oil.

9. Position the rocker arm in the cylinder and install the rocker arm shaft through the rocker arm *with the threaded hole facing out.* Install the rocker arm shaft bolt and tighten to specifications (**Table 3**).

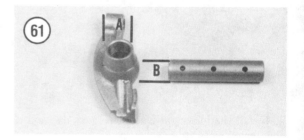

CAUTION
If the rocker arm shaft is installed in the wrong direction, it cannot be removed.

CYLINDER

Removal

1. Remove the cylinder heads as described in this chapter.

2. Remove the head gasket.

3. Loosen the cylinder by tapping around the perimeter with a rubber or plastic mallet.

4. Pull the cylinder straight up (**Figure 62**) and off the piston and cylinder studs.

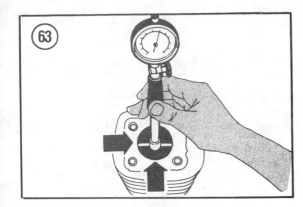

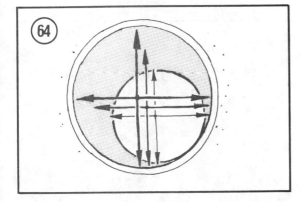

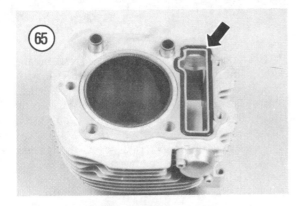

NOTE
Be sure to keep the cam chain wired up to prevent it from falling into the lower crankcase.

5. Stuff clean shop rags into the crankcase opening to prevent objects from falling into the crankcase.
6. Repeat Steps 2-5 for the opposite cylinder.

Inspection

1. Wash the cylinder bore in solvent to remove any oil and carbon particles. The bore must be cleaned thoroughly before attempting any measurement or incorrect readings may be obtained.
2. Measure the cylinder bores with a cylinder gauge (**Figure 63**) or inside micrometer at the points shown in **Figure 64**.
3. Measure in 2 axes—in line with the piston pin and at 90° to the pin. If the taper or out-of-round is greater than specifications (**Table 1** or **Table 2**), the cylinders must be rebored to the next oversize and new pistons and rings installed. Rebore both cylinders even if only one is worn.

NOTE
The new pistons should be obtained first before the cylinders are bored so that the pistons can be measured; each cylinder must be bored to match the piston that will be used in it. Piston-to-cylinder clearance is specified in **Table 1** *and* **Table 2**.

4. If the cylinder(s) are not worn past the service limits, check the bore carefully for scratches or gouges. The bore still may require boring and reconditioning.
5. If the cylinders require reboring, remove all dowel pins and O-rings from the cylinders before leaving them with the dealer or machine shop.

NOTE
After having the cylinders rebored, wash them thoroughly in hot soapy water. This is the best way to clean the cylinder of all fine grit material left from the bore job. After washing the cylinder, run a clean white cloth through the bore; it should show no traces of dirt or other debris. If the rag is dirty, the cylinder is not clean and must be rewashed. After the cylinder is thoroughly cleaned, dry and then lubricate the cylinder walls with clean engine oil to prevent the cylinder liners from rusting.

6. Check the 2 cylinder O-rings. See **Figure 65** and **Figure 66**. Replace the O-rings if worn or damaged.

Installation

1. If the base gasket is stuck to the bottom of the cylinder it should be removed and the cylinder surface cleaned thoroughly.
2. Check that the top cylinder surface is clean of all old gasket material.
3. Install the 2 locating dowels onto the cylinder head.
4. Install a new cylinder base gasket to the crankcase. Make sure all holes align.
5. Install a piston holding fixture under the piston.
6. Carefully install the cylinder onto the cylinder studs (**Figure 62**) and slide it down over the piston. Lubricate cylinder bore and piston liberally with engine oil prior to installation.

> *NOTE*
> *Once the cylinder is placed over the studs, run the cam chain and wire up through the cylinder.*

7. Compress each ring as it enters the cylinder with your fingers or by using aircraft type hose clamps of appropriate diameter.

> *CAUTION*
> *Don't tighten the clamp any more than necessary to compress the rings. If the rings can't slip through easily, the clamp may gouge the rings.*

8. Remove the piston holding fixture and push the cylinder all the way down.
9. Repeat Steps 1-8 for the opposite cylinder.
10. Install the cylinder heads and camshafts as described in this chapter.

PISTONS AND PISTON RINGS

Piston
Removal/Installation

1. Remove the cylinder heads and cylinders as described in this chapter.
2. Stuff the crankcase with clean shop rags to prevent objects from falling into the crankcase.
3. Lightly mark the piston with an "F" (front) or "R" (rear) so they will be installed into the correct cylinder.
4. Remove the piston rings as described in this chapter.
5. Before removing the piston, hold the rod tightly and rock piston as shown in **Figure 67**. Any rocking motion (do not confuse with the normal sliding motion) indicates wear on the piston pin, rod bushing, pin bore or, more likely, a combination of all three. Mark the piston and pin so that they will be reassembled into the same set.
6. Remove the circlips from the piston pin bores (**Figure 68**).

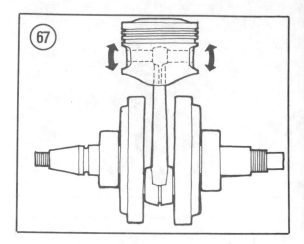

7. Heat the piston and pin with a small butane torch. The pin will probably drop right out. If it doesn't, heat the piston to about 140° F (60° C), i.e., until it is too warm to touch, but not excessively hot. If the pin is still difficult to push out, use a homemade tool as shown in **Figure 69**.
8. Inspect the piston as described in this chapter.
9. Coat the connecting rod bushing, piston pin and piston with assembly oil.
10. Place the piston over the connecting rod. If you are installing old parts, make sure the piston is installed on the correct rod as marked during removal. The "EX" on the front piston should face to the front of the engine and the "EX" on the rear piston should face to the rear of the engine.
11. Insert the piston pin and tap it with a plastic mallet until it starts into the connecting rod bushing. Hold the rod so that the lower end does not take any shock. If the pin does not slide easily, heat the piston as described during removal or use the home made tool (**Figure 69**) but eliminate the piece of pipe. Drive the pin in until it is centered in the piston.
12. Install *new* circlips in the piston bores.

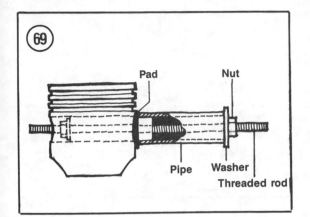

Pad   Nut

Pipe   Washer

Threaded rod

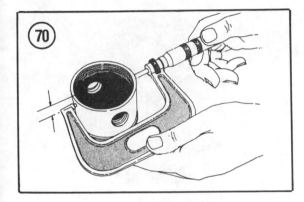

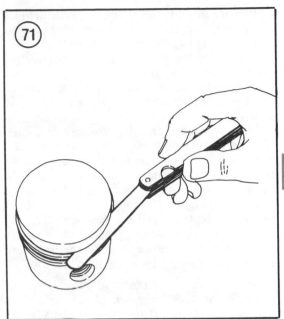

4

13. Install rings as described in this chapter.

14. Repeat Steps 1-13 for the opposite piston.

Piston Inspection

1. Carefully clean the carbon from the piston crown with a soft scraper. Do not remove or damage the carbon ridge around the circumference of the piston above the top ring. If the pistons, rings and cylinders are found to be dimensionally correct and can be reused, removal of the carbon ring from the top of the piston or the carbon ridges from the cylinders will promote excessive oil consumption.

CAUTION
Do not wire brush piston skirts.

2. Examine each ring groove for burrs, dented edges and wide wear. Pay particular attention to the top compression ring groove, as it usually wears more than the others.

3. Measure piston-to-cylinder clearance as described under *Piston Clearance Measurement* in this chapter.

4. If damage or wear indicates piston replacement is necessary, select a new piston as described under *Piston Clearance Measurement* in this chapter.

Piston Clearance Measurement

1. Make sure the piston and cylinder walls are clean and dry.

2. Measure the inside diameter of the cylinder at a point 1/2 in. (13 mm) from the upper edge with a bore gauge.

3. Measure the outside diameter of the piston at the specified height from the lower edge of the piston (**Table 1** or **Table 2**) 90° to piston pin axis (**Figure 70**).

4. Subtract the piston diameter from the bore diameter; the difference is piston-to-cylinder clearance. Compare to specifications in **Table 1** or **Table 2**. If clearance is excessive, the piston should be replaced and the cylinder rebored. Purchase the new piston first; measure its diameter and add the specified clearance to determine the proper cylinder bore diameter.

Piston Ring
Removal/Installation

WARNING
The edges of all piston rings are very
sharp. Be careful when handling them
to avoid cut fingers.

1. Measure the side clearance of each ring in its groove with a flat feeler gauge (**Figure 71**) and compare with the specifications listed in **Table 1** or **Table 2**. If the clearance is greater than specified, the rings must be replaced. If the clearance is still excessive with the new rings, the piston must be replaced.

2. Remove the old rings with a ring expander tool or by spreading the ring ends with your thumbs and lifting the rings up evenly (**Figure 72**).

3. Using a broken piston ring, remove all carbon from the piston ring grooves.

4. Inspect grooves' carefully for burrs, nicks or broken or cracked lands. Replace piston if necessary.

5. Check end gap of each ring. To check ring, insert the ring into the bottom of the cylinder bore and square it with the cylinder wall by tapping with the piston crown. The ring should be pushed into the cylinder about 5/8 in. (15 mm). Insert a feeler gauge as shown in **Figure 73**. Compare gap with **Table 1** or **Table 2**. Replace ring if gap is too large. If the gap on the new ring is smaller than specified, hold a small file in a vise, grip the ends of the ring with your fingers and enlarge the gap.

NOTE
The oil control ring expander spacer is unmeasurable. If the oil control ring rails show wear, all 3 parts of the oil control ring should be replaced as a set.

6. Roll each ring around its piston groove as shown in **Figure 74** to check for binding. Minor binding may be cleaned up with a fine-cut file.

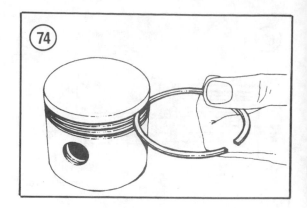

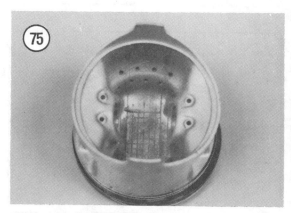

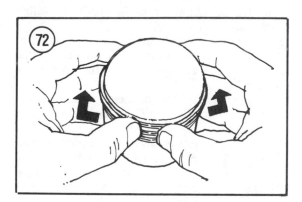

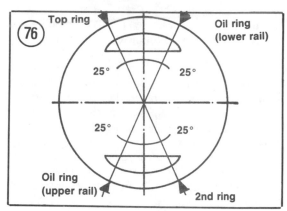

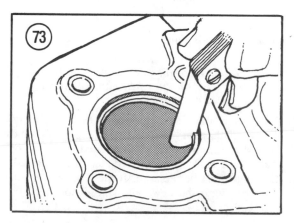

7. Check the oil control holes in the piston (**Figure 75**) for carbon or oil sludge buildup. Clean the holes with a small diameter drill bit.

8. Install the piston rings in the order shown in **Figure 76**.

NOTE
Install all rings with the manufacturer's markings facing up.

9. Install the piston rings—first the bottom, then the middle, then the top ring—by carefully spreading the ends with your thumbs and slipping the rings over the top of the piston. Remember that the piston rings must be installed with the marks on them facing toward the top of the piston or there is the possibility of oil pumping past the rings.

10. Make sure the rings are seated completely in their grooves all the way around the piston and that the end gaps are distributed around the piston as shown in **Figure 76**. It is important that the ring gaps are not aligned with each other when installed to prevent compression pressure from escaping.

11. If installing oversize compression rings, check the number to make sure the correct rings are being installed. The ring numbers should be the same as the piston oversize number.

12. If new rings are installed, measure the side clearance of each ring (**Figure 71**) in its groove and compare to dimensions in **Table 1** or **Table 2**.

OIL PUMP/STRAINER

Removal/Installation

The oil pump on all models can be removed with the engine mounted in the frame; this procedure is shown with the engine removed for clarity.

1. Remove the rotor as described in Chapter Seven.

2. Remove the oil pump cover (**Figure 77**).

3. Remove the oil pump sprocket bolt (A, **Figure 78**) and slide the sprocket (B, **Figure 78**) off of the oil pump. Lift the sprocket up and remove it and the drive chain.

4. Remove the bolts securing the oil pump housing (**Figure 79**) to the crankcase and remove it.

5. Remove the Allen bolts securing the oil line (**Figure 80**) and remove it.

6. Remove the 4 O-rings and dowel pin from the left-hand crankcase. See **Figure 81** and **Figure 82**.

7. Remove the oil pump drive sprocket with a universal type puller. See **Figure 83**.

NOTE
*The oil pump drive sprocket is damaged during removal; a new sprocket **must** be installed during reassembly.*

8. Inspect all parts as described in this chapter.

9. Installation is the reverse of these steps; note the following:

a. Position a *new* oil pump drive sprocket onto the crankshaft. Install the sprocket by driving it into place with a piece of pipe as shown in **Figure 84**.

b. Tighten the oil pump housing bolts and the oil pump driven sprocket bolts to 7.2 ft.-lb. (10 N•m).

c. Install the oil pump cover and push the cover chain guide (if so equipped) toward the front of the engine while tightening the cover bolts (**Figure 85**). This will take up slack in the drive chain.

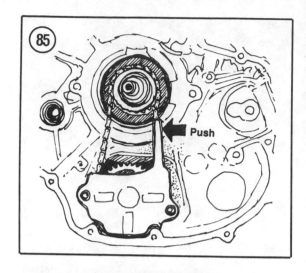

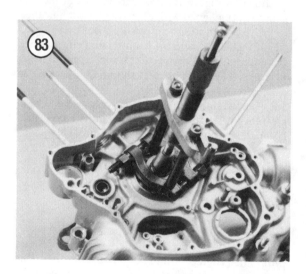

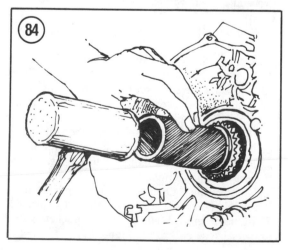

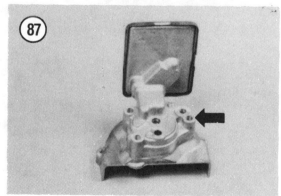

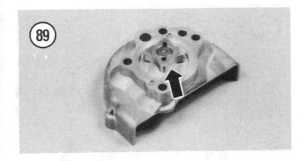

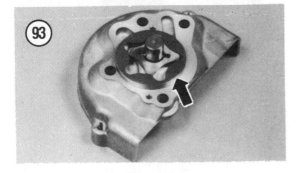

Disassembly/Inspection/Assembly

This procedure describes disassembly and inspection of the oil pump assembly. If any part is worn or damaged, the entire pump assembly must be replaced.

1. Inspect the outer housing for cracks.
2. Remove the bolt (**Figure 86**) securing the oil pump case. Separate the strainer cover (**Figure 87**) from the main housing.
3. Remove the outer (**Figure 88**) and inner (**Figure 89**) rotors from the top housing.
4. Remove the rotor pin (**Figure 90**) and remove the inner housing cover (**Figure 91**).
5. Remove the 2 inner housing alignment pins (**Figure 92**).
6. Remove the outer (**Figure 93**) and inner (**Figure 94**) rotors from the main housing.
7. Remove the rotor pin (**Figure 95**).
8. Clean all parts in solvent and thoroughly dry with compressed air.
9. Assemble the 2 rotor assemblies as shown in **Figure 96**. Replace the oil pump assembly if the rotors appear worn or damaged in any way. If not, proceed to Step 10.

4

10. Install the outer rotors in their respective housings and check the clearance between the housing and the rotor (**Figure 97**) with a flat feeler gauge. The clearance should be within the specifications in **Table 1** or **Table 2**. If the clearance is greater, replace the oil pump.

11. Check the strainer screen (**Figure 98**) for tearing or other damage; replace the oil pump assembly if the strainer is damaged.

12. Check the pump shaft (**Figure 99**) for wear or damage.

NOTE
Proceed with Step 13 only when the above inspection and measurement steps have been completed and all parts are known to be good.

13. Coat all parts (**Figure 100**) with fresh engine oil prior to assembly.

14. Assemble the main housing as follows:
   a. Install the pin (**Figure 95**) through the pin hole in the pump shaft.
   b. Align the slot in the inner rotor with the pin and install the inner rotor onto the main housing (**Figure 94**).
   c. Install the outer rotor (**Figure 93**).
   d. Install the 2 outer housing alignment pins (**Figure 92**).

15. Assemble the inner housing as follows:
   a. Install the inner housing (**Figure 91**).
   b. Install the pin (**Figure 90**) through the pin hole in the pump shaft.
   c. Align the slot in the inner rotor with the pin and install the inner rotor into the inner housing (**Figure 89**).
   d. Install the outer rotor (**Figure 88**).

16. Install the oil strainer cover onto the inner housing (**Figure 87**). Install and tighten the oil pump housing attachment screw (**Figure 86**).

OIL PRESSURE RELIEF VALVE

Removal/Installation

1. Disassemble the crankcase as described in this chapter.

2. The oil pressure relief valve is located at the front of the right-hand crankcase. See **Figure 101**. Remove it by pulling it straight out of its mounting hole. If the valve is tight, twist it slightly while attempting to pull it out.

3. If disassembly of the valve is required, remove the cotter pin securing the unit and pull the spring and end caps out of the valve housing. Discard the O-ring on the outside of the valve housing.

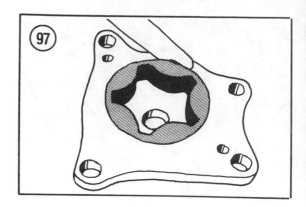

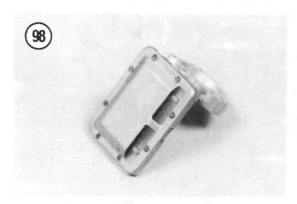

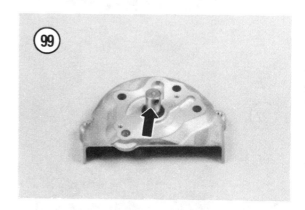

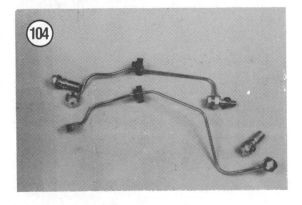

4. Clean all parts in solvent. Inspect all parts for damage or wear. If any part requires replacement the entire oil pressure relief valve must be replaced.

5. Lubricate all parts with *clean* engine oil. Assemble the valve in the reverse order of removal. Secure the spring and end caps with a new cotter pin.

NOTE
Measure the length of the new cotter pin and compare it to the old one. The new cotter pin must be cut to the same length to ensure correct installation.

6. Install the new cotter pin and bend it tightly against the valve housing.

7. Insert the relief valve into the crankcase. Make sure the O-ring does not slide off the valve during installation.

8. Assemble the crankcase as described in this chapter.

OIL LINES

Two oil lines feed engine oil from the main engine oil gallery to the cylinder heads. These lines should be inspected once a month to ensure they have not been damaged.

Removal/Installation

1. Put the bike on the centerstand.
2. Disconnect the negative battery cable.
3. Remove the oil line union bolt and washers at the front and rear cylinders (**Figure 102**).
4. Remove the union bolt where both oil lines meet at the right-hand side of the engine (**Figure 103**).
5. Carefully pull the oil line rubber dampers out of the cylinders and remove both oil lines.
6. Inspect the oil lines (**Figure 104**) for any dents or cracks and replace as required. Do not attempt to repair a damaged oil line.
7. Clean the oil lines in solvent and allow to dry before installation.
8. Clean the union bolts and copper washers (**Figure 104**) in solvent. Replace any washer that appears flattened.
9. Installation is the reverse of these steps; note the following:
   a. Align the oil lines carefully in position. The longer oil line goes to the front cylinder.
   b. Install a union bolt with a copper washer on both sides of the oil line connection. Install the bolts finger-tight at this time. The copper washers with the 3 inside tabs fit onto the longest union bolt.

c. Wedge each oil line rubber damper between two cylinder fins.

d. Tighten the union bolts to 14.5 ft.-lb. (20 N•m).

e. Once the pipes are installed, check their routing carefully.

f. After a brief road test, stop the bike and check the pipes for any signs of leakage. Correct any problems before further operation.

OIL LEVEL SWITCH

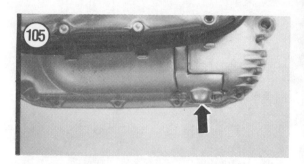

The oil level switch and lamp are designed to alert the rider should the crankcase oil level become low. The oil level switch is located directly below the oil filter housing. The switch can be replaced with the engine in the frame.

Testing

1. Disconnect the oil level switch wire at its bullet or molded connector. Refer to the appropriate wiring diagram at the end of the manual for the wire color code.

2. Connect the oil level switch wire to a good engine ground. Use a suitable jumper lead if necessary. Turn the key switch ON and observe the oil level warning light. If the light comes on, check the engine oil level.

3. If the oil level is low, add the recommended oil as necessary, then repeat this test. If the oil level is correct (but light comes on), replace the oil level switch as described in this chapter.

Removal/Installation

1. Place the bike on the centerstand.

2. Remove the front cylinder exhaust pipe as described in Chapter Six.

3. Drain the engine oil as described in Chapter Three.

4. Disconnect the oil level switch electrical connector.

5. Remove the oil level switch cover (**Figure 105**) and pull the oil level switch out of the crankcase (**Figure 106**).

6. Discard the O-ring on the switch.

7. Installation is the reverse of these steps; note the following:

a. Install a new O-ring on the switch. Coat the O-ring with *clean* engine oil prior to installation.

b. Make sure the area around the switch mounting position is clean of all dirt and other debris.

c. Refill the engine with oil as described in Chapter Three.

NEUTRAL SWITCH

The neutral switch is located underneath the shift lever on the left-hand side of the engine. The neutral switch can be replaced with the engine in the frame. Performance testing of the switch is covered in Chapter Seven.

Removal/Installation

1. Place the bike on the centerstand.
2. Remove the left-hand footrest bar on 1984 models.
3. Drain the engine oil as described in Chapter Three.

4. Slide back the rubber cover and disconnect the electrical connector at the neutral switch (**Figure 107**).
5. Remove the neutral switch by unscrewing it with a socket.
6. Remove and discard the gasket on the switch (**Figure 108**).
7. Installation is the reverse of these steps; note the following:
   a. Install a new gasket on the switch.
   b. Make sure the area around the switch mounting position is clean of all dirt and other debris.
   c. Tighten the neutral switch to 14.5 ft.-lb. (20 N•m).
   d. Refill the engine with oil as described in Chapter Three.

TIMING GEARS

The timing gear for each cylinder is an assembly composed of three gears. The timing gear (front gear) is spring-loaded (A, **Figure 109**) and attached to the intermediate gear (middle gear). See B, **Figure 109**. The cam chain drive gear (C, **Figure 109**) is machined on the backside of the intermediate gear. During this procedure, the gears will be referred to as the timing gear assembly. When aligning the gears, the timing gear (A, **Figure 109**) will be called out separately.

Removal

The procedure for removing the timing gears is the same for the front and rear cylinders. Mark the individual gears and shafts with an "F" and "R" before removal. See **Figure 110**. Note that there are separate installation procedures for the front and rear gears.

1. Remove the engine as described in this chapter.
2. Remove the cylinders as described in this chapter.
3. Remove the timing gear shaft bolt and stopper plate (**Figure 111**).
4. Withdraw the timing gear shaft (**Figure 112**) and remove the timing gear assembly (A, **Figure 113**) and chain (B, **Figure 113**) through the top of the crankcase.
5. To remove either chain tensioner, loosen the tensioner bolt locknut (A, **Figure 114**) and remove the chain tensioner (B, **Figure 114**) through the top of the crankcase.
6. Repeat for the opposite cylinder.

Inspection

1. Wash all parts in solvent and thoroughly dry.

2. Check the gear teeth (A, **Figure 115**) for wear; replace if necessary.

3. Check the shaft (**Figure 112**) for wear or scoring. The shaft surface should show no appreciable wear marks. Replace the shaft if necessary. If the shaft is worn, inspect the shaft bore in the crankcase for wear also.

4. Check the timing chains (**Figure 116**) for wear; replace if necessary. If a timing chain is worn, check the chain drive gear on the backside of the intermediate gear (B, **Figure 115**) and the camshaft sprocket. If any one of the three parts (chain, gear or sprocket) is worn, replace all three as a set.

5. Check the chain tensioner pad (**Figure 116**) and bolt for excessive wear. Replace both parts if necessary.

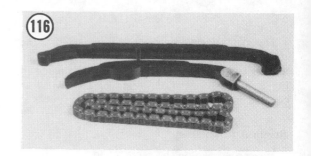

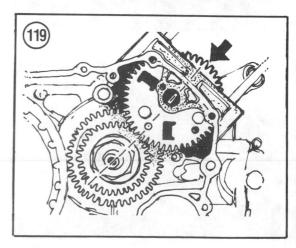

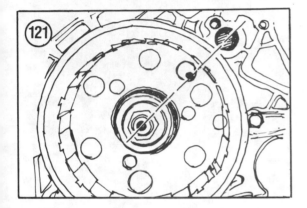

Installation

Front cylinder

1. Remove the clutch assembly if you have not previously done so.

2. Install the camshaft chain tensioner assembly into the crankcase and tighten the securing bolt. See **Figure 114**.

3. Install the timing chain on the cam chain drive gear (B, **Figure 115**).

4. Insert the timing gear/timing chain assembly into the crankcase. Do not engage the gear assembly with the crankshaft.

5. See **Figure 117**. Insert a punch through the timing gear alignment hole.

6. Pry the timing gear with the punch so that its teeth align with the teeth on the intermediate gear (B, **Figure 109**). Then remove the punch.

7. After aligning the gear teeth, lower the timing gear assembly so that it engages with the crankshaft drive gear (**Figure 118**). The timing mark on the timing gear must align with the timing mark on the cam chain drive gear (**Figure 119**).

8. Install the timing gear shaft (**Figure 120**). Secure it with the stopper plate and bolt.

Rear cylinder

1. Install the camshaft chain tensioner assembly into the crankcase and tighten the securing bolt. See **Figure 114**.

2. See **Figure 121**. Hold the chain already installed and rotate the crankshaft so that the flywheel timing hole aligns with the timing gear shaft hole.

3. Install the timing chain on the cam chain drive gear (**Figure 122**).

4. Align the timing mark on the timing gear assembly (**Figure 123**) with the timing gear shaft hole and insert the timing gear/timing chain assembly into the crankcase. Do not engage the gear assembly with the flywheel.

5. See **Figure 124**. Insert a punch through the timing gear alignment hole.

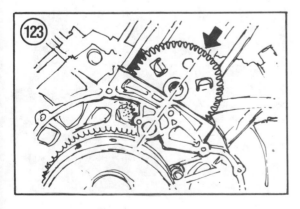

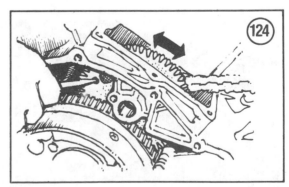

6. Pry the timing gear with the punch so that its teeth align with the teeth on the intermediate gear (B, **Figure 109**).

7. After aligning the gear teeth, lower the timing gear assembly so that it engages with the flywheel drive gear. The timing mark on the timing gear must align with the timing hole on the flywheel.

8. Install the timing gear shaft. Secure it with the stopper plate and bolt.

Both cylinders

1. Reinstall the cylinders and engine as described in this chapter.

PRIMARY DRIVE GEAR

Removal/Installation

1. Remove the engine as described in this chapter.
2. Pry the lockwasher tab away from the primary drive gear nut.
3. Place a copper or lead washer between the cam chain drive and intermediate gears (**Figure 125**) to lock the gears while you loosen the primary drive gear nut (**Figure 126**).
4. Remove the front cylinder as described in this chapter.
5. Remove the front cylinder timing gear assembly as described in this chapter.
6. Remove the primary drive gear nut (**Figure 127**) and lockwasher (**Figure 128**).
7. Remove the washer (**Figure 129**) and remove the cam chain drive/primary drive gear assembly (**Figure 130**).
8. Remove the Woodruff key (**Figure 131**).
9. Disassemble the cam chain drive and primary drive gears (**Figure 132**) by pulling them apart. Remove the 6 springs and 6 pins from the primary drive gear slots (**Figure 133**).
10. Inspect the cam chain drive and primary drive gears; replace them if necessary.
11. Check the springs and pins for wear or damage; replace them as a set if any one is worn or damaged.

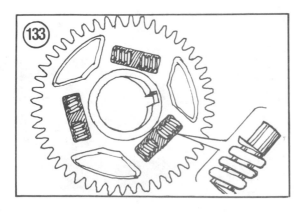

12. Installation is the reverse of these steps; note the following.

13. Install 2 pins and 2 springs in each slot in the primary drive gear (**Figure 133**). Push both springs in each slot as far away from each other as possible.

14. Align the drive dogs on the backside of the cam chain drive gear with the slots in the primary drive gear and install the drive gear. The dot on the cam chain drive gear should align with the dot on the primary drive gear. See **Figure 134**.

15. Make sure the Woodruff key (**Figure 131**) is installed on the crankshaft.

16. Tighten the primary drive gear nut to specifications (**Table 3**).

4

CRANKCASE

Service to the lower end requires that the crankcase assembly be removed from the motorcycle frame and disassembled (split).

Disassembly

1. Remove the engine as described in this chapter. Remove all exterior assemblies from the crankcase. Set the engine on the workbench.

2. Remove the shift fork-guide bar stopper plate (**Figure 135**) from the right-hand crankcase.

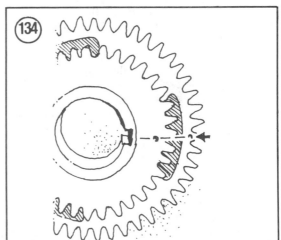

3. Remove the neutral switch from the left-hand crankcase.

4. Loosen by 1/2 turn all numbered bolts (No. 1-14) in the left-hand crankcase half (**Figure 136**). Work in sequence, starting with the highest number first. The numbers are stamped into the case next to each bolt hole.

5. Turn the crankcase around.

6. Loosen by 1/2 turn all numbered bolts (No. 15-19) in the right-hand crankcase. Work in sequence, starting with the highest number first (**Figure 136**). After loosening all bolts, remove them from the left- and right-hand crankcase halves.

NOTE
Bolt No. 15 uses a copper washer. Do not lose it.

7. Carefully tap around the perimeter of the crankcase with a plastic mallet (do not use a metal hammer) to help separate the 2 case halves.

8. As you separate the crankcase halves, the transmission and crankshaft assemblies should stay in the left-hand crankcase. Check the right-hand crankcase to make sure no transmission shims are stuck to the bearings. If found, reinstall them immediately in their original position.

9. Remove the red O-ring (**Figure 137**).

10. Remove the black O-ring and dowel pin (**Figure 138**) located underneath the crankshaft.

11. Remove the 3 dowel pins. See **Figure 139** and **Figure 140**.

12A. *Chain-drive models:* Remove the middle driven gear assembly from the crankcase.

12B. *Shaft-drive models:* Remove the middle driven gear (**Figure 141**). Removal of the drive shaft assembly is not required unless it is damaged or the left-hand crankcase requires replacement. If necessary, take the crankcase half to a dealer and have it removed. Special tools and procedures are required.

13. Remove the transmission, shift forks and shift drum assemblies from the left-hand crankcase half as described in Chapter Five.

14. Remove the crankshaft assembly as described in this chapter.

Inspection

1. Thoroughly clean the inside and outside of both crankcase halves with cleaning solvent. Dry with compressed air. Make sure there is no solvent residue left in the cases as it will contaminate the new engine oil. Lubricate the bearings with oil to prevent rust formation.

2. Make sure all oil passages are clean; blow them out with compressed air.

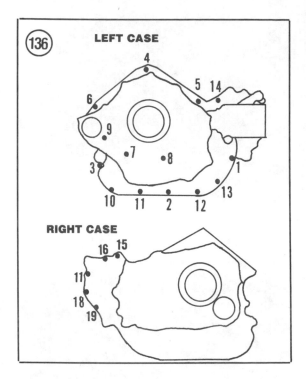

3. Check the crankcases for cracks or other damage. Inspect the mating surfaces of both halves. They must be free of gouges, burrs or any damage that could cause an oil leak.

4. Make sure the cylinder studs are not bent and the threads are in good condition. Make sure they are screwed into the crankcase tightly. Do not remove the covers from the cylinder studs.

5. Inspect the crankcase bearings as described in this chapter.

6A. *Chain-drive models*: Inspect the middle driven gear assembly for wear or damage. If the unit requires disassembly for parts replacement or further inspection, refer all service to a dealer as a press is required to compress and remove the spring unit.

> *WARNING*
> *Do not attempt to disassemble the middle driven gear assembly without the use of a suitable press. Serious injuries may result from the use of improper tools and service techniques.*

6B. *Shaft-drive models*: Inspect the middle driven gear for wear or damage.

Crankcase Bearings
Inspection/Replacement

1. After cleaning the crankcase halves in cleaning solvent and drying with compressed air, lubricate the bearings with engine oil.

2. Rotate the bearing inner race and check for play or roughness. Replace the bearing if it is noisy or if it does not spin smoothly.

3. To remove crankcase bearings:
  a. Heat the crankcase to approximately 200-260° F (95-125° C) in an oven or on a hot plate. Do not heat the crankcase with a torch as this type of localized heating may warp the case.
  b. Wearing a pair of work gloves for protection, remove the case from the oven and place it on wood blocks for support. Drive out the bearing with a suitable size drift placed on the outside bearing race. A large socket works well for bearing removal.

> *NOTE*
> *The main bearings are installed in a steel sleeve that is part of the crankcase (Figure 142). When attempting to remove these bearings, the sleeve should also be supported with wood blocks on the opposite side to prevent its being driven out with the bearing.*

4. Before installing new bearings, clean the bearing housing and oil passages with solvent. Dry thoroughly with compressed air.

5. Install new crankcase bearings by reversing the removal steps, noting the following:

   a. The two crankshaft bearings are not interchangeable. The left-hand bearing has a groove in the outer race; the right-hand bearing does not.

   b. Installation of the bearings is made easier by first placing the bearings in a freezer for approximately 30 minutes. Then reheat the crankcase half and install the bearing by driving it squarely into position. If the bearing cocks in its bore, remove it and reinstall. It may be necessary to refreeze the bearing and reheat the case half.

   c. Lubricate the bearing races with clean engine oil after installation.

Assembly

1. Prior to installation, coat all parts with assembly oil or engine oil.
2. Install the middle drive gear assembly as described in this chapter (if removed).
3. Install the crankshaft as described in this chapter.
4. Place the left-hand crankcase on wood blocks as shown in **Figure 143**.
5. Install the shift drum, shift forks and transmission assemblies as described in Chapter Five.
6. Install the 2 O-rings in the left-hand crankcase as follows:

   a. Red O-ring (**Figure 137**).

   b. Black O-ring (**Figure 138**) and small dowel pin.

7. Install the 3 crankcase half locating dowel pins. See **Figure 139** and **Figure 140**.
8. Clean the crankcase mating surfaces of both halves with contact cleaner.
9. Make sure the case half sealing surfaces are perfectly clean and dry.
10. Apply a light coat of Yamabond No. 4 liquid gasket sealer (**Figure 144**) to the sealing surfaces of each half. Make the coating as thin as possible.

> *NOTE*
> *Always use the correct type of gasket sealer—avoid thick and hard-setting materials.*

11. Align the right-hand crankcase bearings with the left-hand assembly. Join both halves and tap together lightly with a plastic mallet—do not use a metal hammer as it will damage the case.
12. Apply oil to the threads of all bolts. Install all bolts in both crankcase halves and tighten in two stages to a final torque as follows:

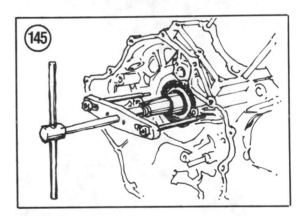

   a. 6 mm bolts—7.2 ft.-lb. (10 N•m).

   b. 10 mm bolts—28 ft.-lb. (39 N•m).

Tighten bolts in the correct sequence. See **Figure 136**. The torque pattern is indicated by the bolt number next to the bolt hole.

> *NOTE*
> *Bolt No. 15 uses a copper washer.*

13. Install all engine assemblies that were removed.
14. Install the engine as described in this chapter.

CRANKSHAFT AND CONNECTING RODS

Removal/Installation

1. Disassemble the crankcase as described in this chapter.

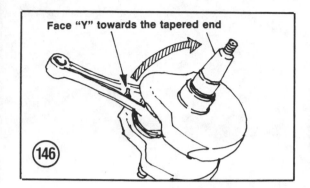

Face "Y" towards the tapered end

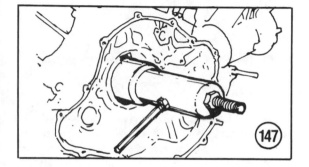

2. Remove the transmission assemblies as described in Chapter Five.

3. Remove the middle driven gear as described under *Crankcase Disassembly* in this chapter.

4. Remove the oil pump drive sprocket as described under *Oil Pump* in this chapter.

NOTE
The oil pump drive sprocket will be damaged during removal; a new sprocket must be installed during reassembly.

5. Remove the crankshaft from the left-hand crankcase bearing with a universal type puller as shown in **Figure 145**.

6. Remove the connecting rod cap bolts and separate the rods from the crankshaft. Mark each rod cap and bearing insert so that they can be reinstalled in their original position.

7. Install by reversing these removal steps; note the following.

8. Install the bearing inserts into each connecting rod and cap. Make sure they are locked in place correctly.

CAUTION
If the old bearings are reused, be sure they are installed in their exact original positions.

9. Lubricate the bearings and crankpins with assembly oil and install the rods so that the letter

"Y" on each rod faces the tapered end of the crankshaft (**Figure 146**). Apply molybdenum disulfide grease to the threads of the connecting rods. Install the caps and tighten the cap nuts evenly, in a couple of steps, to 35 ft.-lb. (48 N•m).

CAUTION
*On the final tightening sequence, if a torque of 31 ft.-lb. (43 N•m) is reached, **do not stop** tightening until the final torque value is achieved. If the tightening is interrupted between 31-34 ft.-lb. (43-48 N•m), loosen the nut to less than 31 ft.-lb. (43 N•m) and tighten to the final torque value in one step.*

10. Install the crankshaft in the left-hand crankcase bearing using the Yamaha crankshaft installation puller (TLU-90900-57-01) and puller adapter No. 10 (TLU-90900-69-00). See **Figure 147**. When installing the crankshaft, align the front and rear connecting rods with their respective cylinder position (**Figure 148**). Continue to check this alignment until the crankshaft is completely installed.

CAUTION
Do not attempt to install the crankshaft without using the special tools described in Step 10. Do not knock the crankshaft into position with a hammer as this may force the crankshaft out of alignment. If you do not have the special tools, have a Yamaha dealer install the crankshaft for you.

Connecting Rod Inspection

1. Check each rod for obvious damage such as cracks and burns.

2. Check the piston pin bushing for wear or scoring.

3. Take the rods to a machine shop and have them checked for twisting and bending.

4. Examine the bearing inserts (**Figure 149**) for wear, scoring or burning. They are reusable if in good condition. Make a note of the bearing size (if any) stamped on the back of the insert if the bearing is to be replaced; a previous owner may have used undersize bearings.

5. Remove the connecting rod bearing bolts and check them for cracks or twisting. Replace any bolts as required.

6. Check bearing clearance as described in this chapter.

**Connecting Rod Bearing
Clearance Measurement**

> *CAUTION*
> *If the old bearings are to be reused, be sure that they are installed in their exact original location.*

1. Wipe bearing inserts and crankpins clean. Install bearing inserts in rod and cap (**Figure 150**).
2. Place a piece of Plastigage on one crankpin parallel to the crankshaft.
3. Install rod and cap. Tighten nuts to 35 ft.-lb. (48 N•m).

> *CAUTION*
> *Do not rotate crankshaft while Plastigage is in place.*

4. Remove rod cap.
5. Measure width of flattened Plastigage according to the manufacturer's instructions (**Figure 151**). Measure at both ends of the strip. A difference of 0.001 in. (0.025 mm) or more indicates a tapered crankpin; the crankshaft must be reground or replaced.
6. If the crankpin taper is within tolerance, measure the bearing clearance with the same strip of Plastigage. Correct bearing clearance is specified in **Table 1** and **Table 2**. Remove Plastigage strips.
7. If the bearing clearance is greater than specified, use the following steps for new bearing selection.
8. The connecting rods and caps are marked "4" or "5" (**Figure 152**).
9. The crankshaft is marked on the left-hand counterbalancer with a set of 2 numbers (**Figure 153**). The numbers relate to the crankshaft connecting rod journals, reading from left to right.
10. To select the proper bearing insert number, subtract the crankshaft connecting rod journal number (Step 9) from the connecting rod and cap number (Step 8). For example, if the connecting rod and cap number is 4 and the crankshaft connecting rod journal is 2, 4 - 2 = 2. The new bearing insert should be coded 2.

11. After new bearings have been installed, recheck clearance with Plastigage. If the clearance is out of specifications, either the connecting rod or the crankshaft is worn beyond the service limit. Refer the engine to a dealer or qualified specialist.

Crankshaft Inspection

1. Clean crankshaft thoroughly with solvent. Clean oil holes with rifle cleaning brushes; flush thoroughly and dry with compressed air. Lightly oil all journal surfaces immediately to prevent rust.
2. If the surface on all journals is satisfactory, take the crankshaft to your dealer or local machine shop. They can check out-of-roundness, taper and wear on the journals. They can also check crankshaft alignment and inspect for cracks. Check against measurements given in **Table 1** or **Table 2**.
3. Inspect the cam chain and primary chain drive sprockets. If they are worn or damaged, the crankshaft will have to be replaced. Also inspect the condition of both chains; replace if necessary.

MIDDLE DRIVE GEAR

Because special tools and procedures are required, refer all service to a qualified Yamaha specialist.

STARTER GEARS

**Removal/Installation
1981-1983 XV750 and XV920; 1984-1985 XV700)**

Refer to **Figure 154** for this procedure.
1. Remove the left side crankcase cover.
2. Remove the circlip and remove the starter motor drive gear and spring clip.

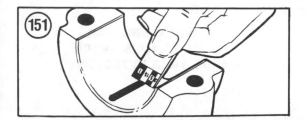

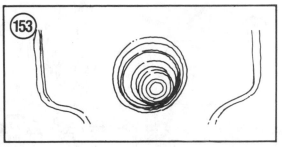

3. Remove the idler gear shaft and remove the following parts in order:
   a. Idler wheel.
   b. Spring.
   c. Idler gear No. 2 and spring clip.
   d. Idler gear No. 1.
   e. Washer.
4. Inspect the teeth on the starter driven gear and on the idler gear. Look for chipped or missing teeth. Check for uneven or excessive wear on the gear faces. Replace if necessary.
5. Installation is the reverse of these steps.

Removal/Installation
1986-1987 XV700; 1988-on XV750;
XV1000 and XV1100)

Refer to **Figure 155**.
1. Disconnect the electrical starter cable at the starter.
2. Remove the drive lever cover and its gasket.
3. Remove the left side crankcase cover.
4. Loosen the drive lever collar screw.
5. Referring to **Figure 155**, remove the following in order:
   a. Starter gear shaft and O-ring.
   b. Starter wheel.
   c. Spring.
   d. Idler gear.
   e. Drive lever shaft.
   f. Idler gear.
   g. Spacer.
6. Remove the circlip. Then remove the starter clutch and circlip.
7. At the crankcase cover, remove the drive lever screw and the solenoid securing nut.
8. Remove the solenoid screws and pull the solenoid out of the crankcase cover. Remove the solenoid gasket.

9. Remove the drive lever collar, then remove the drive lever and spring.
10. Inspect the teeth on the starter driven gear and on the idler gear. Look for chipped or missing teeth. Check for uneven or excessive wear on the gear faces. Replace if necessary.
11. Installation is the reverse of these steps.

BREAK-IN

Following cylinder servicing (boring, honing, new rings, etc.) and major lower end work, the engine should be broken in just as if it were new. The performance and service life of the engine depends greatly on a careful and sensible break-in. For the first 500 miles, no more than one-third throttle should be used and speed should be varied as much as possible within the one-third throttle limit. Prolonged, steady running at one speed, no matter how moderate, is to be avoided, as is hard acceleration.

Following the 500-mile service, increasingly more throttle can be used but full throttle should not be used until the motorcycle has covered at least 1,000 miles and then it should be limited to short bursts until 1,500 miles have been logged.

During the break-in period, oil consumption will be higher than normal. It is therefore important to frequently check and correct the oil level. At no time, during break-in or later, should the oil level be allowed to drop below the bottom line on the inspection window; if the oil level is low, the oil will become overheated resulting in insufficient lubrication and increased wear.

500-mile Service

It is essential that the oil and filter be changed after the first 500 miles. In addition, it is a good idea to change the oil and filter at the completion of break-in (about 1,500 miles) to ensure that all of the particles produced during break-in are removed from the lubrication system. The small added expense may be considered a smart investment that will pay off in increased engine life.

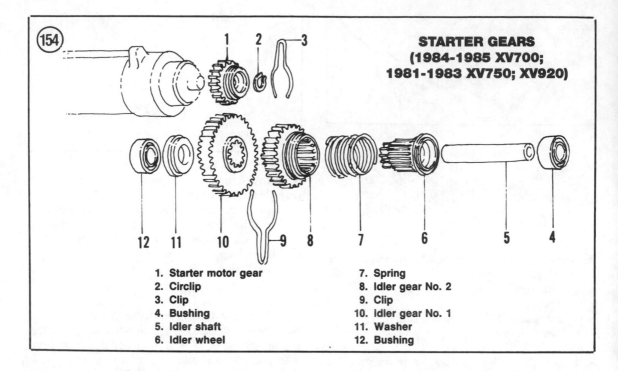

**STARTER GEARS
(1984-1985 XV700;
1981-1983 XV750; XV920)**

1. Starter motor gear
2. Circlip
3. Clip
4. Bushing
5. Idler shaft
6. Idler wheel
7. Spring
8. Idler gear No. 2
9. Clip
10. Idler gear No. 1
11. Washer
12. Bushing

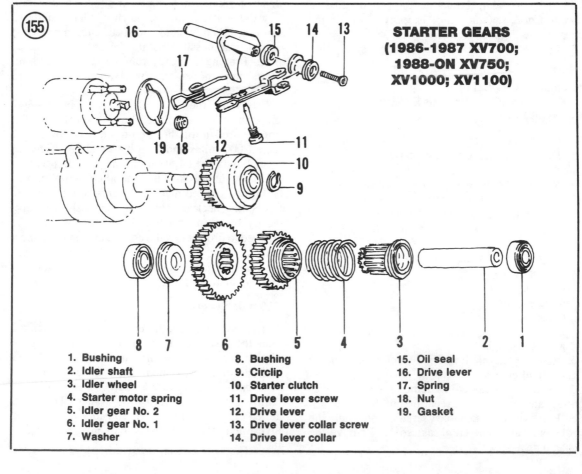

**STARTER GEARS
(1986-1987 XV700;
1988-ON XV750;
XV1000; XV1100)**

1. Bushing
2. Idler shaft
3. Idler wheel
4. Starter motor spring
5. Idler gear No. 2
6. Idler gear No. 1
7. Washer
8. Bushing
9. Circlip
10. Starter clutch
11. Drive lever screw
12. Drive lever
13. Drive lever collar screw
14. Drive lever collar
15. Oil seal
16. Drive lever
17. Spring
18. Nut
19. Gasket

Table 1 ENGINE SPECIFICATIONS (XV700 AND XV750)

Item	Specifications in. (mm)	Wear limit in. (mm)
General		
Type	4-stroke, air-cooled, V-twin	
Number of cylinders	2	
Bore and stroke		
XV700	3.16 × 2.72 (80.2 × 69.2)	
XV750	3.268 × 2.72 (83.0 × 69.2)	
Displacement		
XV700	42.65 cu. in. (699 cc)	
XV750	45.64 cu. in. (748 cc)	
Compression ratio		
XV700	9.0:1	
XV750	8.7:1	
Cylinders	Aluminum alloy with cast iron liners	
Warp limit	0.001 (0.03)	
Bore		
XV700	3.157 (80.2)	
XV750	3.268 (83.0)	
Taper	—	0.002 (0.05)
Out-of-round	—	0.0004 (0.01)
Piston/cylinder clearance		
XV700	0.0016-0.0024 (0.040-0.060)	
XV750	0.0016-0.0024 (0.040-0.060)	
Pistons		
Diameter		
XV700	3.155-3.157 (80.155-80.157)	
XV750	3.266-3.267 (82.95-82.97)	
Measuring point		
XV700	0.354 (9.0)	
XV750	0.374 (9.5)	
Piston rings		
Number per piston		
Compression	2	
Oil control	1	
Ring end gap		
Top and second		
XV700	0.008-0.016 (0.2-0.4)	
XV750 (1981-1983)	0.012-0.020 (0.3-0.5)	
XV750 (1988-on)	0.008-0.016 (0.2-0.4)	
Oil (side rail)		
XV700	0.008-0.027 (0.2-0.7)	
XV750 (1981-1983)	0.012-0.035 (0.3-0.9)	
XV750 (1988-on)	0.012-0.020 (0.3-0.5)	
Ring side clearance		
XV700		

(continued)

Table 1 ENGINE SPECIFICATIONS (XV700, XV750) (continued)

Item	Specifications in. (mm)	Wear limit in. (mm)
Top	0.0016-0.0031 (0.04-0.08)	
Second	0.0012-0.0028 (0.03-0.07)	
XV750		
Top and second	0.0016-0.0031 (0.04-0.08)	
Oil control		
XV700, XV750	0-0.0015 (0.04)	
Crankshaft		
Runout	—	0.0008 (0.02)
Connecting rod bearing clearance	0.0012-0.0021 (0.030-0.054)	
Connecting rod big-end side clearance	0.0146-0.0187 (0.370-0.474)	
Camshaft		
Runout	—	0.001 (0.03)
Bearing clearance		
XV700	0.0008-0.0024 (0.020-0.061)	
XV750 (1981-1983)	0.0008-0.0021 (0.020-0.054)	
XV750 (1988-on)	0.0008-0.0024 (0.020-0.061)	
Lobe height		
Intake	1.5421 (39.17)	1.5362 (39.02)
Exhaust	1.5433 (39.20)	1.5374 (39.05)
Lobe width		
XV700		
Intake	1.2689 (32.23)	
Exhaust	1.2701 (32.26)	
XV750 (all)	1.2598 (32.00)	1.2539 (31.85)
Cam cap inside diameter	0.9843-0.9851 (25.000-25.021)	
Cam journal outside diameter	0.9827-0.9835 (24.96-24.98)	
Rocker arms and shafts		
XV700		
Shaft clearance	0.0003-0.0013 (0.009-0.033)	
Rocker arm inside diameter	0.5512-0.5518 (14.000-14.018)	
Rocker arm shaft outside diameter	0.5505-0.5508 (13.985-13.991)	

(continued)

Table 1 ENGINE SPECIFICATIONS (XV700, XV750) (continued)

Item	Specifications in. (mm)	Wear limit in. (mm)
XV750		
Shaft clearance	0.0004-0.0017 (0.010-0.043)	0.0039 (0.1)
Rocker arm inside diameter	0.5512-0.5518 (14.000-14.018)	0.533 (14.05)
Rocker arm shaft outside diameter	0.5502-0.5508 (13.975-13.991)	0.549 (13.95)
Valves		
Valve stem outer diameter		
Intake	0.3140-0.3145 (7.975-7.990)	
Exhaust	0.3133-0.3140 (7.960-7.975)	
Valve guide inner diameter	0.3150-0.3160 (8.0-8.012)	
Stem-to-guide clearance		
Intake	0.0004-0.0015 (0.010-0.037)	0.0039 (0.1)
Exhaust	0.0010-0.0020 (0.025-0.052)	0.0039 (0.1)
Valve seat width	0.051 ±0.0039 (1.3 ±0.01)	0.08 (2.0)
Valve face width	0.083 (2.1)	
Valve stem runout (maximum)	—	0.0012 (0.03)
Margin thickness	0.051 ±0.0079 (1.3 ±0.2)	0.028 (0.7)
Head diameter		
Intake	1.693-1.701 (43.00-43.02)	
Exhaust	1.457-1.465 (37.00-37.02)	
Valve springs		
Outer free length	1.756 (44.6)	
Inner free length	1.783 (45.3)	
Oil pump		
Tip clearance	0.0012-0.0035 (0.03-0.09)	
Side clearance	0.0012-0.0031 (0.03-0.08)	

4

Table 2 ENGINE SPECIFICATIONS (XV920, XV1000 AND XV1100)

Item	Specifications in. (mm)	Wear limit in. (mm)
General		
Type	4-stroke, air-cooled, V-twin	
Number of cylinders	2	
Bore and stroke		
XV920	3.62×2.72 in. (92.0×69.2 mm)	
XV1000	3.74×2.72 in. (95.0×69.2 mm)	
XV1100	3.74×2.95 in. (95.0×75.0 mm)	
Displacement		
XV920	56.14 cu. in. (920 cc)	
XV1000	59.86 cu. in. (981 cc)	
XV1100	64.86 cu. in. (1,063 cc)	
Compression ratio	8.3:1	
Cylinders	Aluminum alloy with cast iron liners	
Warp limit	0.001 (0.03)	
Bore		
XV920	3.661 (92.0)	
XV1000, XV1100	3.74 (95.0)	
Taper		0.002 (0.05)
Out-of-round		0.0004 (0.01)
Piston/cylinder clearance	0.0018-0.0026 (0.045-0.065)	
Pistons		
Diameter		
XV920	3.622 (92.0)	
XV1000, XV1100	3.738 (94.965)	
Measuring point	0.575 (14.6)	
Piston rings		
Number per piston		
Compression	2	
Oil control	1	
Ring end gap		
XV920		
Top and second	0.008-0.016 (0.2-0.4)	
XV1000, XV1100		
Top	0.012-0.020 (0.3-0.5)	
Second		
XV1000	0.008-0.016 (0.2-0.4)	
XV1100	0.012-0.018 (0.3-0.45)	
Oil (side rail)		
XV920RH, RJ, XV1000	0.012-0.035 (0.3-0.9)	
XV920J, K, MK	0.012-0.024 (0.3-0.6)	
XV1100	0.008-0.0276 (0.2-0.7)	
Ring side clearance		
Top	0.0016-0.0031 (0.04-0.08)	
Second	0.0012-0.0028 (0.03-0.07)	
Crankshaft		
Runout	—	0.0008 (0.02)
Connecting rod side clearance	0.0146-0.0187 (0.370-0.474)	
Connecting rod oil clearance	0.0012-0.0021 (0.030-0.054)	
Camshaft		
Runout	—	0.001 (0.03)
Oil clearance		
XV920	0.0008-0.0021 (0.020-0.054)	
XV1000, XV1100	0.0008-0.0024 (0.020-0.061)	
		(continued)

Table 2 ENGINE SPECIFICATIONS (XV920, XV1000 AND XV1100) (continued)

Item	Specifications in. (mm)	Wear limit in. (mm)
Lobe height		
Intake	1.5421 (39.17)	1.5362 (39.02)
Exhaust	1.5433 (39.20)	1.5374 (39.05)
Lobe width		
XV920 (all)	1.2598 (32.00)	1.2539 (31.85)
XV1000, XV1100		
Intake	1.2665 (32.17)	
Exhaust	1.2705 (32.27)	
Cam cap inside diameter		
XV920		
Front cylinder	0.9448-0.9456 (23.997-24.018)	
Rear cylinder	0.9843-0.9851 (25.000-25.021)	
XV1000, XV1100	0.09843-0.9851 (25.000-25.021)	
Camshaft outside diameter		
XV920		
Front cylinder	0.9440-0.9435 (23.98-23.96)	
Rear cylinder	0.9835-0.9830 (24.98-24.97)	
XV1000	0.9440-0.9432 (23.98-23.95)	
XV1100	0.9826-0.9834 (24.96-24.98)	
Rocker arms and shafts		
XV920		
Shaft clearance	0.004-0.0017 (0.010-0.043)	0.0039 (0.1)
Rocker arm inside diameter	0.5512-0.5518 (14.000-14.018)	0.533 (14.05)
Rocker arm shaft diameter	0.5502-0.5508 (13.975-13.990)	0.549 (13.95)
XV1000, XV1100		
Shaft clearance	0.0003-0.0013 (0.009-0.033)	
Rocker arm inside diameter	0.5512-0.5518 (14.000-14.018)	
Rocker arm shaft outside diameter	0.5505-0.5508 (13.985-13.991)	
Valves		
Valve stem outer diameter		
Intake	0.3140-0.3145 (7.975-7.990)	
Exhaust	0.3133-0.3140 (7.960-7.975)	
Valve guide inner diameter		
Intake and exhaust	0.3150-0.3160 (8.0-8.012)	
Stem-to-guide clearance		
Intake	0.0004-0.0015 (0.010-0.037)	0.0039 (0.1)
Exhaust	0.0010-0.0020 (0.025-0.052)	0.0039 (0.1)
Valve seat width		
Intake & exhaust	0.051 ±0.0039 (1.3 ±0.01)	0.08 (2.0)
Valve face width		
Intake & exhaust	0.083 (2.1)	
Valve stem run-out maximum	(0.03)	0.0012

(continued)

4

Table 2 ENGINE SPECIFICATIONS (XV920, XV1000 AND XV1100) (continued)

Item	Specifications in. (mm)	Wear limit in. (mm)
Margin thickness		
Intake & exhaust	0.051 ±0.0079 (1.3 ±0.2)	0.028 (0.7)
Head diameter		
XV920RH, RJ		
Intake	1.693-1.701 (43.00-43.02)	
Exhaust	1.457-1.465 (37.00-37.02)	
XV920J, K, MK;		
XV1000; XV1100		
Intake	1.850-1.858 (47.00-47.20)	
Exhaust	1.540-1.548 (39.00-39.02)	
Valve springs (XV920, XV1000)		
Outer free length		
Intake & exhaust	1.756 (44.6)	
Inner free length		
Intake & exhaust	1.783 (45.3)	
Valve springs (XV1100)		
Outer free length		
Intake & exhaust	1.789 (45.33)	
Inner free length		
Intake & exhaust	1.708 (43.39)	
Oil pump		
Tip clearance	0.0012-0.0035 (0.03-0.09)	
Side clearance	0.0012-0.0031 (0.03-0.08)	

Table 3 ENGINE TIGHTENING TORQUES

	ft.-lb.	N•m
Cylinder nut (XV750 & XV920)		
No. 1	36	50
No. 2	46	64
Cylinder nut (XV700, XV1000 and XV1100)	36	50
Cylinder head nut		
XV750, XV920	29	40
XV700, XV1000, XV1100	25	35
Cylinder head bolt	14	20
Cam sprocket cover	7	10
Cam sprocket	40	55
Camshaft bushing	14	20
Rocker arm cover	7	10
Rocker arm shaft	27	38
Rocker arm shaft/oil delivery pipe	14	20
Oil delivery pipe	14	20
Valve adjuster locknut	19	27
Cam chain tensioner bolt	7	10
Cylinder bolt	7	10
Cam chain guide (rear)		
Bolt	6	8
Nut	9	12
Starter motor	7	10
Timing gear shaft stopper plate	7	10
		(continued)

Table 3 ENGINE TIGHTENING TORQUES (continued)

	ft.-lb.	N•m
Flywheel nut		
1981-1983	112	155
1984-on	125	175
Primary drive gear		
XV750	50	70
XV700, XV920, XV1000, XV1100	80	110
Clutch boss	50	70
Crankshaft end cover	9	12
Oil pump cover	7	10
Oil pump sprocket	9	12
Oil pump	7	10
Neutral switch	14	20
Shift fork guide bar sprocket	5	7
Crankcase bolts		
M10	28	39
M6	7	10
Connecting rod nut	35	48
Engine drain plug	31	43
Oil level switch	7	10

Table 4 SHAFT DRIVE UNIT TIGHTENING TORQUES

	ft.-lb.	N•m
Drive shaft nut	80	110
Bearing housing (XV750, XV920)		
Bolt	16	23
Nut	16	23
Bearing housing (XV700, XV1000, XV1100)		
Bolt	18	25
Oil drain screw	16	23
Bearing retainer*	80	110

* Left-hand threads.

Table 5 ENGINE MOUNT TIGHTENING TORQUES

Item	ft.-lb.	N•m
All engine mount fasteners		
XV750, XV920RH, RJ	39	54
XV920J, K, MK	50	70
XV700, XV1000, XV1100		
Front engine mount bracket	46	64
All others	40	55

CHAPTER FIVE

CLUTCH AND TRANSMISSION

CLUTCH

The clutch on the Yamaha XV is a wet multi-plate type which operates immersed in the engine oil.

All clutch parts can be removed with the engine in the frame. Refer to **Table 1** or **Table 2** for specifications on all clutch components and **Table 3** for all tightening torques. **Tables 1-3** are found at the end of the chapter.

Removal

This procedure is shown with the engine partially disassembled. Engine disassembly is not necessary for clutch removal. Refer to **Figure 1A** or **Figure 1B**.

1. Place the bike on the centerstand.
2. Drain the engine oil as described in Chapter Three.
3. Loosen and slide the cover away from the clutch lever adjustment nut at the handlebar and slacken the clutch cable (**Figure 2**).
4. Remove the clutch adjuster cover (**Figure 3**).
5. Loosen the clutch adjuster locknut and turn the adjuster (**Figure 4**) counterclockwise 2-3 turns.
6. See **Figure 5**. Remove the following from the right-hand side.

a. Rear brake pedal (A).
b. Footpeg assembly (B).
c. Left-hand footrest bar, if so equipped.

7. Remove the Allen bolts securing the right-hand side cover (**Figure 6**) in place and remove it.

8A. *All models except XV1100:* Perform the following:

a. Remove the 6 pressure plate screws (**Figure 7**) and springs (**Figure 8**).
b. Remove the pressure plate (**Figure 9**).
c. Remove the clutch plate (**Figure 10**) and friction disc (**Figure 11**). Continue until all plates are removed. Stack plates in order.
d. Remove the washer (**Figure 12**), clutch release bearing (**Figure 13**) and outer pushrod (**Figure 14**).

8B. *XV1100:*Perform the following:

a. Remove the plate washer screws (1, **Figure 1B**).
b. Remove the plate washer (2, **Figure 1B**) and the clutch spring (3, **Figure 1B**).
c. Remove the spring seat (4, **Figure 1B**).
d. Remove the clutch pressure plate (5, **Figure 1B**).
e. Remove the washer (6, **Figure 1B**), clutch release bearing (7, **Figure 1B**) and pushrod (8, **Figure 1B**).

9. Straighten out the locking tab on the clutch nut and remove the clutch nut (**Figure 15**).

(1) A

**CLUTCH
(EXCEPT XV1100)**

1. Screw
2. Washer
3. Spring
4. Pressure plate
5. Washer
6. Bearing
7. Pushrod
8. Nut
9. Lockwasher
10. Clutch plate
11. Friction plate
12. Ring
13. Clutch plate
14. Spring
15. Seat plate
16. Clutch boss
17. Washer
18. Clutch housing
19. Long pushrod

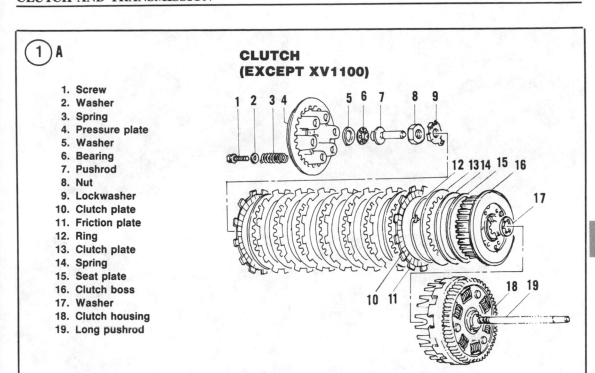

5

(1) B

**CLUTCH
(XV1100)**

1. Screw
2. Plate Washer
3. Clutch spring
4. Spring seat
5. Pressure plate
6. Washer
7. Bearing
8. Pushrod
9. Nut
10. Lockwasher
11. Clutch plate
12. Friction disc
13. Ring
14. Clutch plate
15. Spring
16. Seat plate
17. Clutch boss
18. Washer
19. Clutch housing
20. Long pushrod

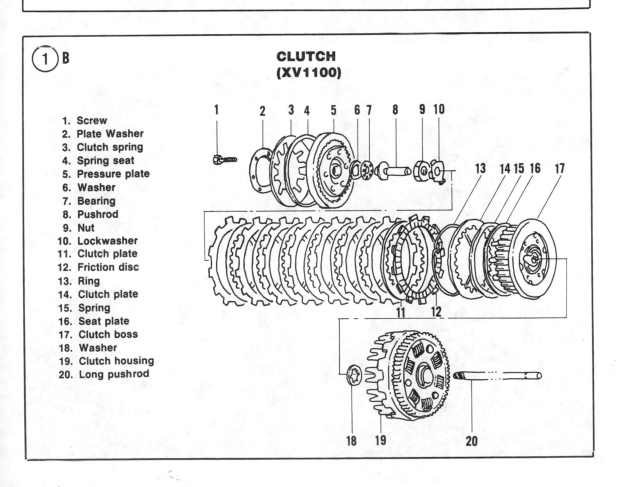

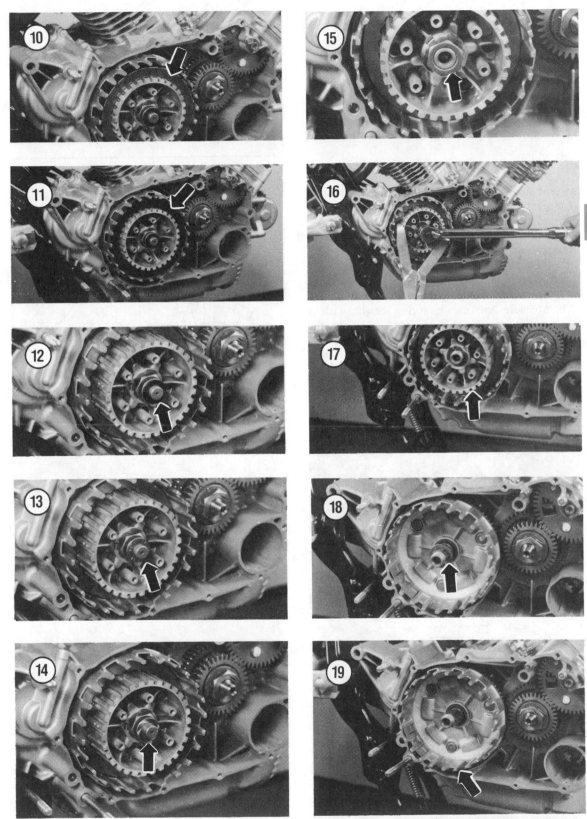

NOTE
To keep the clutch housing from turning, use the "Grabbit" special tool available from Joe Bolger Products, Inc., Barre, MA 01005. See **Figure 16**.

10. Remove the clutch boss (**Figure 17**).
11. Remove the washer (**Figure 18**) and clutch housing (**Figure 19**).
12. Remove the pushrod (**Figure 20**).

Inspection

1. Clean all clutch parts in a petroleum-based solvent such as kerosene, and thoroughly dry with compressed air.
2A. *All models except XV1100:* Measure the free length of each clutch spring as shown in **Figure 21**. Replace any springs that are too short (**Table 1**).
2B. *1986-on XV1100:* Perform the following.
  a. Inspect the clutch spring (3, **Figure 1B**) for bends or cracks. Replace if necessary.
  b. Measure the clutch spring height with a vernier caliper (**Figure 22A**). Replace the clutch spring if the minimum height is too short (**Table 2**).
  c. Place the clutch spring on a flat surface, such as a piece of glass, and measure its flatness

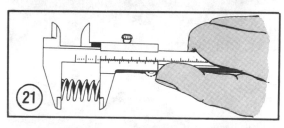

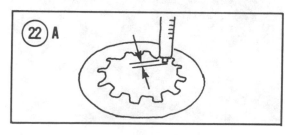

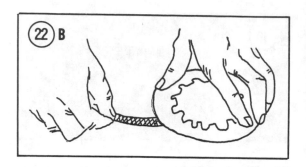

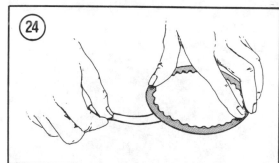

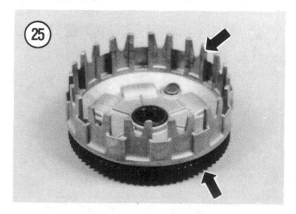

with a feeler gauge (**Figure 22B**). Replace the clutch spring if the warpage exceeds the standard limit in **Table 2**.

   d. Inspect the spring seat (4, **Figure 1B**) for wear, bending or damage. Replace if necessary.

3. Measure the thickness of each friction disc at several places around the disc as shown in **Figure 23**. See **Table 1** or **Table 2**. Replace all friction discs if any one is found too thin. Do not replace only 1 or 2 discs.

4. Check the clutch metal plates for warpage as shown in **Figure 24**. If any plate is warped more than specified (**Table 1** or **Table 2**) replace the entire set of plates. Do not replace only 1 or 2 plates.

5. Check the teeth on the clutch housing. Replace if necessary.

6. Inspect the clutch hub outer housing (**Figure 25**) and the clutch boss assembly (**Figure 26**) for cracks or galling in the grooves where the clutch friction disc tabs slide. They must be smooth for chatter-free clutch operation.

7. Inspect the shaft splines (**Figure 27**) in the clutch boss assembly. If damage is slight, remove any small burrs with a fine-cut file; if damage is severe, replace the assembly.

NOTE
*The clutch boss is a subassembly with a built-in damper located inside the first clutch plate. A circlip (**Figure 28**) holds the assembly together. Do not disassemble this unit unless there is severe clutch chatter.*

8. Inspect the clutch release bearing (**Figure 29**). Replace all 3 parts if damaged.

9. Inspect the long pushrod (**Figure 30**) by rolling it on a flat surface, such as a piece of glass. Any clicking noise detected indicates that the rod is bent and should be replaced.

10. Inspect the clutch nut, lockwasher and washer for wear or damage (**Figure 31**). Replace as necessary.

11. Inspect the pressure plate (**Figure 32**) for signs of wear or damage; replace if necessary.

Installation

1. Coat all parts with clean engine oil.

2. Install the long pushrod (**Figure 20**). Insert the rod's shorter end into the shaft first.

3. Install the clutch housing (**Figure 19**). Make sure it meshes properly with the primary drive gear.

> *NOTE*
> *While installing the clutch housing, slightly rotate it back and forth until the gears mesh properly. Push it on until it bottoms.*

4. Install the thrust washer (**Figure 18**).

5. Install the clutch boss (**Figure 17**).

6. Install the lockwasher (**Figure 33**). Make sure the locking taps on the lockwasher are inserted into the slots in the pressure plate.

7. Install the clutch nut (**Figure 15**) and tighten to specifications (**Table 3**) using a torque wrench and holding tool to keep the clutch hub from turning. See **Figure 16**. Bend up the lockwasher against one side of the nut.

8. Install the short pushrod into the transmission mainshaft (**Figure 14**). Then install the bearing (**Figure 13**) and washer (**Figure 12**) onto the end of the pushrod.

9. Install the friction discs (**Figure 11**) and clutch plates (**Figure 10**). Refer to **Figure 1A** or **Figure 1B** for plate installation order.

10A. *All models except XV1100:* Perform the following:

  a. Install the pressure plate (**Figure 9**).

  b. Install the springs (**Figure 8**) and bolts (**Figure 7**) and tighten in a crisscross pattern to 5.8 ft.-lb. (8 N•m).

10B. *XV1100:* Perform the following.

  a. Mesh the pressure plate splines (5, **Figure 1B**) with the clutch boss splines (17, **Figure 1B**) and install the pressure plate.

  b. Install the spring seat (4, **Figure 1B**) and the clutch spring (3, **Figure 1B**).

  c. Install the plate washer (2, **Figure 1B**) and bolts. Tighten the bolts to 7.2 ft.-lb. (10 N•m) in a crisscross pattern.

11. Install the clutch cover (**Figure 6**) with a new gasket. Tighten the cover screws securely.

12. Continue installation by reversing Steps 1-5.

13. Adjust the clutch as described in Chapter Three.

14. Refill the crankcase with the recommended type and quantity of engine oil. Refer to Chapter Three.

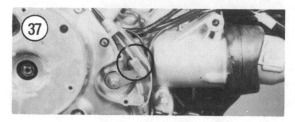

CLUTCH CABLE

Replacement

In time, the cable will stretch to the point where it can no longer be adjusted and will have to be replaced.

1. Remove the seat.
2. Remove the fuel tank as described in Chapter Six.
3. Loosen and slide the cover away from the clutch lever adjustment nut at the handlebar. Then loosen the adjustment nut (**Figure 34**) and remove the cable from the hand lever.

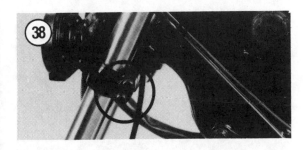

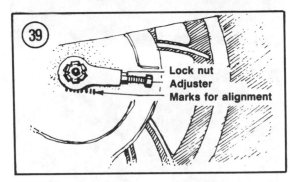

Lock nut
Adjuster
Marks for alignment

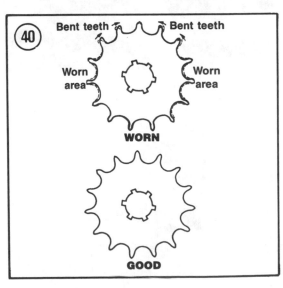

Bent teeth — Bent teeth
Worn area — Worn area
WORN

GOOD

4. Remove the clutch cable adjuster cover (**Figure 35**).
5. Loosen the clutch cable adjuster locknut and turn the adjuster counterclockwise 2-3 turns. See **Figure 36**.
6. Disconnect the clutch cable at the adjuster (**Figure 37**). Pull the cable out of the engine.

> *NOTE*
> *Prior to removing the cable, make a drawing of the cable routing through the frame. It is very easy to forget how it was, once it has been removed. Replace it exactly as it was, avoiding any sharp turns.*

7. Remove the cable from the frame and replace with a new one. Make sure the cable fits into the cable clamp on the left-hand side (**Figure 38**).
8. Adjust the clutch as described in Chapter Three.

DRIVE SPROCKET (CHAIN-DRIVE MODELS)

Removal/Installation

1. Place the bike on the centerstand.
2. Remove the shift lever and left side cover.
3. Remove the rear axle nut cotter pin and loosen the axle nut.
4. Loosen the drive chain adjusters (**Figure 39**) to allow slack in the drive chain.
5. Have an assistant apply the rear brake to keep the drive sprocket from turning. Remove the sprocket bolts.
6. Move the rear wheel slightly forward and remove the drive chain from the sprocket. Remove the drive sprocket from the engine.
7. Installation is the reverse of these steps; note the following:
   a. Tighten the drive sprocket bolts to 7.2 ft.-lb. (10 N•m).
   b. Adjust the drive chain as described in Chapter Three.

Inspection

Inspect the teeth of the sprocket. If the teeth are visibly worn (**Figure 40**), replace the sprocket with a new one.

If the sprocket requires replacement, the drive chain and rear sprocket are probably worn also. Refer to Chapter Nine.

SHIFT MECHANISM

Refer to **Figure 41** for this procedure.

Removal/Inspection/Installation

1. Remove the shift lever and the left-hand foot peg. See **Figure 42**.

2. On 1984 models, remove the left-hand footrest bar (**Figure 43**).

3. Loosen the clutch cable adjuster at the handlebar (**Figure 34**).

4. Drain the engine oil as described in Chapter Three.

5. Remove the Allen bolts securing the left-hand crankcase cover and remove it.

6. Disengage the shift lever from the shift drum and remove it from the crankcase (**Figure 44**).

7. Disassemble the shift shaft by performing the following:

   a. Remove the washers from both ends of the shift shaft assembly. See **Figure 45**.

   b. Remove the circlip and slide the stopper lever assembly (**Figure 46**) off the shaft.

   c. Remove the washer (**Figure 47**) and circlip (**Figure 48**) and disconnect the return spring (**Figure 49**).

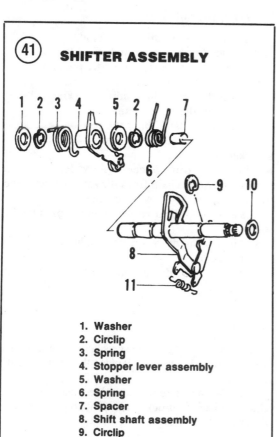

41 SHIFTER ASSEMBLY

1. Washer
2. Circlip
3. Spring
4. Stopper lever assembly
5. Washer
6. Spring
7. Spacer
8. Shift shaft assembly
9. Circlip
10. Washer
11. Spring

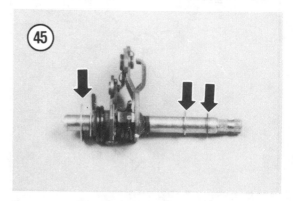

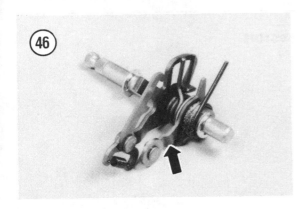

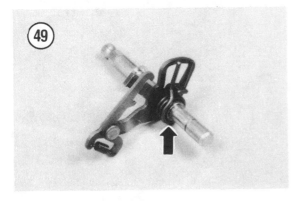

8. Examine the shift shaft assembly spindle for damage. If the spindle is bent or damaged in any way, it must be replaced.

9. Assemble the shift shaft assembly in the order shown in **Figure 41**. Install the washers on both ends of the shift shaft (**Figure 45**).

10. Insert the end of the spindle into the engine crankcase opening.

11. Pull the shift lever down (**Figure 44**) and install the shift mechanism all the way. **Figure 50** shows the installed assembly.

12. Reverse Steps 1-5 to complete installation. Refill the engine with the correct type and quantity of oil as described in Chapter Three.

TRANSMISSION

The crankcase must be disassembled as described in Chapter Four to gain access to the transmission components.

Removal/Installation

Refer to **Figure 51** for this procedure.

1. Perform Steps 1-12 of *Crankcase Disassembly* in Chapter Four.

2. Slide off the middle gear (**Figure 52**) and first gear (**Figure 53**) from the drive axle.

3. Remove the shift fork guide bar (**Figure 54**).

4. Remove the drive axle fourth gear and the No. 3 shift fork. See **Figure 55**.

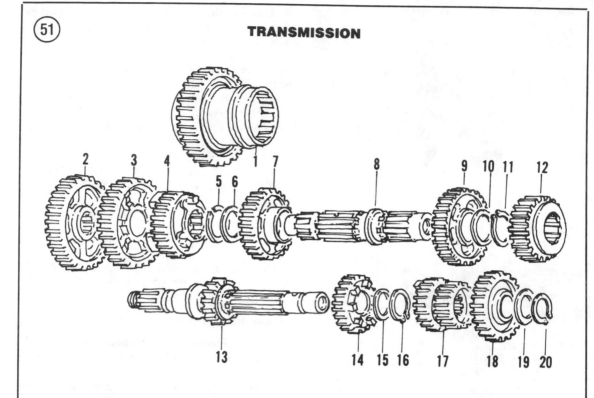

TRANSMISSION

1. Middle driven gear (shaft-drive models)
2. Middle drive gear
3. Drive axle 1st gear
4. Drive axle 4th gear
5. Circlip
6. Washer
7. Drive axle 3rd gear

8. Drive axle
9. Drive axle 2nd gear
10. Washer
11. Circlip
12. Drive axle 5th gear
13. Main shaft
14. Main shaft 4th gear

15. Washer
16. Circlip
17. Main shaft 2nd/3rd gear
18. Main shaft 5th gear
19. Washer
20. Circlip

5. Remove the No. 2 shift fork (**Figure 56**).

6. Remove the main shaft and drive axle shaft at the same time. See **Figure 57**.

7. Remove the No. 1 shift fork and the drive axle fifth gear. See **Figure 58**.

8. Remove the shift drum (**Figure 59**).

9. Inspect the transmission assembly as described in this chapter.

> *NOTE*
> *Prior to installing any components, coat all bearing surfaces with assembly oil.*

10. Install the shift drum into the left-hand crankcase (**Figure 59**).

> *NOTE*
> *When installing the shift forks, the number on each shift fork (**Figure 60**) must face toward the left-hand crankcase.*

5

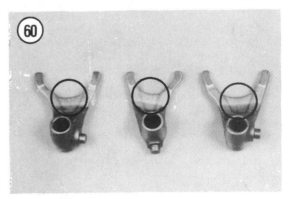

11. Insert the No. 1 shift fork into the drive axle fifth gear (**Figure 61**). Then install the shift fork/gear assembly into the left-hand side crankcase, making sure to center the gear over the crankcase bearing. See **Figure 62**.

12. Position the No. 1 shift fork so that its pin seats in the shift drum groove (**Figure 62**).

13. Install the drive axle and main shaft assemblies into the left-hand crankcase at the same time (**Figure 57**).

14. Install the No. 2 shift fork onto the second/third combination drive axle gear (**Figure 56**). Position the No. 2 shift fork so its pin seats in the shift drum groove.

15. Insert the No. 3 shift fork into the drive axle fourth gear (**Figure 63**). Then slide the shift fork/gear combination onto the drive axle. Position the No. 3 shift fork so its pin seats in the shift drum groove. See **Figure 55**.

16. Install the shift fork guide bar so it goes through all 3 shift forks and seats properly in the guide bar boss in the crankcase. See **Figure 54**.

17. Install the drive axle first gear (**Figure 53**) and middle gear (**Figure 52**).

18. Assemble the crankcase as described in Chapter Four.

Main Shaft Disassembly/Assembly

Refer to **Figure 51** for this procedure.

NOTE
During disassembly, place all parts in a container such as an egg carton to keep the gears in order.

1. Remove the circlip and washer (**Figure 64**).
2. Remove fifth gear (**Figure 65**).
3. Remove second/third gear combination (**Figure 66**).
4. Remove the circlip and washer and slide off fourth gear (**Figure 67**).

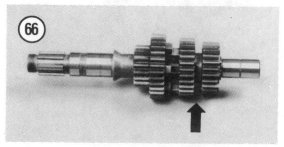

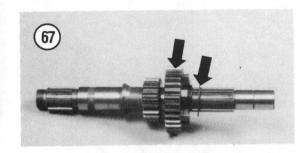

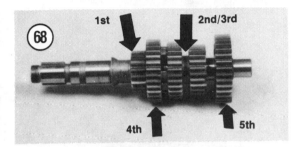

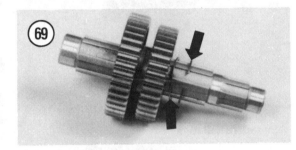

5. Inspect the main shaft assembly as described in this chapter.

6. Assemble by reversing these removal steps. Refer to **Figure 51** and **Figure 68** for correct placement of the gears. Make sure that all circlips are seated correctly in the main shaft grooves.

7. Make sure each gear engages properly with the adjoining gear where applicable.

Drive Axle Disassembly/Assembly

Refer to **Figure 51** for this procedure.

> *NOTE*
> *During disassembly, place all parts in a container such as an egg carton to keep the gears in order.*

> *NOTE*
> *Some gears were removed from the drive axle during transmission removal. Inspect these gears as described later in this chapter.*

1. Remove the circlip and washer (**Figure 69**).
2. Slide off fourth gear (**Figure 70**).
3. Remove the circlip and washer and slide off second gear (**Figure 71**).
3. Inspect the drive axle assembly as described in this chapter.
4. Assemble by reversing these removal steps. Refer to **Figure 51** and **Figure 72** for correct placement of the gears. Make sure that all circlips are seated correctly in the drive axle grooves.
5. Make sure each gear engages properly with the adjoining gear where applicable.

Inspection

1. Clean all parts in cleaning solvent and thoroughly dry.
2. Inspect the gears visually for cracks, chips, broken teeth and burnt teeth. Check the lugs

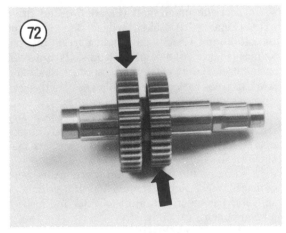

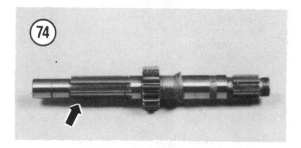

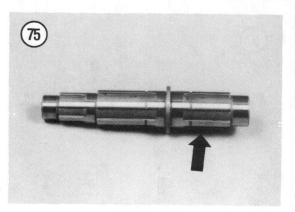

(**Figure 73**) on ends of gears to make sure they are not rounded off. If lugs are rounded off, check the shift forks as described in this chapter. More than likely, one or more of the shift forks is bent.

> *NOTE*
> *Defective gears should be replaced. It is a good idea to replace the mating gear even though it may not show as much wear or damage. Remember that accelerated wear to new parts is normally caused by contact from worn parts.*

3. Inspect all free-wheeling gear bearing surfaces for wear, discoloration and galling. Inspect the mating shaft bearing surface also. If there is any metal flaking or other visible damage, replace both parts.

4. Inspect the main shaft (**Figure 74**) and drive axle (**Figure 75**) shaft splines for wear or discoloration. Check the mating gear internal splines (**Figure 76**) also. If no damage is apparent, install each sliding gear on its respective shaft and work the gear back and forth to make sure the gear operates smoothly.

5. Check all circlips and washers. Replace any circlips that may have been damaged during operation or removal as well as any washers that show wear.

6. If some of the transmission components were damaged, make sure to remove the shift drum and shift forks as described in this chapter and inspect all components carefully.

SHIFT DRUM AND FORKS

Removal/Installation

Remove and install the shift forks and shift drum as described under *Transmission Removal/Installation* in this chapter.

Inspection

1. Inspect each shift fork for signs of wear or cracking (**Figure 77**). Examine the shift fork at the point where it contacts the slider gear. This surface should be smooth with no signs of wear or damage. Make sure the forks slide smoothly on the shaft (**Figure 78**). Make sure the shaft is not bent. This can be checked by removing the shift forks from the shaft and rolling the shaft on a piece of glass. Any clicking noise detected indicates that the shaft is bent.

2. Check grooves in the shift drum (**Figure 79**) for wear or roughness.

3. Check the shift drum bearing (**Figure 80**). Make sure it operates smoothly with no signs of wear or damage.

4. Check the cam pin followers in each shift fork. They should fit snugly but not too tightly. Check the end that rides in the shift drum for wear or burrs. Replace as necessary.

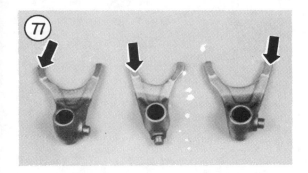

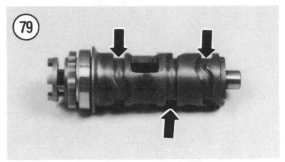

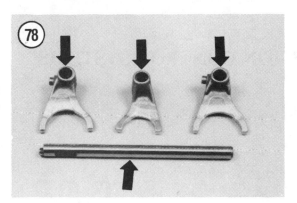

Table 1 CLUTCH SPECIFICATIONS (XV700, XV750, XV920, XV1000)

Item	Standard in. (mm)	Minimum in. (mm)
Friction plate (8 pcs)	0.12 (3.0)	0.11 (2.8)
Clutch plate (7 pcs)	0.063 (1.6)	
Warp limit	0.001 (0.04)	
Clutch spring free length (5 pcs)	1.62 (41.2)	1.58 (40.2)
Pushrod bend limit		0.02 (0.5)

Table 2 CLUTCH SPECIFICATIONS (XV1100)

Item	Standard in. (mm)	Minimum in. (mm)
Friction plate (8 pcs)	0.12 (3.0)	0.11 (2.8)
Clutch plate (7 pcs)	0.079 (2.0)	
Warp limit	0.001 (0.04)	
Pushrod bend limit		0.02 (0.5)
Clutch spring height		0.256 (6.5)
Warp limit		0.004 (0.1)

Table 3 CLUTCH TIGHTENING TORQUES

	ft.-lb.	N·m
Clutch hub	50.5	70
Shift fork guide bar screw	5	7
Neutral switch	14.5	20
Clutch push screw	9	12

CHAPTER SIX

FUEL, EXHAUST AND EMISSION CONTROL SYSTEMS

The fuel system consists of the fuel tank(s), shutoff valve with fuel filter, two Hitachi constant velocity carburetors, fuel pump (XV1000 and XV1100) and an air cleaner.

The exhaust system consists of two exhaust pipes, a crossover pipe and two mufflers.

Some models are equipped with emission control systems to comply with state and Federal regulations. These systems are discussed in this chapter.

Information about fuel grade and engine and carburetor adjustments that would affect the emission control system is found behind either the left-hand or right-hand side cover (**Figure 1**). This information must be observed to ensure that your motorcycle will comply with Federal and state regulations.

This chapter includes service procedures for all parts of the fuel, exhaust and emission control systems. **Table 1** and **Table 2** are at the end of the chapter.

AIR CLEANER

The air cleaner must be cleaned frequently. Refer to Chapter Three for specific procedures and service intervals.

CARBURETORS

Basic Principles

An understanding of the function of each of the carburetor components and their relationship to one another is a valuable aid for pinpointing a source of carburetor trouble.

The carburetor's purpose is to supply and atomize fuel and to mix it in correct proportions with the air that is drawn in through the air intake. At the primary throttle opening (idle), a small

amount of fuel is siphoned through the pilot jet by the incoming air. As the throttle is opened further, the air stream begins to siphon fuel through the main jet and needle jet. The tapered needle increases the effective flow capacity of the needle jet because, as it is lifted, the needle occupies less area of the jet. In addition, the amount of cutaway in the leading edge of the throttle valve (or vaccuum cylinder) aids in controlling the fuel-air mixture during partial throttle openings.

At full throttle, the carburetor venturi is fully open and the needle is lifted far enough to permit the main jet to flow at full capacity.

Service

Major carburetor service (removal and cleaning) should be performed every 20,000 miles (32,000 km) or when poor engine performance and/or hesitation is observed. Alterations in jet size, cylinder cutaway, etc., should be attempted only if you're experienced in this type of "tuning" work; a bad guess could result in costly engine damage or poor performance.

> *NOTE*
> *Check with local authorities for regulations concerning emissions. Changing carburetor settings is not allowed in many areas.*

If after servicing the carburetors and making adjustments as described in this chapter the motorcycle does not perform correctly (and assuming that other factors affecting performance are correct, such as ignition timing and condition, valve adjustment, etc.), the motorcycle should be checked by a dealer or a qualified performance tuning specialist.

Standard carburetor specifications are in **Table 1** at the end of this chapter.

Removal/Installation

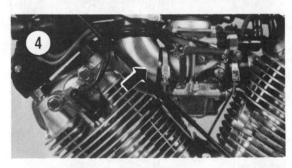

1. Remove the fuel tank as described in this chapter.
2. *1984-on:* Remove the mixture control valve/air induction system as described in this chapter.
3. *XV1100:* Refer to *Coasting Enricher System (Vacuum Line Routing)* in this chapter and disconnect the vacuum lines before removing the carburetor. Tag all hoses so that they can be reconnected correctly during installation.
4. Lift the carburetor cable lever on the right-hand carburetor and disconnect the throttle cable (**Figure 2**). Lift the carburetor cable lever on the left-hand carburetor and disconnect the choke cable (**Figure 3**).
5. Label and disconnect all vacuum and air lines at the carburetors.
6. Remove the left- and right-hand intake hoses at the carburetors. See **Figure 4**.
7. Loosen the intake manifold clamp screws (**Figure 5**) and slide the clamps away from the carburetors.
8. Rotate the carburetors until they are clear of the intake manifolds and remove the carburetors.

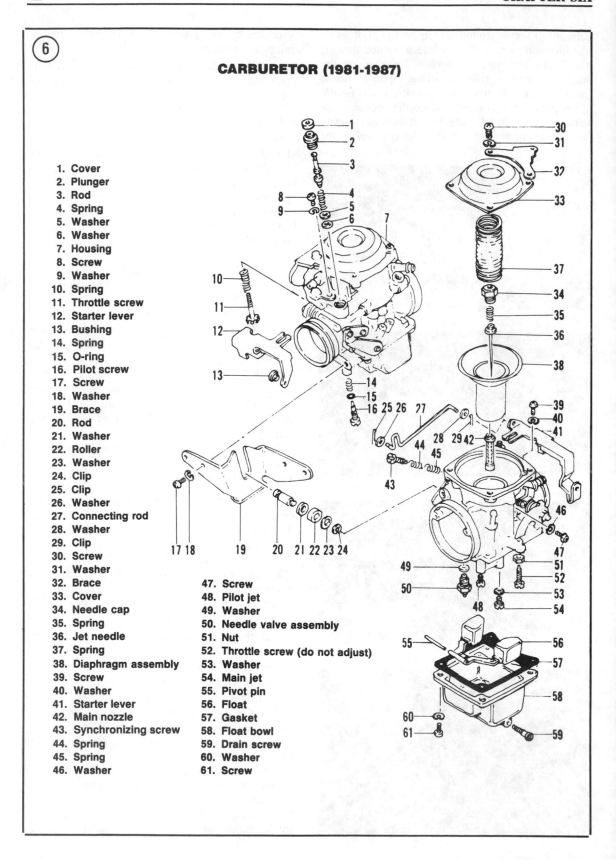

CARBURETOR (1981-1987)

1. Cover
2. Plunger
3. Rod
4. Spring
5. Washer
6. Washer
7. Housing
8. Screw
9. Washer
10. Spring
11. Throttle screw
12. Starter lever
13. Bushing
14. Spring
15. O-ring
16. Pilot screw
17. Screw
18. Washer
19. Brace
20. Rod
21. Washer
22. Roller
23. Washer
24. Clip
25. Clip
26. Washer
27. Connecting rod
28. Washer
29. Clip
30. Screw
31. Washer
32. Brace
33. Cover
34. Needle cap
35. Spring
36. Jet needle
37. Spring
38. Diaphragm assembly
39. Screw
40. Washer
41. Starter lever
42. Main nozzle
43. Synchronizing screw
44. Spring
45. Spring
46. Washer
47. Screw
48. Pilot jet
49. Washer
50. Needle valve assembly
51. Nut
52. Throttle screw (do not adjust)
53. Washer
54. Main jet
55. Pivot pin
56. Float
57. Gasket
58. Float bowl
59. Drain screw
60. Washer
61. Screw

NOTE
Drain the gasoline from the carburetor assembly and place it in a clean heavy-duty plastic bag to keep it clean until it is worked on or reinstalled.

9. While the carburetors are removed, examine the intake manifolds on the cylinder head and the intake hoses for any cracks or damage that would allow unfiltered air to enter the engine. Replace any worn or damaged parts.

10. Install by reversing these removal steps; note the following.

11. Prior to installing the carburetor assembly, coat the inside surfaces of both intake manifolds with Armor All or rubber lube. This will make it easier to install the carburetor throats into the manifolds.

12. Be sure the throttle and choke cables are correctly positioned in the frame—not twisted or kinked and without any sharp bends. Tighten the locknuts securely.

13. Adjust the throttle cable as described in Chapter Three.

14. Adjust the choke cable as described in this chapter.

Disassembly/Cleaning/Inspection/Assembly (1981-1987)

Refer to **Figure 6** for this procedure.

It is recommended that only one carburetor be disassembled and cleaned at one time. This will prevent mixing of parts.

All components that require cleaning can be removed from the carburetor body without removing the carburetors from the mounting plates. *Do not* separate the carburetors as misalignment will occur on assembly. If one carburetor body must be replaced, have a dealer or qualified specialist do the job.

CAUTION
When cleaning the carburetor assembly, do not turn the pilot adjustment screw as it has has been preset at the factory; changing the basic setting will actually detune the carburetor. Carburetor adjustments which can be performed by the amateur mechanic are described in Chapter Three.

1. Remove the diaphragm cover (**Figure 7**) and pull out the spring (**Figure 8**) and diaphragm (**Figure 9**).

2. Remove the 4 screws securing the float bowl (**Figure 10**) and remove it and its gasket.

3. Remove the float pivot pin (**Figure 11**) and remove the float together with the needle valve (**Figure 12**).
4. Remove the needle seat and gasket (**Figure 13**).
5. Remove the main jet and washer (**Figure 14**).
6. Remove the main nozzle (**Figure 15**).

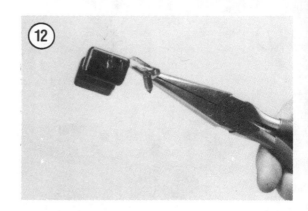

> *NOTE*
> *Further disassembly is neither necessary nor recommended. If the throttle or choke shafts are damaged, take the carburetor body to a dealer for replacement.*

7. Clean all parts, except rubber or plastic parts and gaskets, in a good grade of carburetor cleaner. This solution is available at most automotive or motorcycle supply stores in a small, resealable tank with a dip basket . If it is tightly sealed when not in use, the solution will last for several cleanings. Follow the manufacturer's instructions for correct soaking time (usually about 1/2 hour).

8. Remove all parts from the cleaner and blow dry with compressed air. Blow out the jets with compressed air. *Do not* use a piece of wire to clean them as minor gouges in a jet can alter the flow rate and upset the air-fuel mixture.
9. If the floats are suspected of leaking, put them in a small container of a non-caustic solution and push them down. If the floats sink or if bubbles appear (indicating a leak), the floats must be replaced.
10. Check the needle seat O-ring. If it appears cracked or worn, replace it.
11. Check the float needle (**Figure 16**) and seat contact areas closely. Both contact surfaces should appear smooth without any gouging or other apparent damage. Replace both needle and seat as a set if any one part is worn or damaged.

12. Repeat Steps 1-11 for the other carburetor. Do not mix the parts—keep them separate.

13. Assemble by reversing these disassembly steps; note the following:

   a. After installing the main nozzle, make sure it seats in the carburetor housing correctly (**Figure 17**).

   b. When installing the diaphragm, make sure to position the tab on the diaphragm (**Figure 18**) correctly into the recess in the carburetor body.

   c. After installing the carburetor, check the fuel level as described in this chapter.

Disassembly/Cleaning/Inspection/ Assembly (1988-on)

Refer to **Figure 19** for this procedure.

It is recommended that only one carburetor be disassembled and cleaned at one time. This will prevent mixing of parts.

All components that require cleaning can be removed from the carburetor body without removing the carburetor from the mounting plates. *Do not* separate the carburetors as misalignment will occur on assembly. If one carburetor body must be replaced, have a dealer or qualified specialist do the job.

> *CAUTION*
> *When cleaning the carburetor assembly, do not turn the pilot adjustment screw as it has been preset at the factory; changing the basic setting will actually detune the carburetor. Carburetor adjustments which can be performed by the amateur mechanic are described in Chapter Three.*

1. Remove the diaphragm cover (**Figure 20**) and pull out the spring (A, **Figure 21**) and diaphragm (B, **Figure 21**).

2. Remove the screws securing the float bowl (**Figure 22**) and remove it and its gasket.

3. Remove the float pivot pin (**Figure 23**) and remove the float along with the needle valve.

4. Remove the needle seat and gasket.

5. Remove the main jet (A, **Figure 24**) and washer (B, **Figure 24**).

6. Remove the main nozzle (C, **Figure 24**).

7. Remove the pilot jet (D, **Figure 24**).

8. Remove the screws securing the coasting enrichener cover. Remove the cover, outer spring, diaphragm, holder, pushrod and inner spring (**Figure 25**).

> *NOTE*
> *Further disassembly is neither necessary nor recommended. If the throttle shaft is damaged, take the carburetor body to a dealer for replacement.*

9. Clean all parts, except rubber or plastic parts and gaskets, in a good grade of carburetor cleaner. This solution is available at most automotive or motorcycle supply stores in a small, resealable tank with a dip basket. If it is kept tightly sealed when not in use, the solution will last for several cleanings. Follow the manufacturer's instructions for correct soak time (usually 1/2 hour).

10. Remove all parts from the cleaner and blow dry with compressed air. Blow out the jets with

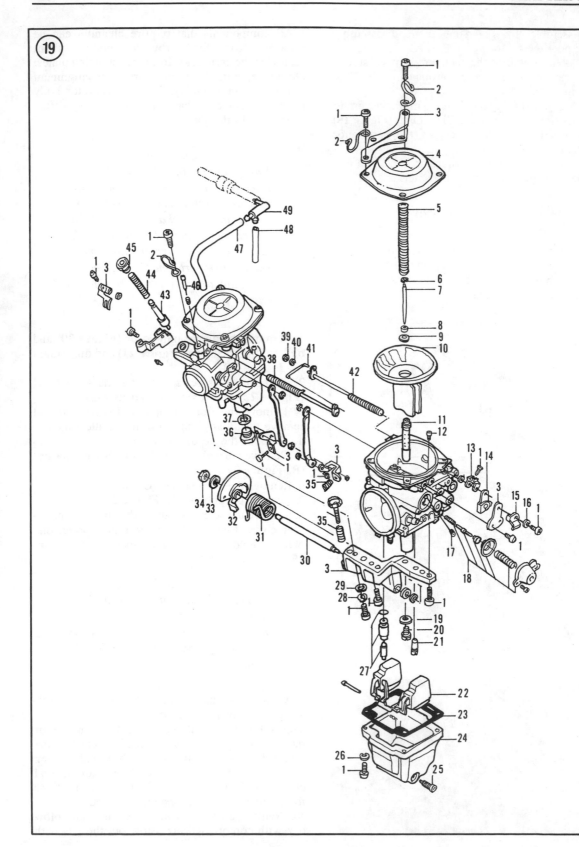

CARBURETOR (1988-ON)

1. Screw
2. Cable clamp
3. Brace
4. Top cover
5. Spring
6. Clip
7. Jet needle
8. Ring
9. Seal
10. Diaphragm assembly
11. Main nozzle
12. Pilot air jet No. 1
13. Bracket
14. Tab
15. Clamp
16. Lockwasher
17. Screw
18. Coasting enrichener assembly
19. Washer
20. Main jet
21. Pilot jet
22. Float
23. Gasket
24. Float bowl
25. Drain screw
26. Washer
27. Needle valve assembly
28. Lockwasher
29. Washer
30. Throttle shaft
31. Spring
32. Throttle wheel
33. Lockwasher
34. Nut
35. Spring
36. Plug
37. Gasket
38. Spring
39. Nut
40. Lockwasher
41. Rod
42. Spring
43. Starter plunger
44. Spring
45. Nut
46. Pilot screw
47. Tube
48. Tube
49. Elbow fitting

6

compressed air. *Do not* use a piece of wire to clean them as minor gouges in a jet can alter the flow rate and upset the air-fuel mixture.

11. If the floats are suspected of leaking, put them in a small container of a non-caustic solution and push them down. If the float sinks or if bubbles appear (indicating a leak), the float(s) must be replaced.

12. Check the needle seat O-ring. If it appears cracked or worn, replace it.

13. Check the float needle seat (**Figure 16**) and seat contact areas closely. Both contact surfaces should appear smooth without any gouges or other apparent damage. Replace both the needle and seat as a set if any one part is worn or damaged.

14. Repeat Steps 1-13 for the other carburetor. Do not mix the parts—keep them separate.

15. Assemble by reversing these disassembly steps; note the following:

   a. After installing the main nozzle, make sure it seats in the carburetor housing correctly.

   b. When installing the diaphragm, make sure to position the tab on the diaphragm (**Figure 26**) correctly into the recess in the carburetor body.

   c. After installing the carburetor, check fuel level as described in this chapter.

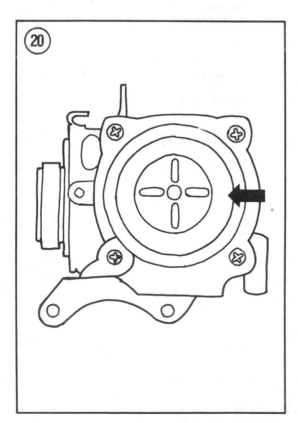

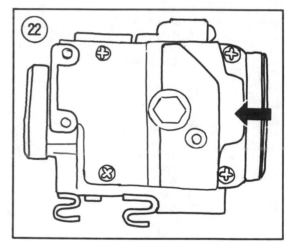

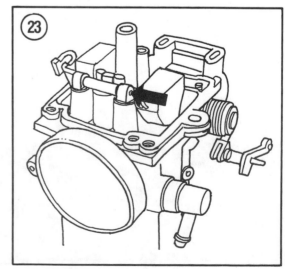

COASTING ENRICHENER SYSTEM 1986-ON XV1100 AND 1988-ON XV750

Refer to **Figure 27** for 1986-1987 XV1100 models or **Figure 28** for 1988-on XV750 and XV1100 models.

The carburetors on these models are equipped with a coasting enrichener system. When the throttle is opened, air is forced to the pilot jet through passages A and B. When the throttle is off, vacuum at the carburetor joint increases and actuates the enrichener diaphragm which shuts off the air through passage B. This action increases the fuel mixture at the pilot outlet and reduces afterburning.

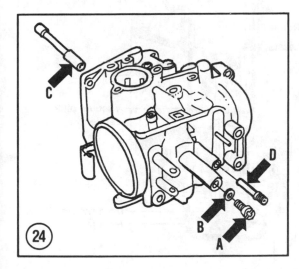

(24)

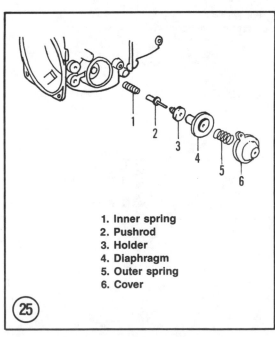

1. **Inner spring**
2. **Pushrod**
3. **Holder**
4. **Diaphragm**
5. **Outer spring**
6. **Cover**

(25)

Refer to **Figure 29** for 1986-1987 XV1100 models for this procedure. On 1988-on models, the coasting enrichener assembly is incorporated into the carburetor body and is not a separate unit that can be removed as an assembly.

1. Remove the carburetor as described in this chapter.

2A. On 1986-1987 XV1100 models, perform the following:

    a. Remove the screws securing the coasting enrichener system to the carburetor housing and remove it.

    b. Remove the O-ring.

2B. On 1988-on models, remove the screws securing the coasting enrichener cover. Remove the cover, outer spring, diaphragm, holder, pushrod and inner spring (**Figure 25**).

3. Inspect the enrichener diaphragm for tears or other damage. Replace the coasting enrichener system if necessary.

4. On 1986-1987 XV1100 models, check the O-ring for wear or damage. Replace if necessary.

5. Install by reversing these steps. Adjust the throttle cables as described in Chapter Three.

Coasting Enrichener System Vacuum Line Routing

Refer to **Figure 30** for 1986-1987 XV1100 models or **Figure 31** for 1988-on XV750 and XV1100 models.

Refer to these illustrations when removing or installing the carburetor or when reconnecting the carburetor vacuum lines.

(26)

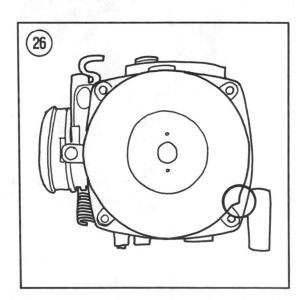

6

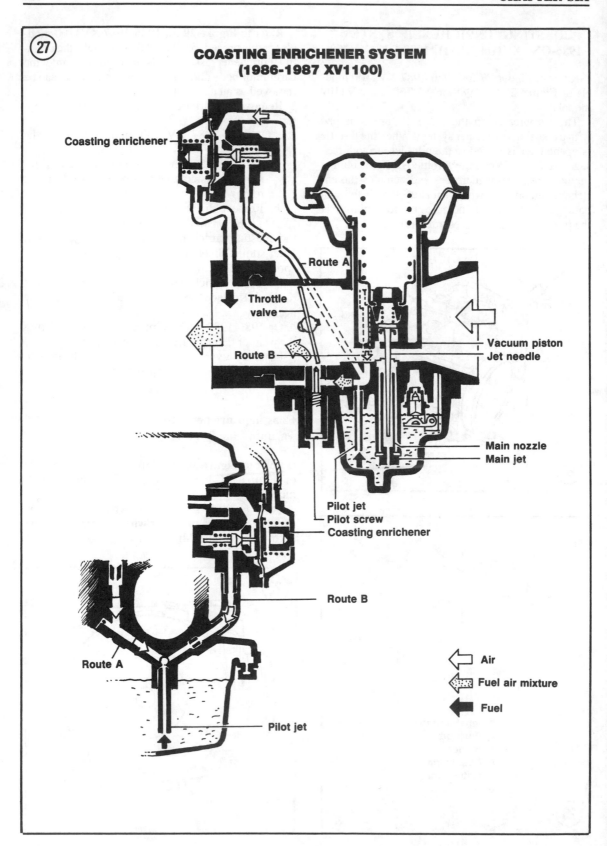

**COASTING ENRICHENER SYSTEM
(1986-1987 XV1100)**

Coasting enrichener

Route A

Throttle
valve

Route B

Vacuum piston
Jet needle

Main nozzle
Main jet

Pilot jet
Pilot screw
Coasting enrichener

Route B

Route A

Pilot jet

Air

Fuel air mixture

Fuel

FUEL LEVEL MEASUREMENT

The bike must be *exactly level* for this measurement to be accurate. Place pieces of wood or shims under either side of the centerstand or place a suitable size jack under the engine and position the bike so the carburetor assembly is level from side to side.

Use either the Yamaha special level gauge (part No. 90890-01312-00, **Figure 32**) or a piece of clear vinyl tubing with an inside diameter of 0.24 in. (6 mm). The tubing should be long enough to reach from one side of the carburetor assembly to the other.

> *WARNING*
> *Before starting any procedure involving gasoline, have a class B fire extinguisher rated for gasoline or chemical fires within reach. Do not smoke, allow anyone to smoke or work where there are open flames. The work area must be well-ventilated.*

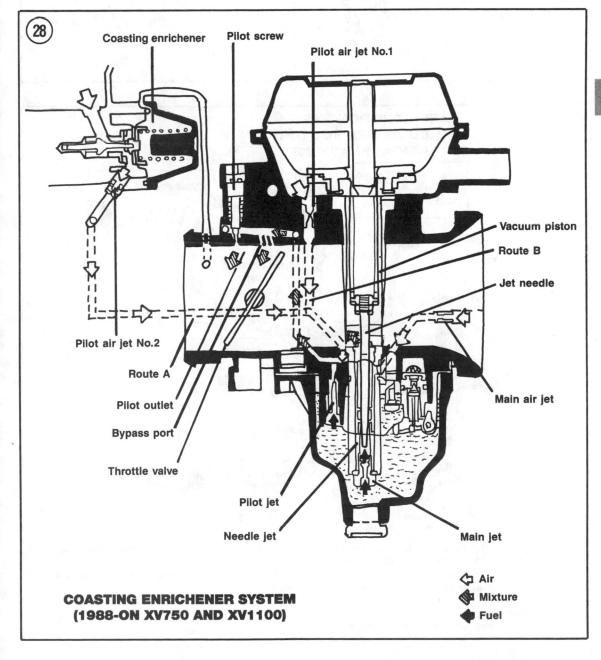

COASTING ENRICHENER SYSTEM (1988-ON XV750 AND XV1100)

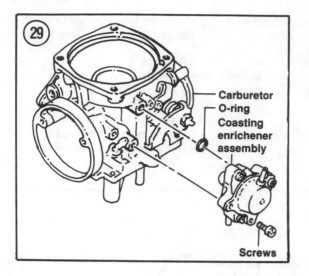

Carburetor
O-ring
Coasting
enrichener
assembly

Screws

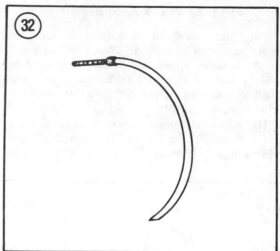

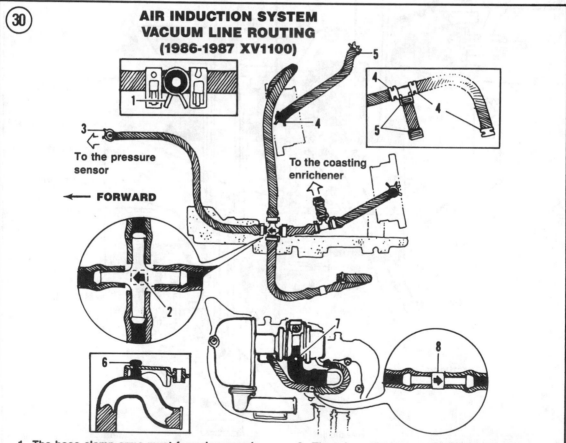

AIR INDUCTION SYSTEM VACUUM LINE ROUTING (1986-1987 XV1100)

To the pressure sensor

← FORWARD

To the coasting enrichener

1. The hose clamp arms must face downwards.
2. The arrow on the T-connection must face towards the pressure sensor.
3. The hose clamp arms must face towards the front of the bike.
4. The hose clamp arms must face to the inside.
5. The hose clamp arms must face to the outside.
6. The tab on the hose must fit into the square hole.
7. The white mark must face towards the air-cut valve.
8. The connector arrow must face towards the air-cut valve.

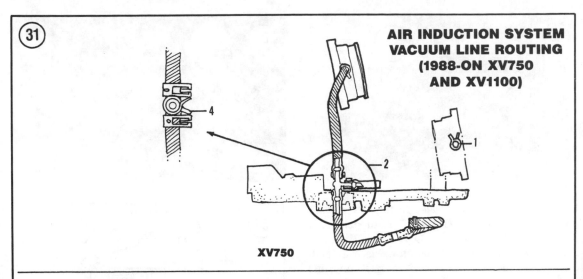

(31)

**AIR INDUCTION SYSTEM
VACUUM LINE ROUTING
(1988-ON XV750
AND XV1100)**

XV750

6

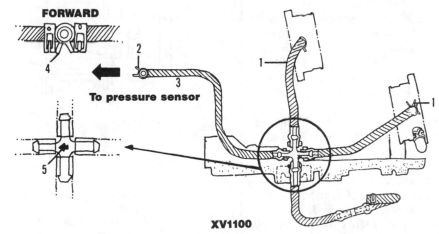

XV1100

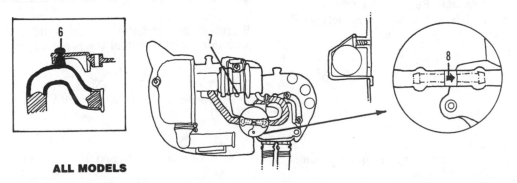

ALL MODELS

1. The hose clamp arms must face inside.
2. The hose clamp arms must face toward the front of the bike.
3. To pressure sensor.
4. The hose clamp arms must face downward.
5. The arrow on the T-connection must face toward the pressure sensor.

6. The tab on the hose must fit into the square hole.
7. The white mark must face toward the air-cut valve.
8. The connector arrow must face toward the air-cut valve.

1. Turn the fuel shutoff valve to the ON or RES position. On XV1000 and XV1100 models, turn the handlebar fuel switch to ON.

2. Start with the front carburetor. Place a small container under the carburetor to catch any fuel that may drip from the float bowl.

3. Insert the level gauge adapter and hose into the carburetor. **Figure 33** shows the level gauge adapter holes for each carburetor.

4. Loosen the float bowl drain screw (**Figure 34**). When the screw is loosened fuel will flow into the tube. Make sure to hold the loose end up or the fuel will flow out of the tube.

5. Start the engine and let it run for 2-3 minutes. This is necessary to make sure the fuel level is at the normal operating level in the float bowl.

6. Hold the loose end of the tube up against the front carburetor body next to the throttle stop screw (**Figure 35**). Check the fuel level in the tube. It should be within the specifications in **Table 2**.

7. Tighten the drain screw (**Figure 34**) and hold both ends of the tube at the same height so fuel will not drain out. Remove the tube from the carburetor float bowl nozzle. Immediately wipe up any spilled fuel on the engine.

> *WARNING*
> *Do not let any fuel spill on the hot exhaust system.*

8. Repeat Steps 2-7 for the rear carburetor. Record the measurement.

9. If the fuel level is incorrect, remove and partially disassemble the carburetor assembly. Adjust the float as follows.

10. Adjust the float tang on affected carburetor(s). Adjust by carefully bending the tang on the float arm (**Figure 36**). Bend the float tang upward very slightly to lower the fuel level; bend the float tang downward to raise the fuel level. If the float level is set too high, the result will be a rich air-fuel mixture. If it is set too low, the mixture will be too lean.

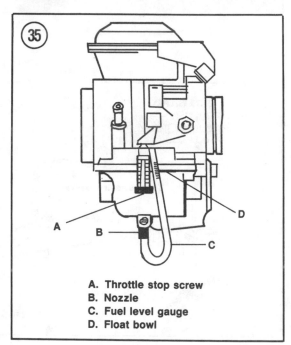

A. Throttle stop screw
B. Nozzle
C. Fuel level gauge
D. Float bowl

11. Install the carburetor assembly and repeat this procedure until both fuel levels are correct.

> *CAUTION*
> *The floats on both carburetors must be adjusted to the correct position (**Table 2**) to maintain the same air-fuel mixture to each cylinder.*

CHOKE CABLE ADJUSTMENT

1. Operate the choke lever (**Figure 37**) and check for smooth operation of the cable and choke mechanism.

2. Slide the lever all the way to the closed position. Then pull the choke arm (**Figure 38**) at the carburetor to make sure it is at the end of its travel. If you can move the choke arm an additional amount, it must be adjusted as follows.

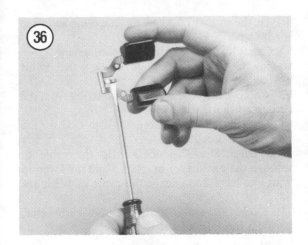

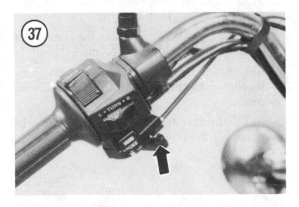

3. Loosen the choke cable clamping screw (**Figure 38**) and move the cable sheath *up* until the choke lever is fully closed. Hold the choke lever in this position and tighten the cable clamping screw (**Figure 38**).

4. Slide the choke lever all the way to the fully open position.

5. If proper adjustment cannot be achieved using this procedure, the cable has stretched and must be replaced. Refer to *Choke Cable Replacement* in this chapter.

REJETTING CARBURETORS

Do not try to solve a poor running engine problem by rejetting the carburetors if all of the following conditions hold true.

1. The engine has held a good tune in the past with the standard jetting.

2. The engine has not been modified (this includes the addition of accessory exhaust systems).

3. The motorcycle is being operated in the same geographical region under the same general climatic conditions as in the past.

4. The motorcycle was and is being ridden at average highway speeds.

If those conditions all hold true, the chances are that the problem is due to a malfunction in the carburetor or in another component that needs to be adjusted or repaired. Changing carburetor jet size probably won't solve the problem. Rejetting the carburetors may be necessary if any of the following conditions hold true.

1. A non-standard type of air filter element is being used.

2. A non-standard exhaust system is installed on the motorcycle.

3. Any of the top end components in the engine (pistons, cam, valves, compression ratio, etc.) have been modified.

NOTE
When installing accessory engine equipment, manufacturers often enclose guidelines on rejetting the carburetors.

4. The motorcycle is in use at considerably higher or lower elevations or in a considerably hotter or colder climate than in the past.

5. The motorcycle is being operated at considerably higher speeds than before and changing to colder spark plugs does not solve the problem.

6. Someone has previously changed the carburetor jetting.

7. The motorcycle has never held a satisfactory engine tune.

NOTE
If it is necessary to rejet the carburetors, check with a dealer or motorcycle performance tuner for recommendations as to the size of jets to install for your specific situation.

THROTTLE CABLE REPLACEMENT

The 1981-1987 models are equipped with one throttle cable. The 1988-on models have 2 cables.
1. Remove the seat and fuel tank.
2. Loosen the throttle cable adjustment screw (A, **Figure 39**). Then remove the screws (B, **Figure 39**) securing the upper and lower right-hand switch/throttle housing together.
3. Separate the housing from the handlebar and disengage the throttle cable(s) from the throttle grip.
4. On 1988-on models, remove the air cleaner as described in Chapter Three.
5A. On 1981-1987 models, at the carburetor, hold the lever up with one hand and disengage the cable end (**Figure 40**). Slip the cable out through the carburetor bracket.
5B. On 1988-on models, at the carburetor, perform the following:
   a. Mark each throttle cable as "front" or "rear" cable so the new ones will be installed in the correct position.
   b. Loosen the front cable locknut (A, **Figure 41**) and turn the adjuster (B, **Figure 41**) all the way toward the cable sheath.
   c. Loosen the rear cable locknut (C, **Figure 41**) and turn the adjuster (D, **Figure 41**) all the way toward the cable sheath.
   d. Rotate the throttle wheel and disengage the throttle cables from the throttle wheel and cable bracket.

NOTE
The piece of string attached in the next step will be used to pull the new throttle cable(s) back through the frame so it will be routed in exactly the same position as the old cable.

6. Tie a piece of heavy string or cord to the end of the throttle cable at the carburetor. Wrap this end with masking or duct tape. Do not use an excessive amount of tape as it must be pulled through the frame during removal. Tie the other end of the string to the frame.
7. At the throttle grip end of the cable, carefully pull the cable (and attached string) out through the frame. Make sure the attached string follows the same path as the cable through the frame.
8. Remove the tape and untie the string from the old cable.
9. Lubricate the new cable as described in Chapter Three.

10. Tie the string to the new throttle cable and wrap it with tape.
11. Carefully pull the string back through the frame, routing the new cable through the same path as the old cable.
12. Remove the tape and untie the string from cable and the frame.
13. On 1988-on models, repeat Steps 6-12 for the other throttle cable.
14A. On 1981-1987 models, slip the cable in through the carburetor bracket. Hold the lever up with one hand and engage the cable end (**Figure 40**).
14B. On 1988-on models, at the carburetor, perform the following:
   a. Note the marks made prior to removal on each throttle cable ("front" or "rear").
   b. Install the end of the cable into the correct slot in the throttle wheel and bracket.
   c. Temporarily tighten the locknut on each throttle cable to hold the throttle cables in place.
15. Attach the throttle cable(s) to the throttle grip and assemble the housing onto the handlebar.

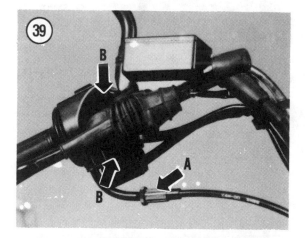

16. Install the screws (B, **Figure 39**) securing the upper and lower right-hand switch/throttle housing together.

17. Operate the throttle grip and make sure the carburetor linkage is operating correctly and with no binding. If operation is incorrect or there is binding, carefully check that the cable(s) is attached correctly and there are no tight bends in the cable.

18. On 1988-on models, install the air cleaner as described in Chapter Three.

19. Install the fuel tank and seat.

20. Adjust the throttle cable(s) as described in Chapter Three.

21. Place the motorcycle on the centerstand. Have an assistant push down on the rear end to raise the front wheel off the ground. Start the engine and let it idle. Turn the handlebar from side-to-side and

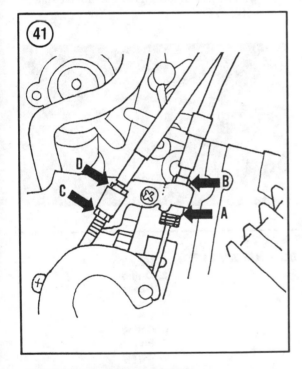

do not operate the throttle. If the engine speed increases as the handlebar assembly is turned, the throttle cable is routed incorrectly. Shut the engine off, remove the seat and fuel tank and recheck the cable(s) routing.

WARNING
Do not ride the bike until the cable(s) routing is correct.

21. Test ride the bike slowly at first and make sure the throttle is operating correctly.

CHOKE CABLE REPLACEMENT

1. Remove the seat and fuel tank.

2. Remove the screw securing the choke lever at the handlebar (**Figure 42**). Then slip the lever and cable out of the left-hand switch housing.

3. Loosen the choke cable clamp screw and remove the cable end from the choke lever (**Figure 38**).

NOTE
The piece of string attached in the next step will be used to pull the new choke cable back through the frame so it will be routed in the exact same position.

4. Tie a piece of heavy string or cord to the end of the choke cable at the carburetor. Wrap this end with masking or duct tape. Tie the other end of the string to the frame.

5. At the grip end of the cable, carefully pull the cable (and attached string) out through the frame loop, past the electrical harness and from behind the headlight housing. Make sure the attached string follows the same path as the cable through the frame and behind the headlight.

6. Remove the tape and untie the string from the old cable.

7. Tie the string to the new choke cable and wrap it with tape.

8. Carefully pull the string back through the frame, routing the new cable through the same path as the old cable.

9. Remove the tape and untie the string from the cable and the frame.

10. Lubricate the new cable as described in Chapter Three.

11. Attach the new cable to the choke linkage and tighten the choke cable clamp screw (**Figure 38**).

12. Attach the new cable to the choke lever. Then install the choke lever and cable on the left-hand switch housing.

13. Operate the choke lever and make sure the carburetor choke linkage is operating correctly and with no binding. If operation is incorrect or there is binding carefully check that the cable is attached correctly and that there are no tight bends in the cable.

14. Adjust the the choke cable as described in this chapter.

15. Install the fuel tank and seat.

FUEL SHUTOFF VALVE
(EXCEPT XV1000 and XV1100)

Troubleshooting

There are 3 positions on the shutoff valve (**Figure 43**).

a. *ON:* Fuel flows when the engine is running but stops when the engine is not running.

b. *RES (reserve):* Fuel flows when the engine is running but stops when the engine is not running. The RES position should only be used when there is not enough fuel in the tank to operate in the ON position. If the engine runs out of fuel when in the ON position, turn to PRI (prime) to allow fuel to flow to the carburetors. Then start the engine and turn the shutoff valve to RES. Refill the tank as soon as possible, then switch back to ON.

c. *PRI (prime):* In the position, fuel flows whether the engine is running or not. The PRI position should be used only when the fuel tank is empty. First, fill the tank with fresh gasoline. Then turn the shutoff valve to the PRI position to allow the carburetors to fill with fuel. Start the engine and turn the shutoff valve to ON.

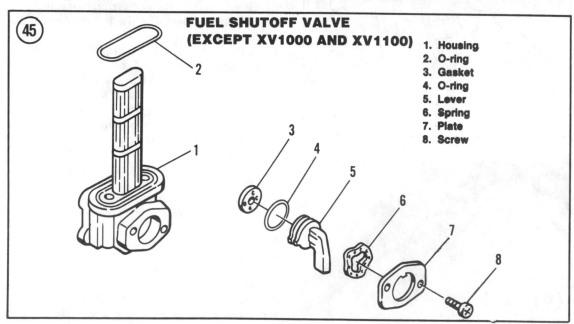

FUEL SHUTOFF VALVE (EXCEPT XV1000 AND XV1100)
1. Housing
2. O-ring
3. Gasket
4. O-ring
5. Lever
6. Spring
7. Plate
8. Screw

CAUTION
Never leave the shutoff valve in the PRI position.

While there is no OFF position on the valve, fuel will not flow through the valve in the ON or RES position without engine vacuum to open the valve. If there is fuel in the tank but it will not flow in the ON or RES position, check the vacuum line (**Figure 44**) from the shutoff valve to the rear carburetor intake manifold. If this line is not connected properly or is leaking, the fuel shutoff valve cannot operate properly.

Removal/Cleaning/Installation

The fuel filter removes particles which might otherwise enter the carburetors and cause the float needle to remain in the open position.

Refer to **Figure 45** for this procedure.

1. Remove the fuel tank as described in this chapter.
2. Set the fuel tank on a protective pad or blanket and position it so fuel will not spill out when the shutoff valve is removed.
3. Remove the screws securing the shutoff valve to the tank. Remove the valve and gasket.
4. Clean the filter with a medium soft toothbrush and carefully blow out with compressed air.
5. If the valve has been leaking, remove the screws securing the lever fitting plate and disassemble the valve assembly. Inspect all components for cracks or corrosion on all sealing surfaces. Inspect the O-ring; replace any part if its condition is doubtful.
6. Reassemble and install the valve. Turn the tank to the position in which it sits on the bike. Check the area around the valve carefully to make sure no fuel is leaking.
7. Install the fuel tank and seat.

FUEL FILTER
(XV1000 and XV1100)

These models have a separate fuel filter that cannot be cleaned. If dirty, a new filter must be installed.

Removal/Installation

1. Remove the seat.
2. Remove the right-hand side cover (**Figure 46**).
3. Disconnect the negative battery cable.
4. Remove the fuel filter cover (**Figure 47**).
5. Disconnect the flexible fuel lines from the fuel filter (**Figure 48**). Plug the ends of the fuel lines with golf tees.
6. Install by reversing these removal steps. The arrow stamped on the fuel filter must point toward the fuel pump.
7. After installation is complete, thoroughly check for fuel leaks.

FUEL PUMP
(XV1000 and XV1100)

Fuel pump performance testing is covered in Chapter Seven.

Removal/Installation

1. Remove the right-hand side cover (**Figure 46**).
2. Disconnect the negative battery cable.
3. Remove the fuel pump chrome cover (**Figure 49**).
4. Remove the fuel filter cover (**Figure 47**).
5. Disconnect the fuel pump electrical connector (**Figure 50**).
6. See **Figure 51**. Disconnect the fuel inlet (A) and outlet (B) flexible fuel lines from the fuel pump. Plug the ends of the fuel lines with golf tees to prevent fuel leakage.
7. Remove the fuel pump from the frame.
8. Install by reversing these removal steps.
9. After installation is complete, thoroughly check for fuel leaks.

FUEL TANK
(EXCEPT XV1000 AND XV1100)

Removal/Installation

1. Place the bike on the centerstand.
2. Disconnect the battery negative lead.
3. Remove the clip or rear bolts securing the fuel tank.
4. Turn the fuel shutoff valve to the ON or RES position (**Figure 43**). Lift up the rear of the tank and disconnect the fuel and vacuum lines at the shutoff valve. On 1984 and later models sold in California, disconnect the carbon canister hose at the back of the tank.
5. Pull the tank to the rear and remove it.

> *NOTE*
> *Whenever removing the tank, make sure to store it in a safe place away from open flame or objects that could fall and damage the tank.*

6. Install by reversing these removal steps.

FUEL TANK
(XV1000 AND XV1100)

This procedure describes removal and installation of the main and sub-fuel tanks.

Removal/Installation

1. Remove the seat.
2. Remove the left- and right-hand side covers.
3. Disconnect the negative battery cable.
4. Remove the main fuel tank bolt (**Figure 52**).

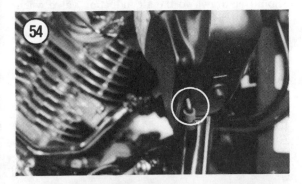

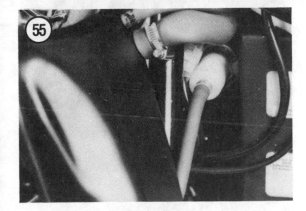

5. On California models, lift up the rear of the main tank and disconnect the carbon canister hose.
6. Remove the sub-fuel tank attaching bolt (**Figure 53**) and lift the tank away from the bike.
7. Remove the fuel line from the lower fitting on the sub-fuel tank (**Figure 54**). Attach a piece of fuel line to the fitting on the sub-fuel tank and place the loose end in a clean sealable metal container (suitable for gasoline storage). Drain both the main and sub-fuel tanks. If the fuel is kept clean it can be reused. Open the fuel filler cap to speed up the flow of fuel.
8. Lift the main fuel tank up slightly. Then loosen the clamps on the fuel and vent lines and remove both lines from the main fuel tank.
9. To remove the sub-fuel tank (if necessary), loosen the clamps on the fuel and vent lines (**Figure 55**) and disconnect both lines from the sub-fuel tank.
10. Install by reversing these removal steps; note the following.
11. Spray a small amount of WD-40 (or equivalent) onto the inside ends of the fuel and vent lines. This will make installation of the lines a little easier. Make sure they are completely installed onto the fittings on the main fuel tank. Tighten the clamps securely.
12. Check for fuel leaks.

CRANKCASE BREATHER SYSTEM

To comply with air pollution standards, the crankcase breather system (**Figure 56**) draws

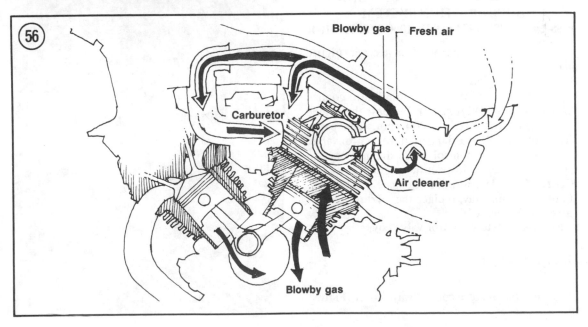

blowby gases from the crankcase and recirculates them into the fuel-air mixture and thus into the engine to be burned.

Inspection

Make sure all hose clamps are tight. Check all hoses for deterioration and replace as necessary.

MIXTURE CONTROL VALVE (1981-1983 XV750; 1984 AND 1985 XV700)

Inspection/Replacement

1. Remove the fuel tank as described in this chapter.

2A. *XV700*—Remove the mixture control valve cover.

2B. *XV750*—Remove the left-side engine mounting bracket cover.

3. Start the engine.

4. Place a piece of paper on the mixture control valve intake side (**Figure 57**). Increase the engine speed to approximately 5,000 rpm. The paper should be drawn toward the mixture control valve.

5. If the mixture control valve did not operate correctly in Step 4, inspect the vacuum lines (A, **Figure 58**) for deterioration. Replace if necessary. If the lines are okay, replace the mixture control valve (B, **Figure 58**).

6. Reinstall the fuel tank.

MIXTURE CONTROL VALVE AND AIR INDUCTION SYSTEM (1988-ON XV750, 1984-ON XV1000 AND XV1100)

1. Remove the mixture control valve cover (**Figure 59**).

2. Start the engine.

3. Place a piece of paper on the mixture control valve intake side (**Figure 60**). Increase the engine speed to approximately 5,000 rpm. The paper should be drawn toward the mixture control valve.

4. If the mixture control valve did not operate correctly in Step 3, inspect the vacuum lines (A, **Figure 61**) for deterioration. Replace if necessary. If both lines are okay, replace the mixture control valve (B, **Figure 61**).

5. Reinstall mixture control valve cover.

Air Induction System
Inspection

1. Remove the mixture control valve cover (**Figure 59.**)

2. Start the engine.

3. Place a piece of paper on the intake side of the air induction air filter (**Figure 62**). Increase the engine speed to approximately 5,000 rpm, then quickly close the throttle.

4. Repeat Step 3 two or three times. The paper should be drawn to the air induction valve when the throttle is closed.

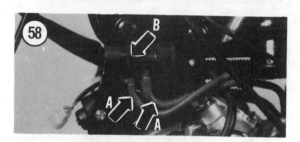

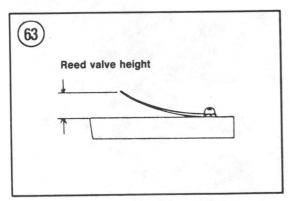

Reed valve height

5. If the air induction valve did not operate correctly in Step 4, perform the following steps.

6. Referring to **Figure 62**, remove the following:
   a. Hose (A).
   b. Hose (B).
   c. Reed valve case (C).

7. Remove the screws securing the reed valve case and separate it.

8. Remove the reed valve assembly. Measure the height of the reed valve as shown in **Figure 63**. The correct height is 0.3 in. (7.7 mm). Replace the reed valve assembly if necessary.

9. Remove the air filter cover (A, **Figure 64**) and remove the air filter. Clean the air filter by blowing it with compressed air.

10. Reinstall all parts removed in Steps 6-9 and retest the air induction valve. If the valve still doesn't perform as described, replace it.

Removal/Installation

1. Remove the mixture control valve cover (**Figure 59**).

2. Label and disconnect all vacuum hoses and tubes.

3. Remove the screws (B, **Figure 64**) securing the mixture control valve/air induction system assembly to the bike and remove it.

4. Installation is the reverse of these steps.

EXHAUST SYSTEM

Removal/Installation (1981-1983)

1. Place the bike on the centerstand.

2A. On all models except XV920RH and RJ (chain-drive), remove the muffler as follows:
   a. Loosen the rear cylinder exhaust pipe clamp at the muffler (**Figure 65**).
   b. Loosen the front cylinder exhaust pipe clamp at the muffler (**Figure 66**).
   c. Remove the rear muffler bolts and footpegs (**Figure 67**) and remove the muffler assembly.

2B. See **Figure 68**. Remove the left- and right-hand mufflers on XV920RH and RJ models as follows:
   a. Loosen the exhaust pipe clamp bolts at the front and rear cylinder mufflers.
   b. Loosen the muffler mounting bolts at the rear of the mufflers and and remove the mufflers.

3. Remove the Allen bolts securing the front exhaust pipe flange at the front cylinder head (**Figure 69**) and remove the exhaust pipe and gasket. Repeat for the rear cylinder exhaust pipe (**Figure 70**).

4. Install by reversing these removal steps; note the following.

5. Install a new gasket into each exhaust port in the cylinder head. In addition, check the gaskets between the exhaust pipes and mufflers. Replace any gasket as required.

6. Install all parts and secure fasteners finger-tight only. Then tighten the exhaust flange bolts securely and work back to the mufflers. This will minimize exhaust leak at the cylinder heads. Tighten all bolts securely.

Removal/Installation (1984-on)

1. Place the bike on the centerstand.
2. Remove the muffler as follows:
   a. Loosen the rear cylinder exhuast pipe clamp at the muffler.
   b. Loosen the front cylinder exhaust pipe clamp at the muffler (**Figure 71**).
   c. Remove the rear muffler bolts and footpegs (**Figure 72**) and remove the muffler assembly.
3. Remove the Allen bolts securing the front exhaust pipe flange at the front cylinder head (**Figure 73**) and remove the exhaust pipe and gasket. Repeat for the rear cylinder exhaust pipe.

4. Install by reversing these removal steps; note the following.

5. Install a new gasket into each exhaust port in the cylinder head. In addition, check the gaskets between the exhaust pipes and mufflers. Replace any gasket as required.

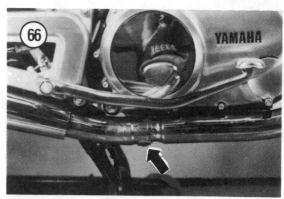

6. Install all parts and secure fasteners finger-tight only. Then tighten the exhaust flange bolts securely and work back to the mufflers. This will minimize exhaust leak age at the cylinder heads. Tighten all bolts securely.

Exhaust System Care

The appearance of the exhaust system greatly enhances any motorcycle. More importantly, the exhaust system is a vital key to the motorcycle's operation and performance. As the owner, you should periodically inspect, clean and polish the exhaust system. Special chemical cleaners and preservatives compounded for exhaust systems are available at most motorcycle shops.

Severe dents which cause flow restrictions require the replacement of the damaged part.

Problems occurring within the exhaust pipes are usually due to rust from the collection of water in the pipe. Periodically, or whenever the exhaust pipes are removed, turn the pipes to drain any trapped water.

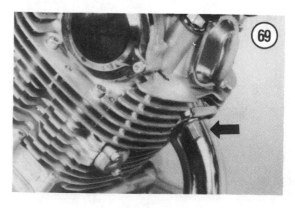

68

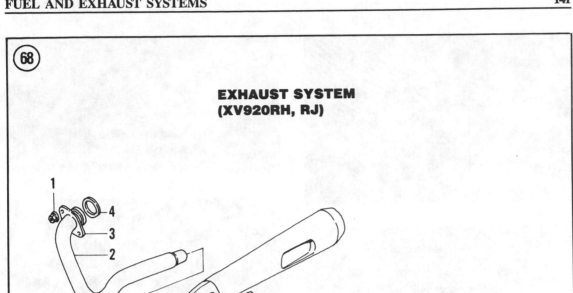

**EXHAUST SYSTEM
(XV920RH, RJ)**

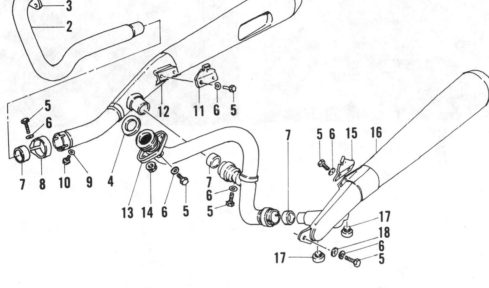

6

1. Nut
2. Exhaust pipe
3. Clamp
4. Gasket
5. Screw
6. Washer
7. Gasket
8. Band
9. Nut
10. Bolt
11. Bracket
12. Muffler
13. Exhaust pipe
14. Nut
15. Bracket
16. Muffler
17. Stopper
18. Washer

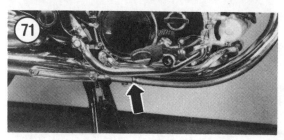

Table 1 CARBURETOR SPECIFICATIONS

Item	XV700	XV750H, J, K, MK
Manufacturer	Hitachi	Hitachi
Model	HSC40	HSC40
I.D. mark	42X-00	4X7-00
Main jet		
Both	122	
Cylinder 1	—	128
Cylinder 2	—	132
Main air jet	50	50
Jet needle		
Both	Y-32	—
Cylinder 1	—	Y-23
Cylinder 2	—	Y-22
Pilot jet	42	41
Pilot air jet	190	185
Pilot screw	Preset	Preset
Starter jet	40	40
Idle speed (rpm)	950-1,050	950-1,050

Item	XV750U-on	XV750UC-on
Manufacturer	Mikuni	Mikuni
Model	BST40	BST40
I.D. mark	3AL01	3CM00
Main jet	122.5	122.5
Main air jet	80	80
Jet needle	5DL12	5DL12
Pilot jet	40	40
Pilot air jet	60	60
Pilot screw	Preset	Preset
Starter jet	35	35
Idle speed (rpm)	950-1,050	950-1,050

Item	XV920RH, RJ	XV920J, K, MK	XV1000
Manufacturer	Hitachi	Hitachi	Hitachi
Model	HSC40	HSC40	HSC40
I.D. mark	5H1-00	10L-00	42H-00
Main jet			
Cylinder 1	126	126	124
Cylinder 2	124	128	132
Main air jet	50	50	50
Jet needle			
Both	Y-22	—	—
Cylinder 1	—	Y-25	Y-34
Cylinder 2	—	Y-24	Y-32
Pilot jet	41	41	40
Pilot air jet	180	195	190
Pilot screw	Preset	Preset	Preset
Starter jet	40	40	40
Idle speed (rpm)	950-1,050	950-1,050	950-1,050

6

(continued)

Table 1 CARBURETOR SPECIFICATIONS (continued)

Item	XV1100S, T	XV1100SC, TC
Manufacturer	Hitachi	Hitachi
Model	HSC40	HSC40
I.D. mark	1TE	1TF
Main jet		
Cylinder 1	122	122
Cylinder 2	128	128
Main air jet	50	50
Jet needle		
Cylinder 1	Y-33	Y-33
Cylinder 2	Y-33	Y-33
Pilot jet	40	40
Pilot air jet	100	100
Pilot screw	Preset	Preset
Starter jet	40	40
Idle speed (rpm)	950-1,050	950-1,050
Item	**XV1100U-on**	**XV1100UC-on**
Manufacturer	Mikuni	Mikuni
Model	BST40	BST40
I.D. mark	3CF00	3CG00
Main jet		
Cylinder 1	122.5	122.5
Cylinder 2	125	125
Needle jet	Y-4	Y-4
Jet needle		
Cylinder 1	5DL8	5DL8
Cylinder 2	5DL8	5DL8
Pilot jet	40	40
Pilot air jet		
No. 1	60	60
No. 2	140	140
Pilot screw	Preset	Preset
Starter jet	35	35
Idle speed (rpm)	950-1,050	950-1,050

Table 2 FUEL LEVEL SPECIFICATIONS

Year	in.	mm
1981-1983		
No. 1 carburetor (left)	0.04 ±0.04	1.0 ±1.0
No. 2 carburetor (right)	0.08 ±0.04	2.0 ±1.0
1984-1987	0 ±0.04	0 ±1.0
1988-on	0.06-0.10	1.5-2.5

ELECTRICAL SYSTEM

The electrical system includes the following:
a. Charging system.
b. Ignition system.
c. Starting system.
d. Lighting system.
e. Directional signal system.
f. Horn.

This chapter discusses each system in detail. Refer to Chapter Three for routine ignition system maintenance. Electrical system specifications are in **Table 1**. **Tables 1-4** are at the end of the chapter.

CHARGING SYSTEM

The charging system consists of the battery, alternator and a solid state rectifier/voltage regulator. See **Figure 1** (1981-1983) or **Figure 2** (1984-on).

The alternator generates an alternating current (AC) which the rectifier converts to direct current (DC). The regulator maintains the voltage to the battery and load (lights, ignition, etc.) at a constant voltage regardless of variations in engine speed and load.

Testing

Whenever the charging system is suspected of trouble, make sure the battery is fully charged before going any further. Clean and test the battery as described in Chapter Three. If the battery is in good condition, test the charging system as follows.

1A. On 1981-1983 models, remove the right-hand side cover.

1B. On 1984-on models, perform the following:
   a. Remove the right hand side cover.
   b. Remove the battery case cover (**Figure 3**).
   c. Disconnect the negative battery cable (**Figure 4**). Slide the battery out of its box slightly and disconnect the positive battery cable.
   d. Sit the battery on a wooden box placed next to the motorcycle.
   e. Reconnect the battery cables.

2. Connect a 0-15 DC voltmeter to the battery as shown in **Figure 5**. Connect the positive voltmeter terminal to the positive battery terminal and the negative voltmeter terminal to ground.

NOTE
Do not disconnect either the positive or negative battery cables; they are to remain in the circuit as is.

3. Start the engine and accelerate to approximately 2,000 rpm. Voltage should read 14.5 ±0.5 volts on XV750 and XV920 models or 14.8 ±0.5 volts on all other models.

4. If charging voltage is lower than specified, check the alternator and voltage regulator/rectifier. It is less likely that the charging voltage is too high;

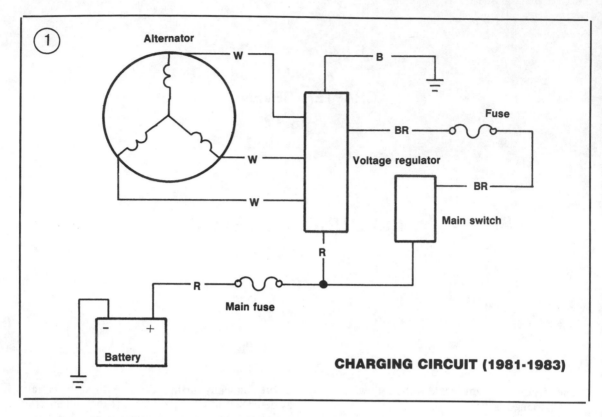

① **CHARGING CIRCUIT (1981-1983)**

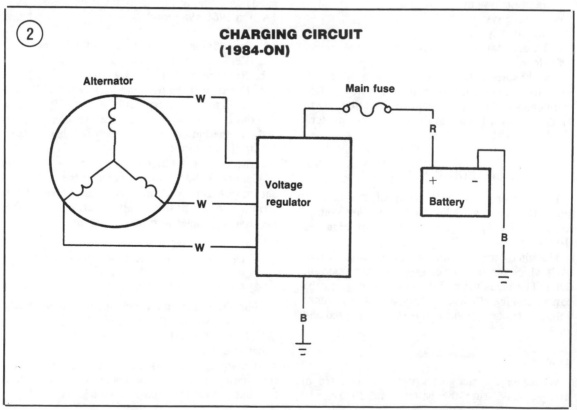

② **CHARGING CIRCUIT
(1984-ON)**

however, in that case the regulator is probably faulty. Test the separate charging system components as described in this chapter.

ALTERNATOR

An alternator is a form of electrical generator in which a magnetized field called a rotor revolves within a set of stationary coils called a stator. As the rotor revolves, alternating current is induced in the stator. The current is then rectified and used to operate the electrical accessories on the motorcycle and for charging the battery.

Stator Checks

1. Remove the left-hand side cover. On 1981-1983 models, remove the tool kit and the tool kit holder.
2. Disconnect the alternator connector (white wires).
3. Using an ohmmeter, measure the resistance between the alternator terminals (**Figure 6**). **Figure 7** shows the alternator/coil assembly removed. However, it is not necessary to remove the assembly to perform this test. Set the ohmmeter to ohms × 1. Check each white wire against the other white wires. The reading should be 0.5 ohm.
4. If the reading is not close to specification, check the electrical wires to and within the terminals. If they are okay, then there is an open or short in the coils and the stator must be replaced.
5. Next, connect the ohmmeter between a good engine ground and alternately to each white wire. No continuity should be noted between ground and any

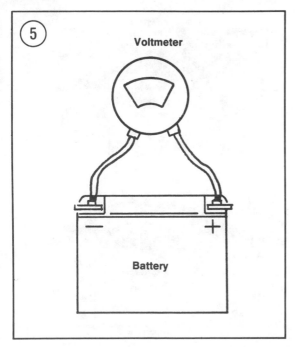

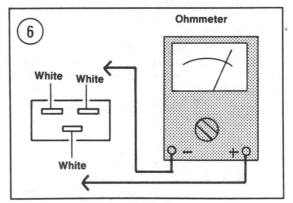

wire. If continuity is present, the alternator stator or alternator wire(s) is shorted to ground. Repair the shorted wire(s) or replace the alternator assembly.

Stator Removal/Installation

1. Place the bike on its centerstand.
2. Disconnect the negative battery cable.
3. Disconnect the stator coil wires.
4A. On 1981-1983 models, remove the shift lever and the left-hand foot peg assembly. See **Figure 8**.
4B. On 1984-on models, remove the left-hand side engine brace, gear shift and foot peg assembly (**Figure 9**).
5. Remove the clutch adjuster cover and disconnect the clutch cable at the engine (B, **Figure 10**).
6. Disconnect the neutral indicator switch wire (**Figure 11**).
7. Carefully pull the wire harness from the frame and remove the wires from the frame. Note the path of the wire harness during removal; it must be routed the same during installation.
8. Remove the Allen screws securing the alternator cover/coil assembly (A, **Figure 10**).
9. Remove the alternator cover/coil assembly and electrical cables. **Figure 12** shows the cover/coil assembly.
10. Remove the screws securing the stator (**Figure 13**) and remove the stator from the engine.
11. Install by reversing these removal steps; note the following.
12. Make sure the electrical wire harness is routed through the frame exactly as before.
13. Clean all wire connectors with electrical contact cleaner.

Inspection

1. Inspect the alternator cover/coil assembly for wear or cracking.
2. Check the electrical wires on the stator for any opens or poor connections. Also check the stator's insulating material for cracking. If the stator appears damaged in any way, test the assembly as described under *Stator Testing* in this chapter.

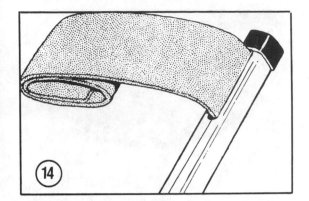

Rotor Removal/Installation

1. Remove the alternator cover as described under *Stator Removal/Installation* in this chapter.

2. Place a strap wrench (**Figure 14**) on the rotor to keep it from turning. Then remove the nut (**Figure 15**) and washer securing the rotor.

> *NOTE*
> *When the rotor is removed in Step 3, six springs and six pins may fall out from the cam chain drive gear positioned behind the rotor. Store these components in a plastic bag.*

3. Install the Yamaha rotor puller (Part No. TLU-90901-05-20) or a similar puller, onto the rotor as shown in **Figure 16**. Make sure to thread the bolts completely into the rotor threads. Use a wrench on the puller and tap on the end of it with a brass mallet until the rotor disengages. Remove the puller and rotor.

4. Remove the cam chain drive gear (A, **Figure 17**) from the rotor (B, **Figure 17**) if attached. Remove the pins and springs from the rotor (**Figure 18**).

5. Remove the Woodruff key from the crankshaft if necessary.

6. Installation is the reverse of these steps; note the following.

7. Install the Woodruff key in the crankshaft.

8. The three slots machined in the back of the rotor each house two springs and two pins. To assemble, install a single pin in each spring and install them into the rotor. See **Figure 18**.

9. On the backside of the rotor, push the two springs in each individual slot as far apart as possible. Then align the punch mark on the cam chain drive gear with the mark on the rotor (**Figure 19**) and install the drive gear into the rotor. During installation, it is necessary to push the drive dogs on the backside of the drive gear between the springs in each slot in the rotor (**Figure 20**).

> *CAUTION*
> *Carefully inspect the rotor for small bolts, washers or other metal "trash" that may have been picked up by the magnets. These small metal bits can cause severe damage to the alternator stator assembly.*

10. Turn the crankshaft to align the crankshaft Woodruff key with the timing mark on the rear cylinder intermediate gear. Then install the rotor, making sure to align the keyway in the rotor with the Woodruff key. Check that the rotor timing hole aligns with the timing gear shaft hole as shown in **Figure 21**. If the alignment is incorrect, remove the rotor and repeat this procedure.

7

NOTE
*If the rotor is being installed with the timing gears removed, refer to **Timing Gears**, Chapter Eight, for further information on timing gear installation.*

11. Install the rotor washer and nut. Place a strap wrench on the rotor and tighten the nut to 112 ft.-lb. (151 N•m).

12. Reconnect the clutch cable and adjust it as described in Chapter Three.

Rotor Testing

The flywheel is a permanently magnetized and cannot be tested except by replacement with a flywheel known to be good. A flywheel can lose magnetism from old age or a sharp blow. If defective, the flywheel must be replaced; it cannot be remagnetized.

VOLTAGE REGULATOR/RECTIFIER

Varying engine speeds and electrical system loads affect alternator output. The voltage regulator controls alternator output by varying the field current through the rotor windings. Before making any voltage regulator test, be sure that the battery is in good condition and is at or near full charge. See Chapter Three for battery testing.

Testing

1. Disconnect the battery negative cable from the battery.

2. Remove the left-hand side cover and disconnect the regulator/rectifier terminal connector. The regulator/rectifier assembly is shown in **Figure 22**.

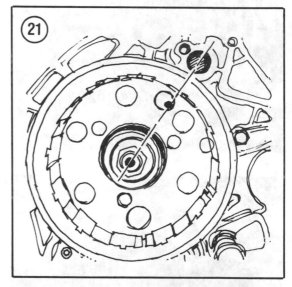

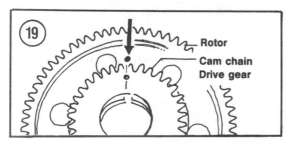

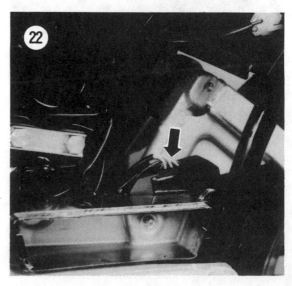

Rotor
Cam chain
Drive gear

CAUTION
If the rectifier is subjected to overcharging it can be damaged. Be careful not to short-circuit or incorrectly connect the battery positive and negative leads. Never directly connect the rectifier to the battery for a continuity check.

3. Measure the resistance between each of the following terminals with an ohmmeter (**Figure 23**). Record each of the measurements:

  a. D and A.
  b. D and B.
  c. D and C.
  d. A and E.
  e. B and E.
  f. C and E.

NOTE
*Depending on the internal polarity of the ohmmeter, the actual readings obtained may be the exact opposite of those specified in **Figure 23**. However, the readings must be very high (no continuity) with the meter connected one way and very low (continuity) when the leads are reversed.*

4. Reverse the ohmmeter leads, then repeat Step 3. Each set of measurements must be high with the ohmmeter connected one way and low with the ohmmeter leads reversed. It is not possible to specify exact ohmmeter readings, but each set of measurements should differ by a factor of not less than 10.
5. Even if only one of the elements is defective, the entire unit must be replaced; it cannot be serviced.

IGNITION SYSTEM

All XV models are equipped with a fully transistorized ignition system. This solid state system, unlike breaker point systems, provides a longer life for components and delivers a more efficient spark throughout the entire speed range of the engine. Ignition timing and advance are maintained without adjustment. Ignition timing procedures given in Chapter Three can be used to determine if the ignition system is operating properly.

Figure 24, **Figure 25** and **Figure 26** are diagrams of the ignition circuit.

When the crankshaft-driven reluctor passes one of the pick-up coils, a pulse is generated within the pick-up coil. This pulse (electrical current) flows to

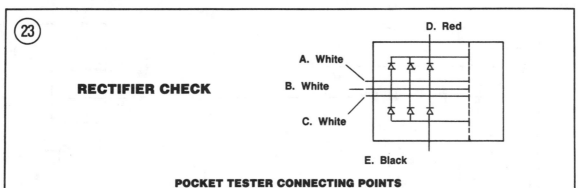

(23) **RECTIFIER CHECK**

A. White
B. White
C. White
D. Red
E. Black

POCKET TESTER CONNECTING POINTS

Positive	Negative	Correct test results
D	A	Continuity
A	D	Infinity
D	B	Continuity
B	D	Infinity
D	C	Continuity
C	D	Infinity
A	E	Continuity
E	A	Infinity
B	E	Continuity
E	B	Infinity
C	E	Continuity
E	C	Infinity

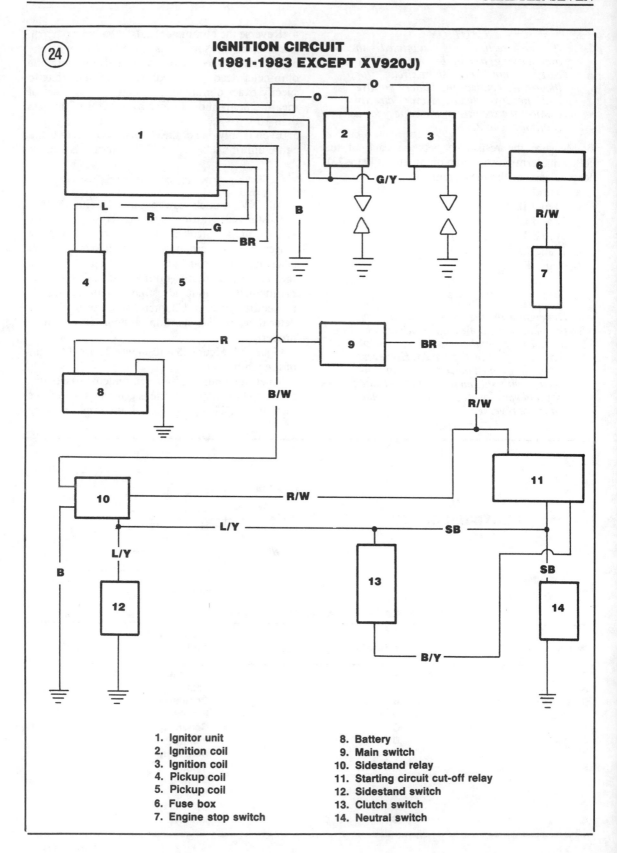

**IGNITION CIRCUIT
(1981-1983 EXCEPT XV920J)**

1. Ignitor unit
2. Ignition coil
3. Ignition coil
4. Pickup coil
5. Pickup coil
6. Fuse box
7. Engine stop switch
8. Battery
9. Main switch
10. Sidestand relay
11. Starting circuit cut-off relay
12. Sidestand switch
13. Clutch switch
14. Neutral switch

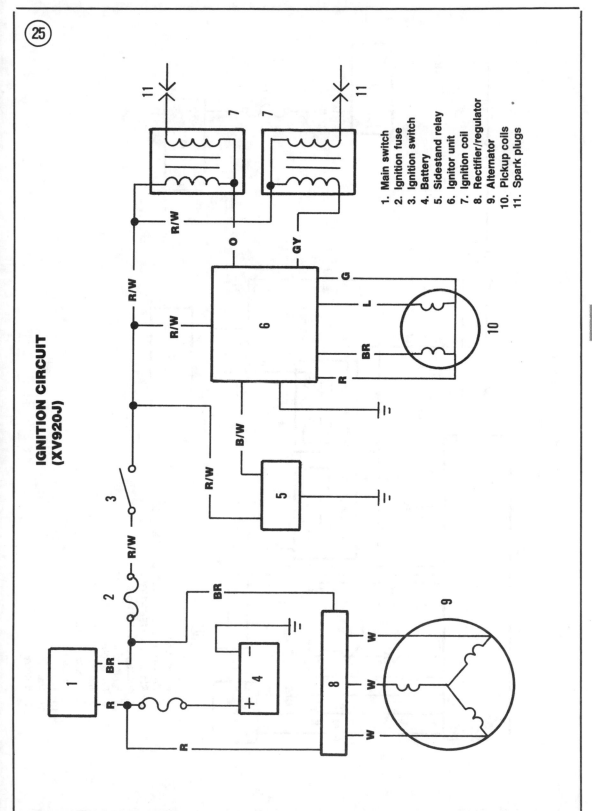

IGNITION CIRCUIT (XV920J)

1. Main switch
2. Ignition fuse
3. Ignition switch
4. Battery
5. Sidestand relay
6. Ignitor unit
7. Ignition coil
8. Rectifier/regulator
9. Alternator
10. Pickup coils
11. Spark plugs

7

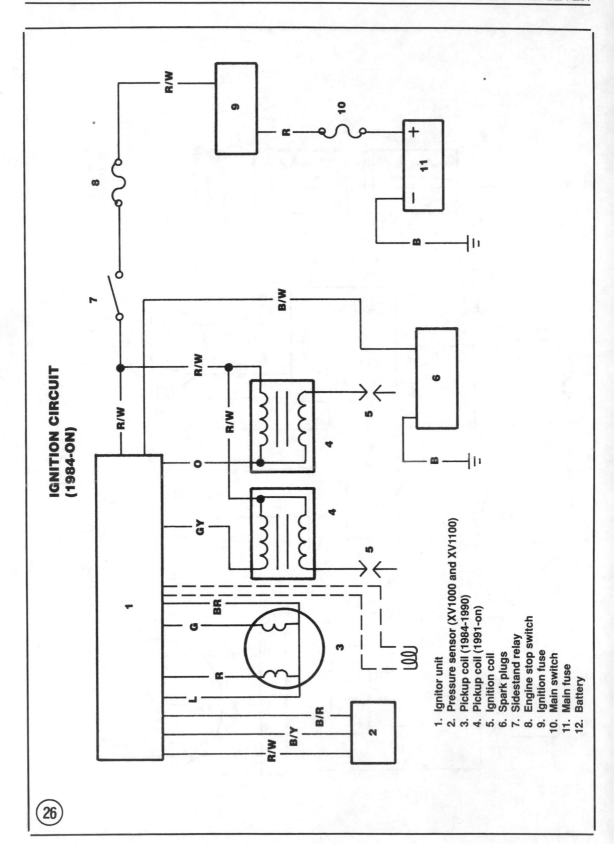

IGNITION CIRCUIT (1984-ON)

1. Ignitor unit
2. Pressure sensor (XV1000 and XV1100)
3. Pickup coil (1984-1990)
4. Pickup coil (1991-on)
5. Ignition coil
6. Spark plugs
7. Sidestand relay
8. Engine stop switch
9. Ignition fuse
10. Main switch
11. Main fuse
12. Battery

26

the switching and distributing circuits in the ignitor unit. The ignitor unit then stops the flow of current from the battery through the ignition coil primary winding. The magnetic field that has built up in the coils collapses. When this happens, a very high voltage is induced in the secondary winding of the ignition coil. This voltage is sufficient to jump the gap at the spark plug of one cylinder, causing the plug to fire. The same sequence of events happens to the other cylinder when the reluctor passes by the other pick-up coil.

The ignitor unit is also controlled by the sidestand relay and switch. When the sidestand is down, the ignition control unit is grounded through the sidestand relay. The engine cannot be started when the sidestand is down unless the transmission is in NEUTRAL. The sidestand relay and sidestand switch are covered separately in this chapter as they are also a part of the starting system.

Precautions

Certain measures must be taken to protect the transistorized ignition system. Instantaneous damage to the semiconductors in the system will occur if the following precautions are not observed.
1. Never connect the battery backwards. If the battery polarity is wrong, damage will occur to the voltage regulator, alternator and ignitor unit.

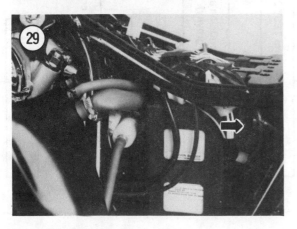

2. Do not disconnect the battery while the engine is running. A voltage surge will occur which will damage the voltage regulator and possibly burn out the lights.
3. Keep all connections between the various units clean and tight. Be sure that the wiring connectors are pushed together firmly.
4. Do not substitute another type of ignition coil or battery.
5. Each unit is mounted on a rubber vibration isolator. Always be sure that the isolators are in place when replacing any units.

Troubleshooting

Problems with the electronic ignition system are usually limited to the production of a weak spark or no spark at all. Test procedures for troubleshooting the ignition system are described in the diagnostic chart in **Figure 27**.

Before beginning actual troubleshooting read the entire test procedure (**Figure 27**). When required, the diagnostic chart will refer you to a certain chapter and procedure for service information. Basic ignition system and spark plug troubleshooting information can be found in Chapter Two and Chapter Three.

IGNITOR UNIT

Replacement

1A. *1981-1983 models*—Remove the seat and fuel tank.
1B. *1984-on models*—Remove the seat, left-side cover and the luggage box. On XV1000 and XV1100 models, remove the sub-fuel tank as described in Chapter Six.
2. Disconnect the electrical wire connectors at the ignitor unit. Then remove the screws securing the ignitor unit and remove it. See **Figure 28** (1981-1983) or **Figure 29** (1984-on).
3. Install by reversing these removal steps. Before connecting the electrical wire connectors at the ignitor unit, make sure the connectors are clean of any dirt or moisture.

Testing

The ignitor unit should be tested by a mechanic familiar with the Yamaha transistorized ignition. Improper testing of a good unit can damage it.

IGNITION COIL

Removal/Installation

1. Place the bike on its centerstand.

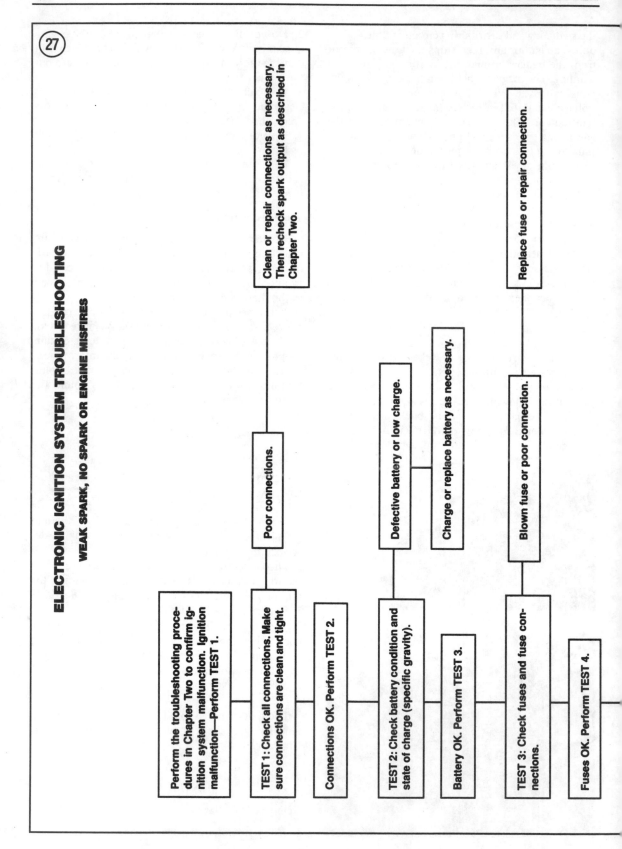

27

ELECTRONIC IGNITION SYSTEM TROUBLESHOOTING

WEAK SPARK, NO SPARK OR ENGINE MISFIRES

Perform the troubleshooting procedures in Chapter Two to confirm ignition system malfunction. Ignition malfunction—Perform TEST 1.

TEST 1: Check all connections. Make sure connections are clean and tight.

Poor connections. → Clean or repair connections as necessary. Then recheck spark output as described in Chapter Two.

Connections OK. Perform TEST 2.

TEST 2: Check battery condition and state of charge (specific gravity).

Defective battery or low charge. → Charge or replace battery as necessary.

Battery OK. Perform TEST 3.

TEST 3: Check fuses and fuse connections.

Blown fuse or poor connection. → Replace fuse or repair connection.

Fuses OK. Perform TEST 4.

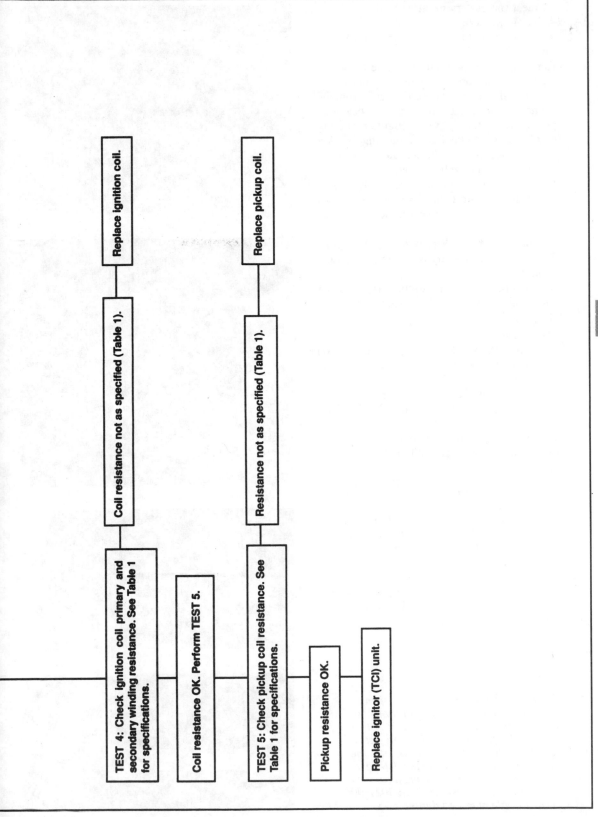

7

2. Disconnect the battery negative lead.

3A. *1981-1983 models*:

   a. Remove the fuel tank as described in Chapter Six.

   b. Remove the screw securing the left-side engine mounting bracket cover (at front cylinder). Lift the cover up to disengage it from the frame. Remove the cover, then repeat this procedure on the right-side engine mounting bracket cover. The front mounting bracket cover is secured by the left- and right-side covers and can now be removed.

   c. Without disconnecting any vacuum hoses, remove the mixture control valve (**Figure 30**) from its mounting bracket on the left side of the engine.

   d. Disconnect the spark plug leads (A, **Figure 31**) and the coil primary wires at the electrical connectors.

   e. Remove the 2 nuts (B, **Figure 31**) securing each coil to the frame and remove the coils (**Figure 32**).

3B. *1984-on models*:

   a. Disconnect the spark plug leads (A, **Figure 31**) and the coil primary wires at the electrical connector.

   b. On XV1000 and XV1100 models, disconnect the pressure sensor from the top of the ignition coil cover.

   c. Remove the ignition coil cover screws. Then remove the cover (**Figure 33**) and the ignition coils.

> *NOTE*
> *The ignition coils on 1984 and later models have dampers installed on the backside of each coil. Do not lose then during removal.*

4. Install by reversing these removal steps; note the following. Make sure to correctly connect the primary electrical wires to the coils and the spark plug leads to the correct spark plug.

Testing

> *NOTE*
> *Resistance tests can only detect open or shorted windings in the ignition coil. Replace the coil if resistance is not as specified. If, however, the coil resistance is within specifications, and the coil is still suspected as being defective, the coil should be tested using a Yamaha Electro Tester part No. 90890-03021-00 or a suitable magneto analyzer.*

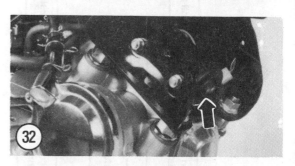

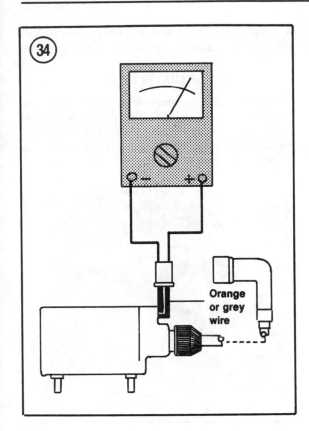

Orange
or grey
wire

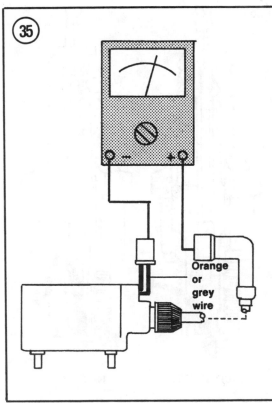

Orange
or
grey
wire

The ignition coil is a transformer which develops the high voltage necessary to jump the spark plug gap. The only maintenance required is that of keeping the electrical connections clean and tight and occasionally checking to ensure the coil is mounted securely.

To check coil primary and secondary winding resistance, proceed as follows:

1. Disconnect the coil primary wires. Disconnect the spark plug leads from the spark plugs.

2. Calibrate an ohmmeter on the R ×1 scale. To check primary winding resistance, connect the meter between the coil primary wires (**Figure 34**).

3. Next, calibrate the ohmmeter on the R ×100 scale. To check secondary winding resistance, connect the meter between the orange or gray primary wire and the spark plug terminal (**Figure 35**). If secondary resistance is higher than specification, be sure to check the spark plug cap resistance before replacing the coil. Remove the spark plug cap from the spark plug lead by turning it counterclockwise while pulling it away from the lead.

NOTE
If checking secondary winding resistance with the spark plug lead removed, be sure to factor in the spark plug cap resistance. Spark plug cap resistance is 5000 ohms on all models and is added into coil secondary resistance specifications.

4. Compare the results in Step 2 and Step 3 with the specifications in **Table 1**. Replace the ignition coil(s) if not within specification.

5. Inspect the spark plug leads for cracked insulation or other damage. The spark plug leads are available for replacement on 1981-1983 models. On 1984-on models, the ignition coil must be replaced if the spark plug lead is damaged or defective.

PICKUP COIL

Removal/Installation

1. Remove the alternator cover as described in this chapter.

NOTE
Figure 36 shows the early (prior to 1991) 4-wire pickup coil assembly. On 1991-on models, a new 2-wire pickup coil is used. The early and late coils are similar, however, and are located in the same place.

2. Remove the screws securing the pickup coil assembly (**Figure 36**) and remove it.

3. Installation is the reverse of these steps. Install the alternator cover as described in this chapter.

4. Check the ignition timing. Refer to Chapter Three.

NOTE
*The ignition timing is not adjustable. If the timing is incorrect when checked by the procedures given in Chapter Three, refer to **Ignition System Troubleshooting** in this chapter.*

Testing

1. On 1981-1983 models, remove the seat and fuel tank. On 1984-on models, remove the seat, left-side cover and luggage box. On XV1000 and XV1100 models, remove the sub-fuel tank as described in Chapter Six.

NOTE
On 1981-1990 models, the pickup coil has a 4-wire connector. On 1991-on models, the pickup coil has a 2-wire connector.

2. Disconnect the pickup coil connector from the ignitor assembly. See **Figure 28** (1981-1983) or **Figure 29** (1984-on).

3A. *1981-1990 models*—Connect an ohmmeter between the brown and green (No. 1 cylinder) pickup coil wires in the 4-wire connector. **Figure 37** shows the connector with the alternator cover and pickup coil removed. Note the reading, then connect the meter between the red and blue wires (No. 2 cylinder). Note the reading and compare with the specifications in **Table 1**.

3B. *1991-on models*—Connect the ohmmeter between the gray and black pickup coil wires in the 2-wire connector. Note the reading and compare with the specifications in **Table 1**.

4. If resistance is not within specification, replace the pickup coil assembly as described in this chapter.

SPARK PLUGS

The spark plugs recommended by the factory are usually the most suitable for your machine. If riding conditions are mild, it may be advisable to go to spark plugs one step hotter than normal (**Figure 38**).

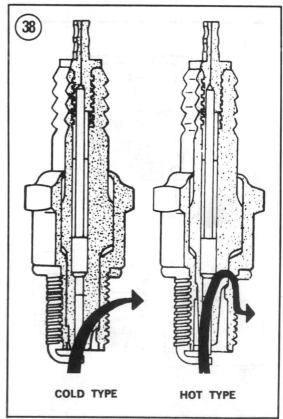

COLD TYPE   HOT TYPE

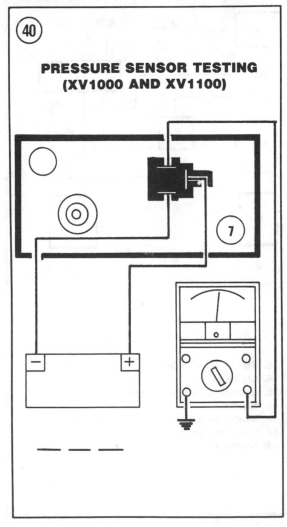

**PRESSURE SENSOR TESTING
(XV1000 AND XV1100)**

Unusually severe riding conditions may require slightly colder plugs. See Chapter Two and Chapter Three for details.

PRESSURE SENSOR
(XV1000 and XV1100)

A pressure sensor is installed in the ignition circuit (**Figure 26**) to control the ignition timing advance.

Testing/Replacement

1. Disconnect the intake tube and remove the pressure sensor from the ignition coil cover (**Figure 39**).
2. Check that the pressure intake tube is clear of all obstructions before starting Step 3.
3. Connect a 12 volt battery and voltmeter to the pressure sensor as shown in **Figure 40**. The output voltage should be 3 ± 0.03 volts.
4. If the pressure sensor failed the test in Step 3, replace it with a new unit.
5. Install the pressure sensor by reversing Step 1. Make sure the intake tube is attached securely to the pressure sensor.

STARTING SYSTEM

The starting system on 1981-1983 models, consists of the starter motor, starter solenoid, starter circuit cutoff relay, starter cutout relay, sidestand relay, sidestand switch, neutral switch, starter button and related wiring.

On 1984-on models, the starting system consists of the starter motor, starter relay, starter safety unit (relay assembly), solenoid switch (XV1000), sidestand relay (except 1991-on), sidestand switch, neutral switch, starter button and related wiring.

The starting system is shown in **Figures 41-45**. When the starter button is pressed, it engages the solenoid switch which closes the circuit. Electric current then flows from the battery to the starter motor.

> *CAUTION*
> *Do not operate the starter for more than 5 seconds at a time to prevent overheating the starter motor. Allow it to cool for approximately 10 seconds, then resume cranking.*

When the engine stop switch and the main switch are turned ON, the engine can only be started if the transmission is in NEUTRAL, or if the clutch lever is pulled in (transmission in gear) and the sidestand is up.

If the above conditions are not met, the starting circuit is disabled and the starter will not operate.

7

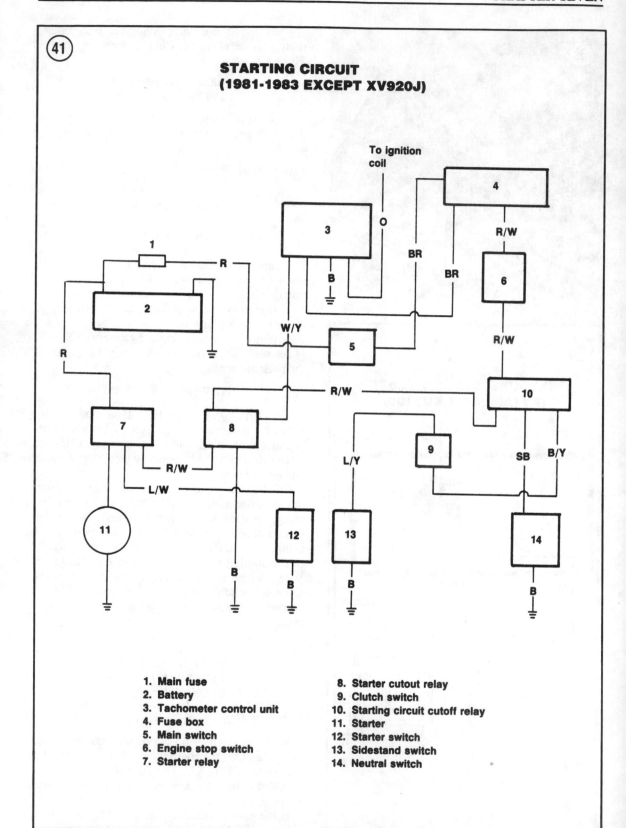

**STARTING CIRCUIT
(1981-1983 EXCEPT XV920J)**

1. Main fuse
2. Battery
3. Tachometer control unit
4. Fuse box
5. Main switch
6. Engine stop switch
7. Starter relay
8. Starter cutout relay
9. Clutch switch
10. Starting circuit cutoff relay
11. Starter
12. Starter switch
13. Sidestand switch
14. Neutral switch

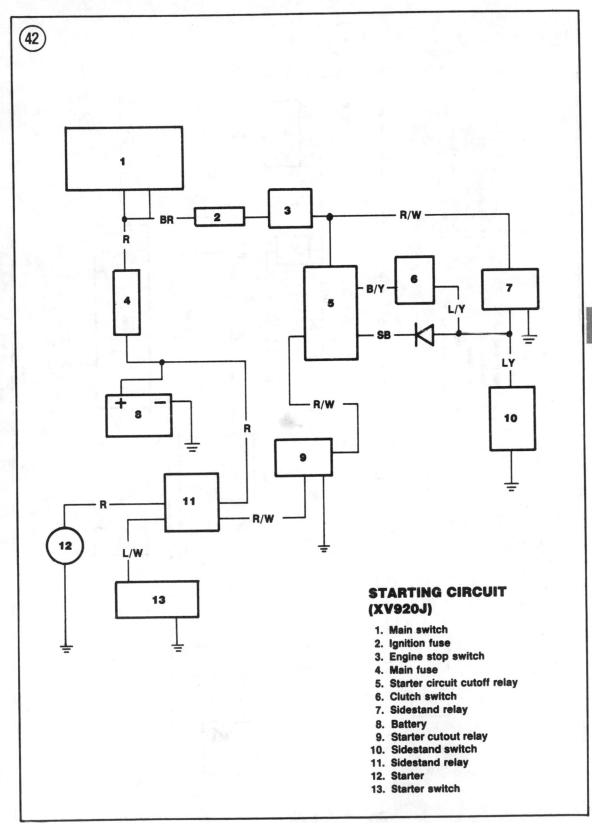

STARTING CIRCUIT (XV920J)

1. Main switch
2. Ignition fuse
3. Engine stop switch
4. Main fuse
5. Starter circuit cutoff relay
6. Clutch switch
7. Sidestand relay
8. Battery
9. Starter cutout relay
10. Sidestand switch
11. Sidestand relay
12. Starter
13. Starter switch

7

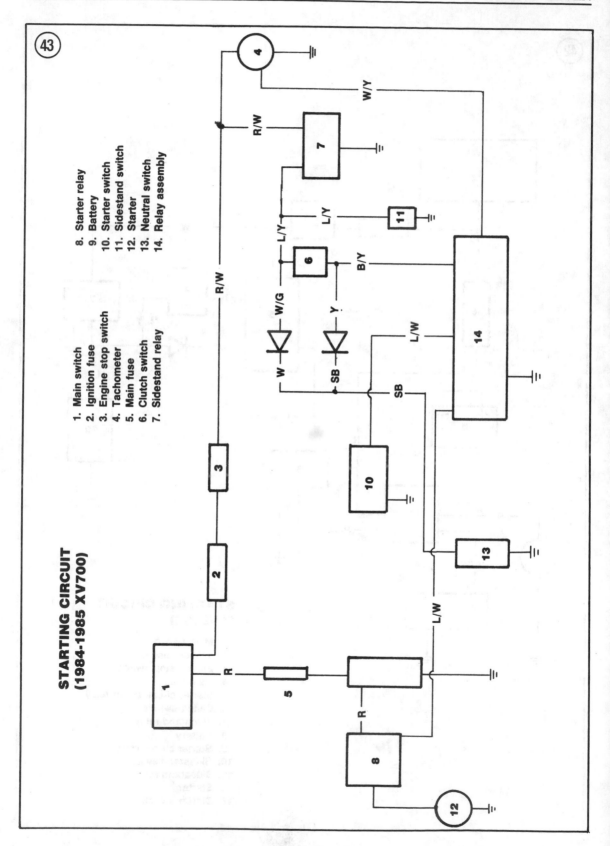

STARTING CIRCUIT
(1984-1985 XV700)

1. Main switch
2. Ignition fuse
3. Engine stop switch
4. Tachometer
5. Main fuse
6. Clutch switch
7. Sidestand relay
8. Starter relay
9. Battery
10. Starter switch
11. Sidestand switch
12. Starter
13. Neutral switch
14. Relay assembly

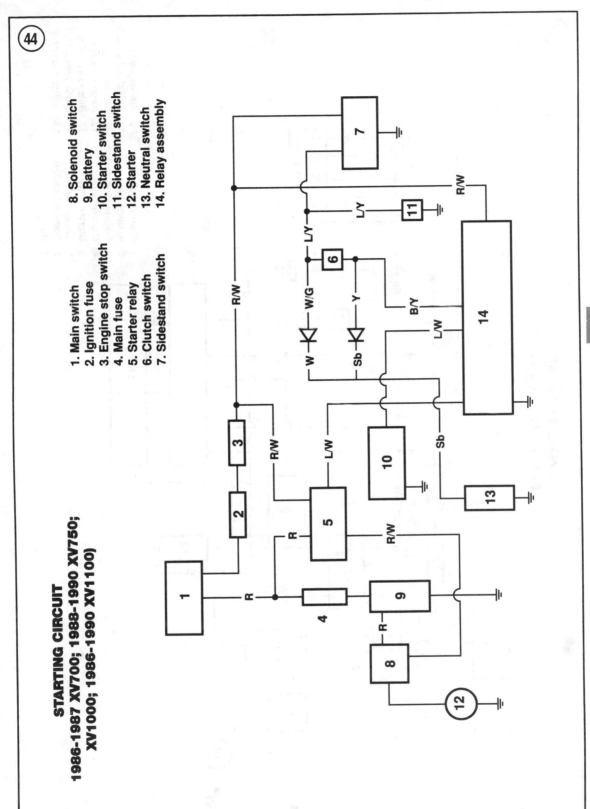

STARTING CIRCUIT
1986-1987 XV700; 1988-1990 XV750;
XV1000; 1986-1990 XV1100)

1. Main switch
2. Ignition fuse
3. Engine stop switch
4. Main fuse
5. Starter relay
6. Clutch switch
7. Sidestand switch

8. Solenoid switch
9. Battery
10. Starter switch
11. Sidestand switch
12. Starter
13. Neutral switch
14. Relay assembly

7

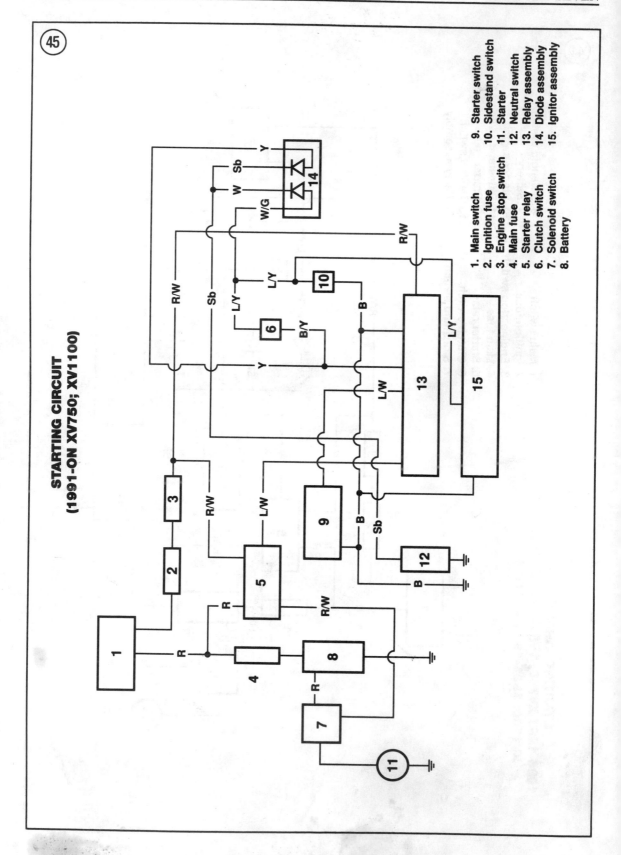

STARTING CIRCUIT
(1991-ON XV750; XV1100)

1. Main switch
2. Ignition fuse
3. Engine stop switch
4. Main fuse
5. Starter relay
6. Clutch switch
7. Solenoid switch
8. Battery
9. Starter switch
10. Sidestand switch
11. Starter
12. Neutral switch
13. Relay assembly
14. Diode assembly
15. Ignitor assembly

The starter gears are covered in Chapter Four. **Table 2**, at the end of the chapter, lists possible starter problems, probable causes and the most common remedies.

Starter Removal/Installation

1. Place the bike on the centerstand.
2. Make sure the ignition switch is in the OFF position.
3. Disconnect the negative lead from the battery.
4. On 1986-on models, remove the drive lever cover (**Figure 46**).

5. Pull back on the rubber boot and disconnect the electrical wire (**Figure 47**).
6. Remove the starter gears as described in Chapter Four.
7. Remove the bolts securing the starter to the crankcase and remove the starter (**Figure 48**).
8. Installation is the reverse of these steps, noting the following.
9. Inspect the starter O-ring and replace if damaged. Grease the starter O-ring (**Figure 49**) and insert the starter into the crankcase. Do not damge the O-ring during installation.
10. Tighten the starter motor bolts to 7.2 ft.-lb. (10 N•m).
11. Install the starter motor gear (with circlip attached) onto the end of the starter motor. Position the circlip into the channel in the crankcase.

Starter Disassembly/Inspection/Assembly

Starter overhaul is best left to an expert. This section will tell you if repairs are necessary.
    Refer to **Figure 50** (1981-1982 models) or **Figure 51** (1983-on models) as appropriate during this procedure.
1. Remove the starter motor case screws and separate the case.
2. Clean all grease, dirt and carbon dust from the armature, case and end covers.

> *NOTE*
> *Do not immerse brushes or the wire windings in solvent or the insulation might be damaged. Wipe the windings with a cloth slightly moistened with solvent and dry thoroughly.*

3. Pull back the brush springs and remove the brushes from their guides. Measure the length of

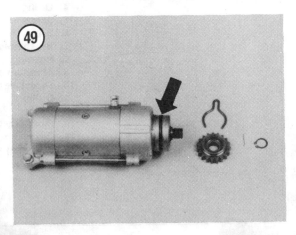

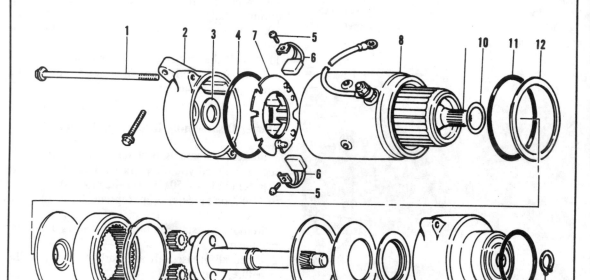

STARTER MOTOR
(1981-1982 MODELS)

1. Bolt
2. End cover
3. Thrust washer
4. O-ring
5. Screw
6. Brush
7. Brush holder assembly
8. Housing
9. Armature shaft
10. Thrust washer
11. O-ring
12. Gasket
13. Front bracket assembly
14. O-ring
15. Snap ring

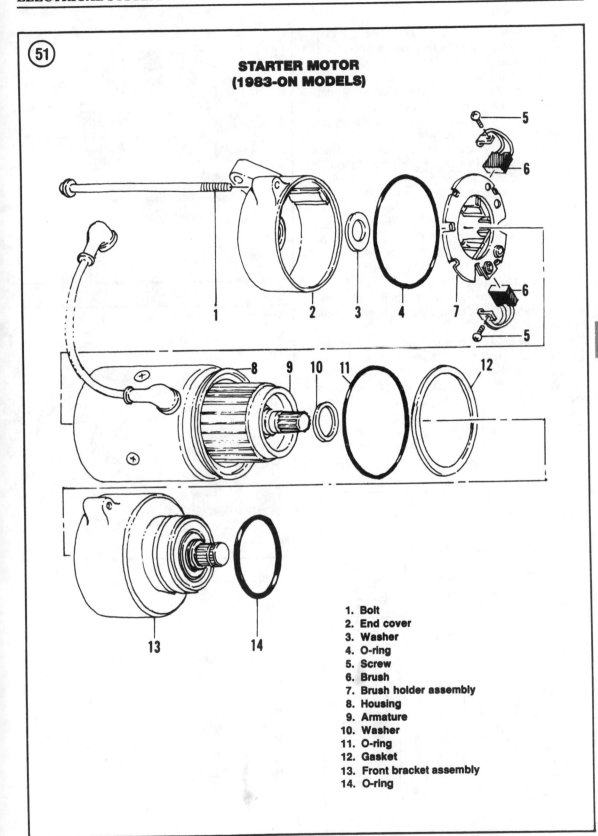

**STARTER MOTOR
(1983-ON MODELS)**

1. Bolt
2. End cover
3. Washer
4. O-ring
5. Screw
6. Brush
7. Brush holder assembly
8. Housing
9. Armature
10. Washer
11. O-ring
12. Gasket
13. Front bracket assembly
14. O-ring

7

each brush with a vernier caliper (**Figure 52**). If they are worn to less than 0.33 in. (8.5 mm), replace them.

4. Check spring tension. Replace springs if their condition is in doubt.

5. Inspect the commutator. The mica in a good commutator is below the surface of the copper bars (**Figure 53**). A worn commutator is indicated by the copper and mica being level with each other. A worn commutator can be undercut, but it requires a specialist. Take the job to a dealer or electrical shop.

6. Inspect the commutator bars for discoloration. Pairs of discolored bars indicate grounded armature coils.

7. Use an ohmmeter to check continuity between commutator bars (**Figure 54**). There should be continuity between pairs of bars. Also check for continuity between commutator bars and the shaft (**Figure 55**). There should be no continuity and if the test indicates continuity, a short is indicated. If the armature fails either of these tests, the starter should be replaced.

8. Inspect the field coil by checking continuity from the cable terminal to the motor case with an ohmmeter; there should be no continuity. Also check from the cable terminal to each brush wire; there should be continuity. If the unit fails either of these tests, the starter motor assembly must be replaced.

9. Check the armature front and rear bearings. If worn or damaged, replace the starter motor assembly.

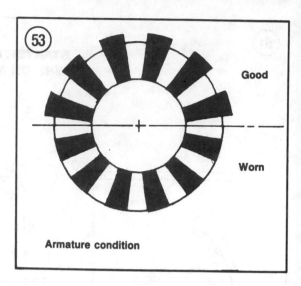

Good

Worn

Armature condition

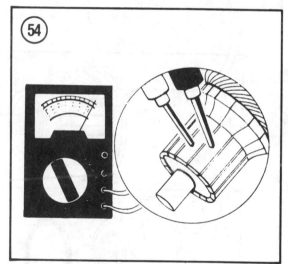

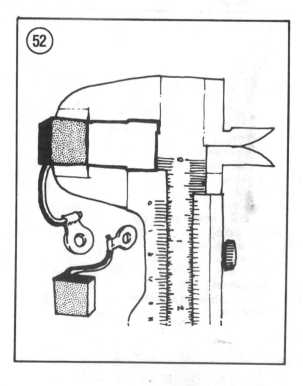

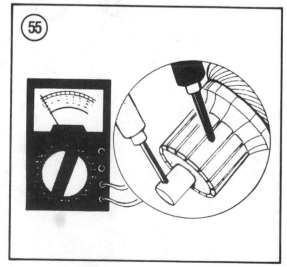

10. Assembly is the reverse of disassembly, noting the following. When the armature is inserted through the case, make sure each of the 2 brushes contact the commutator evenly. Then attach the cable terminal to the end cover and install the end cover.

Starter Relay Removal/Installation

1984-1985 XV700; 1981-1983 XV750; XV920

1. Remove the right-hand side cover.
2. Disconnect the negative battery cable from the battery.
3. Disconnect the positive battery cable and the solenoid-to-starter motor cable from the solenoid. See **Figure 56**.
4. Disconnect the blue/white and red (XV700) or red/white and blue/white (XV750 and XV920) wires from the solenoid.

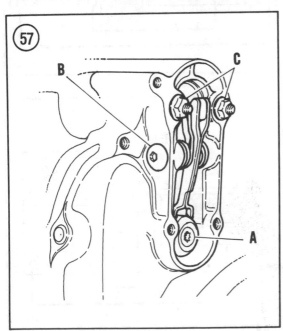

5. Remove the solenoid from its rubber holder (**Figure 56**).
6. Reverse Steps 1-5 to install the solenoid. Make sure all electrical connections are clean and tight.

Starter Solenoid Removal/Installation

1986-1987 XV700; 1988-on XV750; XV1000; XV1100

1. Remove the right-hand side cover.
2. Disconnect the negative battery cable from the battery.
3. Remove the starter drive lever cover (**Figure 46**) and gasket.
4. Disconnect the starter cable (**Figure 47**, typical) from the starter motor.
5. Remove the drive lever collar screw (A, **Figure 57**).
6. Remove the drive lever pivot screw (B, **Figure 57**).
7. Remove the 2 solenoid mounting nuts (C, **Figure 57**).
8. Remove the 2 screws securing the solenoid cover to the crankcase cover. Remove the solenoid cover, solenoid and gasket.
9. Reverse Steps 1-8 to install the solenoid while noting the following. Tighten the solenoid mounting nuts (C, **Figure 57**) to 71 in.-lb. (8 N•m). Install a new solenoid gasket. Apply a suitable thread-locking compound to the threads of the drive lever pivot screw (B, **Figure 57**). Tighten the screw to 88 in.-lb. (10 N•m).

Troubleshooting (1981-1983 XV750 and XV920)

The starter circuit cutoff relay, starter cutout relay and sidestand relay are located under the seat in various positions. See **Figure 58**. Therefore, the

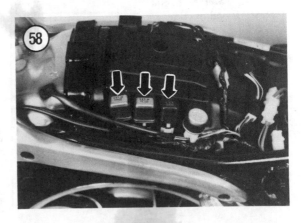

7

relays are identified by markings, relay color code, number of wires and wire color in the following troubleshooting sections.

Starting circuit cutoff relay test

The starting circuit cutoff relay prevents current flow to the starting motor unless the transmission is in NEUTRAL, or the clutch lever is depressed (transmission in gear) and the sidestand is in the UP position.

On early models the relay is marked 4H7; on later models the relay is marked 12R. The relay has no color code and is connected to 4 wires: 2 red/white, 1 sky blue and 1 black/yellow.

1. Place the motorcycle on its centerstand.
2. Remove the seat.
3. Remove the starting circuit cutoff relay from its rubber holder, then disconnect the relay connector.
4. Check the resistance of the relay coil by connecting an ohmmeter between the terminals shown in **Figure 59**. The resistance should be 100 ohms.
5. Next, connect an ohmmeter and a 12-volt battery to the relay as shown in **Figure 60**. With the battery connected, the ohmmeter should indicate zero ohms. With the battery disconnected the ohmmeter should indicate infinity.

> *NOTE*
> *The resistance specified in Step 6 (9.5 ohms) is based on the use of a Yamaha Pocket Tester part No. 90890-03112. The actual resistance measured may vary between ohmmeters from different manufacturers.*

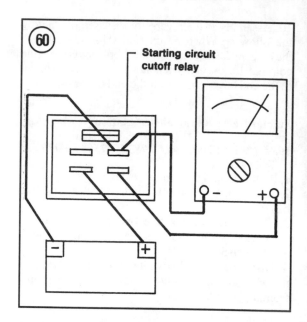

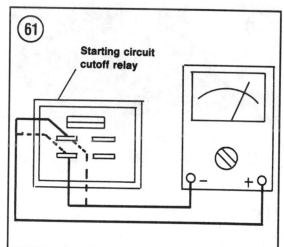

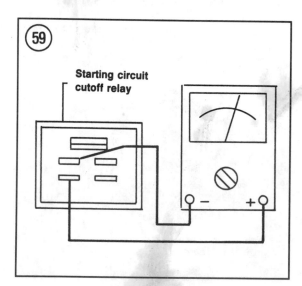

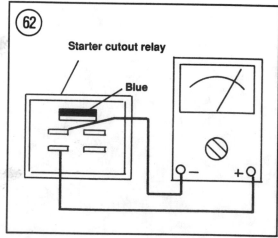

6. Next, connect the ohmmeter between the relay terminals shown in **Figure 61**. Resistance should be 9.5 ohms.

7. Replace the starting circuit cutoff relay if it failed any test (Steps 4-6).

Starter cutout relay test

The starter cutout relay prevents damage to the starter motor and gears by disabling the starting circuit after the engine starts. After the engine starts, a signal from the tachometer control unit causes the starter cutout relay to switch OFF, preventing current flow to the starter motor.

The starter cutout relay and the sidestand relay are both color-coded blue and marked 4U8, so the starter cutout relay must be identified by the connecting wires. The starter cutout relay is connected to a plug which has 2 red/white wires, 1 white/yellow wire

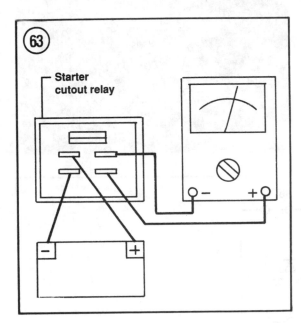

Starter cutout relay

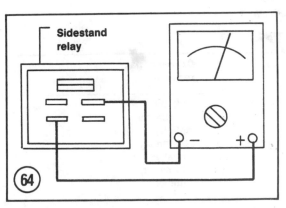

Sidestand relay

and 1 black wire. Refer to the following for removing and testing the starter cutout relay.

1. Place the motorcycle on its centerstand.

2. Remove the seat.

3. Remove the starter cutout relay from its rubber holder, then disconnect the relay connector.

4. Measure the resistance of the relay coil windings by connecting an ohmmeter between the relay terminals shown in **Figure 62**. The resistance should be 100 ohms.

5. Next, connect an ohmmeter and a 12-volt battery to the relay as shown in **Figure 63**. With the battery connected, the ohmmeter should indicate infinity. With the battery disconnected, the ohmmeter should indicate zero ohms.

6. Replace the starter cutout relay if it failed any test (Steps 4 and 5).

Sidestand relay test

The sidestand relay and the starter cutout relay are both color-coded blue and marked 4U8, so the sidestand relay must be identified by the connecting wires. The sidestand relay is connected to a plug which has 1 black/white wire, 1 red/white wire, 1 blue/yellow wire and 1 black wire. Refer to the following for removing and testing the sidestand relay.

1. Place the motorcycle on its centerstand.

2. Remove the seat.

3. Remove the sidestand relay from its rubber holder, then disconnect the relay connector.

4. Connect the ohmmeter to the black and blue/yellow terminals. When the sidestand is up, the ohmmeter should indicate zero ohms. When the sidestand is down, the reading should be infinity.

5. Next, measure the resistance between the terminals shown in **Figure 64**. The resistance should be 100 ohms.

6. Connect the ohmmeter and a 12-volt battery to the sidestand relay as shown in **Figure 65**. With the battery connected, the ohmmeter should indicate infinity. With the battery disconnected, the ohmmeter should indicate zero ohms.

7. Replace the sidestand relay if it fails any test (Steps 4-6).

Starter relay test

1. Disconnect the starter motor cable from the relay. See **Figure 56**.

2. Connect a voltmeter between a good engine ground and the starter motor terminal of the relay.

7

3. Turn the main switch ON, the stop switch to RUN and shift the transmission to NEUTRAL.

4. Push the starter button. The relay should "click" and the voltmeter should indicate battery voltage. If not, first make sure the starter cutout relay and starting circuit cutoff relay are operating properly as outlined in this chapter. If so, replace the starter relay.

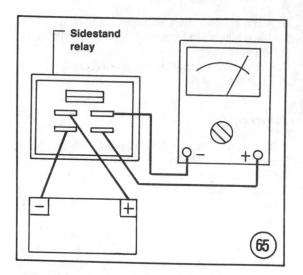

Diode test

1. Remove the seat.

2. Disconnect the diode block (**Figure 66**) from the wiring harness.

3. Check each diode and resistor in the diode block with an ohmmeter. Referring to **Figure 67**, check the diode between the indicated wires. Replace the diode if it fails any test.

Neutral switch test

1. Place the motorcycle on its centerstand.

2. Remove the left side cover.

3. Remove the luggage box, if so equipped.

5. Disconnect the blue neutral switch wire at its connector.

6. Connect an ohmmeter between a good engine ground and the blue neutral switch wire.

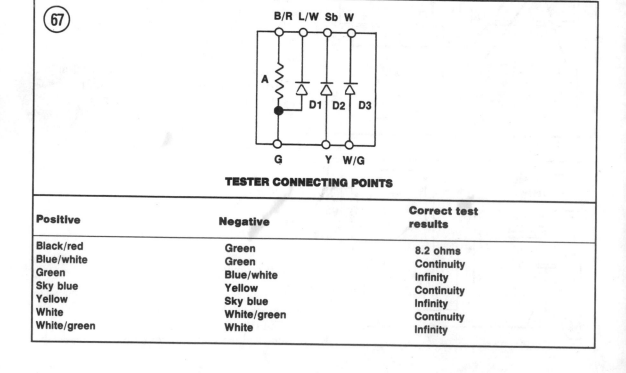

TESTER CONNECTING POINTS

Positive	Negative	Correct test results
Black/red	Green	8.2 ohms
Blue/white	Green	Continuity
Green	Blue/white	Infinity
Sky blue	Yellow	Continuity
Yellow	Sky blue	Infinity
White	White/green	Continuity
White/green	White	Infinity

7. Shift the transmission into NEUTRAL. The ohmmeter should indicate zero ohm. Next, shift into FIRST gear. The ohmmeter should indicate infinity.

8. Replace the neutral switch if it does not perform as specified.

Sidestand switch test

1. Place the motorcycle on its centerstand. Remove the seat and left side cover.

2. Remove the luggage box on models so equipped.

3. Disconnect the sidestand switch connector. The connector contains 2 wires—black and blue/yellow.

4. Connect an ohmmeter between the sidestand switch wires. With the sidestand in the up position, the ohmmeter should indicate zero ohm. With the sidestand down, the ohmmeter should indicate infinity.

5. Replace the sidestand switch if it does not perform as specified. Reverse Steps 1 and 3 to complete assembly.

Clutch switch test

1. Place the motorcycle on its centerstand.

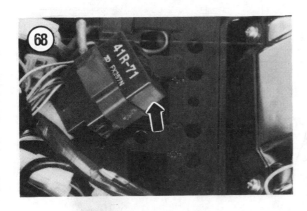

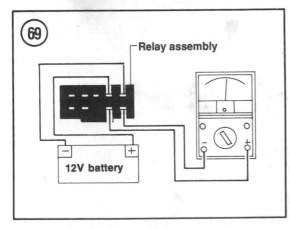

2. Remove the headlight assembly as described in this chapter.

3. Locate the black/yellow and blue/yellow 2-wire connector inside the headlight shell. Disconnect the clutch switch at the 2-wire connector.

4. Connect an ohmmeter between the black/yellow and blue/yellow wires (switch side).

5. With the clutch lever pulled in, the ohmmeter should indicate zero ohm. With the lever out, the ohmmeter should indicate infinity.

Starter switch test

1. Place the motorcycle on its centerstand.

2. Remove the headlight assembly as described in this chapter.

3A. *XV920*—Locate the red/white and black/white 2-wire connector located inside the headlight shell. Disconnect the starter switch at the 2-wire connector.

3B. *XV750*—Locate the blue/white starter switch connector inside the headlight shell. Disconnect the switch.

4A. *XV920*—Connect an ohmmeter between the red/white and black/white wires in the switch side of the connector.

4B. *XV750*—Connect an ohmmeter between a good engine ground and the blue/white wire in the switch side of the connector.

5. Push the starter button while noting the ohmmeter. Zero ohm should be noted. Release the button and note the meter. The ohmmeter should indicate infinity. If not, replace the starter switch.

Troubleshooting (XV700; 1988-on XV750; XV1000; XV1100)

Relay assembly (starter safety unit) test

1. Place the motorcycle on its centerstand and remove the seat.

2. Remove the relay assembly (**Figure 68**) from its mounting bracket. Disconnect the relay from the wiring harness.

3. Connect a 12-volt battery and ohmmeter to the relay as shown in **Figure 69**.

    a. With the battery connected, the ohmmeter should indicate zero ohm.

    b. With the battery disconnected, the ohmmeter should indicate infinity.

4. Replace the relay assembly if the test results are not as specified.

Sidestand relay test (except 1991-on models)

1. Place the motorcycle on its centerstand, then remove the seat and left side cover.
2. Disconnect and remove the sidestand relay (A, **Figure 70**).

3. Connect a 12-volt battery and ohmmeter to the relay as shown in **Figure 71**.
   a. With the battery connected, the ohmmeter should indicate infinity.
   b. With the battery disconnected, the ohmmeter should indicate zero ohm.

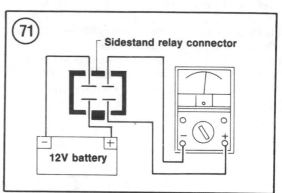

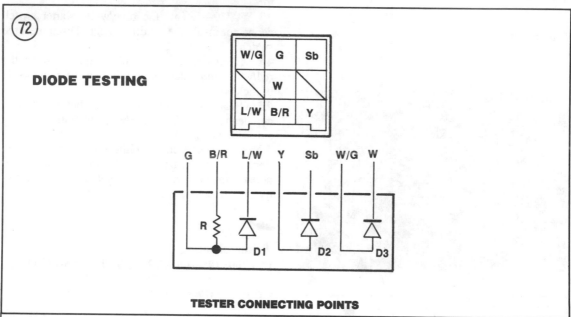

DIODE TESTING

TESTER CONNECTING POINTS

Positive	Negative	Correct test results
Green	Blue/white	0 ohms[1]
Blue/white	Green	Infinite[2]
Yellow	Sky blue	0 ohms[1]
Sky blue	Yellow	Infinite[2]
White/green	White	0 ohms[1]
White	White/green	Infinite[2]
Green	Black/red	8.2 ohms

1. Scale ohms×1000.
2. Scale ohms×1.

4. Replace the sidestand relay if the test results are not as specified.

Diode test

1. Place the motorcycle on its centerstand and re-move the seat.
2. Disconnect and remove the diode assembly (B, **Figure 70**).
3. Measure the resistance at each of the wire connections as indicated in **Figure 72**. Record each reading.
4. Replace the diode assembly if all test results are not as specified in **Figure 72**.

Neutral switch test

1. Place the motorcycle on its centerstand.
2. Remove the left side cover.
3. On XV1000 and XV1100 models, unfasten the sub-fuel tank and set it aside without disconnecting any fuel hoses. See Chapter Six.
4. Remove the luggage box on XV700 and XV750 models.
5. Disconnect the blue neutral switch wire at its connector. The neutral switch is located where shown in **Figure 73**.
6. Connect an ohmmeter between a good engine ground and the blue neutral switch wire.
7. Shift the transmission into NEUTRAL. The ohmmeter should indicate zero ohm. Next, shift into FIRST gear. The ohmmeter should indicate infinity.

8. Replace the neutral switch if it does not perform as specified.

Sidestand switch test

1. Place the motorcycle on its centerstand. Remove the seat and left side cover.
2. On XV700 and XV750 models, remove the luggage box. On XV1000 and XV1100 models, remove the sub-fuel tank as described in Chapter Six. It is not necessary to disconnect the fuel hoses from the sub-fuel tank.
3. Disconnect the sidestand switch connector. The connector contains 2 wires—black and blue/yellow. The sidestand switch is located where shown in **Figure 74**.
4. Connect an ohmmeter between the sidestand switch wires. With the sidestand in the up position, the ohmmeter should indicate zero ohm. With the sidestand down, the ohmmeter should indicate infinity.
5. Replace the sidestand switch (**Figure 74**) if it does not perform as specified. Reverse Steps 1 and 2 to complete assembly.

Clutch switch test

1. Place the motorcycle on its centerstand.
2. Remove the headlight assembly as described in this chapter.
3. Locate the black/yellow and blue/yellow 2-wire connector inside the headlight shell. Disconnect the clutch switch at the 2-wire connector.
4. Connect an ohmmeter between the black/yellow and blue/yellow wires in the switch side of the connector.
5. With the clutch lever pulled in, the ohmmeter should indicate zero ohm. With the lever out, the ohmmeter should indicate infinity.

Starter switch test

1. Place the motorcycle on its centerstand.
2. Remove the headlight assembly as described in this chapter.
3. Locate the blue/white and black 2-wire connector located inside the headlight shell. Disconnect the starter switch at the 2-wire connector.
4. Connect an ohmmeter between the blue/white and black wires in the switch side of the connector.
5. Push the starter button while noting the ohmmeter. Zero ohm should be noted. Release the button and note the meter. The ohmmeter should indicate infinity.

7

Starter relay test (1984-1985 XV700 models)

NOTE
The following test procedure assumes that all other starter system components are functioning properly. If necessary, test other components as described in this chapter before failing the starter relay.

Figure 75 shows a typical starter relay installation on 1984-1985 XV700 models. These models are not equipped with a starter solenoid.

1. Place the motorcycle on its centerstand and remove the right side cover.
2. Remove the relay mounting fasteners.
3. Disconnect the starter motor cable from the relay.
4. Connect an ohmmeter between the 2 large relay terminals.
5. Turn the main switch ON, the stop switch to RUN and shift the transmission into NEUTRAL.
6. Push the starter button while noting the ohmmeter. The relay should "click" and the ohmmeter should indicate zero ohm. If not, continue at Step 7.
7. Disconnect the blue/white wire and battery cable from the relay. Check the resistance between the blue/white wire terminal and the battery side terminal. If the resistance exceeds 1 ohm, replace the relay.

Starter relay test (1986-1987 XV700; 1988-on XV750; XV1000; XV1100)

1. Place the motorcycle on its centerstand and remove the seat.
2. Remove the relay (**Figure 76**) from its mounting bracket. Disconnect and remove the relay.
3. Connect a 12-volt battery and ohmmeter to the relay as shown in **Figure 77**.
4. With the battery connected, the ohmmeter should indicate zero ohm. With the battery disconnected, the ohmmeter should indicate infinity.
5. Replace the starter relay if it does not perform as specified.

Starter solenoid test (1986-1987 XV700; 1988-on XV750; XV1000; XV1100)

1. Place the motorcycle on its centerstand.
2. Remove the seat and right side cover.
3. Disconnect the positive battery cable and starter motor cable from the solenoid.
4. Connect an ohmmeter between the positive battery terminal and starter motor cable terminal on the

solenoid. Then, connect a suitable jumper lead to the positive battery terminal and red wire connector at the main fuse.
5. Turn the main switch ON, the stop switch to RUN and shift the transmission into NEUTRAL.
6. Push the starter button while noting the ohmmeter. The solenoid should "click" and the ohmmeter should indicate zero ohm. If not, continue at Step 7.
7. Disconnect the black solenoid wire. Check the resistance between the black wire terminal on the solenoid and a good ground. If resistance exceeds 1 ohm, replace the solenoid.

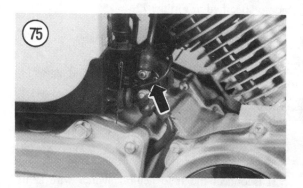

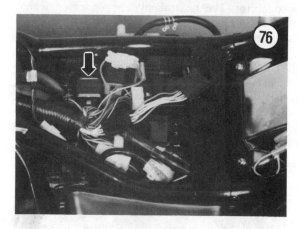

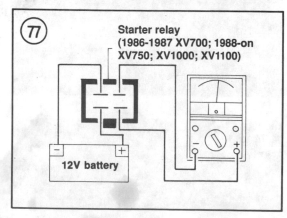

Starter relay
(1986-1987 XV700; 1988-on
XV750; XV1000; XV1100)

12V battery

LIGHTING SYSTEM

The lighting system consists of the headlight, taillight/brakelight combination, directional signals, warning lights and speedometer and tachometer illumination lights. If a light doesn't work, check the bulb. If the bulb is good, check all

Headlight Replacement

WARNING
*If the headlight has just burned out or been turned off it will be **hot**! Don't touch the bulb until it cools off.*

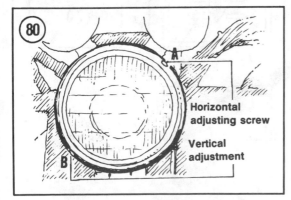

Horizontal
adjusting screw

Vertical
adjustment

1. Remove the mounting screws (A, **Figure 78**) on each side of the headlight housing.
2. Pull the trim bezel and headlight unit out and disconnect the electrical connector from the bulb.
3. Remove the bulb cover (**Figure 79**).

CAUTION
During the next step, do not touch the bulb glass with your fingers because traces of oil on the bulb will drastically reduce the life of the bulb. Clean any traces of oil from the bulb with a cloth moistened in alcohol or lacquer thinner.

4. Turn the bulb holder counterclockwise and remove the bulb.
5. Install by reversing these steps.
6. Adjust the headlight as described under *Headlight Adjustment*.

Headlight Adjustment

Adjust the headlight horizontally and vertically according to the Department of Motor Vehicles regulations in your area.
1. *Horizontal adjustment*—Turn the screw clockwise to move the beam to the left and counterclockwise to move the beam to the right. See B, **Figure 79** (1981-1983) or A, **Figure 80** (1984-on).
2. *Vertical adjustment*—On 1981-1983 models, loosen the screw (**Figure 81**) and turn the headlight shell up or down to adjust the beam. On 1984-on models, turn the screw clockwise to move the beam up and counterclockwise to move the beam down (**Figure 80**).

Headlight Relay Testing
(1981-1983 Except XV920 Shaft Drive)

1. Place the motorcycle on the centerstand.
2. Remove the seat.
3. Disconnect the headlight relay connector. It contains 4 wires—1 black, 1 white, 1 red/yellow and 1 blue/black. The relay is marked 3H5 and is color coded yellow.

4. Set the ohmmeter scale to read ohms ×10. Measure the resistance between the terminals shown in **Figure 82**. It should read 100 ohms.

5. Connect an ohmmeter and 12-volt battery to the headlight relay switch as shown in **Figure 83**. Set the ohmmeter to read ohms ×1. Results should be as follows:

    a. Battery connected: 0 ohms.

    b. Battery disconnected: Infinity.

6. Set the ohmmeter scale to read ohms ×1. Measure the resistance between the terminals shown in **Figure 84**. It should be 9.5 ohms. Now switch the ohmmeter leads and retest. The reading should be infinite.

7. If the headlight relay fails any of the tests in Steps 4-6, pull it out of its holder and insert a new one.

Taillight Replacement

All models are equipped with 2 double-filament bulbs in the taillight/brakelight assembly for safety.

Remove the screws securing the lens (**Figure 85**) and take the lens off. Wash the inside and outside of the lens with a mild detergent, rinse thoroughly and wipe dry. Wipe off the reflective base surrounding the bulbs with a soft cloth. Replace the bulbs (**Figure 86**) and install the lens; do not overtighten the screws or the lens may crack.

Directional Signal Light Replacement

Remove the 2 screws securing the lens (**Figure 87**) and take the lens off. Wash the inside and outside with a mild detergent. Replace the bulb (**Figure 88**). Install the lens; do not overtighten the screws or the lens may crack.

Speedometer and Tachometer Illumination Bulb Replacement

XV920J

Refer to *Computerized Monitor System* in this chapter.

All other models

1. Disconnect the speedometer cable (**Figure 89**).

2. Remove the bolts securing the speedometer/tachometer brace and pull it away from the steering head.

3. Remove the outside cover to gain access to the blown bulb.

4. Remove the bulb from the connector and install a new one.

5. Installation is the reverse of these steps.

SWITCHES

Front Brake Light Switch Replacement

Pull the protective cap back from the switch. Disconnect the switch and the electrical connectors. See **Figure 90**. Install the new switch, connect the wires and install the protective cap.

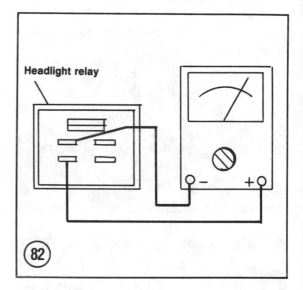

Headlight relay

(82)

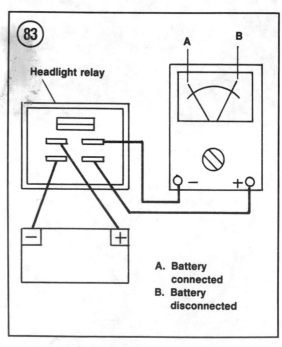

(83)

Headlight relay

A. Battery connected
B. Battery disconnected

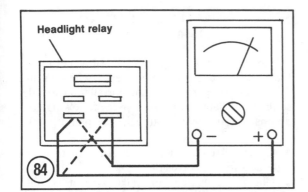

Headlight relay

Rear Brake Light Switch Replacement

1. Remove the right-hand side cover.
2. Unhook the spring from the brake arm.
3. Unscrew the switch housing and locknut from the right-hand side. See **Figure 91** (1981-1983) or **Figure 92** (1984-on).
4. Disconnect the electrical wires.
5. Reverse Steps 1-4 to install. Adjust the switch as described in this chapter.

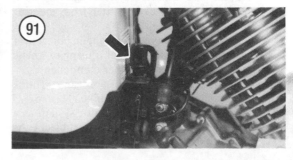

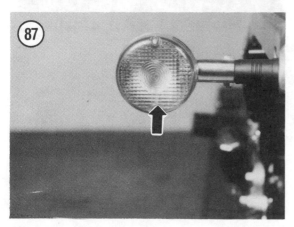

Rear Brake Light
Switch Adjustment

1. Turn the ignition switch to the ON position.
2. Depress the brake pedal. Brake light should come on just as the brake begins to work.
3. To make the light come on earlier or later, hold the switch body and turn the adjusting nut as required.

Sidestand Switch Replacement

With the bike resting on the centerstand and the sidestand up, remove the sidestand switch screws (**Figure 93**). Then disconnect the switch electrical connector and remove the switch. Reverse to install.

Flasher Relay Replacement

Remove the seat. Disconnect the flasher relay (**Figure 94**) and replace it with a new unit.

COMPUTERIZED MONITOR
SYSTEM (XV920J)

This system monitors 7 separate functions on the XV920. If one of these fails, the system provides a continuous warning until the problem is located and repaired.

Service

Because the monitor system is computerized, all service and repair should be entrusted to a qualified specialist. For example, improper handling of the gold plated wire connector units could damage the microcomputer or electrical components. When performing service on your XV920J observe the following general cautions:

a. When replacing bulbs, use only bulbs of the correct wattage. Do not replace a burned-out bulb with one of too high or too low wattage just to get by. Incorrect wattage bulbs will damage the computer system. **Table 3** lists correct bulb sizes.
b. When washing your bike, cover the computerized monitor system tightly with a plastic cover to prevent water from entering the unit.
c. Do not place any type of magnetic object near the display panel. Be careful if using magnetic screwdrivers to service other components.
d. Do not install any type of accessory lighting equipment anywhere on the bike.
e. Treat the computerized monitor system as a precision instrument. Never subject the system to any types of hard knocks or shock.

FUEL PUMP TESTING
(XV1000 AND XV1100)

The fuel pump system consists of a fuel pump, fuel pump controller and fuel reserve switch (**Figure 95**). Fuel pump removal and installation are described in Chapter Six. Observe the following conditions when troubleshooting the fuel pump system.

1. Check all connections to make sure they are tight and free of corrosion.
2. Check the battery to make sure it is fully charged. Fuel pump troubleshooting is divided into 3 separate test procedures, depending on the problem experienced.

a. Test 1: Fuel pump fails to operate after engine is started.
b. Test 2: Fuel pump fails to operate for 5-second intervals when the carburetor fuel

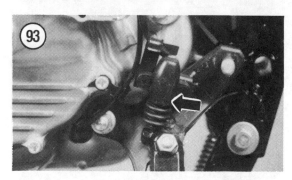

level is low (main and engine stop switch turned to ON and fuel switch turned to RES).

c. Test 3: After fuel warning light comes on, fuel pump does not stop after 30 seconds.

Test 1

1. Start engine and check voltage at the fuel pump light blue wire (**Figure 96**). Interpret results as follows:

a. More than 11 volts: Check fuel pump as described under *Fuel Pump Function Test* in this chapter. If fuel pump is damaged, replace it.

b. Less than 11 volts: Have a dealer check the rear cylinder ignition coil spark gap. If gap is correct, proceed to Step 2. If gap is incorrect, proceed to Step 3.

2. Check the fuel pump controller (**Figure 97**) ground lead with an ohmmeter. Reading should be 0 ohms. Interpret results as follows:

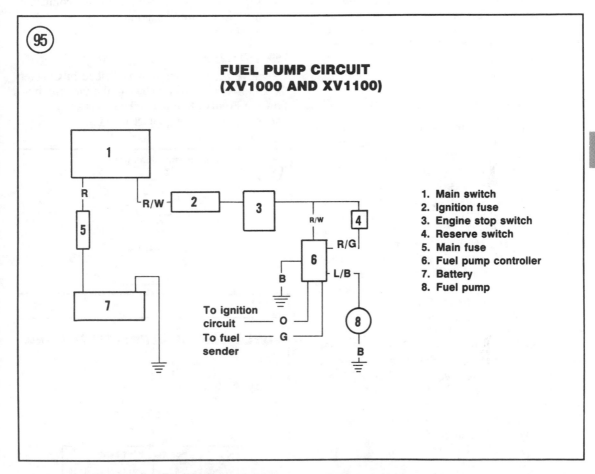

**FUEL PUMP CIRCUIT
(XV1000 AND XV1100)**

1. Main switch
2. Ignition fuse
3. Engine stop switch
4. Reserve switch
5. Main fuse
6. Fuel pump controller
7. Battery
8. Fuel pump

a. Ground reading correct: Check the fuel pump controller as described later in this chapter. Replace controller if damaged.

b. Ground reading incorrect: Repair connector or replace controller unit.

3. Check the voltage at the red/white igniter unit connector wire. Reading should be 12 volts. Interpret results as follows:

a. Reading incorrect: Check the wiring for breaks or bad connections.

b. Reading correct: Check the igniter unit as described in this chapter under *Ignition System Troubleshooting*.

c. Check the main fuse as described in this chapter. Repair or replace the damaged part.

d. Have a dealer check the stop/main switch assembly. Repair or replace as required.

Test 2

1. Turn the main engine switch ON (do not start the engine). Measure the voltage at the fuel pump blue/black wire. Interpret results as follows:

a. 11 volts or less: Perform Step 2.

b. More than 11 volts: Perform Step 3.

2. Measure the voltage at the pump controller red/white wire. Interpret results as follows:

a. 12 volts: Check the fuel pump controller ground lead with an ohmmeter. Reading should be 0 ohms. If reading is correct, check the fuel pump controller as described in this chapter. Replace controller if damaged. If reading is incorrect, repair connector or replace controller unit.

b. No voltage: Check the engine stop/main switch and main fuse as described in this chapter. Repair or replace the damaged part.

3. Turn the fuel reserve switch to RES and measure the voltage at the fuel pump blue/black wire. Interpret results as follows:

a. 11 volts or more: Check fuel pump as described in this chapter.

b. Less than 11 volts: Perform Step 2.

Test 3

1. Start the engine and ground the fuel sender green wire. After approximately 30 seconds, check the voltage at the fuel pump controller blue/black wire. Interpret results as follows:

a. 11 volts or more: Check the resistance at the fuel sender green and black wires with an ohmmeter set on ohms×100. Resistance should be 1,100 ±200 ohms. If resistance is correct, proceed to Step 2. If resistance is incorrect, replace the fuel sender unit.

b. No voltage: Check all fuel pump electrical connectors. If okay, check the fuel pump as described in this chapter.

2. Check the fuel pump controller ground lead with an ohmmeter. Connect the ohmmeter positive lead to the wire and the negative lead to ground. Reading should be 0 ohms. Interpret results as follows:

a. Ground reading correct: Check the fuel pump controller as described in this chapter. Replace controller if damaged.

b. Ground reading incorrect: Repair connector or replace controller unit.

Fuel Pump Test

Remove the fuel pump as described in Chapter Six. Connect a 12-volt battery to the fuel pump as shown in **Figure 98**. If the fuel pump is good, it will vibrate slightly. If not, replace it.

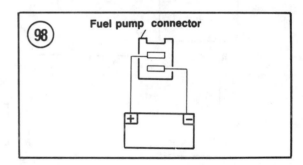

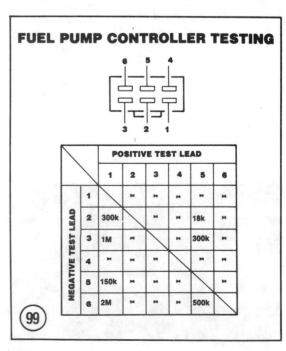

Fuel Pump Controller
Testing/Replacement

1. Remove the seat.
2. Disconnect the fuel pump controller electrical connector (**Figure 96**) and remove the controller.
3. Use an ohmmeter to check for resistance at each of the test terminals. See **Figure 99** and **Figure 100**.
4. If the fuel pump controller fails any test in Step 3, it must be replaced.
5. Install by reversing these removal steps.

Fuel Reserve Switch

1. Remove the headlight as described in this chapter.
2. Disconnect the fuel reserve switch electrical connector. It contains 2 wires: red/white and red/green.
3. Set an ohmmeter on R×1. Connect the ohmmeter's positive lead to the red/white wire and the negative lead to the red/green wire.
4. Interpret results as follows:
   a. With the fuel reserve switch turned to RES, the reading should be 0 ohms.
   b. With the fuel reserve switch turned to ON, the reading should be infinity.
5. If the fuel reserve switch failed either of the tests in Step 4, the right-hand switch assembly (**Figure 101**) should be replaced.

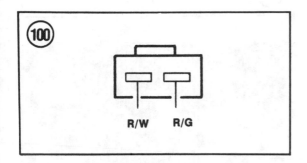

R/W   R/G

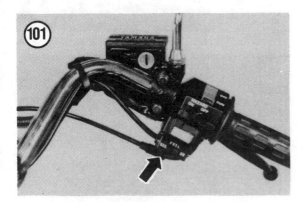

FUEL WARNING LIGHT SYSTEM
(XV700, 1988-ON XV750, XV1000
AND XV1100)

Troubleshooting

The fuel gauge warning light (mounted on the tachometer dial) will light when the fuel level is low. If the fuel warning light comes on and the fuel level is okay or if the light does not operate correctly, perform the following.
1. Check the fuel warning light bulb; replace if necessary. If the bulb is okay, proceed to Step 2.

NOTE
The fuel sender tested in Step 2 is mounted on the fuel tank.

2. Using a voltmeter, check the voltage at the fuel sender connector. The fuel sender connector uses 2 wires (green and black). The voltage should be 12 volts. If the voltage is incorrect, check the fuel sender as described in this chapter. If the voltage is correct, check the following:
   a. Fuses.
   b. Battery (Chapter Three).
   c. Have a Yamaha dealer check the main switch assembly.

Fuel Sender Troubleshooting

1. Remove the fuel tank as described in Chapter Six.

WARNING
Drain the gasoline in a container approved for gasoline storage.

WARNING
Perform Step 2 away from all open flames.

2. Remove the fuel sender mounting bolts and remove the sender from the fuel tank.
3. Place the fuel sender on a workbench so that it sits in its installed position. Attach an ohmmeter to the fuel sender electrical connector. Switch the ohmmeter to R×100.
4. Raise the fuel sender weight to the following height:
   a. XV700 and XV750: 1.65 in. (42 mm).
   b. XV1000 and XV1100: 0.86 in. (22 mm).
With the weight positioned at the correct height, the ohmmeter should read 1.1 ±0.2 K ohms at 68° F. If the reading is incorrect, replace the fuel sender.
5. Reverse to install the fuel sender. Use a new gasket during installation. Then fill the tank partway and check for leaks.

7

LIGHTING SYSTEM

Fuel Warning Light Troubleshooting (1986-1987 XV700, 1988-on XV750 and XV1100)

The fuel gauge warning light (**Figure 102**) will come on when the fuel level drops below 0.7 gal. (XV700) or 0.8 gal. (XV1100). If the fuel warning light comes on and the fuel level is okay or if the light does not operate correctly, perform the following.

1. Check the fuel warning light bulb. Replace if necessary. If the bulb is okay, proceed to Step 2.
2. Turn the main switch to ON and the engine stop switch to RUN. Then push the starter button. The fuel warning light bulb should light. If the light is on, proceed to Step 3. If the light did not come on, check the following.
   a. Diode—see *Diode Testing* in this chapter.
   b. Main fuse—see *Fuses* in this chapter.
   c. Battery—see Chapter Three.
   d. Have a Yamaha dealer check the main switch.
3. Check the fuel sender electrical connections. The fuel sender is mounted on the fuel tank. If the connections are tight and correct, the fuel sender may be faulty. Check it as described in this chapter.

HORN

Removal/Installation

1. Disconnect the horn electrical connector.
2. Remove the bolts securing the horn.
3. Installation is the reverse of these steps.

Testing

1. Disconnect horn wires from harness.
2. Connect horn wires to 12-volt battery. If the horn is good, it will sound. If it doesn't, replace it.

FUSES

Whenever a fuse blows, find out the reason for the failure before replacing the fuse. Usually, the trouble is a short circuit in the wiring. This may be caused by worn-through insulation or a disconnected wire shorting to ground. Fuse ratings are listed in **Table 4**.

> *CAUTION*
> *Never substitute metalfoil or wire for a fuse. Never use a higher amperage fuse than specified. An overload could result in fire and complete loss of the bike.*

There are 5 fuses used on the XV models. The main fuse is located underneath the seat and the remaining 4 are located in the fuse panel.

If the main fuse blows, raise the seat and separate the rubber fuse holder. Remove the fuse and replace it with one of the same amperage. See **Figure 103** (1981-1983) or **Figure 104** (1984-on).

On 1981-1983 models, the remaining fuses are located on the lower steering crown. Remove the cover and replace the blown fuse (**Figure 105**).

On 1984-on models, the remaining fuses are located underneath the indicator light panel. Remove the panel (**Figure 106**) and replace the blown fuse.

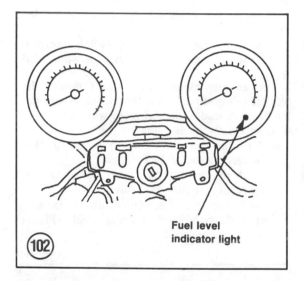

Fuel level
indicator light

(102)

Tables are on the following pages.

7

Table 1 ELECTRICAL SPECIFICATIONS*

System voltage	12
Pickup coil resistance	
Prior to 1991	155 ohms
1991-on	202 ohms
Ignition coil resistance	
1981-1983	
Primary windings	2.7 ohms
Secondary windings	8,500 ohms
1984-on	
Primary windings	4.2 ohms
Secondary windings	13,200 ohms
Spark plug cap resistance	5,000 ohms
Charging voltage	
1981-1983	14-15 volts @ 2,000 rpm
1984-on	14 volts @ 5,000 rpm
Armature coil resistance	0.5 ohm
Starter brush wear limit	0.22 in. (5.5 mm)

All resistance specifications are ± 15% at 68° F (20° C).

Table 2 STARTER TROUBLESHOOTING

Symptom	Probable cause	Remedy
Starter does not start	Low battery	Recharge battery
	Worn brushes	Replace brushes
	Defective relay	Repair or replace
	Defective switch	Repair or replace
	Defective wiring connection	Repair wire or repair connection
	Internal short circuit	Repair or replace defective component
Starter action is weak	Low battery	Recharge battery
	Pitted relay contacts	Clean or replace
	Worn brushes	Replace brushes
	Defective connection	Clean and tighten
	Short circuit in commutator	Replace armature
Starter runs continuously	Stuck relay	Replace relay
Starter turns; does not turn engine	Defective starter clutch	Replace starter clutch

Table 3 REPLACEMENT BULBS

Item	Wattage
Headlight	12V 60/55W
Tail/brakelight	12V 8/27W
Meter light	
1982 XV920 (shaft drive)	12V 2W
All other models	12V 3.4W
Indicator lights	
1981-1983	12V 3.4W
1984-1985	12V 4.0W
1986-on	12V 3.0W
(continued)	

Table 3 REPLACEMENT BULBS (continued)

License light	
XV750	12V 8W
1982 XV920 (shaft drive)	12V 3.8W
All other models	*
Flasher/running light	
XV700, XV1000, XV1100	12V 27W
1982 XV920 (shaft drive)	12V 27W × 4/8W
All other models	*

*Not specified.

Table 4 FUSES

	Amperage
Main	
1982 XV920 (shaft drive)	30
All others	20
Headlight	15
Signal	15
Ignition	10
Tail	10

7

FRONT SUSPENSION AND STEERING

This chapter discusses service operations on suspension components, steering, wheels and related items. Specifications (**Table 1**) and tightening torques (**Table 2**) are at the end of the chapter.

FRONT WHEEL

Removal/Installation

1. Place a wooden block under the crankcase to lift the front wheel off the ground.

> *NOTE*
> *If the front wheel can be raised enough to provide sufficient clearance to remove the wheel, removal of the front fender is not required. However, if removal of the front fender is necessary, perform Step 2 and Step 4.*

2. Disconnect the brake hose(s) at the front fender (**Figure 1**).
3. Disconnect the speedometer cable (**Figure 2**) at the front wheel and pull it through the front fender bracket.
4. Remove the bolts securing the fender to the fork tubes and carefully pull the fender out (**Figure 3**).
5. Remove the cotter pin and axle nut (**Figure 4**). Discard the cotter pin.
6. Loosen the axle pinch bolt(s). See **Figure 5**.

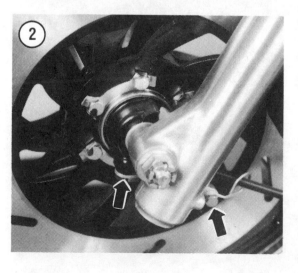

NOTE
It is not necessary to completely remove the axle pinch bolt(s).

7. Push the axle out with a drift or screwdriver and remove it from the right (shaft-drive) or left (chain-drive) side. See **Figure 6**.

8. Pull the wheel forward to disengage the brake disc(s) from the caliper(s). Then turn the caliper(s) outward to provide clearance for the wheel and remove it.

9. Remove the spacer from the seal in the left-hand or right-hand side of the wheel. See **Figure 7**.

10. Remove the speedometer drive from the seal in the left-hand or right-hand side of the wheel (**Figure 8**).

11. Remove the wheel.

CAUTION
Do not set the wheel down on the disc surface as it may be scratched or warped. Either lean the wheel against a wall or place it on a couple of wood blocks.

NOTE
*Insert a piece of wood in the caliper(s) in place of the disc (**Figure 9**). That way, if the brake lever is inadvertently squeezed, the piston will not be forced out of the cylinder. If this does happen, the caliper(s) might have to be disassembled to reseat the piston and the system will have to be bled. By using the wood, bleeding the brake is not necessary when installing the wheel.*

12. While servicing the wheel assembly, install the spacer, speedometer drive gear, washer and nut on the axle to prevent their loss.

Inspection

1. Remove any corrosion on the front axle with a piece of fine emery cloth.

2. Measure the radial runout of the wheel rim with a dial indicator as shown in **Figure 10**. If runout exceeds 0.08 in. (2.0 mm), check the wheel bearings. If the wheel bearings are okay, examine the wheel rim. The stock Yamaha aluminum wheel cannot be serviced, but must be replaced if damaged. On spoked wheels, refer to *Wheels* in this chapter for information on spoke tightening and wheel truing.

3. Check the rims for cracks or damage as described in this chapter.

Installation

1. Lightly grease the lips of both front wheel seals (**Figure 11**) and the seal in the speedometer gear case.

2. Insert the spacer in the left-hand or right-hand side seal (**Figure 12**).

3. Insert the speedometer gear case into the wheel. Make sure the notches in the gear case (**Figure 13**) align with the speedometer drive dogs (**Figure 14**).

4. *Carefully* insert the disc(s) between the brake pads when installing the wheel.

5. Make sure the locating slot in the speedometer gear case is aligned with the boss on the fork tube (**Figure 15**).

6. Insert the axle. Then install the washer and axle nut and tighten the nut to specifications (**Table 2**).

7. Apply the front brake and compress the front forks several times to make sure the axle is installed correctly without binding the forks. Then tighten the axle pinch bolt(s) to specifications (**Table 2**).

8. Install a *new* axle cotter pin.

> *WARNING*
> *Never reuse a cotter pin on the axle shaft; always install a new one.*

9. After the wheel is installed, completely rotate it and apply the brake several times to make sure the wheel rotates freely.

10. Install the front fender (if removed), making sure to secure the brake hose clamp(s). See **Figure 1**.

11. Install the speedometer cable.

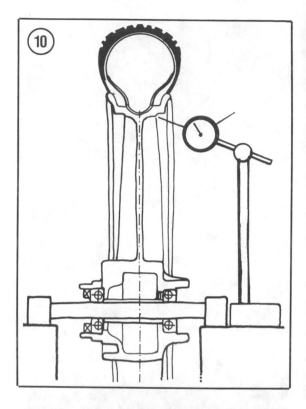

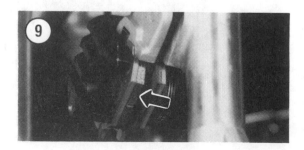

NOTE
Rotate the wheel slowly when inserting the cable so that it will engage properly.

FRONT HUB

Refer to **Figure 16**, **Figure 17** or **Figure 18** for this procedure.

Disassembly

1. Remove the front wheel as described in this chapter.
2. Remove the spacer (**Figure 12**) and speedometer drive gear.
3. Remove the wheel cover (**Figure 19**), if so equipped.
4. Remove the right-hand (**Figure 20**) and left-hand oil seals.
5. Remove the speedometer gear case retainer and dog (**Figure 14**).
6. Remove the wheel bearings, spacer and spacer flange. Tap the bearing out with a soft aluminum or brass drift.

CAUTION
Tap only on the outer bearing race. The bearing will be damaged if struck on the inner race.

Inspection

1. Clean bearings thoroughly in solvent and dry with compressed air.

8

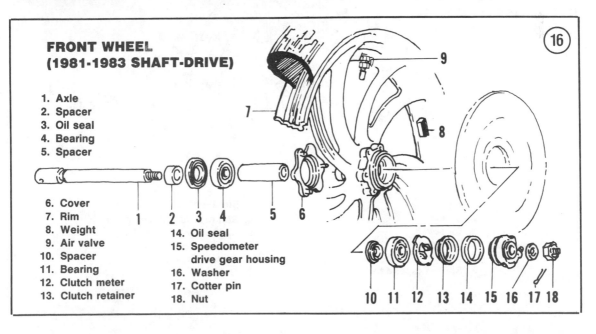

FRONT WHEEL
(1981-1983 SHAFT-DRIVE)

1. Axle
2. Spacer
3. Oil seal
4. Bearing
5. Spacer
6. Cover
7. Rim
8. Weight
9. Air valve
10. Spacer
11. Bearing
12. Clutch meter
13. Clutch retainer
14. Oil seal
15. Speedometer drive gear housing
16. Washer
17. Cotter pin
18. Nut

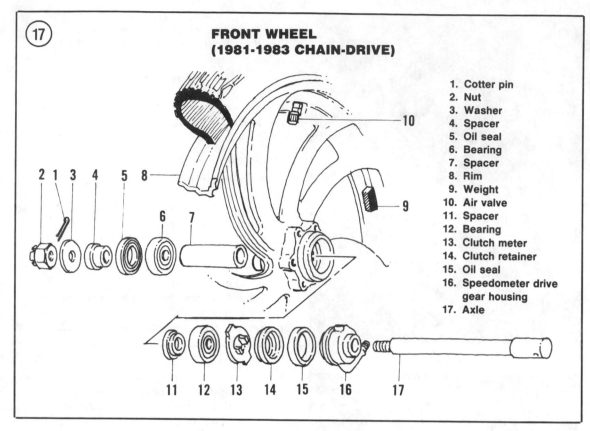

⑰ **FRONT WHEEL**
(1981-1983 CHAIN-DRIVE)

1. Cotter pin
2. Nut
3. Washer
4. Spacer
5. Oil seal
6. Bearing
7. Spacer
8. Rim
9. Weight
10. Air valve
11. Spacer
12. Bearing
13. Clutch meter
14. Clutch retainer
15. Oil seal
16. Speedometer drive
    gear housing
17. Axle

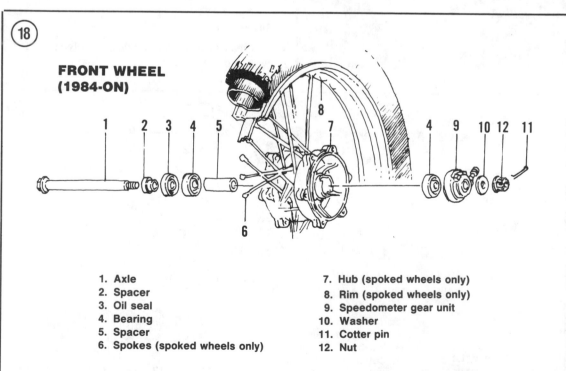

⑱ **FRONT WHEEL**
(1984-ON)

1. Axle
2. Spacer
3. Oil seal
4. Bearing
5. Spacer
6. Spokes (spoked wheels only)
7. Hub (spoked wheels only)
8. Rim (spoked wheels only)
9. Speedometer gear unit
10. Washer
11. Cotter pin
12. Nut

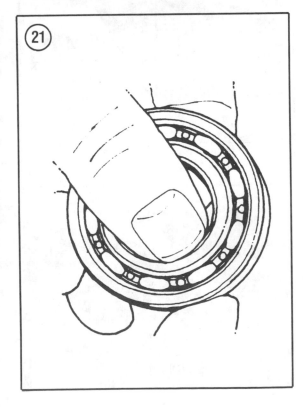

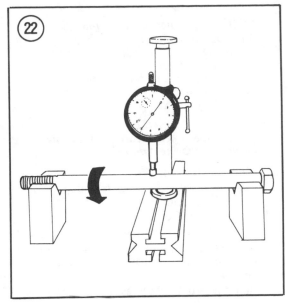

WARNING
Do not spin the bearing with the air jet while drying. Hold the inner race with your hand. Because the air jet can spin the bearing race at higher speeds than it was designed for, the bearing may disintegrate and possibly cause severe injuries.

2. Clean the inside and outside of the hub with solvent. Dry with compressed air.

3. Turn each bearing by hand (**Figure 21**), making sure it turns smoothly. Check balls for evidence of wear, pitting or excessive heat (bluish tint). Replace bearings if necessary; always replace as a complete set.

4. Check the axle for wear and straightness. Use V-blocks and a dial indicator as shown in **Figure 22**. If the runout is 0.008 in. (0.2 mm) or greater, the axle must be replaced.

Assembly

NOTE
If installing sealed bearings, it is not necessary to grease the bearings as described in Step 1. Instead, proceed to Step 2.

1. Pack the bearings thoroughly with multipurpose grease. Work the grease between the balls thoroughly.

2. Pack the wheel hub and axle spacer with multipurpose grease.

3. Install the right-hand wheel bearing and the spacer. Install the spacer flange and install the left-hand bearing.

8

CAUTION
*Tap the bearings squarely into place and tap on the outer race only. Use a socket (**Figure 23**) that matches the outer race diameter. Do not tap on the inner race or the bearing might be damaged. Be sure that the bearings are completely seated.*

NOTE
Install the wheel bearings with the sealed side facing outward.

4. Install the left-hand oil seal.
5. Install the speedometer gear case dog, retainer and oil seal in the hub.
6. Lubricate the oil seal lips with grease.
7. Disassemble the speedometer gear case and lubricate the gears and sliding faces with a lightweight lithium soap base grease. Reassemble the gear case.
8. Install the front wheel as described in this chapter.

WHEEL BALANCE

An unbalanced wheel results in unsafe riding conditions. Depending on the degree of unbalance and the speed of the motorcycle, the rider may experience anything from a mild vibration to a violent shimmy and loss of control.

On aluminum wheels, weights are attached to the rim (**Figure 24**). On spoke wheels, weights are clamped to the spokes (**Figure 25**). Weights for both aluminum and spoke wheels can be purchased from most motorcycle dealers or motorcycle supply stores.

NOTE
Be sure to balance the wheel with the brake discs attached as they also affect the balance.

Before attempting to balance the wheels, check to be sure that the wheel bearings are in good condition and properly lubricated. The wheel must rotate freely.
1. Remove the wheel as described in this chapter or in Chapter Nine.
2. Mount the wheel on a fixture such as the one shown in **Figure 26** so it can rotate freely.
3. Give the wheel a spin and let it coast to a stop. Mark the tire at the lowest point.
4. Spin the wheel several more times. If the wheel keeps coming to rest at the same point, it is out of balance.
5. Tape a test weight to the upper (or light) side of the wheel.

6. Experiment with different weights until the wheel, when spun, comes to rest at a different position each time.
7. Remove the test weight and install the correct size weight. See **Figure 24** or **Figure 27**.

WIRE WHEEL SERVICE

Spoke Inspection and Replacement

Wire wheel spokes loosen with use and should be checked periodically. The "tuning fork" method for checking spoke tightness is simple and works well. Tap the center of each spoke with a spoke wrench (**Figure 28**) or the shank of a screwdriver and listen for a tone. A tightened spoke will emit a clear, ringing tone and a loose spoke will sound flat or dull. All the spokes in a correctly tightened wheel will emit tones of similar pitch but not necessarily the same precise tone. The tension of the spokes does not determine wheel balance.

Bent, stripped or broken spokes should be replaced as soon as they are detected, as they can destroy an expensive hub.

Unscrew the nipple from the spoke and depress the nipple into the rim far enough to free the end of

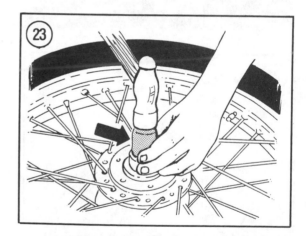

the spoke; take care not to push the nipple all the way in. Remove the damaged spoke from the hub and use it to match a new spoke of identical length. If necessary, trim the new spoke (at the threaded end) to match the original and dress the end of the threads with a thread die. Install the new spoke in the hub and screw on the nipple; tighten it until the spoke's tone is similar to the tone of the other spokes in the wheel. Periodically check the new spoke; it will stretch and must be retightened several times before it takes a final set.

Spoke Adjustment

If all spokes appear loose, tighten all on one side of the hub, then tighten all on the other side. One-half to one turn should be sufficient; do not overtighten.

After tightening the spokes, check rim runout to be sure you haven't pulled the rim out of shape.

One way to check rim runout is to mount a dial indicator on the front fork or swing arm so that it bears against the rim.

If you don't have a dial indicator, improvise one as shown in **Figure 29**. Adjust the position of the bolt until it just clears the rim. Rotate the rim and note whether the clearance increases or decreases. Mark the tire with chalk or light crayon at areas that produce significantly large or small clearances. Clearance must not change by more than 2 mm (0.08 in.).

To pull the rim out, tighten spokes which terminate on the same side of the hub and loosen spokes which terminate on the opposite side of the hub (**Figure 30**). In most cases, only a slight amount of adjustment is necessary to true a rim. After adjustment, rotate the rim and make sure another area has not been pulled out of true. Continue adjustment and checking until runout is less than 2.0 mm (0.08 in.).

Rim Replacement

The rim can be bent by hitting rocks, curbs, potholes, etc. A bent rim should be replaced

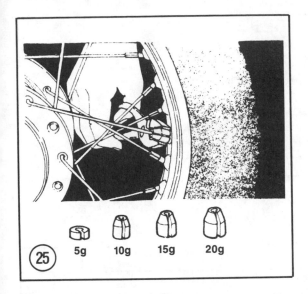

(25)   5g   10g   15g   20g

(26)

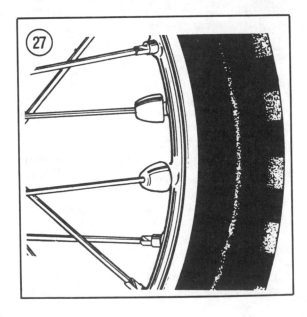

(27)

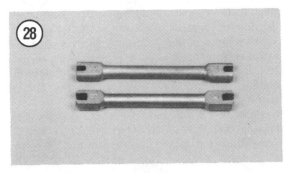

(28)

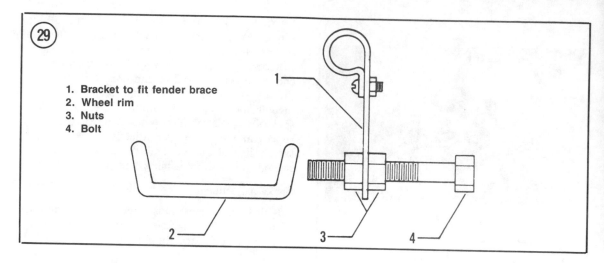

1. Bracket to fit fender brace
2. Wheel rim
3. Nuts
4. Bolt

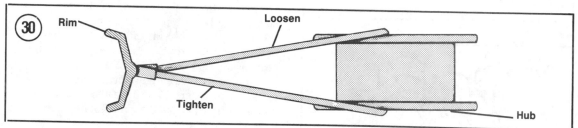

immediately. A bent or dented wheel creates very dangerous handling characteristics.

If the spokes are not bent or damaged also, they may be reused. This procedures describes how to replace the rim without removing the spokes.

1. Remove the tire as described in this chapter.
2. Securely fasten the spokes together with wire, string or tape at each point where they cross.
3. Place the replacement rim on top of the old rim and align the nipple holes of both rims. This is to make sure the replacement rim is the correct one. When the rims are aligned correctly, mark one spoke and its corresponding nipple hole on the new rim.
4. Remove the nipples from the spokes using a spoke wrench. If they are coated with dirt or rust, clean them in solvent and allow to dry. Then check the nipples for signs of cracking or other damage. Spoke nipples in this condition can strip when the wheel is later trued. Replace nipples as necessary.
5. Lift the hub and spokes out of the old rim, making sure not to knock the spokes out of alignment.
6. Position the hub and spokes into the new rim, making sure to align the marks made in Step 3. Then insert the spokes into the rim until they are all in place.

7. Place a drop of oil onto the threaded end of each spoke and install the nipples. Thread the nipples halfway onto the spokes (before they make contact with the rim).
8. Lift the wheel and stand it up on the workbench. Check the hub to make sure it is centered in the rim. If not, reposition it by hand.
9. With the hub centered in the rim, thread the nipples until they just seat against the rim. True the wheel as described in this chapter.

Seating Spokes

When spokes loosen or when installing new spokes, the head of the spoke should be checked for proper seating in the hub. If it is not seated correctly, it can loosen further and may cause severe damage to the hub. If one or more spokes require reseating, hit the head of the spoke with a punch. True the wheel as described in this chapter.

NOTE
To prevent the punch from damaging the chrome on the spoke head, apply strips of tape to the end of the punch before using it.

TIRE CHANGING

The wheels used on all models can easily be damaged during tire removal. Special care must be

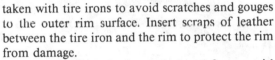

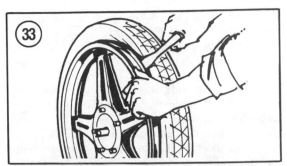

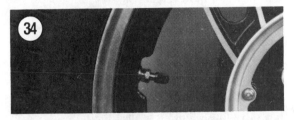

taken with tire irons to avoid scratches and gouges to the outer rim surface. Insert scraps of leather between the tire iron and the rim to protect the rim from damage.

The stock cast wheels are designed for use with either tubeless or tube-type tires. Spoked wheels are designed for tube-type tires only. Tire removal and installation are basically the same for tube and tubeless tires; where differences occur they are noted. Tire repair is different and is covered in separate procedures.

When removing a tubeless tire, take care not to damage the tire beads, inner liner of the tire or the wheel rim flange. Use Yamaha tire levers or flat-handled tire irons with rounded ends.

Removal

1. Remove the valve core to deflate the tire.
2. Press the entire bead on both sides of the tire into the center of the rim.
3. Lubricate the beads with soapy water.
4. Insert the tire iron under the bead next to the valve (**Figure 31**). Force the bead on the opposite side of the tire into the center of the rim and pry the bead over the rim with the tire iron.

NOTE
Insert scraps of leather between the tire irons and the rim to protect the rim from damage.

5. Insert a second tire iron next to the first to hold the bead over the rim. Then work around the tire with the first tool prying the bead over the rim (**Figure 32**). On tube-type tires, be careful not to pinch the inner tube with the tools.

6. On tube-type tires, use your thumb to push the valve from its hole in the rim to the inside of the tire. Carefully pull the tube out of the tire and lay it aside.

NOTE
Step 7 is required only if it is necessary to completely remove the tire from the rim, such as for tire replacement or tubeless tire repair.

7. Turn the wheel over. Insert a tire tool between the second bead and the same side of the rim that the first bead was pried over (**Figure 33**). Force the bead on the opposite side from the tool into the center of the rim. Pry the second bead off the rim, working around the wheel with 2 tire irons as with the first.
8. On tubeless tires, inspect the rubber O-ring where the valve stem seats against the inner surface of the wheel. Replace it if it's starting to deteriorate or has lost its resiliency. This is a common cause of air loss.

Installation

1. Carefully inspect the tire for any damage, especially inside.
2. A new tire may have balancing rubbers inside. These are not patches and should not be disturbed. A colored spot near the bead indicates a lighter point on the tire. This spot should be placed next to the valve stem (**Figure 34**). In addition, most tires have directional arrows on the side of the tire that indicate which direction the tire should rotate. Make sure to install the tire accordingly.

8

3. On tube-type tires, inflate the tube just enough to round it out. Too much air will make installation difficult. Place the tube inside the tire.

4. Lubricate both beads of the tire with soapy water.

5. Place the backside of the tire into the center of the rim. On tube-type tires, insert the valve stem through the stem hole in the wheel. The lower bead should go into the center of the rim and the upper bead outside. Work around the tire in both directions (**Figure 35**). Use a tire iron for the last few inches of bead (**Figure 36**).

6. Press the upper bead into the rim opposite the valve (**Figure 37**). Pry the bead into the rim on both sides of the initial point with a tire tool, working around the rim to the valve.

7. On tube-type tires, wiggle the valve to be sure the tube is not trapped under the bead. Set the valve stem squarely in its hole before screwing on the valve nut to hold it against the rim.

8. Check the bead on both sides of the tire for an even fit around the rim.

9. On tube-type tires, inflate the tire slowly to seat the beads in the rim. It may be necessary to bounce the tire to complete the seating.

10. On tubeless tires place an inflatable band around the circumference of the tire. Slowly inflate the band until the tire beads are pressed against the rim. Inflate the tire enough to seat it, deflate the band and remove it.

> *WARNING*
> *Never exceed 56 psi (4.0 kg/cm²) inflation pressure as the tire could burst causing severe injury. Never stand directly over the tire while inflating it.*

11. Inflate the tire to the required pressure (Chapter Three). Tighten the valve stem locks and screw on the cover cap.

12. Balance the wheel assembly as described in this chapter.

TIRE REPAIRS

Tubeless Tires

Patching a tubeless tire on the road is very difficult. If both beads are still in place against the rim, a can of pressurized tire sealant may inflate the tire and seal the hole. The beads must be against the wheel for this method to work. Another solution is to carry a spare inner tube that can be temporarily installed and inflated. This will enable you to get to a service station where the tire can be correctly repaired. Be sure that the tube is designed for use with a tubeless tire.

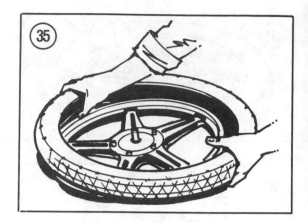

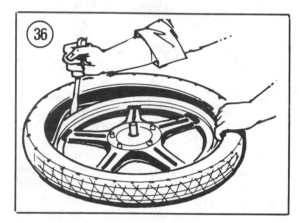

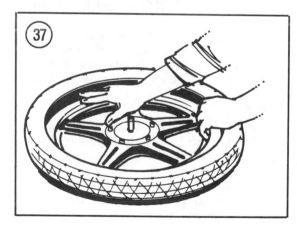

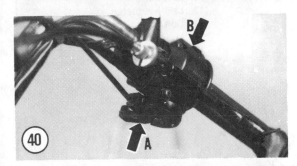

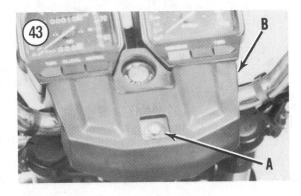

The motorcycle tire industry recommends that tubeless tires be patched from the inside. Therefore, do not patch the tire with an external type plug. If you find an external patch on a tire, it is recommended that it be patch-reinforced from the inside.

Due to the variations of material supplied with different tubeless tire repair kits, follow the instructions and recommendations supplied with the repair kit.

Tube-type Tires

Every rider will eventually experience trouble with a tire or tube. Repairs and replacement are fairly simple and every rider should know the techniques.

Patching a motorcycle tube is only a temporary fix. A motorcycle tire flexes so much that the patch could rub right off. However, a patched tube should get you far enough to buy a new tube.

Due to the variations of material supplied with different tube-type tire repair kits, follow the instructions and recommendations supplied with the repair kit.

HANDLEBAR

Removal/Installation

1. Place the bike on the centerstand. Remove the rear view mirrors (A, **Figure 38**).
2. Disconnect the brake fluid level warning wire at the master cylinder (if so equipped). Remove the 2 bolts (B, **Figure 38**) securing the master cylinder and lay it on the fuel tank. It is not necessary to disconnect the hydraulic brake line.

> *CAUTION*
> *Cover the fuel tank with a heavy cloth or plastic tarp to protect it from accidental spilling of brake fluid. Wash any spilled brake fluid off any painted or plated surface immediately, as it will destroy the finish. Use soapy water and rinse thoroughly.*

3. Slide back the clutch adjuster cover. Then slacken the clutch cable and disconnect it at the hand lever (**Figure 39**).
4. Disconnect the choke cable (A, **Figure 40**).
5. Separate the 2 halves of the left-hand switch assembly (B, **Figure 40**).
6. Separate the 2 halves of the start switch assembly (**Figure 41**). Disconnect the throttle cable from the twist grip.
7. Remove the cover (**Figure 42**), then remove the screw (A, **Figure 43**) and remove the handlebar cover (B, **Figure 43**), if so equipped.

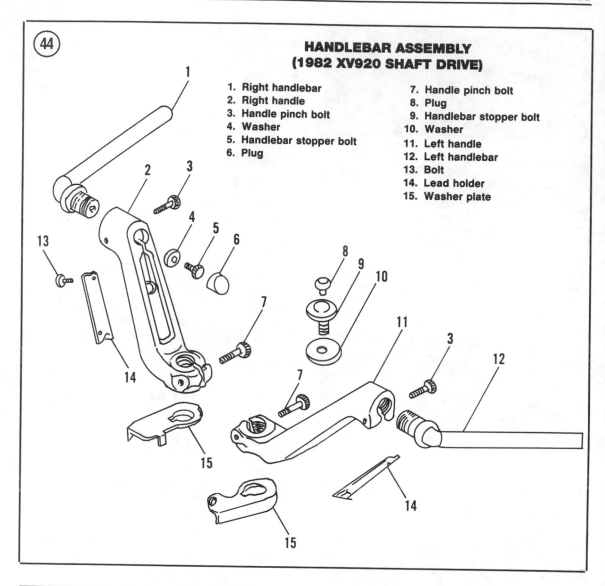

**HANDLEBAR ASSEMBLY
(1982 XV920 SHAFT DRIVE)**

1. Right handlebar
2. Right handle
3. Handle pinch bolt
4. Washer
5. Handlebar stopper bolt
6. Plug
7. Handle pinch bolt
8. Plug
9. Handlebar stopper bolt
10. Washer
11. Left handle
12. Left handlebar
13. Bolt
14. Lead holder
15. Washer plate

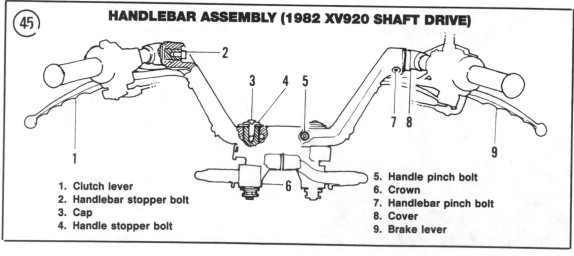

HANDLEBAR ASSEMBLY (1982 XV920 SHAFT DRIVE)

1. Clutch lever
2. Handlebar stopper bolt
3. Cap
4. Handle stopper bolt
5. Handle pinch bolt
6. Crown
7. Handlebar pinch bolt
8. Cover
9. Brake lever

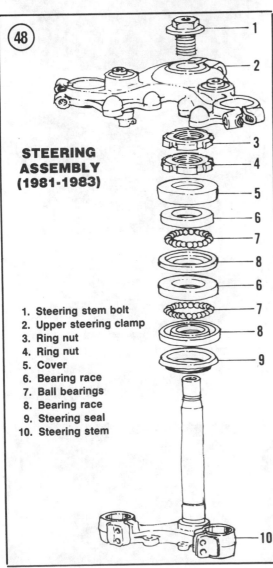

**STEERING
ASSEMBLY
(1981-1983)**

1. Steering stem bolt
2. Upper steering clamp
3. Ring nut
4. Ring nut
5. Cover
6. Bearing race
7. Ball bearings
8. Bearing race
9. Steering seal
10. Steering stem

8. Remove the clamps securing electrical cables to the handlebar.

9A. *1982 XV920 shaft drive:*Referring to **Figure 44** and **Figure 45**, perform the following:

   a. Remove the bolt cap and bolt.

   b. Loosen the pinch bolt and remove the handlebar assembly.

   c. Repeat for the opposite side.

9B. *All other models*: Remove the 4 handlebar clamp Allen bolts (**Figure 46**) and remove the handlebar.

10. Install by reversing these steps; note the following:

   a. Tighten all fasteners to the specifications in **Table 2**.

   b. Make sure the "UP" mark on the master cylinder clamp (**Figure 47**) faces up.

   c. On 1982 XV920 shaft drive models, adjust the handlebar as described in this chapter.

HANDLEBAR ADJUSTMENT (1982 XV920 SHAFT DRIVE)

Refer to **Figure 44** and **Figure 45** for this procedure.

WARNING
Never attempt to adjust the handlebar more than one notch from the standard position (there are 3 adjustment positions each for vertical and horizontal adjustment). Always adjust both sides to the same position. Failure to observe these precautions will cause an uneven steering condition and possible loss of steering control.

Vertical Adjustment

1. Remove the handlebar cover.
2. Remove the handlebar stopper and pinch bolts.
3. Rotate the grip bar either up or down one notch from standard position to adjust. After adjustment, tighten the handlebar stopper and pinch bolts to specifications in **Table 2**.
4. Repeat for the opposite side.

Horizontal Adjustment

1. Remove the handlebar cover.
2. Remove the handlebar bolt cap and stopper bolt. Then loosen the pinch bolt.
3. Pull the handlebar up to disengage it from the handle crown and turn one notch either forward or backward from standard position to adjust.
4. Reinstall the handlebar and tighten all bolts to specifications in **Table 2**.
5. Repeat for the opposite side.

8

STEERING HEAD

Refer to **Figure 48** and **Figure 49** for this procedure.

Disassembly

1. Place the bike on the centerstand.
2. Remove the fuel tank as described in Chapter Six.
3. Remove the front wheel as described in this chapter.
4. Disconnect the speedometer cable (**Figure 50**).
5. Remove the headlight as described in Chapter Seven.
6A. On 1981-1983 models, remove the front fuse box cover (**Figure 51**). Then unplug the fuse box assembly and remove it from the lower steering crown (**Figure 52**).
6B. On 1984-on models, remove the front cover (**Figure 53**).
7. Disconnect and remove the horns.

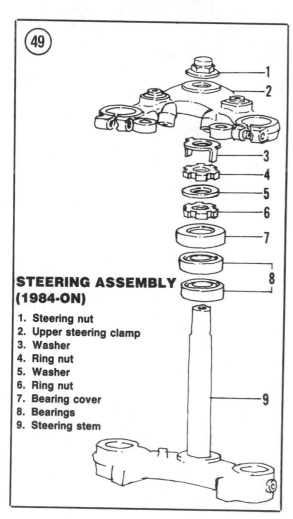

STEERING ASSEMBLY (1984-ON)

1. Steering nut
2. Upper steering clamp
3. Washer
4. Ring nut
5. Washer
6. Ring nut
7. Bearing cover
8. Bearings
9. Steering stem

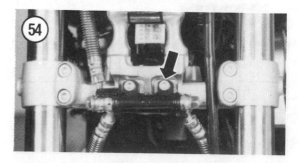

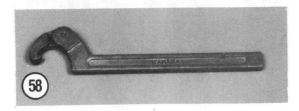

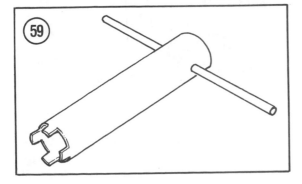

8. Remove the master cylinder and brake line clamp bolts (**Figure 54**) at the steering head. Do not disconnect the hoses or it will be necessary to bleed the brake system.

9. Remove the front turn indicators and the headlight shell (**Figure 55**).

10. Remove the handlebar as described in this chapter.

11. Remove the bolts securing the computer monitor system (XV920J) or the speedometer/tachometer unit (all other models) and lay it over the fuel tank. See **Figure 56**.

> *NOTE*
> *Be very careful when handling the computer monitor system; it is easily damaged. Refer to **Computer Monitor System** in Chapter Seven for further information.*

12. Loosen the upper and lower fork clamp bolts and remove the forks as described in this chapter.

13. See **Figure 57**. Remove the steering stem bolt (A) and loosen the pinch bolt (B). Then remove the upper fork bridge (C).

14. Remove the washer on 1984-on models.

15. Remove the adjusting nuts with a spanner wrench (**Figure 58**) or use an easily improvised unit (**Figure 59**). On 1984-on models, a washer is installed between the 2 adjusting nuts.

16. Remove the upper bearing cover.

17A. *1981-1983*: Pull the steering stem out of the frame (**Figure 60**). On these models, upper and lower bearings are loose ball bearings so be ready to catch them as they fall out. Remove all bearings that are held in the steering head by grease.

> *NOTE*
> *On 1981-1983 models, there are total of 38 ball bearings used: 19 in the top and 19 in the bottom. The bearings should not be intermixed because if worn or damaged, they must be replaced in sets. However, balls in both sets are the same size.*

17B. *1984-on*: Pull the steering stem out of the frame. Remove the upper bearing from the frame tube and slide the lower bearing off of the steering stem.

8

Inspection

1. Clean the bearing races in the steering head and all bearings with solvent.

2. Check for broken welds on the frame around the steering head. If any are found, have them repaired by a competent frame shop or welding service familiar with motorcycle frame repair.

3A. *1981-1983*: Check the balls for pitting, scratches or discoloration indicating wear or corrosion. Replace the bearing if damage is visible.

3B. *1984-on*: Check the bearings for pitting, scratches, or discoloration indicating wear or corrosion. Replace them in sets if any are bad.

4. Check the upper and lower races in the steering head for pitting, galling and corrosion. If any of these conditions exist, replace the races as described in this chapter.

5. Check steering stem for cracks and check its race for damage or wear. Replace if necessary.

Bearing Race Replacement

The headset and steering stem bearing races are pressed into place. Because they are easily bent, do not remove them unless they are worn and require replacement. Take old races to the dealer to ensure exact replacement.

To remove a headset race, insert a hardwood stick into the head tube and carefully tap the race out from the inside (**Figure 61**). Tap all around the race so that neither the race nor the head tube are bent. To install a race, fit it into the end of the head tube. Tap it slowly and squarely with a block of wood (**Figure 62**).

Assembly

Refer to **Figure 48** or **Figure 49** for this procedure.

1. Make sure the steering head bearing races are properly seated.

2A. *1981-1983*:
   a. Apply a coat of wheel bearing grease to the lower bearing race cone on the steering stem and fit 19 ball bearings around it.
   b. Apply a coat of wheel bearing grease to the upper bearing race cone and fit 19 ball bearings around it (**Figure 63**).

2B. *1984-on*:
   a. Lubricate the bearings thoroughly with wheel bearing grease.
   b. Slide the lower bearing onto the steering stem.
   c. Place the upper bearing into the upper bearing race cone.

3. Insert the steering stem into the head tube. Hold it firmly in place.

4. Install the upper bearing race (1981-1983) and upper bearing cover (all models).

5A. *1981-1983*:
   a. Install the lower adjusting nut and tighten it to approximately 18 ft.-lb. (25 N•m). Then loosen it 1/4 turn.
   b. Holding the lower adjusting nut with a wrench, install the upper adjusting nut and tighten it securely.

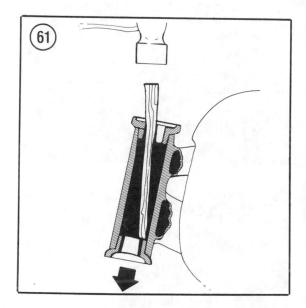

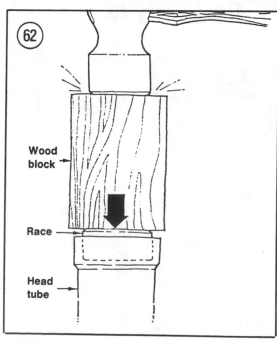

Wood block

Race

Head tube

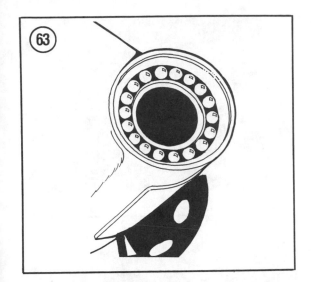

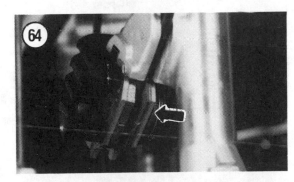

5B. *1984-on*:

   a. Install the lower adjusting nut and tighten it to 36 ft.-lb. (50 N•m).

   b. Loosen the lower adjusting nut completely. Then retighten it to 2.2 ft.-lb. (3 N•m).

   c. Install the washer.

   d. Install the upper ring nut. Tighten it finger-tight.

   e. Install the washer.

6. Continue assembly by reversing *Removal* Steps 1-13. Tightening torques are in **Table 2**.

7. After the total assembly is completed, check the stem for looseness or binding; readjust if necessary.

Steering Stem Adjustment

If play develops in the steering system, it may only require adjustment. However, don't take a chance on it. Disassemble the stem as described under *Steering Head Assembly* in this chapter. Inspect the parts and replace any that are damaged, then reassemble as described in this chapter.

FRONT FORKS

The Yamaha front suspension consists of 2 spring-controlled, hydraulically dampened telescopic forks. Before suspecting major trouble, drain the front fork oil and refill with the proper type and quantity; refer to Chapter Three. If you still have trouble, such as poor damping, a tendency to bottom or top out or leakage around the rubber seals, follow the service procedures in this section.

To simplify fork service and to prevent the mixing of parts, the legs should be removed, serviced and installed individually.

Removal/Installation

1. Place the motorcycle on the centerstand.

2. Remove the front wheel as described in this chapter.

3. Remove the brake caliper(s) as described in Chapter Ten.

NOTE
*Insert a piece of wood in the caliper(s) (**Figure 64**) in place of the disc. That way, if the brake lever is inadvertently squeezed, the piston will not be forced out of the caliper. If it does happen, the caliper might have to be disassembled to reseat the piston. By using the wood, bleeding the brake is not necessary when installing the wheel.*

4. Remove the top rubber cap (**Figure 65**).

5. Remove the air valve cap (**Figure 66**) and depress the valve to release fork air pressure.

Repeat on opposite fork. On models equipped with an air line connecting both fork tubes, only one air valve is used.

6. *1982-1983 XV920 shaft drive, XV1000 and XV1100:*Disconnect the air line at one fork tube air joint bracket (**Figure 67**).

7. Loosen the pinch bolts (**Figure 68**) on the upper fork bridge bolts.

> *NOTE*
> *Step 8 describes how to loosen the fork cap while the forks are still held in the triple clamps.*

8A. *1981-1983 XV750 and 1981-1982 XV920 chain drive:*The spring seat and spring are held inposition bya wire ring (**Figure 69**). To remove the wire ring, have an assistant depress the spring seat (A, **Figure 70**) with a suitable size drift while you pry the wire ring (B, **Figure 70**) out of its groove in the fork with a small screwdriver. When the wire ring is removed, slowly release tension from the spring seat and remove it together with the fork spring.

8B. *XV700, 1983 XV920 (except Midnight Virago), XV1000 and XV1100:*Loosen the fork cap with a 17 mm Allen wrench.

> *NOTE*
> *An alternative to using a 17 mm Allen wrench is to use a 17 mm bolt head; hold the bolt with locking pliers as shown in* ***Figure 71***.

8C. *1983 XV750 and XV920 Midnight Virago:* Loosen the fork tube cap and remove it.

8D. *XV920 shaft drive:*

  a. Turn the adjuster cover (**Figure 72**) to the No. 1 position (**Figure 72**).

  b. Loosen the fork tube cap pinch bolt (**Figure 72**).

  c. Remove the fork tube cap.

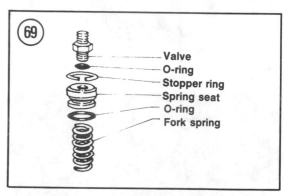

Valve
O-ring
Stopper ring
Spring seat
O-ring
Fork spring

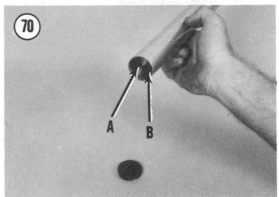

A   B

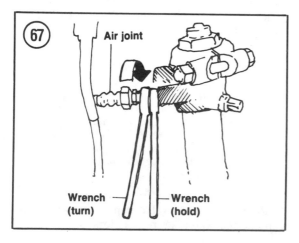

Air joint

Wrench (turn)   Wrench (hold)

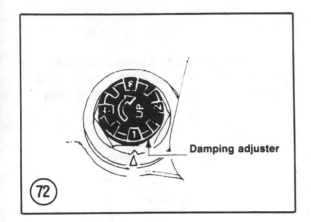

(72) Damping adjuster

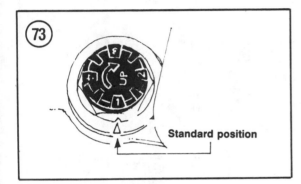

(73) Standard position

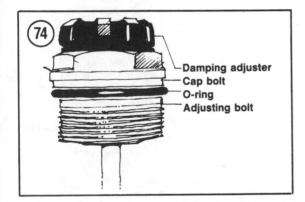

(74) Damping adjuster
— Cap bolt
— O-ring
— Adjusting bolt

(75)

CAUTION
*The fork tube cap is fitted with a damper adjustment rod (**Figure 74**). When handling the fork cap, make sure not to bend or damage the rod in any way as this will cause improper fork operation.*

9. On 1984-on models, remove the lower fork bridge cover (**Figure 75**).

10. Loosen the lower fork bridge bolts. See **Figure 76** or **Figure 77**.

11A. *XV700, XV750 and 1981-1982 XV920 chain drive*—Remove the fork tube. It may be necessary to slightly rotate the tube while removing it.

11B. *1983 XV920 and XV920 Midnight Virago, XV1000 and XV1100:*

   a. Withdraw the fork tube 3-4 inches.

   b. Remove the rubber spacer and air joint bracket.

   c. Remove the fork tube. On XV920 Midnight models, remove the O-rings and fork tube cover as the fork tube is withdrawn.

11C. *1982 XV920 shaft drive:*

   a. Withdraw the fork tube 3-4 inches.

   b. Remove the rubber spacer and the air joint bracket. Then, pry the ring clip out of the fork tube (**Figure 78**) and slide the clip up and off the fork tube. Remove the fork tube.

12. Repeat for the opposite side.

13. Install by reversing these removal steps, noting the following.

8

(76)

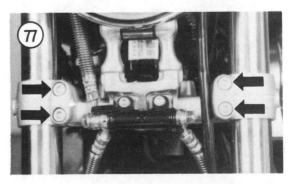

(77)

14. On models so equipped, examine the air joint bracket, rubber spacer, O-rings and clip for any wear or damage. Replace as necessary.

15. Tighten the fasteners to specification (**Table 2**).

16. *XV750 and 1981-1982 XV920 chain drive—* Install the fork spring and spring seat. Have an assistant compress the spring seat and install a new wire stopper ring. Make sure the wire ring seats fully in the groove in the fork tube before releasing the spring seat.

17. *1982 XV920 shaft drive—*Insert the end of the cap/rod assembly into the semicircular hole in the top of the damper rod. Push the fork cap down and screw the cap on. Tighten to 22 ft.-lb. (30 N•m).

> *CAUTION*
> *Do not force the cap/rod assembly during installation or when tightening the cap or you may damage it. If the cap/rod is not inserted into the top of the damper rod correctly, the cap/rod will protrude too far out of the fork tube. The cap/rod is inserted into the damper rod correctly when the cap/rod sits on the fork tube collar.*

18. If it is necessary to bleed the brake caliper(s), refer to Chapter Ten.

Disassembly

Refer to **Figures 79-82** for this procedure.

1. The fork cap was loosened during the removal procedure. Remove the fork cap.

2. Remove the fork spring.

3. Pour the oil out and discard it. Pump the fork several times by hand to expel most of the remaining oil.

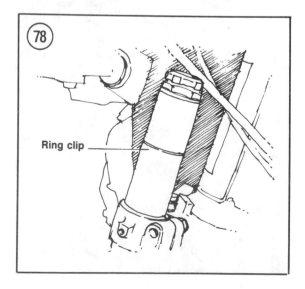

(78) Ring clip

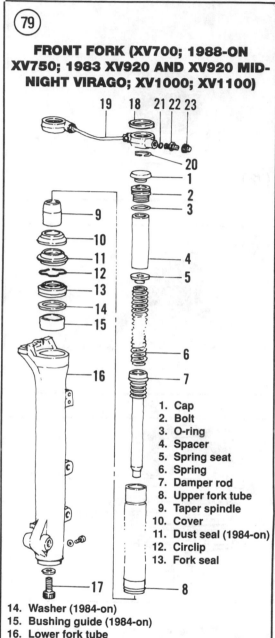

(79)

FRONT FORK (XV700; 1988-ON XV750; 1983 XV920 AND XV920 MID-NIGHT VIRAGO; XV1000; XV1100)

1. Cap
2. Bolt
3. O-ring
4. Spacer
5. Spring seat
6. Spring
7. Damper rod
8. Upper fork tube
9. Taper spindle
10. Cover
11. Dust seal (1984-on)
12. Circlip
13. Fork seal
14. Washer (1984-on)
15. Bushing guide (1984-on)
16. Lower fork tube
17. Bolt
18. Rubber spacer (1983 XV920, XV920 Midnight Virago; XV1000; XV1100)
19. Air joint bracket (1983 XV920, XV920 Midnight Virago; XV1000; XV1100)
20. Ring clip (1983 XV920, XV920 Midnight Virago; XV1000; XV1100)
21. O-ring (1983 XV920, XV920 Midnight Virago; XV1000; XV1100)
22. Air valve (1983 XV920, XV920 Midnight Virago; XV1000; XV1100)
23. Cap (1983 XV920, XV920 Midnight Virago; XV1000; XV1100)

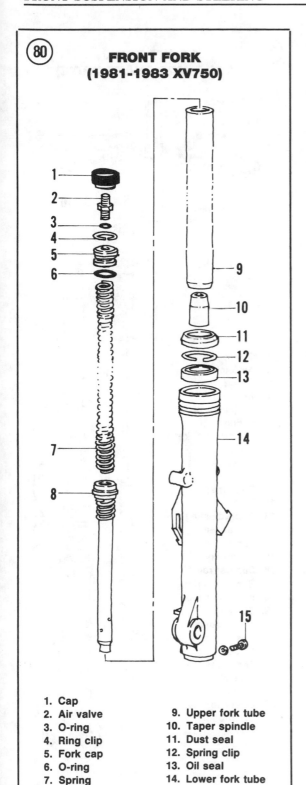

80

FRONT FORK
(1981-1983 XV750)

1. Cap
2. Air valve
3. O-ring
4. Ring clip
5. Fork cap
6. O-ring
7. Spring
8. Damper rod
9. Upper fork tube
10. Taper spindle
11. Dust seal
12. Spring clip
13. Oil seal
14. Lower fork tube
15. Bolt

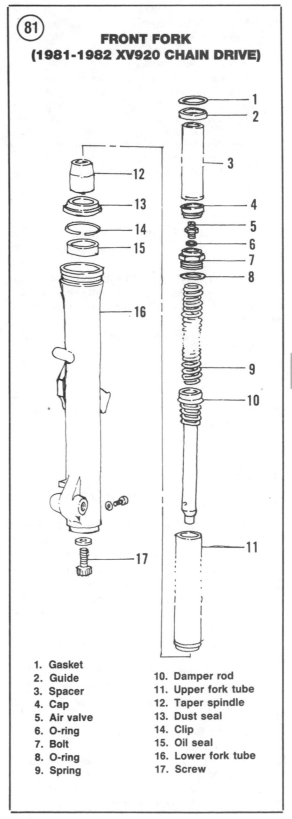

81

FRONT FORK
(1981-1982 XV920 CHAIN DRIVE)

1. Gasket
2. Guide
3. Spacer
4. Cap
5. Air valve
6. O-ring
7. Bolt
8. O-ring
9. Spring
10. Damper rod
11. Upper fork tube
12. Taper spindle
13. Dust seal
14. Clip
15. Oil seal
16. Lower fork tube
17. Screw

8

NOTE
Further disassembly of the XV700, 1988-on XV750, 1982 XV920 shaft drive, XV1000 and XV1100 front forks is not recommended. Further disassembly requires special tools as well as access to a torch to head the slider for complete removal of all parts. During assembly, special tools are also required to seat the seals and metal slides. Because the operation of the front forks is critical to steering and safety, refer further service to a dealer or qualified specialist.

4. Remove the rubber boot from the notch in the lower fork tube and slide it off of the upper fork tube.

5. Clamp the slider in a vise with soft jaws.

6. Remove the Allen bolt (**Figure 83**) at the bottom of the slider and pull the fork tube out of the slider.

7. Remove the oil lock piece (**Figure 84**), the damper rod and rebound spring (**Figure 85**).

8. Remove the snap ring from the groove in the lower fork tube.

9. Remove the oil seal by prying it out with a flat-blade screwdriver. Remove the oil seal slowly to prevent damage to the fork tube.

Inspection

1. Thoroughly clean all parts in solvent and dry them.

2. Check upper fork tube exterior for scratches and straightness. If bent or scratched, it should be replaced.

3. Check the lower fork tube for dents or exterior damage that may cause the upper fork tube to hang up during riding conditions. Replace if necessary.

4. Carefully check the damper rod and the piston ring (**Figure 86**) for wear or damage.

5. Check the damper rod for straightness. **Figure 87** shows one method. The rod should be replaced if the runout is 0.008 in. (0.2 mm) or greater.

6. Measure the uncompressed length of the fork spring. Replace the spring if it is too short. See **Table 1** for specifications.

7. Check the O-ring on the fork cap. Replace if worn or damaged.

8. Any parts that are worn or damaged should be replaced. Simply cleaning and reinstalling unserviceable components will not improve performance of the front suspension.

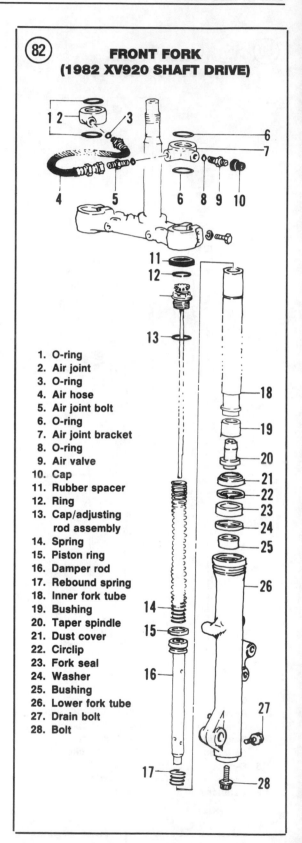

(82) **FRONT FORK (1982 XV920 SHAFT DRIVE)**

1. O-ring
2. Air joint
3. O-ring
4. Air hose
5. Air joint bolt
6. O-ring
7. Air joint bracket
8. O-ring
9. Air valve
10. Cap
11. Rubber spacer
12. Ring
13. Cap/adjusting rod assembly
14. Spring
15. Piston ring
16. Damper rod
17. Rebound spring
18. Inner fork tube
19. Bushing
20. Taper spindle
21. Dust cover
22. Circlip
23. Fork seal
24. Washer
25. Bushing
26. Lower fork tube
27. Drain bolt
28. Bolt

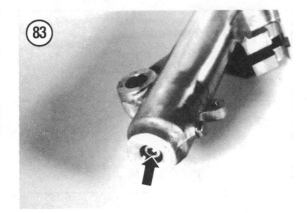

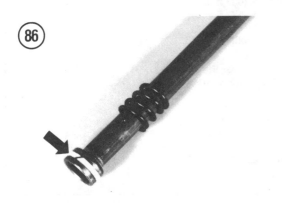

Assembly

NOTE
For XV700, 1982 XV920 shaft drive,
XV1000 and XV1100 models, begin re-
assembly with Step 5.

1. Install the oil seal and snap ring in the lower fork tube.

NOTE
Make sure the seal seats squarely and
fully in the bores of the tube.

2. Install the rebound spring onto the damper rod. Insert the damper rod into the fork tube (**Figure 85**) and install the oil lock piece (**Figure 84**).

3. Apply a light coat of oil to the outside of the fork tube and install it into the lower fork tube (**Figure 88**). Apply Loctite Lock N' Seal to the threads of the Allen bolt and install it (**Figure 89**).

4. Slide the rubber boot into place on the lower fork tube.

5. Fill fork tube with fresh fork oil. Carefully fill each fork tube as listed in **Table 1**.

NOTE
To measure the correct amount of fluid,
use a plastic baby bottle. These have
measurements in fluid ounces (oz.) and
cubic centimeters (cc) on the side.

6. Insert the spring with the small coil diameter facing down toward the axle.

7. Install the fork tube and cap as described in this chapter.

8. Pressurize the fork as described in Chapter Eleven.

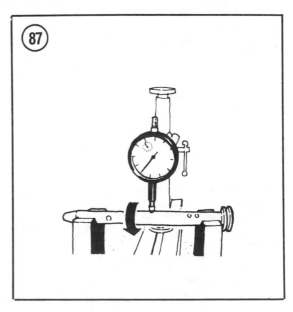

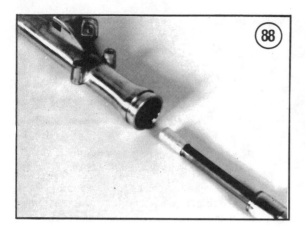

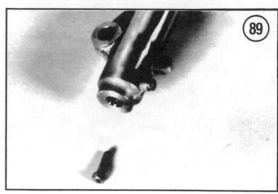

Table 1 FRONT SUSPENSION AND STEERING SPECIFICATIONS

Steering head	
Type	
1981-1983	Ball bearing
1984-on	Tapered roller bearing
Number of balls in steering head	
(1981-1983)	
Upper	19
Lower	19
Size of steering balls	1/4 in.
Front fork	
Front fork travel	5.91 in. (150 mm)
Spring free length	
XV700, XV1000, XV1100	20.2 in. (513 mm)
XV750	25.0 in. (635 mm)
XV920 (chain drive)	22.7 in. (577.5 mm)
XV920 (1982 shaft drive)	24.6 in. (624.7 mm)
XV920 (1983)	Not specified
Oil weight	SAE 10W
Air pressure	See Chapter Eleven
Front wheel runout	0.079 in. (2 mm)
Front fork oil capacity	
XV700 (1984-1985)	13.7 oz. (405 cc)
XV700 (1986-1987), XV750 (1988-on)	13.4 oz. (396 cc)
XV750	9.4 oz. (278 cc)
XV920 (chain drive)	8.9 oz. (264 cc)
XV920 (1982-1983 shaft drive)	10.2 oz. (303 cc)
XV1000, XV1100	13.1 oz. (372 cc)

Table 2 FRONT SUSPENSION TIGHTENING TORQUES

Item	ft.-lb.	N·m
Front axle		
XV700, XV1000, XV1100	75	105
XV750, XV920 (chain drive)	77	107
XV920 (shaft drive)	80	110
Front axle pinch bolt/nut	14	20
Steering crown and steering stem bolts		
1981-1983		
M8	14	20
M14	39	54
Steering crown and steering stem nut		
1984-on		
M22	80	110
Steering crown and front forks		
Upper	14	20
Lower		
1981-1983	14	20
1984-on	17	23

8

REAR SUSPENSION AND FINAL DRIVE

This chapter includes repair and replacement procedures for the rear wheel, chain-drive and shaft-drive units and rear suspension components.

Specifications (**Table 1**) and tightening torques (**Table 2**) are at the end of the chapter.

REAR WHEEL

Refer to **Figure 1** (chain-drive) or **Figure 2** (shaft/drive) for this procedure.

Removal/Installation

1. Place the bike on the centerstand so that the rear wheel clears the ground.
2. *Chain-drive models*: Remove the rear fender bolts and raise the fender away from the wheel.
3. Remove the cotter pin and nut securing the brake rod. Unscrew the rear brake adjusting nut (**Figure 3**) and disconnect the brake rod.

NOTE
*Install the spring, nut and cotter pin back onto the brake rod to prevent their loss (**Figure 4**).*

4. Remove the cotter pin and nut securing the brake torque rod and disconnect it (**Figure 5**).
5. Remove the cotter pin and loosen the rear axle nut (**Figure 6**). Discard the cotter pin; never reuse a cotter pin.

6. Loosen the axle pinch bolt (**Figure 7**) on shaft-drive models.
7. Withdraw the axle from the right-hand side. Note the spacer between the brake hub and swing arm. See **Figure 8**.
8A. *Chain-drive models*: Slide the wheel to the right to disengage it from the drive chain case and remove the wheel (**Figure 9**).
8B. *Shaft-drive models*: Slide the wheel to the right to disengage it from the hub drive splines and remove the wheel (**Figure 10**). Remove the spacer (**Figure 11**).
9. If the wheel is going to be off for any length of time or if it is to be taken to a shop for repair, install the chain adjusters (if so equipped) and axle spacers on the axle along with the axle nut to prevent losing any parts.
10. Install by reversing these removal steps, noting the following:
   a. *Chain-drive models*: Make sure that the rear wheel hub clutch damper fits into the drive chain clutch hub.
   b. *Shaft-drive models*: Make sure that the wheel hub splines (**Figure 12**) engage with the final drive (**Figure 13**).
   c. Prior to tightening the axle nut, install the brake torque link (**Figure 5**) and tighten the nut to specifications in **Table 2**.

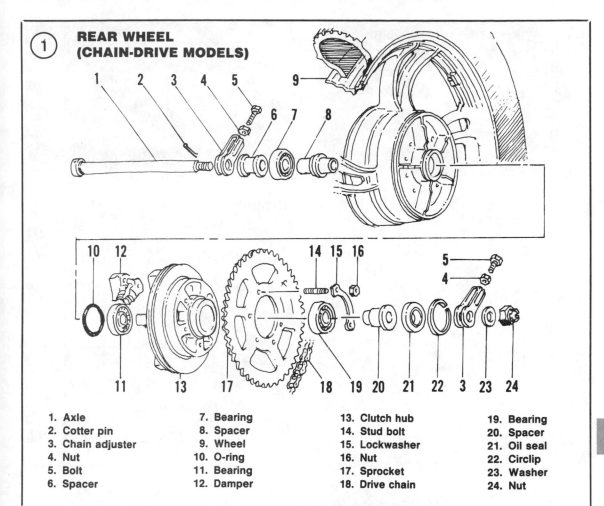

① REAR WHEEL (CHAIN-DRIVE MODELS)

1. Axle	7. Bearing	13. Clutch hub	19. Bearing
2. Cotter pin	8. Spacer	14. Stud bolt	20. Spacer
3. Chain adjuster	9. Wheel	15. Lockwasher	21. Oil seal
4. Nut	10. O-ring	16. Nut	22. Circlip
5. Bolt	11. Bearing	17. Sprocket	23. Washer
6. Spacer	12. Damper	18. Drive chain	24. Nut

9

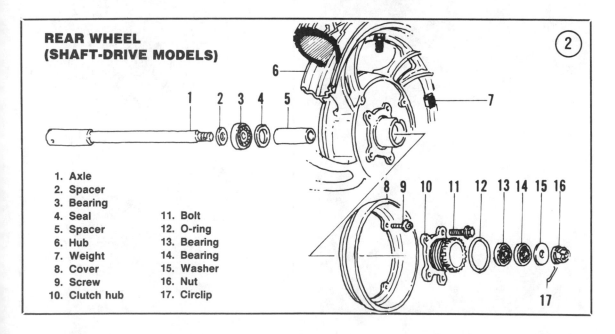

REAR WHEEL (SHAFT-DRIVE MODELS) ②

1. Axle	
2. Spacer	
3. Bearing	
4. Seal	11. Bolt
5. Spacer	12. O-ring
6. Hub	13. Bearing
7. Weight	14. Bearing
8. Cover	15. Washer
9. Screw	16. Nut
10. Clutch hub	17. Circlip

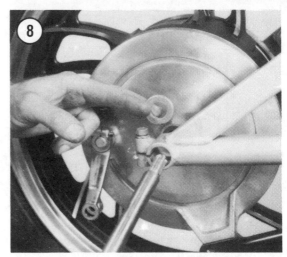

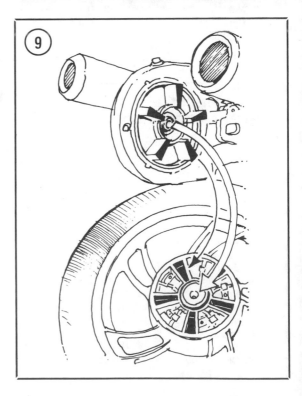

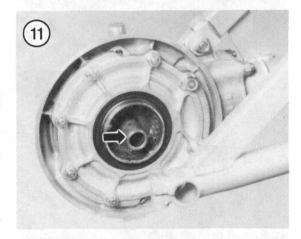

d. Tighten the pinch bolt on shaft-drive models to specifications in **Table 2**.

e. Tighten the axle nut to specifications in **Table 2**. Install a new axle nut cotter pin.

f. Adjust the rear brake pedal free play as described in Chapter Three.

g. Rotate the wheel several times to make sure it rotates freely and that the brake works properly.

h. Adjust the drive chain, if so equipped, as described in Chapter Three.

Inspection

Measure the axial and radial runout of the wheel with a dial indicator as shown in **Figure 14**. The maximum allowable axial and radial runout is 0.08 in. (2.0 mm). If the runout exceeds this dimension, check the wheel bearing condition. If the wheel bearings are okay, check the wheel rim for damage. Cast wheels cannot be serviced but must be replaced if damaged. For wire wheels, refer to the wheel and spoke information in Chapter Eight.

Inspect the wheel for signs of cracks, fractures, dents or bends. If it is damaged in any way, it must be replaced.

WARNING
Do not try to repair any damage to the rear wheel as it will result in an unsafe riding condition.

Check axle runout as described under *Rear Hub Inspection* in this chapter.

REAR HUB

Disassembly

Refer to **Figure 1** or **Figure 2** for this procedure.

1. Remove the rear wheel as described in this chapter.

2. Pull the brake assembly straight out of the wheel (**Figure 10**).

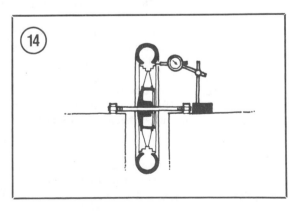

3. *Chain-drive models*: To remove the left-hand clutch hub bearings, perform the following:

   a. Pull the clutch hub (**Figure 1**) out of the wheel assembly.

   b. Remove the circlip, oil seal and spacer from the left-hand side.

   c. Insert a soft aluminum or brass drift into the right-hand side of the clutch hub. Tap the bearing out of the hub with a hammer, working around the perimeter of the outer race.

4. *Shaft-drive models*: Remove the bolts securing the clutch hub (**Figure 15**) to the wheel and remove it.

5. To remove the right-hand bearing (**Figure 16**), insert a soft aluminum or brass drift into the left-hand side of the hub and place the end of the drift on the outer bearing race. Tap the bearing out of the hub with a hammer working around the perimeter of the bearing.

6A. *Shaft-drive models*: Remove the spacer flange and spacer. Then remove the 2 left-hand bearings using the method described in Step 5.

6B. *Chain drive models*: Remove the spacer. Then remove the left-hand bearing using the same method described in Step 5. Remove the O-ring from the left-hand side.

Inspection

1. Do not clean sealed bearings. Non-sealed bearings can be cleaned in solvent and thoroughly dried with compressed air. *Do not* spin the bearing with the air jet while drying.

2. Clean the inside and outside of the hub with solvent. Dry with compressed air.

3. Turn each bearing by hand (**Figure 17**). Make sure bearings turn smoothly. On non-sealed bearings, check the balls for evidence of wear, pitting or excessive heat (bluish tint). Replace bearings if necessary; always replace as a complete set. When replacing the bearings, be sure to take your old bearings along to ensure a perfect matchup.

4. Check the axle for wear and straightness. Use V-blocks and a dial indicator as shown in **Figure 18**. If the runout is 0.008 in. (0.2 mm) or greater, the axle should be replaced.

5. Check the brake drum (**Figure 19**) for any scoring or damage. If damage is apparent, refer to Chapter Ten for further inspection and service.

Assembly

1. Blow any dirt or foreign matter out of the hub prior to installing the clutch hub and right-hand side bearing.

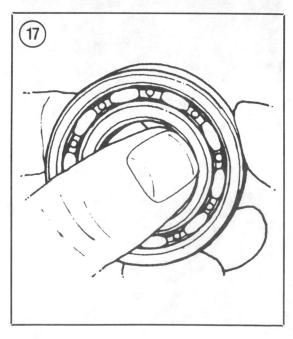

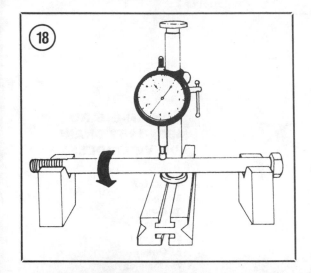

2. *Shaft-drive models*: Replace the clutch hub O-ring if worn or damaged.
3. Pack the hub with multipurpose grease.

NOTE
When performing Step 4, refer to **Figure 1** *or* **Figure 2** *for correct bearing and spacer alignment.*

CAUTION
*Tap the bearings squarely into place and tap only on the outer race. Use a socket (**Figure 20**) that matches the outer race diameter. Do not tap on the inner race or the bearings will be damaged. Be sure to tap the bearings until they seat completely.*

4. Install the right-hand bearing (**Figure 16**), spacer flange (shaft-drive models) and the spacer.

NOTE
*Install the right-hand side bearing with the sealed side facing outward (**Figure 20**).*

5. Install the left-hand bearing(s) into the hub.
6. *Chain-drive models*: Install the bearing in the clutch hub. Then install the spacer, oil seal and circlip.

NOTE
Tap the oil seal into the hub using a socket that matches the outer bushing diameter.

7. Install the clutch hub (**Figure 15**). On shaft-drive models, tighten the bolts securely.
8. Install the rear wheel as described in this chapter.

9

CLUTCH HUB AND DRIVE CHAIN ASSEMBLY (XV920 CHAIN DRIVE)

Refer to **Figure 1** and **Figure 21** for this procedure, which applies to chain-driven XV920 models.

Removal/Installation

1. Remove the rear wheel as described in this chapter.
2. Remove the left-hand rear foot peg assembly.
3. Remove the left-hand muffler assembly as described in Chapter Six.
4. Remove the shift lever.
5. Loosen the upper chain guard boot clamps (A, **Figure 22**) and slide the boots toward the wheel.
6. Remove the front sprocket cover (B, **Figure 22**).

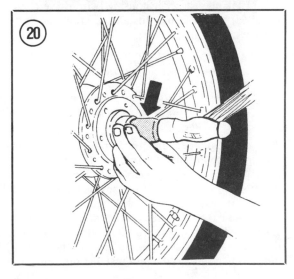

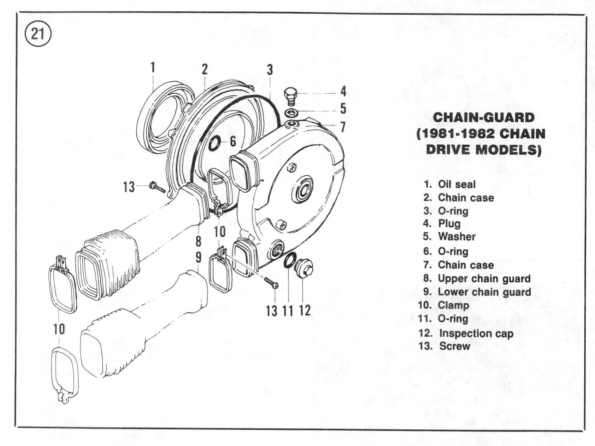

(21)

CHAIN-GUARD
(1981-1982 CHAIN
DRIVE MODELS)

1. Oil seal
2. Chain case
3. O-ring
4. Plug
5. Washer
6. O-ring
7. Chain case
8. Upper chain guard
9. Lower chain guard
10. Clamp
11. O-ring
12. Inspection cap
13. Screw

7. Loosen the rear lower chain guard boot clamp (C, **Figure 22**) and slide the chain guard forward.

8. Rotate the rear sprocket by hand to expose the chain link. Disconnect the chain using a chain breaker.

9. Remove the chain by pulling it out of the lower chain guard.

10. Remove the bolts securing the top and bottom chain guards to the swing arm and remove them.

11. Remove the screws securing the sprocket housing (D, **Figure 22**) and remove it.

12. Remove the bolts securing the sprocket retaining ring to the sprocket housing and remove it.

13. Remove the sprocket assembly from the housing.

14. Inspect the clutch hub assembly as described in this chapter.

15. Installation is the reverse of these steps; note the following.

16. Install the sprocket into the sprocket housing. Then install the chain through the top sprocket housing hole, onto the sprocket and back out through the lower sprocket housing hole.

17. Lightly lubricate the sprocket retaining ring O-ring with chain grease. Then install the O-ring onto the retaining ring.

18. Install the retaining ring onto the sprocket housing. Make sure the O-ring does not slip off the retaining ring during installation. Tighten the retaining ring screws securely.

19. Install the sprocket housing (with drive chain installed) to the frame. Install the attaching bolts loosely.

NOTE
Do not allow the drive chain to become dirty as it hangs down from the sprocket housing. Lay papers underneath the bike to help keep the chain clean.

20. Slip the upper chain guard and its clamps over the upper chain run. Repeat for the lower chain guard. Install the chain guard bolts loosely.

21. Install the chain over the engine sprocket and secure the chain with an old chain link or wire. Then rotate the rear sprocket so that the chain ends stop at the point of original disassembly. Remove the old chain link or wire and install a new chain link, using a universal chain installation tool.

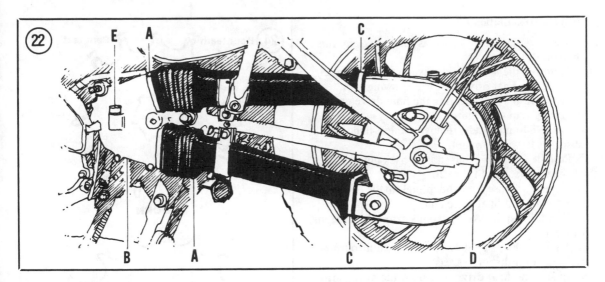

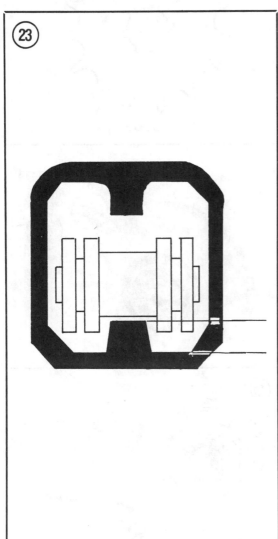

22. Install the front sprocket cover (B, **Figure 22**).
23. Connect the chain guard boots to the front sprocket cover and to the rear chain housing. Tighten the boots securely with their clamps.
24. Refill the chain housing with the correct type and quantity of chain lube. See Chapter Three.

Inspection

1. Clean all parts thoroughly in solvent.
2. Examine the chain guards for wear or damage. Measure the height of the internal chain guard ribs as shown in **Figure 23**. If the rib height is less than 0.157 in. (4 mm), replace the chain guard.
3. Check each O-ring for wear or damage; replace if necessary.
4. Check the chain guard breather (E, **Figure 22**) for obstructions. Clean as required.
5. Check the rear sprocket housing and sprocket retaining ring for wear or damage; replace if necessary.
6. Inspect the teeth on the front and rear sprockets. If the teeth are visibly worn (**Figure 24**), replace both sprockets and the drive chain. Never replace any one sprocket or chain as a separate item; worn parts will cause rapid wear of the new component. Refer to *Drive Chain Adjustment* in Chapter Three.

WHEEL BALANCING

For complete information refer to Chapter Eight.

TIRE CHANGING

Refer to *Tire Changing* in Chapter Eight.

FINAL SHAFT DRIVE UNIT

These procedures apply to shaft-drive models.

Removal/Installation

1. Remove the rear wheel as described in this chapter.

2. Remove the 4 nuts and washers (A, **Figure 25**) securing the final drive unit to the swing arm.

3. Remove the bolt securing the final drive unit to the swing arm (B, **Figure 25**).

4. On 1984-on models, remove the left-hand shock absorber lower acorn nut.

5. Pull the final drive unit straight back until it is free of the engine. See **Figure 26**.

6. Wipe the grease from the splines on the end of the drive shaft and final drive unit.

7. Check the splines of both units carefully for signs of wear.

8. Pack the splines with multipurpose molybdenum disulfide grease.

9. Install the final drive unit onto the swing arm. Make sure that the splines of the drive shaft engage properly with the final drive unit.

10. Install the 4 nuts and washers and tighten to specifications in **Table 2**.

11. Install the bolt and nut and tighten to specifications.

12. Install the rear wheel as described in this chapter.

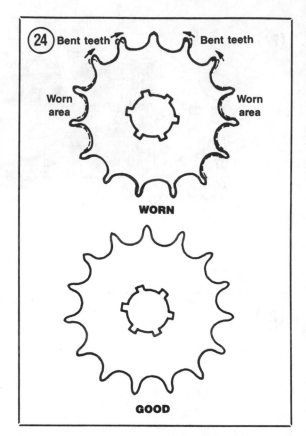

**Disassembly/Inspection/
Troubleshooting**

Although it may be possible for you to disassemble the final drive unit for inspection, you cannot replace the bearings or seals without special tools. If there is trouble in the final drive unit, it is best to remove the unit and take it to a dealer or qualified specialist for overhaul. They are also better equipped to check and adjust gear lash.

Inspect the exterior of the unit for signs of wear, cracks, damage or oil leakage. If any damage is present or there are signs of leakage, take the unit in for further service.

SWING ARM

Refer to **Figures 27-29** for this procedure.

Removal/Installation

1. Place the bike on the centerstand.

2. Remove the rear wheel as described in this chapter.

3A. On 1981-1983 models, perform the following:
  a. Remove the mufflers (**Figure 30**) as described in Chapter Six.
  b. See **Figure 31**. Remove the shift lever (A) and the left-hand front foot peg (B).

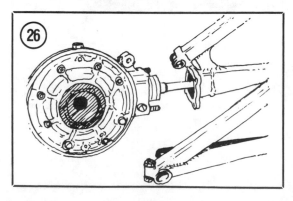

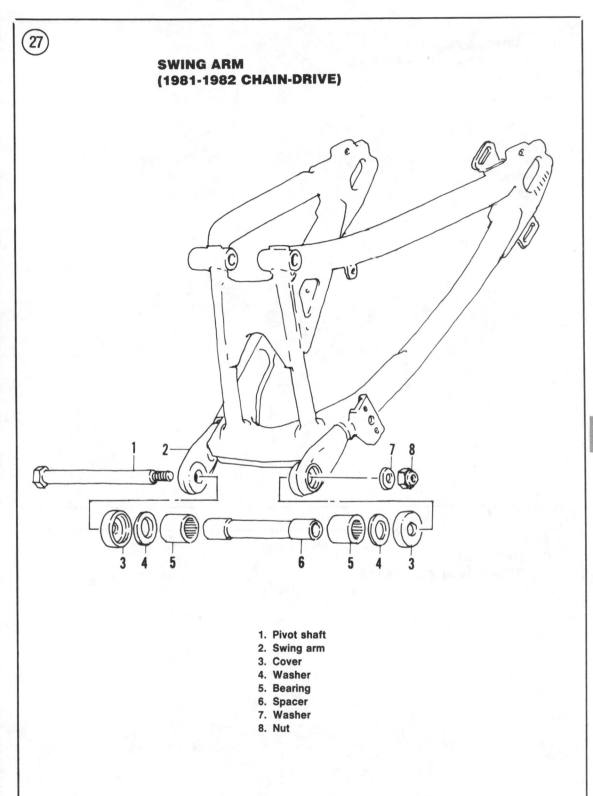

**SWING ARM
(1981-1982 CHAIN-DRIVE)**

1. Pivot shaft
2. Swing arm
3. Cover
4. Washer
5. Bearing
6. Spacer
7. Washer
8. Nut

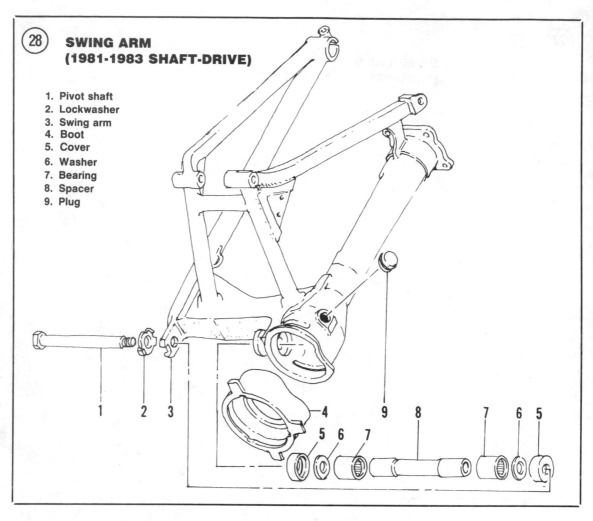

(28) **SWING ARM
(1981-1983 SHAFT-DRIVE)**

1. Pivot shaft
2. Lockwasher
3. Swing arm
4. Boot
5. Cover
6. Washer
7. Bearing
8. Spacer
9. Plug

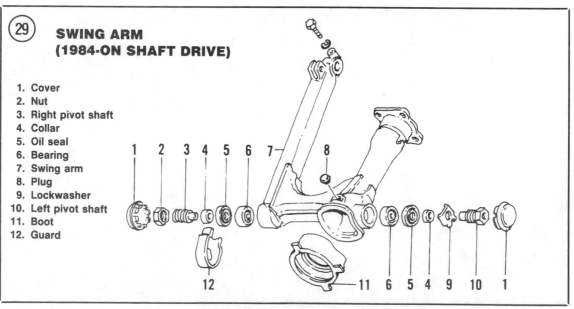

(29) **SWING ARM
(1984-ON SHAFT DRIVE)**

1. Cover
2. Nut
3. Right pivot shaft
4. Collar
5. Oil seal
6. Bearing
7. Swing arm
8. Plug
9. Lockwasher
10. Left pivot shaft
11. Boot
12. Guard

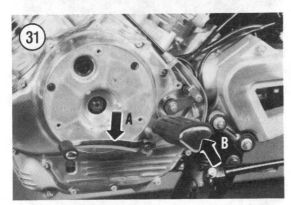

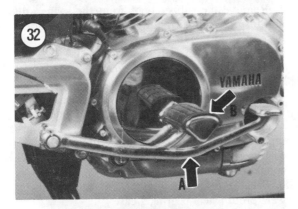

c. See **Figure 32**. Remove the rear brake pedal (A) and the right-hand front foot peg (B).

d. Remove the left-hand and right-hand engine braces. See **Figure 33**.

e. On shaft-drive models, slide the rubber boot (**Figure 34**) away from the engine.

3B. On 1984-on models, remove the left- and right-hand pivot covers (**Figure 35**).

4. Remove the drive chain or final drive unit as described in this chapter.

5. On shaft-drive models, remove the bolts (**Figure 36**) securing the drive shaft to the middle gear housing.

6. Disconnect the shock absorber(s) at the swing arm.

7A. *1981-1982 chain-drive models:*

a. Remove the swing arm pivot shaft nut.

b. Withdraw the pivot shaft from the right-hand side.

c. Remove the swing arm.

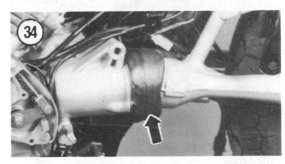

9

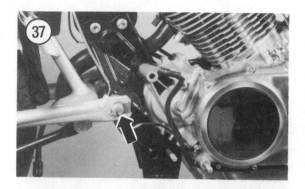

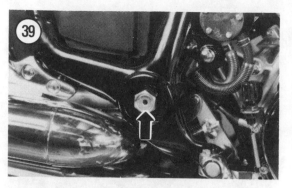

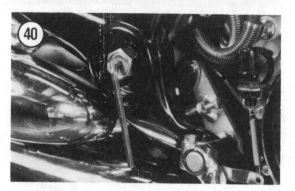

7B. *1981-1983 shaft-drive models*:
  a. Pry back the lockwasher tab on the right-hand side.
  b. Loosen and remove the swing arm pivot shaft (**Figure 37**).
  c. Remove the swing arm.

7C. *1984-on models*:
  a. Pry back the lockwasher tab on the left-hand side.
  b. Remove the left-hand pivot shaft (**Figure 38**).
  c. Remove the lock nut (**Figure 39**) and remove the right-hand pivot shaft.
  d. Remove the swing arm.

8. Installation is the reverse of these steps; note the following.

9A. On 1981-1983 models, tighten the swing arm pivot shaft to the specifications in **Table 2**.

9B. On 1984-on models, perform the following:
  a. Install a new left-hand pivot shaft lockwasher.
  b. Tighten the left-hand pivot shaft (**Figure 38**) to 72 ft.-lb. (100 N•m). Bend over the tab on the lockwasher to lock the pivot shaft.
  c. Tighten the right hand pivot shaft (**Figure 40**) to 4 ft.-lb. (5-6 N•m). To secure the right-hand pivot shaft, tighten the locknut (**Figure 39**) to 72 ft.-lb. (100 N•m). Make sure the pivot shaft does not turn when tightening the locknut.

10. After the swing arm is installed, check the side clearance as described in this chapter.

Inspection

1. Remove the rubber boot from the swing arm and inspect it for tears or deterioration; replace if necessary.

2. Remove the oil seals and bearings.

3. Thoroughly clean the bearings in solvent and dry with compressed air.

4. Turn each bearing by hand. Make sure bearings turn smoothly. Check the balls for evidence of wear or pitting. Replace if necessary. Always replace both bearings at the same time.

5. If bearings have been replaced, the grease seals should be replaced also.

6. Pack the bearings with a lithium base, waterproof wheel bearing grease.

7. Install the bearings into the swing arm.

> *CAUTION*
> *Tap the bearings squarely into place and tap on the outer race only. Do not tap on the inner race or the bearings might be damaged. Be sure that the bearings are completely seated.*

Adjustment

1981-1983

Calculate the swing arm side clearance as shown in **Figure 41**. If the side clearance is not

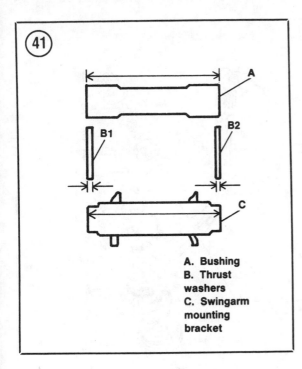

A. Bushing
B. Thrust washers
C. Swingarm mounting bracket

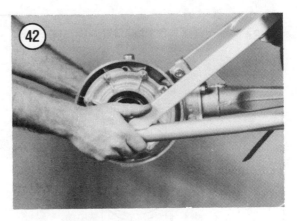

0.004-0.012 in. (0.1-0.3 mm), install new thrust washer(s) of the appropriate thickness. Thrust washers of various thicknesses are available from Yamaha dealers.

1984-on

1. This adjustment must be performed with the lower shock absorber mounts disconnected from the swing arm.
2. Grasp the swing arm at the rear (**Figure 42**) and attempt to move it from side to side. No noticeable movement should be observed. If movement occurs, proceed to Step 3.
3. Remove the pivot shaft cap from the right-hand side of the swing arm (**Figure 35**).
4. Loosen the pivot shaft locknut (**Figure 39**) and tighten the pivot shaft (**Figure 40**) to 4 ft.-lb. (5-6 N•m).
5. Tighten the locknut to 72 ft.-lb. (100 N•m).

> *NOTE*
> *When tightening the locknut, make sure the pivot shaft does not turn.*

6. Repeat Step 2. If movement is still noticeable, the swing arm bearings are probably worn. Replace them as described in this chapter.

SHOCK ABSORBERS

The rear shocks are spring controlled and hydraulically damped. Spring preload can be adjusted on all models; see Chapter Eleven.

Removal/Inspection/Installation (1981-1983)

Refer to **Figure 43**.
1. Remove the fuel tank as described in Chapter Six.
2. Remove the rear wheel as described in this chapter.
3. Remove the cotter pin and remove the lower shock absorber pivot shaft (**Figure 44**).
4. Remove the shock absorber adjuster unit (**Figure 45**) from the frame. Do not disconnect any lines or cables.
5. Remove the front shock absorber bolt (**Figure 46**).
6. Remove the shock absorber by pulling it carefully to the rear of the bike. Do not damage any hoses or cables during removal.
7. Inspect the shock absorber for oil leakage at the O-rings and along the body. If oil leakage occurs at an O-ring connection, have a dealer or qualified specialist replace the O-ring. If the oil leakage is from the shock absorber body, replace the shock absorber.
8. Installation is the reverse of these steps; note the following.
9. Install a new cotter pin at the bottom shock absorber pivot pin.
10. Turn the shock adjuster to the standard setting (**Figure 47**). Then check the shock absorber cable free play by hand. If the free play is excessive, turn the cable adjusters (**Figure 48**) as necessary.
11. Adjust the shock absorber as described in Chapter Eleven.

Removal/Inspection/Installation (1984-on)

Removal and installation of the rear shocks is easier if they are done separately. The remaining unit will support the rear of the bike and maintain the correct relationship between the top and

9

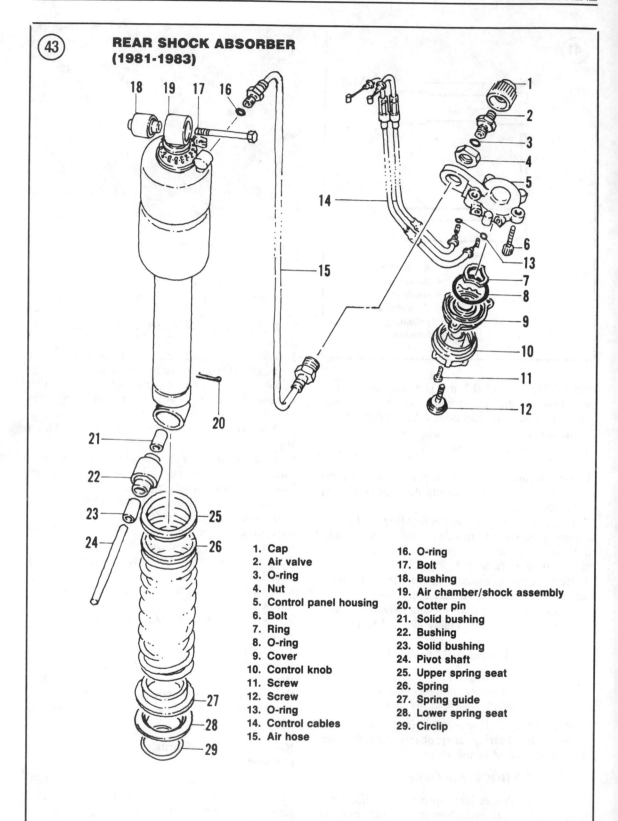

**REAR SHOCK ABSORBER
(1981-1983)**

1. Cap
2. Air valve
3. O-ring
4. Nut
5. Control panel housing
6. Bolt
7. Ring
8. O-ring
9. Cover
10. Control knob
11. Screw
12. Screw
13. O-ring
14. Control cables
15. Air hose
16. O-ring
17. Bolt
18. Bushing
19. Air chamber/shock assembly
20. Cotter pin
21. Solid bushing
22. Bushing
23. Solid bushing
24. Pivot shaft
25. Upper spring seat
26. Spring
27. Spring guide
28. Lower spring seat
29. Circlip

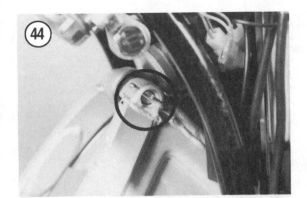

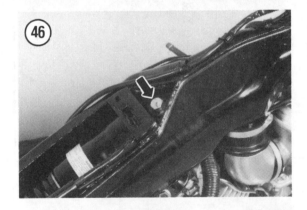

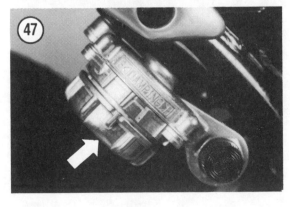

bottom mounts. If both shock absorbers must be removed at the same time, cut a piece of wood the same length as the shock absorber. Drill two holes in the wood the same distance apart as the bolt holes. Install the wood support after one shock absorber is removed. This will allow the bike to be easily moved around until the shock absorbers are reinstalled or replaced.

1. Place the bike on the centerstand.
2. Turn the lower shock adjuster (**Figure 49**) clockwise to its softest setting. Repeat for the opposite side.
3. Remove the upper and lower nuts and bolts (**Figure 50**).
4. Pull the shock off.
5. Check the shock absorber body for any signs of oil leakage. Replace the shock if necessary.
6. Install by reversing these removal steps. Torque to specifications in **Table 2**.
7. Adjust the shock absorbers as described in Chapter Eleven.

Table 1 REAR SUSPENSION SPECIFICATIONS

Shock absorber	
Spring free length	
XV700, XV1000	8.8 in. (223 mm)
XV750	6.57 in. (167 mm)
XV920 (chain drive)	6.77 in. (172 mm)
XV920 (shaft drive)	6.60 in. (168.5 mm)
XV1100	8.5 in. (216.5 mm)
Swing arm side play	
1981-1983	0.008-0.012 in. (0.1-0.3 mm)
1984-on (limit)	0.04 in. (1.0 mm)
Rear wheel runout	0.079 in. (2 mm)
Drive chain (XV920 chain drive)	
Type	DID 630DS
Number of links	90
Free play	1/4-7/16 in. (7-10 mm)

Table 2 REAR SUSPENSION TIGHTENING TORQUES

Item	ft.-lb.	N·m
Rear axle		
XV700, XV1000, XV1100	75	105
XV750, XV920 (chain drive)	77	107
XV920 (shaft drive)	80	110
Swing arm pivot shaft		
1981-1983		
XV750, XV920 (chain drive)	56	78
XV920 (shaft drive)	58	80
1984-on		
Left-side bolt	72	100
Right-side bolt	4.0	5.5
Right-side nut	72	100
Shock absorber bolt		
1981-1983	32	45
1984-on		
At frame	14	20
At swing arm	22	30

CHAPTER TEN

BRAKES

The brake system consists of either a single or dual disc unit on the front and a drum brake on the rear. This chapter describes repair and replacement procedures for all brake components.

Refer to **Table 1** for brake specifications. **Table 1** and **Table 2** are at the end of the chapter.

FRONT DISC BRAKES

The front disc brake is actuated by hydraulic fluid controlled by the hand lever on the right-hand side of the handlebar. As the brake pads wear, the brake fluid level drops in the master cylinder reservoir and automatically adjusts for pad wear. However, brake lever free play must be maintained as described in Chapter Three.

When working on a hydraulic brake system, it is necessary that the work area and all tools be absolutely clean. Any tiny particles of foreign matter or grit on the caliper assembly or the master cylinder can damage the components. Also, sharp tools must not be used inside the caliper or on the caliper piston. If there is any doubt about your ability to correctly and safely carry out major service on the brake components, take the job to a Yamaha dealer or brake specialist.

When adding brake fluid use only a type clearly marked DOT 3 or DOT 4 and use it from a sealed container. Brake fluid will absorb moisture which greatly reduces its ability to perform correctly, so it is a good idea to purchase brake fluid in small containers and discard what is not used.

Whenever *any* component has been removed from the brake system the system is considered "opened" and must be bled to remove air bubbles. Also, if the brake feels spongy, this usually means there are air bubbles in the system and it must be bled. For safe brake operation, refer to *Bleeding the System* in this chapter for complete details.

> *CAUTION*
> *Disc brake components rarely require disassembly, so do not disassemble unless absolutely necessary. Do not use solvents of any kind on the brake system internal components. Solvents will cause the seals to swell and distort. When disassembling and cleaning brake components (except brake pads), use new brake fluid as a cleaning agent.*

MASTER CYLINDER

Removal/Installation

1. Loosen the nut securing the right-hand mirror to the handlebar and remove it.

CAUTION
Cover the fuel tank, front fender and instrument cluster with a heavy cloth or plastic tarp to protect them from accidental spilling of brake fluid. Wash any spilled brake fluid off any painted or plated surfaces immediately, as it will destroy the finish. Use soapy water and rinse completely.

2. Pull back the rubber boot and remove the brake-light switch (**Figure 1**). On 1982 XV920 shaft drive models, disconnect the electrical connector at the master cylinder.

3. Drain the master cylinder as follows:
   a. Attach a hose to the brake caliper bleed screw (**Figure 2**).
   b. Place the end of the hose in a clean container (**Figure 3**).
   c. Open the bleed screw (**Figure 2**) and operate the brake lever to drain all brake fluid from the master cylinder reservoir.
   d. Close the bleed screw and disconnect the hose.
   e. Discard the brake fluid.

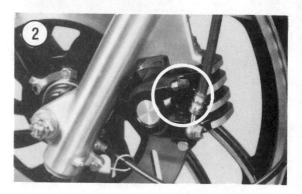

3. Remove the union bolt securing the brake hose to the master cylinder (**Figure 4**). Remove the brake hose and both copper sealing washers. Cover the end of the hose to prevent the entry of foreign matter and moisture. Tie the hose end up to the handlebar.

4. Remove the front brake lever, if necessary.

5. Remove the 2 clamping bolts and clamp securing the master cylinder (**Figure 5**) to the handlebar and remove the master cylinder.

6. Install by reversing these removal steps; note the following:

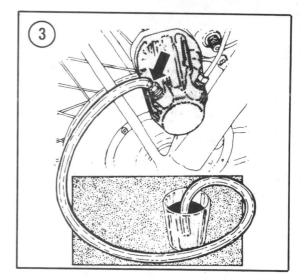

   a. Install the master cylinder clamp with the "UP" mark facing upward (**Figure 5**).
   b. Tighten the upper clamp bolt first, then the lower bolt.
   c. Install the brake hose onto the master cylinder. Be sure to place a copper sealing washer on each side of the hose fitting and install the union bolt. Tighten the union bolt to 19 ft.-lb. (26 N•m).
   d. Bleed the brake system as described in this chapter.

Disassembly

Refer to **Figures 6-9**.

1. Remove the master cylinder as described in this chapter.

2. Remove the screws securing the reservoir cap and diaphragm. Pour out the remaining brake fluid and discard it. *Never* reuse brake fluid.

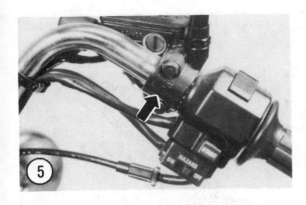

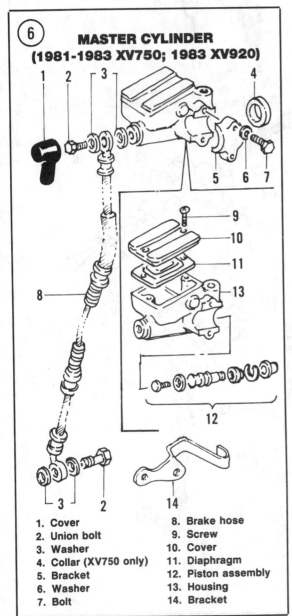

MASTER CYLINDER
(1981-1983 XV750; 1983 XV920)

1. Cover
2. Union bolt
3. Washer
4. Collar (XV750 only)
5. Bracket
6. Washer
7. Bolt
8. Brake hose
9. Screw
10. Cover
11. Diaphragm
12. Piston assembly
13. Housing
14. Bracket

3. Remove the rubber boot from the area where the hand lever actuates the internal piston.

4. Use snap ring pliers to remove the internal snap ring from the groove in the master cylinder body.

5. Remove the piston, return valve, spring cup and return spring.

6. On 1982 XV920 shaft drive models, remove the fluid level switch from the master cylinder body (if necessary).

Inspection

1. Clean all parts in fresh brake fluid. Inspect the cylinder bore and piston contact surfaces for signs of wear or damage. If either part is less than perfect, replace it.

2. Check the end of the piston for wear caused by the hand lever. Replace the entire piston assembly if any portion of it shows damage.

3. Inspect the pivot hole in the hand lever. If worn, it must be replaced.

4. Make sure the passages in the bottom of the brake fluid reservoir are clear. Check the reservoir cap and diaphragm for damage and deterioration. Replace if necessary.

5. Inspect the threads in the master cylinder body where the brake hose union bolt screws in. If the threads are damaged or partially stripped, replace the master cylinder body.

6. Check the hand lever pivot lug on the master cylinder body for cracks. Replace the master cylinder body if necessary.

NOTE
Yamaha recommends replacing the piston seals, dust seals, and rubber cap whenever the master cylinder is disassembled.

Assembly

1. Soak the new cups in fresh brake fluid for at least 15 minutes to make them pliable. Coat the inside of the cylinder with fresh brake fluid prior to assembling the parts.

CAUTION
When installing the piston assembly, do not allow the cups to turn inside out as they will be damaged and allow brake fluid to leak within the cylinder bore.

2. Position the spring with the tapered end facing toward the primary cup. Position the primary cup so the open end will go in first (toward the spring). Install the spring, primary cup and piston assembly into the cylinder.

10

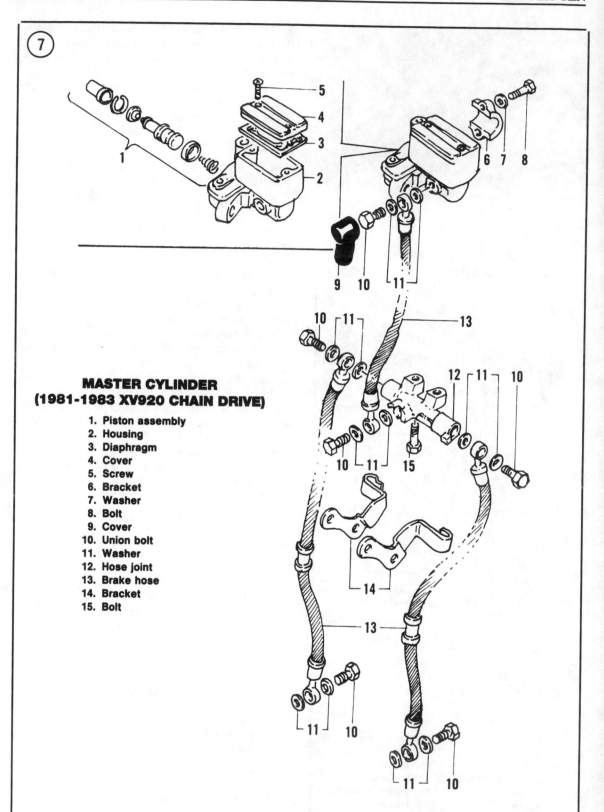

⑦

MASTER CYLINDER
(1981-1983 XV920 CHAIN DRIVE)

1. Piston assembly
2. Housing
3. Diaphragm
4. Cover
5. Screw
6. Bracket
7. Washer
8. Bolt
9. Cover
10. Union bolt
11. Washer
12. Hose joint
13. Brake hose
14. Bracket
15. Bolt

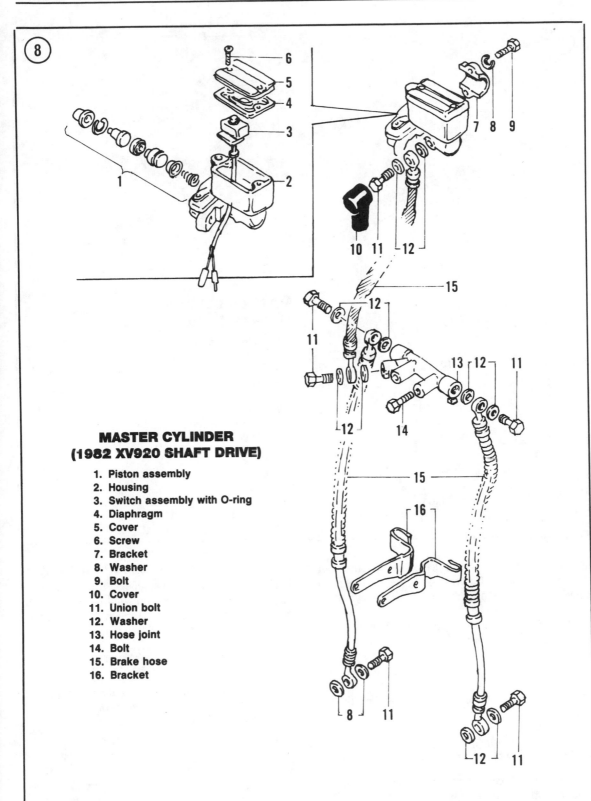

**MASTER CYLINDER
(1982 XV920 SHAFT DRIVE)**

1. Piston assembly
2. Housing
3. Switch assembly with O-ring
4. Diaphragm
5. Cover
6. Screw
7. Bracket
8. Washer
9. Bolt
10. Cover
11. Union bolt
12. Washer
13. Hose joint
14. Bolt
15. Brake hose
16. Bracket

10

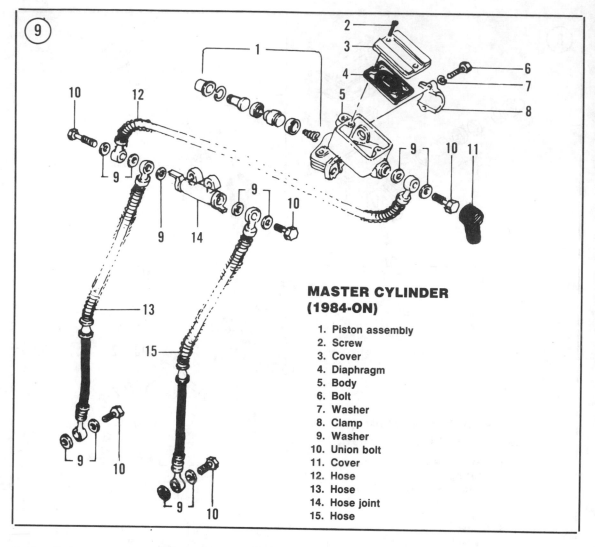

**MASTER CYLINDER
(1984-ON)**

1. Piston assembly
2. Screw
3. Cover
4. Diaphragm
5. Body
6. Bolt
7. Washer
8. Clamp
9. Washer
10. Union bolt
11. Cover
12. Hose
13. Hose
14. Hose joint
15. Hose

3. Install the master cylinder piston assembly in the order shown in **Figures 6-9**. Make sure the snap ring is firmly seated in the groove in the cylinder.

4. Slide on the rubber boot.

5. Install the diaphragm and cover. Do not tighten the screws at this time as fluid will have to be added later.

6. Install the brake lever onto the master cylinder body.

7. Install the master cylinder as described in this chapter.

FRONT BRAKE
PAD REPLACEMENT

There is no recommended mileage interval for changing the friction pads on the disc brakes. Pad wear depends greatly on riding habits and conditions. The pads should be checked for wear at the intervals specified in Chapter Three. On 1981-1982 chain-drive models, check for brake wear through the caliper inspection window (**Figure 10**). Always replace all pads as a set. On dual-disc models, replace both sets of pads (two per disc).

CAUTION
Watch the pads more closely as they begin to wear. If pad wear happens to be uneven for some reason, the backing plate may come in contact with the disc and cause damage.

The front brake on all models is basically the same but has different parts and is assembled differently according to model. To simplify the service procedures, the brake designs have been divided into groups and given a type designation. These groups are *not* recognized by Yamaha; they are used here only for ease of presentation.

The Type I front brake (**Figure 11**) is used on 1981-1983 XV750 and 1983 XV920 models, Type II (**Figure 12**) is used on XV920 chain drive models, Type III (**Figure 13**) is used on 1982 XV920 shaft drive models, and Type IV (**Figure 14**) is used on all 1984-on models.

It is not necessary to disassemble the caliper or open the hydraulic brake fluid lines to replace the brake pads.

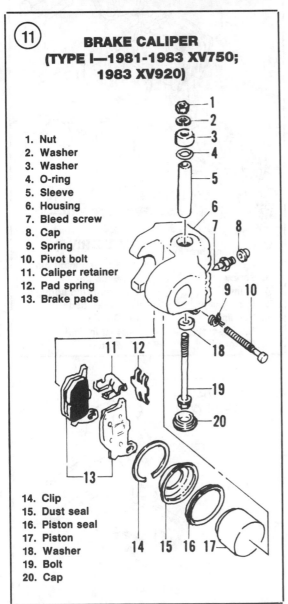

BRAKE CALIPER (TYPE I—1981-1983 XV750; 1983 XV920)

1. Nut
2. Washer
3. Washer
4. O-ring
5. Sleeve
6. Housing
7. Bleed screw
8. Cap
9. Spring
10. Pivot bolt
11. Caliper retainer
12. Pad spring
13. Brake pads
14. Clip
15. Dust seal
16. Piston seal
17. Piston
18. Washer
19. Bolt
20. Cap

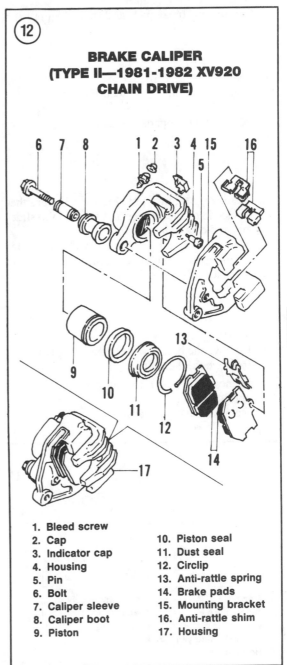

BRAKE CALIPER (TYPE II—1981-1982 XV920 CHAIN DRIVE)

1. Bleed screw
2. Cap
3. Indicator cap
4. Housing
5. Pin
6. Bolt
7. Caliper sleeve
8. Caliper boot
9. Piston
10. Piston seal
11. Dust seal
12. Circlip
13. Anti-rattle spring
14. Brake pads
15. Mounting bracket
16. Anti-rattle shim
17. Housing

10

1. Remove the front wheel as described in Chapter Eight.

2A. *Type I:*
   a. Pinch the end of the retaining spring with pliers (**Figure 15**) to open it; remove the pad retaining spring.
   b. Remove the pin (**Figure 16**).
   c. Remove the brake pads and shim (**Figure 17**).

2B. *Type II:*
   a. Remove the brake pad securing screw.
   b. Remove the brake pads, shim and pad spring.
   c. Repeat on the opposite side.

2C. *Type III:*
   a. Remove the cotter pin (**Figure 13**) from the backside of the caliper and remove the slide pin and caliper housing.
   b. Remove the pad retaining pin clip and pad retaining pin from the caliper.
   c. Repeat on the opposite side.

2D. *Type IV:*
   a. Remove the brake caliper cover (**Figure 18**).
   b. Remove the 2 circlips.
   c. Remove the pad retaining pin and the pad spring.
   d. Remove the brake pads.

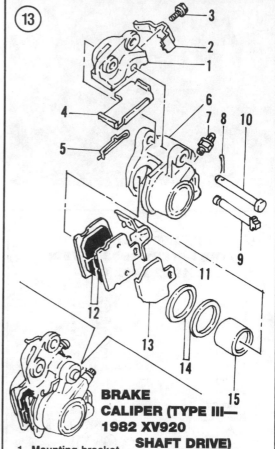

BRAKE CALIPER (TYPE III—1982 XV920 SHAFT DRIVE)

1. Mounting bracket
2. Plate
3. Screw
4. Shim
5. Spring clip
6. Housing
7. Bleed screw
8. Cotter pin
9. Pad retaining pin
10. Slide pin
11. Anti-rattle spring
12. Brake pads
13. Spring
14. Piston seal
15. Piston

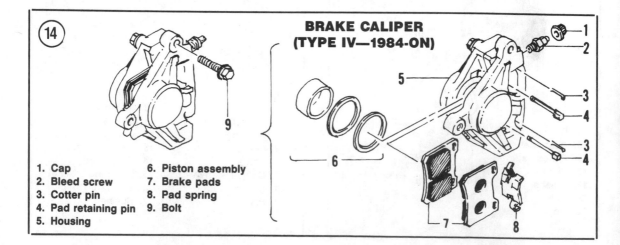

BRAKE CALIPER (TYPE IV—1984-ON)

1. Cap
2. Bleed screw
3. Cotter pin
4. Pad retaining pin
5. Housing
6. Piston assembly
7. Brake pads
8. Pad spring
9. Bolt

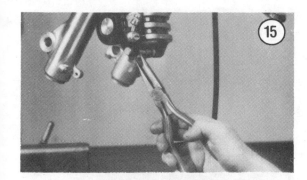

3. Clean the pad recess and the end of the piston with a soft brush. Do not use solvent, a wire brush or any hard tool which would damage the cylinder or piston.

4. Lightly coat the end of the piston with disc brake lubricant.

5. When new pads are installed in the caliper, the master cylinder brake fluid level will rise as the caliper piston is repositioned. Clean the top of the master cylinder of all dirt and foreign matter. Remove the cap (**Figure 19**) and diaphragm. Slowly push the caliper piston into the caliper. Constantly check the reservoir to make sure brake fluid does not overflow. Remove fluid, if necessary, prior to it overflowing. The piston should move freely. If it does not, and there is evidence of it sticking in the cylinder, the caliper should be removed and serviced as described under *Caliper Rebuilding* in this chapter.

6. Push the piston (**Figure 20**) in to allow room for the new pads.

7A. *Type I:*Install the following new parts in order:
   a. Brake pads (**Figure 21**).
   b. Pad retainer.
   c. Pad spring.
   d. Pad retaining pin (**Figure 16**) and retaining spring. Make sure the retaining spring engages the groove (**Figure 22**) in the retaining pin completely.
   e. Repeat on opposite side (dual caliper models).

7B. *Type II:*Install the following new parts in order:
   a. Brake pads and shims.
   b. Pad spring.

10

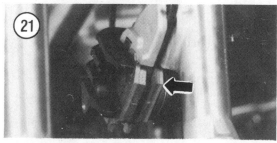

c. Pad securing screw.

7C. *Type III:* Install the following new parts in order:
   a. Brake pads and shim.
   b. Retaining spring.
   c. Pad retaining pin and clip.
   d. Pad retaining pin clip. Make sure the retaining
      pin clip engages the groove in the retaining pin
      completely.

7D. *Type IV:* Install the following new parts in order:
   a. Brake pads.
   b. Pad spring.
   c. Pad retaining pin.
   d. Circlips.
   e. Cover (**Figure 18**).

8. Install the front wheel as described in Chapter
Eight.

9. Spin the front wheel and activate the brake lever
as many times as it takes to refill the cylinder in the
caliper and correctly position the pads.

10. Refill the master cylinder reservoir, if necessary,
to maintain the correct fluid level. Install the diaphragm and top cap.

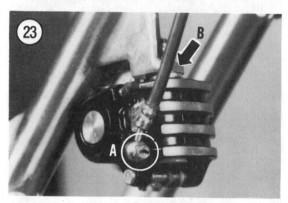

> *WARNING*
> *Use brake fluid from a sealed container
> clearly marked DOT 3. Other types may
> vaporize and cause brake failure. Al-
> ways use the same brand name; do not
> intermix brake fluids, as many brands
> are not compatible.*

> *WARNING*
> *Do not ride the motorcylce until you are
> sure the brake is operating correctly. If
> necessary, bleed the brake as described
> in this chapter.*

11. Bed the pads in gradually for the first 50 miles
by using only light pressure as much as possible.
Immediate hard application will glaze the new friction pads and greatly reduce the effectiveness of the
brake.

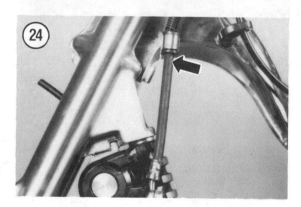

FRONT CALIPER

Removal/Installation

Refer to **Figures 11-14**.

1. Drain the master cylinder as follows:
   a. Attach a hose to the brake caliper bleed screw
      (**Figure 2**).
   b. Place the end of the hose in a clean container
      (**Figure 3**).
   c. Open the bleed screw (**Figure 2**) and operate
      the brake lever to drain all brake fluid from
      the master cylinder reservoir.
   d. Close the bleed screw and disconnect the
      hose.
   e. Discard the brake fluid.

2. Remove the front wheel as described in Chapter
Eight.

3. Remove the union bolt (A, **Figure 23**) and
copper sealing washers attaching the brake hose to
the caliper. Cap the end of the brake hose and tie it
up to the fender to prevent the entry of moisture
and dirt.

4. Remove the bolt(s) (B, **Figure 23**) securing the caliper assembly to the lower fork leg and remove it.

5. Repeat on the opposite side (if so equipped).

6. Installation is the reverse of removal; note the following:

a. Torque the caliper attaching bolts to specifications in **Table 2**.

b. Install the brake hose using new copper washers.

c. Tighten the union bolt to specifications in **Table 2**.

d. Bleed the brakes as described in this chapter.

WARNING
Do not ride the motorcycle until you are sure that the brakes are operating properly.

Caliper Rebuilding

If the caliper leaks, the caliper should be rebuilt. If the piston sticks in the cylinder, indicating severe wear or galling, the entire unit should be replaced. Rebuilding a leaky caliper requires special tools and experience.

Caliper service should be entrusted to a dealer, motorcycle repair shop or brake specialist. Considerable money can be saved by removing the caliper yourself and taking it in for repair.

The factory recommends that the internal seals of the caliper be replaced every two years.

FRONT BRAKE HOSE REPLACEMENT

The factory-recommended brake hose replacement interval is every 4 years, but it is a good idea to replace brake hoses whenever signs of cracking, leakage or damage are apparent.

Refer to **Figures 11-14**.

CAUTION
Cover the front wheel, fender and fuel tank with a heavy cloth or plastic tarp to protect them from the accidental spilling of brake fluid. Wash any spilled brake fluid off of any painted or plated surface immediately, as it will destroy the finish. Use soapy water and rinse completely.

1. Drain the master cylinder as follows:

a. Attach a hose to the brake caliper bleed screw (**Figure 2**).

b. Place the end of the hose in a clean container (**Figure 3**).

c. Open the bleed screw (**Figure 2**) and operate the brake lever to drain all brake fluid from the master cylinder reservoir.

d. Close the bleed screw and disconnect the hose.

e. Discard the brake fluid.

2. Remove the union bolt and copper sealing washers securing the brake hose to the caliper and remove it. See A, **Figure 23**.

3. Disconnect the hose from clamp on the fork (**Figure 24**).

4. On models with dual brake calipers, remove the union bolts securing the hoses to the fitting (A, **Figure 25**).

5. Remove the union bolt (**Figure 26**) securing the hose to the master cylinder.

6. Remove the brake hoses.

7. Install new brake hoses, copper sealing washers and union bolts in the reverse order of removal. Be sure to install the new sealing washers in their correct positions. Tighten all union bolts to specifications in **Table 2**.

8. Refill the master cylinder with fresh brake fluid clearly marked DOT 3. Bleed the brake as described in this chapter.

WARNING
Do not ride the motorcycle until you are sure that the brakes are operating properly.

10

FRONT BRAKE DISC

Removal/Installation

1. Remove the front wheel as described in Chapter Eight.

> *NOTE*
> *Place a piece of wood in the caliper(s) (**Figure 27**) in place of the disc. This way, if the brake lever is inadvertently squeezed, the piston will not be forced out of the cylinder. If this does happen, the caliper might have to be disassembled to reseat the piston and the system will have to be bled. By using the wood, bleeding the system is not necessary when installing the wheel.*

2. Straighten the lock tabs on the washers and remove the bolts (**Figure 28**) securing the disc to the wheel.
3. Repeat for opposite side (if so equipped).
4. Install by reversing these removal steps. Install the bolts and tighten to specifications in **Table 2**. Install new lockwashers and bend over the lock tabs after the bolts are tightened.

Inspection

It is not necessary to remove the disc from the wheel to inspect it. Small marks on the disc are not important, but radial scratches deep enough to snag a fingernail reduce braking effectiveness and increase brake pad wear. If these grooves are found, the disc should be resurfaced or replaced.
1. Measure the thickness around the disc at several locations with vernier calipers or a micrometer (**Figure 29**). The disc must be replaced if the thickness at any point is less than the wear limit specified in **Table 1**.
2. Make sure the disc bolts are tight prior to performing this check. Check the disc runout with a dial indicator as shown in **Figure 30**. Slowly rotate the wheel and watch the dial indicator. If the runout is 0.15 mm (0.006 in.) or greater, the disc should be resurfaced. If it cannot be repaired without becoming thinner than specified in **Table 1**, replace it.
3. Clean the disc of any rust or corrosion and wipe clean with lacquer thinner. Never use an oil-based solvent that may leave an oil residue on the disc.

REAR DRUM BRAKE

Disassembly

Refer to **Figure 31** for this procedure.
1. Remove the rear wheel as described in Chapter Nine.

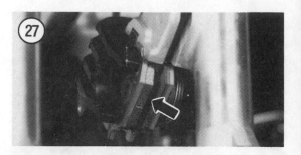

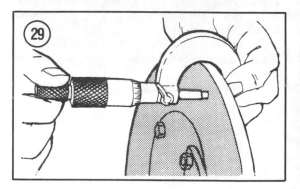

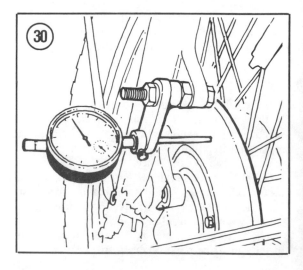

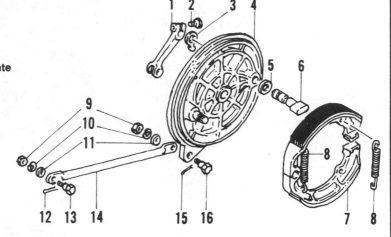

REAR BRAKE

1. Brake arm
2. Bolt
3. Indicator plate
4. Brake backing plate
5. Washer
6. Camshaft
7. Brake shoes
8. Brake springs
9. Nut
10. Lockwasher
11. Flat washer
12. Cotter pin
13. Bolt
14. Brake rod
15. Cotter pin
16. Bolt

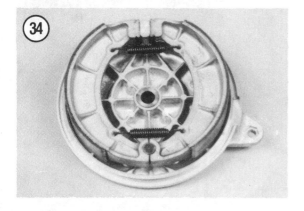

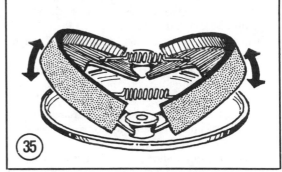

10

2. Pull the brake assembly straight up and out of the brake drum (**Figure 32**).

3. Loosen the clamping bolt (**Figure 33**) and remove the brake arm. Make note of the alignment marks prior to disassembly.

NOTE
Before performing Step 4, mark the left and right shoe positons. If the shoes are to be reused, they must be installed in their original position.

4. Pull the brake shoes (**Figure 34**) and springs up and off the guide pins and camshaft as shown in **Figure 35**.

5. Remove the return springs and separate the shoes. If the shoes will be reused, place a clean shop rag around the linings to protect them from oil and grease.

6. Remove the camshaft and shim.

Inspection

1. Thoroughly clean and dry all parts except the linings.

2. Check the contact surface of the drum (**Figure 36**) for scoring. If there are grooves deep enough to snag a fingernail, the drum should be reground and new shoes fitted. If the drum cannot be repaired without exceeding the diameter specified in **Table 1**, replace it. This type of wear can be avoided to a great extent if the brakes are disassembled and thoroughly cleaned after riding the motorcycle in water, mud or deep sand.

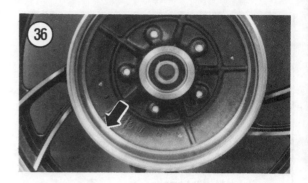

> *NOTE*
> *If oil or grease is on the drum surface, clean it off with a clean rag soaked in lacquer thinner—do not use any solvent that may leave an oil residue.*

3. Use vernier calipers (**Figure 37**) to measure the thickness of each brake shoe. They should be replaced if lining thickness is less than the minimum specified in **Table 1**.

4. Inspect the linings for embedded foreign material. Dirt can be removed with a stiff wire brush. Check for traces of oil or grease. If the linings are contaminated, they must be replaced as a set.

5. Inspect the cam lobe and pivot pin area of the shaft for wear and corrosion. Minor roughness can be removed with fine emery cloth.

6. Inspect the brake shoe return springs for wear or distortion. If they are stretched, they will not fully retract the brake shoes from the drum, resulting in a power-robbing drag on the drums and premature wear of the linings. Replace as necessary and always replace as a pair.

Assembly

1. Assemble the brake by reversing the disassembly steps, noting the following.

2. Grease the camshaft and anchor posts with a light coat of molybdenum disulfide grease; avoid getting any grease on the brake plate where the linings come in contact with it.

3. When installing the brake arm onto the brake camshaft, be sure to align the punch marks on the brake lever and housing. Tighten the bolt securely.

4. Insert the brake panel assembly into the brake drum.

5. Install the rear wheel as described in Chapter Nine.

6. Adjust the rear brake as described in Chapter Three.

REAR BRAKE
PEDAL ASSEMBLY

Removal/Installation

1. Place the motorcycle on its centerstand.

2. Completely unscrew the brake rod adjustment nut (**Figure 38**) and disconnect the rod from the brake arm. Reinstall the adjustment nut and spring on the rod (**Figure 39**) to avoid losing them.

3. Remove the bolt securing the brake pedal to its shaft (**Figure 40**) and remove the pedal.

4. Remove the cotter pin and disconnect the brake actuating arm from the brake pivot shaft. See **Figure 41**.

5. Disconect the brake pedal light switch spring and brake return spring and remove the actuating arm.

6. Withdraw the brake pivot shaft from the frame.

7. Install by reversing these removal steps, noting the following:

   a. Apply grease to the brake pivot lever prior to installing the assembly into the frame.

   b. Install a new cotter pin through the clevis pin. Bend the ends of the cotter pin over completely.

   c. Adjust the rear brake pedal as described in Chapter Three. Adjust the brake light switch as described in Chapter Seven.

BLEEDING THE SYSTEM

This procedure is necessary only when the brakes feel spongy, there is a leak in the hydraulic system, a component has been replaced or the brake fluid is being replaced.

1. Flip off the dust cap from the brake bleeder valve (**Figure 42**).

2. Connect a length of clear tubing to the bleeder valve on the caliper. Place the other end of the tube into a clean container. Fill the container with enough fresh brake fluid to keep the end submerged. The tube should be long enough so that a loop can be made higher than the bleeder valve to prevent air from being drawn into the caliper during bleeding. See **Figure 43**.

> *CAUTION*
> *Cover the front wheel, fender and fuel tank with a heavy cloth or plastic tarp to protect them from the accidental spilling of brake fluid. Wash any spilled brake fluid off of any painted or plated surface immediately, as it will destroy the finish. Use soapy water and rinse completely.*

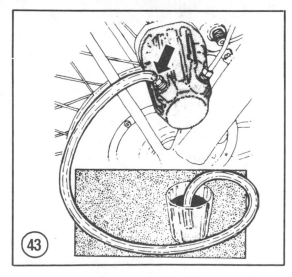

3. Clean the top of the master cylinder of all dirt and foreign matter. Remove the cap and diaphragm (**Figure 44**). Fill the reservoir to about 3/8 in. (10 mm) from the top. Install the diaphragm to prevent the entry of dirt and moisture.

> *WARNING*
> *Use brake fluid from a container clearly marked DOT 3 or DOT 4 only. Others may vaporize and cause brake failure. Always use the same brand name; do not intermix the brake fluids, as many brands are not compatible.*

4. Slowly apply the brake lever several times. Hold the lever in the applied position and open the bleeder valve about 1/2 turn. Allow the lever to travel to its limit. When this limit is reached, tighten the bleeder screw. As the brake fluid enters the system, the level will drop in the master cylinder reservoir. Maintain the level at about 3/8 in. (10 mm) from the top of the reservoir to prevent air from being drawn into the system.

5. Continue to pump the lever and fill the reservoir until the fluid emerging from the hose is completely free of air bubbles. If you are replacing the brake fluid, continue this procedure until fresh brake fluid emerges from the hose.

> *NOTE*
> *If bleeding is difficult, it may be necessary to allow the fluid to stabilize for a few hours. Repeat the bleeding procedure when the tiny bubbles in the system settle out.*

6. Hold the lever in the applied position and tighten the bleeder valve. Remove the bleeder tube and install the bleeder valve dust cap.

7. If necessary, add fluid to correct the level in the master cylinder reservoir. It must be above the level line.

8. Install the cap and tighten the screws.

9. Test the feel of the brake lever. It should feel firm and should offer the same resistance each time it's operated. If it feels spongy, it is likely that air is still in the system and it must be bled again. When all air has been bled from the system and the brake fluid level is correct in the reservoir, double-check for leaks and tighten all fittings and connections.

> *WARNING*
> *Before riding the motorcycle, make certain that the brakes are operating correctly by operating the lever several times. Then make the test ride a slow one at first to make sure the brake is operating correctly.*

Table 1 BRAKE SPECIFICATIONS

Brake fluid	DOT 3 or DOT 4
Front brake	
Disc thickness	
XV750	0.28 in. (7 mm)
XV700, XV920, XV1000, XV1100	0.20 in. (5 mm)
Wear limit	
XV750	0.256 in. (6.5 mm)
XV920	0.117 in. (4.5 mm)
XV700, XV1000, XV1100	Not specified
Pad thickness	
XV700, XV1000, XV1100, XV750 (1988-on)	0.217 in. (5.5 mm)
XV750 (1981-1983)	0.224 in. (5.7 mm)
XV920 (chain drive)	0.433 in. (11 mm)
XV920 (shaft drive)	0.326 in. (6 mm)
Pad wear limit	
XV700, XV1000, XV1100, XV750 (1988-on)	0.0197 in. (0.5 mm)
XV750 (1981-1983)	0.047 in. (1.2 mm)
XV920 (chain drive)	Not specified
XV920 (shaft drive)	0.03 in. (0.8 mm)
Rear brake	
Drum diameter	
XV750	7.087 in. (180 mm)
XV700, XV920, XV1000, XV1100	7.874 in. (200 mm)
Wear limit	
XV750	Not specified
XV700, XV920, XV1000, XV1100	7.91 in. (201 mm)
Lining thickness	0.157 in. (4 mm)
Lining wear limit	0.079 in. (2 mm)
Brake shoe spring free length	2.7 in. (68 mm)

10

Table 2 BRAKE TIGHTENING TORQUES

	ft.-lb.	N•m
Brake disc @ hub	14	20
Brake caliper @ front fork		
XV750, XV920 (chain drive)	19	26
XV920 (shaft drive), XV700, XV1000, XV1100	25	35
Brake hose union bolts	19	26
Rear brake arm bolt/nut	14	20

CHAPTER ELEVEN

SUSPENSION ADJUSTMENT

The front forks must be adjusted to correspond to rear shock absorber adjustment and vehicle load. See **Tables 1-5**. When performing the adjustments in this chapter, make sure not to exceed the air pressures specified in **Table 6**. **Tables 1-6** are at the end of the chapter.

FRONT FORKS

Air Pressure Adjustment

The air pressure in the front forks must be adjusted for various load conditions. See **Tables 1-4**.

1. Place the bike on the centerstand and raise the front wheel off the ground.

2. Attach an air pressure tool to the air fitting (**Figure 1**).

> *NOTE*
> ***Figure 1*** *shows the air pressure tool attached to an air fitting which routes air to both tubes on XV920 (shaft drive), XV1000 and XV1100 models. On all other models, the air pressure must be adjusted at each fork tube.*

3. Inflate to the desired pressure.

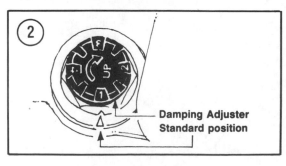

Damping Adjuster
Standard position

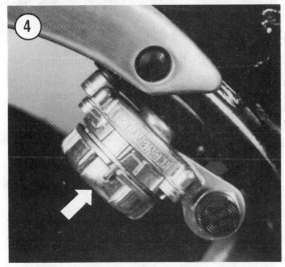

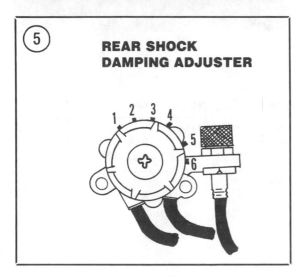

REAR SHOCK DAMPING ADJUSTER

CAUTION
Never exceed the maximum allowable air pressure specified in Table 5. The pressure difference between the two forks should be 1.4 psi (0.1 kg/cm^2) or less. On XV920 (shaft drive), XV1000 and XV1100 models, the forks are connected and so air pressure is automatically the same in each fork.

Damping Adjustment (1982 XV920 Shaft Drive)

These forks are equipped with a damping adjuster to increase or decrease fork damping. The damping adjustment must be set to correspond to front fork air pressure, rear shock absorber adjustment and vehicle load (see **Table 3**). To adjust, turn the damping adjuster (**Figure 2**) by hand to the desired setting. Four damping positions are available. The standard setting is No. 1 (minimum damping). No. 4 provides maximum damping.

WARNING
Always adjust the damping on each fork to the same number (position) or the bike's handling will be unstable.

REAR SHOCK ABSORBERS

The rear shock absorbers must be adjusted to correspond to front fork adjustment and vehicle load. See **Tables 1-4**. On models equipped with an air adjust shock, do not exceed the specified air pressures in **Table 5**.

Air Pressure

1. Place the bike on the centerstand to raise the rear wheel off the ground.
2. Remove the air valve plastic cap.
3. Attach an air pressure tool to the air fitting (**Figure 3**).
4. Inflate to the desired pressure. Reinstall the air cap.

CAUTION
Never exceed the maximum allowable air pressure specified in Table 5.

Damping Adjustment

1981-1983

The damping adjuster can be turned toward the "H" to increase damping (suspension becomes harder) or turned toward the S to decrease damping (suspension becomes softer). Turn the damping adjuster by hand to the desired setting. See **Figure 4** and **Figure 5**.

1984-on XV1000 and XV1100

These shocks are equipped with a damping adjuster to increase or decrease shock damping. The damping adjustment must be set to correspond to front fork air pressure, and vehicle load (see **Table 4**). To adjust, turn the damping adjuster (**Figure 6**) by hand to the desired setting. Four damping positions are available. The standard setting is No. 1 (minimum damping). No. 4 provides maximum damping.

> *WARNING*
> *Always adjust the damping on each shock to the same number (position) or the bike's handling will be unstable.*

> *NOTE*
> *When adjusting the damping, make sure the adjuster is placed in a click position. If not, the damping will automatically be set to the maximum position (No. 4).*

Spring Adjustment (1984-on)

Spring preload on these models can be adjusted by rotating the cam ring at the base of the spring—clockwise to increase preload and counterclockwise to decrease it. See **Figure 7** (XV700) or **Figure 8** (XV1000 and XV1100).

Both cams must be indexed on the same detent.

Table 1 RECOMMENDED SUSPENSION SETTINGS (XV750; 1983 XV920)

Load	Front fork air pressure psi (kg/cm²)	Rear shock absorber air pressure psi (kg/cm²)	Damper adjuster
Rider	5-7 (0.4-0.8)	14-28 (1-2)	1-3
Rider plus passenger	5-7 (0.4-0.8)	43-57 (3-4)	3, 4
Rider plus passenger and/or luggage	5-7 (0.4-0.8)	43-57 (3-4)	4, 5
Maximum vehicle load limit	5.7-17 (0.8-1.2)	57 (4.0)	6

Table 2 RECOMMENDED SUSPENSION SETTINGS (XV920RH, RJ)

Load	Front fork air pressure psi (kg/cm²)	Rear shock absorber air pressure psi (kg/cm²)	Damper adjuster
Rider	5-7 (0.4-0.8)	14-28 (1-2)	1, 2
Rider plus passenger	5-7 (0.4-0.8)	28-42 (2-3)	2, 3
Rider plus passenger and/or luggage	8-14 (0.6-1.0)	42-57 (3-4)	4, 5
Maximum vehicle load limit	11-17 (0.8-1.2)	57 (4.0)	5, 6

Table 3 RECOMMENDED SUSPENSION SETTINGS (1982 XV920 SHAFT DRIVE)

Load	Front fork air pressure psi (kg/cm²)	Damper adjuster	Rear shock absorber air pressure psi (kg/cm²)	Damper adjuster
Rider	5-7 (0.4-0.8)	1	14-28 (1-2)	1, 2, 3
Rider plus passenger	5-7 (0.4-0.8)	2	28-43 (2-3)	3, 4
Rider plus passenger and/or luggage	5-7 (0.4-0.8)	3	42-57 (3-4)	4, 5
Maximum vehicle load limit	11-17 (0.8-1.2)	4	57 (4.0)	6

Table 4 RECOMMENDED SUSPENSION SETTINGS (XV1000)

Load	Front fork air pressure psi (kg/cm²)	Rear shock absorber damper adjuster
Rider	5-7 (0.4-0.8)	1
Rider plus passenger	5-7 (0.4-0.8)	2
Rider plus passenger and/or luggage	5-7 (0.4-0.8)	3
Maximum vehicle load limit	11-17 (0.8-1.2)	4

11

Table 5 RECOMMENDED SUSPENSION SETTINGS (XV1100)

Load	Front fork air pressure psi (Kg/cm²)	Rear shock absorber damper adjuster	Spring seat
Rider	5-7 (0.4-0.8)	1-2	1-2
Rider plus passenger	5-7 (0.4-0.8)	1-2	2-3
Rider plus passenger and/or luggage	5-7 (0.4-0.8)	3-4	3-5
Maximum vehicle load limit	11-17 (0.8-1.2)	4	5

Table 6 SUSPENSION AIR PRESSURE

	Air pressure
Front fork	
XV750, XV920 (shaft drive), XV1000, XV1100	
Standard	5.7 psi (0.4 kg/cm^2)
Minimum	0
Maximum	17 psi (1.2 kg/cm^2)
XV920 (chain drive)	
Standard	5.7 psi (0.4 kg/cm^2)
Minimum	0
Maximum	36 psi (2.5 kg/cm^2)
Rear shock	
All 1981-1983 models	
Standard	14 psi (1.0 kg/cm^2)
Minimum	7 psi (0.5 kg/cm^2)
Maximum	57 psi (4.0 kg/cm^2)

INDEX

12

WIRING DIAGRAMS

1981-1983 XV750 AND 1983 XV920

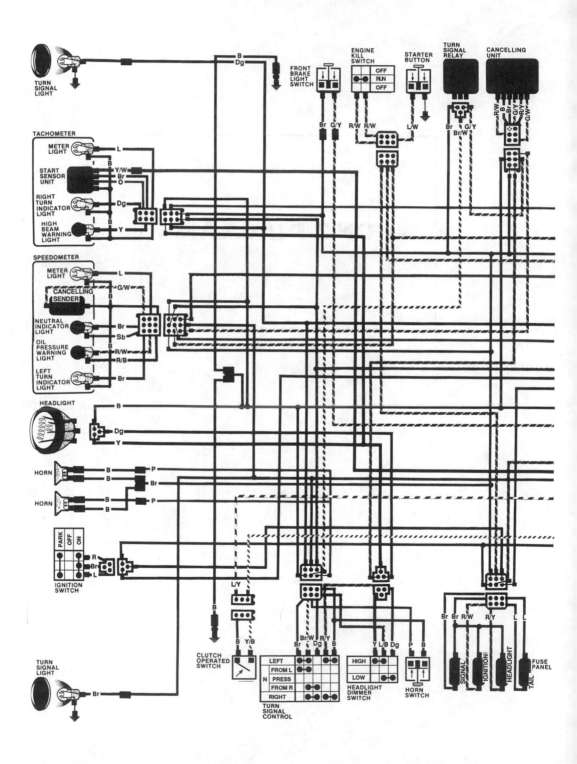

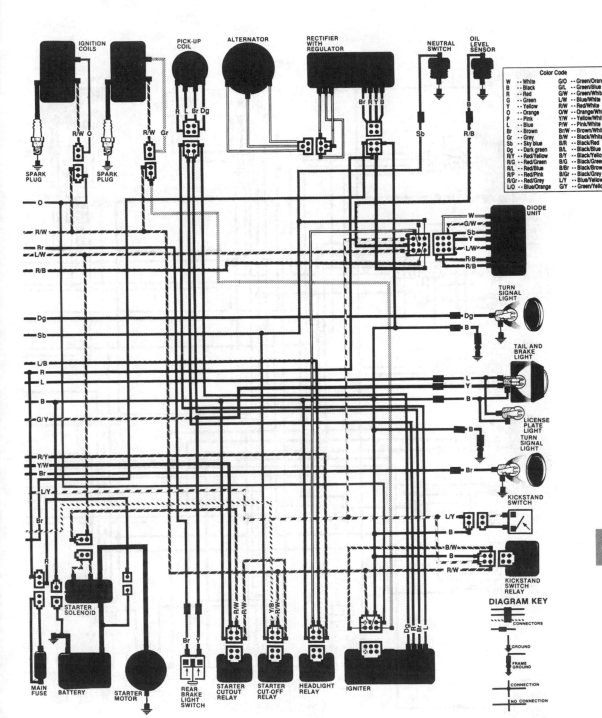

Color Code

W	-- White	G/O	-- Green/Orange
B	-- Black	G/L	-- Green/Blue
R	-- Red	G/W	-- Green/White
G	-- Green	L/W	-- Blue/White
Y	-- Yellow	R/W	-- Red/White
O	-- Orange	O/W	-- Orange/White
P	-- Pink	Y/W	-- Yellow/White
L	-- Blue	P/W	-- Pink/White
Br	-- Brown	Br/W	-- Brown/White
Gr	-- Grey	B/W	-- Black/White
Sb	-- Sky blue	B/R	-- Black/Red
Dg	-- Dark green	B/L	-- Black/Blue
R/Y	-- Red/Yellow	B/Y	-- Black/Yellow
R/G	-- Red/Green	B/G	-- Black/Green
R/L	-- Red/Blue	B/Br	-- Black/Brown
R/P	-- Red/Pink	B/Gr	-- Black/Grey
R/Gr	-- Red/Grey	L/Y	-- Blue/Yellow
L/O	-- Blue/Orange	G/Y	-- Green/Yellow

IGNITION COILS

PICK-UP COIL

ALTERNATOR

RECTIFIER WITH REGULATOR

NEUTRAL SWITCH

OIL LEVEL SENSOR

SPARK PLUG

SPARK PLUG

DIODE UNIT

TURN SIGNAL LIGHT

TAIL AND BRAKE LIGHT

LICENSE PLATE LIGHT

TURN SIGNAL LIGHT

KICKSTAND SWITCH

KICKSTAND SWITCH RELAY

DIAGRAM KEY

CONNECTORS

GROUND

FRAME GROUND

CONNECTION

NO CONNECTION

MAIN FUSE

BATTERY

STARTER MOTOR

STARTER SOLENOID

REAR BRAKE LIGHT SWITCH

STARTER CUTOUT RELAY

STARTER CUT-OFF RELAY

HEADLIGHT RELAY

IGNITER

13

1981-1982 XV920 CHAIN DRIVE

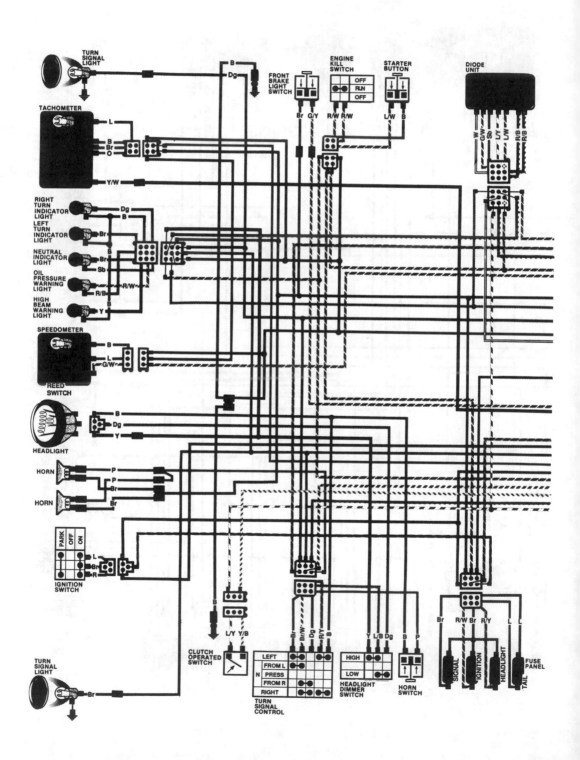

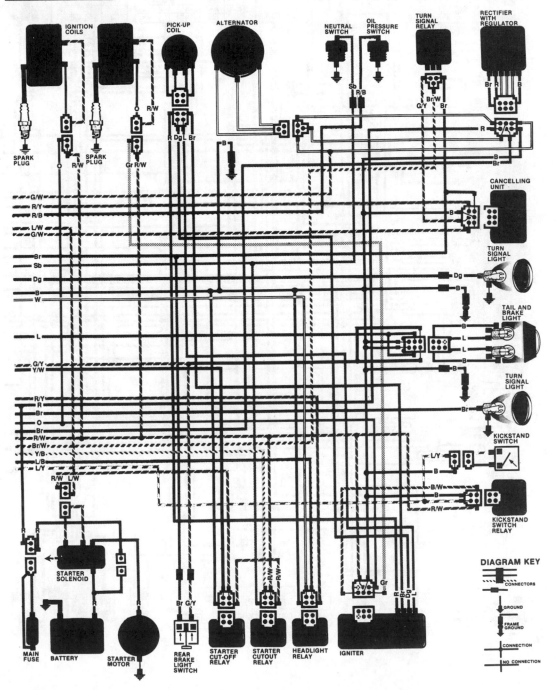

1982 XV920 SHAFT DRIVE

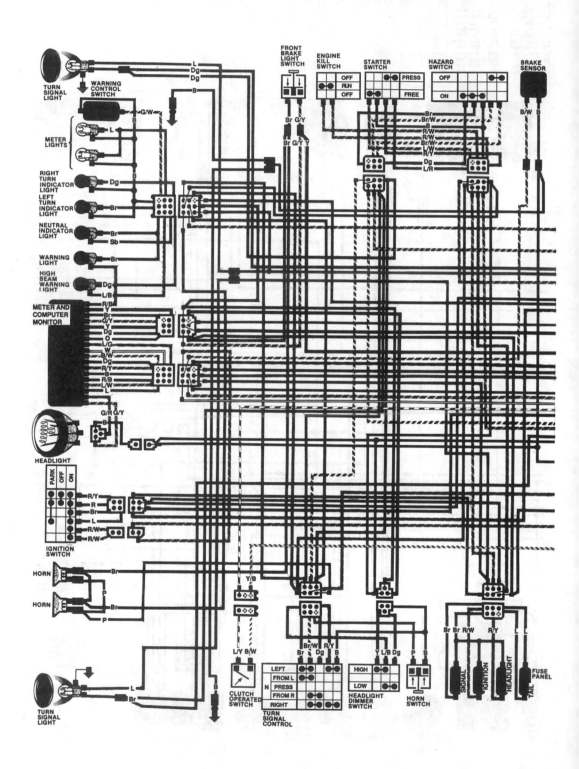

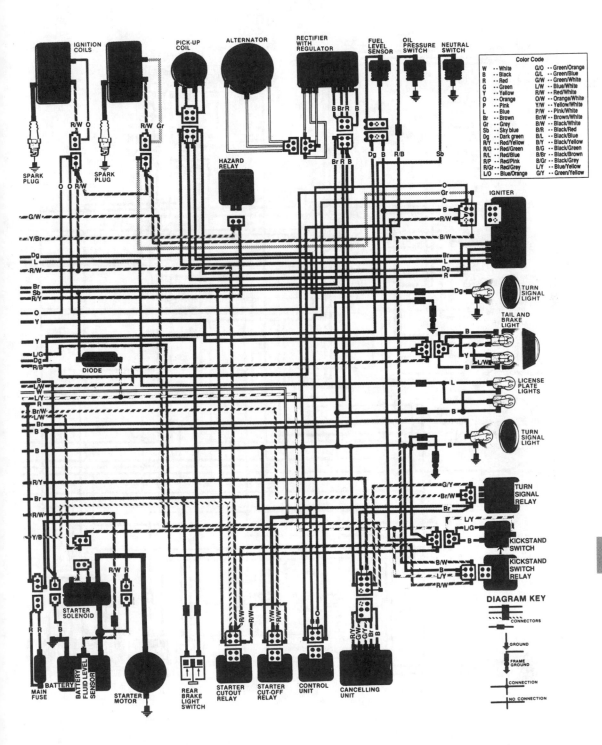

1984-1985 XV700

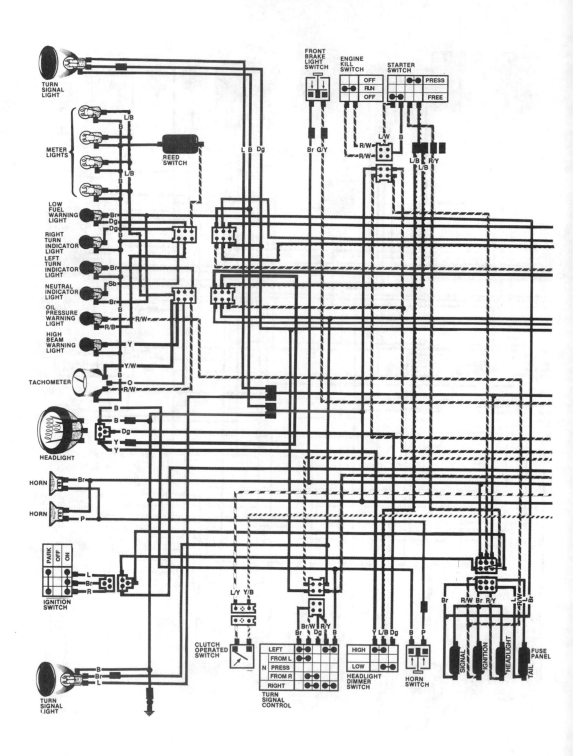

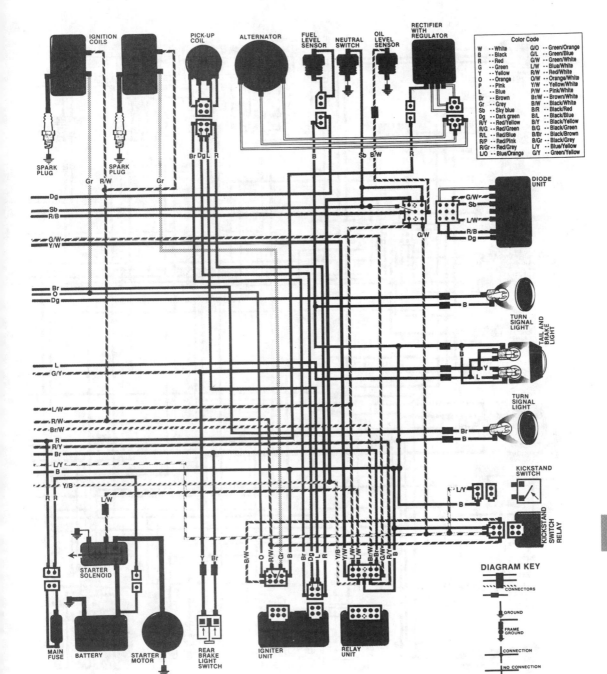

1984-1985 XV1000

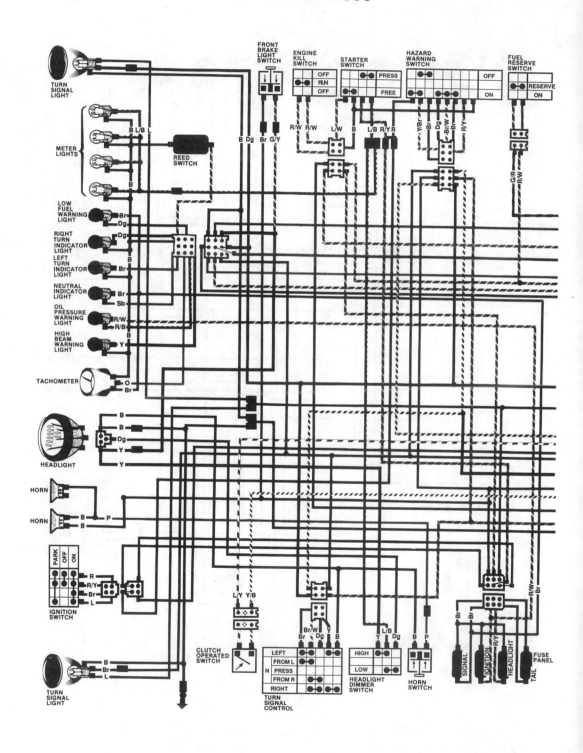

Color Code

W	-- White	G/O	-- Green/Orange
B	-- Black	G/L	-- Green/Blue
R	-- Red	G/W	-- Green/White
G	-- Green	L/W	-- Blue/White
Y	-- Yellow	R/W	-- Red/White
O	-- Orange	O/W	-- Orange/White
P	-- Pink	Y/W	-- Yellow/White
L	-- Blue	P/W	-- Pink/White
Br	-- Brown	Br/W	-- Brown/White
Gr	-- Grey	B/W	-- Black/White
Sb	-- Sky blue	B/R	-- Black/Red
Dg	-- Dark green	B/L	-- Black/Blue
R/Y	-- Red/Yellow	B/Y	-- Black/Yellow
R/G	-- Red/Green	B/G	-- Black/Green
R/L	-- Red/Blue	B/Br	-- Black/Brown
R/P	-- Red/Pink	B/Gr	-- Black/Grey
R/Gr	-- Red/Grey	L/Y	-- Blue/Yellow
L/O	-- Blue/Orange	G/Y	-- Green/Yellow

IGNITION COILS

PICK-UP COIL

ALTERNATOR

FUEL LEVEL SENSOR

NEUTRAL SWITCH

OIL LEVEL SENSOR

RECTIFIER WITH REGULATOR

FUEL PUMP

SPARK PLUG

SPARK PLUG

Gr R/W   BrDgL   R

FUEL PUMP CONTROL UNIT

DIODE UNIT

Q/R

Sb

L/W

R/B

O

R/W

G/W

Dg

TURN SIGNAL LIGHT

TAIL AND BRAKE LIGHT

Dg

L

TURN SIGNAL LIGHT

Y/Br

L/Y

R

Br

Y/W

Br

Y/B

B

R/Y

B

KICKSTAND SWITCH

KICKSTAND SWITCH RELAY

R/W

STARTER SOLENOID

MAIN FUSE

BATTERY

STARTER MOTOR

REAR BRAKE LIGHT SWITCH

PRESSURE SENSOR

STARTER RELAY

IGNITER UNIT

RELAY UNIT

DIAGRAM KEY

CONNECTORS

GROUND

FRAME GROUND

CONNECTION

NO CONNECTION

13

1986-1987 XV700

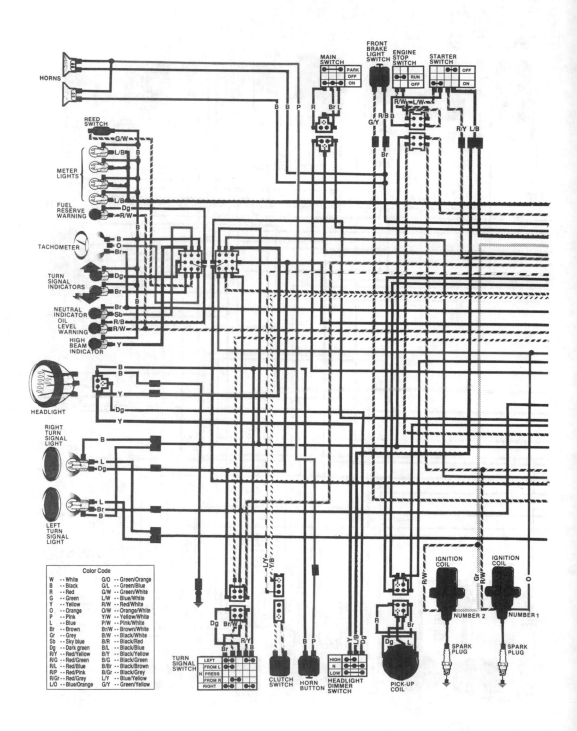

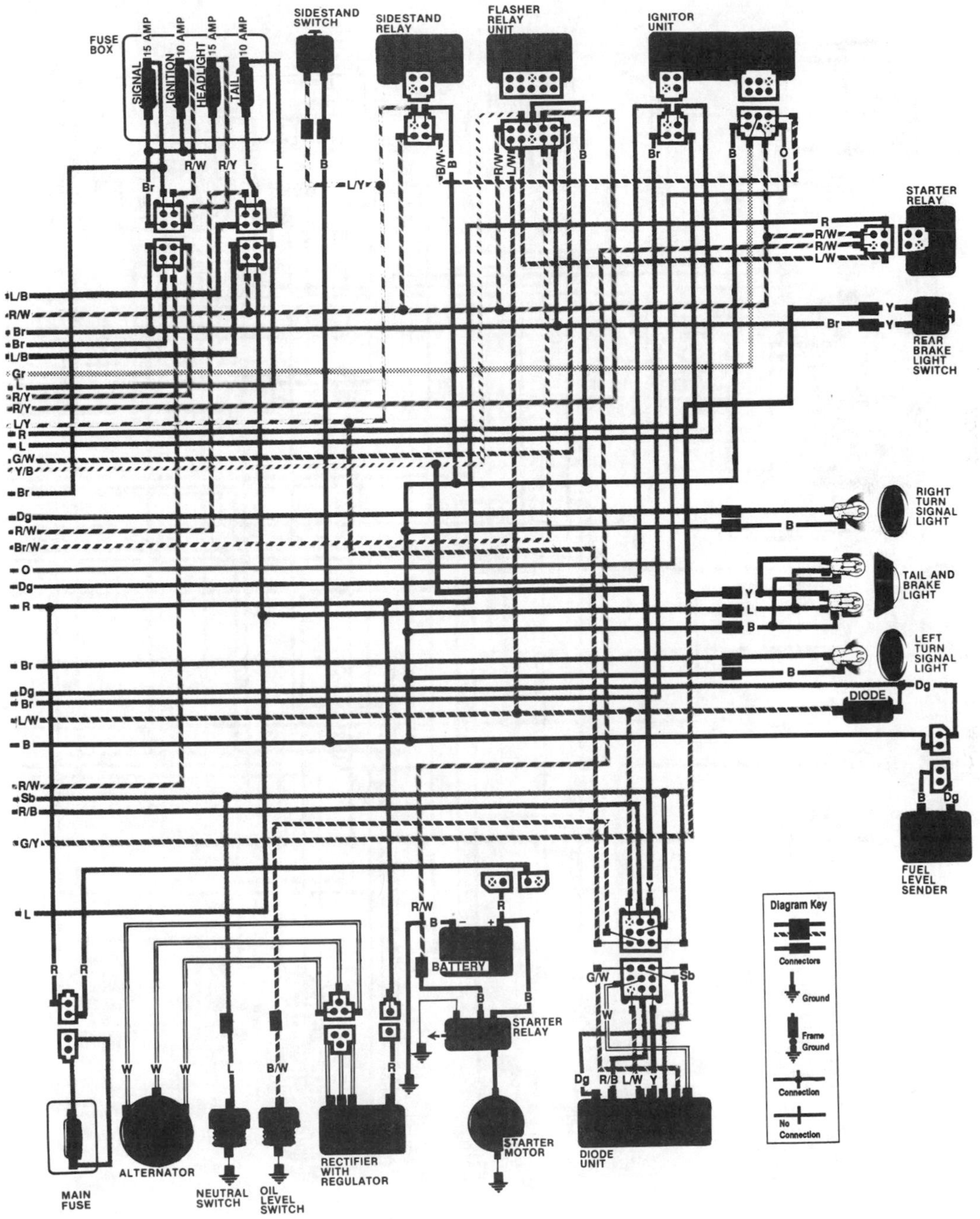
FUSE BOX
SIGNAL 15 AMP
IGNITION 10 AMP
HEADLIGHT 15 AMP
TAIL 10 AMP
SIDESTAND SWITCH
SIDESTAND RELAY
FLASHER RELAY UNIT
IGNITOR UNIT
STARTER RELAY
REAR BRAKE LIGHT SWITCH
RIGHT TURN SIGNAL LIGHT
TAIL AND BRAKE LIGHT
LEFT TURN SIGNAL LIGHT
DIODE
FUEL LEVEL SENDER
BATTERY
STARTER RELAY
STARTER MOTOR
DIODE UNIT
MAIN FUSE
ALTERNATOR
NEUTRAL SWITCH
OIL LEVEL SWITCH
RECTIFIER WITH REGULATOR
Diagram Key
Connectors
Ground
Frame Ground
Connection
No Connection

1986-1987 XV1100

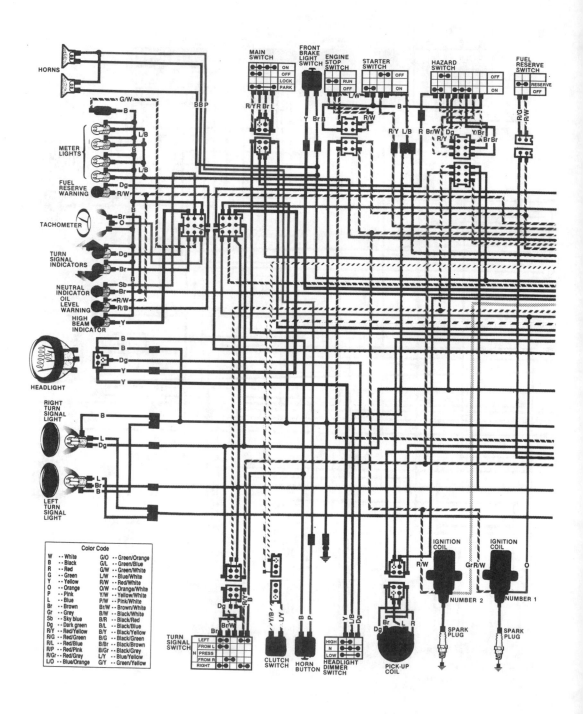

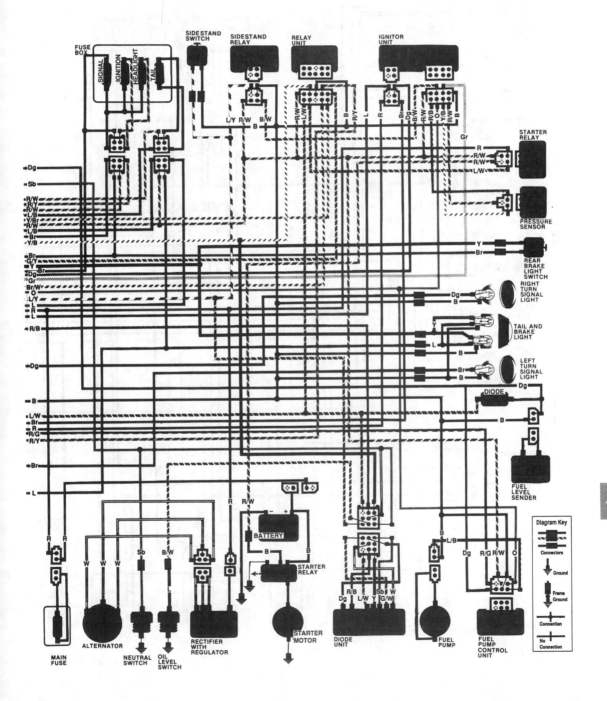

1988-1990 XV750

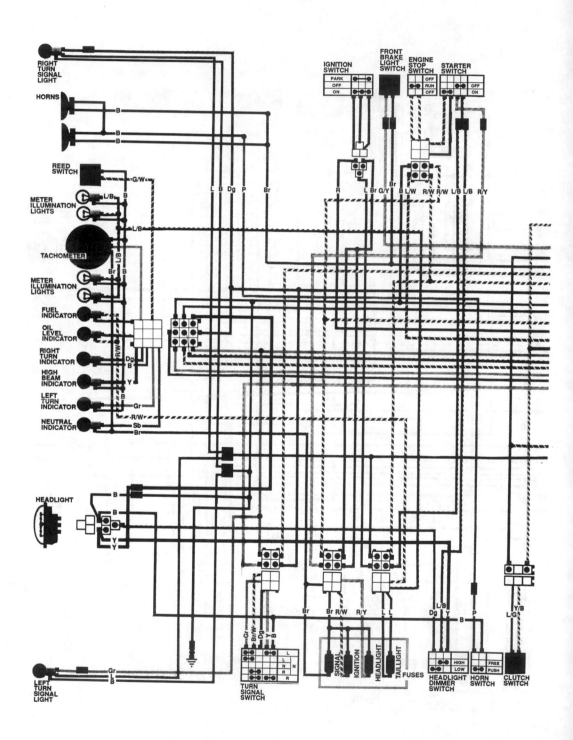

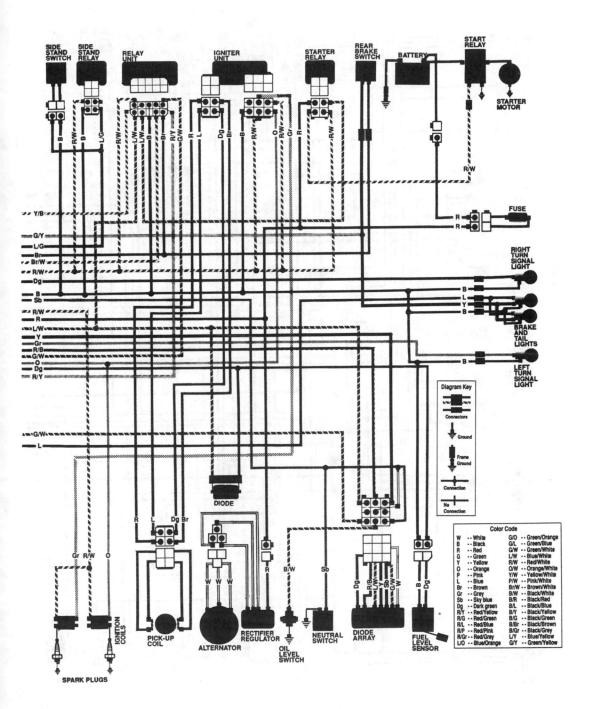

13

1988-1990 XV1100

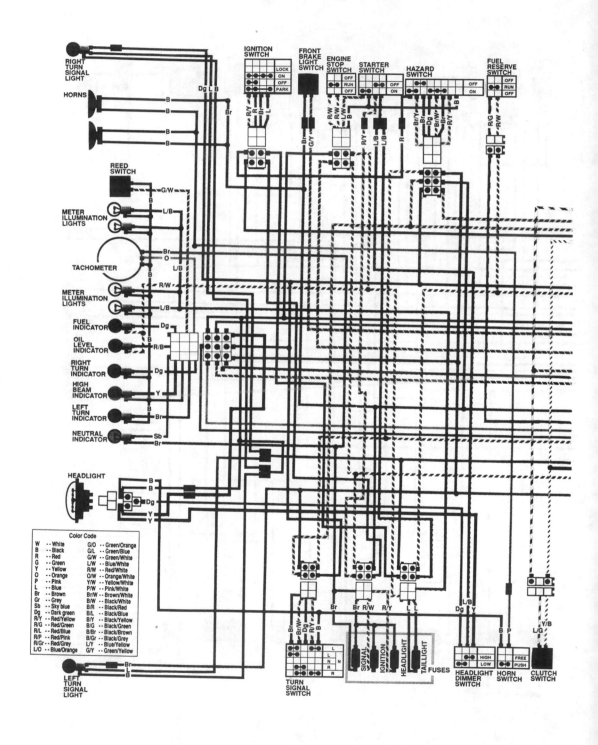

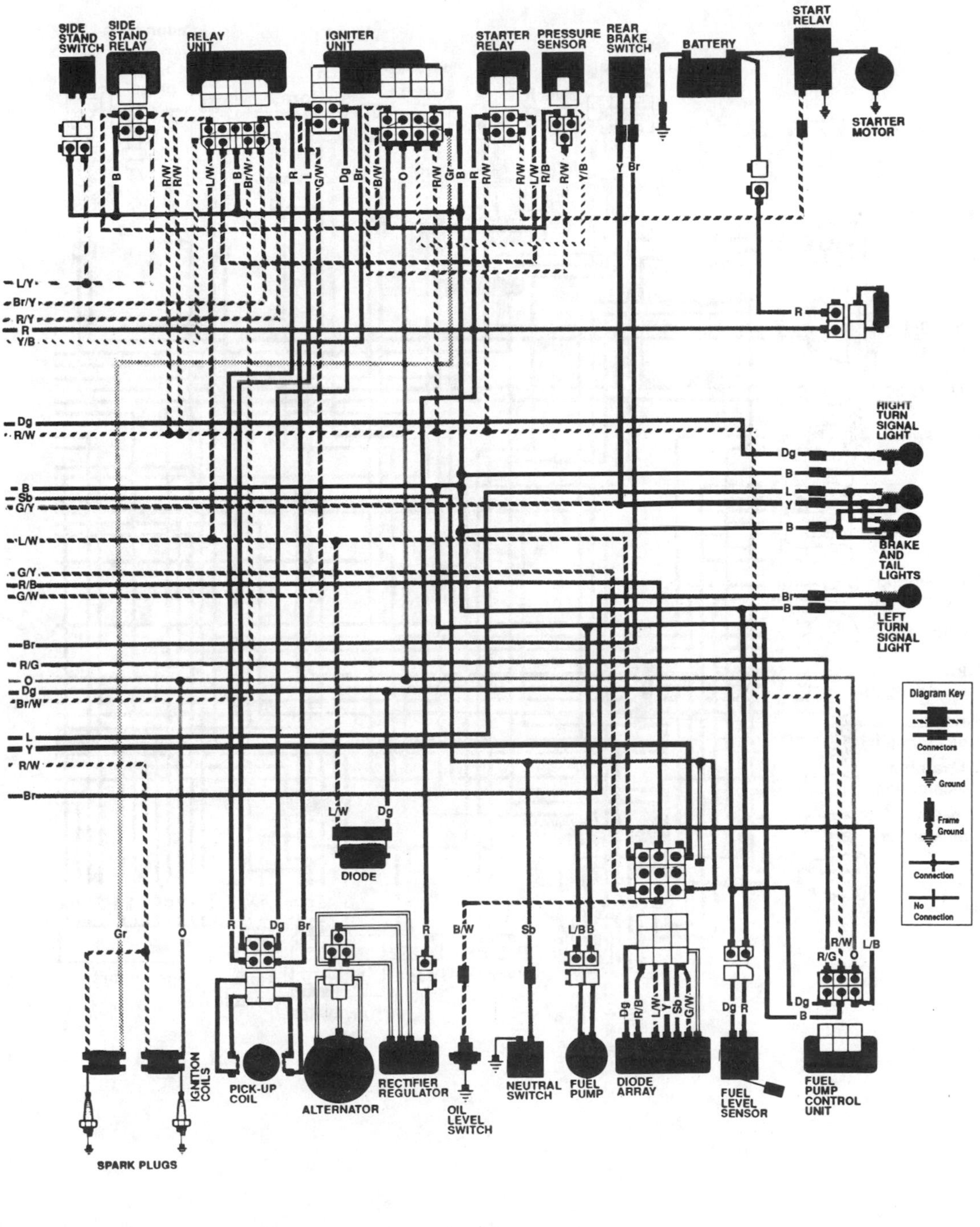

SIDE STAND SWITCH

SIDE STAND RELAY

RELAY UNIT

IGNITER UNIT

STARTER RELAY

PRESSURE SENSOR

REAR BRAKE SWITCH

BATTERY

START RELAY

STARTER MOTOR

RIGHT TURN SIGNAL LIGHT

BRAKE AND TAIL LIGHTS

LEFT TURN SIGNAL LIGHT

Diagram Key

Connectors

Ground

Frame Ground

Connection

No Connection

13

DIODE

SPARK PLUGS

IGNITION COILS

PICK-UP COIL

ALTERNATOR

RECTIFIER REGULATOR

OIL LEVEL SWITCH

NEUTRAL SWITCH

FUEL PUMP

DIODE ARRAY

FUEL LEVEL SENSOR

FUEL PUMP CONTROL UNIT

XV1100 (1992-ON U.K.)

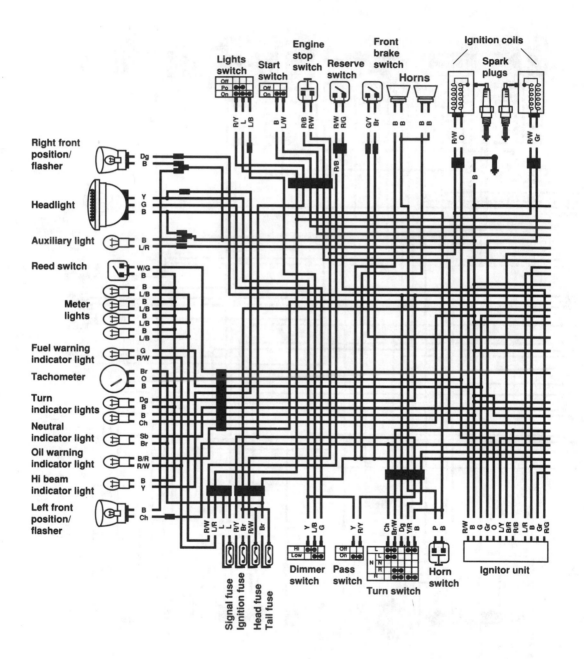

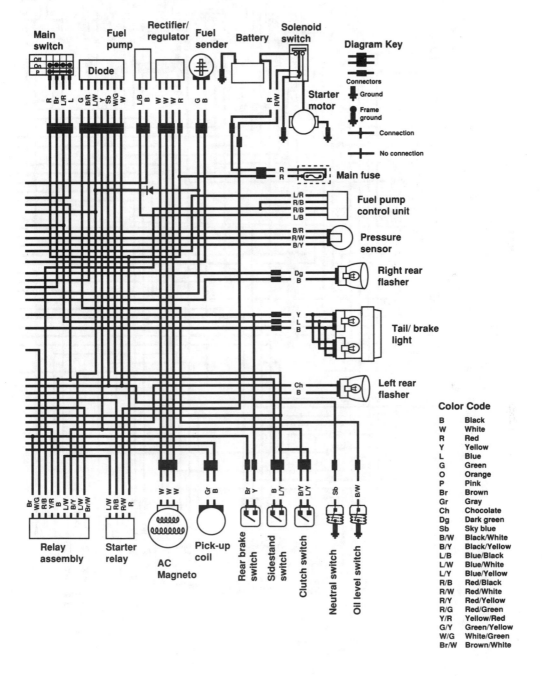

Diagram Key

Connectors

Ground

Frame ground

Connection

No connection

Color Code

B	Black
W	White
R	Red
Y	Yellow
L	Blue
G	Green
O	Orange
P	Pink
Br	Brown
Gr	Gray
Ch	Chocolate
Dg	Dark green
Sb	Sky blue
B/W	Black/White
B/Y	Black/Yellow
L/B	Blue/Black
L/W	Blue/White
L/Y	Blue/Yellow
R/B	Red/Black
R/W	Red/White
R/Y	Red/Yellow
R/G	Red/Green
Y/R	Yellow/Red
G/Y	Green/Yellow
W/G	White/Green
Br/W	Brown/White

13

1991-ON XV750

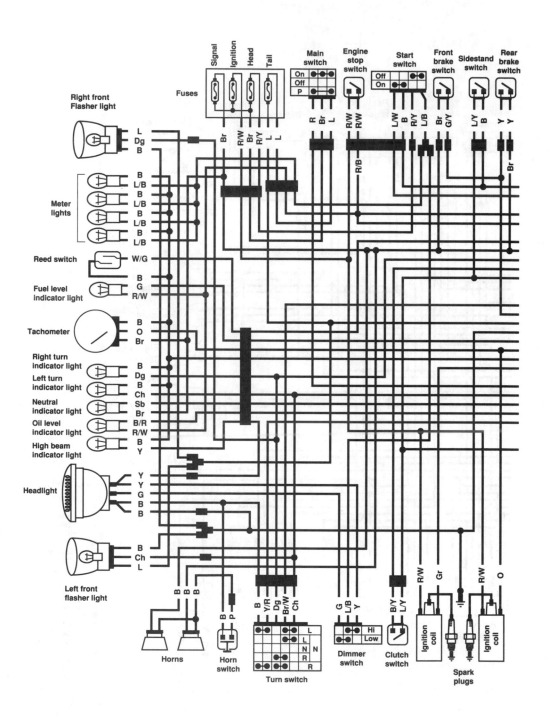

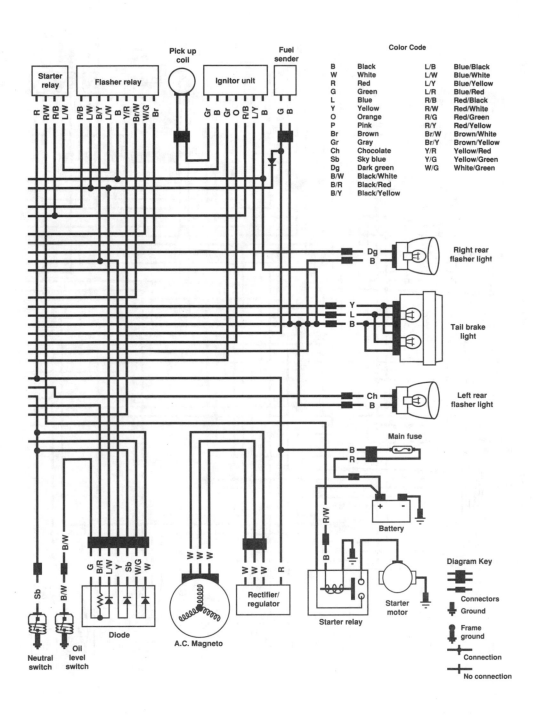

Pick up coil

Fuel sender

Starter relay

Flasher relay

Ignitor unit

Color Code

B	Black	L/B	Blue/Black
W	White	L/W	Blue/White
R	Red	L/Y	Blue/Yellow
G	Green	L/R	Blue/Red
L	Blue	R/B	Red/Black
Y	Yellow	R/W	Red/White
O	Orange	R/G	Red/Green
P	Pink	R/Y	Red/Yellow
Br	Brown	Br/W	Brown/White
Gr	Gray	Br/Y	Brown/Yellow
Ch	Chocolate	Y/R	Yellow/Red
Sb	Sky blue	Y/G	Yellow/Green
Dg	Dark green	W/G	White/Green
B/W	Black/White		
B/R	Black/Red		
B/Y	Black/Yellow		

Right rear flasher light

Tail brake light

Left rear flasher light

Main fuse

Battery

Starter relay

Starter motor

Diagram Key

Connectors
Ground
Frame ground
Connection
No connection

Diode

A.C. Magneto

Rectifier/ regulator

Neutral switch

Oil level switch

13

1991-ON XV1100

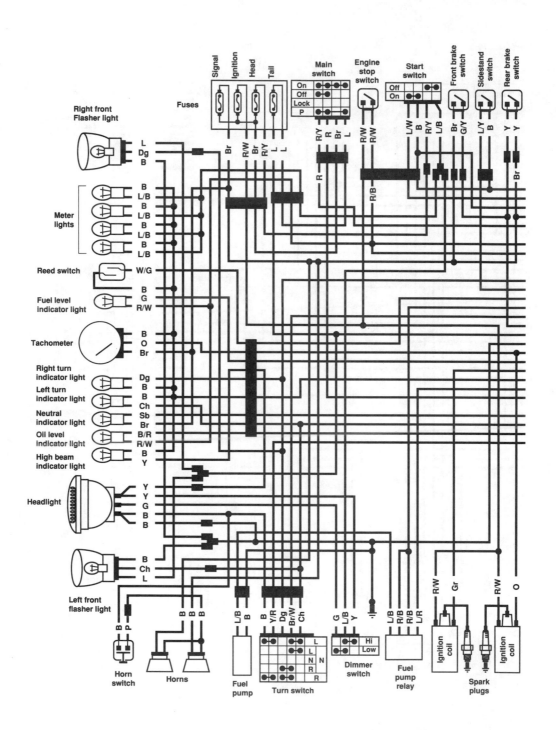

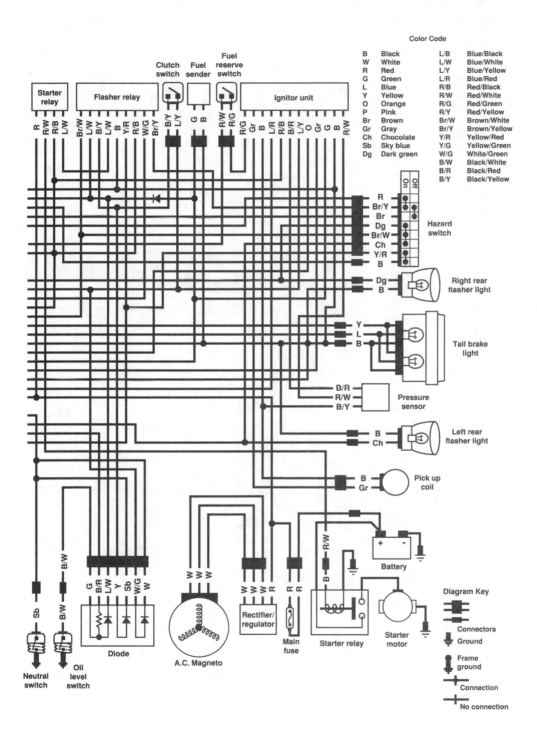

CLYMER™

YAMAHA

XV700-1100 Virago • 1981-1997

▶ ### XV535 Virago • 1987-1997

CONTENTS

QUICK REFERENCE DATA
XV535

TIRE INFLATION PRESSURE (COLD)

Load	psi (kg/cm^2)
Up to 198 lb. (90 kg)	
Front	28 (2.0)
Rear	32 (2.3)
198-max. lb. (90-max kg)*	
Front	28 (2.0)
Rear	36 (2.5)
High-speed riding	
Front	28 (2.0)
Rear	36 (2.5)

* Maximum load: 49-state 507 lb. (230 kg.), Calif. 505 lb. (229 kg.), U.K. 501 lb. (227 kg.).

RECOMMENDED LUBRICANTS

Item	Type
Engine oil	
40° F (5° C) and above	Yamalube 4 or SAE 20W/40
60° F (15° C) and below	Yamalube 4 or SAE 10W/30
Brake fluid	DOT 3
Battery refilling	Distilled water
Fork oil	SAE 10W
Control cables and pivot points	SAE 10W/30 motor oil
Final drive unit	Hypoid gear oil SAE 80 GL-4 or SAE 80W/90

APPROXIMATE REFILL CAPACITIES

Item	Quantity
Engine oil	
With filter change	3.0 U.S. qt. (2.8 L, 2.5 Imp. qt.)
Without filter change	2.7 U.S. qt. (2.6 L, 2.3 Imp. qt.)
Engine rebuild	3.4 U.S. qt. (3.2 L, 2.8 Imp. qt.)
Front forks	7.71 U.S. oz. (228 cc, 8.03 Imp. oz.)
Final gear case	0.20 U.S qt. (0.19 L, 0.17 Imp. qt.)

TUNE-UP SPECIFICATIONS

Ignition timing	Fixed
Valve clearance (cold)	
Intake	0.003-0.005 in. (0.07-0.12 mm)
Exhaust	0.005-0.007 in. (0.12-0.17 mm)
Spark plug	
Type	
U.S.	NGK BP7ES, ND W22EP-U
U.K.	NGK BPR7ES, ND W22EPR-U
Gap	0.028-0.031 in. (0.7-0.8 mm)
Idle speed	1,150-1,250 rpm
Compression pressure (cold at sea level)	
Standard	156 psi (11 kg/cm^2, 1,100 kPa)
Minimum	142 psi (10 kg/cm^2, 1,000 kPa)
Maximum	171 psi (12 kg/cm^2, 1,200 kPa)

REPLACEMENT BULBS

Item	Voltage/Wattage
Headlight	12V 60W/55W
Tail/brakelight	
U.S.	12V 8W/27W
U.K.	12V 5W/21W
Front running light (U.S.)	12V 8W/27W
Auxiliary light (U.K.)	12V 4W
Front flasher	
U.S.	12V 8W/27W
U.K.	12V 21W
Rear flasher	
U.S.	12V 27W
U.K.	12V 21W
Meter light	12V 3.4W
Indicator lights	
High beam	12V 1.7W
All others	12V 3.4W

FUSES

	Amperage
Main	20A
Headlight	10A
Signal	10A
Ignition	10A
Spare	20A & 10A

INTRODUCTION

This portion of this detailed and comprehensive manual covers the U.S. and the U.K. models of the Yamaha XV535 V-twins from 1987-on.

The expert text gives complete information on maintenance, tune-up, repair and overhaul. Hundreds of photos and drawings guide you through every step. The book includes all you will need to know to keep your Yamaha running right.

A shop manual is a reference. You want to be able to find information fast. As in all Clymer books, this one is designed with you in mind. All chapters are thumb tabbed. Important items are extensively indexed at the rear of the book. All procedures, tables, photos, etc., in this manual are for the reader who may be working on the bike for the first time or using this manual for the first time. All the most frequently used specifications and capacities are summarized in the *Quick Reference Data* pages at the front of the manual.

Keep the book handy in your tool box. It will help you better understand how your bike runs, lower repair costs and generally improve your satisfaction with the Yamaha.

CHAPTER ONE

GENERAL INFORMATION

This detailed, comprehensive manual covers the U.S and the U.K. models of the Yamaha XV535 Virago V-twins from 1987-on. **Table 1** lists engine and chassis numbers for models covered in this manual and **Table 2** lists the general specifications.

Table 1 and **Table 2** are found at the end of the chapter.

> *NOTE*
> *This chapter covers all procedures unique to the XV535 Virago V-twins. If a specific procedure is not included in this chapter, refer to Chapter One at the front of this manual for service procedures.*

PARTS REPLACEMENT

Yamaha makes frequent changes during a model year, some minor, some relatively major. When you

order parts from the dealer or other parts distributor, always order by frame and engine numbers. The frame serial number and vehicle identification number (VIN) is stamped on the right-hand side of the steering stem (**Figure 1**). The engine number is stamped on a raised pad on the right-hand side of the crankcase (**Figure 2**) by the rear cylinder. The carburetor number is on the left-hand side of the No. 1 carburetor body just below the top cover.

Write the numbers down and carry them with you. Compare new parts to old before purchasing them. If they are not alike, have the parts manager explain the difference to you. **Table 1** lists engine and frame serial numbers for the models covered in this manual.

> *NOTE*
> *If your Yamaha was purchased second-hand and you are not sure of its model*

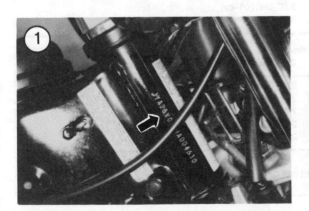

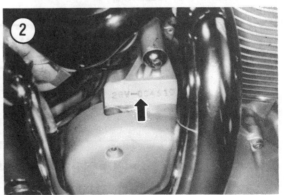

year, use the bike's engine serial number and vehicle identification number (VIN) and the information listed in **Table 1**. Read your bike's engine serial number. Then compare the number with the engine and serial numbers listed in **Table 1**. If your bike's serial number is listed in **Table 1**, cross-reference the number with the adjacent model number and year.

Table 1 ENGINE SERIAL NUMBERS

Model Number and Year	U.S. Models Engine Serial No. Start to End
1987	
XV535T	2GV-000101 to *
XV535TC	2JU-000101 to *
1988	
XV535U	2GV-038101 to *
XV535UC	3BG-000101 to *
1989	
XV535W	2UJ-020101 to *
XV535WC	3BG-002101 to *
1990 **	
XV535A	3JC-007101 to *
XV535AC	3JC-002101 to *
1993	
XV535E	3JC-014101 to *
XV535EC	3JC-020101 to *
1994	
XV535F	3JC-021101*
XV535FC	3JC-025101*
XV535SF	3JC-028101*
XV535SFC	3JC-033101*
1995	
XV535G	3JC-036101*
XV535GC	3JC-039101*
XV535SG	3JC-041101*
XV535SGC	3JC-047101*
1996	
XV535H 3JCS (except California)	3JC-050101-on
XV535HC 3JCT (California)	3JC-053101-on
XV535SH 3JCN (except California)	3JC-055101-on
XV535SHC 3JCP (California)	3JC-060101-on
1997	N/A

Model Number and Year	U.K. Models Engine Serial No. Start to End
1988	2YL-003101 to *
1989	2YL-005101 to *
1990	2YL-0022101 to *
1991	2YL-031101 to *
1992-1997	2YL-*

* Not specified.
** The XV535 was not available in the U.S. in 1991 and 1992.

Table 2 GENERAL SPECIFICATIONS

Engine type	Air-cooled, 4-stroke, SOHC, V-twin
Bore and stroke	2.992 × 2.323 in. (76 × 59 mm)
Displacement	32.64 cu. in. (535 cc)
Compression ratio	9:1
Ignition	Transistor control ignition (TCI)
Carburetion	2 Mikuni carburetors
Air filter	Dry type element
Fuel type	Gasoline: regular unleaded
Fuel tank capacity	
1987-1989 U.S. models and 1988 U. K. models	
Total	2.3 U.S. gal. (8.6 L, 1.9 Imp. gal.)
Reserve	0.5 U.S. gal. (2.0 L, 0.4 Imp. gal.)
1990-on U.S. models and 1989-on U. K. models	
Total	3.6 U.S. gal. (13.5 L, 3.0 Imp. gal.)
Reserve	0.7 U.S. gal. (2.5 L, 0.5 Imp. gal.)
Clutch	Wet, multi-plate
Transmission	5 speeds, constant mesh
Transmission ratios	
1st	2.714
2nd	1.900
3rd	1.458
4th	1.166
5th	0.966
Final reduction ratio	3.071
Starting system	Electric starter only
Battery	12 volt/12 amp hour
Charging system	AC alternator
Chassis dimensions	
Overall length	87.0 in. (2,210 mm)
Overall width	32.1 in. (815 mm)
Overall height	43.3 in. (1,100 mm)
Seat height	27.6 in. (700 mm)
Wheelbase	59.5 in. (1,511 mm)
Ground clearance	5.7 in. (145 mm)
Basic weight	
U.S. models	
1987-1989	
49-state	408 lb. (185 kg)
California	410 lb. (186 kg)
1990-on	
49-state	430 lb. (195 kg)
California	432 lb. (196 kg)
U.K. models	415 lb. (188 kg)
Steering head angle	31°
Trail	4.8 in. (122 mm)
Front suspension	
Telescopic fork	
Travel	5.9 in. (150 mm)
Rear suspension	Dual shock
Travel	3.3 in. (85 mm)
Front tire	3.00S-19 4PR
Rear tire	
1987-1989	140/90-15 70S
1990-on	140/90-15M/C 70S

CHAPTER TWO

TROUBLESHOOTING

Diagnosing mechanical problems is relatively simple if you use orderly procedures and keep a few basic principles in mind. The first step in any troubleshooting procedure is to define the symptoms as closely as possible and then localize the problem. Subsequent steps involve testing and analyzing those areas which could cause the symptoms. A haphazard approach may eventually solve the problem, but it can be very costly in terms of wasted time and unnecessary parts replacement.

> *NOTE*
> *This chapter covers all procedures unique to the XV535 Virago V-twins. If a specific procedure is not included in this chapter, refer to Chapter Two at the front of this manual for service procedures.*

EMERGENCY TROUBLESHOOTING

When the vehicle is difficult to start, or won't start at all, it does not help to wear down the battery and overheat the starter. Check for obvious problems even before getting out your tools. Go down the following list step-by-step. Do each one. If the vehicle still will not start, refer to the appropriate troubleshooting procedures which follow in this chapter.

1. Is there fuel in the tank? On models without a sub-fuel tank, raise the seat and open the main fuel tank filler cap (**Figure 1**). On models with a sub-fuel tank, open the sub-fuel tank filler cap (**Figure 2**) and rock the bike from side to side. Listen for fuel sloshing around.

> *WARNING*
> *Do not use an open flame to check in the tank. A serious explosion is certain to result.*

2. On models so equipped, is the fuel shutoff valve in the ON position?

3. Make sure the fuel reserve switch (A, **Figure 3**) is in the RES position. If there is any doubt about the

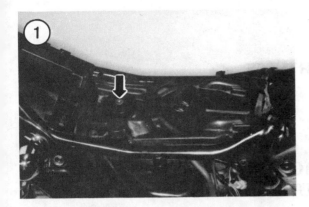

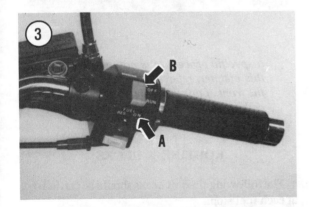

fuel pump operation, refer to Chapter Seven in this section of the manual.

4. Make sure the engine kill switch (B, **Figure 3**) is not stuck in the OFF position or that the wire is not broken and shorting out.

5. Are the spark plug wires (**Figure 4**) on tight? Remove the engine covers and push both on and slightly rotate them to clean the electrical connection between the plugs and the connectors.

6. Is the choke lever (**Figure 5**) in the correct position? Push the lever down for a cold engine and up for a warm engine.

ENGINE STARTING

Follow the *Engine Starting* procedure in Chapter Two in front of this manual noting that the XV535 is equipped with an Ignitor Unit and not a CDI unit.

ENGINE PERFORMANCE

Follow the *Engine Performance* procedure in Chapter Two in front of this manual noting that the XV535 is equipped with a fuel filter.

IGNITION SYSTEM

All XV535 models are equipped with the Transistor Control Ignition system. This system consists of both a pickup unit and an ignitor unit and uses no breaker points or other moving parts. It is non-adjustable, and if any problems arise that you believe to be related to the ignition system, refer to Chapter Seven for ignition system troubleshooting procedures.

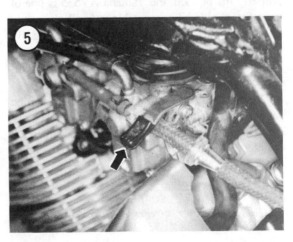

CHAPTER THREE

PERIODIC LUBRICATION, MAINTENANCE AND TUNE-UP

Your bike can be cared for by two methods: preventive and corrective maintenance. Because a motorcycle is subjected to tremendous heat, stress and vibration—even in normal use—preventive maintenance prevents costly and unexpected corrective maintenance. When neglected, any bike becomes unreliable and actually dangerous to ride. When properly maintained, the Yamaha XV535 is one of the most reliable bikes available and will give many miles and years of dependable and safe riding. By maintaining a routine service schedule as described in this chapter, costly mechanical problems and unexpected breakdowns can be prevented.

The procedures presented in this chapter can be easily performed by anyone with average mechanical skills. **Table 1** presents a factory recommended maintenance schedule. **Tables 1-5** are at the end of the chapter.

NOTE
This chapter covers all procedures unique to the XV535 Virago V-twins. If
a specific procedure is not included in this chapter, refer to Chapter Three at the front of this manual for service procedures.

ROUTINE CHECKS

The following simple checks should be carried out at each fuel stop.

Engine Oil Level

Refer to *Engine Oil Level Check* under *Periodic Lubrication* in this chapter.

Tire Pressure

Tire pressure must be checked with the tires cold. Correct tire pressure depends a lot on the load you are carrying. See **Table 2**.

Battery

Remove the frame right-hand side cover and check the battery electrolyte level. The level must be between the upper and lower level marks on the case (**Figure 1**).

For complete details see *Battery Removal/Installation and Electrolyte Level Check* in this chapter.

MAINTENANCE INTERVALS

The services and intervals shown in **Table 1** are recommended by the factory. Strict adherence to these recommendations will insure long life from

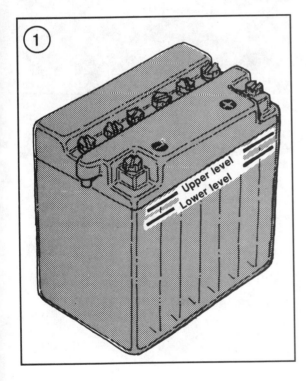

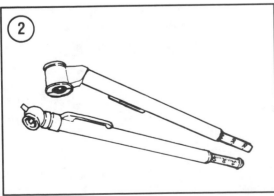

your Yamaha. If the bike is run in an area of high humidity, the lubrication services must be done more frequently to prevent possible rust damage.

For convenient maintenance of your motorcycle, most of the services shown in **Table 1** are described in this chapter. Those procedures which require more than minor disassembly or adjustment are covered elsewhere in the appropriate chapter. The *Contents* and *Index* can help you locate a particular service procedure.

TIRES AND WHEELS

Tire Pressure

Tire pressure should be checked and adjusted to accommodate rider and luggage weight. A simple, accurate gauge (**Figure 2**) can be purchased for a few dollars and should be carried in your motorcycle tool kit. The appropriate tire pressures are shown in **Table 2**.

> *NOTE*
> *After checking and adjusting the air pressure, make sure to reinstall the air valve cap. The cap prevents small pebbles and/or dirt from collecting in the valve stem that could allow air leakage or result in incorrect tire pressure readings.*

BATTERY

> *CAUTION*
> *If it becomes necessary to remove the battery breather tube from the frame when performing any of the following procedures, make sure to route the tube correctly during installation to prevent acid from spilling on parts.*

Removal/Installation and Electrolyte Level Check

The battery is the heart of the electrical system. It should be checked and serviced as indicated (**Table 1**). The majority of electrical system troubles can be attributed to neglect of this vital component.

In order to correctly service the electrolyte level it is necessary to remove the battery from the frame.

The electrolyte level should be maintained between the two marks on the battery case. If the electrolyte level is low, it's a good idea to completely remove the battery so that it can be thoroughly cleaned, serviced, and checked.

1. Remove the seat(s).

2. On 1990-on U.S. models and 1989-on U.K. models, perform the following:

    a. Unhook both fuel lines (A, **Figure 3**) from the clamps on top of the battery cover.

    b. Remove the battery cover (B, **Figure 3**).

3. Unhook the battery strap (A, **Figure 4**).

4. Disconnect the battery vent tube (B, **Figure 4**).

5. Pull the battery part way up out of the battery box to gain access to the battery cable attachment screws.

6. Disconnect the negative (–) battery cable (A, **Figure 5**) from the battery.

7. Disconnect the positive (+) battery cable (B, **Figure 5**).

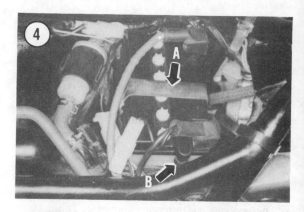

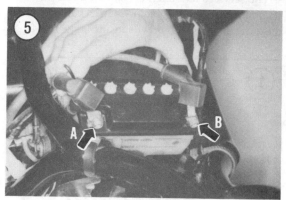

> ### WARNING
> *Protect your eyes, skin and clothing. If electrolyte gets into your eyes, flush your eyes thoroughly with clean water and get prompt medical attention.*

> ### CAUTION
> *Be careful not to spill battery electrolyte on painted or polished surfaces. The liquid is highly corrosive and will damage the finish. If it is spilled, wash it off immediately with soapy water and thoroughly rinse with clean water.*

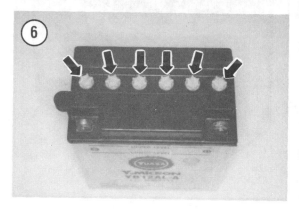

8. Lift the battery out of the battery box and remove it.

9. Rinse the battery off with clean water and wipe dry.

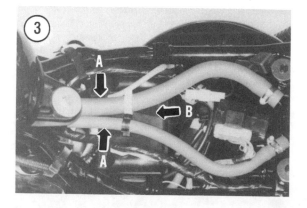

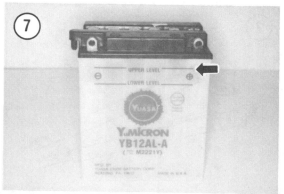

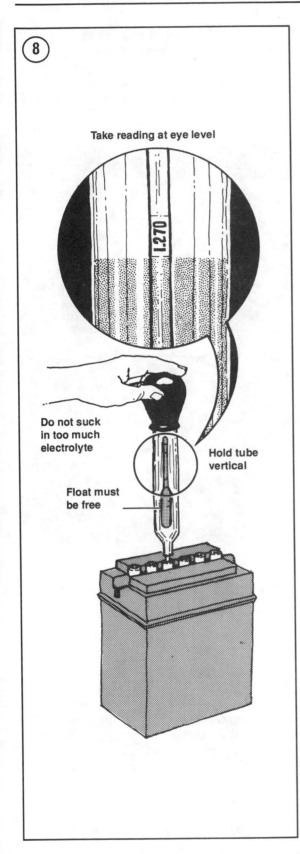

8

Take reading at eye level

I.270

Do not suck
in too much
electrolyte

Hold tube
vertical

Float must
be free

10. Remove the caps (**Figure 6**) from the battery cells and add distilled water. Never add electrolyte (acid) to correct the level. Fill only to the upper battery level mark (**Figure 7**).

11. After the level has been corrected and the battery allowed to stand for a few minutes, check the specific gravity of the electrolyte in each cell with a hydrometer (**Figure 8**). Follow the manufacturer's instructions for reading the instrument. See *Battery Testing* in Chapter Three in the front section of this manual.

> *CAUTION*
> *If distilled water has been added to a battery in freezing or near freezing weather, add it to the battery, dress warmly and then ride the bike for a **minimum of 30 minutes**. This will help mix the water thoroughly into the electrolyte in the battery. Distilled water is lighter than electrolyte and will float on top of the electrolyte if it is not mixed in properly. If the water stays on the top, it may freeze and fracture the battery case, ruining the battery.*

12. After the battery has been refilled, recharged or replaced, install it by reversing these removal steps while noting the following:

    a. Position the battery in the case with the negative (–) terminal on the right-hand side of the bike.

    b. Coat the battery terminals with a thin layer of dielectric grease to retard corrosion and decomposition of the terminals.

    c. Attach the positive (+) cable first then the negative (–) cable.

> *CAUTION*
> *Make sure to reconnect the battery breather tube (B, **Figure 4**) to the battery. If the tube was removed with the battery, make sure to route it in its correct position through the frame.*

NEW BATTERY INSTALLATION

When replacing the old battery with a new one, be sure to charge it completely (specific gravity, 1.260-1.280) before installing it in the bike. Failure to do so, or using the battery with a low electrolyte level will permanently damage the battery. When purchasing a new battery, the correct battery capacity for models covered in this manual is 12 volts/12 amp hours.

NOTE
Recycle your old battery. When you re-place the old battery, be sure to turn in the old battery at that time. The lead plates and the plastic case can be recy-cled. Most motorcycle dealers will ac-cept your old battery in trade when you purchase a new one, but if they will not, many automotive supply stores cer-tainly will. Never place an old battery in your household trash since it is ille-gal, in most states, to place any acid or lead (heavy metal) contents in landfills. There is also the danger of the battery being crushed in the trash truck and spraying acid on the truck operator.

PERIODIC LUBRICATION

Engine Oil Level Check

Engine oil level is checked through the inspection window located at the bottom of the crankcase cover on the right-hand side (**Figure 9**).

1. Place the bike on level ground on the sidestand. Start the engine and let it reach normal operating temperature.
2. Stop the engine and allow the oil to settle.
3. Hold the bike level in the upright position.
4. The oil level should be between the maximum and minimum window marks (**Figure 9**). If necessary, remove the oil fill cap (**Figure 10**) and add the recommended oil listed in **Table 3** to raise the oil to the proper level. Do not overfill.

Engine Oil and Filter Change

The factory-recommended oil and filter change interval is specified in **Table 1**. This assumes that the motorcycle is operated in moderate climates. The time interval is more important than the mileage interval because combustion acids, formed by gaso-line and water vapor, will contaminate the oil even if the motorcycle is not run for several months. If a motorcycle is operated under dusty conditions, the oil will get dirty more quickly and should be changed more frequently than recommended.

Use only a detergent oil with an API rating of SE or SF. The quality rating is on the label of the bottle (**Figure 11**). Try always to use the same brand of oil. Use of oil additives is not recommended. Refer to **Table 3** for correct weight of oil to use under differ-ent temperatures.

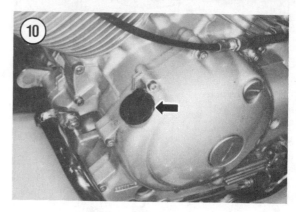

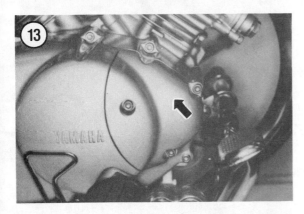

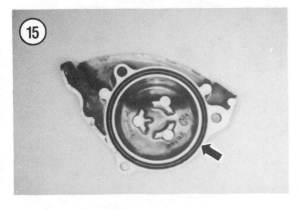

To change the engine oil and filter you will need the following:

   a. Drain pan.

   b. Funnel.

   c. Wrench or socket to remove drain plug.

   d. 3 quarts of oil.

   e. Oil filter element.

NOTE
If you are going to recycle the oil, do not add any other type of chemical (fork oil, brake fluid, etc.) to the oil as the oil recycler will probably not accept the oil.

There are a number of ways to discard the used oil safely. The easiest way is to pour it from the drain pan into a gallon plastic bleach, juice or milk container for recycling or disposal. Do not discard oil in your household trash or pour it onto the ground.

1. Place the motorcycle on the sidestand.

2. Start the engine and run it until it is at normal operating temperature, then turn it off.

3. Place a drip pan under the crankcase and remove the drain plug (**Figure 12**).

4. Remove the oil filler cap (**Figure 10**); this will speed up the flow of oil.

5. Allow the oil to drain for at least 15-20 minutes.

NOTE
Before removing the oil filter cover, thoroughly clean off all dirt and oil around it.

6. Remove the bolts securing the filter cover (**Figure 13**) to the crankcase.

7. Remove the cover and the filter (**Figure 14**). Discard the oil filter and clean out the cover and filter housing with cleaning solvent. Dry parts thoroughly.

8. Inspect the O-ring in the end of the cover (**Figure 15**) and replace if necessary.

NOTE
Prior to installing the cover, clean off the mating surface of the crankcase—do not allow any dirt to enter the oil system.

9. Position the new oil filter with the shoulder end (**Figure 16**) going in first and install the filter.

10. Reinstall the filter cover to the crankcase and tighten the bolts to 7.2 ft.-lb. (10 N•m).

11. Install the drain plug and gasket and tighten to 31 ft.-lb. (43 N•m).

12. Fill the crankcase with the correct weight (**Table 3**) and quantity of oil (**Table 4**).

13. Screw the oil filler cap on securely.

14. Start the engine and allow it to idle. Check for leaks.

15. Turn the engine off and allow the oil to settle. Check for correct oil level (**Figure 9**); adjust if necessary.

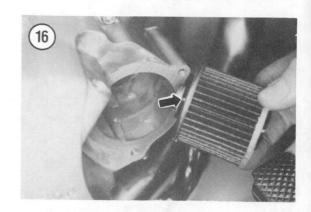

Front Fork Oil Change

1. Place the bike on the sidestand.

> *CAUTION*
> *If the bike has been subjected to frequent rain or moisture or if the bike has been in storage for any period of time, moisture may have passed by the trim cap causing rust. Any rust must be removed prior to removing any upper fork parts during this procedure. If any rust particles drop down into the fork assembly the fork must be removed, disassembled and thoroughly cleaned prior to refilling with fresh fork oil. After removing the trim cap, if rust is present, scrape it clean, blow the rust residue out with compressed air and apply WD-40, or equivalent, then remove the stopper ring and spring seat.*

2. Remove the fork trim cap (A, **Figure 17**).

3. Loosen the top fork tube pinch bolt (B, **Figure 17**).

> *NOTE*
> ***Figure 18*** *is shown with the fork assembly removed for clarity. It is not necessary to remove the fork assembly for this procedure.*

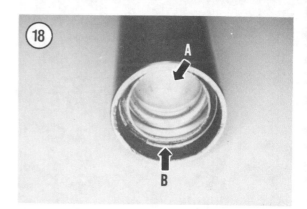

4. The spring seat and spring are held in position by a stopper ring. To remove the stopper ring, have an assistant depress the spring seat (A, **Figure 18**) using a suitable size drift.

5. Remove the stopper ring (B, **Figure 18**) from its groove in the fork with a small screwdriver. Discard the stopper ring as a new one must be installed.

6. When the stopper ring is removed, release tension from the spring seat and remove it.

7. Place a drip pan under the fork and remove the drain screw and washer (**Figure 19**). Allow the oil to drain for at least 5 minutes.

WARNING
Do not allow the fork oil to come in contact with any of the brake compo-nents.

8. Place a shop cloth around the top of the fork tube, the handlebar and the upper fork bridge to catch remaining fork oil while the fork spring is removed. Withdraw the fork spring from the fork tube.

9. With both of the bike's wheels on the ground, have an assistant steady the bike. Then push the front end down and allow it to return. Perform this procedure until all the oil is expelled from the fork tube.

10. Install the drain screw and washer (**Figure 19**) and tighten securely.

11. Fill the fork tube with the correct amount (**Table 4**) and weight (**Table 3**) of fork oil.

NOTE
In order to measure the correct amount of fluid, use a baby bottle. These bottles have measurements in fluid ounces (oz.) and cubic centimeters (cc) imprinted on the side.

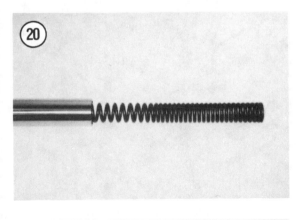

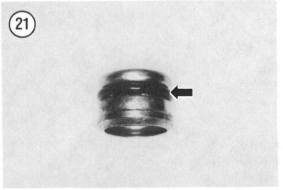

NOTE
Figure 20 is shown with the fork assem-bly removed for clarity. It is not neces-sary to remove the fork assembly for this procedure.

12. Position the fork spring with the narrow pitch coils toward the top and install the fork spring (**Figure 20**).

13. Inspect the O-ring seal (**Figure 21**) on the spring seat; replace if necessary.

CAUTION
Always install a new stopper ring dur-ing assembly. This is necessary in order to hold the spring seat securely in place.

14. Install the spring seat. Have an assistant com-press the spring seat and install a *new* stopper ring. Make sure the stopper ring seats fully in the groove in the fork tube before releasing the spring seat.

15. Install the trim cap.

16. Repeat Steps 2-15 for the opposite side.

17. Road test the bike and check for oil leaks.

PERIODIC MAINTENANCE

Front Disc Brake

The hydraulic brake fluid in the disc brake master cylinder should be checked every month. The disc brake pads should be checked at the intervals speci-fied in **Table 1**. Replacement is described in Chapter Ten.

Disc Brake Fluid Level

The brake fluid on these models is visually moni-tored by observing the fluid level in the reservoir (**Figure 22**). The level is corrected by adding fresh brake fluid.

1. The fluid level in the reservoir should be main-tained above the lower level line (**Figure 22**). If necessary, correct the level by adding fresh brake fluid. Remove the cover screws and cover (**Figure 23**) and lift the diaphragm out of the housing.

WARNING
Use brake fluid from a sealed container and clearly marked DOT 3 only (speci-fied for disc brakes). Others may vapor-ize and cause brake failure. Do not

intermix different brands or types of brake fluid as they may not be compatible. Do not intermix a silicone based (DOT 5) brake fluid as it can cause brake component damage leading to brake system failure.

CAUTION
Be careful not to spill brake fluid on painted or plated surfaces as it will destroy the surface. Wash immediately with soapy water and thoroughly rinse it off.

2. Reinstall all parts and tighten the cover screws securely.

NOTE
If the brake fluid was so low as to allow air in the hydraulic system, the brakes will have to be bled. Refer to Chapter Ten in the front section of this manual.

Disc Brake Pad Wear

Inspect the brake pads for excessive or uneven wear, scoring, and oil or grease on the friction surface.

If any of these conditions exist, replace the pads as described under *Brake Pad Replacement* in Chapter Ten, in this section of this manual.

To inspect, remove the plug (**Figure 24**) on top of the caliper and observe the thickness on each pad. If the pads are worn to a thickness of 0.03 in. (0.8 mm) or less, they must be replaced.

Front Brake Lever Adjustment

An adjuster is provided to maintain the front brake lever free play.

1. Loosen the adjuster locknut (A, **Figure 25**) and turn the adjuster (B, **Figure 25**) to obtain a free play measurement of 0.08-0.20 in. (2-5 mm). Tighten the locknut securely.

NOTE
Free play is the distance the lever travels from the at-rest position to the applied position when the master cylinder is depressed by the lever adjuster.

2. Rotate the front wheel and check for brake drag. Also operate the brake lever several times to make

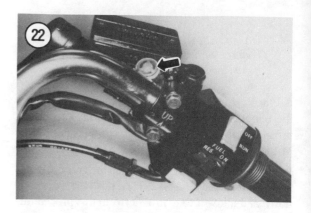

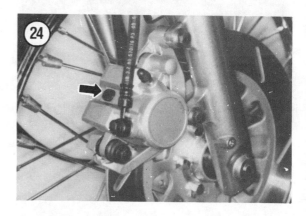

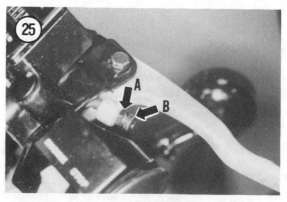

sure it returns to the at-rest position immediately after release.

Rear Brake Pedal Height Adjustment

The rear brake pedal height should be adjusted at the intervals specified in **Table 1** or anytime the brake shoes are replaced.

1. Place the motorcycle on the sidestand.

2. Check to be sure the brake pedal is in the at-rest position.

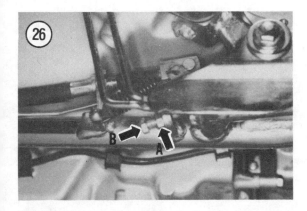

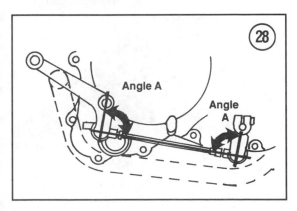

3. The correct height position above the top of the foot peg is 3/4-1 1/4 in. (20-30 mm). To adjust, proceed to Step 4.

4. Loosen the locknut (A, **Figure 26**) and turn the adjusting bolt (B, **Figure 26**) to achieve the correct height. Tighten the locknut securely and adjust the free play, described in Chapter Three in the front section of the manual, and brake light, described in Chapter Seven in this section of the manual.

Gearshift Pedal Adjustment

> *NOTE*
> *The adjuster rod front locknut has left-hand threads.*

1. Loosen the front and rear locknuts (A, **Figure 27**) on the adjuster rod.

2. Turn the adjuster rod (B, **Figure 27**) in either direction until the top of the gearshift pedal is 2.0-2.4 in. (50-60 mm) above the top surface of the footpeg.

3. After the correct height is achieved, check the angle of the change pedal arms. They must be at a 90° angle to the adjuster rod as shown in **Figure 28**. Readjust if necessary to achieve this alignment.

4. Tighten both locknuts securely.

Clutch Adjustment

The clutch cable free play should be adjusted to obtain a free play of 3/32-1/8 in. (2-3 mm) at the intervals specified in **Table 1**.

> *NOTE*
> *If you are unable to achieve the correct amount of free play adjustment using this adjustment procedure, there is an additional adjustment procedure within the clutch mechanism. Refer to Chapter Five in this section of this manual.*

1. At the hand lever, slide back the clutch lever shield (**Figure 29**).

2. Loosen the locknut (A, **Figure 30**) and rotate the adjuster (B, **Figure 30**) for free play adjustment (**Figure 31**).

> *NOTE*
> *If sufficient free play cannot be obtained at the hand lever, additional adjustment can be made at the lower adjuster on the crankcase.*

3. Completely loosen the clutch cable at the handle-bar.

4. At the clutch cable lower adjuster, loosen the locknuts (A, **Figure 32**) and rotate the adjuster (B, **Figure 32**) until the correct amount of free play is achieved. For fine adjustment, repeat Step 2 if necessary.

Throttle Operation/Adjustment

The throttle grip should have 1/8 to 1/4 in. (3-5 mm) of rotational play (**Figure 33**). Make sure there is free play in the cable so the carburetors will be able to close completely when the throttle is let off. If adjustment is necessary, loosen the cable locknut (A, **Figure 34**) and turn the adjuster (B, **Figure 34**) in or out to achieve the proper play. Tighten the locknut securely.

Check the throttle cable from grip to carburetors. Make sure it is not kinked or chafed. Replace it if necessary.

Make sure that the throttle grip rotates smoothly from fully closed to fully open. Check at center, full left and full right position of steering.

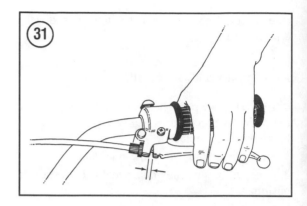

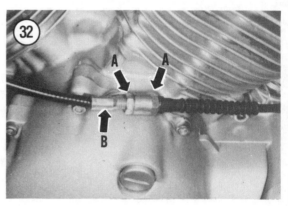

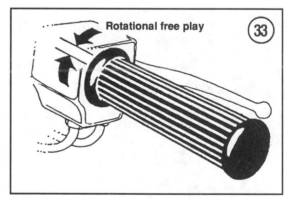

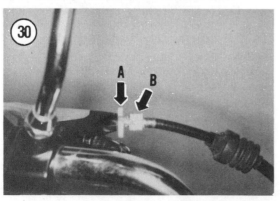

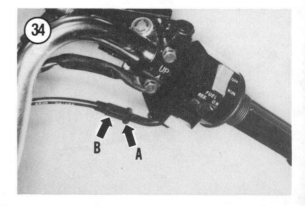

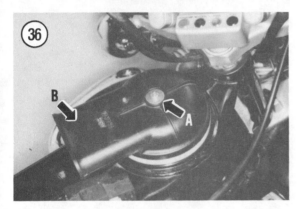

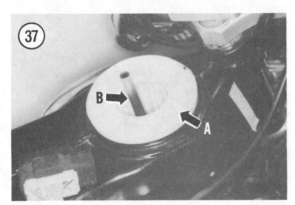

Air Cleaner Removal/Installation

A clogged air cleaner can decrease the efficiency and life of the engine. Never run the bike without the air cleaner installed; even minute particles of dust can cause severe internal engine wear.

The service intervals specified in **Table 1** should be followed with general use. However, the air cleaner should be serviced more often if the bike is ridden in dusty areas.

1. Place the bike on the sidestand.

2. Remove the seat(s).

3A. On 1987-1989 U.S. models and 1988 U.K. models, remove the rear bolt and front bolt on each side, securing the frame top cover and remove the cover (**Figure 35**).

3B. On 1990-on U.S. models and 1989-on U.K. models, remove the sub-fuel tank as described in Chapter Six in this section of the manual.

4. Unscrew the long bolt and remove the bolt and washer (A, **Figure 36**) securing the air cleaner cover.

5. Remove the air cleaner cover (B, **Figure 36**).

6. Remove the air cleaner element (A, **Figure 37**) and long metal tube.

7. Tap the element lightly to remove most of the dirt and dust; then apply compressed air to the *outside* surface of the element.

8. Inspect the element (**Figure 38**) and make sure it is in good condition. Replace if necessary.

9. Clean out the inside of the air box (**Figure 39**) with a shop rag and cleaning solvent. Remove any foreign matter that may have passed through a broken cleaner element.

10. When installing the air cleaner element make sure that the rubber O-ring gasket (**Figure 40**) seats against the air box properly. Also align the hole in the filter with the threaded hole in the lower mount-

ing bracket and install the long metal tube (B, **Figure 37**).

11. Install the cover and position it so the intake lip touches the projection on the frame (**Figure 41**).

12. Install the long bolt and washer and tighten the bolt securely.

13. Install the frame top cover, or sub-fuel tank and the seat(s).

Front Suspension Check

1. Apply the front brake and pump the fork up and down as vigorously as possible. Check for smooth operation and check for any oil leaks.

2. Make sure the upper (A, **Figure 42**) and lower (B, **Figure 42**) fork bridge bolts are tight.

3. Remove the trim caps and check the tightness of the 4 Allen bolts securing the handlebar upper holders (**Figure 43**) and handlebar.

4. Check that the front axle pinch bolt (A, **Figure 44**) and the front axle (B, **Figure 44**) are tight.

> *CAUTION*
> *If any of the previously mentioned bolts and nuts are loose, refer to Chapter Eight, in this section of the manual, for correct procedures and torque specifications.*

Rear Suspension Check

1. Place the bike on the sidestand.

2. Push hard on the rear wheel sideways to check for side play in the rear swing arm bushings or bearings.

> *NOTE*
> *Figure 45 and Figure 46 are shown with the rear wheel removed for clarity.*

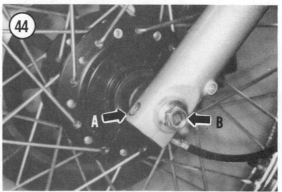

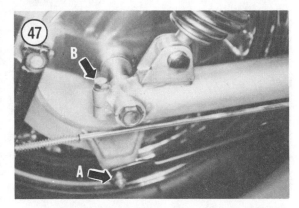

3. Remove the top cover (**Figure 45**) and check the tightness of the upper and lower shock absorber mounting nuts and bolts (**Figure 46**).

4. Check the tightness of the rear brake torque arm bolts (A, **Figure 47**).

5. Make sure the rear axle nut is tight and the cotter pin is still in place (**Figure 48**).

6. Make sure the rear axle pinch bolt (B, **Figure 47**) is tight.

7. Check the tightness of the swing arm pivot bolt (**Figure 49**) and that the tab on the lockwasher is up against one flat of the bolt head.

> *CAUTION*
> *If any of the previously mentioned nuts or bolts are loose, refer to Chapter Nine, in this section of the manual, for correct procedures and torque specifications.*

TUNE-UP

A complete tune-up restores performance and power that is lost due to normal wear and deterioration of engine parts. Because engine wear occurs over a combined period of time and mileage, the engine tune-up should be performed at the intervals specified in **Table 1**. More frequent tune-ups may be required if the bike is ridden primarily in stop-and-go traffic.

Table 5 summarizes tune-up specifications.

Before starting a tune-up procedure, make sure to first have all new parts on hand.

Because different systems in an engine interact, the procedures should be done in the following order:

    a. Clean or replace the air cleaner element.

    b. Adjust valve clearances.

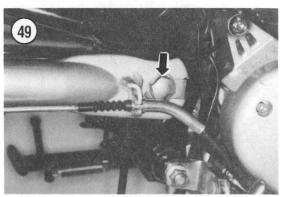

c. Check engine compression.

d. Check or replace the spark plugs.

e. Check the ignition timing.

f. Synchronize carburetors and set idle speed.

Tools

To perform a tune-up on your Yamaha, you will need the following tools:

a. Spark plug wrench.

b. Socket wrench and assorted sockets.

c. Flat feeler gauge.

d. Compression gauge.

e. Spark plug wire feeler gauge and gapper tool.

f. Ignition timing light.

g. Carburetor synchronization tool—to measure manifold vacuum.

Air Cleaner Element

The air cleaner element should be cleaned or replaced prior to doing other tune-up procedures, as described in this chapter.

Valve Adjustment

Valve clearance measurement must be made with the engine cool, at room temperature.

1. Remove the seat.

2A. On 1987-1989 U.S. models and 1988 U.K. models, remove the rear bolt and front bolt on each side securing the frame top cover and remove the cover (**Figure 35**).

2B. On 1990-on U.S. models and 1989-on U.K. models, remove the sub-fuel tank as described in Chapter Six in this section of the manual.

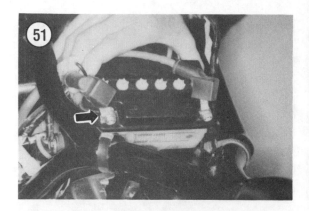

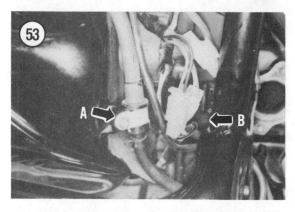

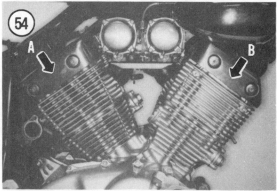

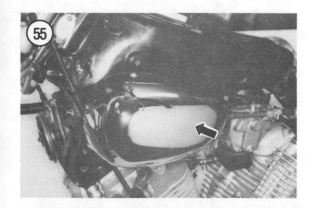

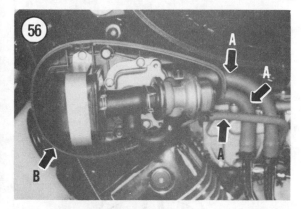

3. Unhook the battery strap (A, **Figure 50**).

4. Disconnect the battery vent tube (B, **Figure 50**).

5. Pull the battery part way up out of the battery box to gain access to the battery cable attachment points.

6. Disconnect the negative (–) battery cable (**Figure 51**) from the battery.

7. Remove the frame right-hand side cover (**Figure 52**).

8. Disconnect the fuel hose from the frame clamp (A, **Figure 53**) and move it out of the way.

9. Carefully pull the starter relay (B, **Figure 53**) from its frame mount and move it out of the way. Do not disconnect the cables from the relay.

10. Remove the battery as described in this chapter.

11. From the rear cylinder, remove the following:
   a. The cylinder head side cover (A, **Figure 54**) from each side.
   b. The spark plug (this makes it easier to turn over the engine by hand).
   c. The intake and exhaust valve adjuster covers.

12. Remove both frame side covers.

13. Remove bolts securing the left-hand side cover (**Figure 55**) and remove the cover.

14A. On models equipped with the air injection system, disconnect the hoses (A, **Figure 56**) from the air injection system and remove the left-hand bracket assembly (B, **Figure 56**) with the system components still attached to it.

14B. On all other models, remove the bracket (**Figure 57**).

15. Remove bolts securing the right-hand side cover (**Figure 58**) and electrical component bracket (**Figure 59**) and move the bracket assembly out of the way.

16. From the front cylinder, remove the following:
   a. The cylinder head side cover (B, **Figure 54**) from each side.
   b. The spark plug (this makes it easier to turn over the engine by hand).
   c. The intake and exhaust valve covers (**Figure 60**).

17. On the left-hand crankcase cover, remove the timing hole cover (A, **Figure 61**) and the crankshaft cover (B, **Figure 61**).

18. Rotate the engine by turning the crankshaft *clockwise*. Use a socket on the bolt (**Figure 62**) located on the left-hand end of the crankshaft. Continue to rotate the crankshaft until the "T" mark on the rotor for the *rear cylinder* (**Figure 63**) is aligned with the crankcase cover stationary pointer as

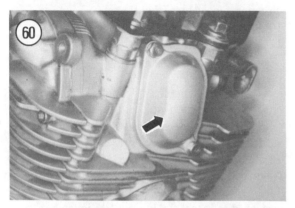

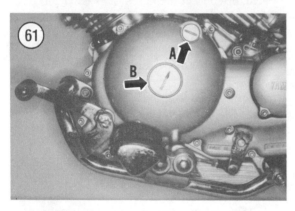

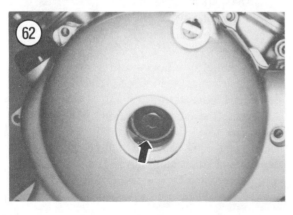

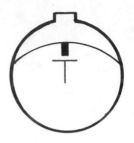

TDC FOR REAR CYLINDER

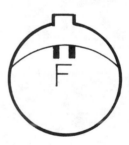

**FIRING RANGE FOR
REAR CYLINDER**

TDC FOR FRONT CYLINDER

viewed through the timing window in the left-hand crankcase cover. The *rear cylinder* is now at top dead center (TDC) on the compression stroke.

19. Check that there is free play in both the intake and exhaust valve for the *rear cylinder*. If not, rotate the crankshaft an additional 360° *clockwise*.

20. The correct clearance is as follows:

    a. Exhaust valves: 0.005-0.007 in. (0.12-0.17 mm).

    b. Intake valves: 0.003-0.005 in. (0.07-0.12 mm).

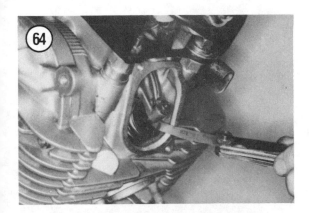

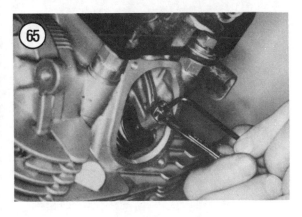

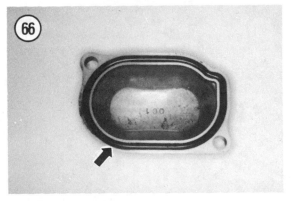

NOTE
The exhaust valves are located next to the exhaust pipes and the intake valves are located next to the carburetor assembly.

21. Insert a feeler gauge between exhaust valve rocker arm adjuster screw and valve stem (**Figure 64**). The clearance is correct when there is a slight drag on the feeler gauge when it is inserted and withdrawn. Repeat for the intake valve.

22. To correct the clearance, perform the following:

    a. Loosen the valve adjuster locknut (**Figure 65**).

    b. Turn the adjuster in or out to obtain the correct clearance.

    c. When the correct clearance is obtained, tighten the locknut securely and recheck the clearance.

    d. Repeat for the opposite valve.

23. Rotate the engine by turning the crankshaft *clockwise*. Use a socket on the nut located on the left-hand end of the crankshaft. Continue to rotate the crankshaft until the slit in the rotor for the *front cylinder* (**Figure 63**) is aligned with the crankcase cover stationary pointer as viewed through the timing window in the left-hand crankcase cover. The *front cylinder* is now at top dead center (TDC) on the compression stroke.

24. Repeat Steps 18-22 to adjust the front cylinder's intake and exhaust valves.

25. Install all items removed in the reverse order of removal. Make sure the O-ring seal (**Figure 66**) is in place in the valve adjuster cover. Replace if necessary.

Correct Spark Plug Heat Range

Spark plugs are available in various heat ranges that are hotter or colder than the spark plugs originally installed at the factory.

Select plugs in a heat range designed for the loads and temperature conditions under which the engine will operate. Using incorrect heat ranges, however, can cause piston seizure, scored cylinder walls or damaged piston crowns.

The standard heat range spark plugs are found in **Table 5**.

Ignition Timing

Timing is set on all models and is not adjustable. The following procedure is used to check ignition timing only.

It is only necessary to check the timing on the rear cylinder. If it is found correct, the front cylinder will automatically be correct.

NOTE
Before starting this procedure, check all electrical connections related to the ignition system. Make sure all connections are tight and free of corrosion and that all ground connections are tight.

1. Place the bike on the sidestand.
2. Remove the timing cover (A, **Figure 61**) on the left-hand crankcase cover.
3. Connect a portable tachometer following the manufacturer's instructions.
4. Connect a timing light to the rear cylinder following the manufacturer's instructions.

CAUTION
When attaching the timing light to the spark plug wire, do not puncture the wire or cap with the timing light probe. This would cause excessive wire resistance from the separation of the wire conductor and/or high-voltage leakage to ground due to damage of the plug wire insulation. In either case, engine miss-firing would result.

5. Start the engine and let it warm up to normal operating temperature. Bring the engine speed to 1,200 rpm and aim the timing light toward the timing marks on the timing plate.

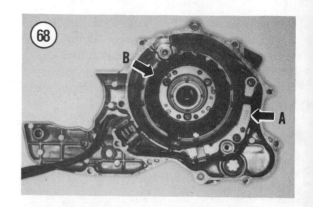

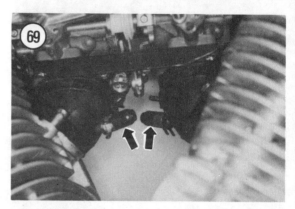

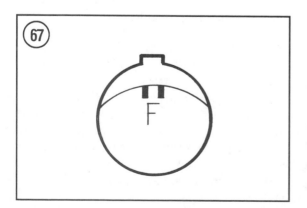

6. The stationary pointer should align with the "F" mark on the timing plate (**Figure 67**). If not, remove the alternator cover as described in Chapter Seven, in this section of the manual, and check the pick-up (A, **Figure 68**) and stator (B, **Figure 68**) assembly screws for tightness. If these are tight, refer to Chapter Seven, in this section of the manual, for ignition system troubleshooting. Ignition timing cannot be adjusted on these models.

Carburetor Synchronization

A vacuum gauge (Chapter One) must be used to synchronize the carburetors.

NOTE
Prior to synchronizing the carburetors, the ignition timing must be checked and the valve clearance properly adjusted.

1. Place the bike on the sidestand.
2. Start the engine and let it reach normal operating temperature. Then turn it off.
3. Disconnect the small vacuum plug cap from each carburetor joint (**Figure 69**).
4. Connect the vacuum gauge to both carburetor vacuum port joints following the manufacturer's instructions.
5. Start the engine and allow it to idle at 1,140-1,250 rpm.

6. The carburetors are synchronized if they have the same gauge readings. If not, turn the synchronizing screw (**Figure 70**) and balance the rear carburetor to the front carburetor until the gauge readings are the same.
7. Rev the engine several times to make sure the readings remain the same.
8. Turn the engine off and disconnect the vacuum gauge from the carburetors.
9. Install the small vacuum plug cap onto each carburetor joint (**Figure 69**) and make sure it is secured in place.

Carburetor Idle Speed Adjustment

Before making this adjustment, the air cleaner must be clean, the carburetors must be synchronized and the engine must have adequate compression. Otherwise this procedure cannot be done properly.

1. Attach a portable tachometer following the manufacturer's instructions.
2. Start the engine and let it warm up to normal operating temperature.
3. Set the idle speed by turning the carburetor throttle stop screw (**Figure 71**) *in to increase* or *out to decrease* idle speed.
4. The correct idle speed is listed in **Table 5**.

Table 1 MAINTENANCE SCHEDULE*	
Initial 600 miles (1,000 km) or 1 month	Change engine oil and oil filter
	Inspect valve clearance, adjust if necessary
	Check front and rear brake lever and pedal free play; adjust if required
	Check front brake pads and rear brake shoe thickness; replace as required
	Adjust clutch lever free play
	Lubricate speedometer and control cables
	Change final gear oil
	Check sidestand switch operation
	(continued)

Table 1   MAINTENANCE SCHEDULE (continued)*

Every 4,400 miles (7,000 km) or 7 months	Inspect valve clearance; adjust if necessary
	Check, clean and regap spark plugs
	Change engine oil and oil filter
	Check crankcase breather hose for tightness and damage
	Inspect fuel lines for deterioration, chafed, cracked or swollen ends; replace if necessary
	Inspect the exhaust system for leaks; tighten bolts and nuts if necessary
	Synchronize the carburetors
	Check idle speed; adjust if necessary
	Check front brake pads and rear brake shoe thickness; replace as required
	Adjust clutch lever free play
	Check oil level in final drive unit
	Lubricate speedometer and control cables
	Clean and inspect air filter element with compressed air, replace if necessary
	Lubricate rear brake pedal, shift lever and sidestand
	Check front fork oil seal for leakage
	Check steering stem for looseness
	Check tire and wheel condition
	Check wheel bearings for smooth operation
	Check battery fluid level and specific gravity; add water if necessary
	Check brake fluid level in master cylinder; add fluid if necessary
Every 8,200 miles (13,000 km) or 13 months	Replace the spark plugs
	Check fluid level in final drive unit; add fluid if necessary
Every 15,800 miles (25,000 km) or 25 months	Lubricate steering stem bearings
	Lubricate swing arm bearings

* This Yamaha factory maintenance schedule should be considered as a guide to general maintenance and lubrication intervals. Harder than normal use and exposure to mud, water, sand, high humidity, etc. will naturally dictate more frequent attention to most maintenance items.

Table 2   TIRE INFLATION PRESSURE (COLD)

Load	psi (kg/cm^2)
Up to 198 lb. (90 kg)	
Front	28 (2.0)
Rear	32 (2.3)
198-max. lb. (90-max kg)*	
Front	28 (2.0)
Rear	36 (2.5)
High-speed riding	
Front	28 (2.0)
Rear	36 (2.5)

* Maximum load: 49-state 507 lb. (230 kg.), Calif. 505 lb. (229 kg.), U.K. 501 lb. (227 kg.)

Table 3   RECOMMENDED LUBRICANTS

Item	Oil Type
Engine oil	
40° F (5° C) and above	Yamalube 4 or SAE 20W/40
60° F (15° C) and below	Yamalube 4 or SAE 10W/30
Brake fluid	DOT 3
Battery refilling	Distilled water

(continued)

Table 3 RECOMMENDED LUBRICANTS (continued)

Item	Oil Type
Fork oil	SAE 10W
Control cables and pivot points	SAE 10W/30 motor oil
Final drive unit	Hypoid gear oil SAE 80 GL-4 or SAE 80W/90

Table 4 APPROXIMATE REFILL CAPACITIES

Item	Quantity
Engine oil	
With filter change	3.0 U.S. qt. (2.8 L, 2.5 Imp. qt.)
Without filter change	2.7 U.S. qt. (2.6 L, 2.3 Imp. qt.)
Engine rebuild	3.4 U.S. qt. (3.2 L, 2.8 Imp. qt.)
Front forks	7.71 U.S. oz. (228 cc, 8.03 Imp. oz.)
Final gear case	0.20 U.S. qt. (0.19 L, 0.17 Imp. qt.)

Table 5 TUNE UP SPECIFICATIONS

Ignition timing	Fixed
Valve clearance (cold)	
Intake	0.003-0.005 in. (0.07-0.12 mm)
Exhaust	0.005-0.007 in. (0.12-0.17 mm)
Spark plug	
Type	
U.S.	NGK BP7ES, ND W22EP-U
U.K.	NGK BPR7ES, ND W22EPR-U
Gap	0.028-0.031 in. (0.7-0.8 mm)
Idle speed	1,150-1,250 rpm
Compression pressure (cold at sea level)	
Standard	156 psi (11 kg/cm^2, 1,100 kPa)
Minimum	142 psi (10 kg/cm^2, 1,000 kPa)
Maximum	171 psi (12 kg/cm^2, 1,200 kPa)

3

CHAPTER FOUR

ENGINE

The engine is a V-twin air-cooled, 4-stroke design. The cylinders are offset (to improve rear cylinder cooling) and set at a 75° angle; the cylinders fire on alternate crankshaft rotations. Each cylinder is equipped with a single camshaft and 2 valves. The crankshaft is supported by 2 main bearings in a vertically split crankcase.

Both engine and transmission share a common case and the same wet sump oil supply. The clutch is a wet-type located inside the right crankcase cover. Refer to Chapter Five in this section of the manual for clutch and transmission service procedures.

This chapter provides complete procedures and information for removal, inspection, service and reassembly of the engine.

Table 1 provides complete specifications for the engine and **Table 2** lists all of the engine torque specifications. **Table 1** and **Table 2** are located at the end of this chapter.

Before beginning work, re-read Chapter One in the front section of this book. You will do a better job with this information fresh in your mind.

ENGINE PRINCIPLES

Figure 1 explains how the engine works. This will be helpful when troubleshooting or repairing the engine.

SERVICING ENGINE IN FRAME

The following components can be serviced while the engine is mounted in the frame (the bike's frame is a great holding fixture for breaking loose stubborn bolts and nuts):

a. Gearshift mechanism.
b. Clutch.
c. Carburetors.
d. Starter motor and gears.

① **4-STROKE PRINCIPLES**

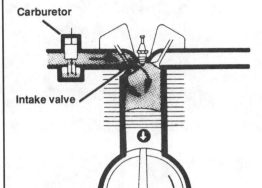

Carburetor

Intake valve

A

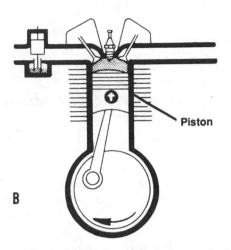

Piston

B

As the piston travels downward, the exhaust valve is closed and the intake valve opens, allowing the new air-fuel mixture from the carburetor to be drawn into the cylinder. When the piston reaches the bottom of its travel (BDC) the intake valve closes and remains closed for the next 1 1/2 revolutions of the crankshaft.

While the crankshaft continues to rotate, the piston moves upward, compressing the air-fuel mixture.

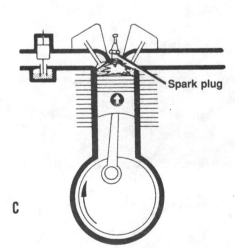

Spark plug

C

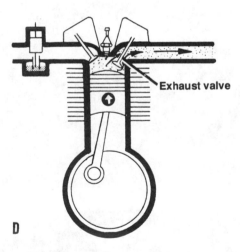

Exhaust valve

D

As the piston almost reaches the top of its travel, the spark plug fires, igniting the compressed air-fuel mixture. The piston continues to top dead center (TDC) and is pushed downward by the expanding gases.

When the piston almost reaches BDC, the exhaust valve opens and remains open until the piston is near TDC. The upward travel of the piston forces the exhaust gases out of the cylinder. After the piston has reached TDC, the exhaust valve closes and the cycle starts all over again.

e. Alternator and electrical systems.

f. Oil pump.

ENGINE

Removal/Installation

1. Drain the engine oil as described in Chapter Three in this section of the manual.

2. Remove the front cylinder head right-hand cover (**Figure 2**) and the rear cylinder head left-hand cover (**Figure 3**).

3. Remove the bolts securing the ignition coil cover (**Figure 4**) and remove the cover.

4. Disconnect the ignition primary coil wire electrical connectors (**Figure 5**). Each connector contains 2 wires: 1 red/white and 1 gray; and 1 red/white and 1 orange.

5. Remove the carburetor assembly as described in Chapter Six in this section of the manual.

6. Remove the exhaust system as described in Chapter Six in this section of the manual.

7. At the clutch hand lever, slide back the clutch lever shield (**Figure 6**).

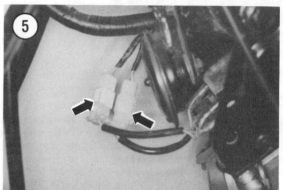

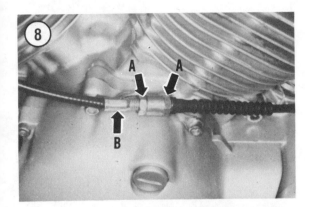

8. Loosen the clutch cable locknut (A, **Figure 7**) and rotate the adjuster (B, **Figure 7**) to allow maximum slack in the clutch cable.

9. At the clutch cable lower adjuster, loosen the locknuts (A, **Figure 8**) and rotate the adjuster (B, **Figure 8**) to allow maximum slack in the clutch cable. Disconnect the clutch cable from the actuating lever.

10. Remove the starter motor as described in Chapter Seven in this section of the manual.

11. Remove the bolts securing the left-hand under cover (**Figure 9**) and remove the cover.

12. Remove the following from the right-hand side:

    a. Right-hand footpeg assembly (**Figure 10**).

    b. Remove the front (**Figure 11**) and rear (**Figure 12**) nuts securing the rear brake pedal and engine guard assembly (**Figure 13**) and remove the assembly.

13. Remove the bolt (**Figure 14**) securing the shift lever arm and slide it off the shift shaft.

14. Remove the left-hand foot peg (A, **Figure 15**).

15. Remove the left-hand footrest bar assembly (B, **Figure 15**).

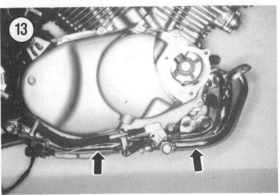

16. Place wood block(s) and a small hydraulic jack under the engine to support it securely.

17. Disconnect the sidestand switch electrical connector.

18. Remove the nuts (**Figure 16**) securing the sidestand and remove the sidestand assembly.

19. Disconnect the spark plug lead (A, **Figure 17**) from each spark plug.

20. Move the drive shaft rubber boot (**Figure 18**) back away from the engine and onto the swing arm.

21. Remove the bolt securing the engine ground cable and disconnect the cable.

22. Carefully pull the stator wire harness from the frame and remove the wires from the frame. Note the path of the wire harness during removal; it must be routed the same during installation.

23. Using a crisscross pattern, loosen then remove the Allen screws securing the left-hand crankcase cover (**Figure 19**). Remove the cover and gasket.

24. Disconnect the neutral switch electrical lead (A, **Figure 20**).

25. Remove the right-hand crankcase lower bolts and remove the starter motor electrical cable and

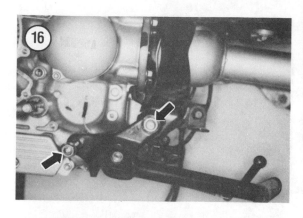

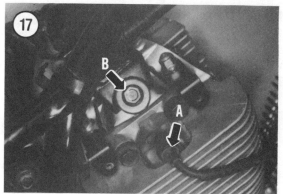

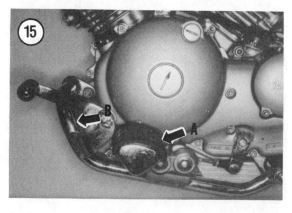

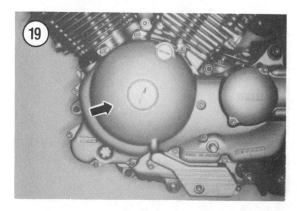

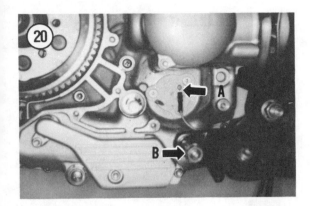

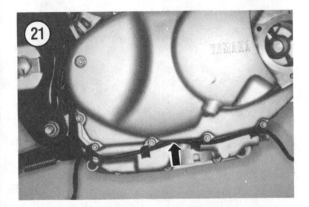

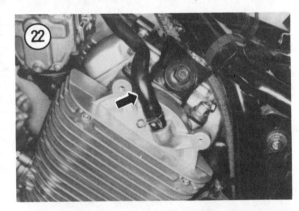

holding straps. Remove the electrical cable (**Figure 21**) from the engine.

26. Disconnect the alternator and the pulse generator electrical connectors.

27. Disconnect the crankcase breather hose (**Figure 22**) from the rear cylinder head.

28. Take a final look all over the engine to make sure everything has been disconnected.

29. Place a stand under the swing arm or tie the bike down to secure it in a vertical position after the engine is removed.

CAUTION
The following steps require the aid of a helper to safely remove the engine assembly from the frame.

30. Make sure the hydraulic jack is still in place and supporting the engine securely.

31. Loosen, but do not remove, all engine mounting bolts and nuts.

32. Remove the rear lower through bolt (B, **Figure 20**).

33. Remove the rear upper bolt (**Figure 23**) on each side.

34. Remove the front upper bolts, washers and nuts (**Figure 24**) securing the front cylinder head to the frame.

35. Remove the rear upper bolts and washers (B, **Figure 17**) securing the rear cylinder head to the frame.

36. Slowly lower the engine and move it forward, then remove the engine from the frame. Using a screwdriver, disengage the drive shaft's universal joint from the output shaft.

37. Take the engine to a workbench for further disassembly.

38. Install by reversing these removal steps, while noting the following:

a. Apply a light coat of molybdenum disulfide grease to the splines of the output shaft and the universal joint prior to engaging these 2 parts.

b. Tighten the engine mounting bolts to the torque specifications in **Table 2**.

c. Fill the engine with the recommended type and quantity of oil as described in Chapter Three in this section of the manual.

d. Adjust the clutch as described in Chapter Three in this section of the manual.

e. Start the engine and check for leaks.

CYLINDER HEADS AND CAMSHAFTS

This section describes removal, inspection and installation procedures for the cylinder head and camshaft components. Valves and valve components are described under a separate heading.

Removal

> *NOTE*
> *This procedure is for the rear cylinder. Removal of the front cylinder is identical, except for differences noted in Step 29.*

1. Remove the engine from the frame as described in this chapter.

2. Remove the exhaust valve adjuster cover (**Figure 25**).

3. Remove the bolts (**Figure 26**) securing the *rear cylinder* side cover and remove the cover.

4. Remove the intake valve adjuster cover.

> *CAUTION*
> *The next steps will position the rear cylinder at top dead center (TDC) on the compression stroke. This is necessary to avoid damage to the camshaft and related parts.*

5. Using the bolt (**Figure 27**) on the left-hand end of the crankshaft, turn the crankshaft *clockwise* until the index mark on the camshaft sprocket aligns with the fixed pointer on the cylinder head (A, **Figure 28**).

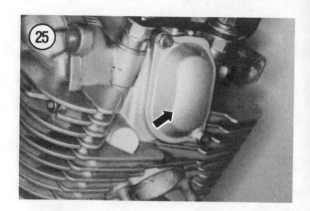

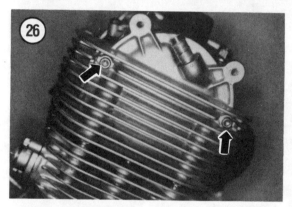

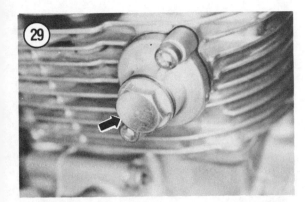

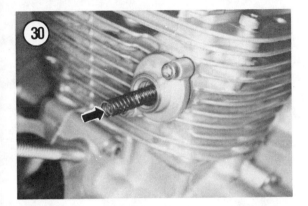

6. Also check that the "T" timing mark on the edge of the alternator rotor is aligned with the centerline of the rear cylinder (pointing straight up toward the timing mark on the camshaft). If the "T" mark is not properly aligned, rotate the crankshaft an additional 360° rotation until alignment is correct.

NOTE
A cylinder at TDC of its compression stroke will have free play in both of its rocker arms, indicating that both the intake and exhaust valves are closed.

7. The rear cylinder piston must be at top dead center (TDC) on the compression stroke.

8. With the crankshaft timing mark on the "T," move both rocker arms to make sure they are loose and have free play. If both rocker arms are not loose; rotate the engine an additional 360° until both rocker arms have free play.

9. Remove the camshaft chain tensioner center bolt (**Figure 29**) and spring (**Figure 30**). Remove the bolts securing the camshaft chain tensioner lifter (**Figure 31**) and remove the tensioner lifter and gasket.

10. Remove both spark plugs. This will make it easier to rotate the engine.

11. Place a wrench on the bolt (**Figure 27**) on the left-hand end of the crankshaft to prevent it from turning, then loosen the camshaft sprocket mounting bolt (B, **Figure 28**).

12. Remove the bolt and the oil baffle plate (C, **Figure 28**) from the sprocket.

NOTE
*If the crankcase is **not** going to be disassembled take note of this possible problem. There is a small locating pin (A, **Figure 32**) that correctly positions the camshaft sprocket to the camshaft. When removing the camshaft sprocket be careful the pin does not work loose as it will fall into the crankcase. If the pin does fall, the crankcase must be split to retrieve the pin.*

13. Carefully slide the camshaft sprocket off the camshaft shoulder and remove the sprocket (B, **Figure 32**) from the drive chain.

14. Remove the locating pin (**Figure 33**) from the end of the camshaft.

15. Tie a piece of wire to the camshaft chain and tie it to an external portion of the engine to prevent the camshaft chain from falling down into the crankcase.

> *CAUTION*
> *If the crankshaft must be rotated with the camshaft removed, pull up on the camshaft chain and keep it taut, make certain that the camshaft chain is properly meshed onto the crankshaft timing sprocket then rotate the crankshaft. If this step is not followed, the chain may become kinked and cause damage to the crankcases, the camshaft chain and the timing sprocket on the crankshaft.*

16. Remove the left-hand bolts (**Figure 34**) securing the cylinder head.

17. Using a crisscross pattern, loosen then remove the nuts and washers securing the engine hanger plates and the cylinder head (**Figure 35**). Don't forget the one nut and washer (**Figure 36**) in the recess on the spark plug side of the cylinder head.

18. Remove the engine hanger plates.

19. Loosen the cylinder head by tapping around the perimeter with a rubber or soft faced mallet. If necessary, *gently* pry the head loose with a broad-tipped screwdriver.

> *CAUTION*
> *Remember the cooling fins are fragile and may be damaged if tapped or pried on too hard. Never use a metal hammer.*

20. Untie the wire securing the camshaft chain to the exterior of the engine and hold onto the end of the wire.

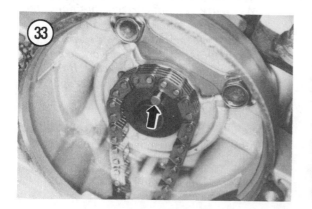

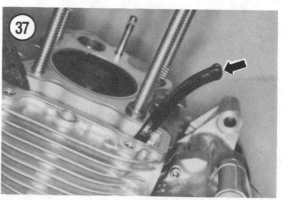

21. Lift the cylinder head straight up and off the crankcase studs. Guide the cam chain through the opening in the cylinder head and retie the wire to the exterior of the engine. This will prevent the drive chain from falling down into the crankcase.

22. Remove the cylinder head gasket and discard it. Don't lose the locating dowels.

23. Remove the camshaft chain slipper on the exhaust side (**Figure 37**).

24. Place a clean shop cloth into the cam chain opening in the cylinder to prevent the entry of foreign matter.

25. Unstake the locking tabs (**Figure 38**) on the camshaft bushing lockwasher.

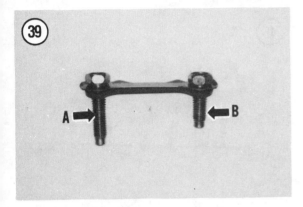

NOTE
*The camshaft bushing bolts are of two different lengths. The long bolt (A, **Figure 39**) is used on the exhaust side and short bolt (B, **Figure 39**) is used on the intake side. The bolts must be installed in this location during installation.*

26. Remove the bolts (A, **Figure 40**) securing the bushing lockwasher (B, **Figure 40**) and remove the lockwasher.

27. Screw a 10 mm bolt (A, **Figure 41**) into the end of the camshaft and withdraw the camshaft and camshaft bushing (B, **Figure 41**).

28. If necessary, remove the self-locking nuts (**Figure 42**) securing the rear exhaust joint to the cylinder head. Remove the exhaust joint and discard the nuts as they cannot be reused.

29. Repeat Steps 2-27 for the front cylinder head, noting the following that are unique to the front cylinder:

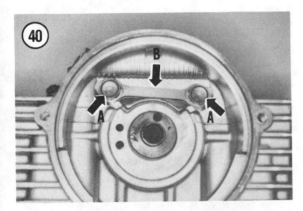

a. Remove the bolt (**Figure 43**) on each side securing the ignition coil assembly to the front cylinder head and remove the coil assembly.

b. Remove the nuts (A, **Figure 44**) and the nuts and washers (B, **Figure 44**) securing the front engine hanger plate to the cylinder head and remove the hanger plate. Note the location of the washers as they must be reinstalled on the same crankcase studs during installation.

c. While observing Step 5, rotate the crankshaft until the slit in the alternator rotor is aligned with the crankcase cover stationary pointer. See **Figure 63** in Chapter Three. The alternator rotor "T" mark is for the rear cylinder.

d. Remove the special long nuts (A, **Figure 45**) and washers securing the cylinder head and the cylinder head cover mounting bracket (B, **Figure 45**). Remove the mounting bracket.

e. The front cylinder camshaft sprocket is not equipped with an oil baffle plate like the one used on the rear cylinder.

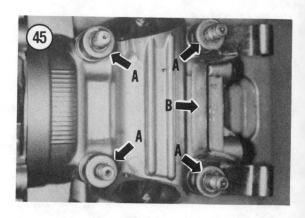

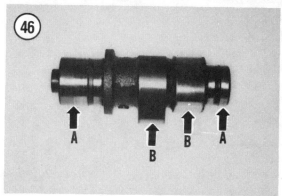

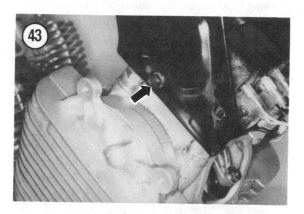

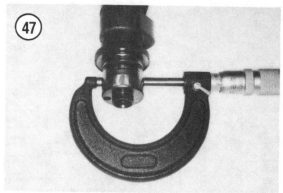

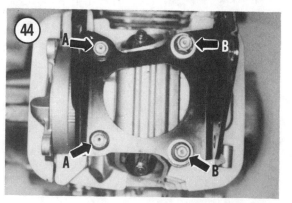

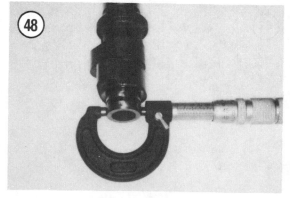

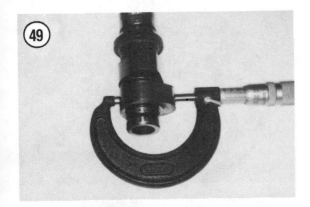

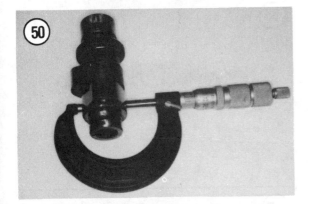

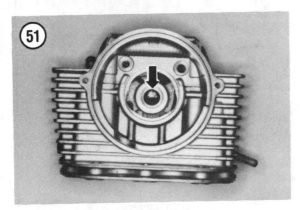

Camshaft Inspection

1. Check the camshaft bearing journals (A, **Figure 46**) for wear or scoring.

2. Using a micrometer, measure the sprocket end of the bearing journal (**Figure 47**) and the opposite journal (**Figure 48**). Compare to dimensions listed in **Table 1**. If any dimension is worn to the service limit dimension or less the camshaft must be replaced.

3. Check the camshaft lobes (B, **Figure 46**) for wear or scoring. The lobes should show no signs of wear or scoring and the edges should be square. Slight damage may be removed with a silicone carbide oilstone. Use No. 100-120 grit stone initially, then polish with a No. 280-320 grit stone.

4. Even though the lobe surface appears to be satisfactory, with no visible signs of wear, each camshaft lobe must be measured as shown in **Figure 49**. Compare to dimensions listed in **Table 1**. If either dimension is worn to the service limit dimension or less the camshaft must be replaced.

5. Also measure the cam lobe width (**Figure 50**) with a micrometer. Compare to dimensions listed in **Table 1**. If either dimension is worn to the service limit dimension or less the camshaft must be replaced.

6. Measure the cam bearing surface inside diameter in the cylinder head (**Figure 51**) and camshaft bushing (**Figure 52**). The bearing surfaces should not be scored or excessively worn. Compare to dimensions listed in **Table 1**. If either dimension is worn to the service limit dimension or less either the cylinder head or the bushing must be replaced.

7. Inspect the camshaft sprocket (**Figure 53**) for wear; replace if necessary.

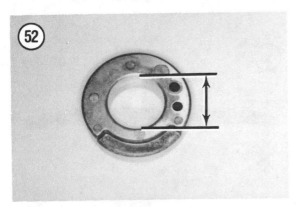

Cylinder Head Inspection

1. Remove all traces of gasket material from the cylinder head and cylinder mating surfaces. Do not scratch the gasket surface.

2. *Without removing the valves,* remove all carbon deposits from the combustion chamber (**Figure 54**) and valve ports with a wire brush. A blunt screwdriver or chisel may be used if care is taken not to damage the head, valves and spark plug threads.

3. Examine the spark plug threads (A, **Figure 55**) in the cylinder head for damage. If damage is minor or if the threads are dirty or clogged with carbon, use a spark plug thread tap (**Figure 56**) to clean the threads following the manufacturer's instructions. If thread damage is severe, refer further service to a dealer or competent machine shop.

4. After the carbon is removed from the combustion chamber and the valve ports (B, **Figure 55**)and the spark plug thread hole is repaired, clean the entire head in cleaning solvent. Blow dry with compressed air.

5. Clean away all carbon from the piston crown. Do not remove the carbon ridge at the top of the piston.

6. Check for cracks in the combustion chamber and exhaust ports. A cracked head must be replaced.

7. Inspect the camshaft bushing seating area (B, **Figure 41**) in the cylinder head for damage, wear or burrs. Clean up if damage is minimal; replace cylinder head if necessary.

8. After the head has been thoroughly cleaned, place a straightedge across the cylinder head/cylinder gasket surface (**Figure 57**) at several points. Measure the warp by inserting a flat feeler gauge between the straightedge and the cylinder head at each location. Maximum allowable warpage is 0.010 in. (0.25 mm). If warpage exceeds this limit, the cylinder head must be replaced.

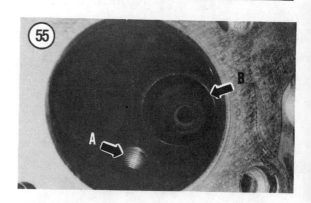

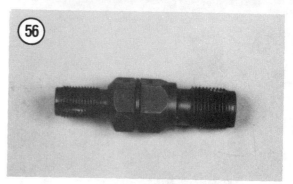

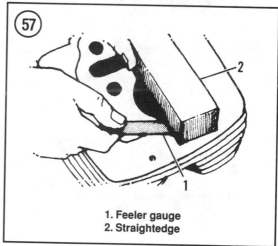

1. Feeler gauge
2. Straightedge

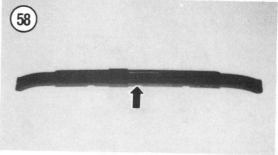

9. Inspect the valve and valve guides as described in this chapter.

10. Inspect the exhaust side camshaft chain guide (**Figure 58**) for excessive wear or separation. Replace if necessary.

11. Inspect the camshaft chain tensioner assembly (**Figure 59**) for wear or damage. If any part is damaged, replace the assembly.

Installation

> *NOTE*
> *This procedure is for the rear cylinder. Installation of the front cylinder is identical, except for differences noted in Step 27. If both cylinder heads have been removed; install the rear cylinder assembly first, then the front cylinder.*

1. Lubricate the camshaft bearing journals and bearing surfaces in the cylinder head and camshaft bushing with molybdenum disulfide grease or assembly oil.

> *NOTE*
> *If both cylinder heads have been disassembled, be sure to install the correct camshaft into the correct cylinder head. The front camshaft is marked with a "2" (**Figure 60**) and the rear camshaft is marked with a "1."*

2. Position the camshaft with the locating dowel hole facing up toward the timing mark in the cylinder head. Install the camshaft and camshaft bushing (B, **Figure 41**) into the cylinder head. After installation, check this basic alignment (**Figure 61**) and realign if necessary.

> *NOTE*
> *The bolts have different lengths. The long bolt (A, **Figure 39**) is used on the exhaust side and short bolt (B, **Figure 39**) is used on the intake side. The bolts must be installed in this location during installation.*

3. Install a new lockwasher (B, **Figure 40**) and the bolts (A, **Figure 40**) in their correct location. Tighten the bolts to the torque specifications in **Table 2**.

4. Stake the locking tabs (**Figure 38**) onto the flat of each bolt.

5. Remove the shop cloth from the cam chain opening in the cylinder.

6. Install the large dowel pin (**Figure 62**) and O-ring seal (**Figure 63**).

7. Position the camshaft chain slipper on the exhaust side with the "UP" mark and arrow (**Figure 64**)

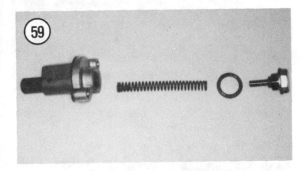

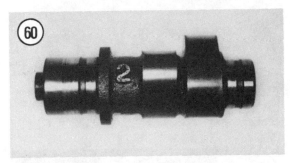

facing up and install the slipper (**Figure 37**). Make sure it is correctly seated in the locator at the lower end.

8. If removed, install the 2 small locating dowels (A, **Figure 65**) and a new cylinder head gasket (B, **Figure 65**).

9. Install the cylinder head onto the crankcase studs. With your fingers, carefully insert the cam chain into the cam chain cavity on the side of the cylinder head while pushing the cylinder head down into position (**Figure 66**).

10. Make sure the upper portion of the exhaust side chain slipper is indexed into the cavity in the cylinder head (**Figure 67**).

11. Tie the wire attached to the cam chain to the exterior of the engine.

NOTE
*If both cylinder heads have been disassembled, be sure to install the correct cylinder head nuts. The front cylinder head uses the larger or longer special nuts (**Figure 68**) while the rear cylinder uses the normal type of nuts.*

12. Install the engine hanger plates (A, **Figure 69**) onto the crankcase studs and install the washers and nuts (B, **Figure 69**). Don't forget to install the one

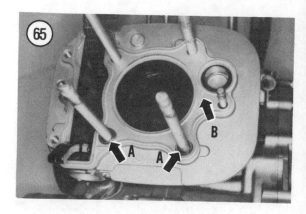

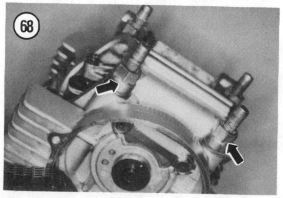

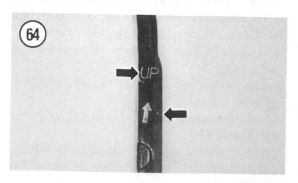

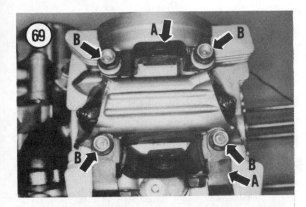

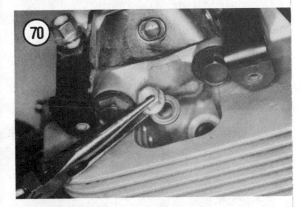

nut and washer (**Figure 70**) in the recess on the spark plug side of the cylinder head.

13. Using a crisscross pattern, tighten the nuts securing the engine hanger plates and the cylinder head (**Figure 71**). Tighten the bolts to the torque specifications in **Table 2**.

14. Install the left-hand bolts (**Figure 34**) securing the cylinder head. Tighten the bolts to the torque specifications in **Table 2**.

15. Make sure the timing mark on the alternator rotor is still aligned correctly to ensure proper valve timing. Perform the following:

   a. Temporarily install the left-hand crankcase cover and hold it in place with several screws.

   b. Remove the timing hole cover and the crankshaft cover.

   c. Observe that the "T" timing mark on the edge of the alternator rotor is aligned with the fixed pointer on the crankcase (**Figure 72**). If alignment is incorrect, use the bolt (**Figure 73**) on the left-hand end of the crankshaft and turn the crankshaft *clockwise* until the "T" timing mark on the edge of the alternator rotor is aligned with the fixed pointer on the crankcase (**Figure 72**).

NOTE
In the following step, the locating pin may want to partially back out of the blind hole in the camshaft due to residual cleaning solvent or engine oil remaining in this receptacle. To help remedy this problem, spray the blind hole in the camshaft with an aerosol electrical contact cleaner, then use compressed air to blow out this blind hole. This will allow the pin to go in the desired amount although it may still stick out farther than necessary at first.

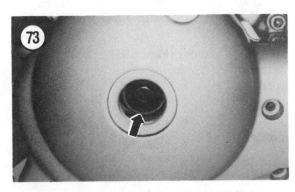

16. Install the locating pin (**Figure 33**) into the end of the camshaft and push it in as far as it will go.

17. Pull the drive chain off the camshaft shoulder.

18. Position the camshaft sprocket with the timing mark facing out and straight up for alignment with the fixed pointer on the top inside surface of the cylinder head.

19. Correctly mesh the sprocket with the drive chain so the index mark on the camshaft sprocket aligns with the fixed pointer on the cylinder head (**Figure 74**) and install the sprocket (B, **Figure 32**) onto the camshaft shoulder while aligning the locating dowel with the sprocket notch (A, **Figure 32**).

> *CAUTION*
> *Very expensive damage could result from improper camshaft and camshaft chain alignment. Recheck your work several times to make sure alignment is correct.*

20. Insert your finger into the camshaft drive chain tensioner hole in the cylinder and press on the drive chain damper. This will take up the slack in the drive chain; make sure the sprocket timing mark is still aligned. If alignment is incorrect, adjust it at this time by repositioning the drive chain on the sprocket, in either direction, until correct alignment is obtained.

21. On the rear cylinder only, install the oil baffle plate (C, **Figure 28**) and bolt (B, **Figure 28**) securing the sprocket.

22. Place a wrench on the bolt (**Figure 73**) on the left-hand end of the crankshaft to prevent it from turning, then tighten the camshaft sprocket mounting bolt to the torque specifications in **Table 2**.

23. Push the tensioner lifter (**Figure 75**) all the way into the tensioner body, then install the tensioner lifter, new gasket and the bolts (**Figure 31**) into the cylinder. Tighten the bolts to the torque specifications in **Table 2**.

24. Install the spring (**Figure 30**) and the center bolt (**Figure 29**). Tighten the center bolt to the torque specifications in **Table 2**.

25. Inspect the large O-ring seal (**Figure 76**) on the side cover and install the side cover and bolts (**Figure 26**). Tighten the bolts securely.

26. Install the engine into the frame as described in this chapter.

27. Repeat Steps 2-26 for the front cylinder head, noting the following that are unique to the front cylinder head:

    a. The front cylinder camshaft sprocket is not equipped with an oil baffle plate like the one used on the rear cylinder.

    b. In Step 15c, the slit in the alternator rotor should align with the crankcase cover stationary pointer.

    c. Install the front hanger plate and install the nuts (A, **Figure 44**) and the nuts and washers (B, **Figure 44**) securing the front engine hanger plate to the cylinder head and tighten the nuts to the torque specification in **Table 2**.

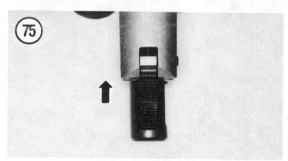

d. Install the ignition coil assembly and the bolt (**Figure 43**) on each side. Tighten the bolts securely.

28. Adjust the valves as described in Chapter Three in this section of the manual.

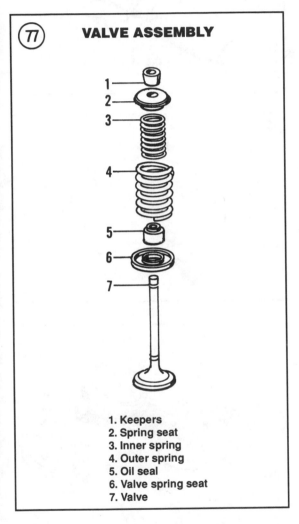

VALVE ASSEMBLY

1. Keepers
2. Spring seat
3. Inner spring
4. Outer spring
5. Oil seal
6. Valve spring seat
7. Valve

VALVES AND VALVE COMPONENTS

Removal

Refer to **Figure 77** for this procedure.

1. Remove the cylinder head as described in this chapter.

> *CAUTION*
> *To avoid loss of spring tension, do not compress the springs any more than necessary to remove the keepers.*

2. Compress the valve springs with a valve compressor tool (**Figure 78**). Remove the valve keepers and release the compression. Remove the valve compressor tool.

3. Remove the valve spring retainer and valve springs (**Figure 79**).

> *NOTE*
> *The valve spring seat and valve stem seal will stay in the cylinder head (**Figure 80**).*

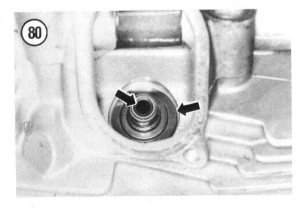

4. Prior to removing the valve, remove any burrs from the valve stem (**Figure 81**). Otherwise the valve guide will be damaged.

5. Mark all parts as they are disassembled so that they will be installed in their same locations.

Inspection

1. Clean valves with a wire brush and solvent.

> *NOTE*
> *The valve contact surface **cannot** be ground as it has a special coating. If defective, the valve(s) must be replaced.*

2. Inspect the contact surface of each valve for burning or pitting (**Figure 82**). Unevenness of the contact surface is an indication that the valve is not serviceable.

3. Measure the valve stem for wear. Compare with specifications given in **Table 1**.

4. Remove all carbon and varnish from the valve guide with a stiff spiral wire brush. Measure each valve guide at top, middle and bottom with a small hole gauge. Compare with specifications given in **Table 1**.

5. Subtract the measurements taken in Step 3 from the measurement taken in Step 4. The difference is the valve-to-valve stem clearance. See **Table 1** for correct clearance. Replace any guide or valve that is not within tolerance. Valve guide replacement is discussed in this chapter.

6. Insert each valve in its guide. Hold the valve just slightly off its seat and rock it sideways in 2 directions. If it rocks more than slightly, the guide is probably worn and should be replaced. If a dial indicator is available, a more accurate measurement can be made as shown in **Figure 83**. Replace any guides that exceed the valve stem-to-guide clearance specified in **Table 1**. If the guides must be replaced, take the cylinder head to a dealer or machine shop.

7. Measure each valve spring free length with a vernier caliper (**Figure 84**). All should be within the length specified in **Table 1** with no signs of bends or distortion. Replace all defective springs in pairs (inner and outer).

8. Measure the tilt of all springs as shown in **Figure 85**. Compare with specifications listed in **Table 1**.

9. Inspect each set of valve springs (**Figure 79**) for wear, distortion or damage. Replace as a set if necessary.

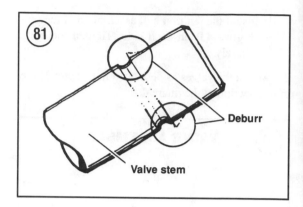

Deburr

Valve stem

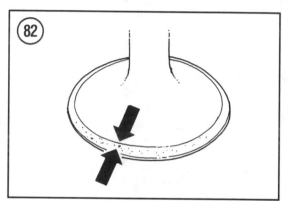

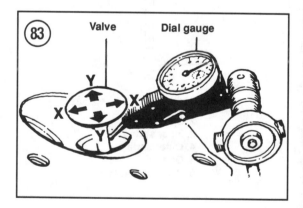

Valve   Dial gauge

Y

X   X

Y

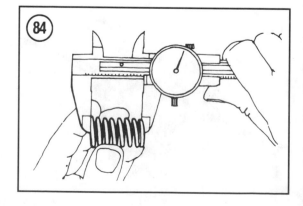

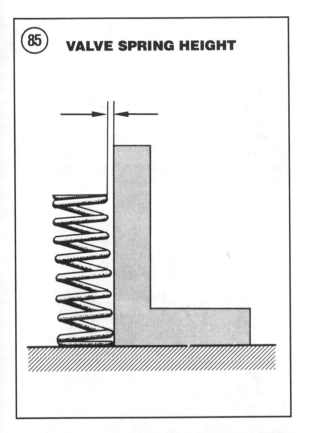

(85) **VALVE SPRING HEIGHT**

10. Check the valve spring retainer and valve keepers. If they are in good condition they may be reused; replace as necessary.

11. Inspect valve seats (B, **Figure 55**). If worn or burned, they must be reconditioned. This should be performed by your dealer or a qualified machine shop. Seats and valves in near-perfect condition can be reconditioned by lapping with a fine carborundum paste. Lapping, however, is always inferior to precision grinding.

Installation

1. Coat the valve stems with molybdenum disulfide grease. To avoid damage to the valve stem seal, turn the valve slowly while inserting the valve into the cylinder head.

2. Install the valve springs with their closer wound coils facing the cylinder head. First install the inner spring (**Figure 86**) and then the outer spring (**Figure 87**).

3. Install the valve spring retainer (**Figure 88**).

CAUTION
To avoid loss of spring tension, do not compress the springs any more than necessary to install the keepers.

4. Compress the valve springs with a compressor tool (**Figure 78**) and install the valve keepers.

5. After the keepers have been installed and the compresssor tool removed, gently tap the end of the valve stem (**Figure 89**) with a soft aluminum or brass drift and hammer. This will ensure that the keepers are properly seated.

(86)

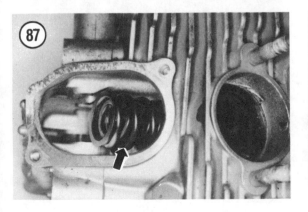

(87)

(88)

Valve Guide Replacement

When valve guides are worn so that there is excessive valve stem-to-guide clearance or valve tipping, the guides must be replaced. This job should only be done by a dealer as special tools are required as well as considerable expertise. If the valve guide is replaced; also replace the respective valve.

Valve Seat Reconditioning

Special valve cutter tools and considerable expertise are required to properly recondition the valve seats in the cylinder head. You can save considerable money by removing the cylinder head(s) and taking just the cylinder head(s) to a dealer or machine shop and have the valve seats ground.

Valve Lapping

Valve lapping is a simple operation which can restore the valve seal without machining if the amount of wear or distortion is not too great.

1. Coat the valve seating area in the head with a lapping compound such as Carborundum or Clover Brand.

2. Insert the valve into the cylinder head.

3. Wet the suction cup of the lapping stick and stick it onto the head of the valve. Lap the valve to the seat by rotating the lapping stick in both directions. Every 5 to 10 seconds, rotate the valve 180° in the valve seat; continue lapping until the contact surfaces of the valve and the valve seat are a uniform grey. Stop as soon as they are, to avoid removing too much material.

4. Thoroughly clean the cylinder head and all valve components in solvent or detergent and hot water to remove all grinding compound. Any compound left on the valves or the cylinder head will end up in the engine and will cause damage.

5. After the lapping has been completed and the valve assemblies have been reinstalled into the head, the valve seal should be tested. Check the seal of each valve by pouring solvent into each of the intake and exhaust ports. The solvent should not flow past the valve seat and the valve head. Perform on all sets of valves. If fluid leaks past any of the seats, disassemble that valve assembly and repeat the lapping procedure until there is no leakage.

6. If the cylinder head and valve components were cleaned in detergent and hot water, apply a light coat

of engine oil to all bare metal surfaces to prevent any rust formations.

ROCKER ARM ASSEMBLIES

The rocker arms and rocker arm shafts are identical (same Yamaha part No.) but they will develop different wear patterns during use. It is recommended that all parts be marked during removal so that they can be assembled in their original position.

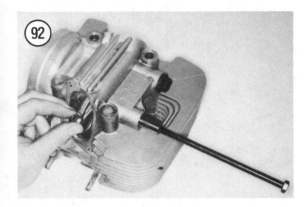

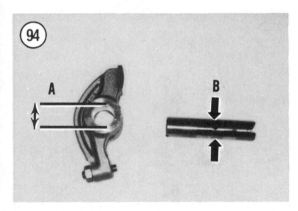

Removal/Inspection/Installation

1. Remove the cylinder head(s) as described in this chapter.

2. Remove the rocker arm shaft bolts and washers (**Figure 90**).

3. Install one of the 10 mm crankcase bolts into the end of the rocker arm shaft (**Figure 91**).

4. Hold onto the rocker arm and withdraw the rocker arm shaft with the bolt (**Figure 92**).

5. Wash all parts in cleaning solvent and thoroughly dry.

6. Inspect the rocker arm pad where it rides on the camshaft lobe and where the adjuster rides on the valve stem (**Figure 93**). If the pad is scratched or unevenly worn, inspect the camshaft lobe for scoring, chipping or flat spots. Replace the rocker arm if defective.

7. Measure the inside diameter of the rocker arm bore (A, **Figure 94**) with an inside micrometer and check against the dimension listed in **Table 1**. Replace if worn to the service limit or greater.

8. Inspect the rocker arm shaft for signs of wear or scoring. Measure the shaft outside diameter (B, **Figure 94**) with a micrometer and check against the dimension listed in **Table 1**. Replace if worn to the service limit or less.

9. Inspect the rocker arm shaft bolt sealing washer (A, **Figure 95**) for damage and replace if necessary.

10. Make sure the rocker arm shaft bolt oil hole (B, **Figure 95**) is clear, clean out if necessary with a piece of wire and compressed air. This hole must be free and clear for proper upper end lubrication.

11. Coat the rocker arm shaft and rocker arm bore with assembly oil or fresh engine oil.

12. Correctly position the rocker arm (**Figure 96**) in the cylinder head and install the rocker arm shaft.

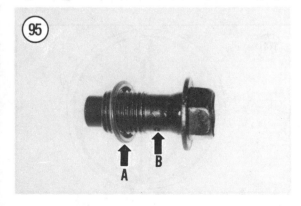

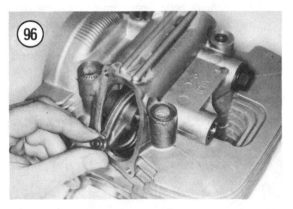

13. Push the rocker arm shaft all the way through the rocker arm until it bottoms out in the cylinder head.

14. Install a sealing washer (**Figure 97**) on the rocker arm shaft bolt and install the bolt.

15. Repeat Steps 3-14 for the other rocker arm assembly.

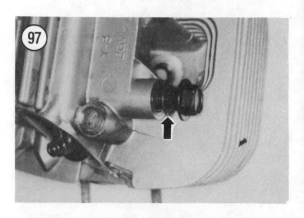

CYLINDER

Removal

1. Remove the cylinder head as described in this chapter.

2. Remove the bolt (**Figure 98**) on the camshaft chain side of the cylinder.

3. Loosen the cylinder by tapping around the perimeter with a rubber or plastic mallet. If necessary, *gently* pry the cylinder loose with a broad-tipped screwdriver.

4. Pull the cylinder straight up and off of the crankcase studs. Work the cam chain wire through the opening in the cylinder and retie the wire to the crankcase so the chain will not fall into the crankcase.

5. Remove the cylinder base gasket and discard it. Remove the small dowel pins from the crankcase studs and the one large dowel pin and O-ring seal.

6. Stuff clean shop cloths into the crankcase opening to prevent objects from falling into the crankcase.

7. Repeat Steps 2-6 for the other cylinder.

Inspection

1. Soak with solvent any old cylinder head gasket material on the cylinder. Use a broad-tipped *dull* chisel and gently scrape off all gasket residue. Do not gouge the sealing surface as oil and air leaks will result.

2. Measure the cylinder bore with a cylinder gauge (**Figure 99**) or inside micrometer at the points shown in **Figure 100**.

3. Measure in 2 axes—in line with the piston pin and at 90° to the pin. If the taper or out-of-round is 0.004 in. (0.10 mm) or greater, the cylinder must be rebored to the next oversize and a new piston and rings installed. Rebore both cylinders even if only one is worn.

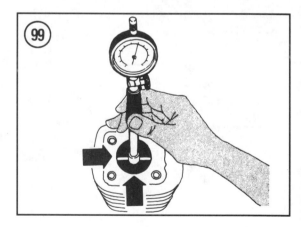

NOTE
The new piston should be obtained be-
fore the cylinder is rebored so that the

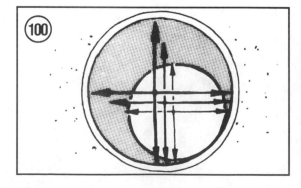

*piston can be measured; slight manu-
facturing tolerances must be taken into
account to determine the actual size and
working clearance. Piston-to-cylinder
wear limit is listed in **Table 1**.*

4. Check the cylinder wall (**Figure 101**) for
scratches; if evident, the cylinder should be rebored.

NOTE
*The maximum wear limit on the cylinder
is listed in **Table 1**. If the cylinder is
worn to this limit, it must be replaced.
Never rebore a cylinder if the finished
rebore diameter will be this dimension
or greater.*

5. Check the cylinder base O-ring (**Figure 102**).
Replace if worn or damaged.

Installation

1. Check that the top surface of the crankcase and
the bottom surface of the cylinder are clean prior to
installing a new base gasket.
2. Install a new cylinder base gasket (A, **Figure
103**).
3. Install the 2 small dowel pins (B, **Figure 103**) and
the large dowel pin and O-ring seal (C, **Figure 103**).
4. Make sure the end gaps of the piston rings are *not*
lined up with each other—they must be staggered.
Lubricate the piston rings and the inside of the
cylinder bore with assembly oil or fresh engine oil.

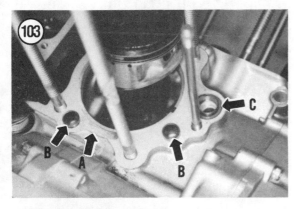

5. Carefully install the cylinder and slide it down
onto the crankcase studs. Guide the camshaft chain
and camshaft tensioner assembly into the camshaft
chain slot in the cylinder.
6. Carefully feed the cam chain and wire up through
the opening in the cylinder and tie it to the engine.
7. Install the cylinder and slide it down onto the
crankcase studs. Guide the camshaft chain and camshaft tensioner assembly into the camshaft chain slot
in the cylinder.
8. Carefully feed the camshaft chain wire up through
the opening in the cylinder and tie the wire to the
exterior of the engine.
9. Start the cylinder down over the piston. Compress
each piston ring with your fingers as it enters the
cylinder (**Figure 104**).
10. Slide the cylinder down until it bottoms out on
the crankcase (**Figure 105**).
11. Repeat Steps 1-10 for the other cylinder.

12. Install the cylinder head as described in this chapter.

PISTONS AND PISTON RINGS

Piston
Removal/Installation

1. Remove the cylinder head(s) and cylinder(s) as described in this chapter.

2. Stuff clean shop cloths into the crankcase opening to prevent objects from falling into the crankcase.

3. Lightly mark the top of the pistons with an "F" (front) or "R" (rear) so they will be installed into the correct cylinder.

4. Remove the piston rings as described in this chapter.

5. Before removing the piston, hold the rod tightly and rock the piston as shown in **Figure 106**. Any rocking motion (do not confuse with the normal sliding motion) indicates wear on the piston pin, piston pin bore or connecting rod small-end bore (more likely a combination of these). Mark the piston and pin so that they will be reassembled into the same set.

6. Remove the clips from each side of the piston pin bore (A, **Figure 107**) with a small screwdriver or scribe. Hold your thumb over one edge of the clip when removing it to prevent the clip from springing out.

7. Use a proper size wooden dowel or socket extension and push out the piston pin.

> *CAUTION*
> *Be careful when removing the pin to avoid damaging the connecting rod. If it is necessary to gently tap the pin to remove it, be sure that the piston is properly supported so that lateral shock is not transmitted to the lower connecting rod bearing.*

8. If the piston pin is difficult to remove, heat the piston and pin with a butane torch. The pin will probably push right out. Heat the piston to only about 140° F (60° C), i.e., until it is too warm to touch, but not excessively hot. If the pin is still difficult to push out, use a homemade tool as shown in **Figure 108**.

9. Lift the piston off the connecting rod and inspect it as described in this chapter.

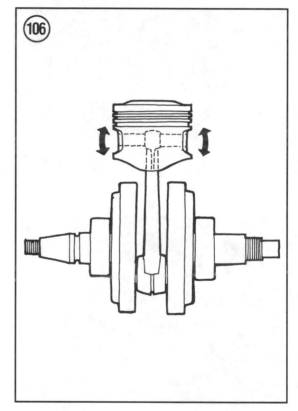

10. If the piston is going to be left off for some time, place a piece of foam insulation tube over the end of the rod to protect it.

11. Apply molybdenum disulfide grease to the inside surface of the connecting rod.

12. Oil the piston pin with assembly oil or fresh engine oil and install it in the piston until its end

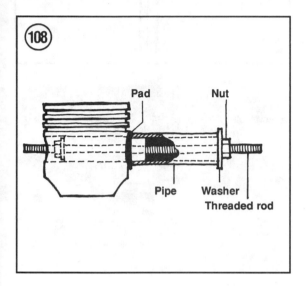

Pad **Nut**

Pipe **Washer**
Threaded rod

extends slightly beyond the inside of the boss (**Figure 109**).

13. Place the piston over the connecting rod with the "EX" mark (**Figure 110**) on the front piston crown directed toward the front of the engine and the "EX" on the rear piston should face toward the rear of the engine.

14. Line up the piston pin with the hole in the connecting rod. Push the piston pin through the connecting rod and into the other side of the piston until it is even with the piston pin clip grooves.

CAUTION
If it is necessary to tap the piston pin into the connecting rod, do so gently with a block of wood or a soft-faced hammer. Make sure you support the piston to prevent the lateral shock from being transmitted to the connecting rod bearing.

NOTE
In the next step, install the clips with the gap away from the cutout in the piston (B, Figure 107).

15. Install *new* piston pin clips in both ends of the pin boss. Make sure they are seated in the grooves in the piston.

16. Check the installation by rocking the piston back and forth around the pin axis and from side to side along the axis. It should rotate freely back and forth but not from side to side.

17. Install the piston rings as described in this chapter.

18. Repeat Steps 1-17 for the other piston.

Piston Inspection

1. Carefully clean the carbon from the piston crown (**Figure 111**) with a chemical remover or with a soft scraper. Do not remove or damage the carbon ridge around the circumference of the piston above the top ring. If the piston, rings and cylinder are found to be dimensionaly correct and can be reused, removal of the carbon ring from the top of the piston or the carbon ridge from the top of the cylinder will promote excessive oil consumption.

CAUTION
Do not wire brush the piston skirts.

2. Examine each ring groove for burrs, dented edges and wide wear. Pay particular attention to the top compression ring groove as it usually wears more than the other grooves.

3. If damage or wear indicates piston replacement, select a new piston as described under *Piston Clearance Measurement* in this chapter.

4. Oil the piston pin and install it in the connecting rod. Slowly rotate the piston pin and check for radial and axial play (**Figure 112**). If any play exists, the piston pin should be replaced, providing the rod bore is in good condition.

5. Measure the inside diameter of the piston pin bore with a snap gauge (**Figure 113**) and measure the outside diameter of the piston pin with a micrometer (**Figure 114**). Compare with dimensions given in **Table 1**. Replace the piston and piston pin as a set if either or both are worn.

6. Check the oil control holes (**Figure 115**) in the piston for carbon or oil sludge buildup. Clean the holes with a small diameter drill bit and blow out with compressed air.

7. Check the piston skirt for galling and abrasion which may have been caused by piston seizure. If light galling is present, smooth the affected area with No. 400 emery paper and oil or a fine oilstone. However, if galling is severe or if the piston is deeply scored, replace it.

8. If damage or wear indicate piston replacement, select a new piston as described under *Piston Clearance Measurement* in this chapter.

Piston Clearance Measurement

1. Make sure the piston and cylinder walls are clean and dry.

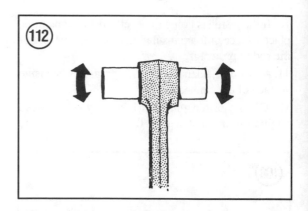

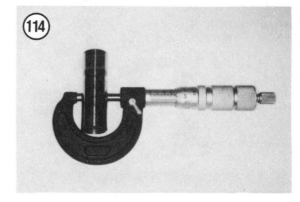

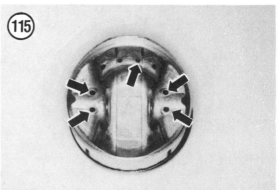

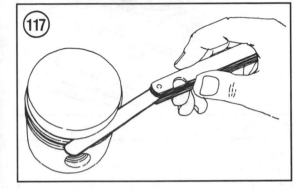

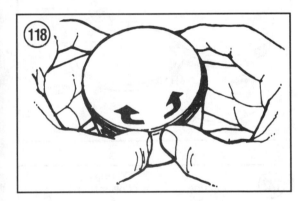

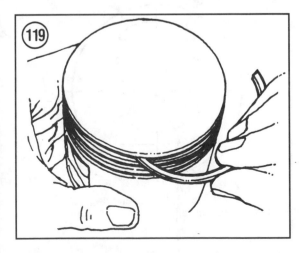

2. Measure the inside diameter of the cylinder bore at a point 1/2 in. (13 mm) from the upper edge with a bore gauge.

3. Measure the outside diameter of the piston across the skirt (**Figure 116**) at right angles to the piston pin. Measure at a distance 0.40 in. (10 mm) up from the bottom of the piston skirt.

4. Subtract the dimension of the piston from the cylinder dimension and compare to the dimension listed in **Table 1**. If clearance is excessive, the piston should be replaced and the cylinder should be re-bored to the next oversize. Purchase the new pistons first; measure its diameter and add the specified clearance to determine the proper cylinder bore diameter.

Piston Ring
Removal/Installation

> *WARNING*
> *The edges of all piston rings are very*
> *sharp. Be careful when handling them*
> *to avoid cutting fingers.*

1. Measure the side clearance of each ring in its groove with a flat feeler gauge (**Figure 117**) and compare to dimensions given in **Table 1**. If the clearance is greater than specified, the rings must be replaced. If the clearance is still excessive with the new rings, the piston must also be replaced.

2. Remove the old rings with a ring expander tool or by spreading the ends with your thumbs just enough to slide the ring up over the piston (**Figure 118**). Repeat for the remaining rings.

3. Carefully remove all carbon buildup from the ring grooves with a broken piston ring (**Figure 119**).

4. Inspect the grooves carefully for burrs, nicks or broken and cracked lands. Recondition or replace the piston if necessary.

5. Check the end gap of each ring. To check the ring, insert the ring, one at a time, into the bottom of the cylinder bore and push it in about 5/8 in. (16 mm) with the crown of the piston to ensure that the ring is square in the cylinder bore. Measure the gap with a flat feeler gauge (**Figure 120**) and compare to dimensions in **Table 1**. If the gap is greater than specified, the rings should be replaced. When installing new rings, measure their end gap in the same manner as for old ones. If the gap is less than specified, carefully file the ends with a fine-cut file until the gap is correct.

NOTE
*The oil control ring expander spacer is
unmeasurable. If the oil control ring
rails show wear, all 3 parts of the oil
control ring should be replaced as a set.*

6. Roll each ring around its piston groove as shown
in **Figure 121** to check for binding. Minor binding
may be cleaned up with a fine-cut file.

NOTE
*Install the compression rings with their
markings facing up.*

7. Install the piston rings—first, the bottom, then the
middle, then the top ring—by carefully spreading
the ends with your thumbs and slipping the rings
over the top of the piston. Remember that the piston
rings must be installed with the manufacturer's
marks on them toward the top of the piston or there
is the possibility of oil pumping past the rings.

8. Make sure the rings are seated completely in their
grooves all the way around the piston and that the
ends are distributed around the piston as shown in
Figure 122. The important thing is that the ring gaps
are not aligned with each other when installed to
prevent compression pressure from escaping.

9. If installing oversize compression rings, check the
number to make sure the correct rings are being
installed. The ring numbers should be the same as
the piston oversize number.

10. If new rings were installed, measure the side
clearance of each ring in its groove with a flat feeler
gauge (**Figure 117**) and compare to dimensions
given in **Table 1**.

OIL PUMP

Removal/Installation

The oil pump can be removed with the engine
mounted in the frame; this procedure is shown with
the engine removed for clarity.

1. Remove the clutch assembly as described in
Chapter Five in this section of the manual.

2. Remove the bolts (**Figure 123**) securing the oil
pump to the crankcase and remove the oil pump
assembly.

3. Remove the small O-ring (A, **Figure 124**) and the
large locating dowel and O-ring (B, **Figure 124**)
from the crankcase.

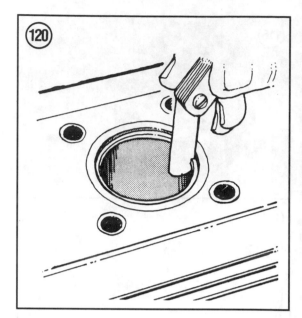

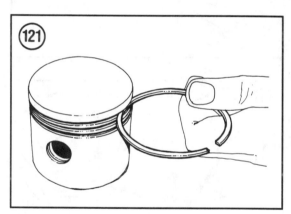

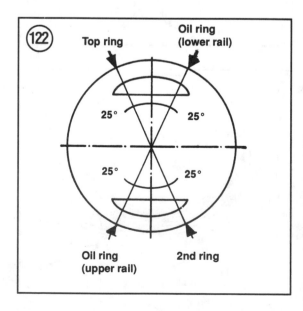

4. Install by reversing these removal steps while noting the following:

    a. Install new O-ring seals.

    b. Install the oil pump mounting bolts and tighten to the torque specification in **Table 2**.

Disassembly/Inspection/Assembly

There are no replacement parts for the oil pump except for the driven gear. If any part(s) is faulty or out of specification, replace the oil pump assembly.

1. Remove the screw and plate (**Figure 125**) securing the oil relief valve in place.

2. Remove the spring (**Figure 126**) and plunger from the oil pump assembly.

3. Remove the Phillips head screw (**Figure 127**) securing the pump cover to the body and remove the cover.

4. Remove the inner and outer rotors and the rotor shaft and dowel pin.

5. Clean all parts in solvent and thoroughly dry.

6. Inspect both rotors (**Figure 128**) for wear and abrasions. If worn or damaged, replace the oil pump assembly.

7. Inspect the oil pump body and cover for cracks (**Figure 129**). If worn or damaged, replace the oil pump assembly.

8. Inspect the teeth on the driven gear (**Figure 130**). Replace the driven gear if the teeth are damaged or any are missing.

9. Coat all parts with fresh engine oil prior to assembly.

10. Install the outer rotor into the oil pump body.

11. Using a flat feeler gauge measure the clearance between the outer rotor and the oil pump body (**Figure 131**). Compare to specifications listed in

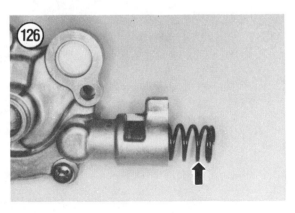

Table 1. If the clearance is worn to the service limit dimension or greater, replace the oil pump assembly.

12. Install the inner rotor into the outer rotor in oil pump body.

13. Using a flat feeler gauge measure the clearance between the inner rotor tip and the outer rotor (**Figure 132**). Compare to specifications listed in **Table 1**. If the clearance is worn to the service limit dimension or greater, replace the oil pump assembly.

14. Install the rotor shaft and dowel pin (**Figure 133**) into the cover.

15. Position the inner rotor with the dowel pin groove facing down and install the inner rotor onto the dowel pin and cover (**Figure 134**).

16. Install the outer rotor onto the inner rotor and align it onto the cover so the body can be installed.

17. Install the body onto the cover and rotor assembly. Align the locating dimple and the recess (**Figure 135**) of the 2 parts and press them together.

18. Install the Phillips head screw (**Figure 127**) securing the pump cover to the body and tighten securely.

19. Install the plunger and the spring (**Figure 126**) into the oil pump assembly.

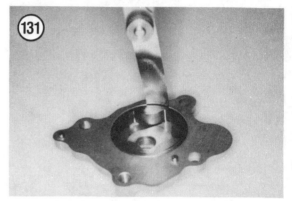

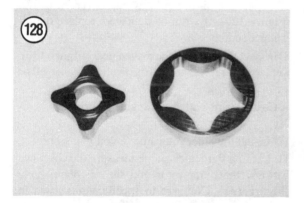

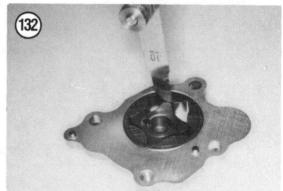

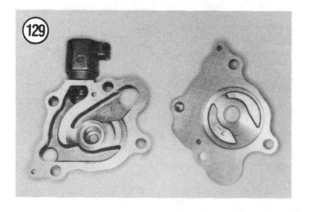

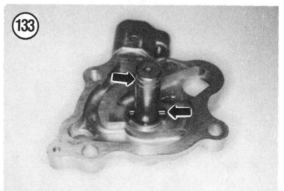

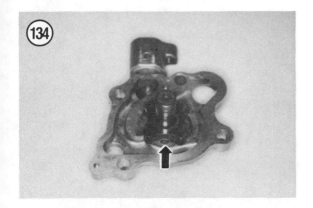

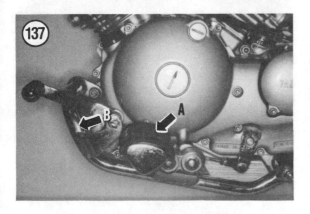

20. Install the plate and screw (**Figure 125**) securing the oil relief valve in place. Tighten the screw securely.

OIL STRAINER

Removal/Inspection/Installation

The oil strainer can be removed with the engine mounted in the frame; this procedure is shown with the engine removed for clarity.

1. Remove the bolt (**Figure 136**) securing the shift lever arm and slide it off the shift shaft.

2. Remove the left-hand foot peg (A, **Figure 137**).

3. Remove the left-hand footrest bar assembly (B, **Figure 137**).

4. Remove the bolt (A, **Figure 138**) securing the oil strainer cover and remove the cover (B, **Figure 138**).

5. Withdraw the oil strainer (**Figure 139**) from the crankcase.

6. Clean the oil strainer and cover in solvent and dry with compressed air.

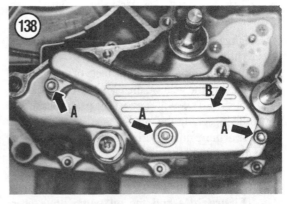

7. Inspect the screen (**Figure 140**) for any broken areas or small holes or damage. If the screen is damaged in any area, replace the strainer.

8. Inspect the O-ring seal (**Figure 141**) on the strainer for deterioration or damage. Replace if necessary.

9. Inspect the O-ring seals (**Figure 142**) on the strainer cover for deterioration or damage. Replace if necessary.

10. Install by reversing these removal steps, while noting the following:

    a. Position the oil strainer with the wing (**Figure 143**) pointing toward the front of the engine and install the strainer.

    b. Make sure all O-ring seals are in place and install the strainer cover. Install the bolts and tighten securely.

PRIMARY DRIVE GEAR

Removal/Installation

1. Remove the engine from the frame as described in this chapter.

2. Remove the clutch assembly as described in Chapter Five in this section of the manual.

3. Temporarily reinstall the clutch outer housing.

4. Straighten the locking tab (A, **Figure 144**) on the primary drive gear lockwasher.

5. Place a shop cloth between the teeth of the primary drive gear and the gear on the backside of the clutch outer housing. This will prevent the gear from rotating while loosening the nut.

6. Loosen the primary drive gear nut (B, **Figure 144**), then remove it.

7. Remove the primary drive gear nut.

8. Remove the lockwasher (**Figure 145**), the holding plate (**Figure 146**) and the oil pump drive gear (**Figure 147**).

9. Remove the clutch outer housing (**Figure 148**).

10. Remove the primary drive gear (**Figure 149**) and the locating key (**Figure 150**) from the crankshaft.

11. Inspect the gears and holding plate (**Figure 151**) for wear or damage. If the gear teeth are worn or damaged they must be replaced.

12. Install by reversing these removal steps while noting the following:

    a. Install the primary drive gear first (A, **Figure 152**), then install the locating key (B, **Figure 152**). This eliminates the problem of the key

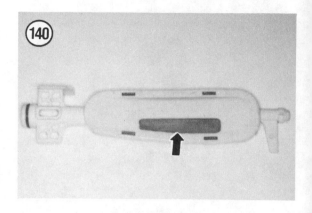

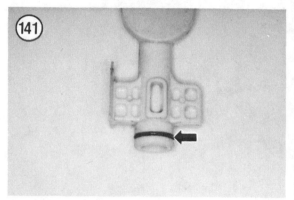

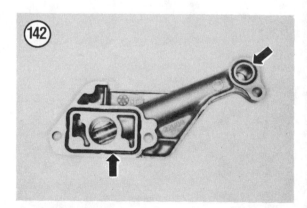

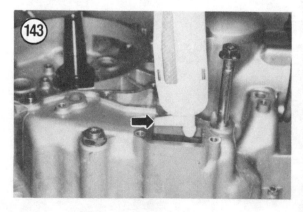

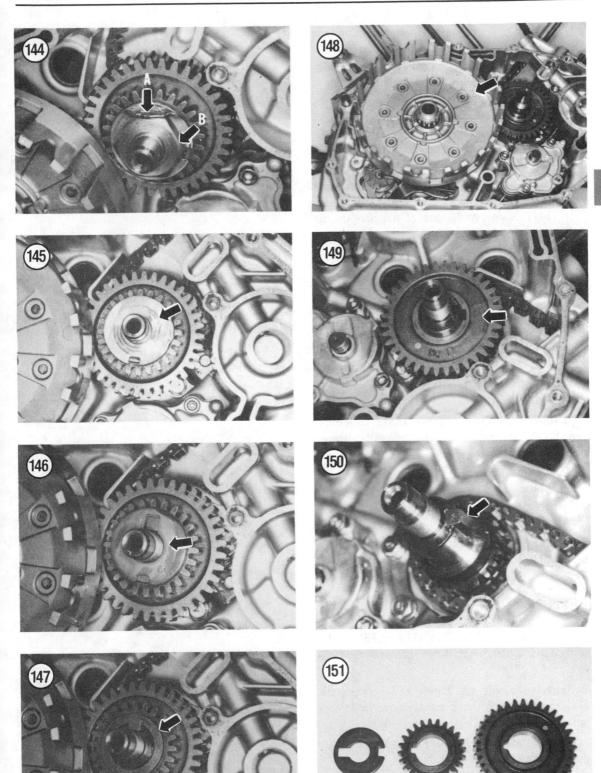

sliding down the keyway when installing the gear onto the shaft.

b. Install the locating tab on the lockwasher (**Figure 153**) into the notch in the holding plate.

c. Place a shop cloth between the teeth of the primary drive gear and the gear on the backside of the clutch outer housing (**Figure 154**). This will prevent the gear from rotating while loosening the nut.

d. Tighten the locknut to the torque specification in **Table 2**. Bend the locking tab (A, **Figure 144**) down against one of the flats on the primary drive gear.

CAMSHAFT DRIVE CHAIN AND DAMPER

Removal/Installation

Front cylinder

1. Remove the primary drive gears as described in this chapter.

2. Remove the bolts (A, **Figure 155**) securing the camshaft drive chain damper and remove the damper unit (B, **Figure 155**).

3. Remove the drive chain (C, **Figure 155**) from the timing sprocket on the crankshaft.

4. Inspect all components as described in this chapter.

5. Install by reversing these removal steps. Install the bolts and tighten to the specification in **Table 2**.

Rear cylinder

1. Remove the alternator rotor (**Figure 156**) as described in Chapter Seven in this section of the manual.

2. Remove the bolts (A, **Figure 157**) securing the camshaft drive chain damper and remove the damper unit (B, **Figure 157**).

3. Remove the drive chain (C, **Figure 157**) from the timing sprocket on the crankshaft.

4. Inspect all components as described in this chapter.

5. Install by reversing these removal steps. Install the bolts and tighten to the specification in **Table 2**.

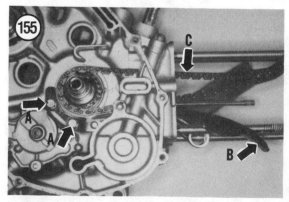

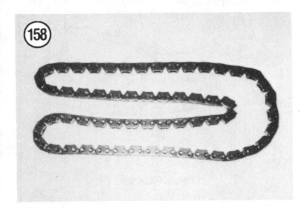

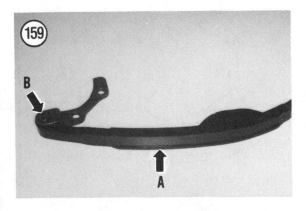

Inspection

1. Inspect the drive chain (**Figure 158**) for wear, stretching or link damage. Replace if necessary.

2. Inspect the damper unit sliding surface (A, **Figure 159**) for excessive wear or damage. Make sure the pivot point (B, **Figure 159**) moves freely. Replace if necessary.

CRANKCASE

Service to the lower end requires that the crankcase assembly be removed from the motorcycle frame and disassembled (split).

Disassembly

1. Remove the engine as described in this chapter. Remove all exterior assemblies from the crankcase. Set the engine on the workbench.

2. Remove the neutral indictor switch (**Figure 160**) from the exterior of the left-hand crankcase half.

3. On the right-hand side, rotate the gearshift drum so the shift cam ramps align with the reliefs in the crankcase. This is necessary so the drum can pass through the crankcase in Step 8.

4. Starting with the right-hand side, loosen in 1/2 turn increments the No. 14 and No. 13 bolts (**Figure 161**). Remove the bolts.

5. Turn the crankcase over with the left-hand side facing up.

6. On the left-hand side, loosen numbered bolts (1-12) in 1/2 turn increments (**Figure 162**). Start with the highest number first. Remove all bolts.

7. Turn the crankcase over with the right-hand side facing up.

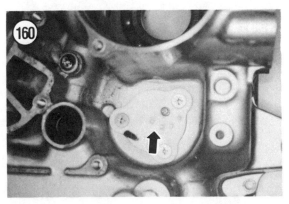

8. Carefully tap around the perimeter of the crankcase with a plastic mallet (do not use a metal hammer) to help separate the 2 case halves. Separate the case halves by pulling the right-hand crankcase up and off the left-hand case half.

9. After separating the crankcase halves, the transmission and crankshaft assemblies should stay with the left-hand crankcase. Check the right-hand crankcase to make sure no transmission shims are stuck to the bearings. If found, reinstall them immediately in their original positions.

10. Remove the 2 small dowel pins and the large O-ring and dowel pin from case halves.

11. Remove the transmission, shift forks and shift drum assemblies from the left-hand crankcase half as described in Chapter Five in this section of the manual.

12. Remove the crankshaft assembly as described in this chapter.

Inspection

1. Remove the screws (**Figure 163**) and remove the oil baffle plate from the right-hand case half.

2. Thoroughly clean the inside and outside of both crankcase halves with cleaning solvent. Dry with compressed air. Make sure there is no solvent residue left in the cases as it will contaminate the engine oil. Lubricate the bearings with oil to prevent rust formation.

3. Make sure all oil passages are clean; blow them out with compressed air.

4. Check the crankcases for cracks or other damage. Inspect the mating surfaces of both halves. They must be free of gouges, burrs or any damage that could cause an oil leak.

5. Make sure the crankcase studs are not bent and the threads are in good condition. Make sure they are screwed into the crankcase tightly.

6. Inspect the crankcase bearings as described in this chapter.

7. Install the oil baffle and the screws (**Figure 163**). Tighten the screws securely.

**Crankcase Bearings
Inspection/Replacement**

1. After cleaning the crankcase halves in cleaning solvent and drying with compressed air, lubricate the bearings with engine oil.

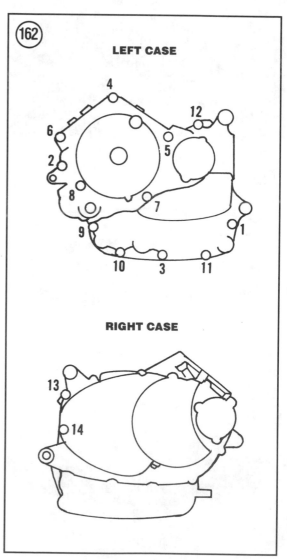

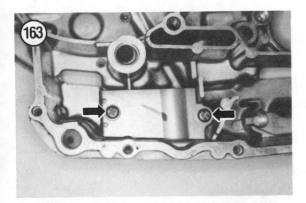

2. Rotate the transmission and bearing inner race and check for play or roughness. Refer to **Figure 164** and **Figure 165**. Replace the bearing if it is noisy or if it does not spin smoothly.

3. Rotate the middle gear shaft bearing inner race (**Figure 166**) and check for play or roughness. Replace the bearing if it is noisy or if it does not spin smoothly.

4. To remove crankcase bearings, perform the following:

a. Heat the crankcase to approximately 205-257° F (95-125° C) in an oven or on a hot plate. Do not attempt bearing removal by heating the crankcases with a torch as this type of localized heating may warp the cases.

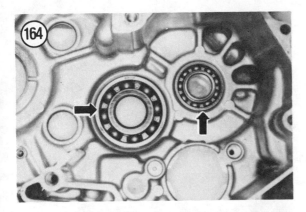

b. Wearing a pair of work gloves for protection, remove the case from the oven and place it on wood blocks for support. Drive out the bearing with a suitable size drift placed on the outside bearing race. A large socket works well for bearing removal.

NOTE
*The main bearings are installed in a steel sleeve that is part of the crankcase (**Figure 167**). Special tools are required to remove and install these bearing and should be entrusted to a Yamaha dealer.*

5. Inspect the crankshaft main bearings (**Figure 168**) for wear (bluish tint) or damage. Replace if necessary.

6. Before installing new bearings, clean the bearing housing and oil passages with solvent. Dry thoroughly with compressed air.

7. Install new crankcase bearings by reversing the removal steps, while noting the following:

a. Installation of the bearings is made easier by first placing the bearings in a freezer for approximately 30 minutes. Then reheat the crankcase half and install the bearing by driving it squarely into position. If the bearing cocks in its bore, remove it and reinstall. It may be necessary to refreeze the bearing and reheat the case half.

b. Lubricate the bearing races with clean engine oil after installation.

Assembly

1. Prior to installation of all parts, coat all parts with assembly oil or engine oil.

2. Install the crankshaft as described in this chapter. Make sure the connecting rods are positioned correctly within the piston opening (**Figure 169**).

3. Place the left-hand crankcase on wood blocks.

4. Install the shift drum, shift forks and transmission assemblies (**Figure 170**) as described in Chapter Five in this section of the manual.

5. Correctly align the gearshift drum so the shift cam ramps align with the reliefs in the right-hand crankcase. This is necessary so the drum can pass through the crankcase in Step 11.

6. Install the large O-ring and dowel pin (**Figure 171**) and the 2 small dowel pins (**Figure 172**) into the left-hand case half.

7. Apply oil to the transmission shafts and crankshaft bearing surfaces.

8. Clean the crankcase mating surfaces of both halves with aerosol electrical contact cleaner.

9. Make sure the case half sealing surfaces are perfectly clean and dry.

> *NOTE*
> *Always use the correct type of gasket sealer—avoid thick and hard-setting materials.*

10. Apply a light coat of Yamabond No. 4 liquid gasket sealer, or equivalent, to the sealing surfaces of the left-hand half. Make the coating as thin as possible.

11. Align the right-hand crankcase bearings with the left-hand assembly. Join both halves and tap together lightly with a plastic mallet—do not use a metal hammer as it will damage the cases (**Figure 173**).

12. Install all bolts in both crankcase halves and tighten in two stages to a final torque listed in **Table**

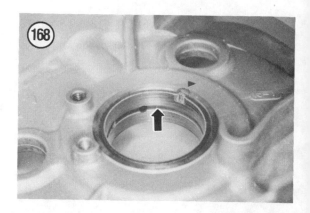

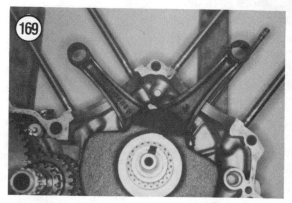

2. Tighten bolts in the correct sequence starting with the lowest number first (**Figure 162**).

13. Install all engine assemblies that were removed.

14. Install the engine as described in this chapter.

CRANKSHAFT AND CONNECTING RODS

Removal/Installation

1. Split the crankcase as described in this chapter.

2. Remove the crankshaft assembly (**Figure 174**) from the left-hand crankcase half.

3. Remove the connecting rod cap bolt nuts (A, **Figure 175**) and separate the rods from the crankshaft.

4. Mark each rod and cap (**Figure 176**) as a set. Also mark them with a "F" (front) and "R" (rear) to indicate from what cylinder they were removed.

5. Mark each rod cap and bearing insert so that they can be reinstalled in their original position.

6. Install by reversing these removal steps while noting the following:

   a. Install the bearing inserts into each connecting rod and cap. Make sure they are locked in place correctly.

   CAUTION
   If the old bearings are reused, be sure they are installed in their exact original positions.

   b. Lubricate the bearings and crankpins with assembly oil and install the rods so that the letter "Y" (B, **Figure 175**) on each rod faces the tapered end of the crankshaft. Apply molybdenum disulfide grease to the threads of the

connecting rod bolts. Install the caps and tighten the cap nuts evenly, in a couple of steps, to the torque specification listed in **Table 2**.

> *CAUTION*
> *On the final tightening sequence, if a torque of 22 ft.-lb. (32 N•m) is reached, do not stop tightening until the final torque value is achieved. If the tightening is interrupted between 22-25 ft.-lb. (32-36 N•m), loosen the nut to less than 22 ft.-lb. (32 N•m) and tighten to the final torque value in one step.*

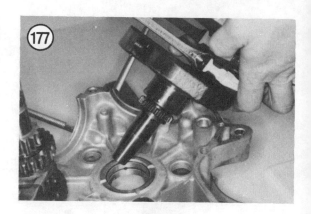

7. Position the crankshaft with the tapered end going into the left-hand crankcase (**Figure 177**) and install the crankshaft in the left-hand crankcase bearing. When installing the crankshaft, align the front and rear connecting rods with their respective cylinder position (**Figure 169**). Continue to check this alignment until the crankshaft is completely installed.

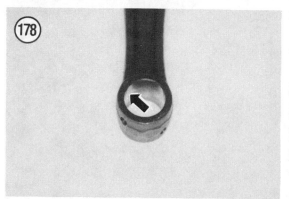

Connecting Rod Inspection

1. Check each rod for obvious damage such as cracks and burns.

2. Check the piston pin bushing (**Figure 178**) for wear or scoring.

3. Take the rods to a machine shop and have them checked for twisting and bending.

4. Examine the bearing inserts (**Figure 179**) for wear, scoring or burning. They are reusable if in good condition. Make a note of the bearing size (if any) stamped on the back of the insert if the bearing is to be discarded; a previous owner may have used undersize bearings.

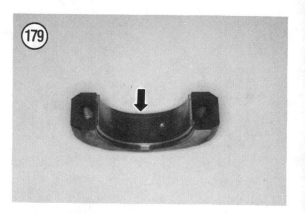

5. Remove the connecting rod bearing bolts (**Figure 180**) and check them for cracks or twisting. Replace any bolts as required and as a set.

6. Check bearing clearance as described in this chapter.

Connecting Rod Bearing and Oil Clearance Measurement

> *CAUTION*
> *If the old bearings are to be reused, be sure that they are installed in their exact original locations.*

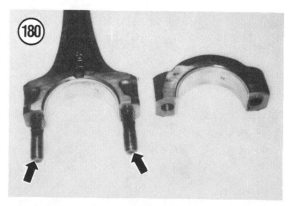

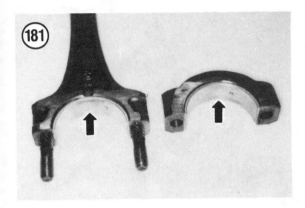

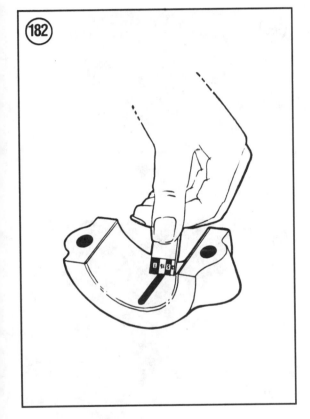

1. Wipe bearing inserts and crankpins clean. Install bearing inserts in rod and cap (**Figure 181**).

2. Place a piece of Plastigage on one crankpin parallel to the crankshaft.

3. Install rod, cap and nuts, then tighten the nuts to 25 ft.-lb. (36 N•m).

CAUTION
Do not rotate crankshaft while Plastigage is in place.

4. Remove nuts and the rod cap.

5. Measure width of flattened Plastigage according to the manufacturer's instructions (**Figure 182**). Measure at both ends of the strip. A difference of 0.001 in. (0.025 mm) or more indicates a tapered crankpin; the crankshaft must be reground or replaced. Use a micrometer and measure the crankpin OD (**Figure 183**) to get an exact journal dimension.

6. If the crankpin taper is within tolerance, measure the bearing clearance with the same strip of Plastigage. Correct bearing clearance is specified in **Table 1**. Remove Plastigage strips.

7. If the bearing clearance is greater than specified, use the following steps for new bearing selection.

8. The connecting rods and caps are marked with a No. 4 or No. 5.

9. The crankshaft is marked on the left-hand counterbalancer with a set of 2 numbers (**Figure 184**). The numbers relate to the crankshaft connecting rod journals, reading from left to right.

10. To select the proper bearing insert number, subtract the crankshaft connecting rod journal number (Step 9) from the connecting rod and cap number (Step 8). For example, if the connecting rod and cap number is 4 and the crankshaft connecting rod journal is 2, 4 - 2 = 2. The new bearing insert should be coded 2.

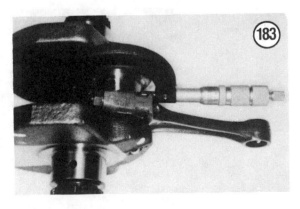

11. After new bearings have been installed, recheck clearance with Plastigage. If the clearance is out of specifications, either the connecting rod or the crankshaft is worn beyond the service limit. Refer the engine to a dealer or qualified specialist.

Connecting Rod Side Clearance Measurement

1. With both connecting rods attached to the crankshaft, insert a flat feeler gauge between the counterweight and the connecting rod big end (**Figure 185**).

2. The specified side clearance is listed in **Table 1**.

3. If the clearance is out of specification, either the connecting rod or the crankshaft is worn beyond the service limit. Refer the engine to a dealer or qualified specialist.

Crankshaft Inspection

1. Clean crankshaft thoroughly with solvent. Clean oil holes with rifle cleaning brushes; flush thoroughly and dry with compressed air. Lightly oil all oil journal surfaces immediately to prevent rust.

2. If the surface on all journals is satisfactory, take the crankshaft to your dealer or local machine shop. They can check out-of-roundness, taper and wear on the journals. They can also check crankshaft alignment and inspect for cracks. Check against measurements given in **Table 1**.

3. Inspect the cam chain sprockets at each end. Refer to **Figure 186** and **Figure 187**. If they are worn or damaged, the crankshaft will have to be replaced. Also inspect the condition of both chains; replace if necessary.

Crankshaft Bearing and Oil Clearance Measurement

1. Wipe bearing inserts in the crankcase and the main bearing journals clean.

2. Use a micrometer and measure the main journal OD (**Figure 188**) at two places. Write these dimensions down.

3. Use a bore gauge and measure the main journal insert ID (**Figure 189**) at two places. Write these dimensions down.

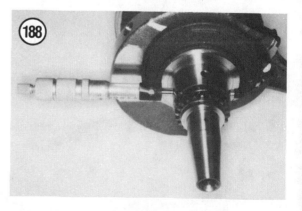

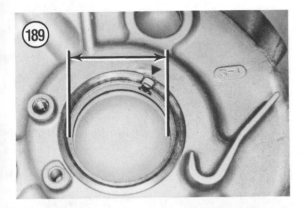

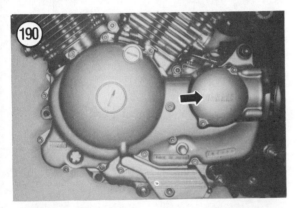

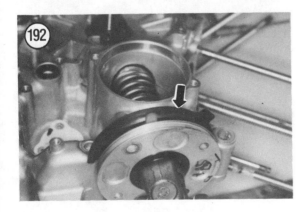

4. To select the proper bearing insert number, subtract the crankshaft OD (Step 2) from the main journal insert ID (Step 3).

5. The oil clearance specification is listed in **Table 1**. If the clearance is out of specifications, either the crankshaft or the bearing insert is worn beyond the service limit. Refer the engine to a dealer or qualified specialist.

MIDDLE DRIVE GEAR

4

Removal/Installation

1. Remove the bolts securing the middle drive gear cover (**Figure 190**) and remove the cover and O-ring gasket.

2. Remove the engine from the frame as described in this chapter.

3. Remove the bolts (**Figure 191**) securing the middle driven gear bearing housing.

4. Remove the bearing housing and shims from the crankcase. Note the location and number of shims (**Figure 192**). They must be reinstalled in the same location.

5. Separate the crankcase as described in this chapter. Do not remove the transmission shaft assemblies.

6. Unstake the nut securing the middle drive gear.

7. Remove the first gear (**Figure 193**) from the transmission drive shaft.

8. Install the "Grabbit," or equivalent onto the transmission drive shaft forth gear (**Figure 194**) this will keep the transmission shaft from rotating while loosening the middle drive gear nut.

9. Loosen, then remove the middle drive gear nut (A, **Figure 195**).

10. Remove the middle drive gear (B, **Figure 195**) and if necessary, remove the transmission drive shaft as described in Chapter Five.

11. Inspect the components as described in this chapter.

12. Install by reversing these removal steps while noting the following:

a. Be sure to install the same number of shims and in the same location (**Figure 192**) as noted during removal.

b. Use the same tool set-up used during removal (**Figure 196**) to keep the transmission shaft from rotating while tightening the middle drive gear nut. Tighten the drive gear nut to the torque specification in **Table 2**.

c. Stake the nut securing the middle drive gear.

d. Tighten the middle driven gear bearing housing bolts to the torque specification in **Table 2**.

e. Make sure the O-ring seal (**Figure 197**) is in place on the middle drive gear cover. Install the cover and tighten the screws securely.

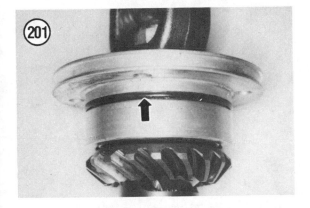

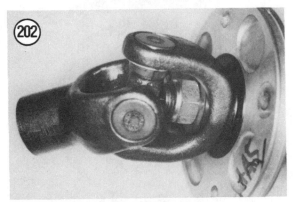

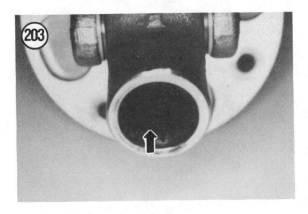

Inspection

Special tools are required to disassemble the driven shaft assembly. Refer this type of work to a Yamaha dealer or competent machine shop.

1. Inspect for chipped or missing teeth on the middle drive (**Figure 198**) and the driven gear (A, **Figure 199**). If either gear is damaged, both the drive and driven gears must be replaced as a set.

2. Inspect the drive gear inner splines (**Figure 200**) for wear or damage. If damaged, both the drive and driven gears must be replaced as a set.

3. Inspect the spring (B, **Figure 199**) for wear, cracks or damage and replace if necessary.

4. Inspect the O-ring seal (**Figure 201**) for deterioration or hardness. Replace if necessary.

5. Move the universal joint (**Figure 202**) back and forth and pull in and out on it. Check for looseness or stiffness, replace if necessary.

6. Inspect the universal joint inner splines (**Figure 203**) for wear or damage. If the splines are damaged, also check the outer splines on the drive shaft for damage. Replace the universal joint if necessary.

STARTER CLUTCH AND REDUCTION GEARS

Removal/Installation

1. Remove the alternator rotor (**Figure 156**) as described in Chapter Seven in this section of the manual.

2. Remove the Woodruff key (**Figure 204**) from the crankshaft.

3. Remove the starter idler gear No. 1 (**Figure 205**) and shaft (**Figure 206**).

4. Slide the idler gear No. 2 (**Figure 207**) from the crankshaft.

5. If necessary, remove the Allen bolts (**Figure 208**) securing the starter clutch assembly to the backside of the alternator rotor and remove the assembly.

6. Inspect the components as described in this chapter.

7. Install by reversing these removal steps while noting the following:.

    a. If removed, apply red Loctite (No. 271) to the bolts prior to installation.

    b. Install the bolts and tighten to the specification in **Table 2**.

Inspection

1. Inspect for chipped or missing teeth on the starter idler gear No. 2 (**Figure 209**) and on the starter idler gear No. 1 (A, **Figure 210**). Replace either gear if necessary.

2. Inspect the starter idler No. 1 shaft (B, **Figure 210**) for wear or damage. Replace if necessary.

3. Inspect the area (**Figure 211**) in the idler gear No. 2 where it rides on the crankshaft for wear or galling. Replace the gear if any damage is evident.

4. Inspect the roller riding surface of the starter idler gear No. 2 for wear or abrasion. Replace the gear if any damage is evident.

5. Check the rollers (**Figure 212**) in the starter clutch for uneven or excessive wear. Replace as a set if any are bad. If damaged, remove the rollers, springs and plungers.

BREAK-IN

Following cylinder servicing (boring, honing, new rings, etc.) and major lower end work, the engine should be broken in just as if it were new. The performance and service life of the engine depends greatly on a careful and sensible break-in. For the first 500 miles, no more than one-third throttle

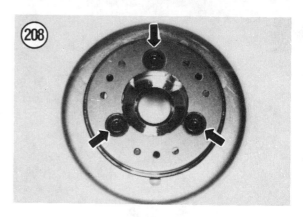

should be used and speed should be varied as much as possible within the one-third throttle limit. Prolonged, steady running at one speed, no matter how moderate, is to be avoided, as is hard acceleration.

Following the 500-mile service, increasingly more throttle can be used but full throttle should not be used until the motorcycle has covered at least 1,000 miles and then it should be limited to short bursts until 1,500 miles have been logged.

The mono-grade oils recommended for break-in and normal use provide a superior bedding pattern for rings and cylinders than do multi-grade oils. As a result, piston ring and cylinder bore life are greatly increased. During this period, oil consumption will be higher than normal. It is therefore important to frequently check and correct the oil level. At no time, during break-in or later, should the oil level be allowed to drop below the bottom line on the inspection window; if the oil level is low, the oil will become overheated resulting in insufficient lubrication and increased wear.

500-Mile Service

It is essential that the oil and filter be changed after the first 500 miles. In addition, it is a good idea to change the oil and filter at the completion of break-in (about 1,500 miles) to ensure that all of the particles produced during break-in are removed from the lubrication system. The small added expense may be considered a smart investment that will pay off in increased engine life.

Table 1   ENGINE SPECIFICATIONS

Item	Specifications in. (mm)	Wear limit in. (mm)
General		
Type	4-stroke, air-cooled, V-twin	
Number of cylinders	2	
Bore and stroke	2.992 × 2.323 in. (76 × 59 mm)	
Displacement	32.64 cu. in. (535 cc)	
Compression ratio	9:1	
Cylinders		
Cylinder liner	Aluminum alloy with cast iron liners	
Warp limit	0.0012 (0.03)	
Bore	2.991-2.993 (75.98-76.02)	
Taper	—	0.002 (0.05)
Out-of-round	—	0.002 (0.05)
Cylinders		
Piston/cylinder clearance	0.0014-0.0022 (0.035-0.055)	0.004 in. (0.1)
		(continued)

Table 1   ENGINE SPECIFICATIONS (continued)

Item	Specifications in. (mm)	Wear limit in. (mm)
Pistons		
Diameter	2.989-2.991 (75.92-75.97)	—
Measuring point	0.14 (3.5)	—
Piston rings		
Number per piston		
Compression	2	—
Oil control	1	—
Ring end gap		
Top	0.012-0.018 (0.30-0.45)	0.028 (0.7)
Top and second	0.012-0.018 (0.30-0.45)	0.031 (0.8)
Oil (side rail)	0.008-0.031 (0.2-0.8)	—
Ring side clearance		
Top	0.001-0.003 (0.03-0.07)	0.005 (0.12)
Second	0.0008-0.0024 (0.02-0.06)	0.005 (0.12)
Crankshaft		
Runout	—	0.0012 (0.03)
Oil clearance	0.0008-0.0020 (0.020-0.052)	—
Connecting rod		
Side clearance	0.011-0.017 (0.27-0.42)	—
Oil clearance	0.001-0.002 (0.026-0.050)	
Camshaft		
Runout	—	0.0012 (0.03)
Oil clearance	0.0008-0.0024 (0.020-0.061)	—
Lobe height		
Intake	1.564 (39.73)	1.560 (39.63)
Exhaust	1.566 (39.77)	1.562 (39.67)
Lobe width		
Intake	1.269 (32.22)	1.229 (31.22)
Exhaust	1.272 (32.30)	1.232 (31.30)
Cam cap inside diameter	1.102-1.103 (28.00-28.02)	—
Camshaft outside diameter	1.100-1.102 (27.96-27.98)	—
Rocker arms and shafts		
Shaft clearance	0.0004-0.0015 (0.009-0.038)	0.0032 (0.08)
Rocker arm inside diameter	0.5512-0.5519 (14.000-14.018)	0.5543 (14.078)
Rocker arm shaft diameter	0.5504-0.5508 (13.980-13.991)	0.5492 (13.950)
Valves		
Valve stem outer diameter		
Intake	0.274-0.275 (6.960-6.990)	0.273 (6.930)

(continued)

Table 1 ENGINE SPECIFICATIONS (continued)

Item	Specifications in. (mm)	Wear limit in. (mm)
Valve clearance outer diameter		
Exhaust	0.273-0.274 (6.930-6.960)	0.272 (6.910)
Valve guide inner diameter		
Intake and exhaust	0.275-0.276 (7.0-7.012)	0.278 (7.05)
Stem-to-guide clearance		
Intake	0.0004-0.0015 (0.010-0.037)	0.0031 (0.08)
Exhaust	0.0010-0.0020 (0.025-0.052)	0.0039 (0.10)
Valve seat width intake & exhaust	0.04-0.05 (1.0- 1.2)	0.055 (1.4)
Valve face width intake & exhaust	0.09 (2.3)	—
Valve stem runout maximum	—	0.0012 (0.03)
Margin thickness intake & exhaust	0.04-0.06 (1.0-1.4)	0.028 (0.7)
Head diameter		
Intake	1.453-1.461 (36.9-37.1)	—
Exhaust	1.256-1.264 (31.9-32.1)	—
Valve springs		
Outer free length		
Intake & exhaust	1.717 (43.6)	—
Inner free length intake & exhaust	1.571 (39.9)	—
Tilt limit intake & exhaust	—	2.5°/0.067 (1.7)
Oil pump		
Tip clearance	0.0-0.005 (0.0-0.12)	0.007 (0.17)
Side clearance	0.001-0.003 (0.03-0.08)	0.003 (0.08)

Table 2 ENGINE TIGHTENING TORQUES

Item	ft.-lb.	N•m
Engine mounting hardware		
Rear upper bolt	40	55
Front upper bolts	40	55
Rear lower through bolt	40	55
Bracket-to-front cylinder head	40	55
Camshaft bushing holder bolts	14	20
Cylinder head bolts and nuts		
Side bolt	14	20
8 mm nut	14	20
10 mm nut	25	35
Cylinder bolt	7.2	10
Camshaft sprocket bolt	40	55
Camshaft chain tensioner		
Mounting bolts	8.7	12
Center bolt	14	20
Camshaft drive chain damper		
mounting bolts	7.2	10
Oil pump mounting bolts	5.1	7
Primary drive gear		
Locknut	50	70
Bearing housing bolts	18	25
Middle drive gear nut	85	120
Starter clutch bearing bolts	14	20
Crankcase bolts		
6 mm	7.2	10
8 mm	17	24
Connecting rod nuts	25	36

4

CHAPTER FIVE

CLUTCH AND TRANSMISSION

CLUTCH

The clutch on the Yamaha XV535 is a wet multi-plate type which operates immersed in the engine oil.

All clutch parts can be removed with the engine in the frame. Refer to **Table 1** for all clutch specifications and **Table 2** for all tightening torques. **Tables 1** and **2** are found at the end of the chapter.

NOTE
This chapter covers all procedures unique to the XV535 Virago V-twins. If a specific procedure is not included in this chapter, refer to Chapter Five in the front of this manual for service procedures.

Removal

Refer to **Figure 1** for this procedure.

Portions of this procedure are shown with the engine remove and partially disassembled. It is not necessary to do so for clutch removal.

1. Place the bike on the sidestand.

2. Drain the engine oil as described in Chapter Three in this section of the manual.

3. At the hand lever, slide back the clutch lever shield (**Figure 2**).

4. Loosen the clutch cable locknut (A, **Figure 3**) and rotate the adjuster (B, **Figure 3**) to allow maximum slack in the cable.

5. At the clutch cable lower adjuster, loosen the locknuts (A, **Figure 4**) and rotate the adjuster (B, **Figure 4**) to allow maximum slack in the cable. Disconnect the clutch cable from the actuating lever.

6. Remove the following from the right-hand side.

   a. Right-hand footpeg assembly (**Figure 5**).

   b. Rear brake pedal and engine guard assembly (**Figure 6**).

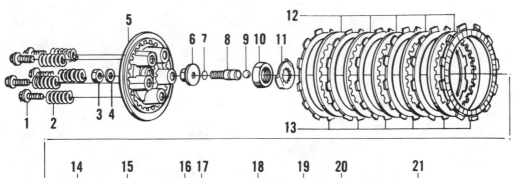

CLUTCH

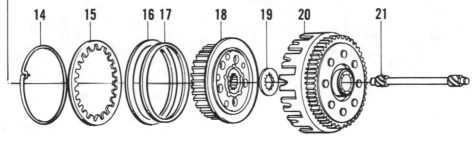

1. Bolt	8. Pushrod No. 1	15. Clutch plate No. 1
2. Spring	9. Steel ball	16. Spring
3. Locknut	10. Clutch nut	17. Spring seat
4. Washer	11. Lockwasher	18. Clutch boss
5. Pressure plate	12. Clutch disc	19. Splined thrust washer
6. Push plate	13. Friction disc	20. Clutch housing
7. O-ring	14. Clutch boss ring	21. Pushrod No. 2

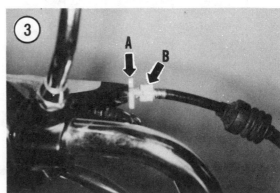

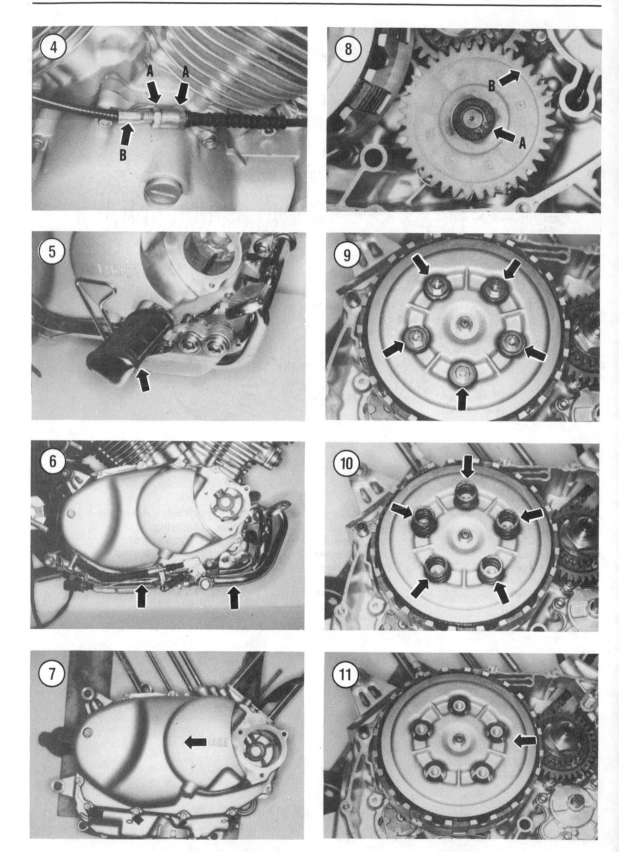

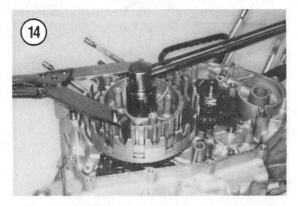

7. Remove the bolts securing the right-hand crankcase cover (**Figure 7**) and remove the cover and gasket. Don't lose the dowel pins.

8. Remove the circlip (A, **Figure 8**) and remove the oil pump drive gear (B, **Figure 8**).

9. Remove the 5 pressure plate screws (**Figure 9**) and springs (**Figure 10**).

10. Remove the pressure plate (**Figure 11**).

11. Remove the clutch plates and friction disc (A, **Figure 12**) and keep them in order.

12. Use a magnetic tool and remove the steel ball from the center of the transmission shaft (B, **Figure 12**).

13. Straighten out the locking tab (A, **Figure 13**) on the clutch nut lockwasher.

NOTE
*To keep the clutch housing from turning, use the "Grabbit" or Yamaha Universal Clutch Holder special tool (part No. YM-91042) on the clutch boss. See **Figure 14**.*

14. Loosen, then remove the clutch nut (B, **Figure 13**) and the lockwasher (**Figure 15**). Discard the lockwasher as a new one must be installed during assembly.

15. Remove the clutch boss (**Figure 16**).

16. Remove the thrust plate (**Figure 17**) and clutch housing (**Figure 18**).

17. Remove the long push rod No. 2 from the center of the transmission shaft.

Inspection

1. Clean all clutch parts in a petroleum-based solvent such as kerosene and thoroughly dry with compressed air.

2. Measure the free length of each clutch spring as shown in **Figure 19**. Replace any springs that are too short (**Table 1**).

3. Measure the thickness of each friction disc (**Figure 20**) at several places around the disc as shown in **Figure 21**. See **Table 1** for specifications. Replace all friction discs if any one is found too thin. Do not replace only 1 or 2 discs.

4. Check the clutch metal plates for warpage as shown in **Figure 22**. If any plate is warped more than

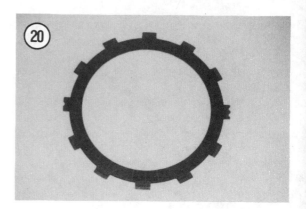

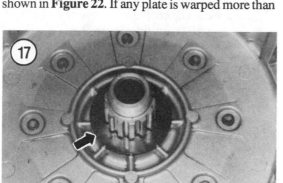

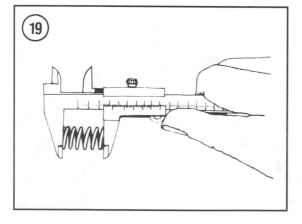

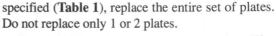

specified (**Table 1**), replace the entire set of plates. Do not replace only 1 or 2 plates.

5. Check the gear teeth on the clutch housing (**Figure 23**). Replace if necessary.

6. Inspect the pressure plate (**Figure 24**) for signs of wear or damage; replace if necessary.

7. Inspect the fingers on the clutch housing (**Figure 25**) and the clutch boss (**Figure 26**) for cracks or galling in the grooves where the clutch friction disc tabs slide (**Figure 27**). They must be smooth for chatter-free clutch operation.

8. Inspect the inner splines (**Figure 28**) in the clutch boss assembly. If damage is only a slight amount, remove any small burrs with a fine cut file; if damage is severe, replace the clutch boss.

NOTE
*The clutch boss is a sub-assembly with a built-in damper located inside the first clutch plate. A large wire clip (**Figure 29**) holds the assembly together. Do not disassemble this unit unless there was severe clutch chatter prior to disassembly.*

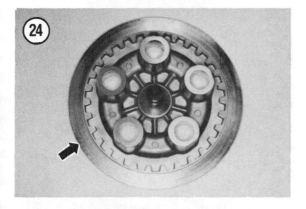

9. Inspect the long push rod No. 2 (**Figure 30**) by rolling it on a flat surface, such as a piece of glass. Any clicking noise detected indicates that the rod is bent and should be replaced.

10. Inspect the clutch nut and splined thrust washer (**Figure 31**) for wear or damage. Replace as necessary.

11. Inspect the end of the pushrod No. 1 (A, **Figure 32**) for wear or damage. If damaged, perform the following:

   a. Remove the nut and washer (**Figure 33**) and remove the pushrod No. 1 and the push plate from the pressure plate.
   b. Inspect the O-ring seal (B, **Figure 32**) on the No. 1 pushrod and replace if necessary.
   c. Reinstall the pushrod No. 1 and push plate into the backside of the pressure plate.
   d. Install the washer and nut. Do not tighten the nut at this time as it must be adjusted after the clutch assembly is installed in the crankcase.

Installation

1. Coat all parts with clean engine oil.

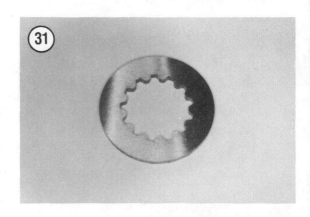

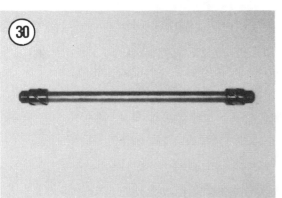

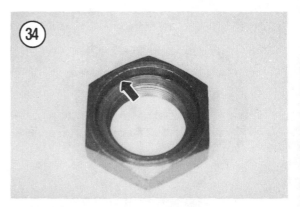

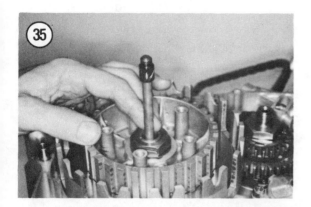

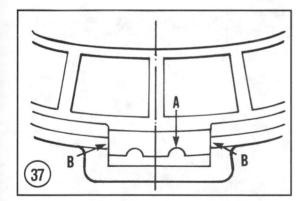

NOTE
While installing the clutch housing, slightly rotate it back and forth until the gears mesh properly. Push it on until it bottoms out.

2. Install the clutch housing (**Figure 18**). Make sure it meshes properly with the primary drive gear.

3. Install the splined thrust washer (**Figure 17**).

4. Install the clutch boss (**Figure 16**).

5. Install the *new* lockwasher (**Figure 15**). Make sure the locking tabs on the lockwasher are inserted into the slots in the pressure plate.

6. Position the clutch nut with the recessed side (**Figure 34**) going on first. Install the clutch nut (B, **Figure 13**) and tighten to specification (**Table 2**) using a torque wrench and holding tool to keep the clutch hub from turning. See **Figure 14**. Bend up the lockwasher (A, **Figure 13**) against one side of the nut.

7. Install the long push rod (**Figure 35**) into the center of the transmission shaft.

8. Install the steel ball (**Figure 36**) into the center of the transmission shaft.

NOTE
*On models so equipped, position the friction discs so the double notches (A, **Figure 37**) align with the embossed marks on the clutch housing (B, **Figure 37**). If the clutch housing is not marked, align all friction disc double notches.*

9. First install a friction disc (**Figure 38**) and then a clutch plate (**Figure 39**). Continue to install the friction discs and clutch plates until all are installed. The last item installed is a friction disc (A, **Figure 12**).

5

10. Make sure all friction discs are aligned as shown in **Figure 40**.

11. Install the pressure plate (**Figure 11**).

12. Install the springs (**Figure 10**) and bolts (**Figure 9**) and tighten in a criss-cross pattern to specifications (**Table 2**).

> *NOTE*
> *The clutch mechanism free play must be adjusted after the clutch assembly has been disassembled even if the No. 1 push rod assembly was not disassembled.*

13. Adjust the clutch mechanism free play as described in this chapter.

14. Make sure the clutch cover dowel pins (A, **Figure 41**) are in place and install a new clutch cover gasket (B, **Figure 41**).

15. Install the clutch cover (**Figure 7**) and tighten the cover screws securely.

16. Install the following onto the right-hand side.

    a. Rear brake pedal and engine guard assembly (**Figure 6**).

    b. Right-hand footpeg assembly (**Figure 5**).

17. Adjust the clutch as described in Chapter Three in this section of the manual.

18. Refill the crankcase with the recommended type and quantity of engine oil; refer to Chapter Three in this section of the manual.

Clutch Mechanism Free Play Adjustment

This adjustment is necessary if there is insufficient freeplay in the clutch cable or if the clutch assembly has been disassembled.

1. If the clutch has *not* been disassembled, perform Steps 1-7 *Clutch Removal* in this chapter.

2. Loosen the pushrod No. 1 locknut (A, **Figure 42**).

3. Push the clutch actuating lever (A, **Figure 43**) on the crankcase cover toward the front of the engine until it stops.

4. With the clutch actuating lever in this position, use a screwdriver to turn the pushrod No. 1 (B, **Figure 42**) in either direction until the mark on the lever is aligned with the match mark on the crankcase cover (B, **Figure 43**).

5. Hold the pushrod No. 1 in this position and tighten the locknut securely.

6. Repeat Step 3 to ensure correct alignment, readjust if necessary.

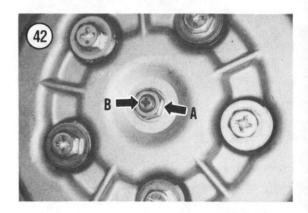

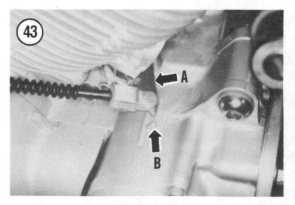

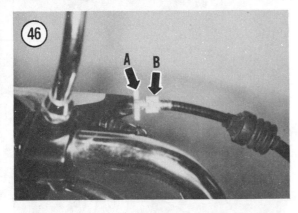

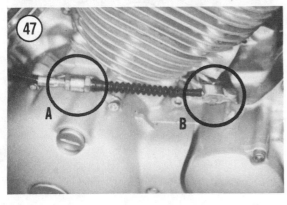

7. Install all items removed.

8. Adjust the clutch as described in Chapter Three in this section of the manual.

CLUTCH CABLE

Replacement

In time, the cable will stretch to the point where it is no longer useful and will have to be replaced.

1. Place the bike on the sidestand.

2. Remove the seat(s).

3A. On 1987-1989 U.S. models and 1988 U.K. models, remove the rear bolt and front bolt on each side securing the frame top cover and remove the cover (**Figure 44**).

3B. On 1990-on U.S. models and 1989-on U.K. models, remove the sub-fuel tank as described in Chapter Six in this section of the manual.

4. At the hand lever, slide back the clutch lever shield (**Figure 45**).

5. Loosen the clutch cable locknut (A, **Figure 46**) and rotate the adjuster (B, **Figure 46**) to allow maximum slack in the cable.

6. At the clutch cable lower adjuster, loosen the locknuts and rotate the adjuster (A, **Figure 47**) to allow maximum slack in the cable.

7. Disconnect the clutch cable from the clutch actuating lever (B, **Figure 47**). Then pull the cable out of the lever.

> *NOTE*
> *Prior to removing the cable, make a drawing of the cable routing through the frame. It is very easy to forget how it was, once it has been removed. Replace it exactly as it was, avoiding any sharp turns.*

8. Carefully remove the cable from the frame clamps and replace with a new one. Make sure the cable fits into the cable clamp on the left-hand side of the frame (**Figure 48**) and upper fork bridge (**Figure 49**).

9. Adjust the clutch as described in Chapter Three in this section of the manual.

SHIFT MECHANISM

Refer to **Figure 50** for this procedure.

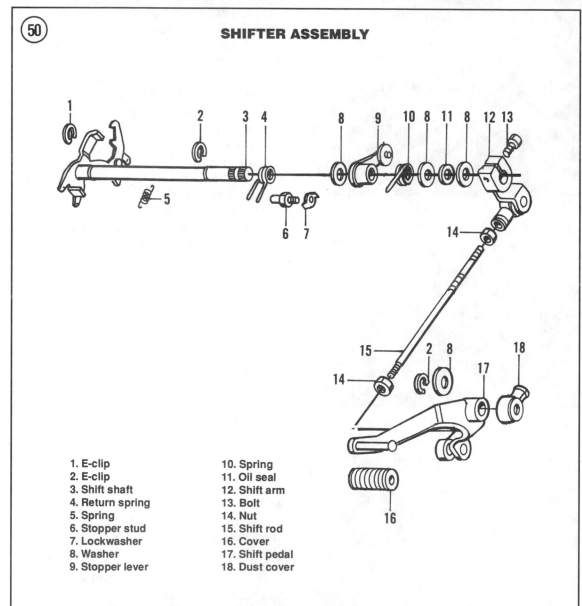

SHIFTER ASSEMBLY

1. E-clip	10. Spring
2. E-clip	11. Oil seal
3. Shift shaft	12. Shift arm
4. Return spring	13. Bolt
5. Spring	14. Nut
6. Stopper stud	15. Shift rod
7. Lockwasher	16. Cover
8. Washer	17. Shift pedal
9. Stopper lever	18. Dust cover

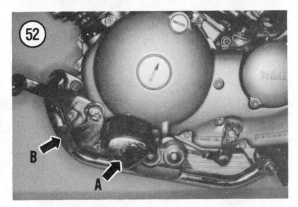

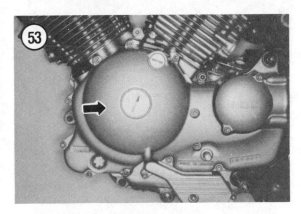

Removal/Inspection/Installation

Portions of this procedure are shown with the engine remove and partially disassembled. It is not necessary to do so for shift mechanism removal and installation.

1. Drain the engine oil as described in Chapter Three in this section of the manual.

2. Remove the bolt (**Figure 51**) securing the shift lever arm and slide it off the shift shaft.

3. Remove the left-hand foot peg (A, **Figure 52**).

4. Remove the left-hand footrest bar (B, **Figure 52**).

5. At the hand lever, slide back the clutch lever shield (**Figure 45**).

6. Loosen the locknut (A, **Figure 46**) and rotate the adjuster (B, **Figure 46**) to allow maximum slack in the cable.

7. At the clutch cable lower adjuster, loosen the locknuts and rotate the adjuster (A, **Figure 47**) to allow maximum slack in the cable.

8. Disconnect the clutch cable from the clutch actuating lever (B, **Figure 47**). Then pull the cable out of the lever.

9. Drain the engine oil as described in Chapter Three in this section of the manual.

10. Remove the bolts securing the left-hand crankcase cover (**Figure 53**) and remove the cover and gasket. Don't lose the dowel pins.

11. Remove the clutch assembly as described in this chapter.

12. On the left-hand side, remove the E-clip (**Figure 54**) and washer (**Figure 55**) from the shift shaft assembly.

13. On the right-hand side, disengage the shift lever (**Figure 56**) from the shift drum and remove the shift shaft assembly from the crankcase (**Figure 57**).

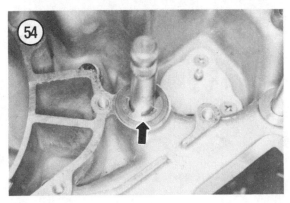

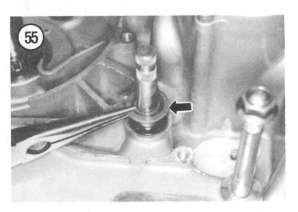

14. Examine the shift shaft spindle assembly for damage. Refer to **Figure 58** and **Figure 59**. If the shaft is bent or damaged in any way, it must be replaced.

15. If necessary, remove the washer (A, **Figure 60**), spring (B, **Figure 60**) and slide the stopper lever assembly (C, **Figure 60**) off the shaft.

16. On the left-hand side, insert the end of the shift shaft spindle into the engine crankcase opening.

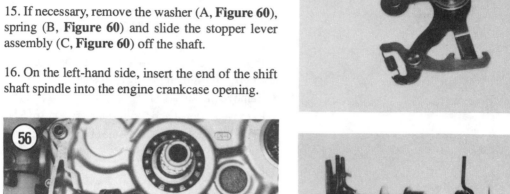

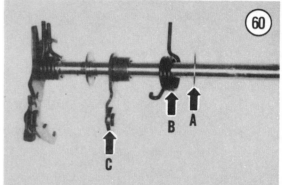

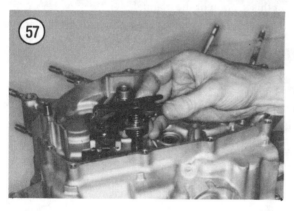

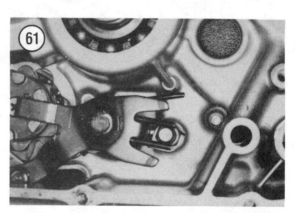

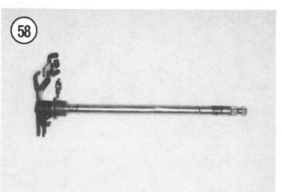

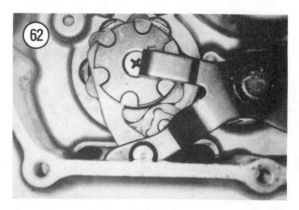

17. Push the shift arm down and install the shift mechanism all the way. **Figure 61** and **Figure 62** shows the installed assembly.

18. Reverse Steps 2-12 to complete installation. Refill the engine with the correct type and quantity of oil as described in Chapter Three in this section of the manual.

TRANSMISSION

The crankcase must be disassembled to gain access to the transmission components.

Removal/Installation

Refer to **Figure 63** for this procedure.

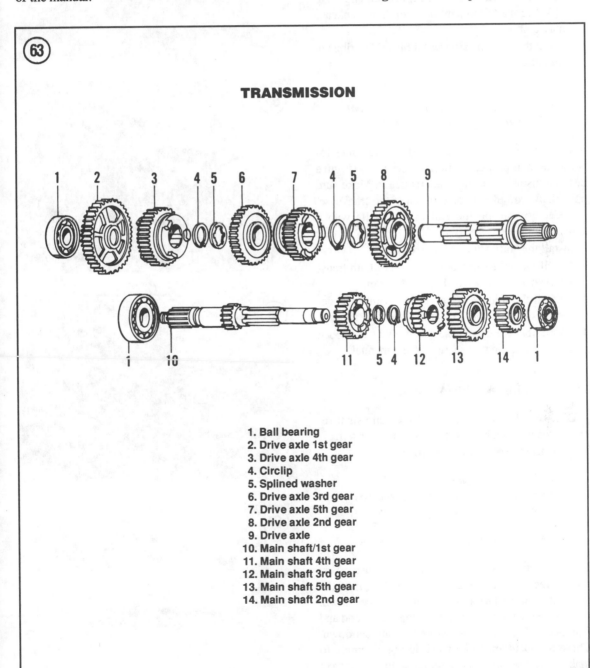

63

TRANSMISSION

1. Ball bearing
2. Drive axle 1st gear
3. Drive axle 4th gear
4. Circlip
5. Splined washer
6. Drive axle 3rd gear
7. Drive axle 5th gear
8. Drive axle 2nd gear
9. Drive axle
10. Main shaft/1st gear
11. Main shaft 4th gear
12. Main shaft 3rd gear
13. Main shaft 5th gear
14. Main shaft 2nd gear

5

1. Separate the crankcase as described in Chapter Four in this section of this manual.

2. Remove the middle driven gear assembly as described in Chapter Four.

3. Withdraw the shift fork shafts and shift forks from both transmission shafts as described in this chapter.

4. Remove the shift drum (**Figure 64**).

5. Remove the main shaft (A, **Figure 65**) and drive axle (B, **Figure 65**) assemblies from the crankcase as an assembly.

6. Inspect the transmission assembly as described in this chapter.

NOTE
Prior to installing any components, coat all bearing surfaces with assembly oil.

7. Properly mesh both transmission assemblies together in their proper relation to each other (**Figure 66**) and install them into the crankcase. Make sure both shafts completely bottom out in the crankcase. If necessary, tap on the end of the shafts with a soft-faced mallet.

8. Install the shift drum (**Figure 64**).

9. Install the shift forks and shafts into both transmission shafts as described in this chapter.

10. Install the middle driven gear assembly as described in Chapter Four in this section of the manual.

11. Assemble the crankcase assembly as described in Chapter Four in this section of the manual.

Main Shaft Disassembly/Assembly

Disassembly and assembly of the main shaft requires the use of a hydraulic press and an insert.

Refer to **Figure 63** for this procedure.

NOTE
*When disassembling the main shaft assembly, place all parts in a container, such as an egg carton (**Figure 67**), to prevent mixing up the gear alignment.*

1. Prior to disassembling the main shaft, use a Vernier caliper and measure the overall length of the gear set (**Figure 68**) and write this number down. Also measure the clearance between the second and fifth gears (**Figure 69**) and write this number down. These numbers are to be used during assembly to make sure the shaft is assembled to the correct clearance and overall length.

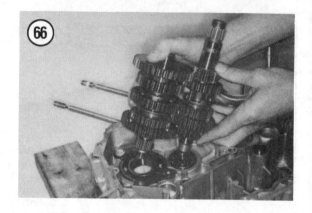

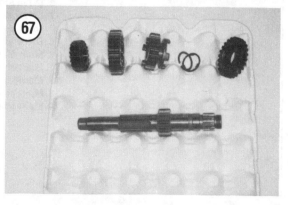

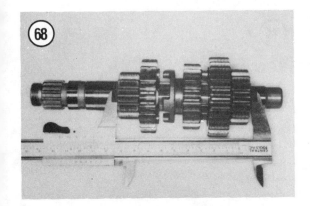

2. Install an insert (A, **Figure 70**) below the fifth gear and install the main shaft assembly in the hydraulic press.

3. While holding onto the main shaft assembly, press the second gear (B, **Figure 70**) off the shaft.

4. Release hydraulic pressure and remove the shaft and insert assembly from the press.

5. Remove the second gear, fifth gear and the insert.

6. Remove the third gear.

7. Remove the circlip, splined washer and slide off the fourth gear.

8. Inspect the main shaft assembly as described in this section.

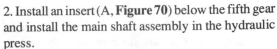

NOTE
Prior to installing any components, coat all bearing surfaces with assembly oil.

9. Install the fourth gear (A, **Figure 71**).

10. Install the splined washer (B, **Figure 71**) and circlip (C, **Figure 71**). Make sure the circlip is seated correctly in the main shaft groove.

11. Install the third gear (**Figure 72**).

12. Install the fifth gear (**Figure 73**).

13. Apply a light coat of molybdenum disulfide grease to the main shaft and to the inner surface of the second gear. This will aid in pressing the second gear onto the shaft.

14. Install the second gear (**Figure 74**) onto the end of the shaft as far as it will go.

15. Install the main shaft assembly in the hydraulic press (**Figure 75**).

16. Install a piece of pipe or socket on top of the second gear (**Figure 76**). The inner diameter of the pipe or socket must be large enough for the end of the main shaft to pass into it without touching.

17. While holding onto the main shaft assembly, start pressing the second gear onto the shaft.

18. Refer to the clearance measured in Step 1 and place the correct thickness flat feeler gauge between the second and fifth gears (**Figure 77**).

NOTE
At the beginning the second gear will press smoothly onto the main shaft and then will usually "jump" several times making a loud cracking noise. This is normal, but when the gear does jump it moves rapidly and will close the clearance between the 2 gears very rapidly. Apply hydraulic pressure slowly.

19. Continue to press the second gear onto the shaft while holding the feeler gauge in place. Press the gear into place until the correct clearance between the gears is achieved as noted in Step 1. If the gear jumps during installation and clamps onto the feeler gauge, the second gear must be pressed back off and then reinstalled until the correct amount of clearance is achieved.

20. After the correct clearance is achieved, release the hydraulic pressure and remove the shaft assembly from the press.

21. Use a Vernier caliper and measure the overall length of the gear set (**Figure 68**). This dimension should be the same as noted in Step 1.

22. Refer to **Figure 78** for correct placement of the gears.

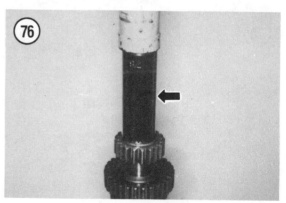

Drive Axle Disassembly/Assembly

Refer to **Figure 63** for this procedure.

NOTE
When disassembling the drive axle as-sembly, place all parts in a container,

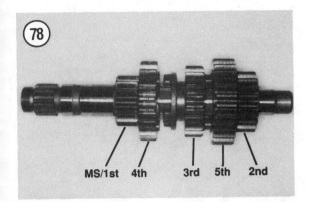

MS/1st   4th   3rd   5th   2nd

*such as an egg carton (**Figure 79**), to prevent mixing up the gear alignment.*

1. Remove the drive axle first gear and forth gear.
2. Remove the circlip and splined washer.
3. Remove the drive axle third gear and fifth gear.
4. Remove the circlip and splined washer.
5. Remove the drive axle second gear.
6. Inspect the drive axle assembly as described in this chapter.

NOTE
Prior to installing any components, coat all bearing surfaces with assembly oil.

7. Install the drive axle second gear (A, **Figure 80**).
8. Install the splined washer (B, **Figure 80**) and circlip (C, **Figure 80**). Make sure the circlip is properly seated in the drive axle groove.
9. Install the drive axle fifth gear (**Figure 81**).
10. Position the drive axle third gear with the dog receptacle side going on last and install the drive axle third gear (**Figure 82**).
11. Install the splined washer (A, **Figure 83**) and circlip (B, **Figure 83**). Make sure the circlip is properly seated in the drive axle groove.
12. Install the drive axle forth gear (**Figure 84**).
13. Install the drive axle first gear (**Figure 85**).
14. Refer to **Figure 86** for correct placement of the gears.
15. Properly mesh both transmission assemblies together (**Figure 87**) to make sure all mating gears are properly aligned.

Inspection

1. Clean all parts in cleaning solvent and thoroughly dry.

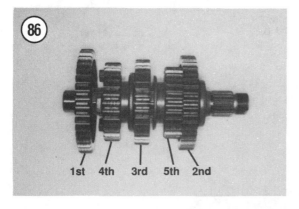

2. Inspect the gears visually for cracks, chips, broken teeth (**Figure 88**). Check the dogs (A, **Figure 89**) on the ends of the gears to make sure they are not rounded off. If the lugs are rounded off, check the shift forks as described later in this chapter. More than likely, one or more of the shift forks is bent.

NOTE
Defective gears should be replaced, and it is a good idea to replace the mating gear even though it may not show as much wear or damage. Remember that accelerated wear to new parts is normally caused by contact from worn parts.

3. Inspect all free wheeling gear bearing surfaces (**Figure 90**) for wear, discoloration and galling. Inspect the mating shaft bearing surface also. If there is any metal flaking or visual damage, replace both parts.

4. Inspect the splines (**Figure 91**) on both shafts for wear or discoloration. Check the mating gear internal splines also (B, **Figure 89**). If no visual damage is apparent, install each sliding gear on its respective shaft and work the gear back and forth to make sure gear operates smoothly.

5. Check all circlips and washers. Replace any circlips that may have been damaged during operation or removal as well as any washers that show wear.

6. If some of the transmission components were damaged, make sure to inspect the shift drum and shift forks as described in this chapter.

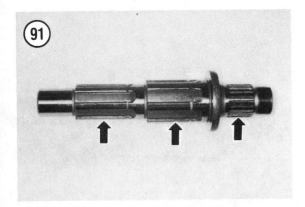

SHIFT DRUM AND FORKS

Removal/Installation

1. Separate the crankcase as described in Chapter Four in this section of the manual.

2. Withdraw the rear long shift fork shaft.

3. Withdraw the front short shift fork shaft.

4. Remove all 3 shift forks from both transmission shafts.

5. Remove the shift drum from the left-hand side crankcase.

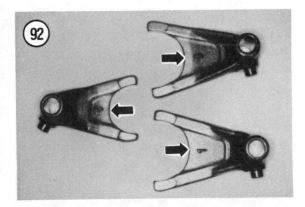

NOTE
*When installing the shift forks, the number on each shift fork (**Figure 92**) must face toward the left-hand side crankcase.*

6. Install the shift drum (**Figure 93**).

7. Insert the No. 1 shift fork into the drive axle fifth gear (A, **Figure 94**) then insert the No. 3 shift fork into the drive axle forth gear (B, **Figure 94**).

8. Insert the No. 2 shift fork into the main shaft third gear (**Figure 95**).

9. Move all shift forks into position so that their pin seats in their respective shift drum groove.

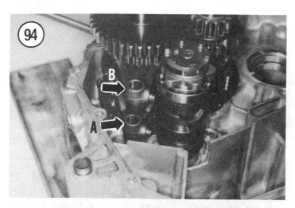

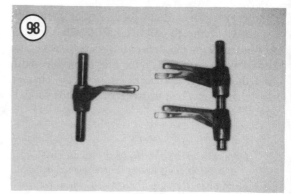

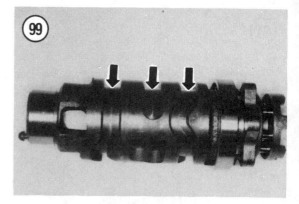

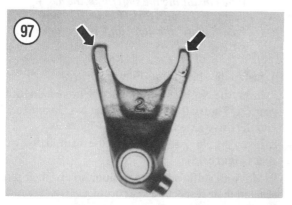

10. Insert the rear long shift fork shaft through the No. 1 and No. 3 shift forks (A, **Figure 96**). Make sure the shaft bottoms out in the crankcase.

11. Insert the front short shift fork shaft into the No. 2 shift fork (B, **Figure 96**). Make sure the shaft bottoms out in the crankcase.

12. Assemble the crankcase assembly as described in Chapter Four.

Inspection

1. Inspect each shift fork for signs of wear or cracking (**Figure 97**). Examine the shift forks at the points where they contact the slider gear. This surface should be smooth with no signs of wear or damage. Make sure the forks slide smoothly on the shaft (**Figure 98**). Make sure the shaft is not bent. This can be checked by removing the shift forks from the shaft and rolling the shaft on a piece of glass. Any clicking noise detected indicates that the shaft is bent.

2. Check grooves in the shift drum (**Figure 99**) for wear or roughness.

3. Check the shift drum bearing (A, **Figure 100**). Make sure it operates smoothly with no signs of wear or damage.

4. Check the ramps and pin in the segment (B, **Figure 100**) for wear or damage, replace if necessary by removing the screw (**Figure 101**) on the end.

5. Check the cam pin followers in each shift fork. They should fit snugly but not too tightly. Check the end that rides in the shift drum for wear or burrs. Replace as necessary.

Table 1   CLUTCH SPECIFICATIONS

Item	Standard in. (mm)	Minimum in. (mm)
Friction plate (6 pcs)	0.114-0.122 (2.9-3.1)	0.102 (2.6)
Clutch plate (5 pcs)	0.060-0.067 (1.1-1.7)	—
Warp limit	—	0.008 (0.2)
Clutch spring (5)		
Free length	1.56 (39.5)	1.52 (38.5)
Pushrod No. 2 bend limit	—	0.02 (0.5)

Table 2   CLUTCH TIGHTENING TORQUES

Item	ft.-lb.	N•m
Clutch nut	50	70
Clutch spring bolts	5.8	8

FUEL, EMISSION CONTROL AND EXHAUST SYSTEMS

This chapter describes complete procedures for servicing the fuel, emission control and exhaust systems. Carburetor specifications are listed in **Table 1**. **Table 1** is at the end of the chapter.

> *NOTE*
> *Where differences occur relating to the United Kingdom (U.K.) models they are identified. If there is no (U.K.) designation relating to a procedure, photo or illustration it is identical to the United States (U.S.) models.*

> *NOTE*
> *This chapter covers all procedures unique to the XV535 Virago V-twins. If a specific procedure is not included in this chapter, refer to Chapter Six in the front section of this manual for service procedures.*

CARBURETOR

Removal/Installation

Remove both carburetors as an assembled unit.

1. Place the motorcycle securely on the sidestand.
2. Remove the seat(s).
3A. On 1987-1989 U.S. models and 1988 U.K. models, remove the rear bolt and front bolt on each side securing the frame top cover and remove the cover (**Figure 1**).
3B. On 1990-on U.S. models and 1989-on U.K. models, remove the sub-fuel tank as described in this chapter.
4. Unhook the battery strap (A, **Figure 2**).
5. Disconnect the battery vent tube (B, **Figure 2**).
6. Pull the battery part way up out of the battery box to gain access to the battery cable attachment screws.
7. Disconnect the negative (–) battery cable (**Figure 3**) from the battery.
8. Remove the right-and left-hand frame and engine side covers.
9A. On models equipped with the air injection system, disconnect the hoses (A, **Figure 4**) from the air injection system and remove the left-hand bracket assembly (B, **Figure 4**) with the system components still attached to it.
9B. On all other models, remove bolts securing the left-hand side cover (**Figure 5**) and remove the bracket (A, **Figure 6**).

10. Disconnect the vent hose (B, **Figure 6**) from each carburetor.

11. Remove bolts securing the right-hand side cover (**Figure 7**) and electrical component bracket (**Figure 8**) and move the bracket assembly out of the way.

12. Remove the bolts securing the rubber intake tube to each cylinder head (**Figure 9**).

13. At the throttle lever, loosen the cable locknut (A, **Figure 10**) and loosen the adjuster (B, **Figure 10**) to allow maximum amount of slack in the throttle cable.

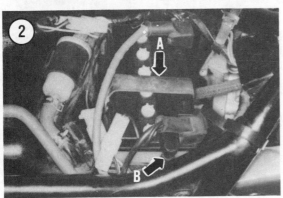

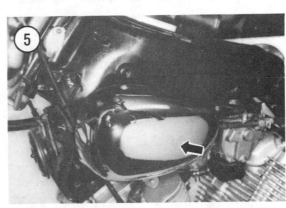

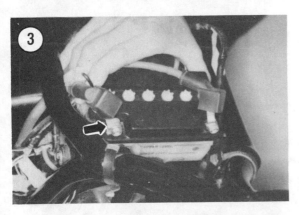

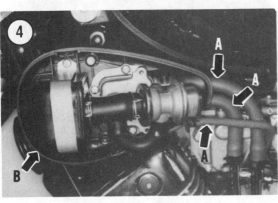

14. Loosen the locknut on the throttle cable (A, **Figure 11**).

15. Open the throttle wheel with your finger and disconnect the throttle cable from the carburetor throttle wheel (B, **Figure 11**).

16. Loosen the hose clamp and disconnect the fuel hose (**Figure 12**) from the carburetor assembly. Insert a golf tee to prevent the dribbling of fuel.

17. Remove the hose clamp screws (**Figure 13**) securing the air filter housing joints to both carburetors. Remove both hose clamps.

18. Push the air filter housing joints up into the air box.

19. Grasp the carburetor assembly and work the assembly out toward the left-hand side. Remove the carburetor assembly from the frame.

CAUTION
Stuff clean shops rags into the intake openings in the cylinder heads to prevent foreign objects from falling into the cylinder heads.

20. While the carburetor assembly is removed, examine the cylinder head intake tubes and the rubber

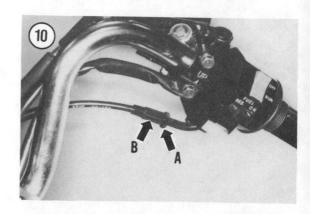
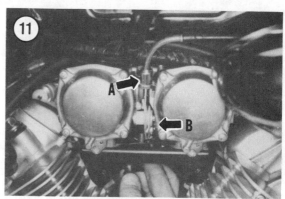
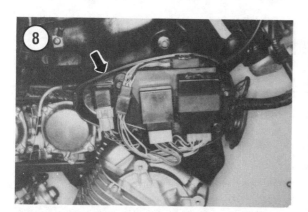
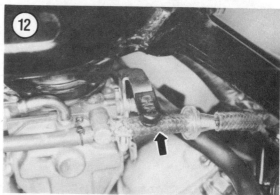

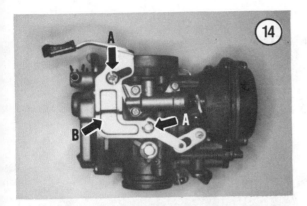

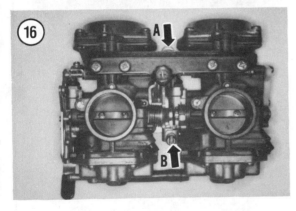

outlet boots on the air filter box for any cracks or damage that would allow unfiltered air to enter the engine. Replace any damaged parts.

21. Install by reverse these removal steps while noting the following:

   a. Make sure the O-ring seal is in place in the rubber intake tube prior to installation. During installation of the carburetor assembly, do not snag the O-ring on the cylinder head surface as the O-ring will either be damaged or may be moved out of position resulting in a vacuum leak.

   b. Make sure the carburetors are fully seated forward in the filter housing joints on both carburetors. Also make sure the joints are correctly seated in the air filter air box.

CAUTION
Make sure the carburetor intake tubes are air tight. Air leaks can cause severe engine damage because of a lean mixture or the intake of dirt and moisture.

   c. Check the throttle cable for correct routing after installation. The cable must not be twisted, kinked or pinched.

   d. Adjust the throttle cable as described in Chapter Three in this section of the manual.

Carburetor Assembly
Separation/Reassembly

The carburetors can be cleaned without separating the individual body assemblies but if necessary, they can be separated as follows.

1. Remove the screw and E-clip (A, **Figure 14**) securing the choke lever and remove the choke lever assembly (B, **Figure 14**). Don't lose the plastic washers that will fall out when the lever is removed.

2. Loosen the screws on the choke lever link (**Figure 15**).

3. Remove the E-clip, spring and remove the choke lever from the assembly.

4. Remove the screws securing the upper bracket and remove the bracket.

5. Remove the screws securing the lower bracket (A, **Figure 16**) and remove the bracket.

6. Move the hose clamps on the fuel line assembly (**Figure 17**) away from both carburetor bodies.

7. Place the carburetor assembly on a piece of plate glass with the vacuum chamber covers facing down.

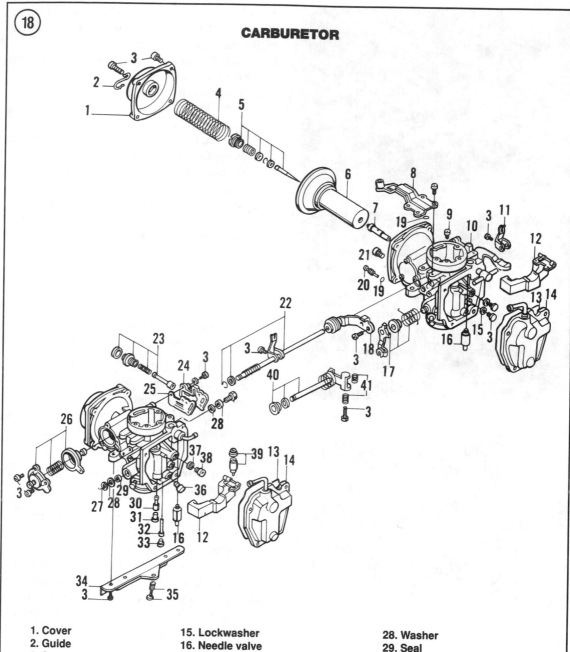

CARBURETOR

1. Cover
2. Guide
3. Screw
4. Spring
5. Jet needle assembly
6. Diaphragm/slide
7. Main jet nozzle
8. Upper bracket
9. Pilot air jet No. 1
10. Carburetor body
11. Float hanger
12. Float
13. O-ring gasket
14. Float chamber

15. Lockwasher
16. Needle valve
17. Throttle lever and
    return spring
18. Choke lever
19. O-ring
20. Drain screw
21. Screw
22. Choke lever assembly
23. Choke assembly
24. Choke plate
25. Gasket
26. Coasting enrichener assembly
27. E-clip

28. Washer
29. Seal
30. Pilot jet
31. Rubber plug
32. Main jet bleed pipe
33. Rubber plug
34. Lower bracket
35. Throttle adjust knob and spring
36. Main jet
37. Washer
38. Main jet holder
39. Needle valve and seat
40. Sychronizing lever assembly
41. Springs

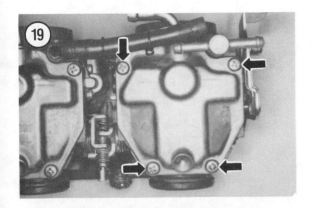

8. Carefully separate the carburetor bodies from each other. Don't lose the small synchronizing screw (B, **Figure 16**) that will usually fall out.

9. Reassemble by reversing these separation steps while noting the following:

   a. Place the carburetor assembly on a piece of plate glass with the inlet side facing down.

   b. Tighten the upper and lower bracket screws securely while pressing down on both carburetors to maintain proper alignment between the 2 carburetors.

   c. Connect the rubber fuel line onto each carburetor body and reposition the hose clamps. Make sure the clamps are positioned correctly to avoid a fuel leak.

Individual Carburetor Disassembly/Assembly

Refer to **Figure 18** for this procedure. It is recommended to disassemble only one carburetor at a time to prevent accidental interchange of parts.

1. Move the hose clamps on the fuel line assembly (**Figure 17**) away from the carburetor to be disassembled.

2. Remove the screws (**Figure 19**) securing the float bowl and remove the float bowl and gasket.

3. Remove the float (**Figure 20**) and the needle valve (**Figure 21**).

4. Remove the main jet (A, **Figure 22**).

5. Remove the main jet nozzle holder screw (B, **Figure 22**) and the washer under it.

NOTE
One of the vacuum cover screws is a Torx head type (size T-27) and a special tool is required to remove it. Use Yamaha special tool U.S. part No. YU-05258, U.K. part No. 90890-05349, or equivalent.

6. Remove the screws (**Figure 23**) and the vacuum chamber cover.

7. Remove the diaphragm spring (**Figure 24**) from the diaphragm.

8. Lift the diaphragm assembly (A, **Figure 25**) out of the carburetor.

9. Unscrew the pilot air jet No. 2 (**Figure 26**).

10. Remove the screws securing the choke chamber and remove the chamber assembly.

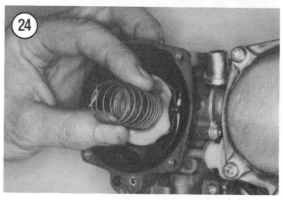

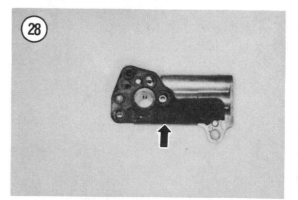

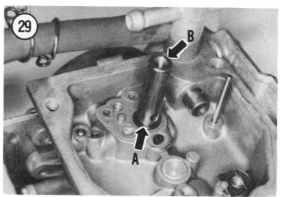

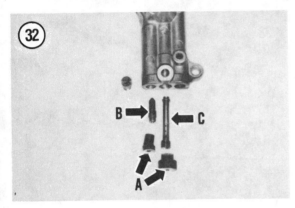

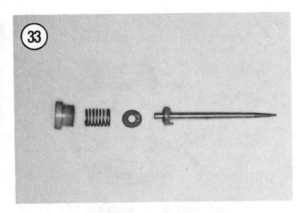

11. Remove the screws securing the jet block assembly (**Figure 27**) and remove it. Remove the gasket (**Figure 28**) and O-ring (A, **Figure 29**).

12. Turn the carburetor over and tap it with your hand. Remove the main jet nozzle (B, **Figure 29**).

13. Remove the screws securing the coasting enricher cover (**Figure 30**) and remove the spring and diaphragm (A, **Figure 31**).

14. Remove the rubber plugs (A, **Figure 32**) from the jet holder assembly.

15. Unscrew the pilot jet (B, **Figure 32**) and the main bleed pipe (C, **Figure 32**).

16. If necessary, remove the screws securing the throttle cable bracket and remove it.

17. Remove the needle valve assembly (**Figure 33**). Don't lose the O-ring seal.

18. Unscrew the pilot air jet No. 1 (A, **Figure 34**).

19. Clean and inspect that carburetor as described in this chapter.

20. Installation is the reverse of these steps while noting the following.

   a. Check the throttle shaft and throttle plate (**Figure 35**) for excessive play or damage. Check the throttle plate screws for looseness. If the throttle shaft and/or plate is damaged, that carburetor body must be replaced as an assembly.

   b. Make sure the O-ring seal is in place on the needle valve assembly prior to installation.

   c. Align the projection (**Figure 36**) on the jet block with the groove (**Figure 37**) on the jet needle and install the jet block. Check to make sure the alignment is correct as shown in **Figure 38**. Tighten the screws securely.

   d. Replace the float bowl seal (**Figure 39**) if deformed or starting to deteriorate or if the bowl has leaked.

6

e. Align the locating tab on the vacuum diaphragm (B, **Figure 25**) with the relief in the
carburetor body. Insert your index finger into
the venturi and hold the slide up to almost the
full open position. This will help eliminate
pinching the diaphragm when the top cover is
installed.

f. Install the cover and tighten the cover screws
securely.

g. Align the locating tab on the coasting enricher
diaphragm (B, **Figure 31**) with the relief in the
carburetor body. Install the spring and cover
and tighten the screws securely.

h. If removed, apply blue Loctite (No. 242) to the
throttle cable bracket screws prior to installation. Tighten the screws securely.

21. Repeat Steps 1-17 for the other carburetor. Do
not interchange parts—keep them separate.

22. After the carburetors have been disassembled the
idle speed should be adjusted and the carburetors
synchronized as described in Chapter Three in this
section of the manual.

Cleaning and Inspection

1. Thoroughly clean and dry all parts. Yamaha does
not recommend the use of a caustic carburetor cleaning solvent. Instead, clean carburetor parts in a petroleum based solvent. Then rinse in clean water.

2. Allow the carburetor to dry thoroughly before
assembly and blow dry with compressed air. Blow
out the jets and needle jet holder with compressed
air.

> *CAUTION*
> *If compressed air is not available, allow*
> *the parts to air dry or use a clean lint-*

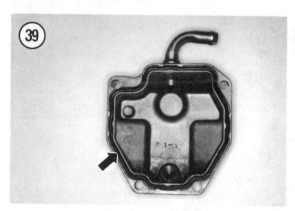

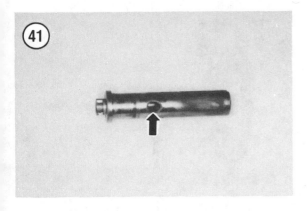

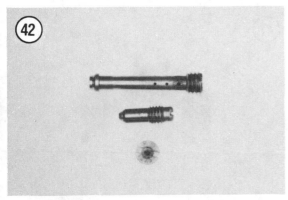

*free cloth. Do **not** use a paper towel to dry carburetor parts, as small paper particles may plug openings in the carburetor body or jets.*

CAUTION
*Do **not** use a piece of wire to clean the jets as minor gouges in the jet can alter flow rate and upset the fuel/air mixture.*

3. Inspect the end of the float valve needle (**Figure 40**) for wear or damage. Also check the inside of the needle valve in the needle valve body. If either part is damaged, replace as a set. A damaged needle valve or a particle of dirt or grit in the needle valve assembly will cause the carburetor to flood and overflow fuel.

4. Inspect all O-ring seals on the needle valve assembly prior to installation. O-ring seals tend to become hardened after prolonged use and heat and therefore lose their ability to seal properly. Replace if necessary.

5. Make sure the holes in the main jet nozzle (**Figure 41**) and all jets are clear (**Figure 42**). Clean out if they are plugged in any way. Replace the main jet nozzle if you cannot unplug the holes.

6. Make sure all openings in the carburetor body are clear. Refer to **Figure 43**, **Figure 44** and B, **Figure 34**. Clean out if they are plugged in any way.

7. Inspect the slide area (**Figure 45**) in the carburetor body. Make sure it is clean and free of any burrs or obstructions that may cause the diaphragm assembly to hang up on during normal operation.

8. Inspect the diaphragm slide (A, **Figure 46**) for scoring and wear. Replace if necessary.

9. Inspect the diaphragm (B, **Figure 46**) for tears, cracks or other damage. Replace the throttle slide assembly if the diaphragm is damaged.

6

10. Inspect the float (**Figure 47**) for deterioration or damage. If the float is suspected of leakage, place it in a container of non-caustic solution and push it down. If the float sinks or if bubbles appear (indicating a leak), the float must be replaced.

CARBURETOR ADJUSTMENTS

Idle Speed, Idle Mixture Adjustment and *Carburetor Synchronization* are covered in Chapter Three in this section of the manual.

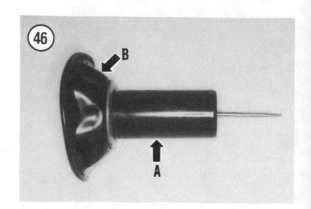

COASTING ENRICHENER SYSTEM

The carburetors on these models are equipped with a coasting enrichener system. When the throttle is opened, air is forced to the pilot air jet through two passageways in the carburetor body. When the throttle is off, vacuum at the carburetor joint increases and actuates the enrichener diaphragm which shuts off the air through one of the passages. This action increases the fuel mixture at the pilot jet outlet and reduces afterburning.

1. Remove the carburetor assembly as described in this chapter.

2. Remove the screws securing the coasting enrichener cover and remove the spring and diaphragm (**Figure 48**).

3. Inspect the enrichener diaphragm for tears or other damage. Replace the diaphragm if necessary.

4. Install by reversing these removal steps.

FUEL LEVEL MEASUREMENT

The fuel level in the carburetor float bowls is critical to proper performance. The fuel flow rate from the bowl up to the carburetor bore depends not only on the vacuum in the throttle bore and the size of the jets, but also on the fuel level. Yamaha gives a specification of actual fuel level, measured from below the piston valve center mark on the float bowl (**Figure 49**) with the carburetors mounted on the motorcycle.

This measurement is more useful than a simple float height measurement because the actual fuel level can vary from bike to bike, even when their floats are set at the same height. Fuel level inspection requires a special Yamaha Fuel Level Gauge (U.S. part No. YM-01312, U.K. part No. 90890-01312) or

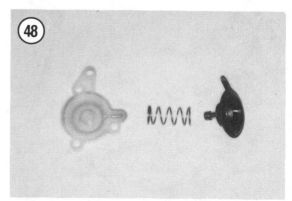

a vinyl tube with an inside diameter of 6 mm (0.24 in.).

The fuel level is adjusted by bending the float arm tang (**Figure 50**).

Inspection/adjustment

Carburetors leave the factory with float levels properly adjusted. Rough riding, a worn needle valve or bent float arm can cause the float level to

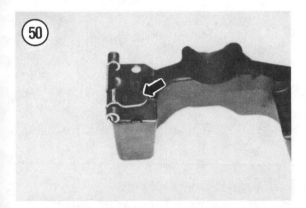

change. To adjust the float level on these carburetors, perform the following.

WARNING
Some gasoline will drain from the car-buretors during this procedure. Work in a well-ventilated area, at least 50 feet from any open flame. Do not allow any-one to smoke. Wipe up spills immedi-ately.

1. Place the motorcycle securely on the sidestand. Make sure the bike and carburetor assembly are in a true vertical position. If necessary, place shims under the sidestand to achieve a true vertical position for the carburetor assembly.

NOTE
Figure 51 *and* ***Figure 52*** *are shown with the carburetor assembly removed for clarity. Do not remove the assembly for this procedure.*

2. Connect the fuel level gauge (U.S. part No. YM-01312, U.K. part No. 90890-01312) or a vinyl tube (with a 0.24 in./6 mm inner diameter) to the drain nozzle on the float chamber (**Figure 51**) on the front carburetor. Secure the gauge so that it is vertical against the float bowl.

3. Loosen the carburetor drain screw. Refer to A, **Figure 52** for the front cylinder or B, **Figure 52** for the rear cylinder.

4. Start the engine and allow it to idle for a few minutes. Turn the engine off.

5. Wait until the fuel in the gauge settles.

6. The fuel level should be 0.53-0.57 in. (13.5-14.5 mm) below the piston valve center mark on the float bowl. Note the reading for the front carburetor.

7. If the fuel level is incorrect, note the dimension for the front carburetor, tighten the drain screw and then repeat this procedure for the rear carburetor. Note the fuel level in the rear carburetor.

8. If the fuel level is incorrect, adjust the float height as follows:

   a. Remove the carburetor assembly as described in this chapter.

   b. Remove the screws (**Figure 53**) securing the float bowl and remove the float bowl and gasket.

   c. Remove the float (**Figure 54**) and the needle valve.

d. Carefully adjust the tang (**Figure 50**) on the float. Bending the float upward very slightly to lower the fuel level; bend the tang downward to raise the fuel level. If the fuel level is set too high, the result with be a rich air-fuel mixture. If it is set too low, the mixture will be too lean.

e. Install the needle valve, float and float bowl.

9. Install the carburetor assembly and repeat this procedure until both fuel levels are correct.

> *CAUTION*
> *The floats on both carburetors must be adjusted to the correct position to maintain the same air-fuel mixture to each cylinder.*

THROTTLE CABLE REPLACEMENT

1. Place the bike securely on the sidestand.

2. Remove the seat.

3A. On 1987-1989 U.S. models and 1988 U.K. models, remove the rear bolt and front bolt on each side securing the frame top cover and remove the cover.

3B. On 1990-on U.S. models and 1989-on U.K. models, remove the sub-fuel tank as described in this chapter.

4. At the throttle lever, loosen the cable locknut (A, **Figure 55**) and loosen the adjuster (B, **Figure 55**) to allow maximum amount of slack in the throttle cable.

5. Remove the screws securing the right-hand switch/throttle housing halves together (C, **Figure 55**).

6. Remove the housing from the handlebar and disengage the throttle cable (D, **Figure 55**) from the throttle grip.

7. Loosen the locknut on the throttle cable (A, **Figure 56**) at the carburetor assembly.

8. Open the throttle wheel with your finger and disconnect the throttle cable from the carburetor throttle wheel (B, **Figure 56**).

9. Disconnect the throttle cable from any clips holding the cable to the frame.

> *NOTE*
> *The piece of string attached in the next step will be used to pull the new throttle cable back through the frame so it will*

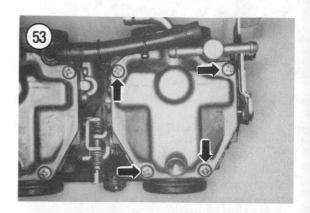

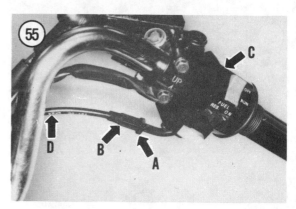

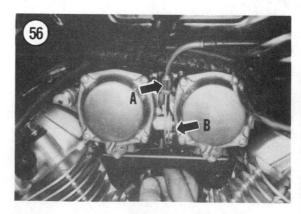

be routed in the exact same position as the old one.

10. Tie a piece of heavy string or cord (approximately 7 ft./2 m) to the carburetor end of the throttle cable. Wrap this end with masking or duct tape. Do not use an excessive amount of tape as it will be pulled through the frame. Tie the other end of the string to the frame.

11. At the throttle lever end of the cable, carefully pull the cable (and attached string) out through the frame. Make sure the attached string follows the same path of the cable through the frame.

12. Remove the tape and untie the string from the old cable.

Installation

1. Lubricate the new cable as described in Chapter Three in the front section of the manual.

2. Tie the string (used during removal) to the new throttle cable assembly and wrap it with tape.

3. Carefully pull the string back through the frame routing the new cable through the same path as the old cable.

4. Remove the tape and untie the string from cable and the frame.

5. Reverse Steps 1-9 of *Removal*, while noting the following:

   a. Operate the throttle grip and make sure the carburetor throttle linkage is operating correctly and with no binding. If operation is incorrect or there is binding, carefully check that the cable is attached correctly and there are no tight bends in the cable.

   b. Adjust the throttle cable as described in Chapter Three in this section of the manual.

   c. Test ride the bike and make sure the throttle is operating correctly.

FUEL SHUTOFF VALVE (1990-ON U.S. MODELS, 1989-ON U.K. MODELS)

Troubleshooting

1. Remove the main fuel tank as described in this chapter.

2. Connect a suitable size piece of tubing to the fuel port.

3. Turn the lever to the ON position.

4. Blow through the tubing and observe the following:

   a. The air goes through the tubing and valve—the valve is operating correctly.

   b. The air *does not* go through the tubing and valve—the valve is faulty and must be replaced.

5. Leave the hose attached and attach a 12 volt battery to the solenoid's electrical connector as follows:

   a. Battery positive (+) to the yellow/blue terminal.

   b. Battery negative (–) to the blue terminal.

6. Blow through the tubing and observe the following:

   a. The air goes through the tubing and valve—the valve is faulty and must be replaced.

   b. The air *does not* go through the tubing and valve—the valve is operating correctly.

Removal/Installation

Refer to **Figure 57** for this procedure.

NOTE
On prior models the main fuel tank was not equipped with a fuel shutoff valve.

WARNING
Some fuel may spill in the following procedure. Work in a well-ventilated area at least 50 feet from any sparks or flames, including gas appliance pilot lights. Do not allow anyone to smoke in the area. Keep a B:C rated fire extinguisher handy.

1. Remove the fuel tank as described in this chapter.

2. If still attached, disconnect the fuel line and vacuum line from shutoff valve.

3. Remove the bolts and washers (A, **Figure 58**) securing the shutoff valve to the fuel tank and remove the valve (B, **Figure 58**).

4. Inspect the shutoff valve mounting O-ring; replace if necessary.

5. Install by reversing these removal steps. Pour a small amount of gasoline in the tank after installing the valve and check for leaks. If a leak is present, solve the problem prior to installing the fuel tank.

FUEL FILTER

All models are equipped with a separate fuel filter that cannot be cleaned. If dirty or clogged, a new filter must be installed. The filter must be periodically replaced (no replacement intervals are specified by Yamaha).

Removal/Installation

1. Remove the seat.

2. Disconnect the inlet (A, **Figure 59**) and outlet (B, **Figure 59**) fuel lines from the fuel filter. Plug the end of the fuel line with golf tees.

3. Remove the fuel filter from the rubber mount and remove the filter (C, **Figure 59**).

4. Install by reversing these removal steps while noting the following:

    a. Install the fuel filter so that the flange end and arrow mark (D, **Figure 59**) face toward the fuel pump.

    b. Check the fuel line clamps for damage; replace if necessary.

    c. After installation is complete, thoroughly check for leaks.

FUEL PUMP

Removal/Installation

1. Remove the seat.

2. Disconnect the battery negative cable.

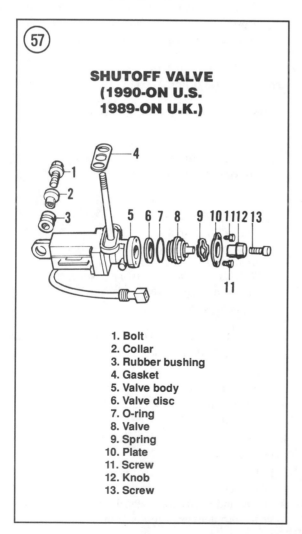

SHUTOFF VALVE (1990-ON U.S. 1989-ON U.K.)

1. Bolt
2. Collar
3. Rubber bushing
4. Gasket
5. Valve body
6. Valve disc
7. O-ring
8. Valve
9. Spring
10. Plate
11. Screw
12. Knob
13. Screw

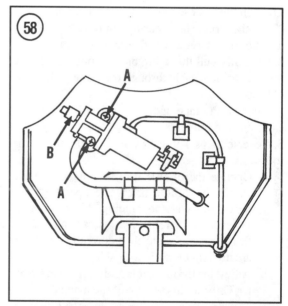

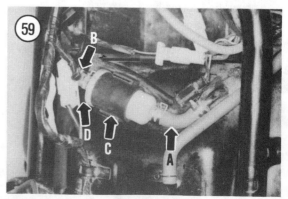

3. Disconnect the fuel pump electrical connector (A, **Figure 60**)

4. Disconnect the fuel inlet and outlet (B, **Figure 60**) lines from the fuel pump. Plug the end of the fuel lines with a golf tee to prevent fuel leakage.

5. Remove the clamping bolts (C, **Figure 60**) securing the fuel pump to the mounting bracket on the fuel tank.

6. Carefully pull the fuel pump (D, **Figure 60**) from the mounting bracket.

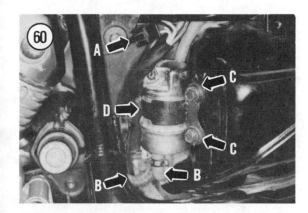

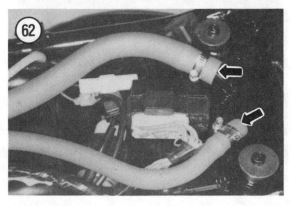

7. Install by reversing these removal steps while noting the following.

    a. Check the fuel line clamps for damage; replace if necessary.

    b. After installation is complete, thoroughly check for fuel leaks.

FUEL TANK(S)

On 1987-1989 U.S. models and 1988 U.K. models, there is one main fuel tank that is mounted within the frame assembly beneath the seat and behind the battery. On 1990-on U.S. models and 1989-on U.K. models, there are two fuel tanks, the main fuel tank that is the same as on prior models as well as an additional sub-fuel tank that is mounted on top of the frame in place of the top cover used on prior years.

WARNING
Some fuel may spill in the following procedures. Work in a well-ventilated area at least 50 feet from any sparks or flames, including gas appliance pilot lights. Do not allow anyone to smoke in the area. Keep a B:C rated fire extinguisher handy.

Sub-Fuel Tank
(1990-on U.S. Models and
1989-on U.K. Models)

1. Place the bike securely on the sidestand.
2. Remove the seat.
3. Disconnect the battery negative cable.
4. Remove the rear bolt, washer and rubber cushion (A, **Figure 61**) and front bolt and washer (B, **Figure 61**) on each side securing the sub-tank to the frame. Don't lose the metal collar within the rubber cushions on the front mounting areas.

NOTE
In the following step, leave the fuel lines attached to the sub-fuel tank.

5. Disconnect both fuel lines (**Figure 62**) from the main fuel tank. Plug the end of both fuel lines with a golf tee to prevent the entry of foreign matter and the loss of fuel.
6. Unhook both fuel lines from the clamps on top of the battery cover.
7. Check to make sure everything is disconnected from the fuel tank and remove it from the frame.

8. If necessary, pour the fuel out of the fuel tank into a container approved for gasoline storage.

9. Check the rubber dampers for wear and damage; replace if necessary.

Main Fuel Tank
Removal/Installation

1. Place the bike securely on the sidestand.

2. Remove both seats(s).

3. Disconnect the battery negative cable.

4. Remove both frame side covers (**Figure 63**).

5. Remove the bolts securing the left-hand rear side cover (**Figure 64**) and remove the cover.

6. On the left-hand side, remove the bolts securing the rear bracket and remove the bracket.

7. On 1990-on U.S. models and 1989-on U.K. models, perform the following:

    a. Disconnect both fuel lines (**Figure 62**) from the main fuel tank. Plug the end of both fuel lines with a golf tee to prevent the entry of foreign matter and the loss of fuel.

    b. Unhook both fuel lines from the clamps on top of the battery cover.

8. Unhook the starter relay (A, **Figure 65**) from the frame mounting bracket and move the relay out of the way.

9. On models so equipped, remove the battery cover.

10. Remove the battery as described in Chapter Three in this section of the manual.

11. Remove the bolts, washers and lockwashers securing the battery box and remove the box from the frame.

12. Disconnect the electrical connectors from the fuse panel and remove the panel.

13. Remove the fuel pump and fuel filter (B, **Figure 65**) from the top and side of the fuel tank as described in this chapter.

14. Remove the bolts securing the fuel tank front mounting bracket and remove the bracket.

15. Remove the bolts, washers and lockwashers (C, **Figure 65**) securing the rear of the fuel tank to the frame.

16. Check to make sure everything is disconnected from the fuel tank and that all mounting bolts are removed.

17A. On 1987-1989 U.S. models and 1988 U.K. models, remove the fuel tank and filler cover (D, **Figure 65**).

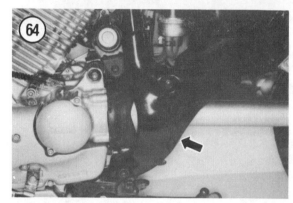

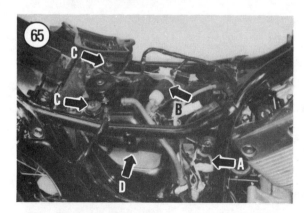

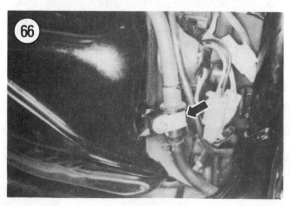

17B. On all other models, remove the fuel tank from the frame.

18. Install by reversing these removal steps while noting the following:

   a. Don't pinch any electrical wires during installation.

   b. Reconnect all hoses and connectors. Make sure all hose clamps are in place and are on tight.

CRANKCASE BREATHER SYSTEM

To comply with air pollution standards, all models are equipped with a closed crankcase breather system. The system routes the engine combustion gases into the air filter air box where they are burned in the engine.

Make sure the hose clamps at each end of the hose are tight. Check the hose for deterioration and replace as necessary.

EVAPORATIVE EMISSION CONTROL (1990-ON CALIFORNIA MODELS)

All models sold in California since 1990 are equipped with an evaporative emission control system to reduce the amount of fuel vapors released into the atmosphere. The system consists of a charcoal canister, a roll-over valve, assorted vacuum lines and modified carburetors and fuel tank.

During engine operation, fuel vapors formed in the fuel tank exit the tank though a roll-over valve and enter the charcoal canister through a connecting hose. The vapors are stored in the charcoal canisters until the bike is ridden at high speed, when the vapors are then passed through a hose to the carburetor and mixed and burned with the incoming fresh air. During low-speed engine operation or when the bike is parked, the fuel vapors are stored in the charcoal canister.

The roll-over valve (**Figure 66**) is installed in line with the fuel tank and charcoal canister. Air and fuel vapor passing through the valve is controlled by an internal weight. During normal riding (or when the fuel tank is properly positioned), the weight is at the bottom of the valve. In this position, the breather passage is open to allow the fuel vapors to flow to the charcoal canister. When the bike is rolled or turned over, the weight moves to block off the pas-

sage. In this position it is impossible for stored fuel vapors to flow to the charcoal canister.

Service to the emission control system is limited to replacement of damaged parts. No attempt should be made to modify or remove the emission control system.

Parts Replacement

When purchasing replacement parts (carburetor and fuel tank), be sure to specify that the parts are for a 1990-on California emission control bike. Parts sold for non-emission control bikes are not compatible with this emission control system.

Inspection/Replacement

Maintenance to the evaporative emission control system consists of periodic inspection of the hoses for proper routing and a check of the canister mounting bracket. Refer to **Figure 67**.

> *WARNING*
> *Because the evaporative emission control system stores fuel vapors, make sure the work area is free of all flame or sparks before working on the emission system.*

1. Whenever servicing the evaporative emission control system, make sure the ignition switch is turned OFF.

2. Make sure all hoses are attached and that they are not damaged or pinched.

3. Replace any worn or damaged parts immediately.

4. The canister is capable of working through the motorcycle's life without maintenance, provided that it is not damaged or contaminated.

Roll-Over Valve Replacement

1. Remove the seat and the frame right-hand side cover.

2. Remove the bolt and washer securing the roll-over valve to the side of the main fuel tank (**Figure 66**).

3. Disconnect the vacuum lines from each end of the roll-over valve and remove the valve.

4. Install by reversing these removal steps. Make sure the roll-over valve is tight.

Canister and Hose
Replacement

1. Label the hoses and fittings prior to disconnecting them.

2. Move the hose clamps off the hoses, then disconnect the hoses from the canister.

3. Remove the bolt, lockwasher and washer securing the canister to the frame.

4. Remove the canister from the frame.

5. To remove the hoses, perform the following:

    a. Remove the tie wraps securing the hoses to the frame and throttle cables.

    b. Disconnect the hoses from the carburetor assembly, fuel tank and canister.

6. Install by reversing these removal steps while noting the following:

    a. Make sure all hoses are connected to the correct fitting.

    b. Make sure the hose clamps and bolts are tight.

AIR INJECTION SYSTEM
(1990-ON U.S. AND
1989-ON U.K. MODELS)

All 1990-on U.S. and 1989-on U.K. models are equipped with an air injection emission control system to reduce the amount of hydrocarbons released into the atmosphere. The system consists of an air cut valve, a reed valve assembly and air and vacuum hoses (**Figure 68**). This system does not pressurize air, but uses the momentary pressure differentials generated by the exhaust gas pulses to introduce fresh air into the exhaust ports. Make sure all air and vacuum hoses are correctly routed and attached as shown in **Figure 69**. Inspect the hoses and replace any if necessary.

Removal/Installation

Refer to **Figure 68**, **Figure 69** and **Figure 70** for this procedure.

NOTE
Prior to removing any hoses, mark the hose and the fitting with a piece of masking tape and identify where the hose goes during installation.

1. Place the bike securely on the sidestand.

2. Remove the seat.

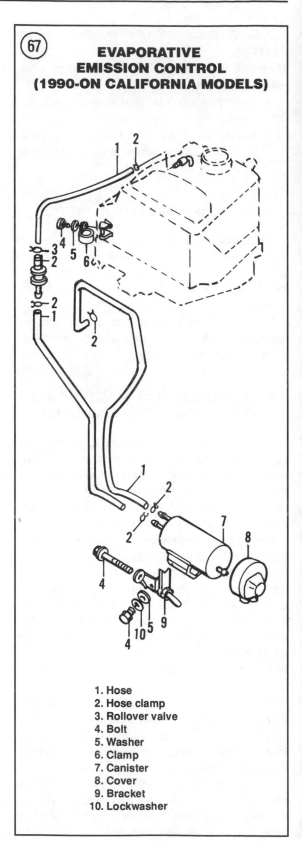

67 **EVAPORATIVE EMISSION CONTROL (1990-ON CALIFORNIA MODELS)**

1. Hose
2. Hose clamp
3. Rollover valve
4. Bolt
5. Washer
6. Clamp
7. Canister
8. Cover
9. Bracket
10. Lockwasher

3. Remove the left-hand cover (**Figure 71**).

4. To remove the air cleaner (**Figure 72**), perform the following:

    a. Remove the bracket screws and remove the bracket and cover.

    b. Disconnect hose No. 2 from the air cleaner and remove the air cleaner.

5. To remove the air cut valve (**Figure 73**), perform the following:

    a. Disconnect hose No. 2 and No. 3 from the air cut valve.

    b. Disconnect the vacuum hose from the air cut valve.

    c. Remove the air cut valve.

6. To remove the reed valve assembly (**Figure 74**), perform the following:

    a. Disconnect hose No. 3, No. 4 and No. 5 from the reed valve assembly.

    b. Remove the mounting screws and remove the reed valve assembly.

7. To remove air pipe No. 1 and No. 2, perform the following:

    a. Disconnect the air pipes from hose No. 4 and No. 5 (**Figure 75**).

    b. Remove the bolt securing the air pipe No. 5 to the rear cylinder (**Figure 76**).

    c. Remove the bolts securing the air pipes to the right-hand crankcase cover (**Figure 77**).

6

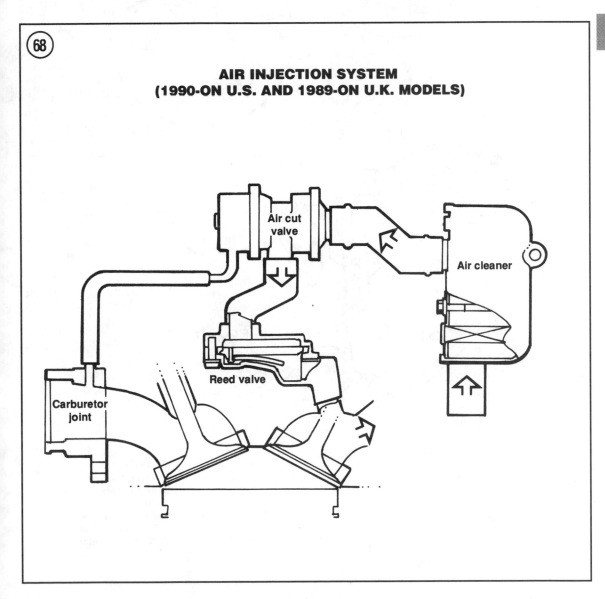

**AIR INJECTION SYSTEM
(1990-ON U.S. AND 1989-ON U.K. MODELS)**

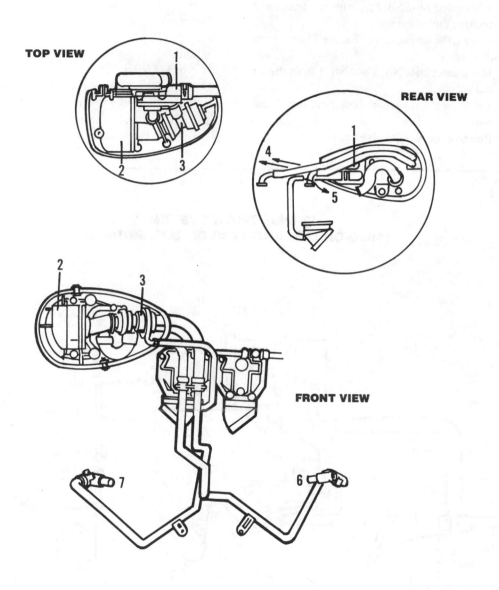

**AIR INJECTION SYSTEM LAYOUT
(1990-ON U.S. AND 1989-ON U.K. MODELS)**

TOP VIEW

REAR VIEW

FRONT VIEW

1. Reed valve
2. Air cleaner
3. Air cut valve
4. To cylinders
5. To air cut valve
6. To front cylinder
7. To rear cylinder

**AIR INJECTION SYSTEM COMPONENTS
(1990-ON U.S. AND 1989-ON U.K. MODELS)**

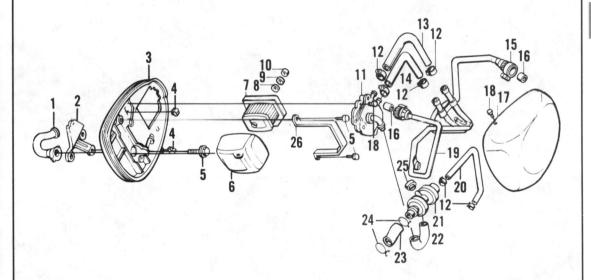

1. Hose No. 1	10. Nut	
2. Mounting bracket	11. Reed valve assembly	19. Air pipe No. 2
3. Bracket	12. Hose clamp	20. Vacuum hose
4. Rubber bumper	13. Hose No. 5	21. Air cut valve
5. Bolt	14. Hose No. 4	22. Air hose No. 3
6. Cap	15. Air pipe No. 1	23. Air hose No. 2
7. Air cleaner	16. Muffler	24. Hose clamp
8. Washer	17. Cover	25. Plug
9. Washer	18. Screw	26. Bracket

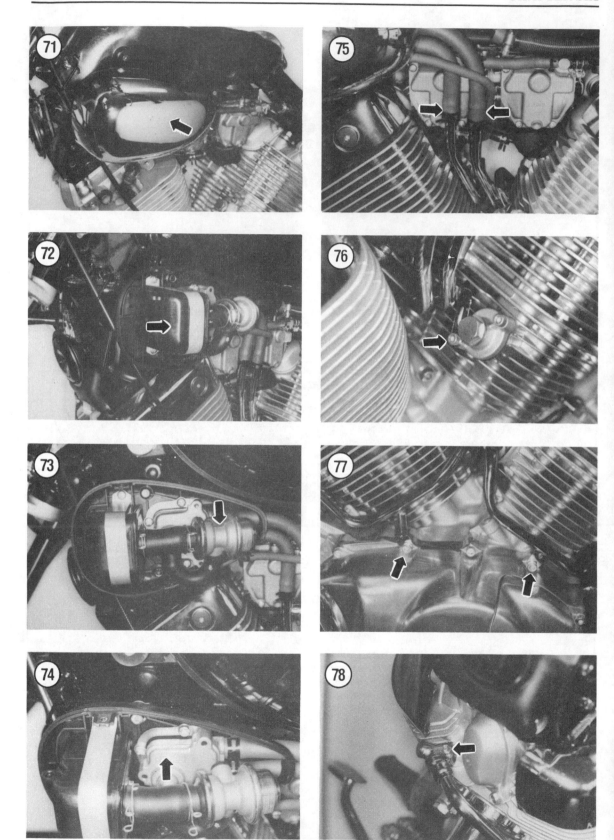

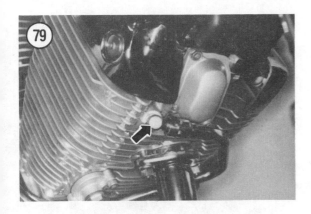

Figure 78 and Figure 79 are shown on the front cylinder. Air pipe attachment to the rear cylinder is identical.

    d. Remove the bolts securing the air pipes to the cylinders. Refer to **Figure 78** and **Figure 79**.

    e. Disconnect the air pipes from the cylinders and remove both air pipes from the engine. Don't lose the small muffler in the fitting where they attach to the cylinders.

8. Install by reversing these removal steps. Be sure to install each hose and pipe onto the correct fitting and tighten the bolts securely.

EXHAUST SYSTEM

Removal/Installation

  Refer to **Figure 80** for this procedure.

1. Place the bike on the sidestand.

2. Remove the nuts (**Figure 81**) securing the front exhaust pipe flange to the front cylinder head.

3. Remove the bolts (A, **Figure 82**) securing the rear exhaust pipe to the rear joint. Leave the rear joint attached to the rear cylinder.

4. Remove the bolt (B, **Figure 82**) securing the right-hand foot peg and muffler to the frame.

5. Remove the bolt, lockwasher and washer (**Figure 83**) securing the muffler chamber to the frame.

6. Carefully move the exhaust system forward to clear the threaded studs on the front cylinder head exhaust port. Pull the exhaust system out of the right-hand side of the frame and remove it from the frame and engine.

7. If replacement of the rear joint is necessary, the rear cylinder head must be removed as described in Chapter Four in this section of the manual. After the

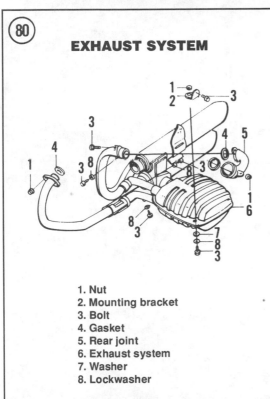

EXHAUST SYSTEM

1. Nut
2. Mounting bracket
3. Bolt
4. Gasket
5. Rear joint
6. Exhaust system
7. Washer
8. Lockwasher

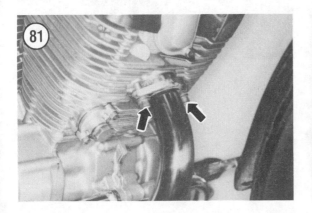

cylinder head is removed, remove the self-locking nuts (**Figure 84**) and remove the rear joint. Install new self-locking nuts and tighten securely.

NOTE
Don't lose the gasket at the front exhaust port and at the rear joint when the exhaust pipe is removed from the engine.

8. Inspect the system as described in this chapter.

9. Be sure to install a new gasket in the front exhaust port in the cylinder head and at the rear joint (**Figure 85**).

10. Install all of the exhaust system components and tighten the fasteners only finger-tight at this time. Make sure the exhaust pipe inlets are correctly seated in the cylinder head exhaust port and at the rear joint.

11. Securely tighten the bolts and nuts securing the front exhaust pipe flange to the cylinder head and to the rear joint, then tighten the bolts and nuts securing the muffler to the frame. This will minimize exhaust leakage at the cylinder head.

12. After installation is complete, start the engine and make sure there are no exhaust leaks. Correct any leak prior to riding the bike.

Inspection

1. Check for leakage where the exhaust pipes attach to the muffler chamber.

2. Inspect the muffler chamber mounting bracket for wear or damage. Replace if necessary.

Maintenance

The exhaust system is a vital key to the motorcycles operation and performance, You should periodically inspect, clean and polish (if required) the exhaust system. Special chemical cleaners and preservatives compounded for exhaust systems are available at most motorcycle shops.

Severe dents which cause flow restrictions require replacement of the damaged part.

To prevent internal rust buildup, periodically remove the system and turn it upside down to drain any trapped moisture.

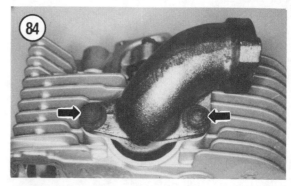

Table 1 CARBURETOR SPECIFICATIONS

Item	1987-1989 U.S.	1990-on U.S.
Manufacturer	Mikuni	Mikuni
Model	BDS34	BDS34
I.D. mark		
49-state	2GV00	3JC10
California	2JU00	3JC00
Main jet		
Both	137.5	—
Front	—	137.5
Rear	—	135
Main air jet	140	140
Jet needle		
Both	—	Y-0
Cylinder 1	5DZ7-1	—
Cylinder 2	5DZ8-1	—
Pilot jet	32.5	35
Pilot air jet		
No. 1	60	70
No. 2	160	170
Pilot screw	Preset	Preset
Starter jet	40	40
Fuel level	0.53-0.57 in.	0.53-0.57 in.
	(13.5-14.5 mm)	(13.5-14.5 mm)
Idle speed	1,150-1,250 rpm	1,150-1,250 rpm

Item	1988 U.K.	1989-on U.K.
Manufacturer	Mikuni	Mikuni
Model	BDS34	BDS34
I.D. mark	2JV00	3BT00
Main jet	135	135
Main air jet	140	140
Jet needle		
Cylinder 1	5DZ10-3	5DZ10-3
Cylinder 2	5DZ9-3	5DZ9-3
Pilot jet	35	35
Pilot air jet		
No. 1	70	70
No. 2	170	170
Pilot screw	2 turns out	2 turns out
Starter jet	40	40
Fuel level	0.53-0.57 in.	0.53-0.57 in.
	(13.5-14.5 mm)	(13.5-14.5 mm)
Idle speed	1,150-1,250 rpm	1,150-1,250 rpm

6

CHAPTER SEVEN

ELECTRICAL SYSTEM

The electrical systems consists of the following systems:

a. Charging system.
b. Ignition system.
c. Starting system.
d. Lighting system.
e. Directional signal system.
f. Horn.

This chapter discusses each system in detail. Refer to Chapter Three for routine ignition system maintenance. Electrical system specifications are found in **Table 1**. **Tables 1-4** are found at the end of the chapter.

> *NOTE*
> *This chapter covers all procedures unique to the XV535 Virago V-twins. If a specific procedure is not included in this chapter, refer to Chapter Seven at the front of this manual for service procedures.*

CHARGING SYSTEM

The charging system consists of the battery, alternator and a solid state rectifier/voltage regulator (**Figure 1**).

The alternator generates an alternating current (AC) which the rectifier converts to direct current (DC). The regulator maintains the voltage to the battery and load (lights, ignition, etc.) at a constant voltage regardless of variations in engine speed and load.

Testing Charging System

Whenever the charging system is suspected of trouble, make sure the battery is fully charged before going any further. Clean and test the battery as described in Chapter Three in this section of the manual. If the battery is in good condition, test the charging system as follows.

1

CHARGING SYSTEM

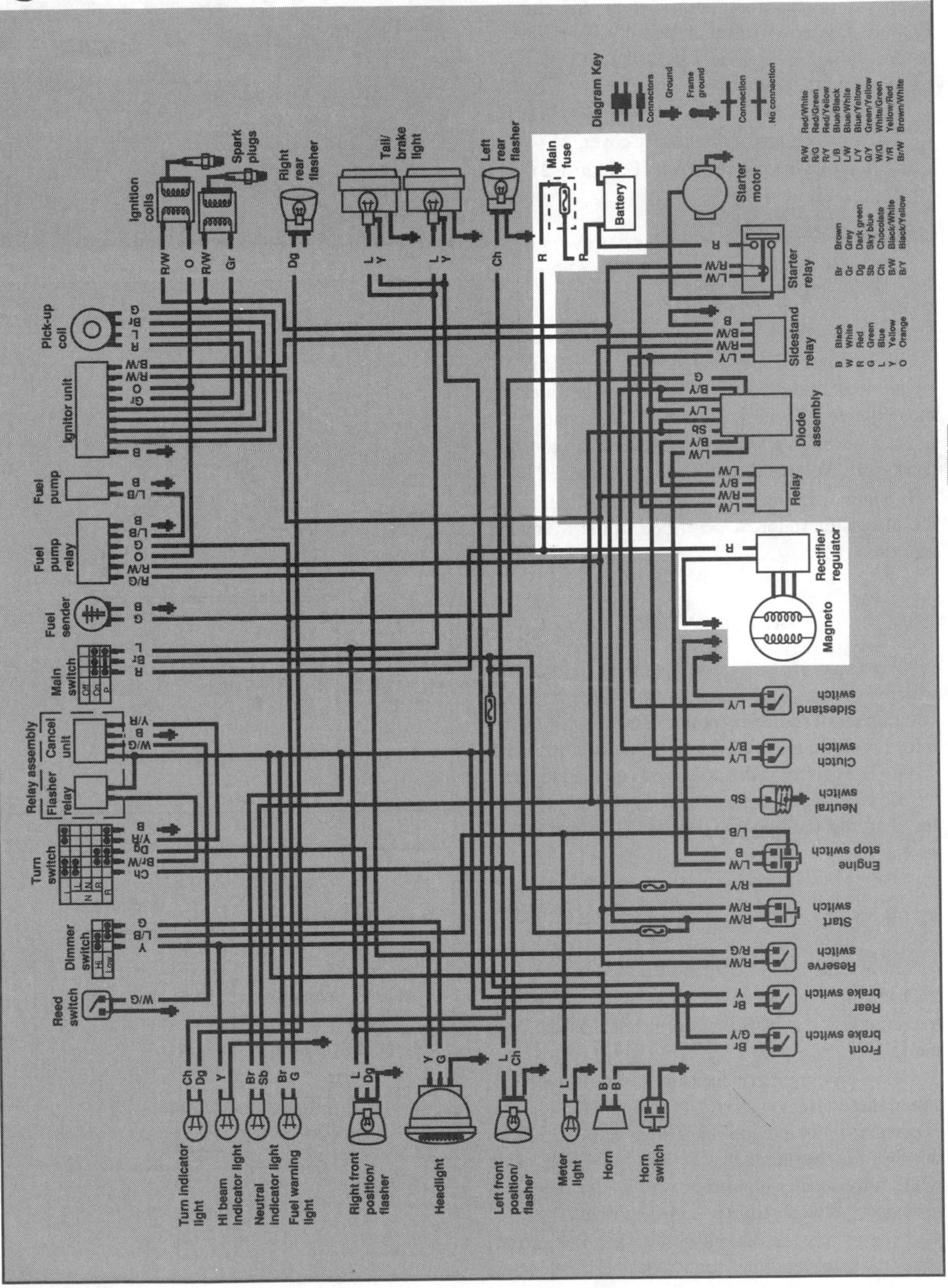

1. Place the bike securely on the sidestand.

2. Remove the seat.

3. Check the fuses as described in this chapter. Replace any blown fuses.

4. On 1990-on U.S. models and 1989-on U.K. models, perform the following:

   a. Unhook both fuel lines (A, **Figure 2**) from the clamps on top of the battery cover.

   b. Remove the battery cover (B, **Figure 2**).

> *NOTE*
> *Do not disconnect either the positive or negative battery cables; they are to remain in the circuit as is.*

5. Connect a 0-20 DC voltmeter to the battery as shown in **Figure 3**. Connect the positive (+) voltmeter terminal to the positive (+) battery terminal and the negative (−) voltmeter terminal to ground.

6. Start the engine and accelerate to approximately 5,000 rpm. Voltage should read 14-15 volts.

7. If charging current is lower than specified, check the alternator stator as described in the following section.

ALTERNATOR

An alternator is a form of electrical generator in which a magnetized field called a rotor revolves within a set of stationary coils called a stator. As the rotor revolves, alternating current is induced in the stator. The current is then rectified and used to operate the electrical accessories on the motorcycle and for charging the battery. The rotor is a permanent magnet.

Stator Checks

1. Remove the frame left-hand side cover.

2. Disconnect the alternator 3-pin electrical connector (containing 3 white wires) located by the fuel pump.

3. Using an ohmmeter, measure the resistance between the alternator terminals (**Figure 4**). It is not necessary to remove the stator assembly to perform this test. Set the ohmmeter to ohms × 1. Check each white wire against the other white. The specified resistance value should be 0.34-0.42 ohms.

4. If the values are not within the specified range, check the electrical wires to and within the connector

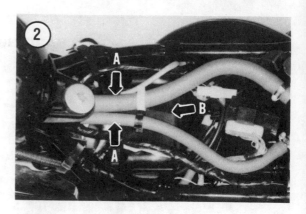

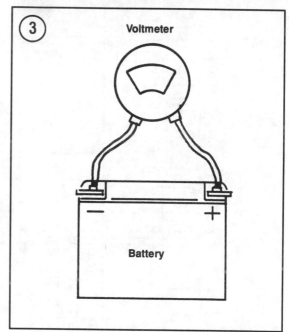

Voltmeter

Battery

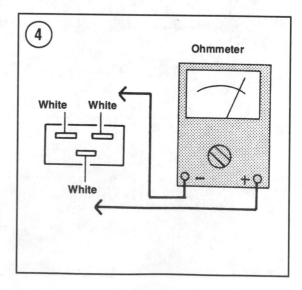

Ohmmeter

White   White

White

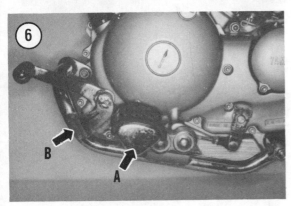

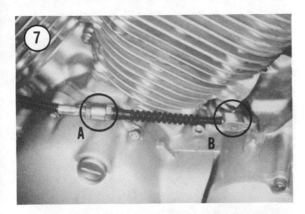

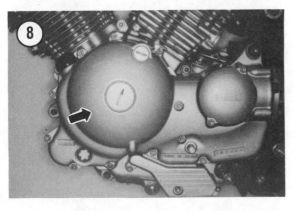

terminals. If they are okay, then there is an open circuit or short in the stator coils and the stator must be replaced as described in this chapter.

Stator
Removal/Installation

1. Place the bike on its sidestand.
2. Remove the frame left-hand side cover.
3. Disconnect the alternator 3-pin electrical connector (containing 3 white wires) located by the fuel pump.
4. On 1990-on U.S. models and 1989-on U.K. models, perform the following:
    a. Unhook both fuel lines (A, **Figure 2**) from the clamps on top of the battery cover.
    b. Remove the battery cover (B, **Figure 2**).
5. Disconnect the negative battery cable as described in Chapter Three in this section of the manual.
6. Remove the bolt (**Figure 5**) securing the shift lever arm and slide it off the shift shaft.
7. Remove the left-hand foot peg (A, **Figure 6**).
8. Remove the left-hand footrest bar (B, **Figure 6**).
9. At the clutch cable lower adjuster, loosen the locknuts and rotate the adjuster (A, **Figure 7**) to allow maximum slack in the cable.
10. Disconnect the clutch cable from the clutch actuating lever (B, **Figure 7**). Then pull the cable out of the lever and move it out of the way.
11. Remove the bolt securing the engine ground cable and disconnect the cable.
12. Carefully pull the stator wire harness from the frame and remove the wires from the frame. Note the path of the wire harness during removal; it must be routed the same during installation.
13. Using a crisscross pattern, loosen then remove the Allen screws securing the alternator cover/coil assembly (**Figure 8**).
14. Remove the alternator cover/coil assembly, gasket and electrical cable. Don't lose the locating dowels.
15. To replace the stator coils, perform the following:
    a. Remove the screws and lockwashers (A, **Figure 9**) securing the stator coil assembly.
    b. Remove the screw and metal retainer (B, **Figure 9**).
    c. Carefully pull the rubber grommets (**Figure 10**) and wiring harness from the cover. Remove the stator coil assembly from the cover.

7

d. Separate the stator wiring harness from the pickup coil harness and remove the stator wiring.

16. Install by reversing these removal steps. Note the following:

   a. Make sure the locating dowels (A, **Figure 11**) are in place and install a new gasket (B, **Figure 11**).

   b. Make sure the electrical wire harness is routed through the frame exactly as before.

   c. Clean all wire connectors with electrical contact cleaner.

Inspection

1. Inspect the alternator cover/coil assembly for wear or cracking.

2. Check the electrical wires on the stator for any opens or poor connectors. Also check the stator's insulating material for cracking. If the stator appears damaged in any way, test the assembly as described under *Stator Testing* in this chapter.

Flywheel (Rotor)
Removal/Installation

The following Yamaha special tools are required for flywheel removal:

   a. Flywheel puller set (U.S. part No. YU-33270) or (U.K. part No. 90890-01362).

   b. Adapter (U.S. part No. YU-33282) or (U.K. part No. 90890-04089).

> *NOTE*
> *This procedure is shown with the engine removed and partially disassembled for clarity. It is not necessary to remove the engine for this procedure.*

1. Remove the alternator stator as described in this chapter.

2. Use a strap wrench (**Figure 12**) on the flywheel to keep it from turning.

3. Remove the flywheel bolt and washer (**Figure 13**) securing the flywheel.

> *CAUTION*
> *Make sure to thread the special tool bolts completely into the flywheel threads to avoid damage to the flywheel as well as the special tool.*

4. Install the previously described Yamaha special tools or a similar puller, onto the flywheel as shown in **Figure 14**.

5. Use a wrench on the puller and tap on the end of the puller jackscrew with a brass mallet until the flywheel disengages. Remove the puller and the flywheel (**Figure 15**).

6. If necessary, remove the Woodruff key from the crankshaft.

7. Installation is the reverse of these steps while noting the following:

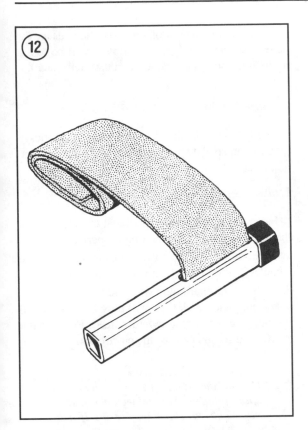

a. If removed, install the Woodruff key (**Figure 16**) in the crankshaft.

> *CAUTION*
> *Carefully inspect the inside of the fly-wheel (**Figure 17**) for small bolts, washers or other metal "trash" that may have been picked up by the magnets. These small metal bits can cause severe damage to the alternator stator assembly.*

7

b. Install the flywheel washer and bolt. Lock the flywheel as in Step 2 during removal. Tighten the flywheel bolt to 58 ft.-lb. (80 N•m).

Flywheel (Rotor) Testing

The flywheel (rotor) is permanently magnetized and cannot be tested except by replacement with a flywheel known to be good. A flywheel can lose magnetism from old age or a sharp blow. If defective, the flywheel must be replaced; it cannot be re-magnetized.

VOLTAGE REGULATOR/RECTIFIER

Varying engine speeds and electrical system loads affect alternator output. The voltage regulator controls alternator output by varying its field current. Yamaha does not provide any test procedures or specifications for the voltage regulator/rectifier.

The voltage regulator is mounted either under the frame behind the engine (**Figure 18**) or under the left-hand trim panel (**Figure 19**).

IGNITION SYSTEM

All XV535 models are equipped with a Transistor Control Ignition (TCI) system. The TCI system consists of both a pickup unit and an ignitor unit and uses no breaker points. It is non-adjustable, but the timing should be checked to make sure all components within the ignition system are operating correctly. The ignition advance circuit is controlled by signals generated by the pickup coils and the advance curve cannot be modified to improve performance. The schematic layout of this ignition system and how it relates to the rest of the bike's electrical systems is shown in **Figure 20**.

Most problems involving failure to start, poor driveability or rough running are caused by trouble in the ignition system:

Note the following symptoms:

a. Engine misses.

b. Stumbles on acceleration (misfiring).

c. Loss of power at high speed (misfiring).

d. Hard starting (or failure to start).

e. Rough idle.

Most of the symptoms can also be caused by a carburetor(s) that is worn or improperly adjusted.

But considering the law of averages, the odds are far better that the source of the problem will be found in the ignition system rather than the fuel system.

Troubleshooting

The following basic tests are designed to quickly pinpoint and isolate problems in the ignition system.

Ignition Spark Test

Perform the following spark test to determine if the ignition system is operating properly.

1. Remove one of the spark plugs as described in Chapter Three in this section of the manual.

2. Connect the spark plug wire and connector to the spark plug and touch the spark plug base to a good ground like the engine cylinder head. Position the spark plug so you can see the electrodes.

> *WARNING*
> *During the next step, do not hold the spark plug, wire or connector or a serious electrical shock may result. If nec-*

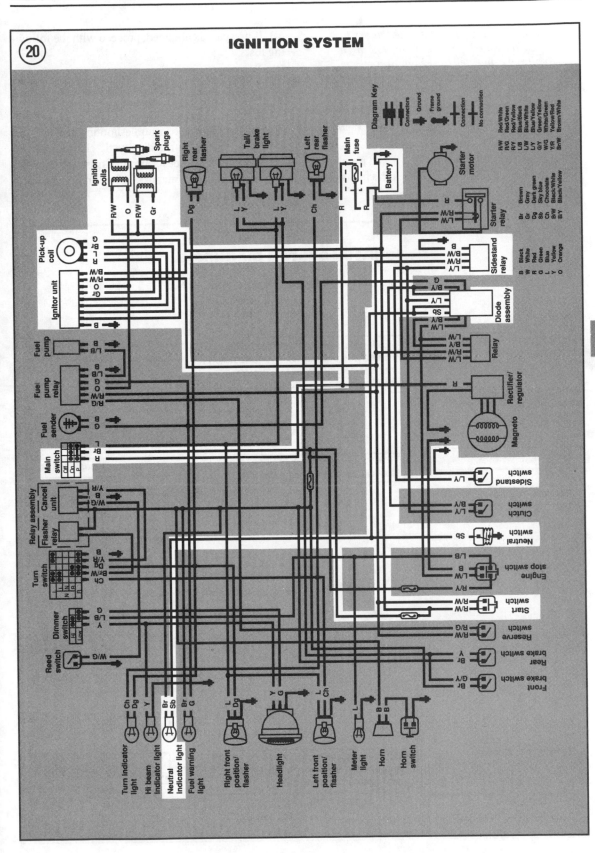

IGNITION SYSTEM

essary, use a pair of insulated pliers to hold the spark plug or wire. The high voltage generated by the ignition system could produce serious or fatal shocks.

3. Crank the engine over with the starter. A fat blue spark should be evident across the spark plug electrodes.

4A. If a spark is obtained in Step 3, the problem is not in the ignitor unit or coil. Check the fuel system and spark plugs.

4B. If no spark is obtained, proceed with the following tests.

Testing

Test procedures for troubleshooting the ignition system are found in the diagnostic chart in **Figure 21**. A multimeter, as described in Chapter One, in the front section of the manual, is required to perform the test procedures.

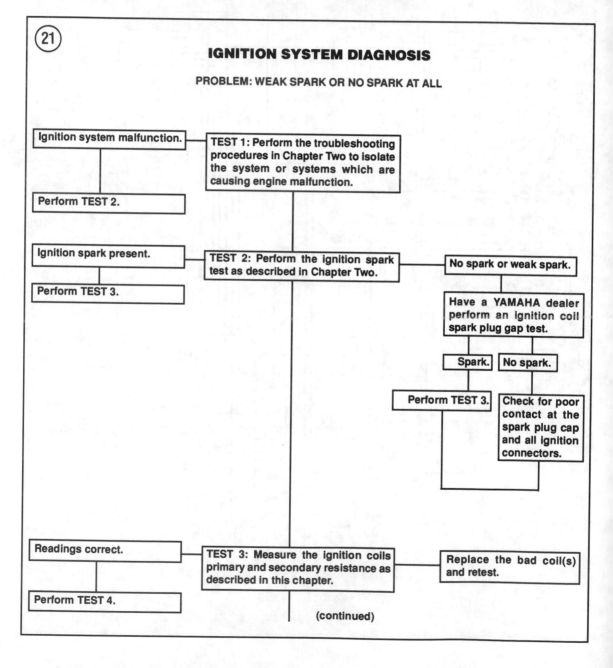

(21)

IGNITION SYSTEM DIAGNOSIS

PROBLEM: WEAK SPARK OR NO SPARK AT ALL

Ignition system malfunction.

Perform TEST 2.

TEST 1: Perform the troubleshooting procedures in Chapter Two to isolate the system or systems which are causing engine malfunction.

Ignition spark present.

Perform TEST 3.

TEST 2: Perform the ignition spark test as described in Chapter Two.

No spark or weak spark.

Have a YAMAHA dealer perform an ignition coil spark plug gap test.

Spark.   No spark.

Perform TEST 3.   Check for poor contact at the spark plug cap and all ignition connectors.

Readings correct.

Perform TEST 4.

TEST 3: Measure the ignition coils primary and secondary resistance as described in this chapter.

Replace the bad coil(s) and retest.

(continued)

the diagnostic chart will refer you to a certain procedure in this chapter for testing.

Pickup Coil Testing

To get an accurate reading, the ignition coils must
be warm (minimum temperature is 20° C [68° F]. If
necessary, start the engine and let it warm up to
normal operating temperature. If you are unable to
start the bike, heat the pickup coil to the proper
temperature with a portable hair dryer.

1. Remove the seat and frame left-hand side cover.

2. Disconnect the battery negative lead as described
in Chapter Three in this section of the manual.

3. Disconnect the pickup coil 4-pin electrical connector (containing 1 red, 1 blue, 1 brown and 1
green) from the ignitor unit. The ignitor unit is
located under the right-hand engine cover (**Figure
22**) behind the fuel pump relay and the flasher relay
assembly.

NOTE
*Connect the ohmmeter to the electrical
connector attached to the wiring harness leading to the pickup coil.*

4. Use an ohmmeter on R × 100 to measure the
pickup coil resistance between the following terminals:

   a. Brown to green.

   b. Red to blue.

5. Compare the pickup coil reading to the specification in **Table 1**. Replace the pickup coil assembly if
it does not meet the test specifications.

6. If the pickup coil is satisfactory, reconnect the
electrical connector and install all removed parts.

Pickup Coil
Removal/Installation

1. Remove the seat and disconnect the battery negative lead as described in Chapter Three in this section
of the manual.

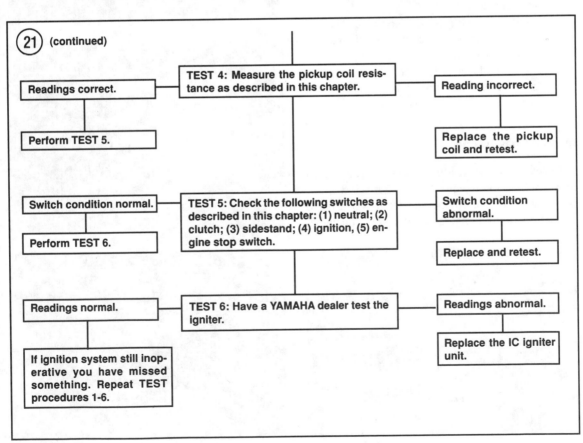

21 (continued)

	TEST 4: Measure the pickup coil resis- tance as described in this chapter.	
Readings correct.		Reading incorrect.
Perform TEST 5.		Replace the pickup coil and retest.
Switch condition normal.	TEST 5: Check the following switches as described in this chapter: (1) neutral; (2) clutch; (3) sidestand; (4) ignition, (5) en- gine stop switch.	Switch condition abnormal.
Perform TEST 6.		Replace and retest.
Readings normal.	TEST 6: Have a YAMAHA dealer test the igniter.	Readings abnormal.
If ignition system still inop- erative you have missed something. Repeat TEST procedures 1-6.		Replace the IC igniter unit.

2. Remove the alternator stator assembly as described in this chapter.

3. Remove the screws and lockwashers (A, **Figure 23**) securing the pickup coil assembly.

4. Remove the screw and metal retainer (B, **Figure 23**).

5. Carefully pull the rubber grommets (**Figure 10**) and wiring harness from the cover. Remove the pickup coil assembly from the cover.

6. Separate the pickup coil wiring harness from the stator coil harness and remove the pickup coil wiring.

7. Follow the pickup coil electrical harness from the coil assembly to the electrical connector on the frame and loosen or remove any clamps or tie wraps securing the harness to the frame.

8. Disconnect the electrical connector from the ignitor unit and remove the pickup coil assembly from the frame.

9. Install by reversing these removal steps while noting the following:

   a. Make sure the rubber grommets are properly seated in the crankcase groove to prevent the entry of moisture.

   b. Apply a dielectric compound to the electrical connectors prior to reconnecting them. This will help seal out moisture.

   c. Make sure the electrical connectors are free of corrosion and are completely coupled to each other.

Ignition Coils Testing

To get an accurate reading, the ignition coils must be warm (minimum temperature is 20° C [68° F]. If necessary, start the engine and let it warm up to normal operating temperature. If you are unable to

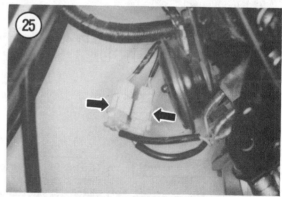

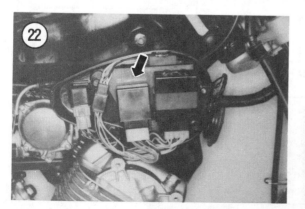

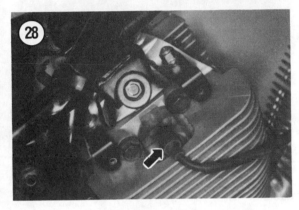

start the bike, heat the coils to the proper temperature with a portable hair dryer.

1. Place the motorcycle on the sidestand. Turn the front wheel to either side to gain access to the cover.

2. Remove the bolts securing the ignition coil cover (**Figure 24**) and remove the cover.

3. Disconnect the ignition primary coil wire electrical connectors (**Figure 25**). Each connector contains 2 wires; (1 red/white and 1 gray) and (1 red/white and 1 orange).

4. Remove the front cylinder head right-hand cover (**Figure 26**) and the rear cylinder head left-hand cover (**Figure 27**)

5. Disconnect the spark plug lead (**Figure 28**) from each spark plug.

6. At each electrical connector, measure the coil primary resistance using an ohmmeter set at R × 1. Connect the ohmmeter test leads to the ignition coil connector as shown in **Figure 29**. The correct primary resistance is listed in **Table 1**.

7. Carefully remove the spark plug cap from each spark plug lead.

8. Measure the secondary resistance using an ohmmeter set at R × 1,000. Measure between the coil's secondary spark plug lead (**Figure 30**) and the gray

7

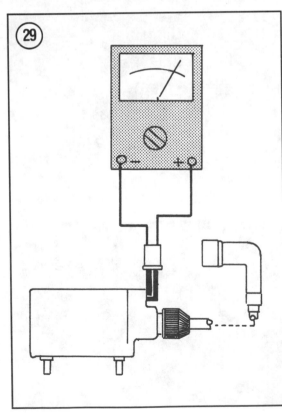

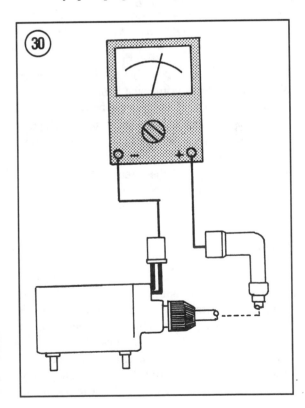

or orange lead. The correct secondary resistance is listed in **Table 1**.

9. Replace the ignition coil(s) if it doesn't test within the specifications in Step 6 and/or Step 8.

10. Reconnect all electrical connections. Make sure the electrical connectors are free of corrosion and are completely coupled to each other.

11. Install all items removed.

Ignition Coil
Removal/Installation

1. Place the motorcycle on the sidestand.

2. Remove the bolts securing the ignition coil cover (**Figure 24**) and remove the cover.

3. Disconnect the ignition primary coil wire electrical connectors (**Figure 25**). Each connector contains 2 wires: 1 red/white and 1 gray; and 1 red/white and 1 orange.

4. Remove the front cylinder head right-hand cover (**Figure 26**) and the rear cylinder head left-hand cover (**Figure 27**).

5. Disconnect the spark plug lead (**Figure 28**) from each spark plug.

> *NOTE*
> *Step 6 and Step 7 are shown with the engine removed from the frame for clarity.*

6. Remove the bolt, lockwasher and washer (**Figure 31**) on each side securing each ignition coil assembly to the front cylinder mounting bracket.

7. Carefully pull the ignition coil assembly (**Figure 32**), spark plug leads and cap out from the mounting bracket and remove both coil assemblies.

8. Install by reversing these removals steps. Make sure the electrical connectors are free of corrosion and are completely coupled to each other.

Ignitor Unit Check

The ignitor unit cannot be tested. If there is a problem within the ignition system and all other components within the ignition system perform within test specifications, then the ignitor unit is probably faulty and should be replaced.

Prior to purchasing a new ignitor unit, have the system checked by a Yamaha dealer. They may perform a "remove and replace" test to see if the igniter unit is faulty. This type of test is expensive if performed by yourself. Remember if you purchase a new ignitor unit and it does *not* solve your particular ignition system problem, you cannot return the ignitor unit for a refund. Most motorcycle dealers will *not* accept returns on electrical and electronic components since they could be damaged internally even though they look okay externally.

Ignitor Unit
Removal/Installation

The ignitor unit is located under the right-hand engine cover behind the fuel pump relay and the flasher relay assembly.

1. Remove the seat and disconnect the battery negative lead as described in Chapter Three in this section of the manual.

2. Remove the right-hand engine cover (**Figure 33**).

3. Remove the bolts securing the electrical panel to the mounting bracket (**Figure 34**).

4. Carefully pull the electrical panel out and turn it around.

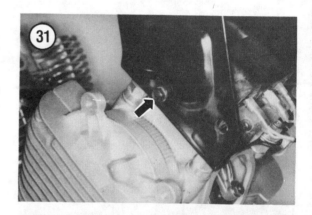

5. Remove the bolts and washers securing the ignitor unit to the electrical panel.

6. Disconnect the electrical wire connectors at the ignitor unit and remove it.

7. Install by reversing these removal steps. Before connecting the electrical wire connectors at the ignitor unit, make sure the connectors are clean of any dirt or moisture.

STARTING SYSTEM

The starting system consists of the starter motor, starter solenoid, starter circuit cutoff relay and the starter switch.

The starting system is shown in **Figure 35**. When the starter button is pressed, it engages the solenoid switch that closes the circuit. The electricity flows from the battery to the starter motor.

CAUTION
Do not operate the starter for more than five seconds at a time. Let it rest approximately ten seconds, then use it again.

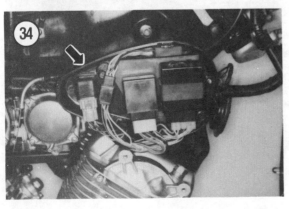

When the engine stop switch and the main switch are turned to ON, the engine can only be started if:

   a. The transmission is in NEUTRAL.

   b. The clutch lever is pulled in (transmission in gear) and the sidestand is up.

If the above conditions are not met, the starting circuit cut-off relay will prevent the starter from operating.

The starter gears are covered in Chapter Four in this section of the manual.

Table 2, at the end of the chapter, lists possible starter problems, probable causes and the most common remedies.

Starter Motor
Removal/Installation

1. Place the bike on the sidestand.

2. Remove the exhaust system as described in Chapter Six in this section of the manual.

3. Make sure the ignition switch is in the OFF position.

4. Disconnect the negative lead from the battery.

NOTE
Figure 36 is shown with the engine partially disassembled for clarity.

5. Pull back on the rubber boot and disconnect the electrical wire (A, **Figure 36**) from the starter motor.

6. Remove the bolts (B, **Figure 36**) securing the starter motor to the crankcase and remove it.

7. Installation is the reverse of these steps. Note the following:

   a. Grease the starter O-ring (A, **Figure 37**) and insert the starter motor into the crankcase and properly mesh it with the starter reduction gears. Do not damage the O-ring during installation.

   b. Tighten the starter motor mounting bolts to 5.1 ft.-lb. (7 N•m).

Starter Motor Disassembly/Assembly

The overhaul of a starter motor is best left to an expert. This section shows how to determine if the unit is defective.

Refer to **Figure 38** for this procedure.

1. Remove the starter motor case bolts and lockwashers (**Figure 39**).

7

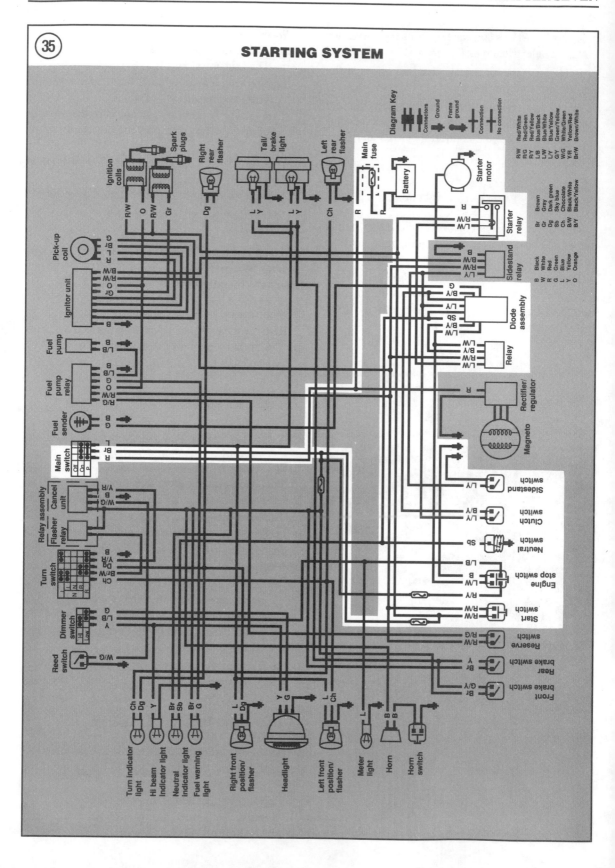

35 STARTING SYSTEM

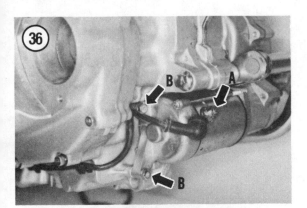

2. Slide off the front cover (B, **Figure 37**).

3. Slide off the rear cover (**Figure 40**) and shims (**Figure 41**). Record the number of shims as the same number must be installed during assembly.

4. Withdraw the armature from the case (**Figure 42**).

5. Clean all grease, dirt, and carbon dust from the armature, case and end covers.

CAUTION
Do not immerse brushes or the wire windings in solvent or the insulation might be damaged. Wipe the windings

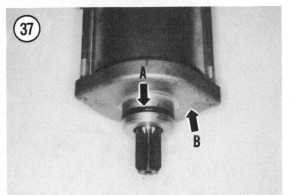

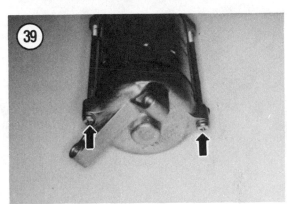

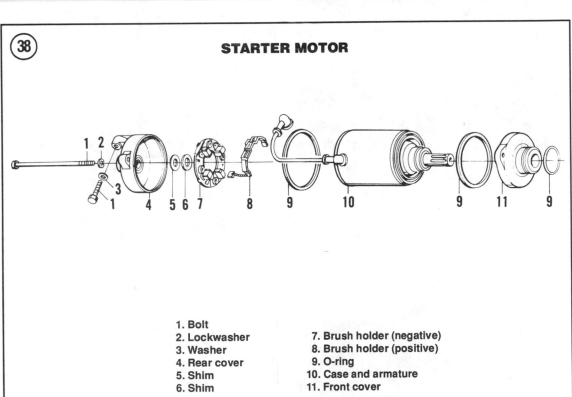

STARTER MOTOR

1. Bolt
2. Lockwasher
3. Washer
4. Rear cover
5. Shim
6. Shim
7. Brush holder (negative)
8. Brush holder (positive)
9. O-ring
10. Case and armature
11. Front cover

with a cloth slightly moistened with solvent and dry thoroughly.

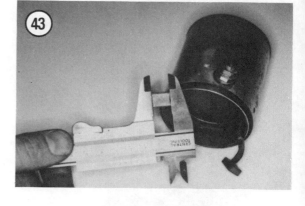

6. Pull back the spring from behind the brushes and remove the brushes from their guides. Measure the length of each brush with a vernier caliper (**Figure 43**). If they are worn to 0.20 in. (5.0 mm) or less, replace them.

7. Check the spring tension by comparing to a new set of springs. Replace if necessary.

8. Inspect the condition of the commutator (**Figure 44**). The mica in a good commutator is below the

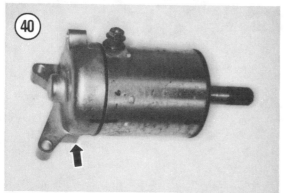

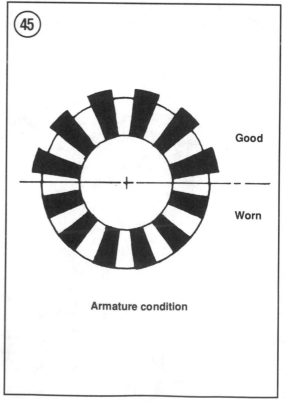

Good

Worn

Armature condition

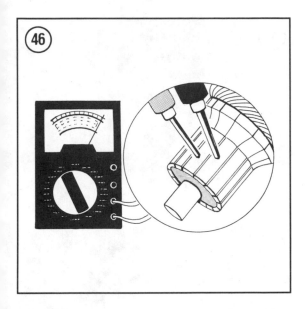

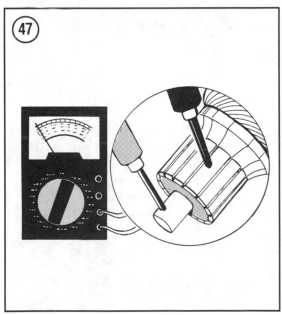

surface of the copper bars (**Figure 45**). A worn commutator is indicated by the copper and mica being level with each other. A worn commutator can be undercut, but it requires a specialist. Take the job to your Yamaha dealer or an electrical repair shop.

9. Inspect the commutator bars for discoloration. If a pair of bars are discolored, that indicates grounded armature coils.

10. Use an ohmmeter and check the electrical continuity between pairs of commutator bars (**Figure 46**) and between the commutator bars and the shaft mounting (**Figure 47**). If there is a short, the armature should be replaced.

11. Inspect the field coil by checking continuity from the cable terminal to the motor case with an ohmmeter; there should be no continuity. Also check from the cable terminal to each brush wire; there should be continuity. If the unit fails either of these tests, the case/field coil assembly must be replaced.

12. Check the bushing in the front end cover (**Figure 48**) and the oil seal and bushing in the rear end cover (**Figure 49**). If worn or damaged, refer it to a Yamaha dealer for further service.

13. Inspect the splines (A, **Figure 50**) on the armature shaft where it meshes with the starter gears. Check for worn or chipped splines.

14. Check the bearing (B, **Figure 50**) on the armature shaft for wear or damage.

15. Inspect the case O-rings (**Figure 51**) for wear, deterioration or damage; replace if necessary.

16. Inspect the stack-up of nuts, washer and insulated washers (**Figure 52**) on the positive brush holder assembly. Replace any damaged part if necessary.

17. Assemble by reversing these removal steps, while noting the following:

7

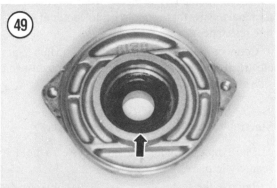

a. Be sure to install the same number of shims (**Figure 41**) on the armature shaft.

b. Align the locating tabs on the brush holder assembly with the notches in the case (**Figure 53**) and install the assembly (**Figure 54**).

c. Align both end covers and align the marks between the covers and the case (**Figure 55**).

d. Install the bolts and lockwashers and tighten securely.

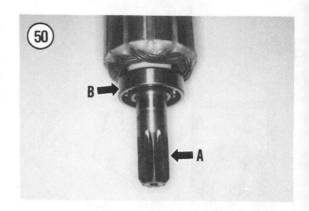

Starter Relay
Removal/Installation

1. Remove the frame right-hand side cover.

2. Pull back the rubber boots and remove the nuts and washers (A, **Figure 56**) securing the cables to the relay.

3. Pull the relay out of its holder (B, **Figure 56**).

4. Installation is the reverse of these steps.

Starting Circuit Cut-Off Relay Testing

1. Place the motorcycle on the sidestand.

2. Remove the right-hand side cover (**Figure 33**).

3. Disconnect the starting circuit cut-off switch 9-pin electrical connector (**Figure 57**). It contains 9 wires (2 blue/white, 1 red/white, 1 black/yellow, 1 black, 1 brown/white, 1 yellow/red, 1 brown and 1 white/green).

4. Set the ohmmeter scale to read ohms × 1. Attach the ohmmeter test leads to the red/white and to the black/yellow terminals on the cut-off relay (not the electrical connector).

5. Connect a 12 volt battery to both blue/white terminals on the cut-off relay. With the battery connected there should be continuity (low resistance).

6. Disconnect the 12 volt battery from the blue/white terminals. Now there should be no continuity (infinite resistance).

7. Connect the starting circuit cut-off switch 9-pin electrical connector and install the engine right-hand side cover.

Starting Circuit Sidestand Switch Testing

1. Place blocks under the motorcycle to hold it securely in place.

2. Remove the seat.

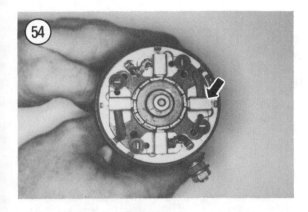

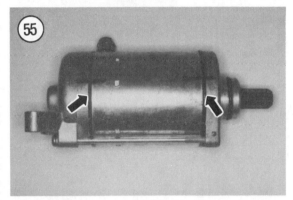

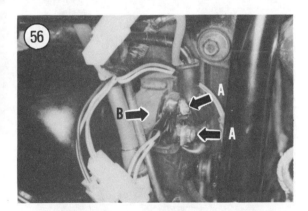

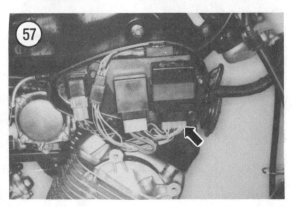

3. Disconnect the starting circuit sidestand relay 2-pin electrical connector located next to the battery. It contains 2 wires (1 black and 1 blue/yellow).

4. Set the ohmmeter scale to read ohms × 1. Connect the ohmmeter test leads to the black and blue/yellow terminals.

5. Raise the sidestand, there should be continuity (low resistance).

6. Lower the sidestand, there should be no continuity (infinite resistance).

7. If the switch tests okay, reconnect the 2-pin electrical connector.

8. To replace the sidestand switch, disconnect the electrical connector. Remove the mounting screws and remove the switch. Reverse to install.

Starting Circuit Neutral Switch Testing

1. Place the motorcycle on the sidestand.

2. Disconnect the starting circuit neutral switch single sky blue electrical connector, located on the left-hand side next to the battery.

3. Set the ohmmeter scale to read ohms × 1. Connect the ohmmeter positive (+) test lead to the sky blue terminal leading to the neutral switch.

4. Ground the ohmmeter negative (−) test lead to the engine.

5. Shift the transmission into NEUTRAL, there should be continuity (low resistance).

6. Shift the transmission into any gear, there should be no continuity (infinite resistance).

7. If the switch tests okay, reconnect the single sky blue electrical connector.

8. To replace the sidestand switch, remove the left-hand crankcase cover as described in Chapter Four in this section of the manual. Disconnect the electrical connector, then remove the mounting screws and remove the switch (**Figure 58**). Reverse to install.

LIGHTING SYSTEM

The lighting system consists of the headlight, taillight/brakelight combination, directional signals, warning lights and speedometer and tachometer illumination lights. In the event of trouble with any light, the first thing to check is the affected bulb itself. If the bulb is good, check all wiring and connections with a test light. **Table 3** lists the replacement bulbs for these components.

7

Headlight Replacement

> *WARNING*
> *If the headlight bulb has just burned out or turned off it will be hot! Don't touch the bulb until it cools off.*

1. Remove the mounting screws (A, **Figure 59**) on each side of the headlight housing.

2. Pull the trim bezel and headlight unit (B, **Figure 59**) out and disconnect the electrical connector (A, **Figure 60**) from the bulb.

3. Remove the bulb cover (B, **Figure 60**).

> *CAUTION*
> *Do not touch the bulb glass with your fingers because traces of oil on the bulb will drastically reduce the life of the bulb. Clean any traces of oil from the bulb with a cloth moistened in alcohol or lacquer thinner.*

4. Turn the bulb holder counterclockwise and remove the bulb.

5. Install by reversing these steps. Be sure to install the bulb cover with the TOP mark (C, **Figure 60**) facing up.

6. Adjust the headlight as described under *Headlight Adjustment* in this chapter.

Headlight Adjustment

Adjust the headlight horizontally and vertically according to the Department of Motor Vehicles regulations in your area.

There are 2 adjustments: horizontal and vertical. To adjust, proceed as follows:

Horizontal adjustment—Turn the top screw (A, **Figure 61**) clockwise to move the beam to the right and counterclockwise to move the beam to the left.

Vertical adjustment—Turn the lower screw (B, **Figure 61**) clockwise to move the beam up and counterclockwise to move the beam down.

Speedometer Illumination Bulb Replacement

1. Disconnect the speedometer cable (**Figure 62**).

2. Remove the bolts securing the speedometer base and pull it away from the steering head.

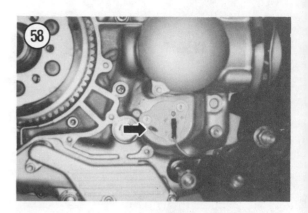

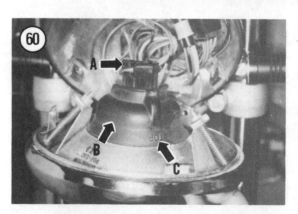

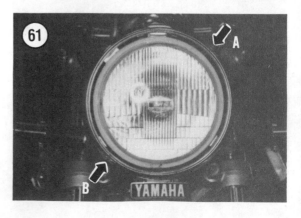

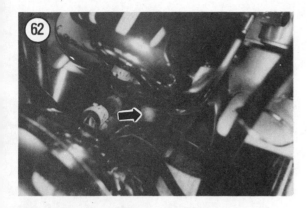

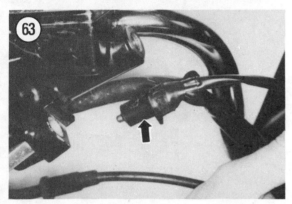

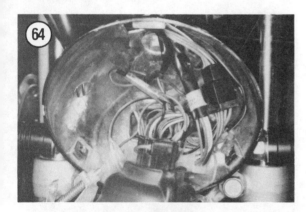

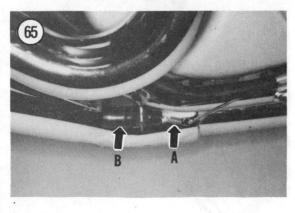

3. Remove the outside cover (as necessary) to gain access to the blown bulb.

4. Remove the bulb from the connector and install a new one.

5. Installation is the reverse of these steps.

SWITCHES

Front Brake Light Switch Replacement

1. Using a small screwdriver or drift, push up in the hole in the base of the master cylinder switch receptacle and withdraw the switch and electrical harness from the master cylinder (**Figure 63**).

2. Remove the headlight and follow the switch's electrical harness into the headlight case (**Figure 64**) and disconnect it.

3. Install the new switch and connect the wires.

Rear Brake Light Switch Replacement

1. Remove the frame right-hand side cover.

2. Unhook the spring (A, **Figure 65**) from the brake arm.

3. Unscrew the switch housing and locknut (B, **Figure 65**) from the mounting bracket.

4. Disconnect the electrical wires.

5. Replace the switch; reinstall and adjust as described in this chapter.

Rear Brake Light Switch Adjustment

1. Turn the ignition switch to the ON position.

2. Depress the brake pedal. Brake light should come on just as the brake begins to work.

3. To make the light come on earlier, hold the switch body (A, **Figure 66**) and turn the adjusting nut (B, **Figure 66**) as required.

Sidestand Switch Replacement

> *NOTE*
> *This procedure is shown with the sidestand assembly removed for clarity. It is not necessary to remove the assembly in order to remove the switch.*

1. Place the bike securely on the sidestand.

2. Remove the sidestand switch screws (**Figure 67**).

3. Disconnect the switch electrical connector and remove the switch.

4. Install the new switch and connect the connector.

Flasher Relay Replacement

1. Remove the right-hand side cover (**Figure 33**).

2. Disconnect the 9-pin electrical connector and remove the flasher relay (**Figure 68**) and replace it with a new unit.

FUEL PUMP TESTING

The fuel pump system consists of a fuel pump, fuel pump controller and fuel reserve switch. Refer to **Figure 69** for 1987-1989 models or **Figure 70** for 1990-1993 models. Fuel pump removal and installation is described in Chapter Six in this section of the manual. Observe the following conditions when troubleshooting the fuel pump system.

1. Check all connections to make sure they are tight and free of corrosion.

2. Check the battery to make sure it is fully charged.

3. Fuel pump troubleshooting is divided into 4 separate test procedures, each dependent upon the problem experienced.

    a. Test 1: Fuel pump fails to operate after engine is started.

    b. Test 2: Fuel pump fails to operate for a 5 second interval when the carburetor fuel level is low and the fuel level indicator does not come on.

    c. Test 3: Fuel pump fails to operate for 5 second intervals when the carburetor fuel level is low and the fuel level indicator comes on.

    d. Test 4: Fuel pump does not stop after 30 seconds when fuel indicator comes on while engine is turned on.

Test 1

1. Remove the right-hand cover (**Figure 33**).

2. Shift the transmission into neutral.

3. Disconnect the fuel pump relay 6-pin electrical connector (**Figure 71**).

4. Connect a 0-20 V DC voltmeter to the wiring harness side of the connector. Connect the positive (+) test lead to the red/white terminals and the negative (–) test lead to ground.

5. Turn the main switch ON and the engine stop switch to RUN.

6. Push the START button and measure the voltage. Interpret results as follows:

    a. Less than 12 volts: check the main switch.

    b. More than 12 volts: proceed to Step 7.

7. Reconnect the 6-pin electrical connector.

8. Remove the headlight as described in this chapter.

9. Within the headlight housing, disconnect the right-hand handlebar switch 9-pin electrical connector.

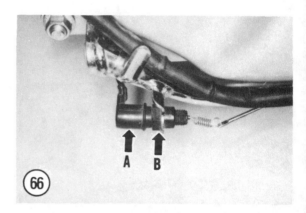

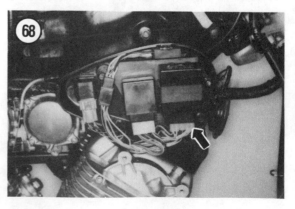

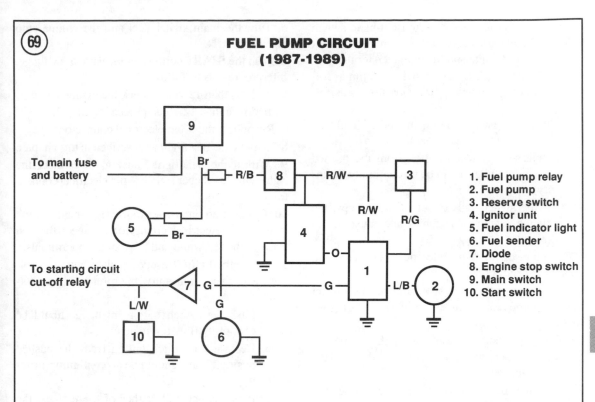

**FUEL PUMP CIRCUIT
(1987-1989)**

1. Fuel pump relay
2. Fuel pump
3. Reserve switch
4. Ignitor unit
5. Fuel indicator light
6. Fuel sender
7. Diode
8. Engine stop switch
9. Main switch
10. Start switch

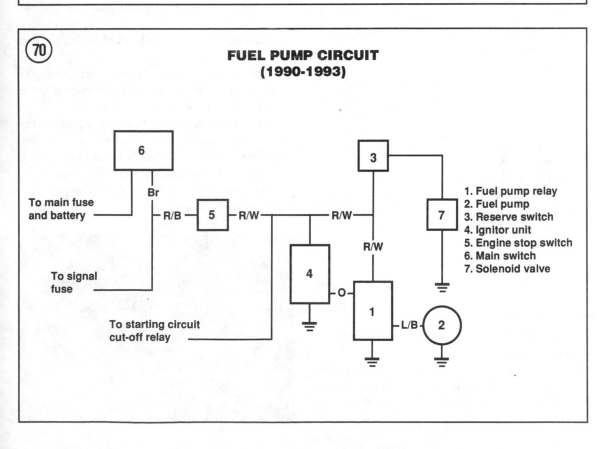

**FUEL PUMP CIRCUIT
(1990-1993)**

1. Fuel pump relay
2. Fuel pump
3. Reserve switch
4. Ignitor unit
5. Engine stop switch
6. Main switch
7. Solenoid valve

7

10. Connect an ohmmeter to the right-hand switch side of the electrical connector. Connect the test leads to the red/white and the red/green terminals.

11. Move the FUEL (reserve) switch button as follows and check continuity. Interpret results as follows:

    a. Push the switch button in: there should be continuity (low resistance).

    b. Release the switch button from the pushed position: there should be no continuity (infinity).

    c. If the switch fails either of these steps, the switch assembly is faulty and must be replaced.

12. Reconnect the 9-pin electrical connector and install the headlight.

13. In the area under the right-hand cover, disconnect the fuel pump relay 6-pin electrical connector (**Figure 71**).

14. On the wiring harness side of the connector, connect a jumper wire between the red/white and the blue/black terminals.

15. Turn the main switch ON and the engine stop switch to the RUN position.

16. Push both the START button and the FUEL (reserve) button at the same time. Interpret results as follows:

    a. Fuel pump operates: Re-check the entire fuel system electrical connections to make sure they are tight and free of corrosion. If all connections are OK, replace the fuel pump relay.

    b. Fuel pump does not operate: replace the fuel pump.

17. Connect the fuel pump relay 6-pin electrical connector. Do not install the right-hand cover if Test 2 is going to be performed.

Test 2

1. If still in place, remove the right-hand cover (**Figure 33**).

2. Shift the transmission into neutral.

3. Disconnect the fuel pump relay 6-pin electrical connector (**Figure 71**).

4. Connect a 0-20 V DC voltmeter to the wiring harness side of the connector. Connect the positive (+) test lead to the red/white terminals and the negative (−) test lead to ground.

5. Turn the main switch ON and the engine stop switch to RUN.

6. Push the START button and measure the voltage. Interpret results as follows:

    a. Less than 12 volts: check the main switch.

    b. More than 12 volts: proceed to Step 7.

7. Reconnect the 6-pin electrical connector.

8. Remove the headlight as described in this chapter.

9. Within the headlight housing, disconnect the right-hand handlebar switch 9-pin electrical connector.

10. Connect an ohmmeter to the right-hand switch side of the electrical connector. Connect the test leads to the red/white and the red/green terminals.

11. Move the FUEL (reserve) switch button as follows and check continuity. Interpret results as follows:

    a. Push the switch button in: there should be continuity (low resistance).

    b. Release the switch button from the pushed position: there should be no continuity (infinity).

    c. If the switch fails either of these steps, the switch assembly is faulty and must be replaced.

12. Reconnect the 9-pin electrical connector and install the headlight.

13. In the area under the right-hand cover, locate the fuel pump relay 6-pin electrical connector (**Figure 71**). Do NOT disconnect it.

14. Carefully insert the positive (+) test lead into the blue/black wire terminal of the connector. Make sure it touches bare metal within the connector.

15. Connect the negative (−) test lead to ground.

16. Turn the main switch ON and the engine stop switch to the RUN position.

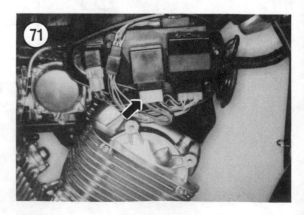

17. Push both the START button and the FUEL (reserve) button at the same time. Interpret results as follows:

   a. Fuel pump input voltage less than 11 volts: replace the fuel pump relay.

   b. Fuel pump input voltage more than 11 volts: Re-check the entire fuel system electrical connections to make sure they are tight and free of corrosion. If all connections are OK, replace the fuel pump.

18. Do not install the right-hand cover if Test 3 is going to be performed.

Test 3

1. Remove the headlight as described in this chapter.
2. Within the headlight housing, disconnect the right-hand handlebar switch 9-pin electrical connector.
3. Connect an ohmmeter to the right-hand switch side of the electrical connector. Connect the test leads to the red/white and the red/green terminals.
4. Move the FUEL (reserve) switch button as follows and check continuity. Interpret results as follows:

   a. Push the switch button in: there should be continuity (low resistance).

   b. Release the switch button from the pushed position: there should be no continuity (infinity).

   c. If the switch fails either of these tests, the switch assembly is faulty and must be replaced.

5. Reconnect the 9-pin electrical connector and install the headlight.
6. If still in place, remove the right-hand cover (**Figure 33**).
7. Shift the transmission into neutral.
8. Disconnect the fuel pump relay 6-pin electrical connector (**Figure 71**).
9. Connect a 0-20 V DC voltmeter to the wiring harness side of the connector. Connect the positive (+) test lead to the red/green terminals and the negative (–) test lead to ground.
10. Turn the main switch ON and the engine stop switch to RUN.
11. Push the START button and measure the voltage. Interpret results as follows:

   a. Less than 12 volts: check the main switch.

   b. More than 12 volts: proceed to Step 12.

12. Reconnect the 6-pin electrical connector.
13. Carefully insert the positive (+) test lead into the blue/black wire terminal of the connector. Make sure it touches bare metal within the connector.
14. Connect the negative (–) test lead to ground.
15. Turn the main switch ON and the engine stop switch to the RUN position.
16. Push both the START button and the FUEL (reserve) button at the same time. Interpret results as follows:

   a. Fuel pump input voltage less than 11 volts: replace the fuel pump relay.

   b. Fuel pump input voltage more than 11 volts for 5 seconds: Re-check the entire fuel system electrical connections to make sure they are tight and free of corrosion. If all connections are OK, replace the fuel pump.

17. Do not install the right-hand cover if Test 4 is going to be performed.

7

Test 4 (1987-1989 models only)

NOTE
1990 and later models are not equipped with a fuel sender, therefor this test cannot be performed on these models.

1. Remove the seat.
2. Disconnect the fuel sender 2-pin electrical connector (1 green and 1 black wire).
3. Connect a jumper wire between the green and black terminals on the wiring harness side of the connector. Make sure the jumper wire stays in place during the remainder of this test.
4. Connect a 0-20 V DC voltmeter to the other side of the connector. Connect the positive (+) test lead to the blue/black terminals and the negative (–) test lead to ground.
5. Turn the main switch ON and the engine stop switch to RUN.
6. Push the START button and measure the fuel pump input voltage. Interpret results as follows:

   a. 0 volts after about 30 seconds: fuel sender is faulty, replace it.

   b. More than 0 volts after about 30 seconds: Re-check the entire fuel system electrical connections to make sure they are tight and free of corrosion. If all connections are OK, replace the fuel pump relay.

7. Reconnect the fuel sender 2-pin electrical connector. Install the right-hand cover.

Fuel Pump Testing

Remove the fuel pump as described in Chapter Six in this section of the manual. Connect a 12-volt battery to the fuel pump as shown in **Figure 72**. If the fuel pump is good, it will vibrate slightly. If not, replace it.

Fuel Reserve Switch

1. Remove the headlight as described in this chapter.
2. Disconnect the fuel reserve switch electrical connector containing 2 wires: red/white and red/green.
3. Connect an ohmmeter's (set on R × 1) red lead to the red/white wire and the black lead to the red/green wire.
4. Interpret results as follows:
   a. With the fuel reserve switch turned to RES, the reading should be 0 ohms.
   b. With the fuel reserve switch turned to ON, the reading should be infinite resistance.
5. If the fuel reserve switch failed either of the tests in Step 4, the right-hand switch assembly should be replaced.

HORN

Removal/Installation

1. Disconnect the horn electrical connector (**Figure 73**).
2. Remove the bolts securing the horn.
3. Installation is the reverse of these steps.

Testing

1. Disconnect horn wires from harness.
2. Connect horn wires to 12-volt battery. If it is good, it will sound.

FUSES

Whenever a fuse blows, find out the reason for the failure before replacing the fuse. Usually, the trouble

is a short circuit in the wiring. This may be caused by worn-through insulation or a disconnected wire shorting to ground. Fuse ratings are listed in **Table 4**.

> *CAUTION*
> *Never substitute aluminum foil or wire for a fuse. Never use a higher amperage fuse than specified. An overload could result in fire and complete loss of the bike.*

There are 4 fuses used on the XV535 models. The fuse panel is located underneath the seat.

If the main fuse blows, raise the seat and separate the rubber fuse holder (**Figure 74**). Remove the fuse and replace it with one of the same amperage.

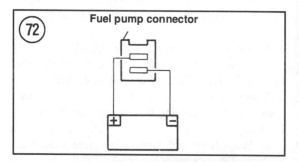
Fuel pump connector

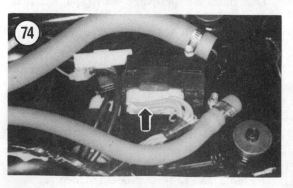

Table 1 ELECTRICAL SPECIFICATIONS

System voltage	12 volts
Pickup coil resistance	140-170 ohms*
Ignition coil resistance	
Secondary	10.6-15.8 K ohms*
Primary	3.8-4.6 ohms*
Charging voltage	14 volts at 5,000 rpm
Armature coil resistance	0.34-0.42 ohms*
Starter brush wear limit	0.20 in. (5.0 mm)

*Test performed to unit at a temperature of 68° F (20° C).

Table 2 STARTER TROUBLESHOOTING

Symptom	Probable cause	Remedy
Starter does not operate	Low battery	Recharge battery
	Worn brushes	Replace brushes
	Defective relay	Repair or replace
	Defective switch	Repair or replace switch
	Defective wiring connection	Repair wire or repair connection
	Internal short circuit	Repair or replace defective component
Starter action is weak	Low battery	Recharge battery
	Pitted relay contacts	Clean or replace
	Worn brushes	Replace brushes
	Defective connection	Clean and tighten
	Short cirouit in commutator	Replace armature
Starter runs continuously	Stuck relay	Replace relay
Starter turns; does not turn engine	Defective starter clutch	Replace starter clutch

Table 3 REPLACEMENT BULBS

Item	Voltage/Wattage
Headlight	12V 60W/55W
Tail/brakelight	
U.S.	12V 8W/27W
U.K.	12V 5W/21W
Front running light (U.S.)	12V 8W/27W
Auxiliary light (U.K. only)	12V 4W
Front flasher	
U.S.	12V 8W/27W
U.K.	12V 21W
Rear flasher	
U.S.	12V 27W
U.K.	12V 21W
Meter light	12V 3.4W
Indicator lights	
High beam	12V 1.7W
All others	12V 3.4W

Table 4 FUSES

	Amperage
Main	20
Headlight	10
Signal	10
Ignition	10
Spare	20 & 10

7

FRONT SUSPENSION AND STEERING

This chapter discusses service operations on suspension components, steering, wheels and related items. Specifications (**Table 1**) and tightening torques (**Table 2**) are found at the end of the chapter.

NOTE
This chapter covers all procedures unique to the XV535 Virago V-twins. If a specific procedure is not included in this chapter, refer to Chapter Eight at the front of this manual for service procedures.

FRONT WHEEL

Removal/Installation

NOTE
It is not necessary to completely remove the axle pinch bolt.

1. Loosen the axle pinch bolt (**Figure 1**).

2. Disconnect the speedometer cable (A, **Figure 2**) at the front wheel.

3. Loosen the front axle.

4. Place a wooden block under the crankcase to lift the front of the bike off the ground.

5. Unscrew the axle (B, **Figure 2**) from the right-hand fork leg and remove it.

6. Pull the wheel forward to disengage the brake disc from the caliper.

7. Remove the wheel.

CAUTION
Do not set the wheel down on the disc surface as it may be scratched or warped. Either lean the wheel against a wall or place it on a couple of wood blocks.

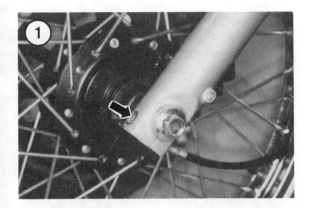

NOTE
Insert a piece of wood in the caliper in place of the disc. That way, if the brake lever is inadvertently squeezed, the piston will not be forced out of the cylinder. If this does happen, the caliper might have to be disassembled to reseat the piston and the system will have to be bled. By using the wood, bleeding the brake is not necessary when installing the wheel.

8. Remove the spacer (**Figure 3**) from the seal in the right-hand side of the wheel.

9. Remove the speedometer drive from the seal in the left-hand side of the wheel.

Inspection

1. Remove any corrosion on the front axle with a piece of fine emery cloth.

2. Measure the radial runout of the wheel rim with a dial indicator as shown in **Figure 4**. If runout exceeds 0.08 in. (2.0 mm), check the wheel bearings. Refer to *Wheels* in Chapter Eight in the front section of this manual for information on spoke tightening and wheel truing.

3. Check the rims for cracks or damage as described under *Rims* in Chapter Eight in the front section of this manual.

Installation

1. Lightly grease the lips of both front wheel seals (**Figure 5**) and the seal in the speedometer gear case.

2. Insert the spacer in the right-hand side seal (**Figure 3**).

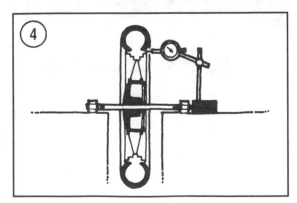

3. Insert the speedometer gear case into the wheel. Make sure to align the notches in the gear case (A, **Figure 6**) with the speedometer drive dogs (B, **Figure 6**).

4. Install the front wheel and *carefully* insert the disc between the pads when installing the wheel.

5. Make sure the locating slot in the speedometer gear case is aligned with the boss on the fork tube. Also make sure the spacer (**Figure 7**) is still in place.

6. Insert the axle and screw it into the right-hand fork leg. Tighten the axle to specifications (**Table 2**).

7. Apply the front brake and compress the front forks several times to make sure the axle is installed correctly without binding the forks. Then tighten the axle pinch bolt to specification (**Table 2**).

8. After the wheel is installed, completely rotate it and apply the brake several times to make sure it rotates freely.

9. Install the speedometer cable.

NOTE
Rotate the wheel slowly when inserting the cable so that it will engage properly.

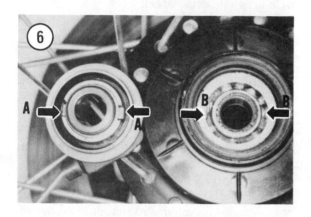

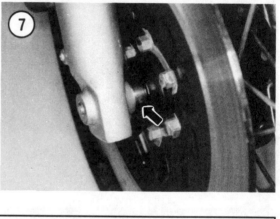

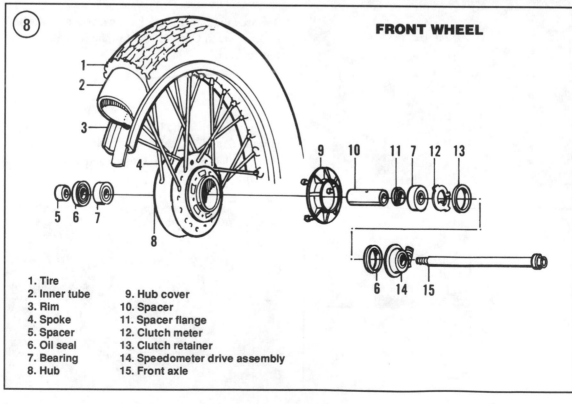

FRONT WHEEL

1. Tire
2. Inner tube
3. Rim
4. Spoke
5. Spacer
6. Oil seal
7. Bearing
8. Hub
9. Hub cover
10. Spacer
11. Spacer flange
12. Clutch meter
13. Clutch retainer
14. Speedometer drive assembly
15. Front axle

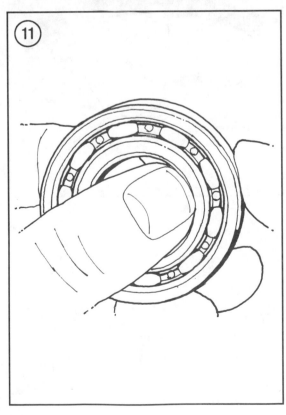

FRONT HUB

Refer to **Figure 8** for this procedure.

Disassembly

1. Remove the front wheel as described in this chapter.

2. If not already removed, remove the spacer (**Figure 3**) from the seal in the right-hand side of the wheel.

3. If not already removed, remove the speedometer drive from the seal in the left-hand side of the wheel.

4. Remove the hub cover (A, **Figure 9**).

5. Remove the right- (**Figure 10**) and left-hand (B, **Figure 9**) oil seals.

6. Remove the speedometer clutch retainer and clutch (C, **Figure 9**).

7. Remove the wheel bearings, spacer and spacer flange. Tap the bearing out with a soft aluminum or brass drift.

> *CAUTION*
> *Tap only on the outer bearing race. The bearing will be damaged if struck on the inner race.*

Inspection

1. Clean bearings thoroughly in solvent and dry with compressed air.

> *WARNING*
> *Do not spin the bearing with the air jet while drying. Instead hold the inner race with your hand. Because the air jet can spin the bearing race at higher speeds than which it was designed, the bearing may disintegrate and possibly cause severe eye injuries.*

2. Clean the inside and outside of the hub with solvent. Dry with compressed air.

3. Turn each bearing by hand (**Figure 11**), making sure it turns smoothly. Check balls for evidence of wear, pitting or excessive heat (bluish tint). Replace bearings if necessary; always replace as a complete set.

4. Check the axle for wear and straightness. Use V-blocks and a dial indicator as shown in **Figure 12**. If the runout is 0.008 in. (0.2 mm) or greater, the axle must be replaced.

8

Assembly

> *NOTE*
> *If installing sealed bearings, it is not necessary to grease the bearings as described in Step 1. Instead, proceed to Step 2.*

1. Pack the bearings thoroughly with multipurpose grease. Work the grease between the balls thoroughly.
2. Pack the wheel hub and axle spacer with multipurpose grease.

> *NOTE*
> *Install the wheel bearings with the sealed side facing outward.*

3. Install the right-hand wheel bearing and the spacer. Install the spacer flange and install the left-hand bearing.

> *CAUTION*
> *Tap the bearings squarely into place and tap on the outer race only. Use a socket (Figure 13) that matches the outer race diameter. Do not tap on the inner race or the bearing might be damaged. Be sure that the bearings are completely seated.*

4. Install the right-hand oil seal.
5. Install the speedometer clutch housing, retainer and oil seal in the hub.
6. Lubricate the oil seal lips with grease.
7. Disassemble the speedometer gear case and lubricate the gears and sliding faces with a lightweight lithium soap base grease. Reassemble it.
8. Install the front wheel as described in this chapter.

HANDLEBAR

Removal/Installation

1. Place the bike on the sidestand.
2. Remove the rear view mirror(s) (A, **Figure 14**).
3. Disconnect the brake light switch electrical connection.

> *CAUTION*
> *Cover the fuel tank with a heavy cloth or plastic tarp to protect it from accidental spilling of brake fluid. Wash any spilled brake fluid off any painted or*

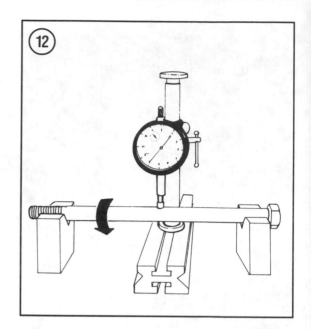

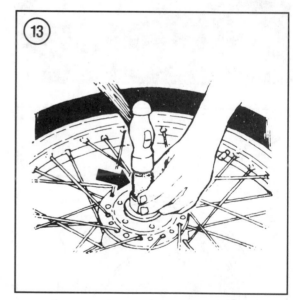

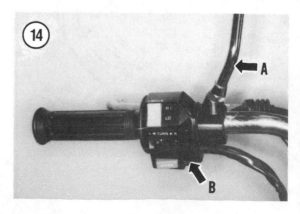

plated surface immediately, as it will destroy the finish. Use soapy water and rinse thoroughly.

4. Remove the 2 bolts (A, **Figure 15**) securing the master cylinder and lay it on the fuel tank. It is not necessary to disconnect the hydraulic brake line.

5. Slide back the clutch cable adjuster cover (**Figure 16**). Then slacken the clutch cable and disconnect it at the hand lever.

6. Remove the screws and separate the 2 halves of the left-hand switch assembly (B, **Figure 14**).

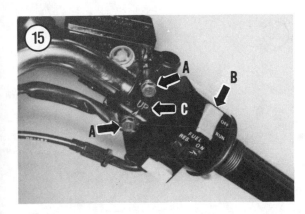

7. Remove the screws and separate the 2 halves of the right-hand switch assembly (B, **Figure 15**). Disconnect the throttle cable from the throttle grip.

8. Remove the bolt covers.

9. Remove the clamps (A, **Figure 17**) securing electrical cables to the handlebar.

10. Remove the 4 handlebar clamp Allen bolts and remove the handlebar upper holders (B, **Figure 17**).

11. Install by reversing these steps. Note the following:

    a. Tighten all fasteners to the specifications in **Table 2**.

    b. Make sure the UP mark on the master cylinder clamp (C, **Figure 15**) is facing up.

STEERING HEAD

Refer to **Figure 18** for this procedure.

Disassembly

1. Place the bike on the sidestand.

2A. On 1987-1989 U.S. models and 1988 U.K. models, remove the rear bolt and front bolt on each side securing the frame top cover and remove the cover.

2B. On 1990-on U.S. models and 1989-on U.K. models, remove the sub-fuel tank as described in Chapter Six in this section of the manual.

3. Remove the front wheel as described in this chapter.

4. Disconnect the speedometer cable (**Figure 19**).

5. Disconnect and remove the horn.

6. Remove the headlight, the front turn indicators and the headlight shell (**Figure 20**).

7. Remove the handlebar (A, **Figure 21**) as described in this chapter.

8. Remove the speedometer unit (B, **Figure 21**) and indicator light assembly (C, **Figure 21**).

9. Remove the front forks as described in this chapter.

10. Remove the steering stem bolt and remove the upper fork bridge (D, **Figure 21**)

11. Remove the ring nut (E, **Figure 21**) with a spanner wrench (**Figure 22**) or use an easily improvised unit (**Figure 23**).

12. Remove the upper bearing cover.

13. Pull the steering stem out of the frame (**Figure 24**). On these models, upper and lower bearings are disassembled ball bearings so be ready to catch them

8

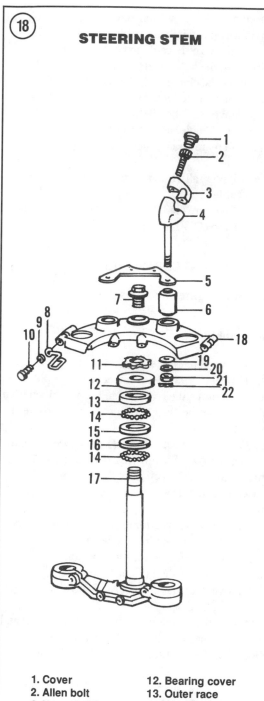

STEERING STEM

1. Cover
2. Allen bolt
3. Upper holder
4. Lower holder
5. Bracket
6. Damper
7. Steering bolt
8. Cable guide
9. Washer
10. Bolt
11. Ring nut
12. Bearing cover
13. Outer race
14. Steel balls
15. Race
16. Race
17. Steering stem
18. Upper fork bridge
19. Washer
20. Lockwasher
21. Nut
22. Clip

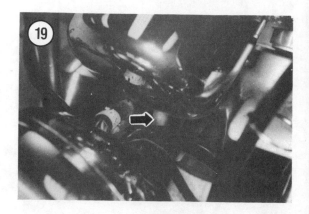

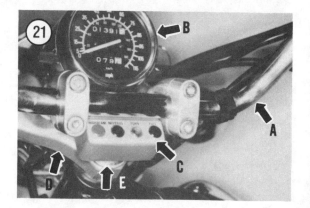

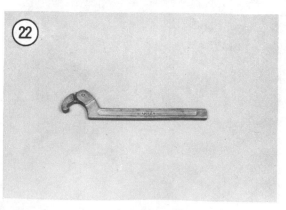

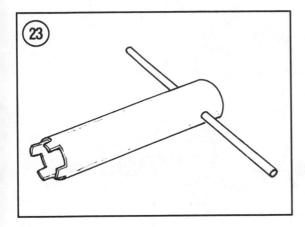

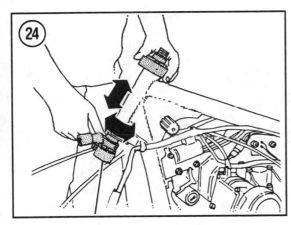

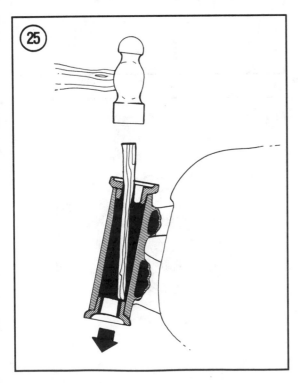

as they fall out. Remove all bearings that are held in the steering head by grease.

NOTE
There is a total number of 38 ball bearings used—19 in the top and 19 in the bottom. The bearings should not be intermixed because if worn or damaged, they must be replaced in sets. However, balls in both sets are the same size.

Inspection

1. Clean the bearing races in the steering head and all bearings with solvent.

2. Check for broken welds on the frame around the steering head. If any are found, have them repaired by a competent frame shop or welding service familiar with motorcycle frame repair.

3. Check the balls for pitting, scratches, or discoloration indicating wear or corrosion. Replace them in sets if any are bad.

4. Check the upper and lower races in the steering head for pitting, galling and corrosion. If any of these conditions exist, replace the races as described in this chapter.

5. Check steering stem for cracks and check its race for damage or wear. Replace if necessary.

Bearing Race Replacement

The headset and steering stem bearing races are pressed into place. Because they are easily bent, do not remove them unless they are worn and require replacement. Take old races to the dealer to ensure exact replacement.

To remove a headset race, insert a hardwood stick into the head tube and carefully tap the race out from the inside (**Figure 25**). Tap all around the race so that neither the race nor the head tube are bent. To install a race, fit it into the end of the head tube. Tap it slowly and squarely with a block of wood (**Figure 26**).

Assembly

Refer to **Figure 18** for this procedure.

1. Make sure the steering head bearing races are properly seated.

2. Apply a coat of wheel bearing grease to the lower bearing race cone on the steering stem and fit 19 ball bearings around it.

3. Apply a coat of wheel bearing grease to the upper bearing race cone and fit 19 ball bearings around it (**Figure 27**).

4. Insert the steering stem into the head tube. Hold it firmly in place.

5. Install the upper bearing race and upper bearing cover.

6. Position the ring nut with the taper side facing downward.

7. Install the ring nut and tighten it to approximately 27 ft.-lb. (38 N•m).

8. Loosen it completely. Then retighten it to 7.2 ft.-lb. (10 N•m).

9. Continue assembly by reversing *Disassembly* Steps 1-10. Tightening torques are found in **Table 2**.

10. After the total assembly is completed, check the stem for looseness or binding—readjust if necessary.

Steering Stem Adjustment

If play develops in the steering system, it may only require adjustment. However, don't take a chance on it. Disassemble the stem as described under *Steering Head* in this chapter.

FRONT FORKS

The Yamaha front suspension consists of a spring-controlled, hydraulically dampened telescopic fork. Before suspecting major trouble, drain the front fork oil and refill with the proper type and quantity; refer to Chapter Three in this portion of the manual. If you still have trouble, such as poor damping, a tendency to bottom or top out or leakage around the rubber seals, follow the service procedures in this section.

To simplify fork service and to prevent the mixing of parts, the legs should be removed, serviced and installed individually.

Removal/Installation

1. Place the motorcycle on the sidestand.

2. Remove the front wheel as described in this chapter.

3. Remove the bolts securing the front fender (**Figure 28**) and remove the fender assembly.

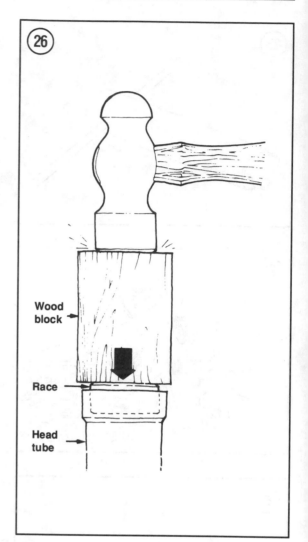

Wood block

Race

Head tube

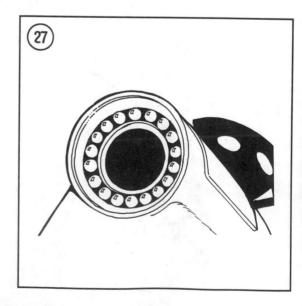

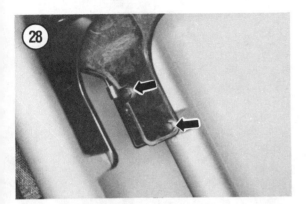

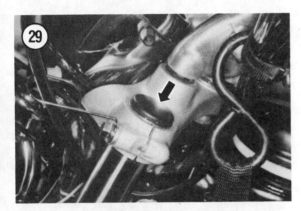

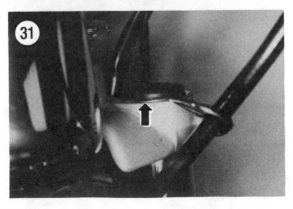

4. Remove the brake caliper as described in Chapter Ten in this portion of the manual.

> *NOTE*
> *Insert a piece of wood in the caliper in place of the disc. That way, if the brake lever is inadvertently squeezed, the piston will not be forced out of the caliper. If it does happen, the caliper might have to be disassembled to reseat the piston. By using the wood, bleeding the brake is not necessary when installing the wheel.*

5. Remove the top trim cap (**Figure 29**).

6. Loosen the upper (A, **Figure 30**) and lower (B, **Figure 30**) fork bridge bolts.

7. Remove the fork tube. It may be necessary to slightly rotate the tube while removing it.

8. Repeat for the opposite side.

9. Install by reversing these removal steps. Note the following:

    a. Push the fork tube up until it is flush with the top surface of the upper fork bridge (**Figure 31**).

    b. Tighten the lower fork bridge bolts only sufficiently to hold the fork assemblies in place.

    c. Install the front axle and tighten it securely. This will hold the fork legs in their correct relation to each other prior to tightening the bridge bolts.

    d. Torque the bolts to specifications in **Table 2**.

    e. Remove the front axle.

Disassembly

Refer to **Figure 32** for this procedure.

> *NOTE*
> *This procedure is best performed with the aid of a helper.*

> *CAUTION*
> *If the bike has been subjected to frequent rain or moisture or if the bike has been in storage for any period of time, moisture may have passed the trim cap causing rust. Any rust must be removed prior to removing any upper fork parts during this procedure. If any rust particles drop down into the fork assembly the fork must be removed, disassembled and thoroughly cleaned prior to refilling*

8

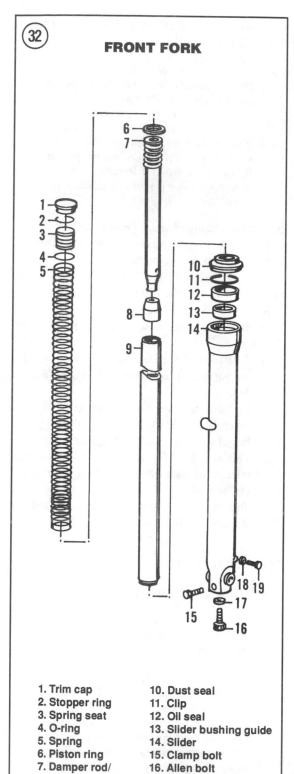

FRONT FORK

1. Trim cap
2. Stopper ring
3. Spring seat
4. O-ring
5. Spring
6. Piston ring
7. Damper rod/
   rebound spring
8. Oil lockpiece
9. Fork tube
10. Dust seal
11. Clip
12. Oil seal
13. Slider bushing guide
14. Slider
15. Clamp bolt
16. Allen bolt
17. Washer
18. Gasket
19. Drain screw

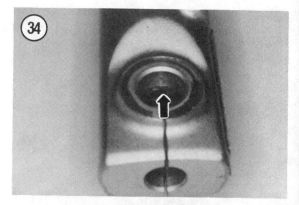

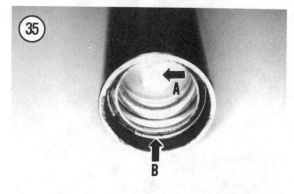

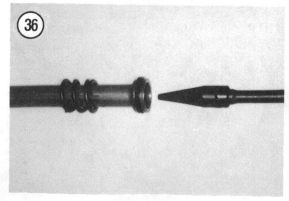

with fresh fork oil. After removing the trim cap, if rust is present, scrape it clean, blow the rust residue out with compressed air and apply WD-40, or equivalent, then remove the stopper ring and spring seat.

1. If not already removed, remove the fork trim cap (**Figure 33**).

2. Turn the fork assembly upside down and place it on a piece of soft wood on the shop floor.

NOTE
The lower Allen bolt had a locking agent applied to the threads during assembly and is usually very difficult to loosen.

3. Have a helper compress the fork slider to exert spring pressure onto the damper rod to prevent it from rotating in Step 4.

4. Loosen the lower Allen bolt (**Figure 34**) with an air driver or impact driver if possible. Remove the Allen bolt and sealing washer. If you are unable to loosen the Allen bolt at this time, it will be loosened in Step 10.

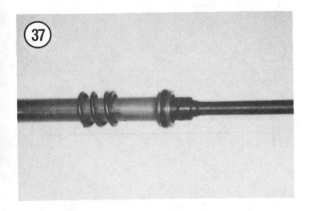

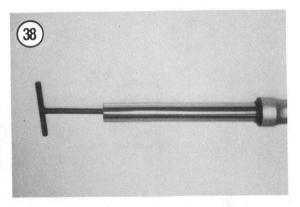

5. The spring seat and spring are held in position by a stopper ring. To remove the stopper ring, have an assistant depress the spring seat (A, **Figure 35**) using a suitable size drift.

6. Remove the stopper ring (B, **Figure 35**) from its groove in the fork with a small screwdriver. Discard the stopper ring as a new one must be installed.

7. When the stopper ring is removed, release tension from the spring seat and remove it.

8. Remove the fork spring and if the Allen bolt was removed, also remove the damper rod.

9. Turn the fork upside down and pour the oil out and discard it. Pump the fork several times by hand to expel most of the remaining oil.

NOTE
The following step requires the use of Yamaha special tools.

10. If you were unable to loosen the lower Allen bolt in Step 4, perform the following:
   a. Install Yamaha special tool Damper Rod Holder (U.S. part No. YM-01300-1, U.K. part No. 90890-01294) onto the T-handle (U.S. part No. YM-01326-1, U.K. part No. 90890-01326).

NOTE
Figure 36 and Figure 37 are shown with the damper rod removed from the fork slider for clarity.

   b. Insert the special tools into the fork tube (**Figure 38**) and carefully drive the holder (**Figure 36**) into the top recess in the damper rod (**Figure 37**). This will hold the damper rod in place while loosening the Allen bolt.
   c. Hold the special tool in place and loosen the Allen bolt (**Figure 34**). Remove the Allen bolt and sealing washer.
   d. Remove the special tool.

11. Remove the dust seal (**Figure 39**) from the slider.

12. Remove the snap ring (**Figure 40**) from the groove in the slider.

13. Pull the fork tube out of the slider.

CAUTION
The oil seal is very stiff and is difficult to remove. Use an oil seal puller if removal is difficult. If necessary, take the fork slider to a Yamaha dealer and have the seal removed to prevent damage to the slider.

8

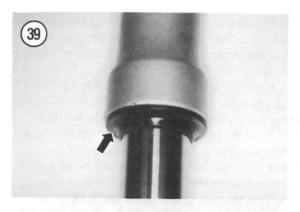

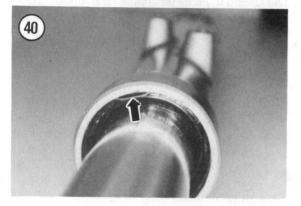

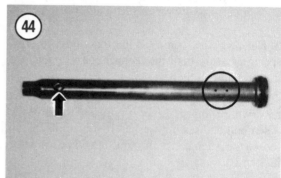

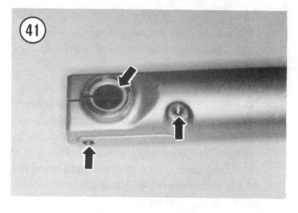

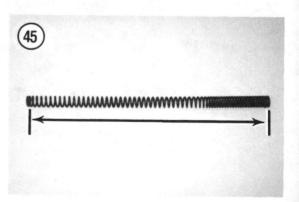

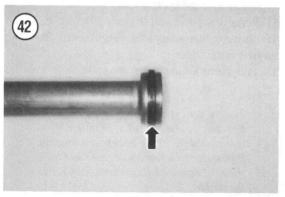

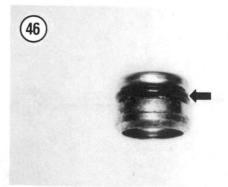

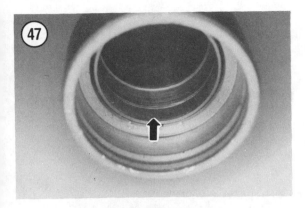

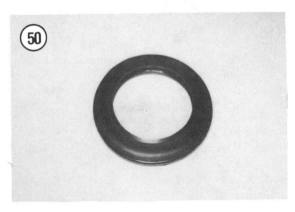

14. Remove the oil seal by prying it out with a flat-tipped screwdriver. Remove the oil seal slowly to prevent damage to the fork slider.

Inspection

1. Thoroughly clean all parts in solvent and dry them.

2. Check upper fork tube exterior for scratches and straightness. If bent or scratched, it should be replaced.

3. Check the fork slider for dents or exterior damage that may cause the upper fork tube to hang up during riding conditions. Replace if necessary.

4. Check the axle bearing surface and the threaded holes in the slider (**Figure 41**) for wear or damage. Replace if necessary.

5. Carefully check the damper rod piston ring (**Figure 42**) for wear or damage.

6. Check the damper rod for straightness. **Figure 43** shows one method. The rod should be replaced if the runout is 0.008 in. (0.2 mm) or greater.

7. Make sure the oil holes in the damper rod are clear (**Figure 44**). Clean out if necessary.

8. Measure the uncompressed length of the fork spring (**Figure 45**). Replace the spring if it is too short. See **Table 1** for specifications.

9. Check the condition of the O-ring (**Figure 46**) on the fork cap. Replace if worn, damaged or starting to deteriorate.

10. Inspect the slider bushing guide (**Figure 47**) for wear or damage. Replace if necessary.

11. Check the oil seal surface (**Figure 48**) of the slider for wear or damage. Clean out if necessary.

12. Thoroughly clean out any rust that may have formed in the top of the fork tube (**Figure 49**). After removing the rust, thoroughly clean the fork tube in solvent to remove all residue that could contaminate the fork oil.

13. Make sure the dust seal (**Figure 50**) is still flexible and the sealing lip is not damaged, replace if necessary.

14. Any parts that are worn or damaged should be replaced. Simply cleaning and reinstalling unserviceable components will not improve performance of the front suspension.

Assembly

Refer to **Figure 32** for this procedure.

8

1. If removed, install the drain screw and washer (**Figure 51**).

2. Apply fork oil to all parts prior to assembly.

3. Install the rebound spring onto the damper rod (**Figure 52**).

4. Insert the damper rod into the fork tube (**Figure 53**) and install the oil lock piece (**Figure 54**).

5. Apply a light coat of oil to the outside of the fork tube and install it into the slider (**Figure 55**). Push it in until it stops.

6. Make sure the sealing washer (**Figure 56**) is in place on the Allen bolt.

7. Apply red Loctite (No. 271) to the threads of the Allen bolt and install it (**Figure 34**).

8. Use the same tool set-up used during removal to keep the damper rod from turning and tighten the Allen bolt to the torque found in **Table 2**.

9. Position the oil seal with the open end facing up (**Figure 57**) and install the oil seal onto the fork tube (**Figure 58**).

NOTE
Some type of fork seal driver is required to install the oil seal. Yamaha sells a fork seal driver set (U.S. part No. YM-

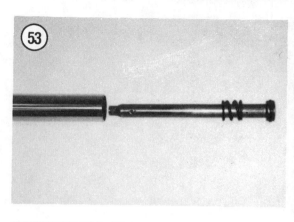

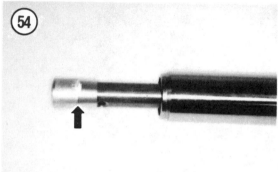

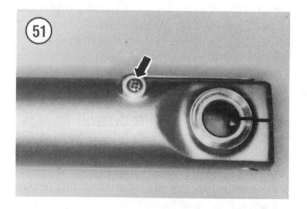

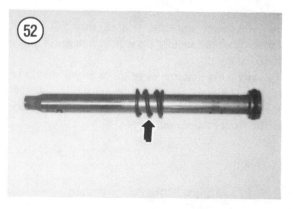

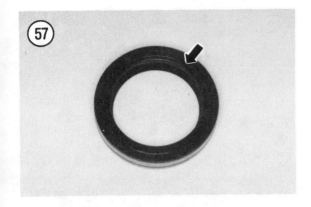

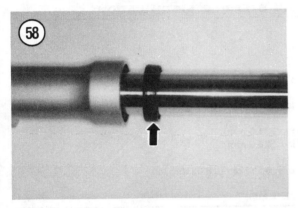

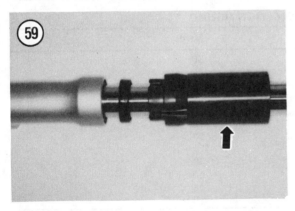

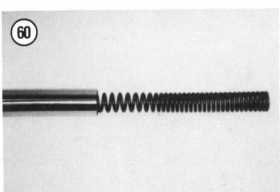

01367 and YM-8010 or U.K. part No. 90890-01367 and 90890-01370). The adjustable fork seal driver shown in **Figure 59** *is made by Suzuki, is universal, and can be used on almost all Japanese fork assembles (including Japanese "Showa" forks equipped on some late model Harleys).*

NOTE
Make sure the seal seats squarely and fully in the bore of the slider.

NOTE
In some cases it may be necessary to drive the oil seal in the final way with a broad tipped flat-bladed screwdriver and hammer being careful not to damage the oil seal.

10. Using a fork seal driver (**Figure 59**), tap the seal into the slider until the clip groove can be seen above the seal.

11. Install the clip (**Figure 40**) and make sure it seats correctly in the slider groove.

12. Install the dust seal and push it down until it completely seats in the slider (**Figure 39**).

NOTE
In order to measure the correct amount of fluid, use a plastic baby bottle. These have measurements in fluid ounces (oz.) and cubic centimeters (cc) on the side.

13. Fill fork tube with fresh fork oil. Carefully fill each fork tube with the type and quantity listed in **Table 1**.

14. Position the fork spring with the closer wound coils going in last (**Figure 60**).

15. Position the spring seat with the O-ring end going in first (A, **Figure 61**) on top of the fork spring.

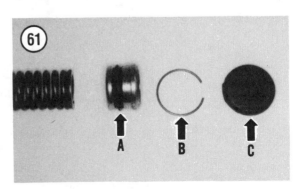

16. Have an assistant depress the spring seat (A, **Figure 62**) using a suitable size drift and install a *new* stopper ring (B, **Figure 62**). Make sure the stopper ring (B, **Figure 61**) is properly seated in the fork tube groove.

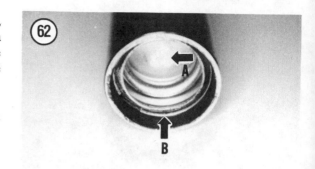

17. After the stopper ring is installed, release tension from the spring seat and remove it.

18. Install the trim cap (C, **Figure 61**).

Table 1   FRONT SUSPENSION AND STEERING SPECIFICATIONS

Steering head	
Number of balls in steering head	
Upper	19
Lower	19
Size of steering balls	1/4 in.
Front fork	
Front fork travel	5.91 in. (150 mm)
Spring free length	
Standard	20.9 in. (531.6 mm)
Wear limit	20.7 in. (526.6 mm)
Oil weight	10
Oil capacity	7.71 U.S. oz. (228 cc, 8.03 Imp. oz.)
Front wheel runout	
Vertical and lateral	0.08 in. (2 mm)

Table 2   FRONT SUSPENSION TIGHTENING TORQUES

Item	ft.-lb.	N•m
Front axle	42	58
Front axle pinch bolt	14	20
Handlebar Allen bolts	14	20
Steering stem ring nut		
Initial tightening	27	38
Final tightening	7.2	10
Steering stem bolt	39	54
Front fork		
Upper bridge bolt	27	38
Lower bridge bolt	14	20
Allen bolts	17	23
Front fender bolts	7.2	10

REAR SUSPENSION AND FINAL DRIVE

This chapter includes repair and replacement procedures for the rear wheel, shaft drive unit and rear suspension components.

Specifications (**Table 1**) and tightening torques (**Table 2**) are found at the end of the chapter.

> *NOTE*
> *This chapter covers all procedures unique to the XV535 Virago V-twins. If a specific procedure is not included in this chapter, refer to Chapter Two at the front of this manual for service procedures.*

REAR WHEEL

Refer to **Figure 1** for this procedure.

Removal/Installation

1. Unscrew the rear brake adjusting nut (**Figure 2**) and disconnect the brake rod from the brake lever.

> *NOTE*
> *Install the spring, nut and cotter pin back onto the brake rod to prevent their loss.*

2. Remove the cotter pin and nut (A, **Figure 3**) securing the brake torque rod and disconnect it from the brake panel.

3. Loosen the axle pinch bolt (B, **Figure 3**).

4. Remove the cotter pin and loosen the rear axle nut (**Figure 4**). Discard the cotter pin; never reuse a cotter pin.

5. Place the bike securely on wood blocks so that the rear wheel clears the ground.

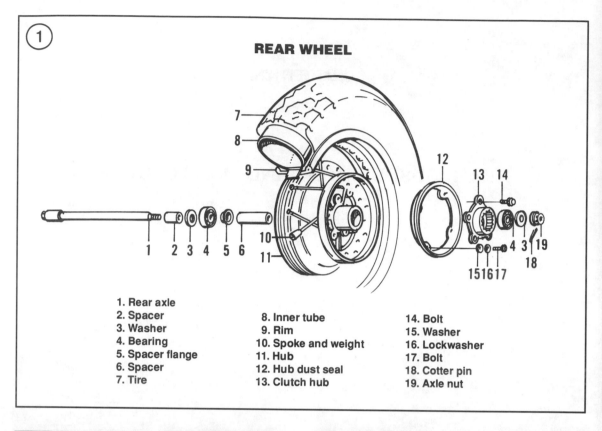

REAR WHEEL

1. Rear axle
2. Spacer
3. Washer
4. Bearing
5. Spacer flange
6. Spacer
7. Tire

8. Inner tube
9. Rim
10. Spoke and weight
11. Hub
12. Hub dust seal
13. Clutch hub

14. Bolt
15. Washer
16. Lockwasher
17. Bolt
18. Cotter pin
19. Axle nut

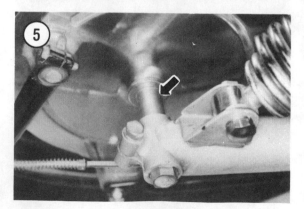

6. Withdraw the axle (C, **Figure 3**) from the right-hand side. Don't lose the spacer (**Figure 5**) between the brake hub and swing arm.

7. Slide the wheel to the right to disengage it from the hub drive splines and remove the wheel.

8. If the wheel is going to be off for any length of time, or if it is to be taken to a shop for repair, install the axle spacer on the axle along with the axle nut to prevent losing any parts.

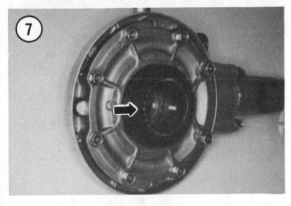

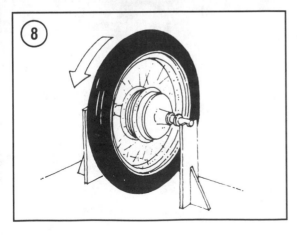

9. Install by reversing these removal steps. Note the following:

   a. Make sure that the wheel hub splines (**Figure 6**) engage with the final drive (**Figure 7**). Apply molybdenum disulfide grease to both splines prior to installation.

   b. Prior to tightening the axle nut, install the brake torque link (A, **Figure 3**) and tighten the nut to specifications in **Table 2**.

   c. Tighten the pinch bolt to specifications in **Table 2**.

   d. Tighten the axle nut to specifications in **Table 2**. Install a new axle nut cotter pin and bend the ends over completely.

   e. Adjust the rear brake as described under *Rear Brake Pedal Free Play* in Chapter Three in the front section of the manual.

   f. Rotate the wheel several times to make sure it rotates freely and that the brake works properly.

Inspection

Measure the axial and radial runout of the wheel with a dial indicator as shown in **Figure 8**. The maximum allowable axial and radial runout is 0.08 in. (2.0 mm). If the runout exceeds this dimension, check the wheel bearing condition. If the wheel bearings are in good condition and no other cause can be found, refer to the wheel and spoke information in Chapter Eight in the front section of the manual.

Inspect the wheel for signs of cracks, fractures, dents or bends. If it is damaged in any way, it must be replaced.

> *WARNING*
> *Do not try to repair any damage to the rear wheel as it will result in an unsafe riding condition.*

Check axial runout as described under *Rear Hub Inspection* in this chapter.

REAR HUB

Disassembly

Refer to **Figure 1** for this procedure.

1. Remove the rear wheel as described in this chapter.

2. Pull the brake assembly straight out of the wheel (**Figure 9**).

3. Remove the bolts securing the clutch hub (A, **Figure 10**) to the wheel and remove it.

4. To remove the right-hand bearing (**Figure 11**). Insert a soft aluminum or brass drift into the left-hand side of the hub and place the end of the drift on the outer bearing race. Tap the bearing out of the hub with a hammer working around the perimeter of the bearing.

5. Remove the spacer flange and spacer. Then remove the left-hand bearing (B, **Figure 10**) using the same method described in Step 4.

Inspection

1. Do not clean sealed bearings. Non-sealed bearings can be cleaned in solvent and thoroughly dried with compressed air. *Do not* spin the bearing with the air jet while drying.

2. Clean the inside and outside of the hub with solvent. Dry with compressed air.

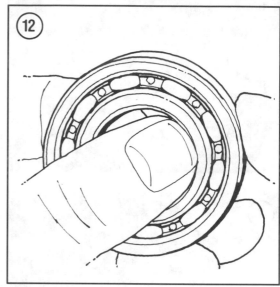

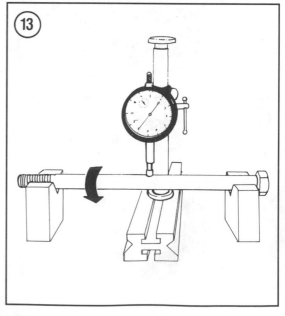

3. Turn each bearing by hand (**Figure 12**). Make sure bearings turn smoothly. On non-sealed bearings, check the balls for evidence of wear, pitting or excessive heat (bluish tint). Replace bearings if necessary; always replace as a complete set. When replacing the bearings, be sure to take your old bearings along to ensure a perfect matchup.

4. Check the axle for wear and straightness. Use V-blocks and a dial indicator as shown in **Figure 13**. If the runout is 0.008 in. (0.2 mm) or greater, the axle should be replaced.

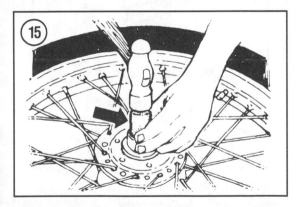

5. Check the brake hub (**Figure 14**) for any scoring or damage. If damage is apparent, refer to Chapter Ten, in the front section of the manual, for further inspection and service.

Assembly

1. Blow any dirt or foreign matter out of the hub prior to installing the clutch hub and right-hand side bearing.
2. Replace the clutch hub O-ring if worn or damaged.
3. Pack the hub with multipurpose grease.

NOTE
*When performing Step 4, refer to (**Figure 1**) for correct bearing and spacer alignment.*

CAUTION
*Tap the bearings squarely into place and tap only on the outer race. Use a socket (**Figure 15**) that matches the outer race diameter. Do not tap on the inner race or the bearings will be damaged. Be sure to tap the bearings until they seat completely.*

NOTE
Install the right-hand side bearing with the sealed side facing outward.

4. Install the right-hand bearing (**Figure 11**), spacer flange and the spacer.
5. Install the left-hand bearing (B, **Figure 10**) into the hub.
6. Install clutch hub (A, **Figure 10**) and tighten the bolts securely.
7. Install the brake assembly into the wheel (**Figure 9**).
8. Install the rear wheel as described in this chapter.

SHAFT DRIVE

Removal/Installation

1. Remove the rear wheel as described in this chapter.
2. Loosen the left-hand lower shock absorber upper nut and remove the lower cap nut (**Figure 16**). Move the shock absorber up and out of the way.

3. Remove the 4 nuts and washers (**Figure 17**) securing the shaft drive unit to the swing arm.

4. Pull the shaft drive unit straight back until it is free.

5. Wipe the grease from the splines on the end of the shaft drive and final drive unit.

6. Check the splines (**Figure 7**) of both units carefully for signs of wear.

7. Pack the splines with multipurpose molybdenum disulfide grease.

8. Install the shaft drive unit onto the swing arm. Make sure that the splines of the shaft drive engage properly with the final drive unit.

9. Install the 4 nuts and washers and tighten to specifications in **Table 2**.

10. Install the rear wheel as described in this chapter.

Disassembly/Inspection/Troubleshooting

Although it may be practical for you to disassemble the final drive for inspection, you cannot replace the bearings or seals (which require bearing removal) without special tools. If there is trouble in the shaft drive unit, it is best to remove the unit and take it to your Yamaha dealer and let them overhaul it. They are also better equipped to check and adjust gear lash.

Inspect the exterior of the unit for signs of wear, cracks, damage, or oil leakage. If any damage is present or there are signs of leakage, take the unit to your Yamaha dealer for service.

REAR SWING ARM

Refer to **Figure 18** for this procedure.

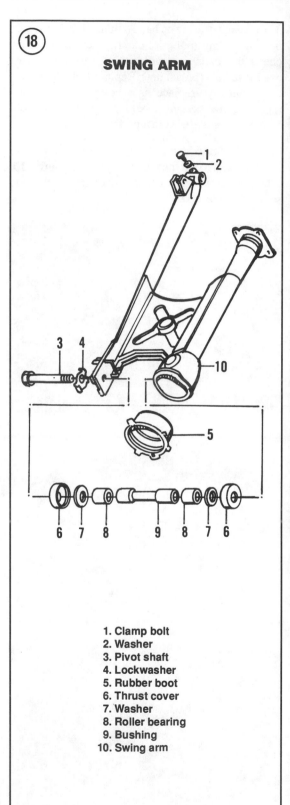

SWING ARM

1. Clamp bolt
2. Washer
3. Pivot shaft
4. Lockwasher
5. Rubber boot
6. Thrust cover
7. Washer
8. Roller bearing
9. Bushing
10. Swing arm

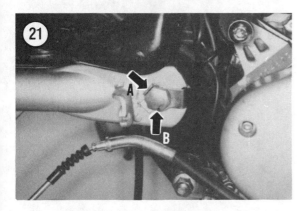

Removal/Installation

1. Place the bike on the sidestand.

2. Remove the exhaust system as described in Chapter Six in this section of the manual.

3. Remove the left-hand rear under cover (**Figure 19**).

4. Remove the rear wheel as described in this chapter.

5. Remove the shock absorbers from the swing arm as described in this chapter.

6. Pull the rubber boot (**Figure 20**) back off the middle driven gear and onto the swing arm.

7. Straighten the locking tab (A, **Figure 21**) on the pivot shaft lockwasher.

8. Loosen, then remove the pivot shaft (B, **Figure 21**).

9. Pull the swing arm straight back and remove it from the frame.

10. Installation is the reverse of these steps. Note the following:

    a. Make sure the washer, oil seal and thrust cover (**Figure 22**) are in place on each side of the pivot area of the frame (**Figure 23**).

    b. Install a new pivot shaft lockwasher and tighten the swing arm pivot shaft to the specifications in **Table 2**.

    c. Bend over the tab on the lockwasher to lock the pivot shaft.

    d. After the swing arm is installed, check free play as described in this chapter.

Inspection

1. Remove the rubber boot from the swing arm and inspect it for tears or deterioration; replace if necessary.

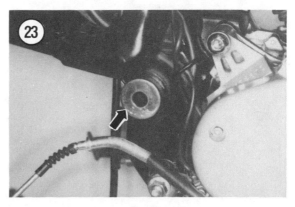

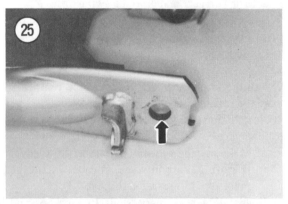

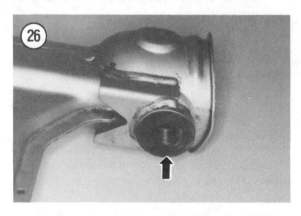

2. On the rear right-hand side of the swing arm, inspect the shock mount, rear axle pinch bolt threads and the rear axle mounting area (**Figure 24**) for wear or damage.

3. On the front right-hand side of the swing arm, inspect the pivot shaft hole (**Figure 25**) for wear or elongation.

4. On the front left-hand side of the swing arm, inspect the pivot shaft threaded hole (**Figure 26**) for wear or damage.

5. Inspect the drive shaft splines (**Figure 27**) for wear or damage.

6. Remove the long bushing from the frame.

7. Remove the oil seals and bearings (**Figure 28**) from the pivot area of the frame.

8. Thoroughly clean the bearings in solvent and dry with compressed air.

9. Turn each bearing by hand. Make sure bearings turn smoothly. Check the balls for evidence of wear or pitting. Replace if necessary. Always replace both bearings at the same time.

10. If bearings have been replaced, the grease seals should be replaced also.

11. Pack the bearings with a lithium base, waterproof wheel bearing grease.

12. Install the bearings into the swing arm.

CAUTION
Tap the bearings squarely into place and tap on the outer race only. Do not tap on the inner race or the bearings might be damaged. Be sure that the bearings are completely seated.

SHOCK ABSORBERS

The rear shocks are spring controlled and hydraulically dampened.

Removal/Inspection/Installation

Removal and installation of the rear shocks is easier if they are done separately. The remaining unit will support the rear of the bike and maintain the correct relationship between the top and bottom mounts. If both shock absorbers must be removed at the same time, cut a piece of wood the same length as the shock absorber. Then drill two holes in the wood the same distance apart as the mounting bolt holes. Install the wood support after one shock absorber is removed. This will allow the bike to be easily moved around until the shock absorbers are reinstalled or replaced.

1. Place the bike on the sidestand.

2. Remove the bolts and the upper trim cover (**Figure 29**).

3. Remove the upper and lower nuts and bolts (**Figure 30**).

4. Pull the shock off.

5. Inspect the shock as follows:
   a. Check the shock absorber body (**Figure 31**) for any signs of oil leakage. Replace the shock if necessary.
   b. Inspect the upper (**Figure 32**) and lower (**Figure 33**) mounts for wear or damage. Replace the shock if necessary.

6. Install by reversing these removal steps. Torque the fasteners to specifications in **Table 2**.

Tables 1-2 are on the following page.

Table 1   REAR SUSPENSION SPECIFICATIONS

Shock absorber	
Spring free length	
Standard	10.5 in. (266 mm)
Wear limit	10.3 in. (261 mm)
Swing arm side play	0.04 in. (1 mm)
Rear wheel runout	
Vertical and lateral	0.08 in. (2 mm)

Table 2   REAR SUSPENSION TIGHTENING TORQUES

Item	ft.-lb.	N•m
Rear axle		
Nut	75	105
Pinch bolt	11	16
Shaft drive unit nuts	30	42
Swing arm pivot shaft	54	70
Shock absorber bolt		
Top bolt	14	20
Right-hand bottom bolt	22	30
Left-hand bottom nut	22	30

CHAPTER TEN

BRAKES

The brake system consists of a single disc unit on the front and drum on the rear. This chapter describes repair and replacement procedure for all brake components.

Refer to **Table 1** for brake specifications. **Tables 1-2** are found at the end of the chapter.

> *NOTE*
> *This chapter covers all procedures unique to the XV535 Virago V-twins. If a specific procedure is not included in this chapter, refer to Chapter Ten at the front of this manual for service procedures.*

FRONT DISC BRAKE

The front disc brake is actuated by hydraulic fluid controlled by the hand lever on the right-hand side of the handlebar. As the brake pads wear, the brake fluid level drops in the master cylinder reservoir and automatically adjusts for pad wear. However, brake lever free play must be maintained. Refer to *Front*

Brake Lever Adjustment in Chapter Three in this section of the manual.

When working on a hydraulic brake system, it is necessary that the work area and all tools be absolutely clean. Any tiny particles of foreign matter or grit on the caliper assembly or the master cylinder can damage the components. Also, sharp tools must not be used inside the caliper or on the caliper piston. If there is any doubt about your ability to correctly and safely carry out major service on the brake components, take the job to a Yamaha dealer or brake specialist.

When adding brake fluid use only a type clearly marked DOT 3 and use it from a sealed container. Brake fluid will draw moisture which greatly reduces its ability to perform correctly, so it is a good idea to purchase brake fluid in small containers and discard what is not used.

Whenever *any* component has been removed from the brake system the system is considered "opened" and must be bled to remove air bubbles. Also, if the brake feels "spongy," this usually means there are air bubbles in the system and it must be bled. For safe brake operation, refer to *Bleeding the System* in Chapter Ten, in the front section of the manual, for complete details.

> *CAUTION*
> *Disc brake components rarely require disassembly, so do not disassemble unless absolutely necessary. Do not use solvents of any kind on the brake systems internal components. Solvents will cause the seals to swell and distort. When disassembling and cleaning brake components (except brake pads) use new brake fluid.*

MASTER CYLINDER

Removal/Installation

1. On models so equipped, loosen the nut securing the mirror to the master cylinder and remove the mirror.

> *CAUTION*
> *Cover the top cover, or fuel tank, front fender and speedometer with a heavy cloth or plastic tarp to protect them from accidental spilling of brake fluid. Wash any spilled brake fluid off any painted or plated surfaces immediately, as it will destroy the finish. Use soapy water and rinse completely.*

2. Using a small screwdriver or drift, push up in the hole in the base of the switch and withdraw the switch and electrical harness from the master cylinder (**Figure 1**).

3. Drain the master cylinder as follows:
   a. Attach a hose to the brake caliper bleed screw (**Figure 2**).
   b. Place the end of the hose in a clean container.
   c. Open the bleed screw and operate the brake lever to drain all brake fluid from the master cylinder reservoir.
   d. Close the bleed screw and disconnect the hose.
   e. Discard the brake fluid.

4. Loosen the screws securing the master cylinder top cover (**Figure 3**). Do not remove the cover at this time.

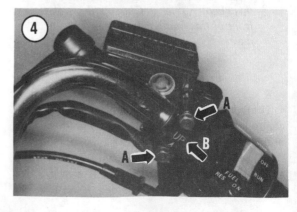

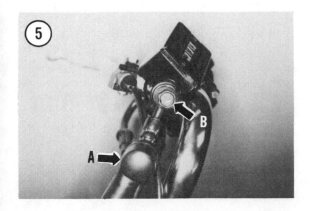

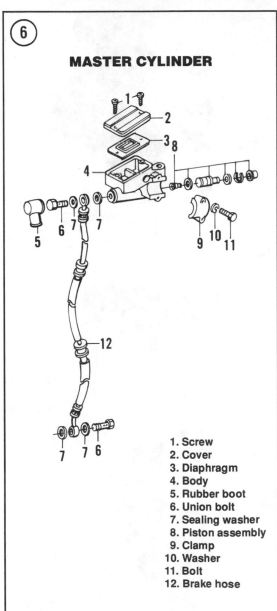

MASTER CYLINDER

1. Screw
2. Cover
3. Diaphragm
4. Body
5. Rubber boot
6. Union bolt
7. Sealing washer
8. Piston assembly
9. Clamp
10. Washer
11. Bolt
12. Brake hose

5. Loosen the 2 clamping bolts (A, **Figure 4**) securing the master cylinder to the handlebar.

6. Slide back the rubber boot (A, **Figure 5**) and loosen the union bolt (B, **Figure 5**) securing the brake hose to the master cylinder.

7. Remove the union bolt, brake hose and both copper sealing washers. Cover the end of the hose to prevent the entry of foreign matter and moisture. Tie the hose end up to the handlebar to prevent the loss of brake fluid.

8. Remove the 2 clamping bolts (A, **Figure 4**) and clamp securing the master cylinder to the handlebar and remove the master cylinder.

9. Install by reversing these removal steps. Note the following:

    a. Install the master cylinder clamp with the arrow facing upward (B, **Figure 4**).

    b. Tighten the upper clamp bolt first, then the lower bolt.

    c. Install the brake hose onto the master cylinder. Be sure to place a copper sealing washer on each side of the hose fitting and install the union bolt and tighten (**Table 2**).

    d. Bleed the brake system as described in Chapter Ten in the front section of this manual.

Disassembly

Refer to **Figure 6** for this procedure.

1. Remove the master cylinder as described in this chapter.

2. Remove the bolt securing the hand lever and remove the lever. Don't lose the small spring (**Figure 7**) within the lever.

3. Remove the screws securing the reservoir cover and diaphragm and remove both of them. Pour out

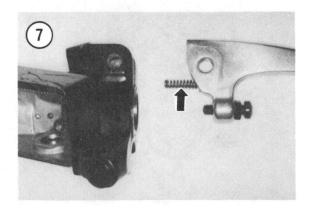

the remaining brake fluid and discard it. *Never* reuse brake fluid.

4. Remove the rubber boot (**Figure 8**) from the area where the hand lever actuates the internal piston.

5. Using snap ring pliers remove the internal snap ring (**Figure 9**) from the cylinder in the master cylinder body.

6. Remove the piston, return valve, spring cup and return spring (**Figure 10**).

Inspection

1. Clean all parts in fresh brake fluid. Inspect the cylinder bore (**Figure 11**) and piston contact surfaces (**Figure 12**) for signs of wear or damage. If either part is less than perfect, replace it.

2. Check the end of the piston (**Figure 13**) for wear caused by the hand lever. Replace the entire piston assembly if any portion of it requires replacement.

3. Inspect the pivot hole in the hand lever and master cylinder body (**Figure 14**). If worn, either part must be replaced.

4. Make sure the passages (**Figure 15**) in the bottom of the brake fluid reservoir are clear. Check the

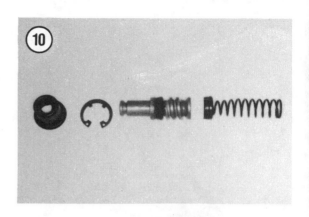

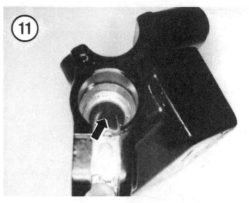

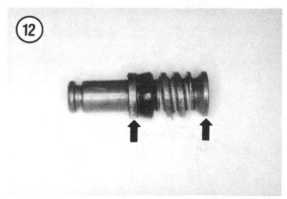

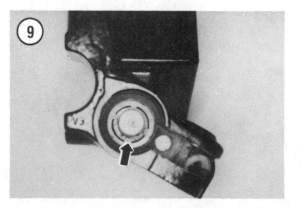

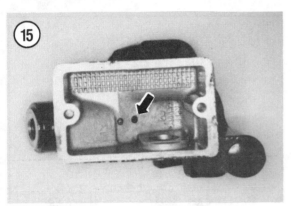

reservoir cap and diaphragm for damage and deterioration. Replace if necessary.

5. Inspect the condition of the threads (**Figure 16**) in the master cylinder body where the brake hose union bolt screws in. If the threads are damaged or partially stripped, replace the master cylinder body.

6. Inspect the dust boot (**Figure 17**) for damage or deterioration. Replace if necessary.

7. Inspect the diaphragm (**Figure 18**) for damage or deterioration. Replace if necessary.

NOTE
*Yamaha recommends replacing the piston assembly (**Figure 19**) whenever the master cylinder is disassembled.*

Assembly

1. Soak the new cups in fresh brake fluid for at least 15 minutes to make them pliable. Coat the inside of the cylinder with fresh brake fluid prior to assembling the parts.

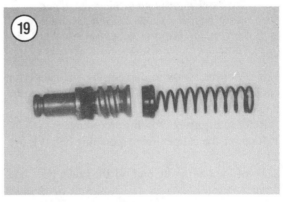

10

CAUTION
When installing the piston assembly, do not allow the cups to turn inside out as they will be damaged and allow brake fluid to leak within the cylinder bore.

2. Position the spring with the tapered end facing toward the primary cup (**Figure 19**). Position the primary cup so the open end will go in first (toward the spring). Install the spring, primary cup and piston assembly into the cylinder (**Figure 10**).

3. Push down on the piston assembly and install the snap ring (**Figure 9**). Make sure the snap ring is firmly seated in the groove in the cylinder.

4. Slide on the rubber boot (**Figure 8**).

5. Install the diaphragm and cover. Do not tighten the screws at this time as fluid will have to be added later.

6. Install the brake lever and spring (**Figure 7**) onto the master cylinder body and tighten the bolt securely.

7. Install the master cylinder as described in this chapter.

FRONT BRAKE PAD REPLACEMENT

There is no recommended mileage interval for changing the friction pads on the disc brakes. Pad wear depends greatly on riding habits and conditions. The pads should be checked for wear at the intervals specified in Chapter Three in this section of the manual and replaced when worn to the minimum thickness listed in **Table 1**. Check for brake pad wear through the caliper inspection window (**Figure 20**). Always replace both pads at the same time.

CAUTION
Watch the pads more closely when they approach the minimum thickness. If pad wear happens to be uneven for some reason, the backing plate may come in contact with the disc and cause damage.

It is not necessary to disassemble the caliper or open the hydraulic brake fluid lines to replace the brake pads.

Refer to **Figure 21** for this procedure.

1. Remove the caliper lower mounting bolt (**Figure 22**).

2. Pivot the caliper up and off the brake pads and disc.

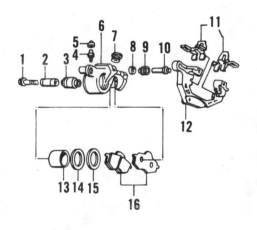

BRAKE CALIPER

1. Bolt
2. Bushing
3. Boot
4. Bleed valve
5. Cap
6. Caliper body
7. Viewing plug
8. Seal
9. Boot
10. Pivot pin
11. Brake pad support
12. Caliper mounting bracket
13. Piston
14. Piston seal
15. Dust seal
16. Brake pads

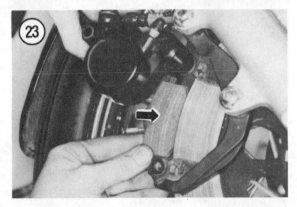

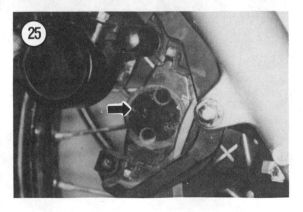

3. Remove both brake pads.

4. Clean the pad recess and the end of the piston with a soft brush. Do not use solvent, a wire brush or any hard tool which would damage the cylinder or piston.

5. Lightly coat the end of the piston with disc brake lubricant.

6. When new pads are installed in the caliper, the master cylinder brake fluid level will rise as the caliper piston is repositioned. Clean the top of the master cylinder of all dirt and foreign matter. Remove the screws, cover and diaphragm (**Figure 3**). Slowly push the caliper piston into the caliper. Constantly check the reservoir to make sure brake fluid does not overflow. Remove fluid, if necessary, prior to it overflowing. The piston should move freely. If it does not, and there is evidence of it sticking in the cylinder, the caliper should be removed and serviced as described under *Caliper Rebuilding* in this chapter.

7. Push the piston back in to allow room for the new pads.

8. Install the inboard disc (**Figure 23**) and make sure it fits correctly into the caliper mounting bracket (**Figure 24**).

9. Install the outboard disc (**Figure 25**) and make sure it fits correctly into the caliper mounting bracket.

10. Pivot the caliper down onto the new pads and install the lower mounting bolt (**Figure 22**). Tighten the bolt to specification in **Table 2**.

11. Spin the front wheel and activate the brake lever as many times as it takes to refill the cylinder in the caliper and correctly position the pads.

12. Refill the master cylinder reservoir, if necessary, to maintain the correct fluid level. Install the diaphragm and top cover and tighten the screws securely.

> *WARNING*
> *Use brake fluid clearly marked DOT 3 from a sealed container. Other types may vaporize and cause brake failure. Always use the same brand name; do not intermix brake fluids, many brands are not compatible.*

> *WARNING*
> *Do not ride the motorcycle until you are sure the brake is operating correctly. If necessary, bleed the brake as described*

10

*under **Bleeding the System** in Chapter Ten in the front section of the manual.*

13. Bed the pads in gradually for the first 50 miles by using only light pressure as much as possible. Immediate hard application will glaze the new friction pads and greatly reduce the effectiveness of the brake.

FRONT CALIPER

Removal/Installation

Refer to **Figure 21** for this procedure.

1. Drain the master cylinder and caliper as follows:
   a. Attach a hose to the brake caliper bleed screw (**Figure 26**).
   b. Place the end of the hose in a clean container.
   c. Open the bleed screw and operate the brake lever to drain all brake fluid from the master cylinder reservoir.
   d. Close the bleed screw and disconnect the hose.
   e. Discard the brake fluid.
2. Remove the union bolt (**Figure 27**) and copper sealing washers attaching the brake hose to the caliper. To prevent the entry of moisture and foreign matter, cap the end of the brake hose and tie it up to the fender.
3. Remove the bolt (**Figure 22**) securing the caliper assembly to the caliper mounting bracket.
4. Pivot the caliper up and off the brake pads. Pull the caliper off the pivot post on the mounting bracket and remove the caliper.
5. To remove the caliper bracket, perform the following:
   a. Remove the mounting bolts (A, **Figure 28**) and remove the bracket (B, **Figure 28**) from the fork slider.
   b. Inspect the brake pad supports (**Figure 29**) for damage or cracks; replace if necessary.
   c. Inspect the pivot pin (**Figure 30**) for wear or damage.
6. Install by reversing these removal steps. Note the following:
   a. Install the brake hose onto the caliper. Be sure to place a copper sealing washer on each side of the hose fitting (**Figure 31**) and install the union bolt and tighten (**Table 2**).
   b. Tighten the bolts to specifications in **Table 2**.

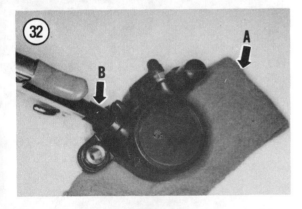

c. Bleed the brake system as described in Chapter Ten in the front section of the manual.

> *WARNING*
> *Do not ride the motorcycle until you are sure that the brakes are operating properly.*

Caliper Rebuilding

If the caliper leaks, the caliper should be rebuilt. If the piston sticks in the cylinder, indicating severe wear or galling, the entire unit should be replaced. Rebuilding a leaky caliper requires special tools and experience.

The factory recommends that the internal seals of the caliper be replaced every two years.

Refer to **Figure 21** for this procedure.

1. Remove the brake caliper as described in this chapter.

> *WARNING*
> *In the next step, the piston may shoot out of the caliper body like a bullet. Keep your fingers out of the way. Wear shop gloves and apply air pressure gradually. Do **not** use high pressure air or place the air hose nozzle directly against the hydraulic line fitting inlet in the caliper body. Hold the air nozzle away from the inlet allowing some of the air to escape.*

2. Pad the piston with shop rags or wood blocks as shown in A, **Figure 32**. Block the exposed housing fluid port holes on the back of the caliper housing. Then apply compressed air through the caliper hose joint (B, **Figure 32**) and blow the piston (**Figure 33**) out of the caliper.

> *CAUTION*
> *In the following step, do not use a sharp tool to remove the dust and piston seals from the caliper cylinder. Do not damage the cylinder surface.*

3. Use a piece of plastic or wood and carefully push the dust seal and the piston seal in toward the caliper cylinder and out of their grooves. Remove the dust and piston seals from the cylinder and discard both seals.

4. Clean all caliper parts and inspect them as described in this chapter.

10

NOTE
Never reuse the old dust seals or piston seals. Very minor damage or age deterioration can make the seals useless.

5. Coat the new dust seal and piston seal with fresh DOT 3 brake fluid.

6. Carefully install the new piston seal (**Figure 34**) and dust seal (**Figure 35**) in the grooves in the caliper cylinder. Make sure the seals are properly seated in their respective grooves.

7. Coat the piston and caliper cylinder with fresh DOT 3 brake fluid.

8. Position the piston with the open end facing out toward the brake pads and install the piston (**Figure 33**) into the caliper cylinder. Push the piston in until it bottoms out.

9. Install the caliper and brake pads as described in this chapter.

Caliper Inspection

1. Clean all parts (except brake pads) with rubbing alcohol and rinse with clean DOT 3 brake fluid. Place the cleaned parts on a lint-free cloth while performing the following inspection procedures.

2. Inspect the seal grooves (A, **Figure 36**) in the caliper body for damage. If damaged or corroded, replace the caliper assembly.

3. Inspect the cylinder walls (B, **Figure 36**) for scratches, scoring or other damage. If rusty or corroded, replace the caliper assembly.

4. Measure the cylinder bore inside diameter with a bore gauge. Replace the brake caliper if the inside diameter is worn. Refer to the standard dimension listed in **Table 1**.

5. Inspect the piston (**Figure 37**) for scratches, scoring or other damage. If rusty or corroded, replace the pistons.

6. Inspect both caliper bodies for damage, replace the caliper body if necessary (**Figure 38**).

7. Inspect the caliper mounting bolt holes on the caliper body. If worn or damaged, replace the caliper assembly.

8. Remove the bleed screw and make sure it is clean and open. Apply compressed air to the opening and make sure it is clear. Clean out if necessary with fresh brake fluid.

9. Inspect the fluid opening (**Figure 39**) in the base of the cylinder bore and make sure it is clean and

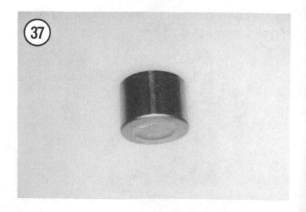

open. Apply compressed air to the opening and make sure it is clear. Clean out if necessary with fresh brake fluid.

10. Inspect the union bolt threads in the caliper for wear or damage. Clean up any minor thread damage or replace the caliper assembly if necessary.

11. The piston seal maintains correct brake pad to disc clearance. If the seal is worn or damaged, the brake pads will drag and cause excessive pad wear and elevate brake fluid temperatures. Replace the

piston and dust seals if the following conditions exist:

    a. Brake fluid leaks around the brake pad.

    b. The piston seal is stuck in the caliper groove.

    c. There is a large difference in inner and outer brake pad wear.

    d. Measure the brake pad friction thickness material with a vernier caliper (**Figure 40**). Replace both brake pads if any one pad is worn to the service limit dimension listed in **Table 1** or less.

FRONT BRAKE HOSE REPLACEMENT

The factory-recommended brake hose replacement interval is every 4 years, but it is a good idea to replace brake hoses whenever signs of cracking, leakage or damage are apparent.

> *CAUTION*
> *Cover the front wheel, fender and top cover or fuel tank with a heavy cloth or plastic tarp to protect it from the accidental spilling of brake fluid. Wash any spilled brake fluid off of any painted or plated surface immediately, as it will destroy the finish. Use soapy water and rinse completely.*

1. Drain the master cylinder and caliper as follows:

    a. Attach a hose to the brake caliper bleed screw (**Figure 26**).

    b. Place the end of the hose in a clean container.

    c. Open the bleed screw and operate the brake lever to drain all brake fluid from the master cylinder reservoir.

    d. Close the bleed screw and disconnect the hose.

    e. Discard the brake fluid.

2. Remove the union bolt (**Figure 27**) and copper sealing washers attaching the brake hose to the caliper.

3. Disconnect the hose from the clamp on the fork (**Figure 41**).

4. Slide back the rubber boot (A, **Figure 42**) and remove the union bolt (B, **Figure 42**) securing the hose to the master cylinder.

5. Remove the brake hose.

6. Install new brake hose, copper sealing washers and union bolts in the reverse order of removal. Be sure to install the new sealing washers in their cor-

10

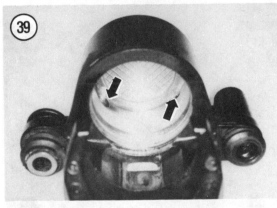

rect positions. Tighten all union bolts to specifications in **Table 2**.

7. Refill the master cylinder with fresh brake fluid clearly marked DOT 3. Bleed the brake as described in Chapter Ten in the front section of the manual.

> *WARNING*
> *Do not ride the motorcycle until you are sure that the brakes are operating properly.*

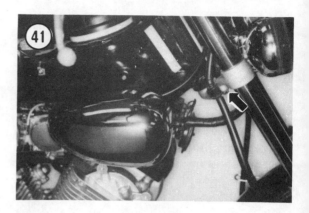

FRONT BRAKE DISC

Removal/Installation

1. Remove the front wheel as described in this chapter.

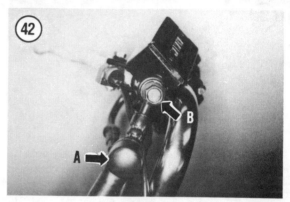

> *NOTE*
> *Place a piece of wood in the caliper in place of the disc. This way, if the brake lever is inadvertently squeezed, the piston will not be forced out of the cylinder. If this does happen, the caliper might have to be disassembled to reseat the piston and the system will have to be bled. By using the wood, bleeding the system is not necessary when installing the wheel.*

2. Straighten the lock tabs on the washers (**Figure 43**) and remove the bolts securing the disc to the wheel.

3. Remove the disc from the hub.

4. Install by reversing these removal steps. Install the bolts and tighten to specifications in **Table 2**. Install new lockwashers and bend over the lock tabs after the bolts are tightened.

Inspection

It is not necessary to remove the disc from the wheel to inspect it. Small marks on the disc are not important, but deep radial scratches, deep enough to snag a fingernail, reduce braking effectiveness and increase brake pad wear. If these grooves are found, the disc should be resurfaced or replaced.

1. Measure the thickness around the disc at several locations with Vernier calipers or a micrometer (**Figure 44**). The disc must be replaced if the thickness at any point is less than specified in **Table 1**.

2. Make sure the disc bolts are tight prior to performing this check. Check the disc runout with a dial indicator as shown in **Figure 45**. Slowly rotate the wheel and watch the dial indicator. If the runout is 0.006 in. (0.15 mm) or greater, the disc must be replaced.

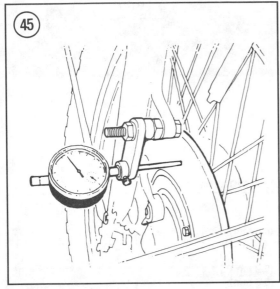

3. Clean the disc of any rust or corrosion and wipe clean with lacquer thinner. Never use an oil based solvent that may leave an oil residue on the disc.

REAR BRAKE PEDAL ASSEMBLY

Removal/Installation

1. Place the motorcycle on its sidestand.

2. Completely unscrew the brake rod adjustment nut (**Figure 46**) and disconnect the rod from the brake arm. Reinstall the adjustment nut, pivot pin and spring on the rod to avoid losing them.

3. Remove the bolts securing the right-hand footpeg and guard assembly (**Figure 47**) to the footpeg bar assembly. Remove the footpeg and guard assembly.

4. Unhook the pedal return spring (A, **Figure 48**) and disconnect the brake light spring or rod (**Figure 49**).

5. Remove the circlip and washer securing the brake pedal to the footpeg bar assembly and remove the pedal (B, **Figure 48**) from the pivot post.

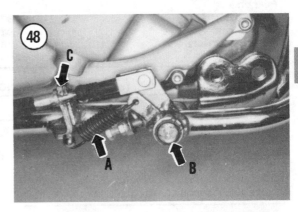

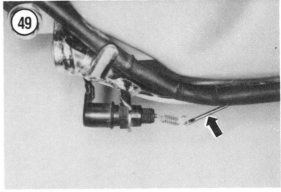

10

6. Unhook the brake cable from the front bracket (C, **Figure 48**) and rear bracket (**Figure 50**) on the swing arm.

7. Remove the brake pedal and cable/rod assembly from the frame.

8. Install by reversing these removal steps, while noting the following:

    a. Apply grease to the brake pivot post prior to installing the assembly into the frame.

    b. Adjust the rear brake pedal as described in Chapter Three in the front section and in this section of the manual.

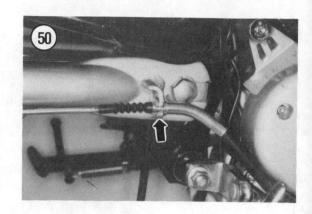

Table 1   BRAKE SPECIFICATIONS

Brake fluid type	DOT 3
Front borake	
Disc thickness (limit)	0.18 in. (4.5 mm)
Disc deflection (limit)	0.006 in. (0.15 mm)
Pad thickness	
New	0.26 in. (6.2 mm)
Wear limit	0.03 in. (0.8 mm)
Rear brake	
Drum diameter	7.87 in. (200 mm)
Wear limit	7.91 in. (201 mm)
Lining thickness	0.16 in. (4 mm)
Wear limit	0.08 in. (2 mm)

Table 2   BRAKE TIGHTENING TORQUES

Item	ft.-lb.	N•m
Master cylinder clamping bolts	6.5	9
Brake hose union bolt	19	26
Caliper		
Mounting bolts	13	18
Caliper bracket mounting bolts	25	35
Brake disc mounting bolts	14	20

INDEX

11

1987-1989 XV535 (U.S.)

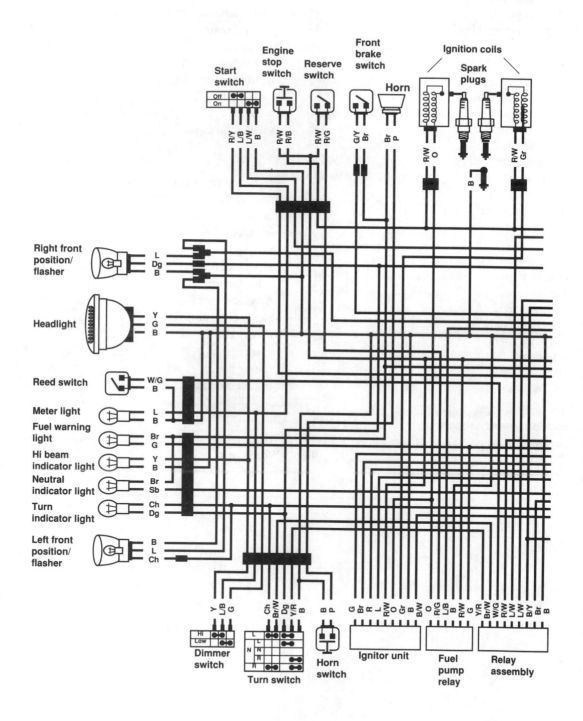

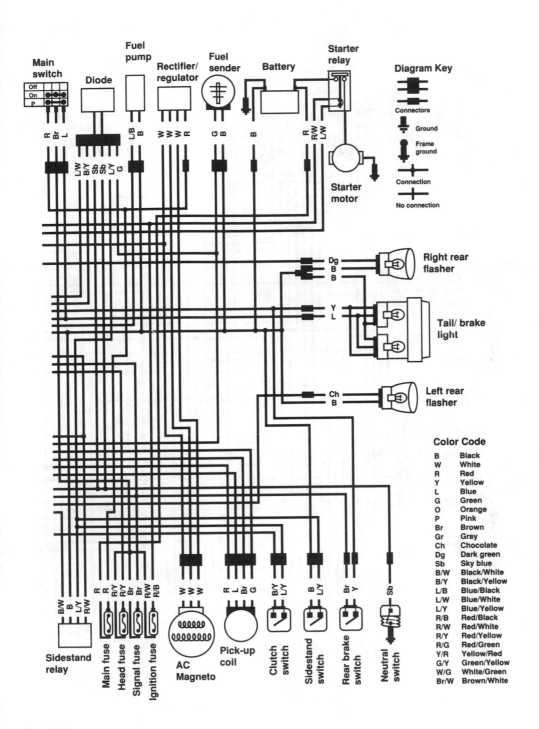

12

1990-ON XV535 (U.S.)

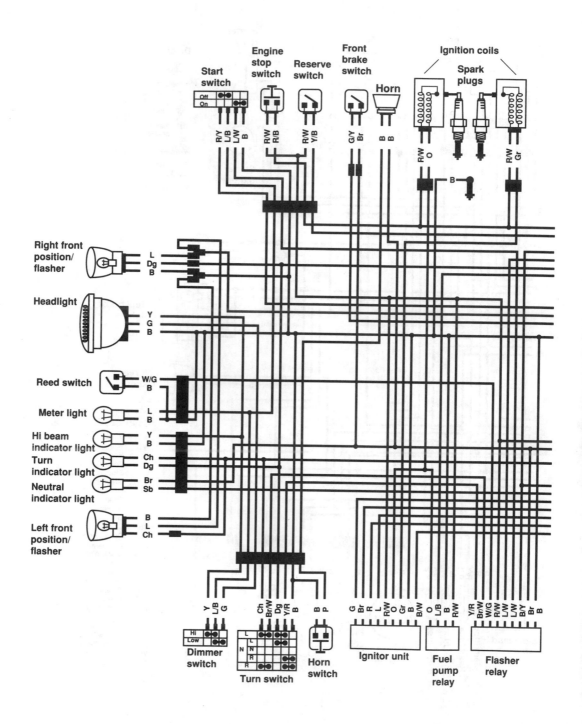

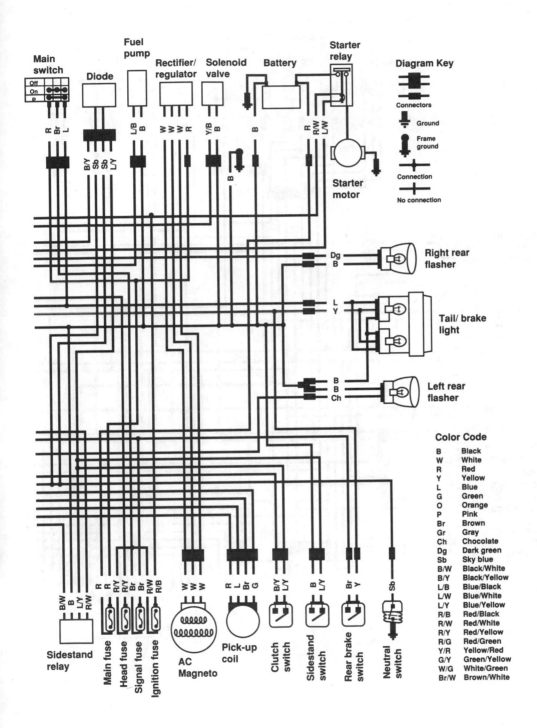

Diagram Key

Connectors

Ground

Frame ground

Connection

No connection

Color Code

B	Black
W	White
R	Red
Y	Yellow
L	Blue
G	Green
O	Orange
P	Pink
Br	Brown
Gr	Gray
Ch	Chocolate
Dg	Dark green
Sb	Sky blue
B/W	Black/White
B/Y	Black/Yellow
L/B	Blue/Black
L/W	Blue/White
L/Y	Blue/Yellow
R/B	Red/Black
R/W	Red/White
R/Y	Red/Yellow
R/G	Red/Green
Y/R	Yellow/Red
G/Y	Green/Yellow
W/G	White/Green
Br/W	Brown/White

12

XV535 (1988-1991 U.K.)

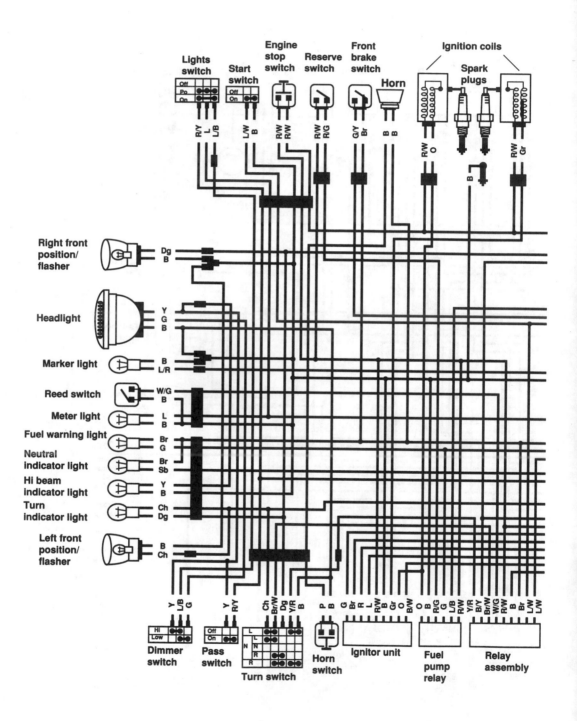

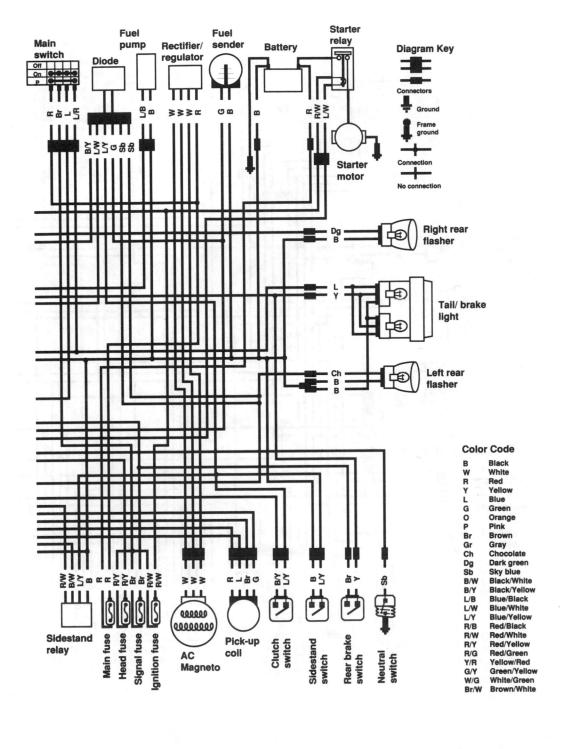

12

XV535 (1992-ON U.K.)

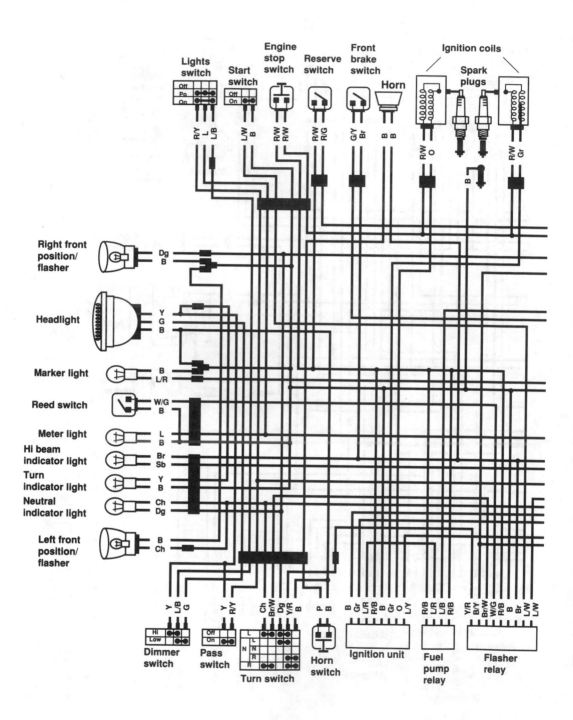

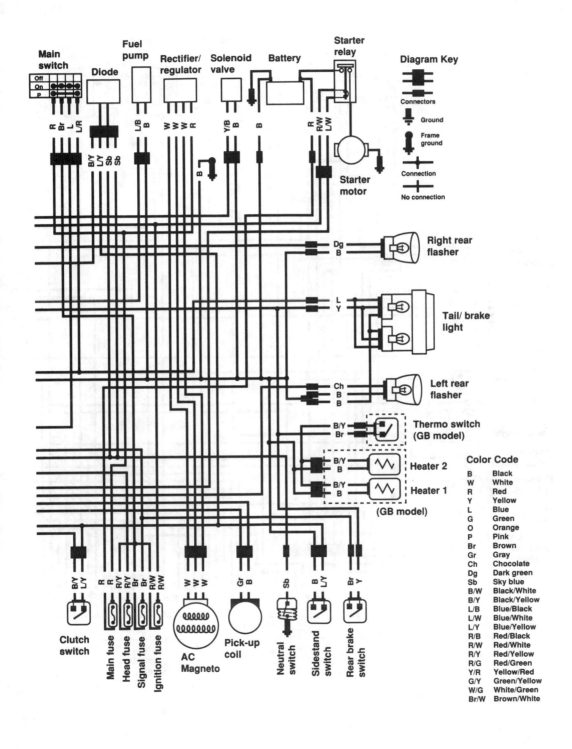

Main switch

Diode

Fuel pump

Rectifier/ regulator

Solenoid valve

Battery

Starter relay

Diagram Key

Connectors

Ground

Frame ground

Connection

No connection

Starter motor

Right rear flasher

Tail/ brake light

Left rear flasher

Thermo switch (GB model)

Heater 2

Heater 1

(GB model)

Color Code

B	Black
W	White
R	Red
Y	Yellow
L	Blue
G	Green
O	Orange
P	Pink
Br	Brown
Gr	Gray
Ch	Chocolate
Dg	Dark green
Sb	Sky blue
B/W	Black/White
B/Y	Black/Yellow
L/B	Blue/Black
L/W	Blue/White
L/Y	Blue/Yellow
R/B	Red/Black
R/W	Red/White
R/Y	Red/Yellow
R/G	Red/Green
Y/R	Yellow/Red
G/Y	Green/Yellow
W/G	White/Green
Br/W	Brown/White

12

Clutch switch

Main fuse

Head fuse

Signal fuse

Ignition fuse

AC Magneto

Pick-up coil

Neutral switch

Sidestand switch

Rear brake switch

XV535 (French & German)

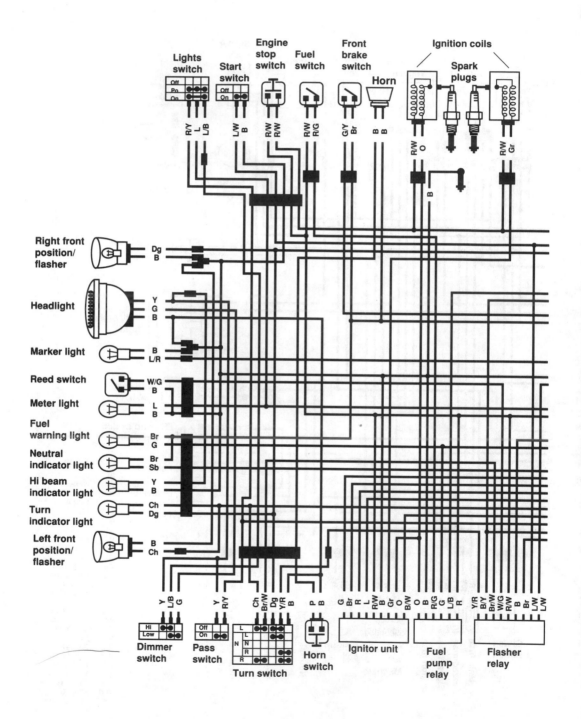

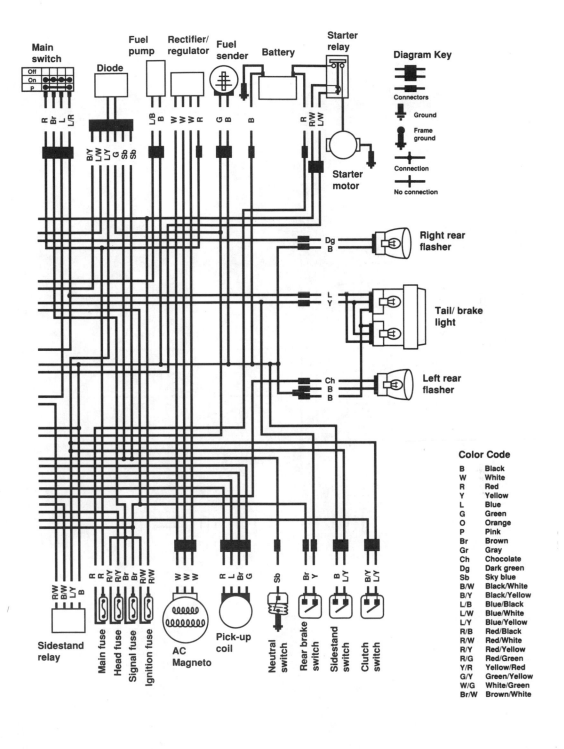

NOTES

NOTES

NOTES

NOTES

NOTES

NOTES

MAINTENANCE LOG

Service Performed   **Mileage Reading**

Oil change (example)	2,836	5,782	8,601		